Trireme *Olympias*
The Final Report

Trireme *Olympias*
The Final Report

Sea Trials 1992–4
Conference Papers 1998

edited by

Boris Rankov

with contributions by

Ronald Bockius, René Burlet, John Coates, Edwin Gifford, John Howarh, Douglas Lindsay, Paul Lipke, Seán McGrail, Robin Oldfield, Anthony J. Papalas, Boris Rankov, Harry Rossiter, André W. Sleeswyk, Timothy Shaw, Andrew Taylor, Alec Tilley, Herman Wallinga, Ford Weiskittel, Brian Whipp, Ian Whitehead and Meph Wyeth

Oxbow Books

Oxford and Oakville

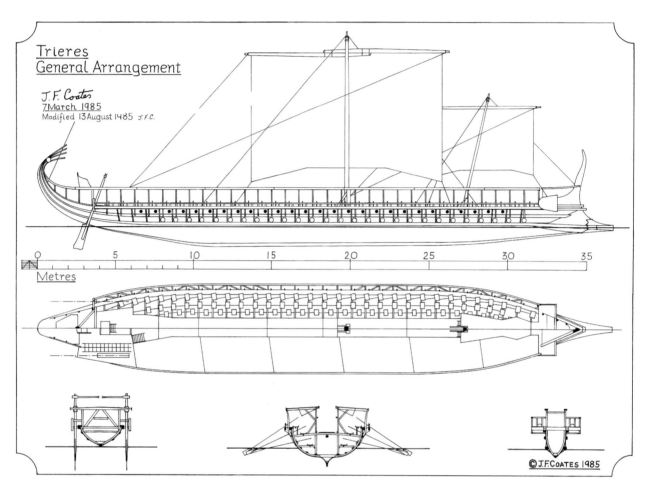

Frontispiece: Plan, elevation and cross-sections of Olympias *(Drawing: John Coates).*

This book is dedicated to the memory of

John Francis Coates
(1922–2010)

and

John Sinclair Morrison
(1913–2000)

Published by
Oxbow Books, Oxford, UK

ISBN 978-1-84217-434-0

This book is available direct from

Oxbow Books, Oxford, UK
(Phone: 01865-241249; Fax: 01865-794449)

and

The David Brown Book Company
PO Box 511, Oakville, CT 06779, USA
(Phone: 860-945-9329; Fax: 860-945-9468)

or from our website
www.oxbowbooks.com

A CIP record is available for this book from the British Library

Library of Congress Cataloging-in-Publication Data

Trireme Olympias : the final report : sea trials 1992-4, conference papers 1998 / edited by Boris Rankov ; with contributions
by Ronald Bockius ... [et al.]. -- 1st ed.
      p. cm.
   Includes bibliographical references.
Summary: "This is the final publication of the Olympias project, which saw the building of a 170-oared Athenian trireme
of the fourth century BC and its operation in five series of sea-trials. The first three sea-trials have already been published
in separate volumes. The rest of the volume is devoted to papers presenting more recent research on the trireme"--Provided
by publisher.
   ISBN 978-1-84217-434-0
   1. Triremes. 2. Olympias (Ship) 3. Triremes--Design and construction. 4. Ships, Ancient--Reconstruction. 5. Ship trials.
I. Rankov, N. B., 1954- II. Bockius, Ronald.
   VM16.T73 2012
   623.82'1--dc23
                                    2011044248

Front Cover: *Olympias* from above, passing through the Corinth Canal on 29th July, 1992
(Photo: Rosie Randolph/Trireme Trust).

Printed in Great Britain by
Short Run Press, Exeter

Contents

List of Figures

Acknowledgements

This volume has taken a very long time to come to fruition, ever since the conference held at Oxford and Henley on Thames in 1998, and my first thanks must go to all the contributors for their infinite patience in awaiting the outcome. I hope they will feel that it has been worth it. I also have to thank, as always, all the members of the Trireme Trust and Trireme Trust USA who rowed on *Olympias* or otherwise contributed to the success of the 1992 sea trials, the 1993 visit to London, and the 1994 sea trials which are reported here, as well as the officers and personnel of the Hellenic Navy without whom none of these would have been possible. The members of the Council of the Trireme Trust, John Allan, the late John Coates, Andrew Morrison, Doug Pattison, John Quenby, Rosie Randolph, Andrew Ruddle, Timothy Shaw, Andrew Taylor, Ford Weiskittel and Frank Welsh, as well as Annis Garfield, Doug Lindsay and the late Sir Charles Willink, have given me unwavering support and assistance since I took over as Chairman in 1996, and they all have my deepest gratitude. Finally, special thanks go to Professor Ted Lendon of the University of Virginia, who read through most of the reports and papers and made several excellent suggestions on how to improve the presentation of this book.

Boris Rankov
Wootton by Woodstock
August, 2010

Introduction and Summaries

Boris Rankov

Introduction

The first three series of sea-trials of the reconstructed Athenian trireme *Olympias*, which took place in 1987, 1988 and 1990 respectively, were each published in separate volumes some years ago (Morrison and Coates 1989; Coates, Shaw and Platis 1990; Shaw 1993); in addition, a report of the latest trials in 1994 was privately published by Timothy Shaw in the same year (Shaw 1994). This volume presents reports of the last two series of trials in 1992 and 1994 (the latter a slightly revised version of the private publication), together with brief accounts of the ship's visit to the Thames in London in 1993 to celebrate the 2,500th anniversary of Greek democracy and of her appearance on the water in 2004 to carry the Olympic flame just before the opening of the Athens Olympics.

Supplementing these reports are a number of papers presented to a conference held at Corpus Christi College, Oxford and the River and Rowing Museum in Henley on Thames from 18th to 20th September, 1998, together with further papers which for various reasons could not be delivered at the conference or were written in its wake. The editor here wishes to express his sincere gratitude for their patience to all the authors who have waited so long for their papers to appear in print. At the same time, the opportunity has been taken to include a number of more recently-written papers which reflect the ongoing research which has been based on the results of the various trials. Those results were summarized by the present author in the new chapter he wrote for the second edition of *The Athenian Trireme*, published in 2000 (Morrison. Coates and Rankov 2000, 231–75). The individual reports and many of the papers which follow may be considered as presenting the raw data and 'showing the working' behind that summary; in particular, Part 2 of the volume explains in detail the argument for canting the oar-rig. The contents of this volume as a whole thus constitute a final report of the *Olympias* sea-trials between 1987 and 1993.

For those interested in the history of the project as a whole, an archive of Trireme Trust papers has been collected and electronically catalogued by John Quenby and Sharon Shellock, and was deposited at the River and Rowing Museum in 2009. This archive includes John Coates' detailed specification, plans and construction notebooks for *Olympias*, together with the letters and papers of John Morrison, John Coates and Timothy Shaw, as well as other items, relating to the ship's design, building and sea trials. The catalogue may now be consulted on-line via the Trireme Trust website (www.triremetrust.org.uk), which also gives details on how to consult the archive.

At the time of writing, *Olympias* herself is on permanent display out of the water near the battle-cruiser *G. Averoff* at the Hellenic Navy Museum in Neo Faliro near the Piraeus (Fig. IS.1). There are, however, plans currently being made to refurbish the ship in Greece and the United States, and for her to be rowed once again in New York City in 2013. If those plans materialise, then there may indeed be more for others to report. In the meantime, this volume offers a wide selection of views and comments on the *Olympias* project, some of them highly critical. Not least amongst these is the report of the 1992 trials (see Shaw 1993, viii) which was compiled by Paul Lipke and other members of Trireme Trust USA, the sister organisation of the original Trireme Trust set up by John Morrison, John Coates and Frank Welsh in 1982. This and other papers later in the volume (notably those of André Sleeswyk and Alec Tilley) which take issue with the *Olympias* design have been included to emphasise that the ship is an hypothetical reconstruction (or a 'floating hypothesis' as Seán McGrail (1992) has so aptly described her), and that approaches and interpretations are possible which differ considerably from those of the Trireme Trust. It should not be assumed that the Trust necessarily accepts any or all of these alternative interpretations; nevertheless, it firmly believes that debate can and should continue.

Summaries of Reports and Papers

The various reports and papers are here summarised as a guide to what the reader may expect to find in this volume, and where.

Figure IS.1. Olympias in her dry-dock and covered shed at the Hellenic Navy Museum, Neo Faliro (Photo: Boris Rankov/ Trireme Trust).

Part 1. The 1992 and 1994 sea trials and other excursions

Paul Lipke of Trireme Trust USA presents a report (pp. 12–39) of the 1992 sea-trials of *Olympias* compiled with the assistance or rowing master **Ford Weiskittel** and ship's carpenters **John Howarth** and **Meph Wyeth**. The introduction (pp. 12–13) explains the genesis of this report in a much longer version originally planned by Ford Weiskittel, who was one of the 1992 rowing masters and is chairman of Trireme Trust USA. Lipke then (pp. 13–16) comments upon the effects of the reduced numbers of oarsmen participating in 1992 compared with earlier trials, and the limits to the accuracy of GPS data available at that time; he offers a summary of the outings undertaken between 22nd July and 8th August, and provides a sample entry from the log kept by trials recorder Andrew Ruddle, giving the reader an excellent insight into the progress of a typical outing, what sorts of exercises were undertaken, and how they were recorded. The next section (pp. 16–21) discusses crew management from Lipke's point of view as one of the team leaders in the ship, rather than from the viewpoint of a rowing master as in previous reports, and notes that this produces different perspectives and insights. John Howarth, Paul Lipke and Meph Wyeth (pp. 21–31) document their work leading the ship's running repair team during the trials, detailing how the 170 oars, the same

number of seats of wooden furniture, and their leather fittings required several hours of maintenance daily both during and after outings. Lipke and Weiskittel, (pp. 32–6) next offer some interpretations of the operation of the ship which differ from those published in previous reports, for instance on the relative importance of the bow rowers, on the timing of the stroke, and on the relative unimportance of the problems caused by the cross-beams or by rowers catching a crab; they also suggest that there is no need to recruit crews entirely from experienced rowers and that it is more realistic to consider 8.3 knots as the fastest sprint speed achieved by *Olympias* than the widely reported 8.9 knots which was achieved only momentarily (if at all). In the next section (pp. 36–7), Lipke and Weiskittel discuss where they consider the project to have gone wrong, citing an excessive focus in the trials on maximum speeds, the use in the ship of unnecessarily thick cross-beams, the location of the thalamian seats higher in the hull than they need to be, and the interpretation of Vitruvius' *interscalmium* as being exactly two cubits, which has restricted the length of the rowing stroke and has led, it is argued, to the unnecessary and impractical proposal that the seats should be canted or skewed outwards in any future reconstruction. They then (pp. 37–9) make suggestions for future research, which include further performance trials, the measurement of drift speed, further testing of the redesigned oars, further experimentation with non-electronic communication, rowing with the oars fitted sternwards of the thole-pin, and more sailing trials; away from the ship they advocate further research into mortise-and-tenon construction, the effects of shipworm, rower physiology, aspects of ship design (including a different type of hogging truss) to be carried out with small-scale models and CAD, and the redesign of the oars. Finally, they comment (p. 39) on a more general problem with the project as a victim of its own success, the expense and complexity of which makes it difficult to construct an alternative, and therefore for other researchers to challenge.

Boris Rankov summarises (pp. 40–2) the visit of *Olympias* to the Thames in London in June 1993, where the ship was rowed up and down the Thames between Hammersmith and Tower Bridge and took part in a ceremony celebrating the 2,500th anniversary of Greek democracy off the Palace of Westminster, during which the Greek Minister of Culture, the Senior Officer of the Hellenic Navy and the Speaker of the House of Commons were welcomed aboard. She also (contrary to regulations) passed through Tower Bridge under sail.

Two complementary reports of the 1994 sea-trials at Poros follow. The first, by trials officer **Timothy Shaw** (pp. 43–9), comprises a summary of findings rather than a day-by-day, outing-by-outing account. He notes that since the previous sea-trials in 1992, the ship's hog had increased, that there were only around 120 useable oars, and that the mainsail needed repairs. He documents the new type of knot suggested by a local fisherman and successfully used on synthetic cord to attach the oars to the tholes, and the measurements taken both on land and in the ship to determine the length of stroke which was being attained. From this he deduces that the oarsystem should be reconfigured by canting the seats as in Cornish gigs in order to allow the oars to pass inside the body of the rower immediately astern. This would enable the maximum possible stroke length to be attained and the effective power of the oarcrew to be increased, so as to bring the ship's performance in line with the ancient evidence. In 1994, the ship was in any case underpowered because only 120 rowers were available, so that the trials focused on experimentation in control and command of the ship without electronic aids and tests to assist in the development of more efficient oars.

The second report, by rowing master **Andrew Taylor** (pp. 50–7), presents some details of the trials which were undertaken with a small, inexperienced crew in a ship which was now hogging badly. Rowing was undertaken on both three and only two levels at a time, and the maximum speeds attained were *c.* 5 knots over two to three minutes, and 6.3 to 7 knots flat out but only momentarily, well short of those in earlier sea-trials. Experiments showed that some at least of the previous underperformance by the thalamian (lowest) level of rowers could be attributed to the narrow oarblades with which they were equipped, and the importance of the ship's trim for fast and effective

rowing was also demonstrated. The ship was effectively rowed backwards at 4.5 knots, and at up to 5.6 knots with a following wind and, contrary to previous experience, no difficulty was experienced with steering the ship in this direction. A crew of 130 was embarked in only 6 minutes, with the ship ready to row 6 minutes later; anchoring took only 4 minutes, and coming off a Mediterranean moor 3 minutes. 100 rowers were recovered from the water onto the ship in 10 minutes. There is thus no doubt that the ship could be cleared for action very rapidly. It was discovered that drift could be minimised by turning the ship broadside to the wind. Techniques for directing the oarcrew without electronic speakers were also investigated. Finally, it is observed (contrary to the conclusions of the 1992 report) that the most experienced rowers were also the most effective; also that, despite appearances, fixed-seat rowing does allow an effective leg-drive

Finally, **Boris Rankov** gives a brief description (pp. 58–60) of what has happened to *Olympias* since the 1994 sea trials, including her last outing, carrying the Olympic torch in 2004 in advance of the Athens Olympic Games.

Part 2. Proposals for a revised design

The second part of the volume consists of a preface and three papers by **Timothy Shaw** and a fourth paper by the designer of *Olympias*, naval architect **John Coates** which are intended to be read together. In these papers, which formed the starting point for the 1998 Oxford/Henley conference and were pre-circulated ahead of it, they present the argument for modifying the *Olympias* design by canting or skewing the oarsystem outboard, so as to remove any restriction on the length of stroke which could be achieved.

Timothy Shaw's preface (p. 62) introduces the rationale for revising the design of *Olympias*. His first paper (pp. 63–7) considers the statement by Xenophon in *Anabasis* 6.4.2 that 'for a trireme, to Heraclea from Byzantium is a long day's voyage under oar' as evidence for the cruising speed of a trireme. Shaw argues that Xenophon's statement suggests that a trireme of the 4th century BC could maintain a cruising speed of between 7 and 8 knots through the water. This would therefore be the performance to be expected of an appropriately modified *Olympias* design.

Shaw's second paper (pp. 68–75) sets out to show that, while the existing *Olympias* could *not* be made to cruise all day from Byzantium to Heraclea at 7 to 8 knots through the water under oar, neither could she, as some have suggested, have sustained this cruising speed under sail alone or with serious wind-assistance under oar. This is because the sea-conditions which the latter would imply would either have damaged the ship or prevented rowing altogether. From this it follows that the rowing rig should be modified to enable the ship to cruise at these speeds under oar.

Shaw's third paper (pp. 76–81) addresses how the *Olympias* design would need to be modified in order to make the ship capable of matching the cruising speed implied by Xenophon. He argues that *Olympias*' cruising speed (about 5.4 knots, with speeds over 7 knots achieved only with exceptional and unsustainable effort) is limited because the stroke attainable by her oarsmen is too short. This can be remedied in two ways: by extending the *interscalmium*, and by canting or skewing the oar-rig outboard so that the length of stroke is limited only by each oarsman's physique. He therefore discusses two possible modifications: Mark IIa with the *interscalmium* extended to 0.98 m but with the oarsmen's seats arranged fore-and-aft as before, and Mark IIb, with the *interscalmium* extended and with the seats skewed outboard by 18.4°. Having calculated the force per man and stroke-rates required in each of these modified designs to match the performance implied by Xenophon, Shaw concludes that a ship with an oar-rig skewed as in Mark IIb would be the more consistent with such a performance.

John Coates (pp. 82–9) then builds on Shaw's conclusions, and on other lessons learnt from the trials of *Olympias*, to propose a modified design for any future trireme reconstruction In order to achieve the extra oar power required for a trireme to cruise at 7 to 8 knots, it will be necessary to increase the *interscalmium* to 0.98 m and skew the rig outboard by 18.4°, as argued by Shaw. Increasing the spacing of the beams (as required by the extension of the *interscalmium*) and raising them slightly will allow the heads of the lowest (thalamian) level of rowers to pass underneath the beams instead of colliding with them (see the critiques of *Olympias* below), while the skewing of the rig will both enable a longer stroke and move the arc swept forward of athwartships, increasing the stroke's effectiveness. Oars will be light and made of spruce, will conform to the longer cubit, and will still be rigged forward of the thole-pins. During construction, the tenons joining the planking will be tapered and cut to fit tightly in the mortices, side planking will be thickened, and the hull will be given a slight sag, so as to counter the hogging which has affected *Olympias*. The proposed changes will extend the length of the ship from 36.8 m to 40 m, while its overall width will be increased from 5.45 m to 5.60 m (reducing the clearance in the Zea ship sheds to 7 cm either side). Displacement will increase by between 5 and 10%; resistance will increase by about 7% at lower speeds, but only about 5% at sprint speeds. With these changes, cruising speeds of 7.5 knots and flat-out speeds of 9.7 knots, as demanded by Shaw's papers, should be attainable.

Part 3. Critiques of Olympias: *for and against*

Three short papers by maritime historians and archaeologists pass some general observations on the *Olympias* project. **René Burlet** (pp. 94–6) notes some of the strengths and successes of the design, which he regards as a realistic hypothesis, but also some of the weaknesses such as the cramped conditions of the thalamians caused by the placing of the cross-beams. He also suggests that fast, long-distance voyages in antiquity must have been done under sail, not under oar, because, as is apparent from later galleys, a 'human engine' cannot maintain high cruising speeds over long distances. **Edwin Gifford** (pp. 97–9) also considers the design of *Olympias* a success, apart from the awkward placing of the cross-beams and its effect on the thalamian rowers. He also emphasises how tightly the design was determined by naval-architectural requirements, even though some maritime archaeologists have found this hard to accept. **Seán McGrail** (p. 100) also expresses approval of the project and suggests that the proposed Mk II design is likely to be as close to authentic as is possible to achieve on the basis of the evidence currently available, but on the basis of that evidence questions the design requirement for the ship to be capable of cruising as fast as 7.5 knots and sprinting at 9 knots (see also the papers by Rankov, Wallinga and Whitehead in Part 4).

The paper by ancient historian **Tony Papalas** (pp. 101–8) aims to reply to some of the published criticisms of *Olympias*, including those of Lucien Basch (1987; 1988; 1990), who suggests that the oars should be of different lengths and questions the length and construction of the hull, and Alec Tilley (1992; 1997), who argues for a trireme design based on his interpretation of the Siren Vase (see his paper, pp. 121–32). Papalas considers Basch to have been overly sceptical and not to have taken sufficient account of the Talos Vase. He also argues that Tilley's reconstruction does not conform to the ancient evidence, although he does agree with Tilley's argument on the basis Herodotus 8.118 that the hold of *Olympias* appears to be too large. Nevertheless, Papalas considers that *Olympias* should be accepted as a generally authentic representation of a Classical Athenian trireme.

André Sleeswyk (pp. 109–20), an historian of technology, takes a far more sceptical view of *Olympias*. He acknowledges the project's demonstration that a three-level oarsystem is practicable as a major achievement, but considers that insufficient attention has been paid in the design to the effects of ramming (for which see now Oldfield's paper, pp. 214–24) and the structure of the hull. He argues that when a trireme rammed a larger vessel, it and the oarcrew are likely to have suffered a significantly more violent retardation than has hitherto been allowed for, and that the rowers should therefore have been seated in such a way as to be able to withstand this. He also argues that Vitruvius' *interscalmium* should have been taken as a clear distance between tholes, which would give the rowers more room and allow for a longer stroke, and that Shaw's suggestion that the oarsystem should be canted or skewed would both reduce the efficiency of the stroke and make it more difficult for the rowers to brace themselves during ramming. He therefore suggests that the ship should have been more sturdily built to allow for a greater overall length and so a longer *interscalmium*, or that Hale's (1996) suggestion that a sliding stroke was employed in antiquity should be adopted. Sleeswyk postulates that the evidence from the

Zea shipsheds would have allowed the reconstruction to be longer than 40 m, that later evidence suggests that a U-shaped hull would have been more appropriate, and that the hull itself should have been more strongly built to withstand ramming. He also argues that it would have been more effective for the *hypozoma* to be an undergirding rather than a hogging truss (see further Sleeswyk's paper below, pp. 207–12), and that for functional reasons the ship should have a higher gangway. Sleeswyk's conception of a trireme thus differs considerably from *Olympias* in detail, if not in its general layout.

The trireme proposed, however, by **Alec Tilley** (pp. 121–32), an experienced sailor and former naval officer, differs from *Olympias* in almost every respect. This is a design based on the Siren Vase in the British Museum, which depicts the ship of Odysseus. The design has been developed in several previous papers by Tilley (1970; 1971; 1973; 1976; 1992; 1997), and in detail in a monograph (2004). Tilley rejects the idea that the Lenormant relief shows a three-level ship, or that ancient depictions which do show three-level ships portrayed triremes. He argues that the three types of trireme rowers – thranites, zygians and thalamians – mentioned in the literary and epigraphic evidence represent different ranks or positions within different parts of the ship. He also believes that the hold of *Olympias* was too large to conform with the evidence of Herodotus 8.118, that there should not have been a central gangway, and that *Olympias* in general was much heavier and higher than is implied by the ancient evidence. Instead, Tilley sees the trireme as a development of a single-level pentekontor, with 30 benches and with three men to a bench, each with his own oar. His proposed arrangement is what he believes to be shown on the Siren Vase: two men on each bench rowing their oars on one side of the ship and the other man rowing his on the opposite side, with the pairs rowing to one side alternating along the ship. Tilley supports his individual arguments in a series of Appendices (including a response to Papalas' criticisms, pp. 104–7) following the main paper.

Part 4. The operation and performance of ancient triremes

The next part of the volume deals with the practicalities of the performance and operation of ancient triremes, and what the ancient evidence tells us about these aspects. It begins with a paper by **John Coates** (pp. 134–41) in which he discusses the requirements for slipping and launching both from shipsheds and from open beaches; the paper was originally written in response to a proposal to reconstruct a shipshed in the Piraeus. Coates explains the need for lateral support from the shed structure (fitted with softwood rubbing-pads) as the ship moves from land to sea and vice versa; how the ship could have been moved (on its keel and without the use of a cradle) by hauling teams stationed within the shed along either side of the groundway using ropes (probably discarded

hypozomata) looped round the ram; and how there would be no need for the slipway to extend into the water, but that a wooden guide would have been required to funnel the stern onto the centre-line of the groundway as it came out of the water. On a beach, a channel would probably have to be dug out to reduce the gradient from a typical 1:5 to something around 1:10 (although such a reduced slope could also have been obtained by hauling out at an oblique angle to the shore); wooden sleepers would then have to be laid down as a groundway, together with bolsters to guide the keel; and lateral support would have to be provided by 'walking shores' (*parastatai*); once ashore, the ship could have been kept upright by supporting it with piles of stones, as described by Homer.

Olympias' sailing master in 1992 and 1994, **Douglas Lindsay** (pp. 142–4), looks at the operation and performance of the ship, mainly under sail. He discusses 'combined sailing', *i.e.* rowing and sailing simultaneously. Running before the wind, in light breezes combined sailing is less effective than rowing alone, while at the other end of the spectrum in stronger winds it becomes impossible once boat speed reaches around 7 knots. Close-hauled, it might be useful at boat speeds of as little as 1 knot, but not at over 5 knots. Under sail alone, the highest speed recorded for *Olympias* is 10.8 knots sailing downwind, and Lindsay estimates that 12 knots should easily be attainable. *Olympias* ghosts well, but suffered from extreme weather-helm when close-hauled. She also sailed well downwind with just the boat-sail, and rode well into or before short waves, but was subject to significant wind-drag. Under oar, in difficult conditions, crew endurance proved to be better than might be expected even without extensive training.

The next three papers offer interpretations of some of the key ancient evidence for the cruising speed of ancient triremes. **Boris Rankov** (pp. 145–51) discusses the only voyage from the ancient world for which both time taken and distance can be established within narrow parameters. Although the voyage in question, undertaken by the Roman consul L. Aemilius Paullus in 168 BC, is reported by the Roman historian Livy, it can be shown beyond reasonable doubt that he is translating directly from the Greek historian Polybius, who knew Paullus personally. Livy quotes a speech of Paullus in which he claimed to have left Brundisium (Brindisi) with his fleet as the sun rose and to have arrived at Corcyra (Corfu) at the ninth hour of the day. From the rest of the speech, we can ascertain that the voyage took place 25 or 26 days before Paullus won the battle of Pydna, which is known to have taken place the day after a lunar eclipse. That establishes the day of the crossing as 28th or 29th May in the modern calendar, and thus the length of the day in question locally as 14 hours 23 minutes. Since the Romans divided the daylight into 12 equal hours which varied according to the time of year, the ninth hour can be calculated as falling between 9 hours 54–56 minutes and 10 hours 42–44 minutes after sunrise. The voyage itself was almost certainly under oar and can only have been either 92, 104 or 117 miles long, depending upon which of the three possible landfalls Paullus chose. Taking the middle landfall as being the most likely and allowing for local winds and currents, the average speed through the water of Paullus' fleet will have been between 6¼ and 7¾ knots, and most probably somewhere in the middle at around 7 knots. Since Paullus' fleet will have consisted of quinqueremes, this implies a slightly faster cruising speed for triremes of around 7½ knots, the same as Shaw's figure, p. 67, based on Xenophon's Byzantium to Heraclea run.

The historian **Herman Wallinga** (pp. 152–4), however, argues for a much lower figure than that based on the Xenophon passage. He believes that Xenophon was happy to minimise the sailing time from Byzantium to Heraclea in order to stress the closeness to those two Greek cities of Kalpes Limen, which lay between them and where Xenophon hoped to found a Greek colony. Wallinga suggests that this is what is likely to have provoked one ancient reader to add the word *mala* ('very') to the phrase 'long day's voyage' in the margin of his copy, from which it passed to some of the manuscripts which have survived. Wallinga therefore discounts the validity of Xenophon's testimony, and prefers instead to accept a figure of between 5.25 and 5.53 knots implied by Thucydides (8.101) in his account of Mindaros' voyage of 95 sea miles from Arginusae to the Dardanelles in 17 to 18 hours in 405 BC.

Another historian, **Ian Whitehead** (pp. 155–60), who acted as Chief Recorder in *Olympias* during the 1987 and 1988 sea trials takes a different approach. He argues that Xenophon's Byzantium to Heraclea voyage would most likely need to be undertaken under both oar and sail, and cannot therefore be used to calculate cruising speed under oar. He also denies that Xenophon's account (*Hell.* 6.2.11–14; 6.2.27–32) of Iphicrates' voyage round the Peloponnese in 373 BC can be used show that voyaging under oar was necessarily faster than voyaging under sail. Instead, he suggests that it was normal for ancient crews to row in contrary or light favourable winds and to sail the rest of the time. It may also have been normal to row in shifts, one level at a time, or even to allow the whole crew to take breaks, while ships in flight normally did so under their boat-sail. From all this, he concludes that the fastest voyages were made under a combination of oar and sail according to changing conditions.

The last two papers in this part of the volume look at some physiological aspects of trireme performance under oar. **John Coates** (pp. 161–4) considers the power output required to match the performance figures implied by Thucydides (3.49) for the dash from Athens to Mytilene in 427 BC and by Xenophon (*Anabasis* 6.4.2) for a 'long day's' voyage, interpreted as 20 hours, of 129 sea miles from Byzantium to Heraclea in the Black Sea in the early fourth century BC, *i.e.* at an average of 6.45 knots. Coates bases his calculations on a rowing efficiency in *Olympias* of 53–55%, as calculated by Timothy Shaw, and a thermal efficiency for the human body as a heat engine of 22–25%. He also draws on figures for sustainable gross

power from a human engine published by Monod (1981), MacFarlane (1981, derived from a study of sugar-cane cutters in Queensland), and Nadel and Bussolari (1988, from measurements taken during the Daedalus project, a four-hour, 119-km man-powered flight from Crete to Santorini). From all these, Coates concludes that intensive training would have enabled a crew to sustain speeds over a period of four hours which were 1.5 times those sustained by untrained crews. The most efficient cycle physiologically would be for the crew to row in shifts of four hours at the oar followed by two hours of rest. Finally, he calculates that a modern untrained crew, rowing in shifts 2/3 on 1/3 off, would have to maintain a cruising speed of 4.5 knots in *Olympias* for their performance to match the speeds implied by Thucydides and Xenophon; in a Mark IIb trireme, they would have to maintain 5.1 knots; in *Olympias*, a trained crew would have to maintain 6.0 knots. The thrust of the paper is thus the need for a Mark IIb oarsystem of greater efficiency than *Olympias*, and for a fully trained and extremely fit crew to row it, if the 6.45 knot average implied by Thucydides and Xenophon are actually to be achieved.

The paper by exercise physiologists **Harry Rossiter** and **Brian Whipp** (pp. 165–8) seeks, like that of Coates to investigate trireme performance under oar from a physiological angle, an approach they refer to as paleo-bioenergetics. They adopt a more severe interpretation than Coates of the sustained cruising speed implied by the ancient sources as being 7.2 knots, and assume that the whole crew would be rowing throughout, rather than in shifts. Also unlike Coates, who considers mainly comparative evidence for human power outputs, they focus on human energy requirements for long-duration rowing: the latter has to be carried out at a rate which does not exhaust muscle glycogen if performance is not to drop off severely. Their calculations suggest that this rate would have been in the region of 80 w per man, whereas *Olympias* (as opposed to a Mark IIb trireme) would require a sustained output of around 115 w per man to cruise at 7.2 knots; of this 115 w, however, only some 62 w would be utilised for actual propulsion, the remaining 53 w being lost through mechanical inefficiencies in the oar-system. It is noted, moreover, that the ability to sustain even 80 w per man would be affected by factors such as diet, heat, fluid intake, the fixed-seat oar-rig, and the physical stature of the rowers. Rossiter and Whipp therefore conclude that the mechanical efficiency of *Olympias'* oar system would have to be significantly improved in a Mark II trireme to achieve a sustainable cruising speed of 7.2 knots, even with the whole crew rowing. This would be difficult, though not impossible, to attain, but would require a crew of outstanding fitness. Their conclusions, based on a slightly different interpretation of the ancient sources and on more recent and different types of physiological studies, are thus nevertheless broadly in line with those of Coates.

Part 5. Aspects of trireme construction and maintenance

This part of the volume begins with the first English translation of a paper by marine archaeologist **Ronald Bockius** (pp. 170–81), which was presented at the Henley/Oxford conference and subsequently published in German (Bockius 2000). Bockius presents the comparative evidence for the *interscalmium*, the distance between thole-pins, in surviving Roman oared shipwrecks. The latter in *Olympias* was based on the implication in a passage of the Roman architect Vitruvius (*De Architectura* 1.2.4) that the distance was normally two cubits, interpreted by Morrison and Coates as being 2 × 0.444 = 0.888 m, *i.e. c.* 89 cms; the ship's sea trials, however, suggested that this was too restrictive of stroke-length to allow optimal performance to be achieved, which has led to a proposed *interscalmium* for Mark II of 0.98m/98 cms based on the cubit shown on the Salamis relief (Shaw, above pp. 76–81; Coates, above, pp. 82–91). The *interscalmia* of one of the late-Roman military shipwrecks found at Mainz (wreck 4) fall within the range of 84 to 92 cms, and of another (wreck 1) within the range of 95 to 96 cms. The *interscalmia* of one of the two military vessels dating from *c.* 100 AD found at Oberstimm in Bavaria (wreck 1) vary between 95 and 99 cm, and in the other (wreck 2) between 94 and 96 cms. Other Roman wrecks from Vechten in the Netherlands, Yverdon in Switzerland and Herculaneum provide figures of between 92 and 112.5 cms, but none of these vessels is thought to be military. Bockius' overall conclusion is that the Roman evidence suggests that there was no absolute standard for the length of the *interscalmium* in oared vessels, and that ancient shipwrights did not necessarily seek to optimise speed by using *interscalmia* longer than those in *Olympias*.

John Coates (pp. 182–4) next considers why ancient warships are known to have regularly 'dried out'. He concludes that while bilge-water and absorption of water by the wooden hull would not have had a significant affect on a ship's speed, it would have reduced her acceleration and agility, the extent of which would be best tested by experiment. He calculates that, in a ship which required drying-out, bilge-water up to the tops of the floors would have been the maximum tolerable before bailing because of the likelihood of straining and damaging the hull, although the sinking effect of this water would counter any loss of stability. It would therefore be practicable and safe to carry out an experiment on the effects of this amount of bilge water on agility in *Olympias* or any similar reconstruction.

In two separate papers, **Paul Lipke** considers the causes of leakage and hull deterioration in ancient triremes. In the first paper, with contributions by **John Coates** (pp. 185–202), he attributes these problems partly to the crushing and slippage of adjacent planks in their hulls, the result of the tendency of long, narrow ships to 'hog' and of tenons being insufficiently tight within their mortises.

These, Lipke suggests, would have limited the practical life of a trireme to between 8 and 14 years. Tightness of tenons would have been affected by the moisture content of planks and tenons during construction, with the tenons needing to be fitted dry so that they would not shrink further after completion. Nevertheless, varying climatic conditions and the cycles of immersion and drying out would inevitably have caused gaps to develop between tenons and their mortises, which would in turn have led to plank-slippage and leakage. Lipke also considers the importance of matching tenons and mortise strength to resist shear forces but notes that crushing of the tenons, and therefore hogging and leakage, were inevitable. The swelling of adjacent planks though initial immersion in water would also have led to their crushing each other through 'compression set', leading to leakage when they were re-immersed after drying; the same problem would have affected tenons within their mortises. This problem would have been worst in the intermediate zone between the underwater planking and the completely dry planking high above the waterline, which is also the zone of the neutral axis of *Olympias* which is subject to the greatest shear forces. Most of the damage would be done within 24–48 hours of relaunch after drying out. Measurements of *Olympias* show that by 1992 she had hogged differentially by 9 cm on the starboard side and 13 cm on the port, *i.e.* that she had twisted. Lipke suggests that these problems might be mitigated by cutting tenons so that their radial planes would be oriented fore-and-aft, as in the Marsala wreck, and by making tenons and planking thicker around the oarports. He nevertheless concludes that more research into the mortise-and-tenon dynamics in shipbuilding is required.

Paul Lipke's second paper (pp. 203–6) investigates the damage caused to wooden hulls by shipworm (*teredo navalis*) and, in contrast to Coates, identifies this as the primary reason for the hauling ashore and drying out of triremes. Ancient galleys of mortise-and-tenon construction would have been particularly susceptible to shipworm, and could have been rendered unseaworthy within a couple of months of an infestation. The only remedy would have been to replace the planking affected. Regular hauling-out would kill off the larvae, but the longer the ship had been in the water, the longer it would have to be dried out – possibly weeks – for this to be effective. Lipke suggests that shipworms were the most likely cause of the leakiness of Nicias' ships at Syracuse in 414/13 BC (Thucydides 7.12.3), and goes as far as to suggest that they were the trireme's greatest weakness. Again, he advocates further research into their impact (on test-sections rather than on *Olympias*!).

This part of the volume concludes with a paper by **André Sleeswyk** (pp. 207–12) on the wooden *cordone* and *contracordone* fitted longitudinally around 17th-century Genoese galleys. These timbers were fitted under tension and compression respectively, so as to prevent the shell from separating from the frames, as a form of permanent frapping. Sleeswyk derives the ancestry of these devices from the *hypozoma* fitted to ancient triremes, which he does not believe acted as an internal hogging truss (contra Morrison, Coates and Rankov 2000, 196), as in *Olympias*, but was a rope fitted longitudinally under tension outside the hull, counterbalanced by an internal wooden *contracodone* under compression. The external rope would have to be supported by passing it at 90° through the hull and the *contracordone* at the bow and stern on opposite sides, and then tensioned within the hull at both places as, Sleeswyk suggests, is described by Apollonius Rhodius (*Argonautica* 1.367–9) and implied by an Athenian inscription (*IG* 1² 73).

Part 6. Recent research

The final part of the volume consists of three papers presenting new research carried out since the 1998 conference. Two of these of papers, by Oldfield and Taylor arise out of an (unsuccessful) 2006 research-grant application to the Arts and Humanities Research Council of the United Kingdom to investigate ancient naval warfare utilising the data produced by the *Olympias* project. The other paper, by Rankov, reflects some of the results of another research project arising out of the *Olympias* project, on *Shipsheds of the Ancient Mediterranean*. This project was funded by the Leverhulme Trust, whose generous support is here gratefully acknowledged, and will eventually be published in full by Cambridge University Press; the paper presented here was originally delivered to the *Tropis X* conference organised by the Hellenic Institute for the Preservation of Nautical Tradition on Hydra, Greece from 27 August to 2 September, 2008, and the editor is grateful to Mr Harry Tzalas for granting his permission to publish a revised version here.

The paper by **Robin Oldfield** (pp. 214–24) is based on his 2007 MSc thesis in the Department of Mechanical Engineering at University College, London, supervised by Professor Simon Rusling. He analyses and models the likely effects of ramming collisions between triremes of similar construction to *Olympias* with the type of performance projected for Coates' modified design (see above). The viable collision headings for an attacking trireme to cripple an opponent without itself becoming stuck are thus established and are found to be limited and relatively narrow, and it is shown that, travelling flat out, a pursuing trireme required a speed advantage of as little as 0.50 knots to be successful. The greater the speed differential, the wider the arcs of successful collision headings, but the greater the absolute speed of the two ships, the greater the deceleration caused to the attacker, with possible adverse effects for its oarcrew.

Boris Rankov's paper (pp. 225–30) notes that the shipsheds excavated by Dragatses and Dörpfeld in 1885, which formed a major basis for the dimensions of the *Olympias* reconstruction were divided by alternating colonnades with intercolumnar spacings of 2.16 m and

3.38–3.39 m respectively. The ratio between these facings is exactly 7:11, which suggests that these sheds were laid out utilising a foot-module of 0.308 m, a variant of a foot-module which has been recognised elsewhere (*e.g.* in the Parthenon) and is known as a 'common foot'. This evidence of modular construction raises the possibility that the sheds were built to take warships which, as has already been suspected, were also built modularly. Rankov argues that the sheds appear to have been laid out to house vessels with an overall breadth of 18 'common' feet (5.544 m) and a breadth:length ratio of 1:7, and which were thus 126 'common' feet (38.8 m) long. This would be 2 m longer than *Olympias* but 0.8 m shorter than the proposed Mark II trireme based on dimensions taken from the Salamis relief (see pp. 76–91); this would not prevent the adoption of the canted or skewed oar-rig proposed for Mark IIb, and might even be a very marginally faster design because of the reduced hull-length.

Finally, **Andrew Taylor** (pp. 231–43) derives the typical acceleration, deceleration and manoeuvring characteristics of a fast, Mark IIb trireme from the mass of data produced by the five sets of *Olympias* trials. He then uses these characteristics and war-gaming techniques to model a series of battle manoeuvres by individual ships and squadrons. These reveal, amongst other things, that an individual ship could come as close as 180 m to another individual ship, or 250 m to a whole line of ships abreast, and still back or turn away without danger of being caught; that triremes could safely circle only 60 m out from a stationary defensive *kuklos*; and that a gap in a line of ships only 150 m long was sufficient to allow an enemy to carry out a successful *diekplous*. This then allows him to develop a tactical paradigm for how a fast fleet might attempt to break up a slow fleet in defensive formation.

Taylor's paper thus provides an example of how the data from *Olympias* could be used in future to model a whole range of trireme tactics, both manually and with the aid of computers. If this volume as a whole provides a stimulus to further research into ancient oared ships and seafaring, then it will have served its purpose. As it went to press, we sadly learned of the death of John Coates on 10th July, 2010 at the age of 88, and it is dedicated to his memory and that of John Morrison.

Bibliography

Basch, L. (1987) Review article on *The Greek Trireme of the Fifth Century BC: discussion of a projected reconstruction* edited by John Coates and Seàn McGrail, and *The Athenian Trireme: the history and reconstruction of an ancient Greek warship* by J. S. Morrison and J. F. Coates. *The Mariner's Mirror* 73.1, 93–105.

Basch, L. (1988) The Eleusis Museum trireme and the Greek trireme. *The Mariner's Mirror* 74.2, 163–197.

Basch, L. (1990) La galère de l'Antiquité. In *Quand voguaient les galères*. Paris, 22–23.

Bockius, R. (2000) Gleichmaß oder Vielfalt? Zum *interscalmium* bei Vitruv (*De architectura* I 2,21 f.). In

Studia Antiquaria. Festschrift für Niels Bantelmann zum 60. Geburtstag. Universitätsforschungen zur prähistorischen Archäologie. Institut für Vor- und Frühgeschichte der Universität Mainz. Bd 63. Bonn, R. Habelt.

Coates, J. F., Platis, S. K. and Shaw, J. T. (eds) (1990) *The Trireme Trials 1988. Report on the Anglo-Hellenic Sea Trials of* Olympias. Oxford, Oxbow Books.

Hale, J. R. (1996) The Lost Technology of Ancient Greek Rowing. *Scientific American* 274, 66–71.

Macfarlane, W. V. (1981) Vie et travail dans les climats chauds. In Scerrer *et al.* 1981, 265–289.

McGrail, S. (1992) Replicas, reconstructions and floating hypotheses. *International Journal of Nautical Archaeology* 21, 353–5.

Monod, H. (1981) Défense énergétique chez l'homme. In Scherrer *et al.* 1981, 107–138

Morrison, J. S. and Coates, J. F. (eds) (1989) *An Athenian Trireme Reconstructed. The British Sea Trials of* Olympias*, 1987.* BAR International Series 486. Oxford, Archaeopress.

Morrison, J. S., Coates, J. F., and Rankov, N. B. (2000) *The Athenian Trireme. The History and Reconstruction of an Ancient Greek Warship.* 2nd ed. Cambridge, Cambridge University Press.

Nadel, E. R. and Bussolari, S. R. (1988) The Daedalus Project: Physiological Problems and Solutions. *American Scientist* (July–August), 351–360.

Scherrer, J. *et al.* (1981) *Précis de physiologie du travail, notions d'ergonomie.* 2nd ed. Paris, Masson et Cie.

Shaw, J. T. (ed.) (1993) *The Trireme Project. Operational Experience 1987–90. Lessons Learnt.* Oxford, Oxbow Books

Shaw, J. T. (1994) *The 1994 Trireme Trials. Research Results and Discussion.* Watlington.

Tilley, A. F. (1970) The ship of Odysseus. *Antiquity* 44, 100–104.

Tilley, A. F. (1971) 'An experiment under oars', *Antiquity* 45, plates 10 and 11.

Tilley, A. F. and Fenwick, V. H. (1973) Rowing in the ancient Mediterranean: a new aspect. *The Mariner's Mirror* 59, 96–9.

Tilley, A. F. (1976) Rowing the trireme – a practical experiment in seamanship. *The Mariner's Mirror* 62.4, 357–369.

Tilley, A. F. (1992) Three men to a room – a completely different trireme. *Antiquity* 66, 599–610.

Tilley, A. F. (1997) Ancient warships – a scientific approach. In Cogar, W. B. (ed.), *New Interpretations in Naval History: selected papers from the Twelfth Naval History Symposium.* Annapolis MD, Naval Institute Press, 1ff.

Tilley, A. F. (2004) *Seafaring in the Ancient Mediterranean. New Thoughts on Triremes and Other Ancient Ships.* BAR International Series 1268. Oxford, Archaeopress.

Part 1

The 1992 and 1994 Sea Trials and Other Excursions

1. *Olympias* 1992 Trials Report

Edited by Paul Lipke

Acknowledgements

Paul Lipke

My thanks go to the Hellenic Navy, the entire *Olympias* trials staff and crew, and particularly to Ben Brungraber, Denis Chagnon, John Coates, Ben Fuller Jr., John Howarth, John Morrison, Seán McGrail, and Ford Weiskittel for their expert advice and support.

Perhaps the most important 'Lesson Learned' in the course of the Trireme Project is that such a huge project only moves forward on the patience, determination and support of the families of the participants. It would be impossible to count their hours of clerical and logistical support, waiting, heat prostration and the many meals they lovingly prepared, and that then grew cold while they waited for their trireme-addicted relative. They did all this with the utmost good nature, in support of obscure historical research and their loved ones having a great deal of fun.

Thus the author has special debts of gratitude to pay to Jane Coates, Mary Morrison, Kati Rankov, Ann Roberts, Nan Shaw, Harriot, Elisabeth and Charlotte Weiskittel, and the mostly-unknown-but-very-appreciated families of the rowers with whom I've been honoured to work.

These chapters are dedicated to my wife Marcelle Lipke, in deep appreciation of her constant good humour and support through 24 years (and counting) of my fascination with the trireme project.

1.1. Introduction: salvaging value from a failed effort to publish a 1992 *Olympias* sea trials report

Paul Lipke and Ford Weiskittel

Nearly two decades ago, we were asked to write and edit the 1992 *Olympias* sea trials report. This remains unfinished due to various complications, other obligations (such as earning a living), and an overly ambitious outline for the work. The envisioned publication was to be written to be valuable to both specialist and non-specialist audiences, and include new data and perspectives in a number of areas.

One advantage of having developed such an expansive outline is that it offers insights into new areas of study. Therefore, in order to advance any future sea trials, historical research, and publications, and to inform readers of some broad concepts worth consideration, below are brief descriptions of the major areas that were to be included in the 1992 report. Some of these topics are considered briefly in the context of other chapters within the publication you have before you.

I. 1992 Aims and performance on the water:

a) Ship position and speed measurements: quality of data from the ship's log and the global positioning system

b) Details of rowing performance in daily outings: Minute-by-minute logs, highlights, including 1 hour of firm, longest row, fastest speed, turning, rowing astern, *etc.*

c) Details of rowing performance on voyage to Corinth and Salamina: route, wind, duration of rows, speed made good, sailing performance

d) Performance comparison with other trials: from sprints to voyages, addressing speed, power and pacing, including tables of adjusted data for earlier trials

e) Operation with partial crews

II. The thesis that *Olympias'* previously published performance data warrants even further caveats than those presented in the Log Summary (see Chapter 1.2: Some Results of Olympias' 1992 trials), due primarily to lack of data and errors in performance of the measuring equipment. This makes suspect any interpretations and debates about *Olympias'* viability *based largely on her top speed*. There are many other, far more valid, reasons to value *Olympias*, her performance and the entire project.

III. Brief commentaries by veteran naval architects and shipwrights who have worked on other historic vessels, replicas and reconstructions. We wanted their insights on how much *Olympias* design 'pushes the envelope' in terms of strength, safety, and hull durability. This proposed chapter was in no way intended to call into question John Coates' extraordinary work designing *Olympias*. Rather we sought to provide non-specialists with a relative sense of how extreme *Olympias* is from an engineering point of view, and how far and in what ways more or less conservative safety and performance standards might affect the design. Could a 'more risky' ship gain materially better performance, and in what parts of the ship might the most effective risks be taken?

a) Useful questions for evaluating the design of any trireme reconstruction in the context of what we have learned.
b) Ship construction and repair:
    i)   Daily maintenance needs of triremes: frequency of repairs, the tools and materials likely carried on board
    ii) Possible battle preparations and likely repair strategies

IV. The evolution of our understanding of the optimum trireme stroke, 'How to row *Olympias*', and how the latter might differ from rowing in a trireme where stroke length is completely unrestricted.

V. The human engine:

a) Rower physiques and the necessary *interscalmium* (the 'room' or space required for a fixed-seat rower to pull effectively)
b) Rower physiology:
    i)   The performance of our rowers in comparison to modern athletic performance
    ii) How fit *Olympias'* oarcrews have been
    iii) Using collected volume of oxygen uptake data and pulse monitors to relate the performance of rowers in the ship to their physiological capacity
    iv) Measuring effective power delivered to the ship
    v)   Predicting ship's performance and crew power output on the basis of this data for a given crew size, gender and fitness

VI. Suggested protocols for future trials

1.2. Some results of *Olympias'* 1992 trials and log summary

Paul Lipke, Andrew Ruddle and Ford Weiskittel, with assistance from Charles Hirschler

The principal efforts of the 1992 sea trials were to explore operations with a reduced crew, crew performance during longer voyages/hours at the oar, and to improve the accuracy of our speed and position data using Global Positioning System (GPS) technology.

1.2.1 Reduced numbers of crew and crew performance

The oarcrew in 1992 numbered approximately 154 (out of a possible complement of 170) at the start of the trials,

and reached a low of 121 on August 8, 1992 (the low numbers resulted in part from a late decision to conduct trials, and therefore a late recruiting effort.) Despite the low numbers, the ship and crew performed well. In fact the reduced 1992 crew rowed better and faster more quickly than the full 1990 crew, especially during the first four training days (this period was followed by a physically demanding voyage leading to cumulative fatigue). Since the 1992 crew was no more fit physically than earlier crews, we believe the improved performance reflects continuing advances in training and coaching methods.

A full hour of non-stop, 'firm' rowing showed what a small crew might do under short-term pressure to perform, *i.e.* in battle. A 156 kilometre (112 nautical mile) voyage to Aegina, Corinth, Salamina and return to Poros tested the small crew's stamina, especially during an 11-hour, non-stop row into headwinds reaching 20 knots with higher gusts.

During much of this long day the crew rowed in rotations of 40 minutes on, 20 minutes off, the thalamian seats being occupied by those who were resting. In such a headwind it was very important to maintain the ship's headway (and thereby her heading) while the oarcrew were swapping seats. This was achieved by reducing the time needed to complete a rotation to well under two minutes (sometimes as little as 80 seconds) and/or by keeping the bow or stern rowing while the balance of the crew changed seats and started up again.

1.2.2 Global Positioning System: accuracy of trials data

Researched by Charles Hirschler, written by Paul Lipke

Previous trials relied primarily on a somewhat inaccurate ship's log for speed measurements (Morrison and Coates 1989, 44–5; Coates, Platis and Shaw 1990, 23–4). Measurements by Dutch log (which involves dropping a buoyant object, such as a wooden block, off the ship's bow and counting the seconds needed for the vessel's length to travel past the block.) and timed runs past measured markers on shore were used to develop an adjusting factor which reduced any recorded reading to 89% of the value displayed. It must be said that almost everyone involved lacked confidence in both the log and the adjusting factor. The 1992 results call for further modest adjustments, but overall greatly increased confidence in the data.

In 1992 Global Positioning Systems used signals from 3–7 orbiting satellites to provide highly accurate measurements of position, speed and distance traveled anywhere on the surface of the earth. It must be said here that GPS accuracy claims fuel stiff competition between manufacturers. Furthermore, there are tensions between users, manufacturers and the military because the latter intentionally introduces random error in the signals in the interests of national security. The introduction of error is called 'selective availability' and is measured by the Horizontal Dilution of Precision (HDOP).

The manufacturer of the Trimble Ensign hand-held GPS used in the 1992 trials claims in their literature that under the best conditions it will determine your two-dimensional position on the globe to within 10 metres (vertical position accuracy is not considered here since *Olympias* is always at sea level). When the signals are being degraded, as they have been (until recently) at virtually all times except during the 1990 Gulf War, GPS accuracy is limited to twice this distance, or 20 metres multiplied by the HDOP.

Typical HDOPs during the 1992 trials consisted of:

Lows of 1.4, *i.e.* accuracy was 20 m x 1.4 = 28 m (92 ft)
Highs of around 3.0, *i.e.* = 60 m (198 ft)
For entire outings, the HDOP averaged 2.1, giving an accuracy of 42 m (138 ft).

An average accuracy of ±138 feet of the position displayed seems realistic. Over distances of a few miles or more such an error is small. Over short distances, *i.e.* for a 2000 metre (1.25 mile) row, assuming an error of up to 42 meters (138 feet) seems reasonable and reduces the usefulness of the GPS for establishing distance traveled.

1.2.3 Speed

Speed resolution is ± one unit of the smallest units displayed per second (*i.e.* if the GPS displays 5.1 knots, actual speed could be 5.2 or 5.0 knots). Speed readings are more accurate under 'selective availability' than position readings because the error factor in the satellites' signals changes gradually over time. This means the built-in error factor does not affect the speed readings which are based on changes in relative positions taken within a few tenths of a second of each other. One of the major factors that typically has significant negative impact on GPS speed accuracy, *i.e.* blockage of the signal by buildings, bridges, and mountains is clearly not a problem on the water.

The published maximum speed record of 8.9 knots (Shaw 1993, 43) achieved during the morning outing on 9th August, 1990 deserves some discussion. The figure of 8.9 knots has since been widely published and quoted as *Olympias's* top speed. It should be said however, that this run had an average speed of 8.3 knots (adjusted) for the last half of the run with a single reading of 8.9 knots at the very end of the run (Table 1.2.1).

Clearly the 8.9 knot (corrected) reading was not sustained for any appreciable period, whereas the 8.3 knot adjusted average is solid.

In 1992, we sought to get a better sense of the accuracy

of the 1990 (and earlier) readings. We received some reassurance, but the peak of 8.9 knots remains a little suspect. For example, the GPS consistently displayed 7.8–7.9 knots for a 2-minute speed run with a reduced oarcrew of about 135. This is consistent with an 8.3 knot average achieved with a full crew in 1990.

The next day, with a reduced crew of 121, a brief peak of 8.2 knots was recorded by the GPS. Given this and other runs with a small crew at speeds well above seven knots, the authors believe a brief peak speed of about 8.5 knots and more sustained speeds of 8.3 knots can be claimed for *Olympias* with confidence. Given the previous uncertainty about the accuracy of the ship's log and the correction factors used in 1990, the GPS readings are reassuring.

This lower number is further strengthened by the speeds recorded in 1988 with a laser tracking system called a geodimeter, which showed that a less well-trained crew was capable of producing a burst of 7.9 knots, with most of the acceleration runs producing speeds from 7.3–7.5 knots (Lowry and Squire 1988, 53–60).

1.2.4 Summary of results of the 1992 trials of *Olympias*

Based on Andrew Ruddle's log
Note: The early days of each set of trials have always focused primarily on crew training and adjustment. This means getting the international crew understand the command language and process on board, learning to row in unison with 169 other people, moving rowers around the ship to find levels and triads within which they row and mesh well, *etc.*

Trials day 1: (22/7/92): max speed of 5.8 Nautical Miles/hour (NM/Hr)
Trials day 2: (23/7/92): max speed of 6.0 NM/Hr
Trials day 3: (24/7/92): max speed of 6.9 NM/Hr, distance covered 6.78 NM
Trials day 4: (25/7/92): max speed of 6.3 NM/Hr

Overview of the Voyage
This was four-day voyage totaling 111.85 NM: 67.8 NM rowing, 7.7 NM rowing/sailing, 24.3 NM sailing; 4.73 NM under tow (through the Corinth Canal). Some long passages were made under oar as a bireme, with rowers pulling in shifts of 40 minutes on, 20 minutes off; rotating rowers between active and inactive seats took well under two minutes. See below for more details.

NB: In the following data set, average speeds were

Table 1.2.1

Strokes/minute (SPM):

SPM:	38		41		42		43		44		45		45		44		45		47		46

Knots:	5.8	6.0	5.9	6.2	6.3	6.6	6.9	7.2	7.4	8.0	8.1	8.0	8.1	8.2	8.1	8.1	8.3	8.5	8.6	8.5	8.9

Minutes-seconds (M-S):

M-S:	0.00		0.30		1.00		1.15		1.30

calculated from the time rowing actually started to time rowing stopped. Time waiting for support vessels and other delays are not included.

Trials day 5: Voyage day one (26/7/92):
Poros to Aegina: 15.77 NM in 4 hrs 16 min time overall, an average of 3.7 knots into wind of 10 knots or less.

Trials day 6: Voyage day two (27/7/92):
Aegina to Corinth: 33.06 NM in 11 hrs, 7 min time overall; rowing 28.33 NM in 9 hrs, 38 min into wind (20–50 degrees off starboard bow with the wind speed averaging 20 knots) for an average of 2.9 knots; tow of 4.73 NM through the Corinth canal.

Trials day 7: Voyage day three (28/7/92): rest day

Trials day 8: Voyage day four (29/7/92):
Corinth to Salamina: 30.73 NM in 8 hrs, 55 min overall for an average for the day of 2.3 knots; rowing and row/sail 20.9 NM (18.7 row and 2.2 row/sail) for 8 hrs and 9 min at an average of 2.56 knots into a 15–20 knot wind 0–35 degrees off the starboard bow and seas of up to 0.75 metre.

Trials day 9: Voyage day five (30/7/92): unplanned rest day

Trials day 10: Voyage day six (31/7/92):
Salamina to Poros: 32.29 NM in 6 hrs, 18 min overall, for an average for the day of 5.1 knots; rowing 5.0 NM in 1 hr 55 min for an average of 2.6 knots in a light wind and a 1-metre swell for approximately 2 NM; sailing 3 hrs 44 min over 21.8 NM for an average of 5.8 knots.
Average speed under oar during voyage:
2.94 knots into a 15–20 knot headwind and seas to 1 metre in height.
Average speed under sail during voyage:
5.8 knots in winds of 7–15 knots for about 2 hrs, and then in winds of 15 to 20 knots for almost two hours.

Trials days 11–12: (1–2/8/92): Rest days

Trials day 13: (3/8/92):
One continuous hour of rowing 'firm' at an average of 5.77 knots with a peak of 7.2 knots after 45 minutes; outing maximum of 7.4 knots during 1 min of firm conducted after the hour of firm; hogging measured at 9 cm to starboard and 13 cm to port.

Trials day 14: (4/8/92):
Outing maximum of 6.6 knots in a series of three 10-minute pieces averaging 5.3 knots at rating 34, 6.0 knots at rating 38, 5.5 knots at rating 39.5; max speed in tests of backing down of 5.3 knots with all three levels after turning around in their seats in 10–15 seconds, with rudders held straight.

Trials day 15: (5/8/92) (with 37 empty seats):
Four 'staircases' of 10 strokes at each rating of 38/40/42/44/46/48 (to train the crew for higher ratings) with averages of 6.3, 6.7, 5.8 and 6.7 knots; backing down exercises with maximums of 2.4 knots with conventional rowing astern, and 3.2 knots with the rowers reversed in

their seats; efforts to scull or row the ship sideways were ineffective.

Inconclusive results were also had in an experiment on the effect of unrestricted stroke length by removing thalamians and every other rower in the top two levels. Surplus zygians and thranites stood in the gangway. The results were inconclusive due to sudden wind increases at key times, failure to measure or record any actual increase in stroke length (if any), and lack of data on wind drift of *Olympias* under various wind speeds and directions with which to calculate corrected speeds. It should also be noted that zygian stoke length is further restricted at the catch in some seats by oar shafts hitting the outrigger brackets, even though the latter have been shaved down to reduce the problem in some cases.

Trials day 16: (6/8/92):
Two speed trials of 2 minutes each, first with both rudders down and a maximum of 7.5 knots about an average of 7.4 knots; then with one rudder hauled out and the other half-immersed, which gave a max of 7.9 knots about an average of 7.9 knots. Turning tests of 1 minute 3 seconds for 180 degrees to port, and a turn to starboard at a full knot faster, which was cut short by an emergency stop.

Trials day 17: (7/8/92):
Four outings were cancelled at the discretion of Capt. Mavrikis, due to on-shore wind and very close mooring of an adjacent cargo ship. This raised questions as to our ability to dock safely if wind strength increased to force 6 (39–49 knots) as forecast. The cancelled outings were the morning outing on Thursday, 6th August, both outings on Friday, 7th August, and the morning outing on Saturday, 8th August. The time ashore was spent completing crew testing of percentage of body fat, 1 and 6 minute ergometer tests, and measurement of optimum stroke length.

Trials day 18: (8/8/92) (with 49 empty seats):
A five-minute piece with a peak of 6.3 knots and an average of 5.9 knots; an 8.2 knot peak at the end of a staircase (of ten strokes per step) averaging 7.5 knots. Turning tests showed that turns taken with an entire inside stern section holding water take 5–10 seconds less but produce drops in speed of 2.5 to 2.9 knots, compared to the drop during those taken without the inside stern rowers holding water of 0.5 to 1 knot.

1.2.5 Sample of the full Log

In the interests of providing readers with the maximum detail and some of the flavour of the trials, the 1992 report was originally to include the minute-by-minute record of each outing or day of the voyage. This proved overly ambitious, as it would involve many hours of transcribing handwritten notes. Here is one short outing's notes, to give a taste of the material available.

Outing 1: AM Wednesday 22/7/92
NB: 'easy' means 'stop rowing.'
Summary: very first outing, rowing with different bireme

configurations, and then whole ship; did one 20 minute piece, one 31 minute piece, and one 27 minute piece, sail assisted.

At pier	2 × single stroke, 2 × 5 strokes; wind negligible
08:01	cast off; five strokes (to clear the buoy), then into continuous row; total distance covered 0.91 NM, speed 2.0 knots up to 4.0 knots maximum; easy at 08:21
08:24	thalamians only, speed approximately 2.5 knots; easy at 08:27; total distance covered 1.02 NM
08:34	thalamians and thranites only, speed 3.2 knots after 1 minute, 3.7 knots after 2 minutes, 4.1 knots after 3 minutes; noticeable improvement when crew counting.
08:39	at distance of 1.49 NM, near the channel, moving turn of 180 degrees in 1 minute
08:42	back to speed of 3.7 knots, rating higher; easy at 08:44; rest
08:55	zygians and thalamians, speed 2.9–3.1 knots at 1 minute,
08:59	easy
09:02	same rowers, speed 2.7 knots after 1 minute, 3.5 knots at 3 minutes
09:06	easy
09:12	all levels row on, speed 4.4 knots after 1 minute, 4.8 knots maximum
09:18	turn; wind now approximately 10 knots, near head
09:24	speed 3.9 knots at 12 minutes
09:27	speed 3.4 at 15 minutes,
09:28	1/2 power, 4.2 knots at 16 minutes,
09:31	speed 3.7 at 19 minutes
09:32	easy and rest
09:41	all row on light, speed 3.4 knots at 2 minutes; some wash
09:46	½ power
09:48	20 strokes at ¾ power, maximum speed 4.8 knots, back to 4.3 knots at ½ power
09:51	20 strokes at ¾ power, range of speeds 5.1–5.8 knots, back to ½ power
09:53	at light by the channel, steady at 4.6 knots, 90 degree turn into the channel, wind about 20 knots head
09:59	¾ pressure, speed 4.9 knots, then back to 4.0 knots, and steady at 3.8 knots
10:06	wash; speed then back to 4.3 knots on counting
10:11	turn
10:12	easy
10:14	foresail set
10:20	mainsail set; wind now dropped, no progress by 10:27
10:29	row on light, speed 3.9 knots at 2 minute; large swells through channel; speed 4.4 knots steady
10:44	through strait and start turn; speed up to 5.8 knots on counts, maximum 6 knots
10:46	sails filling, wind astern
10:48	turn ends
10:51	mainsail braced round to starboard
10:54	speed up to 5.8–6.5 knots on counting
10:55	20 strokes firm, speed 5.6–6.6 knots peak
10:56	emergency stop
11:05	rowers back into seats
11:09	row on
11:11	speed 4.0–4.2 knots
11:13	speed 5.2–5.4 knots on counting
11:14	mainsail up
11:16	easy
11:18	thalamian blades in
11:22	paddle on, top 2 levels, speed 2.6, knots peak of 3.2 knots
11:24	easy
11:31	tie up; total distance covered 7.8 NM

Bibliography

Coates, J. S., Platis, S. K. and Shaw, J. T. (1990) *The Trireme Trials 1988. Report on the Anglo Hellenic Sea Trials of* Olympias. Oxford, Oxbow Books.

Lowry, I. J. and Squire. T. M. (1988) *Trireme Olympias Extended Sea Trials, Poros, 1988.* Cardiff, Maritime Dynamics Ltd/Dept. of Maritime Studies, Cardiff University (unpublished)

Morrison, J. S and Coates, J. F. (eds) (1989) *An Athenian Trireme Reconstructed. The British Sea Trials of* Olympias, *1987.* BAR International Series 486. Oxford, Archaeopress.

Shaw, J. T. (ed.) (1993) *The Trireme Project. Operational Experience 1987–90. Lessons Learnt.* Oxbow Monograph 31. Oxford, Oxbow Books.

Trimble "Ensign" equipment literature and personal communication between Charles Hirschler and the manufacturer

1.3. Training, section leading and crew leadership 1990 and 1992 sea trials

Paul Lipke

Previous publications have presented observations of *Olympias'* rowing masters. Here is the perspective of a member of the trial's 'middle management', the six section leaders, each of whom coaches a team of about 28 rowers. This chapter was originally written as an internal document; to give the reader the flavour of the project; only minimal changes have been made for a broader readership.

1.3.1 Crew management, training and control

In examining the experience of the Trireme Project as it relates to crew command and control in classical times, it is essential to bear in mind some important differences between ancient and modern practice. Classical triremes had a petty officer, a *keleustes*, who was in charge of the crew under oar. The *keleustes* was assisted by the bow officer, the *prorates*, and at least at times, by the piper, the *auletes*. By contrast, this project has divided the ancient role of the *keleustes* between a rowing master and six section leaders. As a result, in order to derive from our work any comprehensive picture of the role of the *keleustes* in ancient times, the work of both the rowing masters and section leaders must be considered.

The project has painfully acquired a body of knowledge

which has enabled us to characterize what makes a good *keleustes*. It is probably fair to say the technical knowledge and skills needed to coach in *Olympias* are likely to be very similar to those needed by the *keleustes* of an ancient trireme: rowing terminology, commands and theory, body mechanics, human physical capacity, battle manoeuvres, *etc.*

The crew management skills might be somewhat different due to substantial and unknowable changes in the psychology of individuals and groups between modern volunteer oarsmen and ancient navies under threat of war. Surprisingly, experience as a coach of eight-oared racing shells or individual athletes does not necessarily constitute good training to be a coach in *Olympias*. The former tends toward autocracy, the other shows too much for concern for individual rowers.

For modern volunteer trireme crews, the ideal *keleustes* would probably be:

i) an experienced rower (sliding and fixed seat) with superb timing
ii) a 'servant leader' with acute powers of observation,
iii) have an excellent sense of humour, including laughing at one's self
iv) have multi-cultural training,
v) have a penchant for consensus and
vi) have the willingness to jump into anyone's seat in order to understand what is happening from their point of view.

The rate at which a trireme crew becomes capable of meaningful performance as well as the absolute level of performance reached may be as much a function of the experience of the rowing masters and section leaders as it is the qualities of the crew and the ship. The 1990 and 1992 crews produced statistically identical power, when it was measured collectively by the ship's performance or totaled from ergometer test results of every crew member. Yet with apparent ease, the 1992 crew averaged nearly six knots in their first piece of rowing 'firm' during their very first row in *Olympias*. By comparison, the 1990 crew took three outings and more visible effort to reach this same speed.

Since the ship's condition and the percentage of crew members with previous experience were essentially the same between years (as was power output) the difference can only be explained by the improvements in crew training and leadership. As it happened, the 1992 trials enjoyed unusually strong unanimity of technique and philosophy among the section leaders, rowing and trials management. It was also the first year the Trireme Trust (UK) followed the Trireme Trust USA's example and built a training mock-up for training its portion of the crew.

1.3.2 The training camps

Many publications have discussed the primary importance of oarcrew recruitment and training to the success of classical navies. In particular it is clear that Athenian supremacy at sea was largely the result of constant training (Thucydides 1.142.6–9). Diodorus (13.39.3) says that

in preparation for meeting the Athenian fleet in battle, Mindarus spent five days "carrying out manoeuveres and training his men."

At the instigation of rowing master Ford Weiskittel, beginning in 1988, the Trireme Trust USA began operating training camps for the 90 or so North American rowers the weekend of departure for Greece. In 1990, nearly half the crew had attended such a training camp, in 1992 there were 54 North American participants. These 2–3 day, intensive programs included:

i) fixed seat rowing racing in 30' lifeboats
ii) training in a specially designed and built training mock-up
iii) crew physiological testing
iv) evening briefings with training videos, common meals and team-building exercises.

During the latter, the cooperative, international nature of the enterprise was stressed, as was the need to work within the inevitable personal and national differences in style and commitment. Future training camps should get experienced fixed seat rowers into sliding-seat 4- or 8=oared racing shells in order to reduce their long layback, and improve their timing and finesse.

The training camps have provided insights into crew effectiveness that may be relevant to trireme operations in classical times, and in general stress the importance of shared mental models, rich contextualization and nourishment of a rowing 'culture' to optimizing oarcrew effectiveness. Those insights include:

i) Such structured, intensive programmes enable non-rowers to learn a surprising amount of the basics and greatly accelerate their learning curve. Many training camp veterans have said they would not want to row *Olympias* without having had that preparation. Such a time period might be just as important to classical men from farming or other pursuits who for a variety of reasons might find themselves in oared warships.
ii) Under such a structured setting, the crew begins to form a cohesive whole. In fact, in 1992 while there were only 54 North Americans in the crew, several English rowers remarked that they thought there were more than 100 because of the Americans' and Canadians' skill, unity, and confidence.
iii) We have no record of on-board duties of the classical-age trireme recruiting officer, the *pentekontarchos* ('captain of fifty') (Morrison and Williams 1968, 268), though they are listed as one of those who "save the city." Perhaps their role, in keeping with their recruiting duties and importance, was as a morale officer and a roaming crew trainer and troubleshooter.

1.3.3 Positive lessons learned in 1992

Contrary to previous trials, the rowing masters and section leaders reached consensus in advance as to the basic components of the stroke, and subsequently taught the same stroke throughout the ship. Problems were addressed in debriefings following virtually every outing. Careful observation of crew problems and brainstorming by rowing masters and section leaders helped enormously.

The coaches were generally more active in addressing problems with seating, personality and technique. Most section leaders actively sought to defuse difficult situations, working closely and confidentially in crew assignments. The importance and effectiveness of these efforts in turning any disruptive individuals or those with particular problems in technique into contributing rowers cannot be overstated.

Section leaders and rowing masters can help rowers enormously if they speak in time with the stroke whenever possible, even when giving general information. Numerous voices of encouragement were heard when this was done.

1.3.4 Increasing stroke length

Stroke length averaged 82–85 cm throughout the ship, a vast improvement over averages of 75 to 77 cm the author observed in much of the crew in 1988. Two triads (port 6 and 7) consistently reached 100 cm or more! The author never had the time to measure the equipment at these positions, but believes this large range resulted from fractional differences in oarport size, seat/thole positions and a serendipitous collection of properly sized rowers. These positions might be worth studying in detail in future trials. In many cases triads were prevented from extending their average further not so much by the thalamian beams as by human backs being in the way and/or zygian oars hitting the oarports or outrigger brackets at the catch.

When rowing space was limited by the back of the person immediately sternward, it could often be increased through careful adjustment of the foot stretchers of the three or four rowers immediately towards the stern. The problem could often be traced to a rower sitting in an 'unfamiliar' seat two or three slots down who had not bothered to adjust the stretcher, particularly if this rower was of noticeably different stature than the slot's regular occupant. If the limits of stretcher adjustment were reached, the rower could be told to sit further forward or aft on the seat. Similarly, if a rower was generally too long-legged or deep in the chest for the ship, the 'damage' to stroke length and rowing comfort could be minimized if the slots immediately either side of this person were filled with smaller-than-average rowers.

Many zygian rowers found their stroke limited by their oarshaft hitting the oarport and stretcher rail. The problem is related to where a rower sits relative to his or her 'room.' To date, rowers have been left to sit as they please, with the result that some rowers sit relatively far back, giving themselves more comfort in greater extension at the catch. Others sit farther forward in order to give those behind them more room. The author has not yet had the time to explore where within the 'room' the optimum position is, but suspects there is an optimum location, and that greater consistency throughout the ship might help iron out some stroke length, comfort and power limitations. In

any case the matter deserves attention in any future trials and in the design of Mark II.

1.3.5 Some negative lessons learned in 1992

The section leaders were encouraged to row as much as the seating plan allowed. While this had many benefits, in some cases section leaders virtually joined the ranks of oarsmen without setting up substitute coaches, so that sections were left without effective leadership. This, combined with slack coaching during the long voyages, meant:

i) technique leveled-off *at best* instead of being continually made more consistent and refined
ii) on average, rowers got sloppy;
iii) complaints took longer to be addressed, and morale generally dipped. More than 10 members of various teams complained about 'disappearing' coaches.

Future trials can correct this and increase the number of people with experience of coaching in *Olympias* by assigning assistant section leaders. In the smaller port and starboard sections forward of the boatmast, one coach and an assistant are probably all that are needed to cover both sides after the first week. The extra section leader and assistant could then move aft to help other sections.

The workload on the rowing masters (and the possibility of having to try and run a set of trials without an experienced rowing master) should be reduced by having more people trained in this position. It is a significant failing that to my knowledge the experienced rowing masters have not written up in detail the process and techniques used to 'master' the ship. From observation and their vociferous comments, it is apparent there is a lot to this process!

The author considers it remarkable (and does not wish to push the odds) that the project has had so few injuries to date, especially given that rowers are not required to stretch and warm up properly before each outing. There should be organized stretching sessions before each outing. The Chief Medical Officer should probably not have regular rowing duties (though some who have filled that slot would doubtless refuse to participate in the trials at all if this were enforced), and should double as a safety officer.

1.3.6 Minimizing delays

Section leaders and their teams need to learn to be flexible in rowing with some triads out of action, even temporarily. Valuable time was wasted with the entire ship waiting for one or two rowers with equipment or other delays.

In many cases, the triads in the immediate vicinity of the problem can wait or row short 'air shots' (*i.e.* going through the motions of rowing a very short stroke with the blade in the air so as to maintain pacing and keep the torso out of the way of the next rower towards the bow) until the problem is solved, then fall in and complete the piece. Section leaders need to have a sense of how long repairs, *etc.* should take if they are to make spot decisions.

Rather than have only "ready" or "not ready" as possible responses to the command query, "Are you ready?" (to start rowing), a third option such as, "two out and ready" (meaning two triads out, but otherwise go ahead) would effectively both reduce the waste and apprise the rowing masters of the situation. It is hard to believe that as a practical matter the classical Athenians would wait for every last seat to be ready when they were rowing day in and day out.

If team leaders managed their own rotations, spares and the filling of empty seats, the rowing masters would not have to stay up late at night handling such details, and the crew management would be more attuned to the particulars of the situation.

For example, two rowers of the same triad fell asleep on the beach one night and came in to the Hellenic Navy base where the training camp was held at 4:55 a.m. (they were neither drunk nor amorously entangled!). They made an effort to get up on time and row hard that same morning, but the rowing masters, not knowing their effort and seeing the hour at which they came on base, rotated this triad out the following day as part of the standard disciplinary procedures. By contrast, two members of another triad spent the entire night drinking, came in at 0700, failed to show up to row that morning, and got off without any discipline what so ever. To say the first pair were angry is an understatement.

1.3.7 Points on section leading

Some section leaders held a quick debriefing with their team after every outing: addressing questions, reviewing progress, hearing complaints/suggestions and generally making themselves available. As a section leader, the author found the comments voiced at these sessions extremely productive and helpful. This author recommends the rowing masters, trials officer *etc.* make a practice of attending these debriefings on a rotating basis; it is a ready source of ideas and observations.

Crew members from teams who did not have leaders following this practice complained on occasion, or addressed section leaders from other parts of the ship asking them to communicate certain points to their section. This particular section leader was then in an awkward position as to whether to talk with the section or transmit the request to the proper section leader. Holding such meetings should be a requirement of all section leaders; if there are no issues to address on a given day, the meeting can be immediately adjourned.

New section leaders should be instructed that it is not always easy to properly interpret what you can see from the gangway, *i.e.* the actions of the oar handles, in a way that always corrects problems with what is happening to the blades in the water. From the gangway, you cannot see the blades in the water. If you climb up on the canopy to observe the blades of a triad that was having difficulty, you disappear and become less accessible to other rowers

in the section. From atop the canopy the section leader cannot see the thalamians or zygians in the triads with the problem, nor can you communicate easily with anyone but a thranite.

The only place a section leader can observe both the blades in the water and all the rowers guiding them is from a crouching position on the outrigger. From this position there is the risk of falling into the forest of moving oar shafts. While in this position, you must also avoid cramping the stroke of any adjacent thranites. Even from such a spot, communication with a zygian or thalamian usually meant relaying instructions through the thranite of the triad. While this author never felt endangered while crouched on the outrigger, it would be wise in Mark II to install a rail or line at the canopy edge which section leaders can use to attached a short safety line and snap ring when they need to be out on the outrigger.

1.3.8 Rowing in the bow

It cannot be emphasized too strongly that the use of the bow as 'the place for poor rowers' is counterproductive. If anything, the bow should have some of the strongest oarsmen. First and foremost, the bow has the only 'clean' water in the ship and therefore has the potential of providing the most power as rated by seat. Rowers from the middle and stern sections (including section leader and one-time rowing master Corny Foster) observed upon moving forward that rowing in the bow was more work. Several said they could apply more power, or the same power through a greater part of the stroke. They perceived the difference as reduced slip and/or reduced tendency of the oar blade to be carried quickly aft (before they could apply power) by the slipstream.

The absence of zygians and/or thalamian beams in the very bow means the first six rowers can have longer, less restricted strokes than any rowers except those in the sternmost positions. Powerful rowers could be very effective in these seats.

The bow is isolated from the stern (*i.e.* command) by distance and the obstructing masts. A rowing master should be aware that what is happening in the stern sections immediately in front of him/her may not be indicative of what is happening (or the effort being made or effectiveness) in the bow. Negative statements and practices serve to further isolate the bow and reduce its effectiveness.

Tests should be conducted to assess the effectiveness of these positions and the applicability of the racing eight 'engine room' theory by swapping sections. Such tests should be conducted before rowers have developed too strong an affinity for a particular seat or part of the ship.

The bow Triad 1 and 2 thalamians were allowed to develop longer strokes and their own rotations. They also had their own emergency escape procedures in the absence of an escape hatch. Bow-triad 1 thalamians had to slowly and carefully climb forward over gear, oar shafts and the *hypozoma* (the ship's steel cable hogging truss) in order to reach the slot at the very end of the gangway. The Triad 3 and Triad 4 port and starboard thalamians taught their zygians to vacate quickly and climbed out (with difficulty) through their slot. Following a swamping (however unlikely) a simple length of pipe or hose with a mouthpiece could save the lives of these rowers.

In general, the foredeck needs to be stronger. It needs to be stronger to handle the impact of crew members handling lines and jumping down to it from the canopy, as often happened. It also needs to be re-designed to give zygians and thalamians more air and elbow room, and if thalamians are still underneath it, should have an escape hatch.

In general the bow thalamians are very short of good air. One actually fell asleep at the oar; maintaining afterwards that it was exhaustion combined with "the inability to get a decent lung-full of air". Karl Anderson (port Triad 1 thalamian) wrote, "Water collects in the ram bilge and begins to stink. This stink, coupled with the fact the 'bathroom' is over your head, becomes almost overpowering at times."

Future trials involving long outings should have a portable toilet, proper bucket with a seat, or other sturdy equipment. Long waits and crowding of the foredeck should be eliminated by the use of a second, stern head with whatever curtaining may be necessary to address the sensitivities of rowers and Hellenic Navy personnel.

Because of the ship's reduced beam in the bow, in the bow-most thalamian positions it is necessary when shipping oars to cross the shafts (rather than sliding them in parallel) and secure the handles close to the exterior of the framing around the opposite *askoma* (the leather sleeve that keeps out seawater). If the grip is positioned within the frame it will push the *askoma* inside out.

During tight power turns the Triad 1 and Triad 2 thalamians on the inside of the turn found it impossible to hold water without crabbing, as the bow tends to be driven under slightly. To quote Karl Anderson again: "My contention is that the first four [thalamian] positions must have good one-minute erg scores. What matters is spirit and strength. You must be able to power out of a crab by yourself. [There is no zygian for these seats and the thranite is too far up to help unless he has very long legs – PL] You must have the strength and ability to wait until one of the other thalamians in the ram can strike their oar and come help you... People 'in the ram' need to like rowing in rough water...you get tossed and turned. When wakes [or swells] approach the ram, the bow-most thranites should track their progress, alerting the thalamians. Before the wake hits, these thalamians shorten their strokes, then sky their blades gently through the return. Then you gradually lengthen out."

In future experiments with tight, fast manoeuvring, the author recommends we experiment with reducing the number of inside rowers holding water to the absolute minimum. Similarly, using the minimum number of rowers *in the stern* to hold water and/or experimenting with having just the outside bow drive the ship around may prove productive.

1.3.9 Miscellaneous

The 1992 voyage was clearly a valuable exercise. But the planned 7 days was too long considering the overall trials period. Even the actual length of 5 days was nearly too much for the crew in light of the overall conditions and the fact that we needed maximum power and productivity for speed trials after the return. In the future, the author believes long day trips or perhaps a voyage of two days and a night could accomplish as much. In any case, the rationale for undertaking the voyage was not consistently applied.

The author believes two outings a day are very effective during the initial trials period (the first week), but after that most days should consist of one longer outing. Such a flexible system would reduce cumulative fatigue, improve crew morale (via more rest) and make higher-level training more effective. Towards the end of the trials period we often had to cut short a good outing when technique and morale were still building in order to "save energy for the afternoon." Given the time it takes to get the crew aboard, fill the empty slots, *etc.*, one outing will impose less 'hurry up and wait' on the crew.

Tightening and adjusting of gear was better than in previous trials, but was still not in keeping with what would most probably have been required in classical times. Future training camps and briefings should include demonstrations and hands-on practice in foot stretcher and thole-strap adjustment, lacing and repairs.

The 1990 repair crew was not aggressively managed initially, as it needs to be, with the result that management had trouble making certain decisions due to lack of information, and maintenance work fell behind. Even when well in hand, the lack of repair crew management in 1990 put an unreasonable burden on two individuals, namely Tony Canavarro and Tom Anderson. It is not enough for the head of the repair crew to undertake work himself, he (or she) needs to orchestrate, communicate and anticipate (this problem was actively corrected in 1992).

Given the considerable challenges we have experienced in communicating with the crew, future trials should attempt to determine how well the ship can operate (after the initial training period) without electronic equipment. A system of whistle signals and ancient Greek commands could be designed and tested, the material being sent out to rowers with their letters of acceptance so they have time to memorize them.

Bibliography

Coates, J. S., Platis, S. K. and Shaw, J. T. (1990) *The Trireme Trials 1988. Report on the Anglo-Hellenic Sea Trials of* Olympias. Oxford, Oxbow Books.

Morrison, J. S and Coates, J. F. (eds) (1989) *An Athenian Trireme Reconstructed. The British Sea Trials of* Olympias, *1987.* BAR International Series 486. Oxford, Archaeopress.

Morrison, J. S. and Willimans, R. T. (1968) *Greek Oared Ships 900—322 B.C.* Cambridge, Cambridge University Press.

Shaw, J. T. (ed.) (1993) *The Trireme Project. Operational Experience 1987–90. Lessons Learnt.* Oxbow Monograph 31. Oxford, Oxbow Books.

1.4. *Olympias* 1992–3 repairs and modifications, with lessons for future reconstructions

John Howarth, Paul Lipke and Meph Wyeth

The development of the trireme and the pentecontor upon which it was based probably took hundreds of years and involved the construction and modification of hundreds of vessels. In each of these 'models,' new ideas could be tested. Furthermore, in aspects other than hull shape, wooden vessels are easily modified, so a single vessel's life typically encompasses various arrangements. Even hull shape can be modified if the need is strong enough. The Trireme Project is attempting to compress the learning curve of ancient shipwrights into a relatively short period of time, and in a single vessel. Because of this, the repair crew is vital not only to the operation of the ship, but to the collection of data and observations relevant to the design and operation of an improved reconstruction.

The repair and modifications crew also feels compelled to point out that *Olympias'* naval architect, John Coates, had the daunting challenge of designing a safe vessel which will not endanger any of the roughly 200 people on board, and whose life span will justify the considerable expense and prestige invested by the Greek government. Furthermore, the Hellenic Navy has to consider the ship's symbolic importance, any long term logistical complications, and the very limited funds available for *Olympias* whenever either of the Trireme Trusts wants to undertake some modification to further test our ideas.

Such a context must unfortunately discourage innovation and radical ideas to some degree. It places a valuable premium on a conservative, safe design, and discourages the sort of design risk-taking that undoubtedly lies behind the success of the triremes of the classical age. We publicly thank John for his unwavering attention to issues of safety and ship longevity.

Starting from the first sea trials in 1987, wear patterns and equipment problems have been one of the main sources of information as to where the design of *Olympias* needs to be modified. As *Olympias* entered her fourth season of sea trials, the passage of time and more ambitious rowing began to uncover defects in the rowing furniture which had not been apparent previously, or had not become problematic.

To get the ship in order during the first week, the repair crew averaged about 18 man-hours a day, each day, not counting oar modifications. Two man-days were spent unlacing the *askomata*, greasing them to get them limber, and then lacing them up again. Other work included making and tying leather thole straps, grommets and thole ropes, installing oars in their proper places, installing the sound system, and fixing furniture. Rowers greased their own oars and leathers, taking just a few seconds as needed during the outings.

Grease is effective only if used in moderation. In their zeal to keep oarstraps well-lubricated, a few rowers applied too much, too often. Consequently, grease sometimes found its way onto places where it did more harm than good, such as oar handles.

Throughout the trials, John Howarth and Meph Wyeth each worked 6–7 hours a day (over and above their rowing) to keep the ship operational and the experiments running. Longer outings, such as those undertaken on the voyage, sometimes required longer repair sessions.

Individual responsibility for the maintenance of rowing equipment was heavily emphasized this year, and contrary to previous experience, we were successful in training many rowers to care for their equipment. One indication of the success was the way foot stretchers were properly adjusted and tightened throughout the ship, sometimes even during rotations of rowers within triads. Rowers learned they could adjust their foot stretcher in less than 60 seconds. Many rowers also learned the best way to get their gear fixed was to show up for repair crew and do it themselves.

1.4.1 Maintenance

John Howarth writes: "I took over the maintenance of *Olympias* because Paul Lipke was overwhelmed with work in the first two days. I was continually engaged in emergency repairs and never got ahead. This meant there was no time to fully examine the ship or do preventative maintenance. This report, therefore, is based on what emergency repairs were undertaken and on general observations. I (Howarth) cannot say whether the initial crew training, voyage or speed trials caused more damage to the ship.

The hull and main timbers received no repair work; they appear to be in excellent condition and there are no obvious problems to anticipate. The only suggested work is the caulking of the seams immediately above the waterline, since the water that came in these dried-out seams when the ship first heeled over under sail in 1992 caused enough concern for the captain to order sail to be substantially reduced.

In 1993, after *Olympias* was freighted to England, three small leaks appeared at the following locations: below port zygian no. 7, below port thalamian no. 10, and below port zygian no. 15, in the fourth plank below the waterline, the latter being the largest leak, but by no means serious. They appeared to come from around the large clench nails, driven through dowels, that hold the planking to the futtock. It is possible that part of the dowel has cracked and come away. If this conjecture proves correct upon inspection after the ship is hauled out, removal of the nail, replacement of the dowel and refastening is straight forward, and does not indicate any serious problems in the hull as a whole.

Douglas Lindsay reported that the sail needed some repair.

The decks, gangway and internal structure are in good condition except for the following:

i)   The storage rack is designed so that downward pressure, from stored equipment and the crew pulling down on it as they move about, pulls the nails out. It was refastened but it needs redesigning. A net would do just as well, would be lighter and less prone to break.

ii) The seats break because people stand on their unsupported edges when climbing to and from the gangway. They are badly designed, and ideally should be completely dismantled in order to repair and replace them. Use of a stronger species, mortise-and-tenon or doweled joints, and additional framing (if it can be added without interfering with the rowing) are three possible improvements.

iii) The zygian stretcher rails tend to split at their stern ends because a) they tend to be stood on more than the stretcher rails of other positions, and b) a weak and unalterable type of joint is used. A beveled notch cut into the zygian beam to hold the stretcher rail's full depth would provide support without relying solely on the weak connection made by the fastening. The easiest, unauthentic reinforcement would appear to be to drill and drive a glued dowel into the stretcher about 2 inches from the end in order to strengthen it across the grain against the frequent downward loading.

iv) This is the first year that significant problems with foot stretchers have appeared. The coaching and training of crews in rowing *Olympias* has finally reached a stage where the process and personnel have become good enough that the rowers are able, within the short period of the sea trials, to learn to apply very substantial leg drive. This stresses the equipment more than has been possible in previous years. Much of the 'breakage' consisted of tired old stretcher ropes breaking, and leather clogs and adjustment pins working loose.

The foot stretcher woodwork displayed some problems, usually because joints worked loose. They were replaced with spares. Extra adjusting holes were drilled in the foot stretcher bar for about six, very short legged thalamians.

The foot stretchers appear to be a very complicated piece of construction, but the author confesses he cannot think of a better one. Since 1987, almost every rower, coach or observer, including John Coates, has tried hard to find simpler, better solution to the problem of where and how rowers feet will be braced. It is difficult to arrange so that the legs of the thranites do not interfere with the loom of the zygian's oar during the stroke, and harder still to find a simple way the stretchers can be adjustable. Of the hundreds of participants, not one has yet claimed to have found an equal, let alone a better solution than that designed for *Olympias*. The only place where some options exist is in the thalamian seats.

v)   The thranite stretcher rails presented one of the two major repair problems on the ship, the other being the oars.

The design of the thranite furniture has to allow for the operation of the zygian oar underneath the thranite stretcher rail. At present the configuration is not strong enough, and the forces have been distributed in such a way that they force joints open, not shut. This is a major weakness and led to the loosening of many of these joints. This can (and did) lead to a domino succession of failures within the thranite file (see below).

The design of the thranite furniture is such that the thrust generated through the feet of the rower is delivered through the stretcher to the crossbar, seat upright and seat (Figs 1.4.1 and 1.4.2). These connections are laid out in such a way that they rely mostly (if not solely) on the strength of the connection between the wood and the copper fastenings, as opposed to relying on wood resisting wood by means of joinery.

More specifically, in Figures 1.4.1 and 1.4.2, the reader can 'see' how thrust is delivered through the rail 'A' into the upper end of the seat upright 'C' (to the right in the figures). These two members are joined by nailing through the seat upright 'C' into the end grain of the stretcher rail 'A.' Nails driven into end grain have very poor holding power and so tend to work loose. Also, since the nails are located near the thin, upper end of the seat upright 'C,' they tend to split the support open. As the joint becomes loose, the problem gets worse.

Thrust is also transmitted to the cross bar 'B,' which is only nailed to the seat upright. The thrust from the rail 'A' tends to drive the seat upright 'C' away from the crossbar, loosening the joint. From the crossbar 'B' the thrust is transmitted to the next stretcher rail 'D.' However, because of the need to leave room for the foot stretcher, stretcher rail 'D' only overlaps cross rail 'B' by a small amount. Thus, the nail securing it is located very near the end of rail 'D,' and is driven downwards and at an angle. It is a very weak connection that cannot resist the force generated by the rowers.

Rowers often generate unequal pressure between the right and left pads of their foot stretcher, and the resulting unequal moments cause the stretcher rail to rotate. [This rotation makes the fastening connecting the end of the rail with the crossbar load *the crossbar* in compression parallel to grain, a direction in which wood is quite strong. *Olympias'* Douglas fir averages 5,850 pounds per square inch (psi) for proportional limit compression strength parallel to grain. By contrast, the twisting of the rail against the fastening loads *the rail* in tension perpendicular to grain, the direction in which wood is weakest (in this case an average of 340. psi for Douglas fir) – PL]. As a result, the rail splits around the nail. This is very difficult to repair.

Lastly, thrust is transmitted to the hull through a weak connection between the raised seat and the gunwale.

The seat configuration cannot transmit all the force from each rower directly to the hull, so that a portion of the force is transmitted through the crossbar to the next stretcher sternwards, and so on down the ship. This domino effect on the seats further aft was clearly demonstrated when the

Figure 1.4.1. Side view of thranite seat and foot gear, showing joinery (Photo: Paul Lipke).

Figure 1.4.2. View of thranite seat and foot gear, looking toward the bow, showing fastenings into end grain and other details (Photo: Paul Lipke).

cross rail of starboard thranite seat no. 5 collapsed and the three seats immediately towards the bow went down with it.

Ideally the joint should have stretcher rail 'A' pushing directly against crossbar 'B' which in turn pushes against stretcher rail 'D.' The seat should then be located directly on top of, and clench fastened to, each member, greatly stiffening the whole thing. This way the joints tend to close themselves and the force is taken more by the wood, not the copper rivets and nails (see Fig. 1.4.3).

Since we cannot reconfigure *Olympias*, a less expensive solution is drawn in Figure 1.4.4.

a) put a dowel protruding down from stretcher rail 'A' to transmit the thrust directly into crossbar 'B' and prevent support 'C' from splitting. This may involve cutting a notch in the foot stretcher.

b) connect crossbar 'B' and stretcher rail 'D' with a dowel to transmit the thrust from 'B' to 'D' (see below)

c) put a block on top of stretcher rail 'D' to stiffen it, either between the seat, the gunwale and the top of 'D,' or onto the stern face of crossbar 'B' and the side of stretcher rail 'D' next to the gunwale. Either of these would be a tricky, time-consuming job with the first being easier if less 'elegant.'

     The ends of each piece are splitting more and more. If they are to survive, they need to be inspected and proper remedial work performed.

vi) By far the worst problem in 1992 was with the oars.

Given that *Olympias* almost always operates with a crew that is largely new to trireme rowing, her oars take a lot of abuse in the first two days or so of each new set of sea trials. This should not obscure the fact that classical triremes would have damaged and broken oars in significant numbers when forced to row during storms, during battles and when training new crews. Even with a seasoned crew, it would be inevitable that rowing long hours each day, as ancient crews did, they would wear oars out.

Thalamian oars are made in one piece and are very strong. Even though the thalamians cannot see their blades, causing their blades to take a lot of abuse, the strength of the design saves them. Apart from minor splits and gouges, thalamian oars are usually either sound or broken beyond repair.

The narrow, 'protective' copper strip around the thalamian blade that was added in recent years has little or no protective effect. In fact, it damages the zygian oars and should be removed. Worse still, a prong of a zygian oar or a second thalamian oar's copper strip can get trapped under one of these strips, bringing the unfortunate rowers involved to a sudden, shocking stop. It can be very difficult to disengage these two oars from on board, and on occasion we have had to climb into the water or the Hellenic Navy's inflatable chase boat to solve the problem.

The 42 main thalamian oars and three spares were modified to increase the gearing (see below). The twelve short thalamian oars positioned in the first three triads at the bow and stern were not modified.

The zygian oars were the hardest hit. The rower cannot see the blades and the design is weak. Zygian blades with tenons through them have been split by the combined radial swelling of the tenon and tangential swelling of the blade. Where they are not split, compression set has loosened some of the tenons in their mortises so that they are starting to fall out. Those blades which are riveted to the shaft without any tenons are in much better shape. As mentioned above, the forks are scuffed and split also by the thalamian copper bands.

Once the oar shaft starts to split towards the handle (from the crotch between the forks) the only answer is to shorten the oar. This converts it to a short zygian blade (of which we now have far too many!). Broken forks are not really repairable, and many blades need renewing. There are many zygian blades with ragged edges and centerline splits, since we were forced to use oars which we rejected in earlier years as being cracked, weakened, *etc.* 34 of the existing 56 zygian blades are damaged.

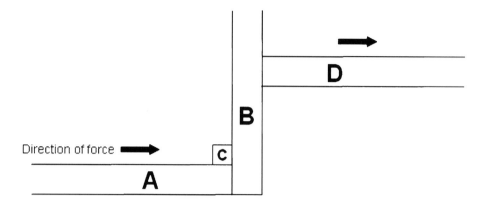

Figure 1.4.3. Suggested stronger layout of stretcher rails and crossbar, viewed from above.

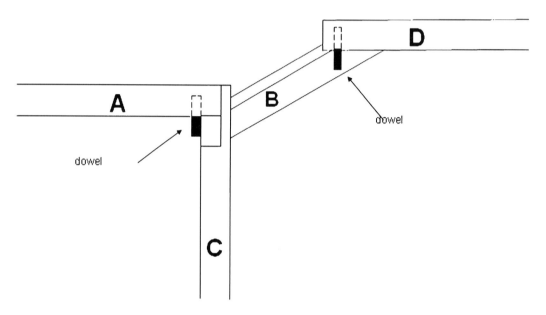

Figure 1.4.4. Proposed use of dowels to stiffen Olympias rowing furniture rails, upright and crossbrace, viewed from inboard.

The ship should have 54 zygian oars, of which the forward six (Triads 1 to 3) are short. However, in practice we found that Triad 4 also required a short oar to prevent the inboard end from catching on the deck support upright at the break in the foredeck. Similar problems appeared with certain rowers in stern Triads 28 and 29.

Thranite oars suffer from the same weaknesses as the zygian blades, except that since the thranites can see what they are doing they are much more able to avoid clashing with others. As a result, they are in much better shape.

All the oars are worn at the thole. This did not appear to contribute to any broken shafts. Broken shafts seem to occur when an oar gets jammed for one reason or another, and then water pressure snaps it. When repaired, these oars are stiffer and do not bend evenly under pressure, so that they simply break at a new weak point.

In the future this author (Howarth) recommends:

a) carrying a full proper set of oars and adequate spares. At the end of 1992 trials the existing oars were so weakened that we were damaging 12–15 oars per outing. If left un-repaired, these oars would have been destroyed.

b) adding sacrificial leather sheath to protect against chafe at the thole and carling.

c) gluing a piece of neoprene (or similar) over the forks to absorb the impact from other blades.

There is no reason, at this point, that replacement oars for *Olympias* should be of the same design as the existing ones, as long as the power characteristics are compatible with the ancient evidence. New oars should be designed assuming we will always have raw crews who will do their share of damage. The more the author (Howarth) thinks about it, the more he realizes an oar is a sophisticated piece of equipment. The author does not have the rowing experience or the technical knowledge to design them,

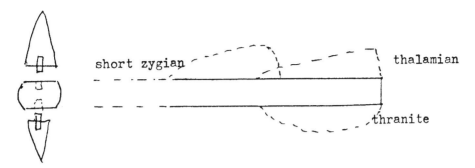

Figure 1.4.5. A proposed standardized shaft with attachable half-blades.

but knows they are a maintenance problem that should be addressed. Here are my thoughts, to be improved upon by someone with the right training and experience:

Design a standard oar shaft which covers all five types of oars, or which can cover them with small modifications, such as moving the pivot point by moving a 'button,' paring down the loom or shortening the shaft. Give the blade end of the shaft flat, parallel sides for the length of all possible blades. Half blades of each type could then be fixed to the shaft with dowels and strong modern adhesives (see Fig. 1.4.5). This design has no forks and is very strong. The blades are thicker at the center than at present because they do not have to fit in between forks. They are therefore stronger, although the whole is slightly heavier.

These oars should be easier and cheaper to make. To repair them you simply saw off the broken blade and attach a new one. There are no metal fittings.

1.4.2 Thalamian oar modifications
by Paul Lipke

In order for the thalamians to contribute more substantially to the ship's progress at high rates of speed, and to equalize their work load relative to other levels, it was necessary to increase the gearing of the thalamian oars and/or increase the blade area. Due to the one-piece design of the thalamian blades, it was not practical with the available resources to increase the load by increasing the blade area. Thus the only alternative was to move the pivot point of the oar closer to the handle. This increase in gearing was highly desirable.

Measurements and photographs taken in 1990 by John Coates showed the thalamian oars were operating 70 mm further inboard than they were designed to do. Their handles were too far inboard because of the shape of the swelling in the oar loom, and the bevel on the carling block supporting the tholepin. John Coates has written in a personal communication:

Timothy [Shaw] and I thought that moving [thalamian oars] 100 mm outboard, *i.e.* 30. mm [further] out

from their originally intended position, would improve thalamian power, observing the relative ease with which those blades slipped in the water, and was a change worth trying.

Once aboard *Olympias* in 1992, the 100 mm movement outboard proved to be impractical. It would have compelled rowers to pull on the oar handle from well off the centreline of the body, and then finish the drive with their *inside* hand cramped against their navel.

Ford Weiskittel, Boris Rankov, Section Leader David Wigg and Paul Lipke each tried to eliminate this cramping and achieve the full 100 mm change by 'rowing through the arc.' This meant rotating the torso to face slightly inboard during the second half of the drive so that at the finish the thalamian's head was actually in the corner formed by the beam and the zygian foot stretcher. It was just possible to do this with limited power application, but we knew it would be impractical to teach in the allotted time, might lead to injuries, and would likely prove impossible for rowers to manage at high power, where the extra length was most important.

By experimenting with different gearings in several thalamian seats, 40 mm was determined to be the maximum possible outboard movement without undue discomfort or risk to the rowers. This gave us just 10 mm movement outboard from John Coates' original design:

Gearing (with blade centre of pressure assumed to be 260 mm from tip):

As designed	2.82
As observed in 1990	2.57
Moved outboard from 1990 position by 40 mm	2.96
If 100 mm outboard movement had been possible	3.11

In the event, the 40 mm change did noticeably increase the work load for the thalamians and tended to increase (very slightly) the clearance between the backs of their hands and the zygian beams. However, this increase in clearance was more than offset by the use of rope thole-straps. The rope was much thicker than the leather that was used in previous years, and so it raised the pivot point and thereby the handle and loom so much that it became necessary to shave off a small portion of the bottom corners of the inboard foot plate and cheek piece for every zygian foot stretcher.

More importantly, the thalamian oar no longer tended to be rolled off square during the recovery because the thick rope thole-strap (sandwiched between the oar shaft and the thalamian carling) created full clearance between the shoulder of the loom and the inboard bevel of the carling block. From the rower's point of view this was a great advantage, far more important than the increase in gearing.

Using only the simplest of hand tools, a thalamian oar modification could be completed in 15–20 minutes, once it was pulled up on deck. In order to have *Olympias* ready to put to sea with all the oars modified, we decided to commandeer part of the oarcrew for a work detail, much as ancient *naupegos* might have done. Modification of all the oars took 84 man hours with 14 people (of uneven woodworking skills) using hand tools and the bandsaws in the Hellenic Navy's two Poros carpentry shops; this figure includes planning, preparation of templates, modification, clean-up, taking oars off the ship and up to the shops, replacing them in the ship with tight *askomata*, *etc.* The short thalamian oars at the ship's ends were not modified, since these rowers were already experiencing slightly restricted strokes due to hitting of the angled (relative to *Olympias'* centerline) oarports at the catch.

The relocation of the thalamian pivot point increased the gearing from 1990 levels by 40 mm, not the 100 mm John Coates had desired. The final result was a pivot point commonly 1050 mm and occasionally 1060 mm outboard of the handle end. This measurement, checked in more than 10 places throughout the ship while rowers were pulling on the oars, held regardless of the configuration of the thole-strap or thole-rope employed.

1.4.3 Oarstraps and grommets

Experiments and difficulties with oarstraps (or thole-straps) have been reported by this project before. In 1992 the effort to solve the problem continued, with experiments using a variety of different configurations made of different types of tanned leather, rawhide and rope.

Quite probably ancient strap-makers had access to a body of leather craft, including such information as preferred animals, seasons and methods of slaughter, types of cuts *etc.*, that we can at best only partly recover. They might also have had the option of inspecting their material at all stages of preparation, from pasture through to tannery. This author [Meph Wyeth] can imagine them laughing to themselves at our bumbling pursuit of what they may have considered to be common knowledge.

An important question I never even thought to ask before is do we know which hide we should be using, *i.e.* sheep, goat, or cow? The project is seeking a tanning/rawhide expert with a kit of different materials (or identical materials with different tanning methods) for further experiments.

Modern athletes do not show much homogeneity of opinion about the relative merits of various materials and configurations of equipment. The classical Athenians may have debated loud and long about the materials, sources, manufacture, *etc.* of their equipment. They may have come up with a number of solutions to the problem of how to attach an oar to a tholepin. The author knows there are any number of ways to lash a Polynesian canoe. All of them will keep it together. Some work better in certain sea conditions, or with certain crews, but they all work.

Leather oarstraps

The 1992 trials continued the use of the single-loop leather straps of previous years on a few oars, and experimented with a double-loop configuration on twelve others. Meph Wyeth recorded dimensions for those we manufactured in 1992 (see Tables 1.4.1 and 1.4.2 below).

As in earlier trials, there were problems with the leather's tendency to stretch. At least when straps were new this necessitated substantial adjustments (*e.g.* removing and retying the strap) as often as once an hour.

To monitor stretch, each strap was measured at manufacture, periodically during the trials, and after the final row. The material used in 1992 varied in thickness from 2.5 to 4 mm, averaging about 3 mm. In previous years, oarstrap leather was about 4 mm thick. Whether this difference affected the straps' tendency to stretch is hard to say. Other factors, such as cut of hide, tanning methods, hide quality, degree of nurture, and the slaughtering methods used on the cows whose hides were exploited may also have promoted stretch. Of the single-loop straps, the longest stretch was l02 mm (from 547 mm to 649 mm), and the shortest 60 mm (from 595 mm to 655 mm). Of the doubles, all of which began life at 685 mm, stretch ranged from 37 mm to 138 mm, averaging about 80 mm.

No pattern for these figures has emerged. Although initially the straps were deployed on both sides, at all three levels, and from bow to stern in an attempt to determine what situations might exert the greatest stress, the results show no consistency. Apparently an individual rower's technique, physical strength *etc.* determine stretch far more than does the disposition of a strap within the ship.

The 'double-half' strap configuration worked well enough for the thalamians, but this may have been due to the difficulty of applying full force to a thalamian oar handle, the reasons for which are discussed elsewhere (see pp. 33–4). The double-half configuration had to be avoided in the upper two levels in order to avoid raising the pivot point and thereby the rowers' hands.

Some crew members found the need for frequent stretch adjustment annoying. Some also reported that the constant stretching made it difficult for them to control their oars. On a positive note, several people found that the leather stabilized after stretching considerably for several days. How well this very distressed material would last once it had reached maximum length is something there was not sufficient time to determine. A longer trial period would be needed before research could address such questions as: if ancient crews used leather straps, how often would they have had to replace them? How many animals of what type would a trireme require for a season's allotment of oarstraps?

Rowers who had double loops said that their oars were continually going off-square. Whether this resulted from stretch, from the dynamics of double loops, or from some combination of the two is hard to determine. On the other hand, the double-half leather strap was preferred by some to the single twist for its ease of installation. Once stretched, leather straps require more time, skill and attention to detail to tighten. Some experienced trireme rowers preferred them, but not all. Some claimed the leather felt more secure and gave better feel or control, others said just the opposite. The strongest rowers generally preferred rope Gallaghers (see below).

Rawhide oarstraps (a.k.a. Oarstraps from Hell)
A verbal communication from Paul Lipke (Athens Airport, 9th August, 1992) assured me [Meph Wyatt] that I was not the first crewperson to have troubles with rawhide. As a student of ancient crafts and cultures, I sometimes enjoy being the vehicle of a tradition; in this case I did not. Either we simply do not have enough understanding of its proper use, the material itself is cursed, or rawhide and *Olympias* are simply not meant for each other.

Of the two model straps received from John Coates of the Trireme Trust, one was softened by soaking it in seawater and placed on the author's oar the night before rowing from Poros to Aegina. Because the rawhide set at an improper angle, the oar having been pulled in for the night, the stiff strap pulled the oar off-square. After one day of rowing the author cut off the strap, the rawhide having become too stiff to slip off over the blade.

The other model was left to soak overnight for installation the next morning. However, an overzealous crewman emptied the soaking pail into the harbour before the author returned. Perhaps this should have been accepted as an omen.

Things got worse. Of the three straps cut from a 25 mm thick piece of rawhide provided by the Trireme Trust USA, two stretched so much from their own weight upon lifting out of the soaking water that they could not be deployed. The third was eaten by the ship's canine mascot.

The plain, one-piece straps having proved unsuccessful, the author decided to try braiding the rawhide, thinking that multiple strands would increase friction and thereby reduce excessive stretching. This experiment resulted in some improvements.

The author made three single-loop braided grommets, one four-strand, one five-strand, one eight-strand. The four-strand grommet was placed on the author's oar for observation. Although it did stretch considerably, the author was able to take up the slack by occasionally pulling out the [removable, thranite] thole-pin and giving

the whole strap a counterclockwise turn or two before reinserting the pin. By 9th August, the author had made ten such turns, and could take no more without shortening the strap's loop too much for the thole pin to fit into it. When installed on 4th August, the four-strand strap had been almost too tight.

Fabricated from scraps as an afterthought, the five-strand grommet did not even survive the setting process. On 7th August, when high winds kept us in port all day, the author put it on an oar (No. 27 starboard zygian), and tied the oar in catch position before going to breakfast. By the time the author returned, pressure from wind-generated chop had stretched the rawhide and broken some of the strands.

The eight-strand grommet (installed on No. 7 Starboard Zygian) turned out to be the most successful of the three, perhaps confirming the hypothesis that increasing the number of strands decreases the amount of stretch.

However, both the zygian who rowed the eight-strand grommet and the author noted that the braided grommets tended to torque the oars slightly, but discernibly, off-square. Because an experimental eight-strand grommet of 'ilihau' (bark of the hau, *hibiscus tiliaceus*) installed on No. 8 port zygian's oar also forced that oar slightly off-square, this author concludes that plaiting, not the material plaited, caused the torsion. This hypothesis may be worth testing in future trials. Perhaps braided oarstraps will prove useful in a different configuration, one that balances opposing torque forces.

Rope grommets
Of the several devices used in 1992, rope grommets proved the most satisfactory to both rowers and maintenance personnel. After some experimentation the author and her helpers installed twelve rope grommets, six single loops and six double loops, on four triads, wrapping them with different colours of tape to indicate their positions in each triad. For 3/8 inch (8 mm) manila line, we found 560–650 mm to be the best length for a single loop grommet, and 1230 mm for a double. (Fig. 1.4.6 top). One thranite (No. 5 starboard) cut his off because he found it pulling his oar off-square, and a zygian (No. 22 starboard) reported that his stretched in the course of a morning's outing. A defective splice apparently caused this stretch. To correct it, the author removed the grommet's top loop from the pin, gave the rope two counter-clockwise turns, and replaced it on the pin. This took up the stretch and solved the problem (Fig. 1.4.6 middle). These rope grommets were deployed on 3rd August, before commencement of speed and maneuvring trials. Considering the material stresses these trials engender, and the inexperience of the chief fabricator, the grommets performed remarkably well. Except for the case noted above, we had no problems with stretch.

Indeed, the grommets' sole apparent drawback is their immutability and the precision of manufacture they demand. If they are a few millimeters too short, even large applications of grease, sweat, and profanity will not loosen them enough to make them useable. If they are too long, there must be enough extra length to give a tight fit with a particular number of extra turns.

In *Olympias*, since the oars do not have sacrificial, protective leathers, the oars have been worn to different diameters at the pivot point. Thus it was impossible to make grommets all of one diameter that were correctly sized for most locations. This task would obviously be easier with new oars if they were more uniform in shaft diameter at the pivot.

Gallaghers

Named for *Olympias* rower Shawn Gallagher, who uses them when rowing in his home waters of Florida, a Gallagher is a length of rope wrapped three times around the oar and the thole pin and tied with a square knot. The turns must be placed so they do not get trapped between the oar and its supporting carling block; for thranites and zygians the lower part of the turn is inboard of the pin, for thalamians the lower turn is positioned outboard of the pin (we found that 1300–1400 mm of 3/8 in. manila sufficed). Because it was faster and easier to cut line than to splice grommets or manufacture leather straps, we decided to use Gallaghers on most of the oars.

The device's advantages derive from its simplicity. It requires neither tools nor expertise nor very much time to rig and adjust. Most crew members seemed to like having this measure of control over their equipment.

By the same token, its drawbacks are of a simple nature; knots can stretch or even break, and not everyone makes good knots. Some rowers complained of having to retie their ropes two or three times each hour, usually because they had not yet learned how to knot them properly.

The author does not know the number of Gallaghers that broke or stretched too much to be usable, but there do not seem to have been many. Those that did were often recycled for light duty jobs such as water bottle lanyards.

Double-loop straps: the date of installation is in the first parentheses. The initial measurement for all double loops was 685 mm. The leather having become twisted and stiff from use, precise final measurements were hard to obtain when they were taken on 8th August. Therefore some of these may err by one or two mm.

1. (29th July) 798mm (No. 11 port thranite)
2. (29th July) 803mm (No. 11 port zygian)
3. (29th July) 762mm (No. 11 port thalamian, later No. 13 port zygian)
4. (29th July) 791mm (No. 20 port zygian)
5. (29th July) 768mm (No. 20 port thalamian)
6. (29th July) 760mm (No. 20 port thranite)
7. lost overboard
8. (29th July) 777mm (No. 24 starboard thalamian, later No. 4 port thranite)
9. (29th July) 722mm (No. 24 starboard zygian, later No. 5 port thalamian)

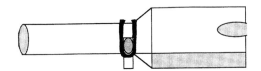

Single loop grommet (manila, rawhide, 'ilihau)

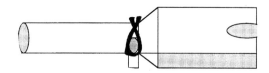

Single loop grommet twisted to remove slack

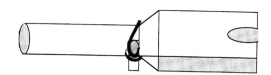

Single loop leather strap

Figure 1.4.6. Top: single loop grommet made of manila, rawhide or 'ilihau; middle: single loop grommet that has been twisted to remove slack; bottom: a single loop leather strap, installed.

10. (29th July) 800mm (No. 24 starboard thranite, later No. 5 port zygian). This double loop grommet was lost. The last measurement was taken on 5th August.
11. (4th August) 767mm (No. 27 port thranite)
12. (4th August) Lost (No. 4 starboard thranite)
13. (4th August) 778mm (No. 27 port zygian)
14. (4th August) 823mm (No. 27 port thalamian)
15. (4th August) 765mm (No. 4 starboard zygian)

During 1992, the hard polypropylene thole-ropes used on some oars tended to wear the oars. The other manila ropes were worn away by the oars. In 1993, the oars wore away the sisal thole-ropes quite significantly. Since we believe the thole-straps should be leather, authenticity is not an issue here, only cost, looks and practicality.

In 1993 a short experiment was conducted by equipping two triads with new, 10 mm sisal, two triads with 12 mm terylene and two triads with 12 mm hempex (a medium polypropylene made to look like hemp). These were chosen simply because they were available.

The results of this short experiment were:

1. Sisal
a. was worn by the oar
b. was fairly easy to tie and did not stretch

Table 1.4.1. Situations and Types of Experimental Oarstraps

Single-loop leather straps	Double-loop leather straps
No. 6 port zygian and thalamian No. 5 port thranite	No. 27 port triad No. 20 Port triad No. 13 port zygian No. 11 port thranite and zygian No. 5 port thranite No. 4 starboard zygian No. 4 port thranite
Single-loop rope grommets (560 mm) No. 22 starboard triad No. 5 starboard triad	**Double-loop rope grommets (1230 mm)** No. 23 port triad No. 16 starboard triad No. 6 starboard thranite
Single-loop braided rawhide grommets 4-strand: No. 6 port thranite 8-strand: No. 7 starboard zygian	**Single-loop 8-strand braided 'ilihau grommet** No. 8 port zygian

Table 1.4.2. Stretch Measurements for Leather Oarstraps

Single-loop straps (in use 28th July-8th August)
A. (initially deployed on No. 6 port thranite, moved to No. 5 port thranite) Initial measurement: 595 mm Final measurement: 655 mm
B. No. 6 port zygian Initial measurement: 547 mm Final measurement: 649 mm
C. No. 6 port thalamian Initial measurement: 545 mm Final measurement: 625 mm

c. tended to un-strand (rope which un-strands does not last)

d. had a natural appearance

2. Soft polypropylene

a. did not wear rope or oar

b. was easy to tie, but stretched

c. had easy-to-seal ends

d. was bright blue in colour

3. Terylene

a. did not wear the oar but the rope suffered from friction burn

b. was beautiful to handle and tie but stretched

c. unstranded easily

d. had a pure white colour

4. Hempex

a. did not wear the oar or rope

b. was easy to tie and did not stretch

c. had easy-to-seal ends

d. had a natural look

The Hempex was regarded as the best rope. I also used it in 8 mm thickness for the foot stretchers.

Previous reports and this one have commented on the difficulties and failures of leather thole straps. Given the difficulties we have had with leather, I wonder if we are using the correct approach. The word 'oarloop' is given in *The Athenian Trireme* as a translation of Thucydides. Crawley's Everyman Edition reads 'thong.' A Penguin translation of Aeschlyus' *The Persians* calls it a thong as well. I would suggest experimenting with a strap, rather than a loop: specifically a long narrow strap with a small loop in one end and a long tail (see Fig. 1.4.6 bottom).

The loop fits closely over the thole pin and the strap is then wound around the oar with the required pattern and tension. Then take one or two turns around the top of the thole pin to take the strain and fasten off the tail end to a fixing point (such as a notch, cleat or whatever) paced astern to maintain tension. This would be easy to make, more authentic, and quicker to fit and adjust than rope.

1.4.4 Repairs while underway

It is possible to undertake many minor repairs to the ship's gear while under oar or sail, thus greatly increasing the ship's operational efficiency. Even a breakage in rowing furniture does not necessarily put the affected triad out of action until the ship is moored.

In 1988, whaleboat rower and trireme section leader Corny Foster introduced the trireme project to the practice of instructing rowers to use 'air shots' when problems need to be addressed in a small part of a vessel moving under oar. A common practice in whaleboat rowing, calling for air shots means the affected rowers continue to 'row' but keep their oars in the air at all times and slightly shorten the length of their stroke. Once air shots are instituted, those rowers who need to stop rowing completely can do so. In this way those rowers just outside the affected area can continue to row normally, since the adjacent rowers are still swinging their bodies in time, and getting their backs out of the way.

In *Olympias*, when a thole strap works loose, a blade breaks, or some other gear failure occurs, there is a short, but intense initial period of confusion. Those around the affected rower are trying to figure out what has happened and/or communicate what has happened to others. This period is greatly abbreviated or eliminated if the effected rowers or section leader call for air shots in three triads, specifically the triad that is directly involved and those just forward and aft of it, *i.e.*, "Air shots, port (or starboard) triads number X, Y and Z." Within a second or two, the affected rower's sense of danger and concern that too many people are talking at once, subsides. This is very helpful since either of these can lead to panic. The situation can then be assessed, and the necessary repairs or adjustments planned.

Most typically, air shots would be needed when a thole strap stretched too much or came untied. In this case, all that would be necessary once air shots were instituted, would be for the affected rower to i) pull their oar in part way, ii) tighten or replace the strap, iii) run the oar out again, and iv) fall in with the rowers doing the air shots. Then all three triads can fall back into rowing normally with the rest of the ship.

If carpentry or the replacement of an oar is required, certain rowers can vacate their seats for the gangway to let the carpenter climb into them to work, or they can simply stop rowing to help swap oars while those around them continue with air shots. Over the past four sets of trials, section leaders, rowers and the ship's carpenters have undertaken a variety of tasks while underway, including driving back into place loose pins, foot clog fastenings, carling blocks, and foot stretcher adjustment pins; and lashing split stretcher rails. It must be said that virtually all of these minor but irritating repairs would be unnecessary in a trireme with more carefully built rowing furniture.

Thranite and zygian oars can be easily replaced with spares using the assistance of a section leader or spare rower working from the gangway or canopy. The damaged oar is run part way in, the strap untied, and then the oar is pulled in by passing the handle end up to the helper on the gangway. The damaged oar and spares are stored out of the way on the canopy. The process is reversed with the new oar the helper passes down.

Replacing a thalamian oar can be accomplished while under oar, but it involves a more complicated procedure which also disrupts more than three triads. The three triads rowing on the opposite side of the ship have to stop rowing also, in order to bring the old oar all the way in and store it in the bilge, then to pass the new oar out the oarport. Since thalamian oars are very strong (p. 23) their replacement was rarely necessary. In any case it was usually easier for the thalamian in question to stop rowing and ship

their oar, allow all the other triads to resume rowing, and then replace the oar when the next rest break was called for the entire crew.

Very occasionally a zygian or thalamian thole pin will work loose. This is due to poor boring during construction. Under way, air shots are called, the rower in question ships their oar, is handed a hammer or mallet, and the pin is driven home again in a few seconds. If the pin is very loose, a few layers of cloth or tape can be wound around the pin before it is hammered back in. As a more permanent repair, undertaken between outings, a nail or dowel can be driven through a pre-drilled hole through the carling block into the pin.

1.4.5 Rowing furniture tolerance: lessons from the 'Seats From Hell'

Note: This passage was written years before the concept of canting the seats (see pp. 76–91) was developed. Despite the great potential of this design change to improve the performance of a trireme reconstruction, much of what follows remains highly relevant.

During the 1992 trials, a number of seats in the bow of *Olympias* seemed to be rather problematic for whomever sat in them. Most typically, problems seemed to occur during the catch of the stroke. For example, in one seat a rower might complain that the catch of the stroke was more restricted than in other seats, in another a thranite might report that the zygian in his/her triad could never fully immerse the blade at the catch, no matter how high and hard the hands came up at the end of the recovery.

The entire crew was then asked to report any 'seats from hell' and from the list of complaints nine authentically bad positions were located. Four of the nine were reported from the aftmost section to starboard, from triads containing disproportionate numbers of veteran trireme rowers. The other problem seats were scattered throughout the ship.

When the nine bad seats were investigated, in all but one case the problem could be traced to slight mis-locations of rowing furniture and/or the outrigger brackets. These mis-locations ranged from 3 to 12 mm off the average, as established by measuring gear from seats that were not problematic. In one case several small errors in rowing furniture placement combined to make a noticeable problem. For the record, the problems (now mostly corrected) are shown in Table 1.4.3.

Olympias's furniture is consistently built. In series-built fleets of ships of the size and complexity of triremes, errors as large as 12 mm in locating internal fittings would not be surprising. Indeed they were almost certainly inevitable, even given the remarkable workmanship demonstrated in excavated ancient ships (Frost 1976; Steffy 1985). The author's hands-on experience in wooden ship building and repair also supports this conclusion.

Yet it cannot be denied that small errors in gear positioning do cause problems in *Olympias*, as shown

Table 1.4.3.

Position	Problem
24 stbd thal	pin too far aft by about 12 mm
27 stbd thal	aft edge of oarport planking not cut away enough and/or pin too far forward for a combined mis-location of 5 mm, also the carling block may be slightly too high
27 stbd zyg	aft edge of oarport planking not cut away enough
24 stbd zyg	carling block about 5 mm too high, restricting the catch. Shaving it down and paring away the thranite stretcher rail helped, but it then became restricted at the catch due to hitting of the outrigger bracket and aft face of the oarport. Is the outrigger bracket is too close or the oarport too small in diameter?
14 port zyg	restricted catch due to close proximity of the outrigger bracket
9 port zyg	carling too high by 4 mm, so the blade was not fully in the water at the catch
14 port zyg	carling too high by 5 mm, so the blade was not fully in the water at the catch
9 port zyg	carling too high by 3 mm, so the blade was not fully in the water at the catch
22 port zyg	oar very heavy. As part of our oar research Conrad McDonnell measured the mass and the moment of inertia for four oars of each type. One zygian oar (neither its location in the ship nor the oar's number were recorded) was much heavier than the others. It was 2.1 kg heavier than four other zygian oars that averaged 8.5 kg, with a moment of inertia 2 kg m² more than the others which averaged 13.0 kg. This heavy oar is presumed to be No. 22 port zygian, or another one like it.

above. This indicates that either the ancient builders kept to very tight tolerances in rowing furniture manufacture and installation, or it indicates a larger problem with *Olympias'* design.

Within the project, there have been discussions as to whether the design of a second, improved trireme reconstruction can be adjusted so that:

i) rowers of a pre-set maximum height are unrestricted by the cross beams or underslung zygian seats
ii) the ship is more tolerant of individual variations in ergonometrics, rowing styles and body types, ideally to the same degree as is typically achieved in a seagoing, fixed-seat pulling boat of the 19th century
iii) equal or even greater inconsistencies in construction do not generate 'seats from hell.'

To achieve these ends, the relative positions (fore and aft and vertically) of the rowers in each triad will probably have to be shifted slightly, a few centimetres in one direction or another. The beams restricting the thalamians, and upon which the zygians sit, would probably be made less deep in section.

These changes sound simple enough to puzzle out, but the interactions and ramifications involved are very complex. A number of the most numerate of the project's participants have come to believe that nothing short of the construction, testing and modification of a full-scale, floating, rowable, adjustable mock-up will make it possible to sort out all the issues without inadvertently creating other problems. This test vessel's initial furniture positioning would be based upon the slight changes indicated by operations with *Olympias*.

If these aims cannot be achieved in such a vehicle, then unless and until the remains of an ancient trireme are excavated and studied, we cannot know if such high tolerances were essential to, and achieved in, ancient triremes.

In the meantime, the argument in favour of the ancient shipwrights achieving very high standards of tolerance in ancient triremes could be summarized as follows:

Hand tools, templates, and 'go' or 'no go' gauges can produce very consistent work, even from rough-sawn or riven material. The design of these ships evolved over many years, and excavated shipwrecks consistently show high standards of workmanship. We know from accounts such as Aristophanes *Birds* 108 that good trireme construction was something to be proud of; this might be one reason why. The opposing view would be:

Excavated shipwrecks like the Kyrenia Wreck, admitting they are not warships, show larger variations in the placement of their parts, especially internal timbers that might be used as reference points, such as framing. The gear in *Olympias* in general is intolerant of individual variations in body type and ergonometrics, and creates problems even when built to tight specifications. If Mark II can be made more tolerant of placement errors it would go a long way to show that the basic configuration of the rowing furniture is correct.

A second, less critical question that comes to mind as a result of the 'seats from hell' is why many problem seats were clustered in one area. Perhaps these more experienced trireme rowers were getting picky. More likely, they had become the catalyst for a longer than average stroke for that part of the ship. In this case the limitations of the rowing furniture with which the ship was designed and built could be expected to be felt more keenly.

Bibliography

Frost. H. (1976) Lilybaeum (Marsala). *Notizie degli scavi di antichità: Serie Ottava 30.*

Steffy, J. R. (1985) The Kyrenia ship: An interim report on its hull construction. *American Journal of Archaeology* 89, 71–101

1.5. Different perspectives on some reported results

Paul Lipke, with assistance from Ford Weiskittel

This chapter explores some of the disagreements in observations and interpretation of events among some project participants created by the ship's compartmentalization, and by participants' varying experience and duties. It closes with a dissenting opinion as to what are *Olympias'* achievable speeds.

1.5.1. The critical context: compartmentalization

Interdisciplinary and cross-cultural efforts were made in the Trireme Project. Even so, the project's large scale meant any assessment of a given situation was highly influenced by one's position, both physically and organizationally. With such a unique project, it would no doubt have been ideal if we'd had the time and energy to invest in creating what experts in organizational learning call a "learning history." In full form, such a history documents how and why Trireme Project participants learned what they learned, how opinions formed, how interpersonal dynamics have influenced the project, *etc.* Learning histories can provide project managers and future historians with invaluable context. Unfortunately, because of the scope and complexity of the project such a history would have consumed, quite literally, thousands of person-hours and pages of text, and so was not within our capabilities. To compensate, the following material is meant to both provide readers with a sense of this missing rich context, and to make some important disagreements as to the meanings of certain events explicit so that readers may judge matters for themselves.

1.5.2. Physical constraints

Physically, an individual's particular field of vision and auditory range greatly skewed their impression of any given event. For reasons explained below, if the rowing masters spent most of their time in the very stern (as was likely in order to be near the captain, helmsman and the emergency sound system) their impression of the crew's freshness was different than if they roamed forward (at least as far as the mainmast) and observed and spoke with the crew in the bow. Similarly, the experiences of section leaders and rowers in the bow were often rather different from those in the stern.

There were a lot of things happening simultaneously with a lot of people in a small, complex space. A rower's observations of the causes of a given problem in their triad were often quite different from those of the section leaders in the gangway who could see larger patterns, which were themselves often different from the assessments of those in command in the stern. It was also easy to misinterpret nuances of the ship's operations without either direct experience in the seat of the persons involved, or repeated close observation of a situation.

1.5.3. Organizational constraints

As in any setting, an individual's context, meaning and level of effort are shaped by the quality and quantity of information and learning, the level of responsibility, and the accuracy and rapidity of any feedback loops. The complexity of the Trireme Project and the number of things happening simultaneously meant there was always an extremely wide range of information levels, responsibility, and feedback effectiveness among the participants.

The debriefing that followed each outing routinely involved listening to the differing accounts of observers and participants, and then piecing together a more accurate, consensus-based picture of what had actually happened. Appropriate decisions about corrective measures, further testing, *etc.* could then be made.

To understand differing views from different organizational levels, it is essential to understand the observers' situations and backgrounds. In *Olympias'* case, these differences often resulted in materially differing points of view and interpretations of data, examples of which are given below. It is important to note a similar comparison could be written between almost *any* two members of the trials leadership, and between rowers from different parts and levels of the ship.

1.5.4. The impact of compartmentalization: two perspectives on four matters

This section summarizes two participants' backgrounds and interpretations of the same issues and or events.

Participant 1
Boris Rankov is a famous, competitive sliding-seat, flat-water rower and a Professor of Ancient History. As one of *Olympias'* two primary rowing masters, he has had responsibility for "the big picture," the successful performance of the ship, powered by its oarcrew. It is unfortunate that after having taken on the substantial task of selecting and organizing the rowers for the 1987 trials, a last minute back injury prevented him from being present that first year. His absence was a loss to those first days on the water, during which the volume and complexity of issues to be addressed put a high premium on a leadership of diverse and deep experience. This complexity is well summarized in his telling contribution to the report of the 1990 trials, 'Rowing *Olympias*: A Matter of Skill' (Rankov 1993). The back injury has also, unfortunately, prevented him from gaining much subsequent experience pulling an oar in *Olympias*: he has rowed briefly one time each in a thranite and zygian seat. As a result, his writings on rowing *Olympias* come from the reports of others, his astute observations and from conversations with rowers and section leaders. From his collegiate rowing background and position of command, he naturally:

i) spent the majority of his time aboard *Olympias* in the stern.
ii) met with co-rowing master Ford Weiskittel nearly every day to assign a specific seat to every rower in the ship.
iii) sat the weakest rowers in the bow, as is the norm in a racing shell
iv) took much of his data, perspectives and details from rowers near the stern, whom he considered to be *Olympias'* stroke rowers

Participant 2

This author, Paul Lipke, is a wood scientist, a wooden boatbuilder, a recreational sliding-seat and open-water, fixed-seat rower who has served in *Olympias* since 1987 as co-organizer of the North American contingent of the oarcrew, director of the pre-trials US training camp, ship's photographer, section leader (in the bow and midship sections) ship's carpenter and a rower in all positions from 1987–1993. Daily, he undertook or supervised the extensive work maintaining and modifying the ship's rowing equipment, and focused on becoming intimately familiar with - and finding solutions for - the particular challenges of individual rowers, sections of rowers, and of the entire oarcrew. From Lipke's ocean rowing background and position as ship's carpenter and section leader he:

i) focused more on how the ship's structure and mechanics influenced the stroke (especially in bow versus stern issues).
ii) focused his energies and time on the rowers in the bow when he perceived the need for a strong bow section leader.
iii) urged rowers under his charge to gravitate towards the seating position in which they felt most productive.
iv) lacked Rankov's heightened awareness of the nuances of timing.

Thus, the difference in perspective between Rankov and Lipke is that of a big-picture management view contrasting with a close-up view of the problems of individual rowers and sections, as influenced by the project's and the ship's management and design. Having summarized their respective perspectives, what follows are some of the most important examples of the different views that arose as a result.

1.5.4.1 Issues of timing

In 'Rowing *Olympias*: A Matter of Skill,' Rankov (1993, 54–5) wrote "The sternmost block of rowers was, in effect, stroking the ship…" If the piped signal for the catch of the stroke was not timed fractionally early to allow time for the sound to travel down the ship, "those in the stern "[took] the full weight of the ship as their oars entered the water. Inevitably, the latter began to tire very quickly." This author's views of the distribution of work between bow and stern and the timing of the piped signal for the catch of the stroke are quite different.

Rowers in the bow would often say the outing was hard work, while stern rowers insisted the same outing was only

a modest work-out. His explanation is that stern rowers worked with their immersed blades in the turbulent race (or 'slipstream') created by dozens of closely-spaced oars further forward pushing water towards the stern. As a result, when seated in the stern, even with almost no effort the author felt his blade slip through the water relatively quickly when the ship was moving at more than about 4½ knots. In the bow the water was relatively undisturbed, and therefore the oar slipped less and the rower was able to make a longer, more sustained pull. Thus the drive of the stroke for a bow oarsman was relatively slow, and the recovery had to be completed relatively quickly. All in all, the stern rowers' period of effort was fractionally shorter than that for rowers in the bow. Ideally the project would have had the capacity to settle the matter by recording the actual energy expended by the same rowers, seated first in the bow and then in the stern, rowing in otherwise identical positions with the same rowing mates, during identical rowing conditions.

Because of the differences, bow to stern, in the relative effort and timing of the stroke's drive and recovery, the best results in timing of the piped signal occurred when Ford Weiskittel, working as rowing master or *auletes*, scanned both sides and the full length of the ship, and then gave the catch and finish signal fractionally ahead of an average point in time derived, more often than not, from the midships sections. If the rowing fell out of time, the rowing masters or *auletes* had to consciously fight the tendency to take a unifying stroke cue off the stern-most rowers.

The author believes the tendency arose: i) from racing-shell rowing traditions in which the stern-most rower is considered the stroke oar, ii) from a tendency for experienced (and often more vocal) racing shell rowers to want to row in the stern for the same reason, iii) from the visual accessibility of stern rowers to the rowing masters, who stood in the stern in order to be near the helmsman and Hellenic Navy's captain, and iv) because it was only at the end of the 1990 trials, at Weiskittel's and this author's instigation, that the project stopped seating the weakest rowers in the bow.

1.5.4.2 Impact of ship's structure on thalamian rowers

Rankov (1993, 52) has written:

> The proximity of the zygian beams to the backs of the potential [crabbing] victim's head has undoubtedly had a psychological effect on all of *Olympias'* thalamians to date, encouraging them to row well within themselves… Moreover, the crossbeams also restrict the maximum length of the thalamian stroke, and therefore, of course, of the stroke at all three levels.

In this author's view, the psychological problem created by the zygian beams, as outlined by Rankov, was largely overcome in 1988 and improved still further later on by improving the training of thalamians. From then on, the vast majority of thalamians did not hold back when rowing due to the crossbeams, and used every part of the space available (Shaw 1993b, 77). Photographs and video-taped records show thalamians touching (and even whacking) both the beam in front and behind themselves with their heads on every stroke. This resulted in minor skin wounds on thalamian foreheads and necks. More tellingly, many had 'recovery bruises' in the small of their backs (from the hands of the rower just forward of their seat). The Medical Report (which see) by Dr. Denis Chagnon documents that 56% of thalamians said they experienced being "bruised or bashed in the back by the rower behind."

This author believes the focus on the zygian beams as thalamian obstructions has tended to overshadow - in trials, crew training and published reports - the fact that *the back* of the rower immediately towards the stern was a more serious obstacle to good rowing. The author found he could often dramatically increase rowing comfort and length of stroke by climbing into the bilge adjacent to the thalamians, and systematically reminding each thalamian to adjust their foot-stretcher position to optimize their own reach and that of the next rower in line. In contrast, if one rower fails to adjust their foot stretcher and sits too far back on their seat, many others are cramped.

Over time our over-attention to the zygian beams has been corrected. The initial design for a second trireme reconstruction includes minor changes to the zygian beams, and more importantly, changing the seat height and athwartship orientations of the rowing gear so as to allow the arc of the thalamian oar handle to clear the back of the next rower. As this publication goes to press, new evidence indicates *trieres* ship-sheds were longer than previously thought, and therefore it may well be possible for a new trireme reconstruction even to avoid canting the rowing furniture.

5.4.3. *Thalamians catching crabs*

Rankov (1993, 51–2) has described problems related to thalamians catching crabs. This description has encouraged some people to question *Olympias'* design and viability as a reconstruction. A somewhat detailed alternative view of thalamian crabbing problems in 1987 (and thereafter) is offered here. This author's direct experience was that:

i)   Zygians instigated thalamian crabs by over-reaching thalamians, not generally by mis-timing the catch of the stroke (as stated by Rankov). The first rowing master, Michael Budd (1989 109), points this out. The thalamian blade most typically continued to dive "irretrievably down into the depths" because it was under-square (tilted off the vertical, with the lower edge further aft than the upper edge) as a result of the oar shaft's shoulder rolling on the mis-shaped thole pin block upon which it rested.

ii)   Thalamian crabs were solved as a serious problem at the suggestion of rower Peter MacLeod, beginning on the third day of trials in 1987 (Budd 1989, 109), not in 1988 as stated by Rankov (1993, 52). They were reduced still further early in 1988 as the rowing masters

and section leaders got better at teaching the requisite techniques and we modified certain equipment. This was accomplished by a) instructing thalamians to keep their blades on the square, b) telling the thranite rowers to keep their blades between the zygian and the thalamian of their triad, especially so the zygian learned not to over-reach the thalamian, c) removing the offending corners of the thalamian's oar pin blocks, and iv) by adding thalamian preventer ropes, primarily as a psychological safety measure. There will be more upon this last point below.

Rankov (1993, 51) is of the opinion that, thalamian crabs in 1987 were "frequent" and: "…invariably accompanied by a harrowing scream which could be heard throughout the ship, shattering the morale of other thalamians. The victims were in real danger..."It is not stated in this passage from what point of view these dangers were perceived and subsequently reported to Rankov. This author's view, from his first hand experience as a 1987 section coach, is that the dangers reported to Rankov were greatly exaggerated:

iii) When the oar handle of a crabbed thalamian blade comes to rest, it actually leaves enough space between the handle and the zygian beam just forward of it for a) the rowers head and neck, b) an air space of an inch of two, and c) the rower's hands. In fact, the thalamian gets 'pinned' when his/her wrists, grasping the oar handle, are fully curled and forced upwards towards their chin. Their shoulders then rise, and their head or neck is pushed back (towards the bow) and up against the beam.

iv) This author was unable to uncover any evidence that a thalamian has ever been more than bruised by catching a crab. There is no mention of such injuries in the 1987 report even though the rowing master, Michael Budd, was a physician. Dr. Denis Chagnon, *Olympias'* medical officer for the 1990–1993 events, told this author in a personal communication in 1998, "I cannot recall ever hearing of or seeing a rower with injuries worse than a bruise that were the result of catching a crab."

v)   This author can remember only one or two occasions when a thalamian offered something approaching a "harrowing scream." Catching a crab usually causes rowers to grunt! Initially, any shouts came from adjacent rowers calling for the entire crew to stop rowing because, since the thalamian rarely "screamed," no one else (*i.e.* the rowing masters) was immediately aware of the problem. By issuing loud safety whistles to all the section leaders and telling the crew that a single long whistle blast meant 'Stop rowing immediately!' the crab 'emergency' communication problem was largely eliminated. As crabs became very rare and our ability to extricate rowers from them adept, it got to the point where most of the time only the 3–6 rowers in the immediate vicinity of the crab had to momentarily stop rowing, and then only if the trapped rower, the triad and/or their section leader determined they needed to stop at all.

vi) Installing safety ropes on thalamian oar handles was largely of psychological value. This is demonstrated by the fact that by 1988 this author observed that most thalamians did not use them after the first few outings, even though the trials management urged their constant use, and insisted on them during high power speed trials, or if rowers were getting tired. The resistance to their use arose because they caused abrasions on rowers' hands. Raw spots causing pain on every stroke are far more troublesome to *Olympias'* rowers than the low risk of catching a crab or the minor bruise that might result.

1.5.4.4 Prior rowing experience among crew members

Rankov (1993, 50) expresses the opinion that the challenges faced by the 1987 trials were significantly aggravated by the fact there were in the crew "too many men and women without rowing experience of any kind."

Recent correspondence between Rankov and Lipke revealed this view to be based on a) Rankov having vetted the 1987 applicants, b) comments to Rankov by 1987 crew member Stephen Walter, and c) Rankov's own observations – in 1988 and later – of crew members without rowing experience.

The view of this author, who was an active coach in 1987 is that the difficulties resulted far more from a totally understandable lack of knowledge on the part of the trials leadership on how to prepare, train and direct a trireme's crew. After all, no one had done so in thousands of years! Rankov writes of "the mistaken belief amongst recruiters that...skills acquired [in modern rowing boats] would not give any significant advantage." It implies that non-rowers can only be allowed some unspecified (by implication quite small) number of seats in a successful trials crew.

There are several points to be made here:

i)   Experienced rowers were critical to the success of the sea trials where all the learning has to be compressed into a few weeks. However Rankov implies, but is too tactful to say outright, how hard it was to get many of them to row in a way that suited *Olympias*! Their experience often came with a lot of mental baggage. In recruiting a modern trireme crew, flexibility of mind can be as important as fitness or experience. We found the more open attitudes of the non-rowers, combined with the more collaborative style of the women in the crew (however historically inaccurate, and whether they were experienced rowers or not) helped open the minds of the experienced rowers.

ii) The present author co-directed, with rowing master Ford Weiskittel, the two-day, intensive training camp given North American rowers before departure for Greece. This training camp, including a training manual sent to participants in advance, detailed briefings, rigorous drills in a 9-seat mock-up of *Olympias*, and in whaleboats, showed it wasn't hard to bring most non-rowers up to a decent standard. We believe one quarter (perhaps more) of our modern oarcrew could be 'raw recruits' without unduly impacting upon the trials. As Rankov rightly says, in classical times the *best* triremes certainly benefited from the vast majority (if not the entirety) of their rowers' extensive prior experience. But based on our experience in *Olympias*, I believe we can assert with confidence that in times of large deployments the average *trieres* of a classical Athenian fleet could have managed reasonably well with significant numbers of inexperienced men, even if battle was relatively near at hand, given an aggressive, if brief, training period.

1.5.4.5. Conclusions

In summary of all these differences, it is quite clear that each of these participant's natural bias and positions strongly influenced what they observed and thought. Through lengthy and often heated discussion, what co-evolved between the Rankov, Lipke, and others was a consensus that:

i)   At higher speeds, a quick firm catch was required. As a result, sternward members of the crew need to be quick and firm at the catch to get solid pressure on the blade at all, and had to be strong and fast to maintain power. It was easier for bow rowers to apply power. Thus, for the ship's maximum performance, some of the most powerful rowers available should be seated in the clean water of the bow where their strength could have a greater impact, as well as distributed throughout the ship. While the bow-stern differences in timing are of the order of fractions of a second, they could still be troublesome due to cumulative fatigue in the bow resulting from the tendency of the rowing masters or *auletes* to forget to take stroke cues from the midships or overall ship's average. In more demanding, longer outings or those with high rates of stroke, this potential was accentuated because the water became still more turbulent in the stern.

ii) The bow section leaders must work actively to reduce the general isolation of the bow caused by the mainmast and boatmast. Simultaneously, the rowing master has to leave his primary location in the stern and get forward as far as the mainmast to be attuned to what is happening before the mast, *and* the forward members of the crew have to work doubly hard both to stay in time with the rest of the ship and to hear what instructions and descriptions of events might be coming from the stern.

How many hours of argument and observation it took to cull out those gems of consensus. How 'biased' reports on *Olympias* would be (and readers mislead!) if such consensus had not generally been actively sought, matured and presented clearly. It is truly a case of lessons learned through sustained commitment to integrity and collaboration.

1.5.5. A note on Olympias' maximum speed

Section 1.2.4 of this Report, 'Some Results of *Olympias'* 1992 trials and Log Summary,' explains the difficulty in assessing the actual speeds reached by the ship. The different methods used produced somewhat different results. In considering the arguments made, this author's view is that the meaningful maximum speed achieved was 8.3 knots, which was sustained for about 1 minute under the crew's truly Herculean effort. The 8.9 knots top speed published elsewhere in this work, and previously publications, was recorded only momentarily, if in fact this number actually represents the ship's speed. This author recalls that *Olympias'* log readings sometimes jumped around quite a bit, and so suspects this number might be one such unreliable spike, resulting perhaps from the sudden drop in oar turbulence as the crew stopped rowing. The author interprets the evidence to show that our meaningful top speed – what we could produce repeatedly in *Olympias* during a single outing, each time sustaining that speed for several minutes at a time as might be required in battle – is in the range of 7.5–8.0 knots.

This viewpoint does not imply any skepticism as to *Olympias'* validity as a highly successful effort to reconstruct the classical Athenian trireme and reproduce its historically acclaimed – and oft-argued – highest speeds. If a second updated reconstruction is ever launched, building on the data and wisdom gleaned from *Olympias*, it will be one that allows rowers to use their brains, legs, back and arms fully to apply their power and skill, and to do so at reasonable stroke rates. In such a case this author believes material improvements in maneuverability, speed, and especially more sustained higher speeds, will be achieved.

Bibliography

Budd, M. (1989) The Rowing Master's story. In Morrison and Coates 1989, 109–10

Coates, J. S., Platis, S.K. and Shaw, J. T. (1990) *The Trireme Trials 1988. Report on the Anglo-Hellenic Sea Trials of* Olympias. Oxford, Oxbow Books.

Lipke, P. (1988) Trials for the trireme. *Archaeology* 41, 22–9

Morrison, J. S and Coates, J. F. (eds) (1989) *An Athenian Trireme Reconstructed. The British Sea Trials of* Olympias, *1987*. BAR International Series 486. Oxford, Archaeopress.

Rankov, N. B. (1993) Rowing *Olympias*: a matter of skill. In Shaw 1993a, 50–7

Shaw, J. T. (ed.) (1993a) *The Trireme Project. Operational Experience 1987–90. Lessons Learnt.* Oxbow Monograph 31. Oxford, Oxbow Books.

Shaw, J. T. (1993b) The meshing of oars in *Olympias*. In Shaw 1993, 75–7

1.6. Where the Trireme Project has gone wrong

Paul Lipke and Ford Weiskittel

1.6.1 Maximum speeds

The project's focus on the top speeds of ancient triremes is wrong. The trials test programs and publications have been overly focused on sprint speeds, primarily as a result of the collegiate racing orientation of the management (ourselves included) and the limitations of *Olympias*. The use of cruising speed as a crucial performance criterion, instead of maximum speed, is both more valuable and valid.

Apollodorus complains of being ordered by Timomachus to tow grain ships more than 70 open sea miles with triremes ([Demosthenes] 50.22.3). This constitutes another very valuable (and perhaps more meaningful) challenging benchmark for the performance of any reconstruction.

1.6.2 Room to row

The project is over-reliant on Vitruvius' text on the *interscalmium* (Vitruvius *De architectura* 1.2.4) as a basis for defining the 'correct' size of each rowing module and therefore the ship as a whole (Coates, Platis and Shaw 1990, 5–6; Morrison, Coates and Rankov 2000, 17, 133, 245–6, 268–9). We believe the project has wasted many hours debating, justifying and writing about this cubit or that, in an attempt to justify a larger ship that would easily accommodate rowers of varying physiques.

Much of the focus on increasing the size of the *interscalmium* and any future trireme reconstruction in general seems predicated on accommodating large, modern (5'10"-6'2") rowers. We ask, how compelling is the rationale for doing so when recruiting shorter rowers has been shown repeatedly to be practical in the USA, where athletes and rowers are especially tall? If recruiting difficulties are driving 'Mark II' design criteria, that should be prominently stated so that future observers and participants will know exactly how and in what way this is impacting the authenticity of any reconstruction.

Furthermore, it is worthwhile to consider Vitruvius in a larger context. Vitruvius, in writing of warships, says warship designs are based on the dimension between rowers. The type of warship is unspecified, it could be a trireme, quinquereme, or some other oared war vessel.

As a general principle, we have no argument with trireme reconstructions using the *interscalmium* concept as a general design principle. However, there are three problems moving forward from this:

i)   We obviously don't have the needed remains of a trireme to measure what that *interscalmium* was.

ii) Many ancient shipbuilding and rowing traditions use modular terms to define vessels without in any way restricting shipwrights from adjusting the size of the module. In the 1950's, wooden shipbuilders of the Nile, Egypt were still using the same two module system for deckbeams as their counterparts 4,500 years before, but the size of the module had changed (Lipke 1984). The lengths of Scandinavian faerings are defined by the number of oar spaces, *i.e.* 'four-oared faerings.' Yet these vary boat to boat, builder to builder, and town to town as needed to suit the physique and work requirements of the builder's client.

iii) it is a big leap to assert that a two cubit *interscalmium* was *exactly* two cubits, no more and no less. A 'nine by twelve room' is almost never exactly 9 feet by 12 feet. If the actual *interscalmium* used was two cubits and a few fingers [1 finger = 19.3 mm], it could easily still be called a two cubit *interscalmium*.

For all these reasons, basing any reconstruction on a measurement of exactly two cubits, regardless of the cubit used, is misleading and can lead to forcing rowers to work within unreasonable constraints. Future design efforts should start from bio-mechanical measurements of rowers. By working from the optimum *interscalmium* dimensions for rowers of given heights and physiques, as archaeology increases the number of measured classical skeletal remains, any proposed trireme reconstructions could become more valid. We are certain the practical 'two cubits' so determined will be close enough to two measured historical cubits to make the above arguments valid.

Such a practical two 'cubit' *interscalmium* may well be found to conform to the cubit purportedly used to build Philon's Arsenal for example, it may conform to other historical data, but it may not. And, if it doesn't so conform we maintain the demands of war, and of crew performance, would have forced the adoption of the 'practical' cubit.

Therefore, the project should avoid canting rowers and their blades (pp. 76–91) as much as possible (even if it creates recruiting difficulties)! Canting rowers, in many ways a brilliant approach, will likely result in ergonomic challenges (and even repetitive motion injuries) for rowers as they spend hours on end in twisting physical exertion, turning their heads to look down the file to stay in time or trying to monitor visual commands from their Rowing Master or *keleustes*. It will probably create other problems we cannot yet anticipate. For each degree of canting, better recruiting and biomechanical measurements are more strongly justified.

Note: In *Olympias*, temporary lowering and testing of four or five thalamian seats and their foot bracing was planned for 1994 by Paul Lipke and John Howarth (pending Hellenic Navy approval) but in the end the former could not attend those trials and no modifications were made.

A bio-mechanical approach would:

i) measure rowers to determine the space through which their bodies move in a fixed-seat stroke over extended rowing periods. This has been done by Ford Weiskittel and others, the data needs to be analyzed in order to:

ii) determine the optimum *interscalmium* for given height and physique.

iii) review skeletal evidence from Herculaneum and Haliae and compare this with our crew's data, considering socio-economic history of the persons whose excavated remains we have, with respect to diet, physique, height *etc*.

iv) compare all the above data to *Olympias*'s, and the Archaic and Doric cubits

v) explore whether such an *interscalmium* is achievable in a ship identical or near to *Olympias* in length with the following reasoning and changes:

    a) lowering of the thalamian seats (using different foot restraints attached directly on the inner hull/framing); and

    b) making the *zyga* truly a shallow, roughly rectangular cross-sectioned *plank* the zygian can sit on directly, thereby gaining additional clearance for the thalamian.

It is not necessary to lower the oarport proportionally, since thalamians are currently rowing with their wrists so low that a few thick-thighed thalamians have had trouble clearing small waves, and all thalamians have trouble clearing large waves during recovery. We have no trireme remains. We cannot know how watertight the ancient Greeks might have been able to make *askomata*. We cannot know what risks classical seamen were willing to take, *i.e.* how low they might have placed thalamian oarports.

The main argument against reducing the depth of the *zyga* has been loss of hull torsional stiffness. Some loss of hull torsional stiffness from reducing the depth of the *zyga* is acceptable since both tenon failure due to moisture cycling and hull shearing forces, and weakness and leakage due to shipworm, can be shown to be far more serious threats to a trireme's effectiveness and life span. These threats are more serious *virtually regardless of the historical/archaeological evidence or naval engineering strength standards chosen*. Even so, any potential strength loss could perhaps be mitigated by changes to other bracing located outboard of the thalamians and zygians and/or alternative arrangements of the adjacent lodging knees.

As a wooden boatbuilder, wood scientist, systems thinker, and student of human nature, Lipke suggests that many factors would take precedent over unmeasurable and subtle torsional forces in the minds of classical shipwrights as they developed triremes using many vessels and years. Far more powerful and immediate feedback loops would be active in shaping shipwrights' decisions such as a) the paramount importance of the apparent power, ease and physical demands (performance) of thousands of rowers, b) the comments of thousands of rowers and their commanders,c) the comments of hundreds of their professional colleagues, *i.e.* the ships' carpenters, d) effectiveness in battle, e) shipworm damage, and f) plank leakage.

Bibliography

Coates, J. S., Platis, S. K. and Shaw, J. T. (1990) *The Trireme Trials 1988. Report on the Anglo-Hellenic Sea Trials of* Olympias. Oxford, Oxbow Books.

Lipke, P. (1984) *The Royal Ship of Cheops: a Retrospective Account of the Discovery, Restoration and Reconstruction, Based on Interviews with Hag Ahmed Youssef Moustafa*. BAR International Series 225. Oxford, Archaeopress.

Morrison, J. S and Coates, J. F. (eds) (1989) *An Athenian Trireme Reconstructed. The British Sea Trials of* Olympias, *1987*. BAR International Series 486. Oxford, Archaeopress.

Shaw, J. T. (ed.) (1993) *The Trireme Project. Operational Experience 1987–90. Lessons Learnt.* Oxbow Monograph 31. Oxford, Oxbow Books.

Morrison, J. S., Coates, J. F. and Rankov, N. B. (2000) *The Athenian Trireme. The History and Reconstruction of an Ancient Greek Warship*. 2nd ed. Cambridge, Cambridge University Press.

1.7. Suggestions for future research in the Trireme Project

Paul Lipke and Ford Weiskittel

The new questions raised by the building and operation of *Olympias* are as important as the answers to old ones provided by sea trials. They identify areas deserving attention. In some cases, they indicate that an entirely new level of understanding about trireme operation has been reached as a result of the work to date. This section summarizes a few of the many remaining research areas that can be addressed both with and without further sea trials.

1.7.1 Research in Olympias

1.7.1.1 Speed and manoeuvring
Difficulties with *Olympias'* measuring equipment have been partially reported previously. New and repeated tests of speed and maneuvring are needed, both with the ship as is and with improved instrumentation on board. These tests will improve the statistical reliability of the project's data as well as advance our understanding of the effective operation of triremes.

1.7.1.2 Drift speed
Additional measurement of the ship's drift speeds at various headings relative to wind direction and strength are needed for the adjustment of earlier and future trials results, and to consider the difficulties of holding position before a battle.

1.7.1.3 Oar designs
Performance and tests to date have indicated areas of improvement for oars at all three levels. New thalamian oars are needed especially to compensate for limitations in the currently possible gearing and water turbulence at higher rates of speed. A new design for these oars has been prepared by Timothy Shaw and John Coates, but tests with prototypes would be valuable before a full set of 54 thalamian oars (plus spares) are ordered.

1.7.1.4 Non-electronic communication
Experiments have been started by Boris Rankov and Ford Weiskittel in non-electronic communication between the *keleustes* and the oarcrew using voice, pipes and/or visual signals. Intra-ship communication is difficult. The noise of the oars, wind, intra-triad communication and the poor acoustics of a hull packed with 170 crew members make it difficult for commands to be heard throughout the ship, especially in the bow.

Due to the brief nature of the trials and the intensive crew training needed, sea trials to date have been largely reliant on amplifying the rowing master's voice so that he/she can be readily heard by the entire crew (especially in the first week.) Clearly electronic amplification was not available in antiquity. Furthermore, in close quarters or a battle situation, it is quite possible for unamplified commands from an adjacent ship to be more audible to those in the bow than those coming from the stern of their own vessel.

Communication without a sound system (using a pipe and/or a second officer standing further forward to relay commands to the bow) has proven to be possible and effective on numerous occasions. The intent should be to conduct future sea trials without using an electronic sound system except in the event of an emergency, and to experiment more with piped and visual signals. This will require the crew to memorize and be attentive to a trireme visual or 'sign' language.

1.7.1.5 Tholepin position
There is continuing controversy about whether a trireme can be safely and more effectively rowed with the oar aft of the thole pin. A series of modifications to the oar furniture have been designed by John Howarth to explore this further.

1.7.1.6 Sailing trials
The sailing performance of triremes, so essential to their effective deployment, could be explored fully through a set of trials specifically devoted to sailing. The Hellenic Navy's lack of an official protocol for the operation of large sea-going sailing vessels, their uncertainties about this unusual ship's sailing performance parameters, and other matters have limited sailing experimentation. A set of sailing trials, with a reduced crew of experienced sailor-rowers and water ballast strapped to the seats of missing crew members has been proposed by sailing master Douglas Lindsay.

Research without a ship

1.7.1.7 Mortise and tenon performance in ship hulls
Testing of mortise and tenon behaviour and strength during moisture cycling and with different configurations is needed along the lines of the limited tests presented (pp. 189–90) especially considering the crucial importance of this technology. Model sections built of historically correct species, tested in a wood testing laboratory would greatly expand our understanding of the limits of triremes.

1.7.1.8 Behaviour in and destruction of hulls by shipworm
More research is required into the behaviour in and destruction of hulls by shipworm (*Teredinidae*) in mortise-and-tenon fastened planking under various conditions of hull construction, wood species, hull coatings, drying cycles and the environment.

1.7.1.9 Crew Physiology
Further testing of the physiology and bio-mechanics of rowing a trireme can be carried out using rowing ergometers, heart monitors and equipment designed to measure volume of oxygen uptake.

1.7.1.10 Trireme design

The design and construction of inexpensive full-scale mock-ups (such as that built by the Trireme Trust USA for about $500) could be used to test trireme design hypotheses and modifications to the oar system. Scale working models and computer-aided design and analysis of the reconstruction can also improve ship performance and our understanding. Alternative hull configurations can be explored via CAD, although the usefulness of this tool is limited due to the inherent difficulty of modelling not only the hull but the three dimensional, biomechanical problems of the arrangement of the rowing furniture and oarcrew.

There is one potentially radical difference between *Olympias* and any future reconstruction that deserves schematic exploration at a minimum, and perhaps preliminary number-crunching. The concept was first raised as a question by Owain Roberts, who designed *Olympias'* sailing rig, was her first sailing master, and has since gone on to reconstruct rigging systems for the 'awning' over Rome's Coliseum, for raising Egyptian monoliths, *etc.* Roberts suggests (personal communication, 1988) making the *hypozoma* (hogging truss) in two parts, one for each side, and raising the middle sections on stanchions (perhaps either side of the gangway) to improve its effective lift against the ship's ends sagging. This might, in turn, allow greater thwartships separation between rowers on different levels, and permit a reduction in the ship's beam, which is already dangerously close to the maximum space between columns in the shipsheds.

1.7.1.11 Re-design and testing of oars

There is a need for re-design and testing of oars using historically correct species, which will affect dimensions, stiffness, balance, and therefore performance.

1.8. A final note: falling victim to our own success

Paul Lipke and Ford Weiskittel

The author dares to suggest that the trireme project has become a victim of its own success. Much of the future research and design of any future reconstruction will require both new blood of a very high technical and academic quality, and a highly interdisciplinary, integrated design effort with a diverse design team, extending well beyond the efforts of the 1998 conference on 'Lessons Learned.' Here's why.

Two men, John Morrison and John Coates, whose combined talents were even more considerable than their intimidating individual brain power, spent many years researching and designing the reconstruction *Olympias*. Their work, supported by many others, has moved our understanding of the trireme to a level probably not seen since the classical age. It is truly remarkable achievement.

It also stands to reason that a design with such a pedigree is not easily invalidated, and alternative designs are rarely well enough developed or technically viable enough to compete with the present project's standard, or to withstand the scrutiny of those who have been deeply immersed in *Olympias*.

Furthermore, this reconstruction has been placed in the hands of a highly competent, diverse, interdisciplinary crew (rowers and management alike) which has further advanced understanding to the point where no one can individually encompass all the learning and specialization.

If recent decades have taught society anything, it is that when it comes to thinking about complex systems, such as *Olympias*, all stakeholders must be engaged and involved for full understanding to emerge so that the project leaps to a much higher level. An interdisciplinary, integrated design effort is essential for any future reconstruction to justify such a vessel's considerable construction and maintenance costs, and to provide the world with a leap forward in understanding of similar magnitude to that provided by *Olympias*.

2. *Olympias* on the Thames, 1993

Boris Rankov

In 1993 *Olympias* was brought to the River Thames in London to take part in a week of events organised by the Hellenic Cultural Centre in London to celebrate 2,500 years of Greek democracy (dating from the reforms of Kleisthenes in 508/7 BC). The ship had been refurbished by the Hellenic navy at a cost of 20 million drachmas (£62,500), and was transported from the Piraeus to Tilbury on her own specially-designed cradle aboard a container vessel, M/V *Arma*. The costs of the visit, an estimated £375,000 at 1993 prices, were borne by various organisations of the Greek and British governments and several individual sponsors and donors from the Greek community in London.

Olympias left Greece in May and was offloaded at Tilbury on Wednesday, 9th June. On the same day, she was towed upstream to West India Dock where, from Thursday, 10th until Saturday, 12th June, she was put on display to the public. On the morning of Sunday, 13th June, she was towed upstream on the tide to Putney Pier, and on the same day the volunteer oarcrew (mainly British, but including several American trireme 'veterans') moved into their accommodation at Hounslow Cavalry Barracks.

As a warship, *Olympias* could not be transferred when under way on the Thames (as a merchant vessel would have been) to the direct control of a river pilot, and so remained throughout under the command of her Hellenic Navy captain, Lt Mavrikis, assisted by a ten-strong Hellenic Navy deck crew as in previous sea trials. Nevertheless, because of the problems of navigating a relatively large vessel on narrow reaches of a tidal river spanned by several bridges, river pilot Chris Livett was aboard in an advisory capacity for all outings. Also aboard throughout was Commander Stavros Platis, HN, who had overseen the ship's construction in Greece.

Since the purpose of the visit was educational, diplomatic and celebratory, no actual trials were planned, and the slightly under-strength volunteer crew had only a few days to practise before the main ceremonies. The first outing took place on the morning of Monday, 14th June (High Tide at Putney: 10.36; Low Tide: 16.19), when the ship was rowed from Putney Pier up the Oxford-Cambridge Boat Race course towards Hammersmith Bridge (1½ miles), back down to the Mile Post, and then back up to Hammersmith. *Olympias* did not, of course, have her masts stepped or on board because of the bridges, but the state of the tide left only about one foot of clearance between the top of the *aphlaston* at the stern and the girders on the underside of Hammersmith Bridge. The ship was inched up to and through the bridge under oar, and this and earlier demonstrations of the ship's turning circle convinced Chris Livett that the ship could be safely manoeuvred on the Tideway, as the tidal reaches of the Thames are known. She was then rowed upstream as far as Chiswick Eyot before turning and covering the 2½ miles back to Putney; the outing was of about 6 miles in total. In the afternoon, during a second outing, the ship was rowed downstream through Putney, Wandsworth, Battersea, Albert and Vauxhall Bridges, and then back up through the bridges to Putney again, a round-trip of about 8 miles.

The following day, Tuesday, 15th June (High Tide at Putney: 11.37; Low Tide: 17.42), was John Morrison's 80th birthday. In the morning outing, because the tide was too high for *Olympias* to pass under the bridges, she was rowed from Putney to Hammersmith and back twice, a total of 6 miles. In the afternoon, with the tide ebbing, she was rowed up through Hammersmith Bridge to Chiswick Eyot and back to Putney, a round trip of 5 miles (Fig. 2.1).

Between outings on Monday and Tuesday, Dr Peter Jones of Friends of the Classics had arranged for some 300 members of that organization, including many distinguished Classicists, to visit the ship at Putney Pier. They were taken aboard and shown round the ship in groups of about 20 at a time by John Morrison and the present writer, some having queued for up to three hours. A particularly distinguished visitor, who was able to stay aboard for one of the outings, was Professor Lionel Casson, whose published work on ancient seafaring had proved invaluable during the early stages of the design of *Olympias*.

Figure 2.1. Olympias *being rowed upstream on the Thames towards Hammersmith Bridge on Tuesday, 15th June, 1993 (Photo: Rosie Randolph/Trireme Trust).*

The first major event of the visit took place on Wednesday, 16th June (High Tide at Putney: 12.34; Low Tide at London Bridge 19.50). Because of the heavy rain, the planned morning outing was cancelled, and in the afternoon the ship was rowed 7 miles downstream through Putney, Wandsworth, Battersea, Albert, Chelsea, Vauxhall and Lambeth Bridges. After a tricky turn, during which the ship narrowly avoided being swept onto the piers of Westminster Bridge by the ebb, which was running at 4–5 knots, she was moored on a pontoon alongside the Albert Embankment and opposite the Houses of Parliament. Here, the Speaker of the House of Commons, the Right Honourable Betty Boothroyd, PC, MP came aboard together with the Greek Minister of Culture, Mrs Dora Bakoyannis, and the Senior Officer of the Hellenic Navy. Following a presentation, they were shown round the ship, and the Speaker was elected an honorary member of the crew and presented with a Trireme Trust T-shirt. Afterwards, a replica of the stele bearing the Eucrates decree of 337/6 BC asserting the principle of democracy together with an image of *Demokratia* crowning *Demos* ('the People'), was presented to the Speaker on the Terrace of the House of Commons; in addition, the Speaker was presented with the Silver Medal of the Aegean Maritime Museum, whose President, Mr George Dracopoulos, had been one of the main sponsors of the visit. Meanwhile, the ship was rowed up past the Houses of Parliament and then

turned and then rowed another 3½ miles downstream on the ebb, again narrowly avoiding the piers of Westminster Bridge and then continuing through Waterloo, Blackfriars, Southwark, London and Tower Bridges. There she was turned and then taken to her mooring for the night at HMS *President* downstream of Tower Bridge.

The next day, Thursday, 17th June (High Tide at London Bridge: 12.42; Low Tide: 19.00) was also a day of display and ceremonial. In the morning, the masts were taken on board and stepped, and the yards raised. The bascules of Tower Bridge were raised to allow the ship to be rowed through upstream and were then lowered behind her. *Olympias* carried on up to London Bridge where she turned to wait for the bascules of Tower Bridge to be raised again. At this point, the sailing master, Douglas Lindsay, asked the captain for permission to lower the sails, and when the bascules were raised *Olympias* sailed through. This turned out to be a unique event, since Lindsay was later informed by the chairman of the Port of London Authority that passing through Tower Bridge under sail had been forbidden ever since the bridge was completed in 1894. The ship then returned to HMS *President* where her masts were unstepped and unshipped. In the afternoon, Mrs Bakoyannis came aboard with the Deputy Mayor of Athens, the Senior Officer of the Hellenic Navy, and Greek Orthodox Archbishop Gregorios of Thyateira and Great Britain, who blessed the ship with Holy Water. The ship was then rowed upstream through Tower Bridge to Upper Tower Bridge Pier, where the distinguished guests were welcomed by the Lord Mayor of London, Sir Francis McWilliams, GBE, who in return received the Silver Medal of the Aegean Maritime Museum. The crew then rowed the ship up through London Bridge and back down again past the guests to HMS *President*. It had originally been intended that the ship should be rowed back to Putney. However, as a result of a low spring tide on the Tuesday night, the ship had come close to grounding at Putney Pier, so it was decided that she should remain at HMS *President* for the rest of the visit.

The results of this enforced change of plan were that the ship was no longer as visible or accessible to the public as she had been at Putney, and that the oarcrew now had to travel for 2½ hours each way to reach the ship from Hounslow Barracks instead of the 1 hour it had taken to Putney. This effectively curtailed further outings, although she was rowed upstream on the afternoon of Sunday, 20th June (Low Tide at London Bridge: 09.09; High Tide: 14.59; Low Tide 21.39) from HMS *President* to the HMS *Chrysanthemum* mooring on the North Bank at Victoria Embankment, between Waterloo and Blackfriars Bridges, so that the crew could join the *Democracy 2500* party on the South Bank. After the party, she was rowed back down to HMS *President*, from where she was towed back to Tilbury the next day, Monday, 21st June, and then shipped back to Greece.

An abiding memory of the visit for the crew was the persistent rain, which fell on every day of the visit except Tuesday and Sunday, and which dripped through the canopy deck and left the rowers permanently drenched; this was not an experience any of the trireme veterans had had in Greece. The demands of ceremonial and publicity, coupled with the problems of navigating on the busy Tideway, meant that no actual trials were even contemplated. Research activities were limited to making bio-mechanical measurements, testing the use of double pipe (*aulos*) for timekeeping, and an experiment with the oars. The measurements, using a special frame designed by Ford Weiskittel continued those begun during the 1992 sea-trials to collect data on movement and length of stroke during fixed-seat rowing. The *aulos* was a reconstruction of an ancient, reeded double-pipe, based on an example from the Temple of Artemis at Brauron and other finds in the British Museum and the National Archaeological Museum at Athens, and made by naval architects Professor Doug Pattison, Roy Collins and Stelios Psaroudakes from University College, London. Unfortunately, as with a

previous reconstruction produced for the 1988 sea-trials by the Department of Music at University of California, Berkeley, the experiment was not a success since conditions made the pipes largely inaudible. Finally, a large-bladed thranite oar was tried in a thalamian seat, and a narrower, thalmian oar in a thranite seat; both were found to work perfectly well, which suggests that there is scope for experimentation with different blade shapes and sizes at all three levels.

There were also some incidental discoveries. The incessant rain ensured that the electronic loudspeaker system failed, as it had done in 1988, and once again it was found that the ship could be effectively controlled by the rowing masters, Ford Wesikittel and the present writer, giving simultaneous instructions from the bow and stern respectively (see Morrison, Coates and Rankov 2000, 255). It was striking, however, how greatly this was facilitated by the absence of masts. This was the first and only occasion on which *Olympias* was rowed with the masts unstepped and left ashore. Without their encumbrance, it was much easier for the rowing masters to see each other clearly, move up and down the ship, and make themselves heard to the crew. This undoubtedly helps to explain why masts were normally put ashore before battle in antiquity (Thucydides 7.24.2; Xenophon *Hellenica* 2.1.9; 6.2.27; Plutarch *Life of Antony* 64.2; Dio Cassius 50.33.5; cf. Polybius 1.61.1; Livy 36.44.2–3).

There is no doubt, however, that the visit's greatest value lay in its publicity impact. The ship's outings were reported daily in the British press and on Greek and British television, as well as further afield. Many thousands of people watched the ship under oar from the banks of the Thames, and public interest in the ship and in Greek antiquity in general was raised significantly. The involvement of the Speaker and the House of Commons in the celebration of Greek democracy was also a clear diplomatic success ahead of Athens' (eventually abortive) bid for the 1996 Olympics. The 1993 excursion to London remains the only occasion to date on which *Olympias* has travelled outside Greece, but provides an indication of how popular and effective such good-will visits by the ship could be.

Bibliography

Morrison, J. S., Coates, J. F., and Rankov, N. B. (2000) *The Athenian Trireme. The History and Reconstruction of an Ancient Greek Warship.* 2nd ed. Cambridge, Cambridge University Press.

3. Report of the 1994 Sea Trials of the Trireme *Olympias*

Timothy Shaw

Introduction

The sea trials of *Olympias* were resumed off the island of Poros, Greece, in July 1994.

These were the sixth in the series arranged by The Trireme Trust with the much-appreciated co-operation of the Hellenic Navy and the Greek Government. The main purposes of these trials were educational and scientific: educational, in giving young people a practical insight into some aspects of life as it may have been lived in classical antiquity; and scientific, in that the oarcrews recruited by The Trireme Trust were asked to perform tests contributing towards a better understanding of the design and the capabilities of ancient triremes and oared ships generally. The main purpose of this report is to draw attention to new findings arising from the 1994 trials: it is not an outing-by-outing account of them.

Organisation of the trials

Matters of a routine nature coming under this heading were covered in Newsletter No. 13 of The Trireme Trust, which gives extensive acknowledgements and names the principal officers acting for The Trireme Trust.

The Trireme Trust's crew

The pulling master was Andrew Taylor.

As the leaders of The Trireme Trust USA did not recruit a contingent, the 1994 crew consisted predominantly of English men and women. A handful of Americans did come and they were most welcome. Although about as many English people were recruited as in any previous trials except the first, the lack of a numerous American contingent was felt in that the number of people rowing at any time scarcely exceeded 120, whereas a full oarcrew numbers 170. The shortfall was regrettable but it did not prevent some useful results from being obtained.

Condition of the ship and oars

Although leakage was negligible, the condition of the hull gave cause for remark as the 'hog' had increased. Details obtained by Andrew Taylor were notified to John Coates, who made appropriate recommendations to the Greek authorities. The 'hog' together with the lightening of the ship caused by the shortfall of about 50 rowers, made it harder for some of the rowers amidships to cover their blades. Putting ballast on board to counter this was considered but not carried out. When the mainsail was briefly lowered it was seen to need some repairs. The 'boat' sail was not lowered and so its condition remained unknown to the Trust. The standing and running rigging appeared to be all right. The flotation bags, air bottles and fire extinguishers were present.

There were enough oars in usable condition for the crew of about 120 rowers. Inevitably a few of the original oars, 7 years old by the time of the trials, were broken as they were in each year of trials. It was clear that some new thranite and zygian oars would be needed the next time a full crew was recruited, and as had been pointed out before, it would be helpful if the thalamian oars were superseded by oars more like those of the two upper levels.

A "new" knot

Perhaps the most intriguing discovery during the 1994 trials was that of a "new" knot – new to the Trireme Trust, that is – for tying the oars to the tholepins. A photograph of the knot is given as Fig. 3.1. The knot was demonstrated to Dick Farmer by a descendant of a long line of Greek fisherfolk, who had visited *Olympias* and had noticed that our oarloops were "wrongly tied".

Doug Lindsay has described how to tie the new knot:

> [The method] calls for a slightly longer thole strap – about one fathom long. Tie a stopper knot in one end. Working from that stopper knot, held close to the oar and tholepin directly in front of the tyer, take three turns round oar and pin, with the underturn inboard of the tholepin so as not

to choke the oar, come up from behind and take a round turn round the stopper knot. From this round turn, lead the tail under the upper part of the three round turns, and make this into a half hitch enclosing the three loops. Pulled tight, it makes a positive knot which is readily adjustable, but allows the three loops to self-equalise the strain on them. A thinner rope, probably no more than 8 mm, will be adequate. Apparently this knot has been used by the locals for generations. I tried it on my oar for the last couple of days of trials, and it performed well.

Although Homer refers to leather thongs for tying oars to tholepins, they have not so far proved satisfactory in *Olympias*, rope grommets being much better. Leather might be strong enough, however, if used in the way now disclosed, and this ought to be tried in any future trials.

Instrumentation

Rates of striking were measured by means of a 'rating' watch using a four-stroke count. The speed of the ship was measured by means of a Trimble Ensign Portable Global Position System or GPS which assessed the ship's rate of change of position by reference to various artificial satellites above the Earth. On the whole the device worked well and there is no need to doubt that its readings were reasonably accurate except when interference was caused by walkie-talkie transmitters on board.

Summary of the tests

The programme of tests described below may fairly be criticised as unambitious. Professor Morrison had obtained from the Greek Admiralty permission for a much fuller programme involving sailing as well as a long-distance row, but the Captain of *Olympias* exercised his discretion and disallowed some of the intended tests.

The tests are described in the order: tests in the barracks, tests in the ship, tests of oars.

Tests in the barracks

In order to throw more light on the internal layout of triremes, with particular reference to the currently-accepted *interscalmium* of 0.98 m, the programme called for measurements of the power, weight, stature, reach and fore-and-aft space occupancy of members of the oarcrew. The rowers are thanked for their co-operation. The results showed – *inter alia* – that the average height of our women rowers, 168 cm, happened to be very close to that reported for ancient Greek men, 167 cm (see for example Shaw 1993, 64). Accordingly it is important to note that when our women rowers were at their full forward reach, which incidentally gave an average stroke length of 1.04 m, the fore-and-aft space they occupied when ready for the catch, measured at the level of their knuckles, averaged 0.99 m. A similar test conducted in the ship and commented on below confirmed and extended these results.

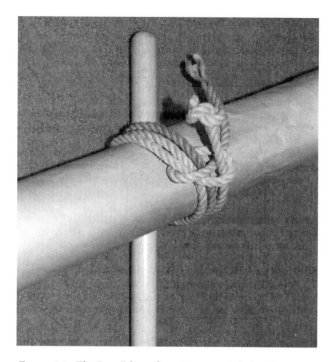

Figure 3.1. The "new" knot for tying oars to tholes; the stopper knot has been pulled clear, for clarity (Photo: Nan Shaw).

Tests in the ship

A test of the space occupancy of a number of the starboard side thranites was conducted. All the starboard side thranite seats from the stern to about the mainmast were occupied and the men and women in them were asked to swing forward with arms stretched until they touched the next person, whilst keeping the blades out of the water by a few inches. Fig. 3.2, which is typical, shows Steve Strong in seat 20 during the test. His right hand overlaps the next man's back, inboard of it. This was possible because of the oar's inboard length and its obliquity, and of course it reflects the fact that the *interscalmium* in *Olympias* is only 0.888 m. If Steve and the next man aft continued to occupy the same fore-and-aft spaces just before the catch in a ship with an *interscalmium* of 0.98 m, the clearance between them would be 9.2 cm. Clearance is important because if crew members are to row long, hard strokes they need to be sure they will not be hit in the back even occasionally, let alone on almost every catch. A calculation is given in Appendix 1 to show that even a clearance of 15 cm. would be insufficient to cover errors of timing of 0.1 second at the catch, at top speed. Also, the writer considers that to rival ancient cruising speeds a modern crew would have to reach a little further forward than was possible for Steve Strong in *Olympias*; this would of course reduce the clearance unless the layout of the oar-rig were altered from that of *Olympias* to allow a rower's oarhandle, when nearest the stern, to pass alongside and *outboard* of the trunk of the next rower aft. On the evidence from our women, this would apply to triremes manned by ancient

Figure 3.2. Steve Strong (thranite) rowing in seat 20 of Olympias *in 1994 (Photo: Nan Shaw).*

Greek men. A plan view showing roughly what is meant is given as Fig. 3.3.

The stroke length implied by ancient cruising speeds is discussed in Appendix 3.

As in previous years the oarcrew was divided into sections each under a team leader who acted as the coach of his or her section under the general direction of the pulling master. Twenty outings were planned. Three were cancelled and others were terminated early because of the wind.

The rowing trials confirmed the practicality of rowing the ship with one level of rowers missing, *i.e.* not even sitting there as ballast, but on the whole the rowing was weak. Not surprisingly, no great speed was obtained, the highest speed indicated by the GPS being 7.1 knots in a tailwind. It was held for a few seconds only.

It was confirmed that the thranite and zygian oars can be used without difficulty in the thalamian level, and that they enable the thalamians to work harder than they can with their usual oars.

An unhistorical feature of the trials to date has been the use of loudspeakers to convey the pulling master's instructions to the oarcrew. The speakers have been a great help particularly during a crew's first few outings, and 1994 was no exception. However it has always been desirable to try working without them, and in 1994 Andrew Taylor devised a method of giving certain orders silently by means of hand signals, which were relayed to the rowers near the bows by Acoris Andipa. This worked well with 120 people. This experiment should be repeated with a full crew in any future trials. Whilst orders may sometimes have been communicated silently in antiquity it

remains not unlikely that at other times orders were given by means of a pipe known as a bosun's 'Call'. Here it may be recalled that Douglas Pattison (at that time Professor of Naval Architecture at University College, London) demonstrated replica *auloi* (pipes) on board *Olympias* in London in 1993.

Very little sailing was permitted, and then only in such light winds that nothing new was learnt.

Tests of oars

Measurements of the moment of inertia and other features of ten oars were made on land as a contribution to the improvement of trireme oar design. No thalamian oar was measured as the existing thalamian oars of *Olympias* are regarded as obsolete. The reasons for this are explained in *The Trireme Project*. In 1990 The Trireme Trust had nine new oars made of spruce to a light design for comparison with the modified original oars, which are made of Douglas fir. Seven of the spruce oars were brought to Poros in 1994 and they were measured alongside one old thranite and two old zygian oars. All these oars were 4.22 m long, *i.e.* 9½ cubits of 0.444 m.

The measurements led to a suggested specification for trireme oars of the enhanced length of 4.66 m, *i.e.* 9½ cubits of 0.49 m. This is given in Appendix 2, below the details of the other oars. It is recommended that one 4.66 m oar should be made from spruce for experimental purposes.

Published papers

In 1993 John Coates and Timothy Shaw each presented a

(Diagrammatic - not to scale)

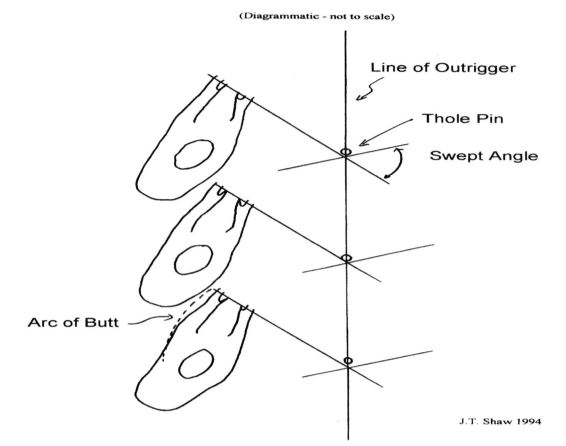

Line of Outrigger

Thole Pin

Swept Angle

Arc of Butt

J.T. Shaw 1994

Figure 3.3. Plan view of Olympias *oar-rig altered to allow the oarhandle to pass alongside and outboard of the trunk of the next rower aft (Drawing: J. T. Shaw).*

paper at one of the Spring Meetings of the Royal Institution of Naval Architects. Both papers were illustrated by drawings by John Coates. The papers were well received, and each was followed by a lively discussion. The papers and discussions were published in different volumes of the transactions as follows:

Coates, J. F. (1994) The Naval Architecture of European Oared Ships. *Transactions of the Royal Institution of Naval Architects, Part B* 136, 175–187

Shaw, J. T. (1993) Rowing in Ships and Boats. *Transactions of the Royal Institution of Naval Architects, Part B* 135, 211–224.

John Coates introduced his paper as follows: "After a brief summary of their history and operational characteristics, some of the main aspects of the naval architecture of European oared ships are discussed, centred upon two types of particular historical importance [These were the Athenian trireme of the 4th century BC and the Mediterranean light galley of the 16th century AD]. This paper is concerned with the effects of oarsystems upon the design, construction and performance of the ships for which they were built. It does not enter into the more general aspects of hulls and rigs on which many books have been written. To keep within the confines of one paper, discussion of many features of these ships has had

to be omitted, in particular armament, rig, manoeuvring and accommodation."

The main headings of John's paper are: Introduction; A Summary Historical Perspective: Oared Ship Operations: Design (Oarpower, Hull Wetted Area and Speed under Oar: Seaworthiness and Speed under Sail; Freeboard and Oar Length: Multi-Rower Oars; Freeboard and Stability: (Constructional Limits); Hull Life, Building Time and Leakage; Acknowledgements.

Timothy Shaw set out to provide the theoretical understanding of rowing geometry, oar mechanics and oarsmanship that is needed alongside other knowledge if the performance of ancient oared ships is to be understood. He has summarised his paper as follows: "The paper discusses the oar-rig of certain oared ships and boats in which each oar is pulled by one man who looks aft (or roughly aft) and is seated. The efficiency and endurance of the human engine are stated and formulae are developed enabling the mean efficiency of the oars of a particular racing eight to be assessed. This leads to an estimate of the efficiency of the oars of the reconstructed trireme *Olympias* which has an oarcrew numbering up to 170. The effects on oar efficiency of variables such as crew's power and ship's resistance are evaluated. Some space is devoted to a reconsideration of a paper on the propulsive efficiency of rowing, published by the Institution in 1927. The paper also contains a short section on the training and control of large oarcrews, a lost art now being rediscovered". In his reply to the Discussion Timothy analysed the merits of a long reach for the catch and those of obtaining the finish by pulling on the oarhandle rather than the footstraps.

Theoretical work

Discussions on the layout of the oar-rig of any future reconstructions of a trireme continued in the light of the studies of the space occupancy of members of the 1994 crew and of the proved effectiveness of the strongly canted and offset oar-rig of fast Cornish gigs. These can reach a speed of 8 knots although they have only 6 rowers. There may thus be merit in similarly canting and offsetting the oar-rig of a trireme. If such a layout could be fitted into a suitable hull it would seem to overcome the restriction of stroke length otherwise associated with the (still) relatively short *interscalmium* of 0.98 m now thought to be characteristic of triremes. With this in mind, the relationship between stroke length and some other parameters implied by a cruising speed of 7½ knots is investigated in Appendix 3, and the suggestion is developed in the writer's three papers elsewhere in this volume.

Appendix 1

Clearance at the catch and errors of timing at top speed

For this calculation some assumptions have to be made. Those chosen are as follows: Top speed is 9.7 knots (say 5.00 m/s), the effective stroke length at the butt is 0.99 m (see Appendix 3 for this), ⅔ of the angle swept by an oar outboard is forward of an athwartships line through the tholepin (thus the angle of attack, when seen in plan, is 90 degrees minus ⅔ of the swept angle when the latter is projected onto a horizontal plane); and the oar is 2½ cubits (1.225 m) long inboard of the pin, 7 cubits (3.43 m) long outboard of it. Also the instantaneous turning point of the oar with respect to undisturbed water is taken to be a little way up the shaft from the neck, say 0.60 m from the tip and so 2.83 m from the pin, and once the blade is covered a man's oarbutt is at the same level as his shoulders, or nearly so, the catch is taken with straight arms, and the seats and stretchers are laid out parallel to the keel or nearly so.

If the oar slopes at 30 degrees to the horizontal in the conditions given above, the angle of attack is 52.9 degrees.

The fore-and-aft component of the momentary rate of the movement of the butt of the oar relative to the ship is then given by:

$$(1.225/2.83)(5.00)\sin^2(52.9); \text{ this is } 1.38\text{m/s}$$

and this will be the speed of movement of the man's shoulders rearwards if he swings straight along a line parallel to the keel. If this speed remained constant it would follow that a distance of 0.15 m would be traversed in 0.109 seconds; but actually the speed will increase. A distance of 0.15 m at the butt implies a swept angle of 7.0 degrees *i.e.* the angle of attack has increased to 59.9 degrees, and if the other conditions are unchanged, the shoulder speed will be 1.62 m/s. Actually it will be a little more as the instantaneous turning point will have moved a little nearer the thole. It is clear that if a rower is late by one tenth of a second in catching the water at the angle given here (*i.e.* about 53 degrees) the rower next aft will certainly be hit in the back if the designed clearance is only 0.15 m. The reader may modify the calculation to show the effect at other speeds, stroke lengths and so on.

Appendix 2

Physical properties of oars

Details of three oars of Douglas fir and seven oars of spruce are given below. The spruce oars were designed by John Coates in consultation with the writer as a result of experience with the original oars of Douglas fir during the 1987 and 1988 trials. They were made by F. Collar of Oxford, belong to The Trireme Trust and were first used in 1990. Modification of the Douglas fir oars was completed during the 1990 trials.

In 1994 the radii of gyration, the moments of inertia about the thole and the positions of the centres of percussion of the ten oars were obtained by experiments using a stopwatch and a bifilar suspension (for details of the method see Lamb 1923, 158–9, 164).

C of G = centre of gravity

The weight "in hand" is calculated as though it acted at the butt, from the overall weight, the inboard length and the distance of the C of G from the thole. The inboard length is taken to be 3ft 7 ins. (1.092 m) in all cases. This dimension was found by the users of spruce oars to be the most convenient in *Olympias*.

MIT = the moment of inertia about the thole, a measure of handiness.

X = the distance of the centre of percussion from the tip of the blade. A positive sign indicates that the centre of percussion is beyond the tip. According to Bourne, the best position for it is within the blade about 6 inches, say 15 cm, from the tip, *i.e.* X = -.15m (Bourne 1925).

The main results are given in Table 3.I.

The old oars and spruce oars nos. 1 and 2 have squared looms. The others have looms of circular cross-section. The old oars had been modified by the Hellenic Navy in accordance with the requirements of John Coates, but the superiority of the spruce oars is clear. It can be concluded that spruce oars 4.66 m long (*i.e.* built in accordance with a cubit of 0.49 m) could be given a satisfactorily low MIT. They could weigh as little as 10 lbf, perhaps less, and as shown below their MIT might be kept as low as 8 kg-m². The adequate rigidity of the existing 4.22 m spruce oars when used by the strongest oarsmen in the 1990 trials gives reason to believe that the 4.66 m oars would not be too

Table 3.1

Spruce oar no.	Wt. lbf	Wt. in hand lbf	Radius of gyration squared m²	Distance of C of G from butt m	MIT kg-m²	X m	Remarks
1	12	7.9	1.48	1.81	10.8	-0.35	
2	12	8.0	1.41	1.82	10.6	-0.46	
3	10½	8.2	1.45	1.94	10.3	-0.57	
4	10	7.8	1.42	1.94	9.7	-0.61	
5	10	7.3	1.45	1.89	9.5	-0.51	
6	9	6.7	1.38	1.90	8.3	-0.61	
7							Missing
8							Missing
9	9	7.2	1.43	1.97	9.0	-0.62	
Old oars							
A	21	10.2	1.45	1.62	18.2	+0.15	Zygian
B	22	9.6	1.38	1.57	17.8	+0.24	Zygian
C	17	7.4	1.46	1.57	13.1	+0.40	Thranite

flexible. The lengthwise dimensions and other desirable properties of a spruce oar 9½ cubits of 0.49 m long can now be specified:

Suggested specification of a spruce oar 4.66 m long

Weight overall: 4.5 kgf (*i.e.* about 10 lbf)
Weight 'in hand' (at the butt): 2.0 kgf (say 4½ lbf)
Gearing 2.8 (*i.e.* 2½ cubits inboard, 7 cubits outboard; this gearing is suitable for fast rowing on fixed seats, and does not entail too steeply-inclined a thranite oar)

From the foregoing, it follows that the centre of gravity must be 0.544 m outboard of the fulcrum and distant 2.886 m from the tip of the blade. Now if the centre of percussion is to be within the blade 0.15 m from the tip it must be 2.736 m from the C of G. From physical principles this distance times that between the C of G and the fulcrum defines the square of the radius of gyration of the oar which is therefore 2.736 × 0.544 *i.e.* 1.488. Our experience with the 4.22 m oars indicates that this should be attainable with 4.66 m oars by careful attention to the taper of the shafts and looms, to the blade area and thickness and so on. The moment of inertia about the thole would then be 4.5 (1.488 + 0.544²) *i.e.* about 8 kg-m². Such an outcome would be most satisfactory. It is recommended that an oar as near as possible to this specification be built for test.

Appendix 3

Cruising at 7½ knots: a note on the implications for stroke length and oar-rig layout

The best evidence we have for the cruising speed of fast triremes is the statement by Xenophon that a trireme under oar could reach Heraclea from Byzantium in "a long day" (see my paper 'From the Golden Horn to Heraclea'

elsewhere in this volume). The least distance between these points, ignoring currents, is about 129 nautical miles. As explained in *The Trireme Project*, it looks as if a speed of 7½ knots or a trifle more will fit the facts (Shaw 1993, 64).

By applying elementary trigonometry and one or two acceptable assumptions it is possible to deduce a quantitative relationship between length of stroke, slip of the oarblades, overall length and gearing of the oars, stroke rate, rhythm factor and speed. One cubit (0.49 m) appears to be a reasonable least value for the fore-and aft slip at the tip of a skilfully-rowed trireme oar; it implies an efficiency of the oars (inertia losses being neglected) of about 0.8 which is not likely to be improved on. If modern oarsmen are anything to go by, the greatest stroke length of which ancient Greek men 167 cm tall, rowing on fixed thwarts, were capable if unrestricted by their rig, was about 1.1 m, measured at the butt; however since 10% of this was probably taken up by lost motion at the ends of the stroke, the effective (*i.e.* powered) length would probably have been about 0.99m. But if the rig was not appreciably canted and offset, the powered stroke length possible within an *interscalmium* of 0.98m would have been restricted to about 0.87 m, as the total movement would be no greater than the *interscalmium* even if the clearance were as little as 0.15 m; and the end losses would be the same, 0.11 m, as with the longer stroke. These two butt-end movements, 0.99 m and 0.87 m, are considered in what follows.

If the speed is 7½ knots and the fore-and-aft slip is 0.49 m and the oars are 4.66 m long with a gearing of 2.8, and ⅔ of the swept angle occurs forward of the pin, the relationship between stroke length, stroke rate and rhythm factor in the region of interest can be tabulated as shown in the first three columns of Table 3.2 reading from the left.

The ratio of rhythm factors at a given stroke rate is 1.17 which is the ratio of distances travelled by the ship during the effective pull.

If at 32 spm the rhythm factor were kept at 3.21 while the effective stroke length was reduced from 0.99 m to 0.87

Table 3.2. Speed 7½ knots.

Stroke Rate	Rhythm factor at length		Mean couple on the oarhandle, newton-metres, at length	
	0.99 m	0.87 m	0.99 m	0.87 m
30	3.42	4.01	215	246
32	3.21	3.76	202	231
34	3.02	3.53	190	218
36	2.85	3.34	180	206
38	2.70	3.16	172	196

m, the speed would fall. It could be restored to 7½ knots by raising the stroke rate by a factor of 1.17 to 37.4 spm. Similar reasoning can be applied to the other cases.

If the effective stroke length were reduced from 0.99 m to 0.87 m but the stroke rate, rhythm factor and slip were unchanged the speed could be restored to 7½ knots only by altering the gearing from 2.8 to 3.18. The ratio of these is (nearly) 99/87. Judging by our experience during the design of existing spruce oars, any increase in gearing beyond 2.8 would bring proportionate difficulties over the balance of the oar.

In all these cases the mean power the crew must apply to the ship, called the mean effective power, is the same because the speed of the ship is the same; but because of differences in stroke rate and rhythm factor the mean couples the rowers have to apply to their oars will differ, as exemplified in the fourth and fifth columns of Table II. If the resistance of the ship at 7½ knots (3.86 m/s) is that of *Olympias* at that speed, say 3100 newtons, the mean effective power (averaged over the duration of the pull plus the run) is 3100×3.86 *i.e.* 11966 W or say 12.0 kW: each oar must therefore exert 70.6 W on the ship, on a continuous average, or 70.6f W averaged during the effective pull only, where f is the rhythm factor. Rhythm factor is defined as:

$$\frac{\text{the duration of the pull plus run}}{\text{the duration of the effective pull}}$$

To calculate the couple we need to know the gross power applied to each oarhandle. It is greater than the effective power because the blade must shift water in order to create the necessary reaction, and the oar's inertia has to be overcome. The gross power can be obtained to a good approximation as follows.

To the quantity of 70.6f W the rower must add about a further 25% on account of the water shifted by the blade, and an amount of about $0.004r^2$ on account of the oar's inertia, r being the stroke rate. Thus the gross power that the rower must exert on the oarhandle, averaged over the duration of the effective pull is about:

$$1.25 \times 70.6f + 0.004r^2 \text{ watts}$$

The mean couple or mean bending stress that the rower applies to the oar during the pull is given by the mean gross power divided by the mean angular velocity of the oar relative to the ship during the effective pull. (This implies a suitable definition of 'mean'). The couples are given in columns 4 and 5 of Table 3.2. From this table some advantages of longer strokes at any given stroke rate are evident: they would put less stress on oars, oarloops and tholepins; by the same token they would require less pull from the rower, and less immersed blade area. These may prove to be critical advantages.

The premises underlying the calculation imply a mean angular velocity for the oar, during the effective pull, of 1.42 radians per second for the stroke length 0.99 m, differing only slightly from that for the length of 0.87 m, which is 1.45 radians per second. Note that because the mean angular velocity for each stroke length is independent of stroke rate and rhythm factor, the immersed blade area must increase with rhythm factor in order to generate sufficient reaction. This may have implications for the static and dynamic balance of the oar.

Having outlined the various options, and mentioned the importance of clearance, the writer invites suggestions as to the choice of length, stroke rate and rhythm most likely to have enabled a fast trireme to sustain 7½ knots for hours on end. He would merely add that if he has assumed too little slip on the blades, he has underestimated the stroke rate required at any particular length and rhythm.

The mean couple expresses the mean bending stress on the oar at the thole. The couple varies during a stroke, its greatest value being considerably higher than the mean.

Acknowledgements and thanks

The Global Positioning System was hired from Regis Electronics. King's School, Canterbury is thanked for the loan of ergometers (contact: Mr. Richard Hooper).

Bibliography

Bourne, G. C. (1925) *A Textbook of Oarsmanship*. Oxford, Oxford University Press.

Lamb, H. (1923) *Dynamics*. 2nd ed. Cambridge, Cambridge University Press.

Shaw, J. T. (ed.) (1993) *The Trireme Project*. Oxford, Oxbow Books.

Trireme Trust *Newsletter* No.13.

4. The Slow Trireme Experience in *Olympias* in 1994

Andrew Taylor

1. Introduction

A variety of reasons have been identified for ancient commentators to record ships or a whole fleet as slow or fast. A summary of the 1994 sea trials alludes to many of those factors associated with the slow trireme classification. The increasing age of *Olympias* has brought a more pronounced hog and generally loosening structure. An under-strength crew reduced the motive power available to drive the ship. A crew of relatively inexperienced rowers, with few veterans from previous trials, compounded the numerical shortfall. An entirely new generation of officers running the oarcrew and experimental trials programme made the trials a fresh start.

However, in terms of experimental archaeology these factors provide performance details in a rather different range from those reported previously. The different style and priorities of a new rowing master also provided a different perspective as well as a new voice in the stern.

2. Comparison of 2-level and 3-level rowing

The reduced number of crew available for the 1994 trials made it relatively easy to compare directly the effects of rowing on two and three levels with essentially the same people rowing. During the first ten days of the trials, the crew had an approximately equal number of sessions rowing on first three, then two levels. Two days at the end of the two weeks were dedicated to achieving the 1994 crew's best performance: 28 July was rowed on two levels and 29 July on three with the crew centrally located between seats 6 and 28.

On both these days *Olympias* was rowed at full achievable speed through the Poros Channel with the time to row from the central square war memorial to the chapel at the eastern end being recorded; in each case the timed course was a maximum effort piece in the middle of 20 minutes of continuous rowing. Average speed and distance run has been estimated from the GPS receiver readings recorded during the timed section. The chart of Poros Harbour and Approaches gives a minimum distance for the fixed distance as 0.52 nautical miles although the actual course steered may have been as much as 0.58 nautical miles. Seating plans, recording who actually rowed, and where, were completed for the two 'race days.' In conjunction with the 6-minute fixed-seat ergometer test results, it is possible to make a detailed comparison of the crew's power output for the two days. These data are summarised in Table 4.1. The average power output in the ergometer tests was 160 Watts; individuals ranged from 328 to 83 W, with 18% of them above 200 W and only one individual above 240 W. The 1994 trials crew were relatively weak and unfit.

Essentially the same people rowed on each day, the slight reduction in number on the second day being due to early departures at the end of the trials. The same set of oars was used in each case with the necessary repositioning happening after rowing on 28 July. Both pieces were completed during the morning outings after 20–25 minutes of warm-up rowing. The light wind was of similar strength and direction on both days, however the channel course was chosen to maximise shelter; the pieces were rowed in essentially still conditions. The time of day was similar with any tide or current through the channel assumed to be the same. Precise courses were not recorded and variation in the track may have sampled different currents as well as varying the total distance covered. For a variety of reasons, return trips through the channel did not provide reliable rowing data. The grouping of the crew into the more severely hogged central section of the ship may have adversely affected performance on the second day.

Towing tests undertaken in 1988 provide measurements of the total power necessary to overcome resistance at a given speed (Coates, Platis and Shaw 1990, 21, 72; Shaw 1993a). The values appropriate to the measured speeds have been included in Table 4.1. The efficiency of the oarsystem and technical ability of the crew to deliver the necessary propulsive power can be estimated by comparing

Table 4.1. Details of the timed rows through the Poros channel comparing Olympias *being rowed on the two upper levels with essentially the same crew rowing on all three levels a day later. A few people sat in thalamian seats on the first day whilst several left before the second day's trials. There is no perceptible difference between the two modes.*

	2-level	3-level
	28 July, 1994	29 July, 1994
Time taken	7 min 25 sec	7 min 56 sec
Speed, if distance 0.56 n.m.	4.5 kn	4.2 kn
Power to overcome resistance	3.6 kW	2.9 kW
GPS distance run	0.607 n.m.	0.668 n.m.
GPS mean speed	4.91 kn	5.05 kn
Power to overcome resistance	4.7 kW	5.1 kW
Crew rowing	119	111
Total ergometer power (average for 6 minutes)	19.0 kW	17.7 kW
Thranite ergometer power	9.15 kW	6.16 kW
Zygian ergometer power	9.00 kW	6.56 kW
Thalamian ergometer power	0.87 kW	5.01 kW

these figures with those measured on the ergometers. The efficiencies range from 19 to 25 % with 2 levels and 16 to 29% with 3 levels rowing; the uncertainty results from the variation in speed estimates. If the crew had spread their efforts more evenly over the 20 minutes of continuous rowing, then we might have expected a 20 % reduction in average power output, as compared with the 6-minute ergometer tests. This would bring the mean efficiency to 28%, more in line with that found in the sprints (see Section 3 below).

There was no perceptible difference in the ability of the oarcrew to propel the ship whether organised on two or three levels. This result confirms that the reasons for the previously reported lack of effective contribution by the thalamian rowers in *Olympias* have been found (Shaw 1993b, 62). Due to the reduced crew numbers in 1994, all the thalamians rowed with wide-bladed oars allowing them to reach the same efficiency as rowers on other levels. The earlier result does not prove that ancient triremes did not have oars at three levels (cf. Tilley 1995). As with the 1990 trials, the average power output of the thalamian rowers, as measured in the ergometer tests, was not significantly different from that of the other two levels (Shaw 1993b). The low average power output of the crew meant that it was not possible to test this conclusion at speeds above 5 knots.

3. Top speed in 1994

On 28 July, three maximal effort sprint runs were undertaken. *Olympias* was accelerated steadily to attain maximum speed, which was then sustained for 45 seconds. Table 4.2 summarises the results.

Run A was conducted in a 10 to 15 knot tail wind. Based on drifting tests John Coates has provided formulae by which to calculate the net resistance/assistance for any true wind (Coates, Platis and Shaw 1990, 32). The wind assistance on the first run will be equivalent to a power contribution of somewhere from 1.3 to 4.4 kW

across the range of estimated wind speeds, which brings the effective power delivered by crew down to a value nearer that produced in the last two runs. Runs B and C were completed in opposite directions in calm water well sheltered from any wind. In total, an hour of rowing had been conducted prior to the last two sprint runs being undertaken, although each was preceded by a short rest.

Each of the sprint runs required approximately two minutes of maximal effort from the crew. Typical athletes will be able to maintain an average power output over two minutes which is approximately twenty percent higher than that maintained over 6 minutes. That is, if the crew had undertaken 2-minute ergometer tests, we would have expected power outputs twenty percent higher than those recorded in the 6 minute tests. On 28 July, 1994 the crew would have delivered a total power equivalent to 22.8 kW. The maximum speeds obtained by the 1994 trials crew required an effective power of 10 kW giving overall efficiency for the crew and oarsystem of 43% in short bursts. This is broadly similar to the 39% transfer coefficient of power from shore to ship quoted by Shaw for the 1990 trials crew performance in similar sprints (Shaw 1993b). Shaw also found that the relative drop in mechanical power with increasing duration was more pronounced in earlier trials crews as compared with standard reference figures. This would tend to reduce the efficiency figure quoted here for the 1994 crew, perhaps also explaining some of the difference from the longer duration pieces discussed above.

4. Sensitivity at the oar handle

In common with oared vessels in general, *Olympias* can accommodate a roll of up to 3 degrees thereby allowing rowers to continue working their oars in both waves and crosswind. When the ship is inclined at 3 degrees from the upright, the rowers on the 'down' side cannot clear waves larger than about 0.2 m from trough to crest, compared with about 0.8 m when the ship is upright. A number of

Table 4.2. Details of sprint runs undertaken on 28 July, 1994. Following a steady acceleration, the crew was asked to maintain their best possible speed for a further 45 seconds. The means of the speeds from the GPS receiver, recorded over the last 45 seconds, are tabulated. The power necessary to overcome water resistance at the speeds noted on the line above have been calculated from Annex F.3 in Coates, Platis and Shaw 1990.

	Run A	*Run B*	*Run C*
Time from start of outing	17 min	74 min	80 min
Rest immediately preceding run	8 min	6 min	3 min
Duration of piece (min:sec)	4:50	3:18	5:15
Stroke rate during last 45 s	44 spm	42 spm	43 spm
Mean of speeds in last 45 s	7.0 kn	6.3 kn	6.3 kn
Oar power to overcome resistance	14.1 kW	9.9 kW	9.9 kW
Peak speed recorded by GPS	7.1 kn	6.4 kn	6.3 kn
Oar power to overcome resistance	14.9 kW	10.4 kW	9.9 kW

factors affect the angle of the oars relative to the rower's position in the ship, effectively the angle the oar loom makes with the mean water level. Change in roll and pitch as people move around the vessel, turning manoeuvres, changes in displacement and hogging, as well as crosswinds, will all affect the relative height at which the oar handle is worked. Increasing wave amplitude requires a larger margin for clearance.

4.1 Displacement for a reduced crew

In 1994 *Olympias* was manned by a crew of 130 (typically with 120 rowing), 70 people less than the designed complement. All the oarcrew, including non-rowing section leaders *etc.*, were weighed: 124 people with a total mass of 8.87 tonnes. To this should be added: the Hellenic Navy personnel also aboard during the trials, six or seven individuals at 0.5 tonnes, and an allowance for drinking water and other personal items, 3 kg per person, thus giving a total crew walk-on weight of 9.8 tonnes. The ship's displacement without crew but with oars and fitted for sailing was measured at 26.12 tonnes in 1990 (Shaw 1993b). Reducing the number of oars aboard by 50, at 9 kg each, and adding the crew mass gives a total displacement for 36.4 tonnes. Subtracting the 50 oars left ashore and the missing 70 crew (75 kg average with 3 kg of kit) from the 1990 overall displacement of 42.25 tonnes, we get a similar figure of 36.3 tonnes.

Olympias' hydrostatic curves indicate a sinkage of 11 mm per tonne for displacements from 30 to 50 tonnes (Shaw 1993b). During the 1994 trials the ship was 5.9 tonnes lighter than designed and consequently rode 65 mm higher in the water. If oar blades are assumed to remain fully immersed, this increase in the height of the wales above the water will increase the angle the loom makes to the horizontal by 2.0 degrees for the thranites. Most of the 3-degree design tolerance was therefore missing in 1994, making it extremely difficult to keep the blades immersed in the troughs of even small waves, on the windward side in a crosswind or on the inside of even a gentle turn.

The end of the oar handle will be 3 cm higher compared with the surrounding structure of the ship when the crew is reduced to the numbers employed in 1994. Most critically, in *Olympias* as currently fitted out, the zygian looms just short of the handle section will rise by 16 mm, leading to their frequently hitting the structure supporting the thranite seats during the power phase of each stroke. The experience of the 1994 trials indicated that we were operating at the lower limit of displacement for which *Olympias* could be rowed in the calm water available at Poros. The ship would need ballasting to be effectively rowed in wave amplitudes over 0.2 m or with fewer crew in calm conditions.

4.2 Crew movement

The sensitivity of skilled rowers to the position of the oar handle as the blade enters the water means they can detect the change in heel associated with a single person moving across the canopy from one side of *Olympias* to the other. Assuming that the person was 75 kg, moved 4.0 m, and that the ship displaced 42 tonnes (full crew) and had a metacentric height of 1.13 m, then these rowers detect and need to compensate for a total roll of just 0.4 degrees. Blind tests with the 1994 oarcrew indicated that rowers, with a wide range of experience, could reliably identify whenever two people moved across the ship at any point along its length, a change in heel of 0.7 degrees (metacentric height 1.3 m, displacement 37 tonnes). Unexpected changes in the height of the oar handle as it is placed in the water degrades the performance of the oarcrew. During critical battle manoeuvres a minimum of non-rowing movement would be essential, and it is little wonder that marines were trained to throw javelins from a seated position.

During the 1992 cruise around the Saronic Gulf, 40-minute periods of rowing were interspersed with 20 minutes of rest, the ship being rowed from the upper two levels only. Following the changeover people would move rapidly to the bow to relieve themselves in buckets stationed on the foredeck. The change in trim that resulted when around ten people joined the toilet queue rendered it nearly impossible for those in the bow section to extract their oars from the water at the end of the stroke. The slight wave chop of around 0.3 m certainly exacerbated the problem. The net effect of moving 800 kg forward by 15 m reduces the trim at the forward tip of the ram by immersing it a further 8 cm. At seat 6, 9.2 m from the bow, this corresponds to a reduction in trim of 4 cm, with the height of the oarhandle dropping by 18 mm compared to the rower and ship structure. Rowers in the stern would have needed a similar increase in height to keep the blade in the water, but they were not sufficiently aggrieved to complain of the effect. Moving even a few troops forward immediately prior to contact would significantly affect oar performance in the critical moments leading up to ramming.

Ancient accounts seldom describe triremes carrying more than 30 to 40 troops in addition to the normal complement. If we allow an average body weight of 75 kg with an extra 25 kg of equipment per person, then 30 additional troops will add an extra 3 tonnes to the ship's displacement. Here we estimate the effect on the oar handle as experienced by the rowers. The extra deck troops will cause a sinkage of 33 mm and decrease the height of the oarhandle by 15 mm. Clearly this was considered acceptable by ancient commanders and is less than that experienced as becoming unacceptable in *Olympias*, but emphasises the narrow range of tolerances under which an oared warship could operate. Carrying 60 extra troops would double the loss in vertical clearance and require strong remedial action even to make rowing possible. Commanders would need to ensure safety in waves of up to perhaps one metre, which would increase the required clearance over that discussed here.

Rowers in *Olympias* have frequently customised their height relative to the oar handle by changing the size of the cushion used. Typically this allows people of widely different heights to row more effectively in the positions constructed for an average individual. Within the context of carrying additional troops, it would be possible to remove the cushions entirely, making rowing possible, but with an attendant loss of efficiency, to say nothing of comfort. Coates proposed the use of variable-height cushions to provide optimal performance in both rough and smooth water (Coates, Platis and Shaw 1990, 81).

4.3 Hogging

The hog of *Olympias* has continued to increase with age. The height above the water of both the thranite outrigger and main upper wale were measured without the crew aboard (Fig. 4.1). The similarity of the hog of the main upper wale to that measured in more detail on the outrigger leads to the conclusion that the basic structure of the ship was causing the hogging. A moderate crosswind blowing from starboard caused the slight heel to port.

The mid-section wales were from 50 to 80 mm higher than the mean for each side, graphically indicating the extent of hogging. This effect is equivalent to the 6-tonne reduction in crew displacement discussed above, with all the negative impact that that implies. Members of the oarcrew who rowed in a variety of positions in *Olympias* commented on the significant difficulties in the centre of the ship as compared to the ends. Toward the ends of the oar wales, heights above the water drop to between 60 and 100 mm below the mean values, which would compound problems associated with carrying crew above the designed complement, *e.g.* thirty additional fighting men. As an oared ship's hog becomes more pronounced, the range of displacements for which the oars can successfully be worked is further reduced.

4.4 Wind-induced heel

As an illustration of the effects of wind induced heel upon the ability of the crew to work the oars, we can investigate the hogging profile (Fig. 4.1) which was measured in the presence of a 15 to 25 knot crosswind. At her mooring *Olympias* was moderately sheltered from this, and so was probably experiencing a lighter wind. In addition, the mooring lines probably resisted a reasonable fraction of the lateral moment.

The mean thranite oar wales were 1.466 m (port) and 1.543 m (starboard) above the water, an average with the ship upright of 1.50 m. The displacement marks, located near seat 7, indicated that the water was 0.86 m (port) and 0.78 m (starboard) above the keel, confirming this 8 cm heel. With a waterline breadth of 3.6 m, this gives a heel angle of 1.3 degrees and an average change in oar angle of 0.9 degrees. In fact, with the hogging as measured in *Olympias*, the oar angles might range from optimal to 4.7 degrees, which for those seats is very near the extreme limits within which a person could row.

If most of the non-rowing crew were repositioned on the windward side of the ship then a moderate wind generated heel could be overcome. Moving 24 crew from a average position on the centre-line to the deck edge, *i.e.* 2 m, would overcome a total heel of 2.2 degrees, which would be sufficient to bring *Olympias* back to a level trim in the crosswind measured. It would be less easy to compensate for crosswinds of greater strength whilst still maintaining a heel angle in which rowing was effective. Use of the sail would tend to impose heel angles large enough to make rowing impossible (see pp. 142–3).

4.5 Manoeuvre-induced heel

Turning a ship inevitably causes it to roll toward the outside of the turn. Tight turns entered at high speed cause *Olympias* to heel considerably. Indeed, during turn diameters of less than about 100 m it is difficult to get the oarblades into the water on the side towards the centre of the turn, even in calm water. Getting the rowers on the inside edge to lean toward the centre of the turn provides some small gains in maintaining trim and therefore helps retain the effectiveness of those who continue rowing on the outside of the curve.

Even in larger-diameter turns, the change in heel of

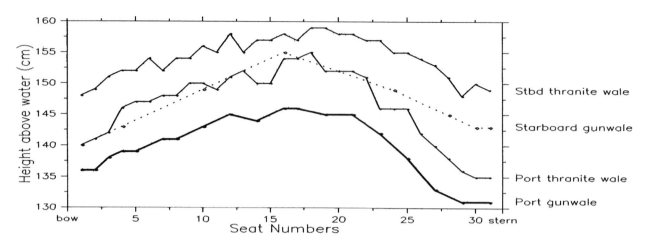

Figure 4.1. Measurement of the hogging profile of **Olympias** *in July 1994. A cross-wind caused the ship to heel to port, a total of 8 cm, as measured by the displacement marks. The outrigger thranite oar wales were measured in detail. Measurements of the upper wale indicate that the overall ship structure was hogged in the same way.*

Olympias, with its attendant change in handle heights, affects an individual's efficiency in placing and extracting the oarblade and therefore his effective oar power. Frequently, the disruption of timing within the oarcrew following the onset of this heel is sufficient to last for the duration of the turn, and this is a significant factor in the loss of boat speed during a turn. A rapid application of helm causes the heel to develop fully between one stroke and the next, thereby maximising the timing problems. We were not able to experiment with less aggressive strategies in 1994. The fact that the heel settled back towards a smaller heel during the turn suggests that such efforts would pay dividends.

An instrument with sufficient accuracy to measure roll to fractions of a degree was not employed in *Olympias* during either the 1992 or 1994 trials, leaving us without detailed quantitative data. As an order of magnitude calculation, if 10 deck crew, 750 kg, were moved 2 m from an average position in the middle of the ship towards the beam at the centre of the turn, they could counterbalance 1.8 degrees of heel; sufficient to overcome heeling problems on the larger diameter turns.

As an illustration of the variation in speed during turns and under a variety of wind conditions, Fig. 4.2 shows three 20-minute sections of rowing during a long session on 23 July, 1994. Annotations on the graphs were logged by the recorder at the time. Typically, the 120-strong oarcrew could maintain 4.5 knots unless disrupted by manoeuvre, wind or boat wash. The lighter than designed displacement made *Olympias* especially sensitive to any change in oar handle heights, and it is our opinion that the resulting loss of timing was the major factor influencing speed loss in all cases except the presence of a head wind. A reduction in speed from 4.5 knots to 2.5 knots represents an 80% loss in effective oar power.

The 1994 trials crew broke no records for particularly rapid or tight turns. With entry speeds of around 4

knots, the crew could achieve a yaw rate of 3 degrees per second.

5. Rowing backwards

Olympias was rowed in reverse for over fifteen minutes on 26 July, 1994, with 4.5 knots being typical of those portions with good timing. A following wind, gusting to 15 knots, boosted this speed to 5.6 knots. Near the end of the run, a gentle 180 degree turn, whilst going astern, was completed in 165 seconds with a final speed of 1.9 knots into the wind. During this piece *Olympias* was pulled backwards, *i.e.* the rowers faced the bows and used the oar of the person in the seat behind. After initial practice, the command to execute a change to or from this mode of rowing was made using a whistle. It typically took from 8 to 12 seconds between the command being given and rowing in the opposite direction being able to commence. The shortest times occurred when the crew were given some warning just preceding the change.

The internal fittings in *Olympias* are not well adapted for pulling the ship backwards. In particular, for most seats there were no strong anchor points on which to brace one's feet, an essential minimum for powerful rowing. During the trials relatively little reverse rowing was practised prior to the piece reported here, with a consequent lack of experience in taking visual timing signals from those in the bows. The mainmast tabernacle and supports for the foredeck also obstructed the sight-lines into the bow. The combination of these factors led to more frequent disintegration of timing than was common when rowing forward at this stage of the trials.

Contrary to previously published reports (Shaw 1993c) there were no problems in controlling the helm whilst moving backwards (including at speeds over 5 knots) or during the 180 degree turn going astern. The helmsman

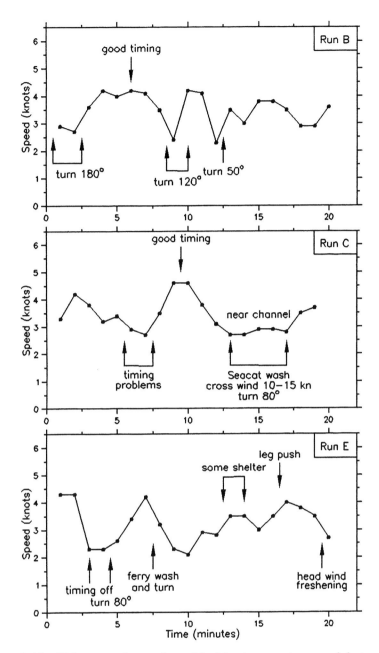

Figure 4.2. Boat speed recorded by GPS receiver during three of the 20-minute sections rowed during a four-hour outing on 23 July, 1994. A one-to-two-minute drink break was provided every 20 minutes. Descriptive notes logged by the recorder during each piece have been added to the graphs. The reduction in speed resulting from the disruptive impact of turns, cross winds, poor timing and boat wash is clearly evident.

described the rudders as feeling 'heavy' but requiring relatively little effort to maintain control. There was no sign of the rudder taking control. Shaw reported that the 1990 trials crew, with two levels rowing could pull the ship in reverse at 4 knots.

6. Boarding and mooring

The following operations were conducted with no particular efforts made to minimise the time taken. Times therefore represent a generous upper limit to that which might have been possible in antiquity:

i) Using one gangway to board the crew of 130 over the stern from the wharf typically took six minutes with people ready to row off in another six to seven minutes. It has previously been reported that a full crew of 200 could be embarked and reach operational readiness in 1 minute 30 seconds, giving some indication of how much some of the times reported here might be reduced (Coates, Platis and Shaw 1990, 37).

ii) Anchoring, backing into a beach, attaching mooring lines to shore and finishing with oars took less than four minutes. Coming off this Mediterranean moor took three minutes, with the operation starting once the last of the oarcrew were aboard. On another occasion it proved possible to slip the stern lines and begin weighing anchor while the final crew members were scrambling aboard.

iii) Around 100 people were recovered from the water in ten minutes. The vast majority climbed onto the ram and then inboard over the bow. It would have been possible to speed this process by stationing assistants at intermediate points along this route. No efforts were made to simulate the extraction from the water of exhausted or injured individuals.

7. Drifting and control of ship orientation

Olympias is blown noticeably to leeward in even fairly light winds. Once the drift speed reaches around 1.5 knots it is possible to point the ship in any desired direction using just the rudders for control. Table 4.3 provides a summary of the final drift speeds reached with the wind at a variety of relative bearings. The Hellenic Navy helmsman usually chose to place the ship broadside to the wind since that minimised drift caused by the wind. The resistance to lateral motion through the water is significantly more than the extra drive due to the increased cross section presented to the wind, a finding similar to that previously published (Coates, Platis and Shaw 1990, 32). From stationary with the bow into a wind gusting to 20 knots, it took 2 minutes, 25 seconds to gain sufficient speed and then turn 90 degrees to drifting beam on. A similar manoeuvre in a wind gusting to 15 knots took 2 minutes 39 seconds.

8. Controlling the oarcrew without electronic speakers

Moderate efforts were made during the 1994 trials to execute and control a variety of manoeuvres without recourse to the electronic amplifier and speakers installed in *Olympias*. As the trials progressed it was possible to run the oar crew in this way with around three people:

i) The rowing master, *keleustes*, near the stern and clearly visible to around two thirds of the oarcrew. The need to immediately acknowledge requests from the helmsman, or captain, and translate these into instructions to the rowers makes the close proximity essential. A vocal relay can also be provided for those rowers in the immediate area of the stern who cannot easily see the rowing master's

Table 4.3. GPS-based estimates of drift with the ship held at a variety of bearings to a 20 knot wind. The rudder provided total control of ship pointing at drift speeds above about 1.5 knots. Boat speeds are probably accurate to a few tenths of a knot, whilst that of the wind is plus or minus about 5 knots.

Ship orientation to wind	Drift speed
Stern to wind	3.4 knots
Wind 45 degrees off stern	2.5 knots
Beam wind	2.6 knots

gestures whilst rowing. Since this group also includes the individuals marked as providing the common timing points for the crew the close proximity makes it easy to provide fine control of the strike rate and hence ship's speed.

ii) A person forward of the mainmast tabernacle (the supporting structure into which the mast is stepped) is essential to relay instructions and hand signals to the more distant and less visible members of the crew in the bow section. This would be an obvious role for an assistant rowing master who may well have been the *pentekontarchos*.

iii) A mobile assistant aft of the mainmast to deal with requests from rowers, emergencies and also to clarify/re-establish communication with the person in the bow. If the deck-crew aboard *Olympias* were more closely integrated with the rowers, as would happen more naturally if, for example, the crew all spoke the same language, then the mobile role of this assistant could be taken by them.

A full-blown whistle in the stern was frequently not heard by those in the bow. On one early occasion, in exasperation, I used a short toot to attract the attention of the bow relay-person (ii). This was assumed by the crew who could hear it to imply an immediate stop. The complete disruption of the oarcrew eventually attracted the relevant attention from the bow section. It is essential that a person is permanently stationed immediately aft of the mainmast, with clear visibility of the rowing master or helmsman, to relay instructions through to those in the bow. With their back to the tabernacle they will not obstruct the view of any of the bow rowers. In addition, this position is the only place from which a single source of sound is audible throughout the oar system, making it a natural position for the *auletes*.

Without a fully developed code of signal instructions, whistles were generally restricted to executing a previously communicated instruction and to attracting the rowers' attention (unique sounds were rapidly established to avoid confusion). The considerable emphasis on looking toward the stern as the means to improve timing had the double benefit of making hand gestures and even mime fairly effective at communicating instructions to the oarcrew. A flute player just aft of the mainmast tabernacle would not be able to provide audible signals whilst also telegraphing mime and hand signals so person (ii) is still required. As a final observation it would not be possible for the bow officer, or *prorates*, to undertake role (iii) with the oarcrew since they would be required to oversee a myriad of other ship operations at just those times when effective communication with the oarcrew was vital, *e.g.* judging distance to a ramming target, anchoring and weighing, marshalling or repelling boarding crews, to name several possible duties.

9. Effective technique and crew skill

Like all effective rowing styles, in whatever context, good

technique in *Olympias* involves placing the blade into the water at maximum reach, drawing it through at a constant depth then extracting it. The fixed seat places relatively more emphasis on a large body motion although, perhaps surprisingly to rowers of modern sliding seat racing shells, it is still possible to deliver substantial power with the legs. Fixed seat does not mean fixed bum, since the hips rotate forward and back with the body causing the leg to bend at the knee joint by up to 45 degrees during the stroke. The feel is like the 'half slide' exercise in a racing shell. This is especially true in the less constricted environment of an ergometer test with the seat firmly tied in place, as compared with conditions in *Olympias*. As a rowing experience, the trireme is definitely constricted although bigger and/or more skilful people tend to create more personal space in which to row. With the restrictions of the slightly short *interscalmium*, every person needs to ensure maximum body lean forward to allow those behind to row at full length. It is possible to deliver a gentle nudge in the back of the person in front to provide any necessary reminders!

Rowing *Olympias* is most critically a question of timing. To achieve this every rower should keep their head up and concentrate on a person as far as possible down the boat. This usually means that they focus on a person on the opposite side which requires clear sight lines down and across in the volume of ship occupied by the rowers' heads; in *Olympias* this involves a minimum of people on the central gangway. To encourage this use of a common timing point, the most visible zygian rowers near the stern were given day-glow armbands on their inboard elbows to clearly attract the eye. Similar armbands on those near the bow would have been a great aid when pulling the ship in reverse.

The thalamians with their view cut off by the cross beam currently have the most restricted sightlines. If their seats were made lower relative to the cross beams by about 150 mm, as has been proposed elsewhere (below, pp. 83, 87), then they could join the rest of the crew in having a view of the sternmost rowers. The addition of racks, in which to store lifejackets immediately below the canopy makes it difficult but not impossible to maintain sight-lines whilst rowing in the thranite seats. Several seats forward of the mainmast have their view restricted by the tabernacle in which the mast is stepped. The crew was divided into sections for coaching and instruction purposes. The restrictions in sight, as well as the ability to speak and move around this tabernacle mean that one boundary between these crew groupings has to occur at the mainmast.

The shortfall in volunteers for the 1994 trials crew meant that anybody willing to travel to Greece was accepted. Few applicants provided ergometer test scores prior to arrival and most of these were not completed with the seat tied in place, thereby allowing use of the legs with a fixed seat. Although all the oarcrew undertook a 6-minute ergometer test under standard conditions early in the trial period,

Table 4.4. Comparison of the years of rowing experience with rowing skill as assessed by section leaders during the 1994 sea trials. Grade A, committed high quality rower; B+, good enthusiastic rower; B- good rower with begrudging attitude; C, technically weak but enthusiastic trier; D, disruptive and negative attitude with minimal ability. Five of the six people with three plus years experience who had rowed on the trireme before and might therefore have been accurately graded based on previous experience were given C or D grades.

Ability as assessed during 1994 trials						
Previous experience	A	B+	B-	C	D	**Totals**
none/some	4	14	6	13	5	42
1 to 2 years	9	11	2	12	7	41
3 plus years	20	10	2	6	1	39
Totals	31	35	10	31	13	122

this could not have been used to ascertain potential rowing ability prior to arrival. Almost everybody did indicate the number of years of previous rowing experience on their application forms. In terms of previous experience, the crew neatly divided into thirds: 'nil,' 'some' or 'none;' one or two years; and three years or more. As a basis for skill assessment, these returns have been compared with the standardised grading of individual ability made by section leaders towards the end of the trials, Table 4.4.

With less than around three years previous rowing experience, in whatever tradition, the actual oarsmanship exhibited by an individual in *Olympias* will tend to cover the full range of ability and the level cannot really be predicted ahead of time. Participation in the sport for longer than this pretty much guarantees skilful and effective rowers. Seventy percent of the most experienced rowers had been rowing for more than five years which would probably be a preferable benchmark of experience from which to reliably guarantee a high fraction of skilled rowers. Although hardly surprising, these conclusions graphically illustrate the years of experience necessary to produce skilled high-performance crews, a fact readily acknowledged in antiquity.

Bibliography

Coates, J. F., Platis S. K., and Shaw, J. T. (1990) *The Trireme Trials 1988: Report on the Anglo-Hellenic Sea Trials of* Olympias. Oxford, Oxbow Books.

Shaw, J. T. (1993) *The Trireme Project: Operational Experience 1987–90. Lessons Learnt.* Oxford, Oxbow Books.

Shaw, J. T. (1993a) The resistance/speed curve of *Olympias*. In Shaw 1993, 45–7.

Shaw, J. T. (1993b) Rowing Olympias: Further lessons of the sea trials. In Shaw 1993, 58–68.

Shaw, J. T. (1993c) Rowing Astern. In Shaw 1993, 69–70

Tilley, A. F. (1995) The performance of the *Olympias* under oar. *The Mariner's Mirror* 81, 207.

5. *Olympias* at the Olympics, 2004

Boris Rankov

After the final series of sea trials in 1994, *Olympias* was cleaned and refurbished, but was unfortunately left in the water for a short period before her hull had been properly protected. As a result, her underwater planking was severely damaged by an attack of shipworm (*teredo navalis*) and in 1995 had to undergo extensive replacement (see Lipke, pp. 203–6 with Fig. 27.1). This was a clear reminder of why such vessels were kept out of the water during antiquity when not in active service. Once repaired, she was put on permanent display at the Hellenic Navy Museum at Neo Faliro, alongside historical vessels including the battlecruiser *G. Averoff*. There, she has been visited by tourists and countless Greek schoolchildren learning about their naval heritage.

Initially, however, she was kept out in the open, and gradually began to deteriorate in ways which had not been anticipated, but which help to explain the purpose of the ancient sheds built to house such ships. The upper timbers of the ship, especially those of the canopy, soon dried out and became brittle, but a more serious problem was caused by exposure to the rains over winter. It would appear that

moisture gradually seeped into the spaces between the tenons and the mortises within the hull, and that this encouraged the growth of fungal spores which had blown from nearby trees. The effects took some time to develop, but by 2002 parts of the hull had been completely eaten away by fungal rot, so that in places it was possible to see the tenons and right through the shell (Fig. 5.1). It was clear that unless action were taken rapidly, the ship would within a few years cease to exist.

A possibility of salvation was offered by Professor Claus von Carnap-Bornheim, the Director of the Archäologisches Landesmuseum at Schloss Gottorf in Schleswig, Germany, who had offered to lend one of his museums' prize exhibits, the oldest surviving Saxon ship found at Nydam, Schleswig to the Danish National Museum in Copenhagen. His idea was to take *Olympias* to Germany, where she would be completely refurbished, and to put her on display and perhaps even conduct sea trials with her at Schloss Gottorf during the months while the Nydam ship was in Denmark. In the meantime, however, the need to repair the ship and a proposal that *Olympias* should carry the Olympic flame for the 2004 Olympics in Athens prompted the Elefsina Shipyards to offer her refurbishment free of charge.

The work was undertaken in 2003 (Fig. 5.2). It was decided that it would be too difficult and expensive to replace the underwater planking with mortise-and-tenon joints, so additional ribs and stringers were inserted internally (Fig. 5.3) to which new strakes could be attached throughout and made watertight with modern caulking. This was extremely successful cosmetically, and from the outside the ship now looked as she had when new. However, the separation of the upper planking, which retained its original mortise-and-tenon monocoque structure, from the lower planking, which was merely bolted to the new ribs, meant that the hull was now much weaker structurally and could not be kept at sea for long periods without further weakening. This nevertheless allowed the ship to perform as a splendid vehicle for the Olympic flame as the Games approached. She was a particularly appropriate

Figure 5.1. The planking of Olympias *affected by fungal rot, June, 2002 (Photo: Boris Rankov/Trireme Trust).*

Figure 5.2. Olympias *during refurbishment at Elefsina Shipyards, July, 2003 (Photo: Boris Reankov/Trireme Trust).*

choice for this as she was not named after the mother of Alexander the Great, as many have believed, but after an actual Athenian trireme of the fourth century BC whose name meant 'Ship of the Olympic Games' (see *IG* 2/32 2 1604.8, dated 378/7 BC), because when the ship was launched in 1987 Greece was already planning her bid for the 1996 Games.

A volunteer oarcrew was recruited in Greece to train in the ship in the month leading up to the opening of the Athens Olympics on 13th August, 2004. She was operated from the Hellenic Navy Museum (Fig. 5.4), and a typical outing involved rowing eastwards along the coast past Mikrolimáno (ancient Mounychia harbour) and Pasalimáni (Zea) and back, a round trip of about 4 nautical miles, perhaps followed by another loop. There were fewer than 120 rowers available, and the lowest (thalamian) level remained unmanned. The ship's original oars had not been replaced during the refurbishment, and those surviving – considerably fewer than the full set of 170 plus 30 spares – were now in poor condition and breaking regularly. Training thus concentrated on producing a well-drilled crew to transport the flame in ceremony.

During an outing on Monday, 19th July, Dr Harry Rossiter of the Faculty of Biological Sciences at Leeds University and the present writer took the opportunity to carry out a small physiological experiment, in which a portable laboratory was used to measure the work done whilst rowing by a small sample of volunteers; the data collected are intended to be of use in building a land-based test-rig which would replicate rowing on the ship and allow experimentation on the physiological aspects of

Figure 5.3. Internal view of Olympias *after refurbishment, July 2003, showing new ribs and stringers attached with bolts (Photo: Boris Rankov/Trireme Trust).*

long-distance rowing in a trireme. During this particular outing, the ship was rowed into and round Pasalimáni/Zea harbour, today a yachting harbour but in the fourth century BC entirely ringed by 196 trireme shipsheds; the latter included those excavated by Iacob Dragatsis and Wilhelm Dörpfeld in 1885 which provided some of the basic dimensions for the *Olympias* reconstruction. It was notable that there was considerable room within the harbour, even today, for the ship to circle and manoeuvre.

Figure 5.4. Olympias *moored at the Hellenic Navy Museum, July, 2004, with Kyrenia 2 alongside, viewed from the battlecruiser* G. Averoff *(Photo: Boris Rankov/Trireme Trust).*

On Wednesday, 11th August, only two days before the opening ceremony of the Games, *Olympias* was rowed into Mikrolimáno and then Pasalimáni accompanied by the *Minos*, a reconstruction of a Minoan oared vessel, and *Kyrenia 2*, a reconstruction of a merchant vessel of the fourth century BC. The three ships then moved on to the Dodecanese dock in the main harbour (Kentrikó Limáni) of the Piraeus (ancient Kantharos), and from there, that evening, *Olympias* carried the Olympic flame, by means of a special torch fixed in the bows, the few hundred metres across the harbour to the Aegina dock.

After the ceremony, *Olympias* was returned to the Hellenic Navy Museum where a roofed shed with removable side-panels was built over her dry dock (see Fig. IS.1) to prevent any recurrence of fungal rot. Since then, she has continued to be on show and carefully maintained in pristine condition by the Hellenic Navy; she has not been returned to the water.

Part 2

Proposals for a Revised Design

6. Preface to the Proposals for a Revised Design

Timothy Shaw

The sea trials of the reconstruction *Olympias* have shown that she is highly manoeuvrable as befits a trireme, that she performs well under sail and that the principle of having oars on three levels is workable. However some disappointment has been expressed over what is seen as her lack of speed under oar (*e.g.* in Shaw 1993). Several reasons for this lack have been put forward but probably the most important one is that nearly all members of the oarcrew are prevented from exercising their natural length of stroke by their proximity to various parts of the ships' structure, not to mention other members of the oarcrew.

After *Olympias* had been constructed evidence was found that her *interscalmium*, that had been set at two cubits of 444 mm, the 'Solonic' cubit, ought probably to have been set at two cubits of about 490 mm, giving the oarcrew about ten percent more room (Morrison 1991). This, with some other modifications, was incorporated in a revised design of a trireme (Coates 1993). During the trials in 1994 the writer devised some experiments briefly described below that led him to conclude that the modifications suggested in 1993 would still not be enough to allow the oarcrew to realise their full potential. However, he noted that if the proposed longer cubit were applied to the inboard length of the oars it would allow the seats of the oarcrew to be moved nearer the midline of the ship, and that if the footrests remained near the shell of the hull, a canted oar-rig would result. He presented a diagram illustrating this (Shaw 1994). He considered that in a new ship such a rig could be so proportioned as to enable all members of the oarcrew to reach past and outboard of each other as they prepared for the catch. In this way a long stroke could be obtained, limited only by the physique of the oarcrew and not calling for any further increase of the *interscalmium*. Unfortunately such a scheme cannot be applied in *Olympias*, but Coates has designed a Mark II trireme that makes use of this idea (see Chapter 10 below).

While the idea of a strongly canted rig is unfamiliar to rowers accustomed to racing in eights, it is well known to those who race Cornish six-oared gigs at the present day. Yet it may be of great antiquity: one of the reliefs brought from Nineveh by Sir Henry Layard about the middle of the nineteenth century and now in the British Museum shows an oared ship of about 700 BC in which the rowers are clearly reaching past and outboard of each other for the catch as they would if the rig were canted. The 'Siren' vase also in the British Museum gives a similar impression.

The long stroke made possible by strongly canting the oar-rig of a Mark II trireme should lead to a large improvement in her cruising and top speeds under oar as compared with those of *Olympias*. Some implications of this are examined in the writer's three papers which follow. The first paper (Chapter 7) employs data from British Admiralty charts and Sailing Directions relevant to the passage from Byzantium to Heraclea, to reveal what sustainable speed of a trireme is entailed by Xenophon's reported statement that the journey could be accomplished by such a ship in 'a long day under oar' The second paper (Chapter 8) deals with the question of whether such a speed could have been sustained without assistance from the wind via the sails. The third paper (Chapter 9) presents a simple mathematical model of rowing and uses it to compare the predicted performance of Trireme Mark IIa (no cant) with that of Mark IIb (canted oar-rig) and of course with that of *Olympias*.

Bibliography

Coates, J. F. (1993) Development of the design. In Shaw 1993, 71–4.

Morrison, J. S. (1991) Ancient Greek Measures of Length in Nautical Contexts. *Antiquity* 65 (no. 247), 298–305.

Shaw, J. T. (ed.) (1993) *The Trireme Project. Operational Experience 1987–90. Lessons Learnt.* Oxford, Oxbow Books.

Shaw, J. T. (1994) *The 1994 Trireme Trials 1994. Research Results and Discussion.* Watlington, The Trireme Trust.

7. From the Golden Horn to Heraclea: duration of the passage in calm weather

Timothy Shaw

1. Summary

One of the pieces of evidence of the speed of an ancient Greek trireme under oar is a statement by Xenophon (*Anabasis* 6.4.2) that for a trireme the passage from Byzantium to Heraclea entailed "a long day under oar". One version makes it "a very long day". The implied speed sets a standard by which any reconstruction of an ancient Greek trireme's hull and oarsystem must be judged.

In this paper data from British Admiralty charts and British Admiralty Sailing Directions (the Black Sea Pilot) are used to assess how long the passage would take in calm weather during the ancient sailing season at cruising speeds 7, 7½ and 8 knots relative to the water. It is assumed that today's conditions are close to those that obtained in antiquity.

Skilful helmsmanship and local knowledge would be required in order to avoid adverse currents wherever possible and to exploit favourable eddies.

The main conclusion is that sustained cruising speeds in the range 7–8 knots are compatible with the statement made by Xenophon and with the calculated performance of a moderately good crew (say at 7½ knots relative to the water) and of an outstandingly good one (nearly 8 knots). The passage would occupy from about 15 to about 17 hours not including any mid-day stoppage. An outstandingly good crew could accomplish more than 90% of the distance in daylight at midsummer, but if a cooler season were essential or the crew slower some part of the voyage would have to be conducted in twilight and/or by moonlight.

2. Discussion

2.1. How long was "a long day"?

Morrison has pointed to Herodotus' use of the word *makremeria* ('long days') and gives reason for thinking that for Herodotus 'a long day' meant the period between sunrise and sunset in summertime (Morrison 1991). Morrison has quoted Brown's Nautical Almanack to show that at the beginning of April and the beginning of September in the latitude of the southern Black Sea the sun is above the horizon for about 12 hours and 40 minutes (in modern hours and minutes) and at midsummer for 15 hours, but that if the hours of twilight before sunrise and after sunset are included, making perhaps "a very long day" the durations extend to 14 hours and 40 minutes in early April and early September and to 17½ hours in midsummer. Of course twilight shades off into darkness in which coastwise navigation would be hazardous. I therefore propose that a little more than half the nominal duration of twilight be added, making "very long days" vary from about 14 hours up to 16½ hours in the absence of help from the moon. On cloudless nights when the moon was full or nearly so, it would have shone brightly all night. That might suggest that "a very long day" could have extended to 24 modern hours or even more. But then we might expect Xenophon to have written not "a (? very) long day" but "a day and a night". What he did write, coupled with the data given above, does not rule out that part of the voyage was sometimes conducted by the light of the moon but does appear to me to rule out a 24 hour "long day". In what follows I seek to show that a moderately good crew in a suitable ship could accomplish the voyage in about 18 hours including an hour's rest at mid-day, and that an exceptionally good one could accomplish it without stopping in 15 hours. I think it is reasonable to conclude that that these durations are consistent with Xenophon's text and with the data from the almanack. The mean speeds while the ship was under way would have been in the range 7 to 8 knots relative to the water.

2.2. Ascent of the Bosporus in normal charted conditions

The information given here is derived from Admiralty Chart No. 1198 and from the *Black Sea Pilot: Admiralty Sailing Directions*. The course is assumed to start at the modern bridge near the mouth of the Golden Horn and to end on the eastern side of the northern exit into the

Table 7.1. Currents and counter currents (eddies) encountered during the preferred course; durations if the ship's speed is 7.5 knots relative to the water.

Nautical Miles	Remarks	Duration in minutes (to nearest 0.5)
0–5.3	Helpful countercurrent Averaging 0.5 knot	40
5.3–5.7	Adverse current of 1.5–2 knots on the port bow during the crossing	4*–4.5*
5.7–6.2	Some help, up to 0.25 knot	4
6.2–8.6	Adverse current of 1.5–2 knots	24–26
8.6–9.9	Helpful eddy of 0.5 knot	10
9.9–10.7	Adverse current of 1–1.5 knots	7.5–8
10.7–11.1	Helpful eddy of 0.25 knot	3
11.1–12.1	Adverse current of 1.5–2 knots	10–11
12.1–12.5	Helpful eddy of 0.25 knot	3
12.5–13.6	Adverse current of 1.5–2 knots	11–12
13.6–14.4	Helpful eddy of 0.25 knot	6
14.4–16.4	Adverse current of 0.5–1 knot	17–18.5

* Allowing for leeway during the crossing

Black Sea. It is described in tabular form. Distances in nautical miles (n.m.) are relative to the land. During the first 5.3 n.m. the recommended course is close to the west bank. It then crosses over and stays near to the east bank as far as the northern exit. I have assumed that during the crossing the ship's heading is at 45 degrees to the adverse stream. The course made good is then at 54.2 degrees to the stream if the adverse current is 1½ knots, or at 57.9 degrees to it if the adverse current is 2 knots. Apparently the stream in the narrows at the crossing can reach 7 knots but presumably not during the sailing season. Exceptionally, the flow may cease. The variations quoted below are presumed to be normal, but wider ones must occur from time to time.

At about 6.75 n.m. the adverse current in the centre of the narrow channel is charted as 1.5–2 knots, increasing to 2–3 knots at about 7.5 n.m. where the strait is wider. This may be an effect of the changing depth. As the ship's course at these points is near the east bank I have felt justified in proposing an adverse current of 1.5–2 knots throughout the stretch from 6.2 to 8.6 n.m. where the ship enters a helpful eddy (Table 7.1).

The total duration is in the range 2 hours 20 minutes to 2 hours 26 minutes depending on the currents encountered.

If the ship's speed through the water is 7 knots the total duration for the 16.4 n.m. is in the range 2 hours 31 minutes to 2 hours 38 minutes; if the speed through the water is 8 knots the range is from 2 hours 10 minutes to 2 hours 16 minutes.

2.3. Conditions of navigation in the southern Black Sea

Here is a summary of the statements in The *Black Sea Pilot* referring to the wind, waves, currents, temperatures and humidities.

The prevailing wind all the year is from the NE but there is a significant proportion of days in which the wind blows from the NW to the SW quarter. Near the coast the wind direction tends to be modified by the land and sea breezes that are well marked in summer. The onshore wind develops in mid-morning. By mid-afternoon it may reach Force 3 to 4 (*i.e.* 7 to 16 knots): it fades soon after dusk. The land breeze is usually weaker and blows offshore from late evening till shortly after sunrise.

On waves the information is limited but shows that slight seas with waves of 0.5 m or less (implying slight winds; see my paper on pp. 68–75 below on 'The performance of ancient triremes in wind and waves') are reported in over 50% of observations in spring and autumn. Waves exceeding 2.5 m are reported in fewer than 10% of observations, though waves of up to 13 m have been reported. In summer, very rough seas do occur, but are unusual, and slight seas with waves 0.5 m or less are reported on over 64% of observations.

Swells are mostly from the NW and NE. In summer they are generally low. Heights of 1 m or less are recorded in about 50% of observations. Swells exceeding 4 m in height are unusual, though in autumn swells up to 15 m can occur in the E (presumably beyond the region of interest here).

There is an anticlockwise current in the Black Sea. According to the *Black Sea Pilot* its velocity along the western part of the southern coast is 0.25 to 0.75 knots in general. It is greatest after the melting of the snows in late spring and early summer. The latest edition of the *Encyclopaedia Britannica* (referring I think to the Black Sea as a whole) gives 40–60 cm/sec (0.78–1.17 knots) as the velocity of circulation near to the shore, but less further out. The *Black Sea Pilot* says the circulation is "weak and inconstant ... Countercurrents ... occur between the main current and the shore in many places."

Humidity: in summer in the S and SE coasts the relative humidity is around 85% in the early morning falling to about 70% in the afternoon.

Table 7.2.

Istanbul	*April*	*May*	*June*	*July*	*August*	*September*
Temp. C	7–16	12–21	16–26	18–28	18–29	15–25
R.H.	81–61	81–60	77–56	77–52	80–51	84–57
Wind, knots	4–8	4–7	4–8	5–10	4–10	3–9
m/s	2–4	2–3½	2–4	2½–5	2–5	1½–4½
Zonguldak	*April*	*May*	*June*	*July*	*August*	*September*
Temp. C	7–14	12–19	15–23	17–25	18–25	15–22
R.H.	76–72	77–74	76–73	75–73	75–71	77–70
Wind, knots	3–5	3–5	2–6	2–6	3–6	3–6
m/s	1½–2½	1½–2½	1–3	1–3	1½–3	1½–3

Table 7.3. Times under oar, Bosporus exit to Heraclea, 210 km with helpful current of 0.5 m/s (1 knot):

Speeds relative to the water, knots	7.0	7.5	8.0
Duration of rowing, hours and minutes	14h 10m	13h 20m	12h 35m

Table 7.4. Total journey time, Golden Horn to Heraclea

Ship's speed relative to the water	7 knots	7.5 knots	8 knots
Duration, hours and minutes			
At weaker Bosporus current	17h 41m	16h 40m	15h 45m
At stronger Bosporus current	17h 48m	16h 46m	15h 51m

Temperature: in July and August, the air temperature reaches its maximum, and mean daily temperatures range between maxima of 25–30 °C and minima of 17–19 °C. The extreme highest temperatures recorded in coastal districts are generally around 38–41 °C but over the open sea the extreme maxima are generally around 27–32 °C.

The ranges of temperature, relative humidity and windspeed at Istanbul and Zonguldak (east of Heraclea/ Eregli) for the months April–September are given in Table 7.2.

In each case the first-given temperature is the mean daily minimum for the month and the other is the mean daily maximum.

Extremes sometimes well beyond these can occur. The first-given R.H. is the average humidity at 0700 and the other is at 1400. The first-given wind is the mean at 0700 and the other is at 1400. Zonguldak is on the south coast further east than Heraclea.

I assume that an ancient trireme would have been steered close enough to the shore to benefit from the faster current there, whose magnitude I take to be 0.5 m/s, the middle of the range given by *Encyclopaedia Britannica*.

The data on the temperature and humidity confirm the importance of ventilating the ship to cool the oarsmen.

The windspeeds confirm that very light winds predominate during the ancient "sailing" season, and bearing in mind the information to be given in my paper on 'The performance of ancient triremes in wind and waves' below it is not surprising that on the whole the waves are low.

2.4. Duration of the voyage after leaving the Bosporus, and total duration

We may take the distance from the northern end of the Bosporus to Heraclea as 113 n.m. (say 210 km). The times taken by the ship to cover this distance at steady speeds of 7, 7.5 and 8 knots relative to the water, given a helpful current of 0.5 m/s (about 1 knot) are given in Table 7.3.

These durations exclude any time spent resting at mid-day.

Adding together the times spent rowing up the Bosporus and in the Black Sea and allowing an hour's rest at mid-day, about half-way into the journey, ignoring any progress that might be made during that rest by virtue of the current and recalling that calm weather is assumed, I obtain the durations given in Table 7.4 for the total journey time:

Say 17h 50m, 16h 50m and 15h 50m respectively.

If there were after all a slight tail wind or onshore wind, not strong enough to raise hampering waves, say a true wind of 4 m/s or 8 knots, it would give virtually no help when the ship was under oar (and if it were from astern it could well cause the men to overheat while they were rowing) but it could drive the ship on at about 4 knots during the hour's rest. This would gain 4 n.m. or about 7.5 km, about 3% of the total distance, reducing the total durations given above by about half an hour. The current of about 1 knot on its own would gain about 1 n.m. worth about 8 minutes.

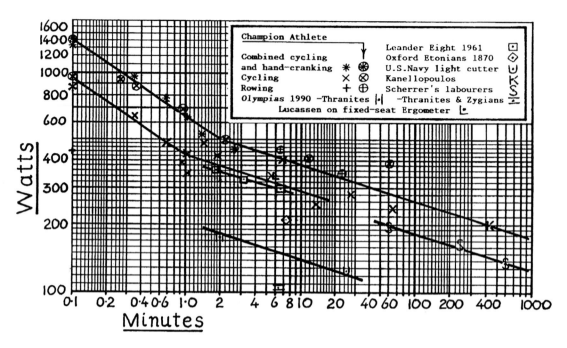

Figure 7.1. The gross mechanical power of athletes of various kinds in relation to the duration of their efforts (from Shaw 1993b, 65, fig. 10.4).

2.5. *Power required*

The power required by *Olympias* at various speeds was deduced by Grekoussis and Loukakis from tank tests of a bare hulled model and their results were reproduced by Lowry and Squire in the form of a graph (Grekoussis and Loukakis 1985; Lowry and Squire 1988). By examining this graph I have found that the power consumption of *Olympias* with rudders partly raised to reduce their resistance can be expressed by the formula:

$$\text{Power in watts} = 155V^3 + 4.13V^5$$

Where V is the speed in m/s.

I suggest that the power required by a Mark II trireme reconstruction would be about 8% more than this because of her probably greater length and displacement. If the whole oarcrew were in action the effective power per man would be 1/170 of this larger quantity but of course each man must do still more because of the inefficiency of the oars and their inertia which both absorb power unavoidably. The man must develop much more power than is absorbed by the ship. If I assign a mean ideal efficiency of 0.78 to the oars (see my paper 'Towards a revised design of a Greek trireme' on pp. 76–81 below) and adopt the formula

$$\text{power in watts absorbed by the trireme oar} = 0.96r + 0.016r^2$$

where r is the rate of striking (Shaw 1993a; for the method of calculating the rates of striking which follow, see the Appendix to this Paper and pp. 76–81 below)

and if I take   r = 25.5 when speed = 7 knots
r = 28.8 when speed = 7.5 knots, and
r = 32.3 when speed = 8 knots

then I find that to the nearest 5 W the gross power to be exerted per oarsman is

115 W at 7 knots
145 W at 7.5 knots, and
180 W at 8 knots

The graph of power a man can exert continuously against the duration of the exercise shows that hardened manual labourers, if kept cool and given adequate sustenance in the form of easily digestible food and drink, could exert 180 watts for just under two hours, 145 watts for about 7½ hours and (if the straight line can be extrapolated) 115 watts for as long as 30 hours (based on the study by Scherrer *et al.* 1981 of sugar-cane cutters in Queensland, Australia; see Shaw 1993b, 65, fig. 10.4 (reproduced here as Fig. 7.1) and the paper by Coates on 'Human mechanical power' on pp. 161–4 below); whereas men of the ability of Kanellos Kanellopoulos, (who in 1988 flew under his own power from Crete to Santorini) could sustain 180 watts for about 13 hours, 170 watts for about 16½ hours (Nadel and Bussolari 1988) (Fig. 7.1). (It is hoped that further information on stamina will become available in the future.)

I retabulate here the duration of the voyage at the three speeds, and at the stronger of the Bosporus currents assumed earlier:

At 7 knots	17 hours 50 min. including an hour's rest
At 7.5 knots	16 hours 50 min. including an hour's rest
At 8 knots	15 hours 50 min. including an hour's rest

From these data it follows that a crew consisting of men whose power and stamina equalled that of modern manual labourers could probably sustain a speed above 7 knots but not as much as 7.5 knots, *i.e.* they could row from Byzantium to Heraclea in a time of about 18 hours (including an hour's stoppage at mid-day). This would involve rowing by the light of the moon for part of the way. A crew of clones of Kanellopoulos could perhaps forgo the mid-day rest and if they did so they might complete the voyage in as little as 15 hours. Such a voyage could be about 90% completed while the sun was up during a few weeks either side of midsummer but at other times the help of the moon would be required.

3. Conclusion

It looks as though a moderately good trireme crew capable of cruising at about 7¼ knots relative to the water, if given appropriate nutrition, a fast and well-ventilated ship, a good set of oars and calm weather, could complete the passage between Byzantium (say the Golden Horn) and Heraclea (modern Eregli) in about 18 hours if they rested for an hour in mid-voyage. (They would probably need to do that.) If they started out at 0400 they would reach their destination at about 2200. An elite crew cruising at nearly 8 knots might not need to stop half way and might then complete the passage in about 15 hours.

It seems reasonable to regard these durations as consistent with Xenophon's "long day". If we are to believe Xenophon (and why not: he had no reason to lie) it follows that the ability to cruise at 7–8 knots (depending on the standard of the oarcrew) is one of the most important criteria by which any ship claiming to be a reconstruction of an ancient Greek fast trireme should be judged.

Appendix

Calculation of rates of striking (See also my paper on 'Towards a revised design of a Greek trireme' below.)

$$nPrLE/60 = 1.08 \times (155V^3 + 4.13V^5)$$

$$V \text{ is in m/s; } 1 \text{ knot} = 0.5148 \text{ m/s}$$

$$n = 170, P = 7,43r, L = 0.99 \text{ m}, E = 0.78$$

The equation shows that:

When	V = 7 knots	r is 25.47 say 25.5 spm
	V = 7.5 knots	r is 28.77 say 28.8 spm
	V = 8 knots	r is 32.32 say 32.3 spm.

Bibliography

Admiralty Chart No. 1198 (The Bosporus) (1995). Taunton, Hydrographer of the Navy.

Black Sea Pilot (Sailing Directions). London, HMSO

Brown's Nautical Almanack 1988 (1988). Glasgow, Brown, Son and Ferguson Ltd.

Grekoussis, C. and Loukakis, T. (1985) *Athenian Trireme Calm Water Tests Without Ram. National Technical University of Athens. Report No. NAL 06–F-1985.* Athens, National Technical University of Athens.

Lowry, I. J. and Squire, T. M. (1988) *Trireme* Olympias *Extended Sea Trials.* Cardiff, UWIST University of Wales College of Cardiff. Unpublished.

Morrison, J. S. (1991) Ancient Greek Measures of Length in Nautical Contexts. *Antiquity* 65 (No. 247), 298–305.

Nadel, E. R. and Bussolari, S. R. (1988) The Daedalus Project: Physiological Problems and Solutions. *American Scientist* (July-August), 351–360.

Scherrer, J. *et al.* (1981) *Précis de physiologie du travail, notions d'ergonomie* (2nd ed. Paris, Masson et Cie.

Shaw, J. T. (1993a) Rowing in Ships and Boats. *Transactions of the Royal Institution of Naval Architects* 194B, 211–22

Shaw, J. T. (1993b) *The Trireme Project. Operational Experience 1987–90. Lessons Learnt.* Oxford, Oxbow Books.

8. The Performance of Ancient Triremes in Wind and Waves

Timothy Shaw

1. Summary

This note argues that ancient triremes did not need help from the sails when they made the fast passage between Byzantium and Heraclea referred to by Xenophon as being achievable in "a long day under oar". Nor would a wind strong enough to offer useful propulsive force all the way in the Black Sea have been helpful in fact: in such a long passage it would have eventually have raised waves high enough to negate the benefit. The main reason for this is the ship's high speed of 7 to 8 knots.

2. Introduction

It is acknowledged that *Olympias* is incapable of cruising all day at 7–8 knots under oar. Her cramped stateroom has been blamed, an explanation that is supported by physiological studies including The Trireme Trust's in 1990 and 1994. These data when coupled with the known resistance/speed curve of *Olympias* confirm that a carefully-selected and well-trained all-male oarcrew whose stature is similar to that attributed to ancient Greek men ought to have enough power and endurance to match the ancient performance with no help from the sails provided that the men have enough stateroom to row at full length. I have argued that a suitably lengthened stateroom can be provided within an *interscalmium* of 0.98 m (two cubits) by strongly 'skewing' the layout of the seats and stretchers (Shaw 1994). This concept has been given detailed expression in Plan 201–12 (Fig. 8.1) which closely resembles Plan 8 (*Olympias*) (Fig. 8.2) apart from the three main changes: the skewed oar-rig, an increase in the height of the *zyga* and a 10% increase in the *interscalmium*.

However, and perhaps not surprisingly, it has been suggested elsewhere that (a) the passage referred to by Xenophon must have been sail-assisted and/or (b) an ancient trireme was not like *Olympias* at all.

As regards (b), I will not go beyond stating that there is massive evidence unrelated to the present discussion that an ancient trireme's hull and main principles of her oarsystem were very like those of *Olympias* and Plan 201–12.

Here, I am concerned with the impact of (a) given that the ship is as shown in Plan 201–12. The question is important, for if (a) were correct, we should no longer be able to insist on a high cruising speed for a trireme under oar, and the case for improving important details of the design would therefore be based on rather weaker evidence than would exist if Xenophon's statement were accepted. We should find ourselves relying not on verifiable or potentially verifiable figures but on a mere opinion that ancient ship designers would not deliberately restrict a crew's length of stroke if they could help it.

This document shows that (a) cannot be true if an ancient trireme was like that depicted in Plan 201–12. As I show in what follows, any tailwind strong enough to offer a useful thrust via the sails at a ship's speed as high as 7 to 8 knots would after blowing for a few hours across a 'fetch' of some scores of kilometres raise waves high enough to hinder the oarsmen, or worse, and so negate the benefit. A passage at that speed under sail alone is ruled out by the fact that if the ship were no more seaworthy than the *Olympias* was for good reasons designed to be, she would be obliged by the waves to seek shelter before reaching Heraclea. A wind on the beam is no help either.

If I am right, it would follow that where the wind, if any, had a long 'fetch', the fastest passages by the triremes were made under oar, and in calm weather, and that when Xenophon said or wrote "under oar" he meant precisely that, not "under sail and oar" and not "under sail". This does not rule out that slower passages by triremes between Byzantium and Heraclea were conducted under sail or under sail and oar in light winds.

3. Discussion

First I discuss the propulsive effect of the wind via the sails, making use of our experiences in *Olympias*. Then I give the effect of the wind on the waves. Then I go into the effect of the waves on the ship and on the rowing, again making use of experience in *Olympias*. I mention the importance of ventilating the ship. The conclusions follow.

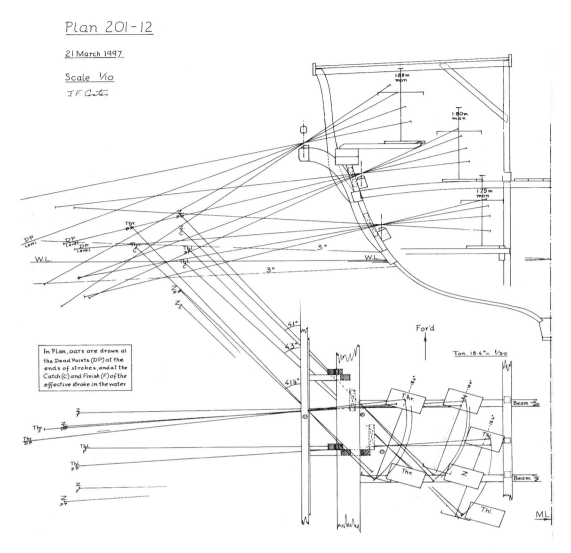

Figure 8.1. Proposed modification to Olympias *oar-rig, with interscalmium of 0.98 m and skewed layout of seats and stretchers (Plan 201–12) (Drawing: John Coates).*

3.1. The propulsive effect of the wind

In my paper 'From the Golden Horn to Heraclea' above, I show that in order to complete the passage between Byzantium and Heraclea in "a long day" a trireme must sustain a speed of between 7 and 8 knots (3.6 to 4.1 m/s) through the water. Here, in order to minimise the number of tables, I deal with the mean of these namely 7½ knots or say 3.9 m/s. While in the Black Sea the ship would be assisted, according to the *Black Sea Pilot*, by an anticlockwise current of ¼ to ¾ knots (13–39 cm/sec), the higher values occurring in spring and early summer. The latest *Encyclopaedia Britannica* says the current amounts to 40–60 cm/sec near the shore but less farther out. I shall assume the ship steers near enough the shore to benefit from a current of 0.5 m/s (1 knot).

Our experiments on sailing *Olympias* have shown that her speed in still water is at best rather less than half the true wind speed, whether the wind is astern or on the beam. A tailwind needs to blow at about 8.5 m/s (16.5 knots, which is Force 4 bordering on 5) if it is to propel the ship under full sail through still water at the postulated 3.9 m/s (7.5 knots) with no help from the oars. A wind on the beam needs a velocity of about 9.8 m/s (19 knots, which is Force 5). The error of the ship's log has been taken into account.

It has long been suggested that the sails could safely be enlarged (Coates, Platis and Shaw 1990, 36). This could reduce the required windspeed by a few percent. On the other hand the proposed improved version of *Olympias* given in Plan 201–12 will probably have a little more resistance, tending to restore the original relationship. In what follows I assume that a tailwind of 8.5 m/s (16.5 knots) or a beam wind of 9.8 m/s (19 knots) will still be required to drive a Mark II trireme through still water at 3.9 m/s (7.5 knots) under sail.

To obtain the propulsive force of gentler winds, such as might, with the help of the oars, enable the ship to continue at 3.9 m/s (7.5 knots), consider the following.

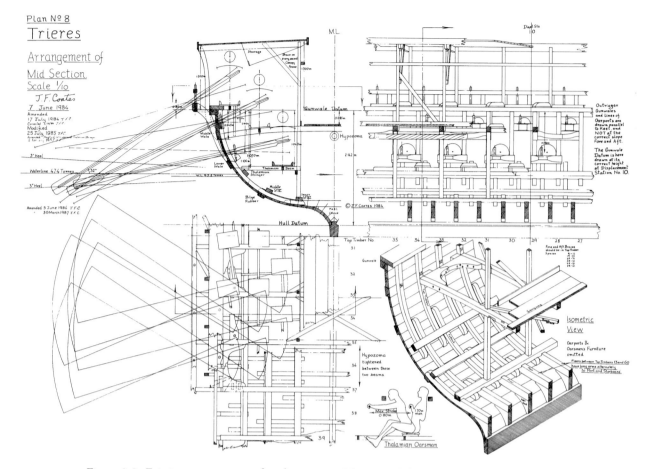

Figure 8.2: Existing arrangement of mid-section in Olympias *(Plan 8) (Drawing: John Coates).*

Take the case of a wind from astern. We may assume that the usual square law of air resistance applies to the sails in this case, and that the same sail area is used irrespective of the strength of the wind as no very strong winds are being considered. Then we have that:

Resistance of the ship at 3.9 m/s (7.5 knots) in still water = propulsive force of an 8.5 m/s (16.5 knots) true wind from astern which is a 4.6 m/s (8.9 knots) wind relative to the ship.

Since the ship must continue to move at 3.9 m/s (7.5 knots) through the water which is itself moving in the same direction at 0.5 m/s (1 knot), a true windspeed of V m/s coming from astern implies a relative wind of (V – 3.9 – 0.5) m/s and a propulsive force proportional to that quantity squared. (The coefficient of proportionality is a constant if the sail area is unchanged.) It follows that when the ship is in the Black Sea the propulsive force of the wind of true speed V is a percentage X of that of a relative wind of 4.6 m/s (8.9 knots) where:

$$X = 100 \left[(V - 3.9 - 0.5)/4.6\right]^2$$

Table 8.1 shows, for example, that when the true wind speed is 5 m/s (9.7 knots) the speed of the relative wind pressing on the sails is only 0.6 m/s (1.2 knots) and this

reduces the oarsmen's burden by only about 2%. The table suggests that higher windspeeds would be much more helpful but this will be true only if the wind has had insufficient time and 'fetch' to raise waves high enough to hamper the oarsmen. Details of the average roughness of the sea caused by steady winds of true velocities 5, 5.5 and 6 m/s (9.7, 10.7 and 11.7 knots) are given in the next section.

I now consider the case of a wind on the beam. To give enough propulsive force to drive the ship at 3.9 m/s (7.5 knots) through the water without help from the oars a beam wind has to be fairly strong. It is perhaps worth re-emphasising the point that it is because the ship's speed is high, *i.e.* about 4.4 m/s (8.5 knots) past the land, that the wind is unhelpful. Suppose the wind's true direction is at 90 degrees to the ship's course. Then the angle by which the direction of the apparent wind differs from the ship's course is that whose tangent is the true wind speed divided by the ship's speed past the land. Table 8.2 gives examples.

To find the wind direction in degrees from the ship's heading a leeway angle of say 7 degrees needs to be subtracted from the tabulated angles. Table 8.2 shows that the ship has to be sailed more and more close-hauled as the

Table 8.1.

True speed of tailwind m/s	Relative speed of tailwind m/s	Propulsive force of the sails as a percentage of that required to maintain the ship's speed at 7.5 knots (3.9m/s)	Balance to be provided by the oars percent
5	0.6	2	98
5.5	1.1	6	94
6	1.6	12	88
7	2.6	32	68
8	3.6	61	39
9	4.6	100	nil

Table 8.2.

True wind speed, m/s	6	7	8	9	10
Apparent wind direction, degrees from the ship's course	53.7	57.8	61.2	63.9	66.3

wind drops. Owain Roberts has written that "*Olympias* will sail well up to 60 degrees off the apparent wind making no more than 7 degrees leeway" (Shaw 1993b, 37). This I take to mean that her course may come as close as 67 degrees from the direction of the apparent wind. According to Table 8.2 this calls for a true windspeed of more than 10 m/s (19.4 knots) if the true wind is at 90 degrees to the course made good. (This exceeds the quantity of 9.8 m/s (19 knots) assumed earlier because the ship's speed is 4.4 m/s (8..5 knots) not 3.9 m/s (7.5 knots)). Dr Basil Greenhill and Peter Allington, have explained that that the use of auxiliary power enables a sailing ship rigged as a schooner to point higher than normal (Greenhill and Allington 1993). On reading that, we might guess that under oar plus sail a trireme could point as much as 5 degrees higher than stated by Roberts. On their next page however, Greenhill and Allington say that "a square-rigged vessel's lack of weatherliness effectively meant that she could not motor-sail to windward." Even if we ignore that, and accept a 5 degree improvement, the windspeed is still required to be as much as 8.3 m/s (16 knots). This windspeed should keep the oarsmen cool but it would also be incompatible with fast rowing, indeed it may prevent all rowing as the ship would heel and probably also roll because of the waves created, even if the wind itself were steady. Coates and Morrison wrote in the first edition of *The Athenian Trireme* that a steady beam wind of 14 knots [which is only 7.2 m/s] would cause [the then unbuilt] *Olympias* to heel about 8 degrees under the action of both sails, or 7 degrees without the boat sail (Morrison and Coates 1986, 223). This would put the thalamian oarports very near the water on the lee side (Coates, Platis and Shaw 1990, 35, fig. 19 gives a good impression of the situation).

If we reduce the windspeed to a level at which the angle of the heel is small enough and the waves low enough to permit hard rowing we find from Table 8.2 that if the ship's

speed is somehow maintained at 4.4 m/s (8.5 knots) the apparent wind is too near the ship's head and its propulsive effect will be nil.

There are a few more points. Suppose the ship steers fairly near the shore and makes use of an offshore (*i.e.* a southerly) wind which has only a short fetch and duration of action on the water. Such a wind however will not arise till the late evening, will blow during the night, and die out soon after sunrise. And even if part of the passage were made by moonlight (which I show above in my paper 'From the Golden Horn to Heraclea' was probably sometimes the case in antiquity) the night would not be long enough for the offshore wind to take the ship very far. An onshore wind, on the other hand, arising about mid-morning and continuing until evening may raise fairly high waves.

3.2. The effect of the wind on the waves

I am indebted to Mr D. J. T. Carter, sometime of the institute of Oceanographic Sciences, Wormley, Surrey, and now of Satellite Observation Services, Godalming, for the information that has enabled me to give the wave heights and other wave data in what follows. His equations are given in his 1982 paper 'Prediction of Wave Height and Period for a Constant Wind Velocity using the JONSWAP Results'. They express and summarise the findings of the Joint North Sea Wave Project of 1969 and they are considered to be applicable to conditions in the south-western part of the Black Sea. They refer to winds measured at a height of 10 m above the mean sea surface, acting for various durations and over various lengths of fetch, over water that is deep enough that the sea floor does not influence the waves, and in the absence of swell. Carter has kindly supplemented this information by means of a personal communication.

Table 8.3. An asterisk means that the sea has reached its full development at the given windspeed, duration and fetch. The wave velocity C is measured with respect to the water which is itself moving at 0.5 m/s (1 knot). A wave having C above 3.9 m/s (7.5 knots) will overtake the ship.

Fetch km	Duration hours	W = 4.5 m/s			W = 5.0 m/s			W = 5.5 m/s		
		H	L	C	H	L	C	H	L	C
50	3.2	0.23	4.1	2.5	0.27	4.7	2.7	0.30	5.2	2.9
100	6.3	0.38	7.4	3.4	0.43	8.3	3.6	0.49	9.3	3.8
150	9.5	0.49*	10.1	4.0	0.58	11.9	4.3	0.65	13.2	4.5
200	12.6	0.49*	10.1	4.0	0.60*	12.5	4.4	0.73*	15.1	4.9

In reality of course the wind does not have a constant velocity but we may still draw valid conclusions from the equations.

I should mention that Carter's equations are not the only ones one might use. Others give somewhat different answers but they are thought to be more appropriate for large oceans such as the North Atlantic than for the limited fetch of westerly winds in the south-western Black Sea.

Carter's equations give us H, the so-called 'significant height' of the waves measured from crest to trough, and the time T that elapses (on average) between successive occasions on which the sea surface rises above its mean level. I have obtained the wavelength L from the formula $L = 1.56\ T^2$ and the wave velocity C from the formula $C = 1.56\ T$. The coefficient 1.56 applies when L is in metres, C is in metres/second and T is in seconds.

The significant height H of the waves is a measure of the average roughness of the sea, and I should make it clear that the quantities given as T, L and C are also averages masking considerable variation. For statisticians it may be mentioned that to a good approximation the elevation of the sea's surface has a Gaussian distribution. The significant wave height is defined as four times the standard deviation of that elevation, *i.e.* at any given location that elevation fluctuates by up to two standard deviations above and two below its mean level for about 95% of the time. If the distribution were truly Gaussian the surface would be found at 2 or more standard deviations away from the mean about 4.6% of the time, 2½ or more standard deviations away about 1.2% of the time, 3 or more standard deviations away about 0.27% of the time and 4 or more standard deviations away only about 0.006% of the time. This means, for example, that if the significant wave height of a fully-developed sea is 0.50 m and the period is 2.58 seconds, then in a time-span of 8 hours, about 7.63 hours will see the passage of about 10,650 waves of up to 0.50 m, but the remaining 22 minutes will see higher waves (distributed at random throughout the whole 8 hours): there will be about 16 minutes' worth of waves between 0.50 and 0.625 m, about 4½ minutes' worth of waves between 0.625 and 0.75 m, and about 1¼ minutes' worth of waves between 0.75 and 1.00 m. A wave of height greater than 1.00 m is unlikely to occur in eight hours if the significant height is 0.50 m, but it is found that every interval of 3 hours is likely to see a wave whose

height is as much as 0.9 m, i.e. 1.8 times the significant height for the given duration or fetch, and windspeed.

We are considering a passage in an easterly direction from the northern exit of the Bosporus along the southern coast of the Black Sea where the 'fetch' of westerly winds increases as the ship proceeds. Since Heraclea is about 113 nautical miles (say 210 km) from the Bosporus, this is the greatest 'fetch' that concerns us if the wind is from the west. I shall present the significant wave heights at 50, 100, 150 and 200 km of fetch, corresponding (by an argument explained below) to durations of about 3.2, 6.3, 9.5, and 12.6 hours respectively. The greatest fetch in the JONSWAP work was 160 km so in quoting for 200 km I am guilty of a slight extrapolation.

To avoid exaggerating the waves I shall discuss a simple case in which the sea is calm initially; but early in the morning as the ship emerges from the Bosporus the wind springs up uniformly all along the course and blows steadily thereafter.

As the ship is to cruise at 3.9 m/s (7.5 knots) through the water its overall speed is 4.4 m/s (8.5 knots) and so it takes 3.2 hours to cover 50 km, 6.3 hours to cover 100 km, 9.5 hours to cover 150 km and 12.6 hours to cover 200 km. Hence in the postulated conditions, by the time the ship reaches the 50 km point the wind will have been blowing for 3.2 hours; when the ship reaches the 100 km point the wind will have been blowing for 6.3 hours, and so on. The propulsive action of the wind will be uniform the whole way. As the durations are fairly short, the waves mostly do not reach their full potential development: the sea is still growing. I have omitted the duration of the mid-day rest the crew may have taken.

As I have assumed a favourable current of 0.5 m/s (1 knot), the windspeeds in relation to the water are reduced by that amount in Table 8.3 which gives the significant wave height H, the mean wavelength L (both in metres) and the mean wave velocity C in m/s. W is the windspeed in m/s relative to the water.

From Carter's formulae I have obtained the data shown in Table 8.3.

I should add that the significant height of waves generated by an 8.5 m/s (16.5 knots) wind relative to the water – one strong enough to propel the ship at 3.9 m/s (7.5 knots) through the water via the sails only – would, at 200 km and 12.6 hours, be about 1.4 m, with a wavelength of about 28 m.

Table 8.4. Height, etc., of the "Three-hour" wave, m. An asterisk means the sea is fully developed. H. L, C and W have the same meanings as in Table 8.3.

Fetch km	Duration hours	W = 4.5 m/s			W = 5.0 m/s			W = 5.5 m/s		
		H	L	C	H	L	C	H	L	C
50	3.2	0.42	5.0	2.8	0.48	5.7	3.0	0.54	6.3	3.1
100	6.3	0.68	9.0	3.7	0.78	10.1	4.0	0.88	11.3	4.2
150	9.5	0.87*	12.2	4.4	1.04	14.4	4.7	1.17	16.0	5.0
200	12.6	0.87*	12.2	4.4	1.08*	15.1	4.9	1.31*	18.3	5.3

As I have explained, some waves must exceed the significant height. The "3 hour" heights are given in Table 8.4. That for an 8.5 m/s (16.5 knot) wind at 200 km, 12.6 hours is 2.5 m. Its wavelength would be about 34 m.

In Table 8.4 the heights H, lengths L and velocities C are 1.8 times, 1.2 times, and 1.1 times those given in Table 8.3 for the same fetch, duration and windspeed. For these factors I am indebted to Carter.

3.3. The effect of the waves on the ship

For reasons explained in *The Trireme Project*, *Olympias* was designed and built to withstand a wave of height 0.8 m and wavelength equal to the waterline length of the ship, about 33 m. Such a wave would not strain the hull. The scantlings of the principal timbers were made the same as those measured by Miss H. Frost at the wreck of a Punic 'long' ship off Marsala. A trireme built in accordance with Plan 201–12 would observe the same criterion. The sills of her thalamian oarports (closed by the *askomata*) would be about 0.3 m above the calm waterline (so that a wave of height 0.6 m would wet them) and those of the zygians about 1.0 m above it. It is believed that ancient Greek triremes were no more seaworthy than this.

Of course the 3-hour wave 2.5 m high and 34 m long for a windspeed of 8.5 m/s (16.5 knots) at a fetch of 200 km and a duration of 12.6 hours would severely strain the ship. Waves of the significant height for those conditions, about 1.4 m, would also strain and damage the hull structure if their heading were similar to that of the ship, as their wavelength, about 28 m, appears long enough that the hull would at times be supported on only one crest. If the hull remained intact and upright such waves would not swamp the ship but they would make rowing impossible.

In the less severe conditions associated with a windspeed of 5.5 m/s (10.7 knots) some waves will eventually rise to a height of about 1.3 m but the wavelength of about 18 m should ensure that the hull is always supported on at least two crests. The ship may therefore survive but as shown below, rowing will still be impossible.

3.4. The effect of the waves on the rowing

Here I should explain that the style of rowing I advocate to enable a fast trireme to attain the highest possible cruising speed in smooth and slight seas is not that of Burlet and Zysberg in which the stroke is short and the depth of immersion of the oarblade is much greater at midstroke than at the catch and finish (Burlet and Zysberg, 1986; cf. Burlet *et al.* 1986; Bondioli *et al.* 1995). The style of Burlet and Zysberg would have to be adopted in rough water but it would not yield the highest speed in smooth and slight seas. For that, one needs a long stroke. The blade is fully immersed as quickly as possible at the catch, thereafter remaining at more-or-less constant depth (if the water is flat) until it is cleanly extracted at the finish. This entails that to a good approximation any given point on the oar moves from catch to finish in a horizontal, circular arc in relation to the ship. The more skilful the oarsmanship, the closer the approximation although a slight increase in depth of immersion towards midstroke does no harm provided that the instantaneous turning point of the oar in relation to undisturbed water is not immersed.

Smooth swells of great height may be compatible with such a style of rowing if the wavelength is so great that the ship rises to them. Such waves certainly occur from time to time in the Black Sea but in the conditions considered here they will be overlain by the short waves whose data has been tabulated.

In what follows I draw on experience gained during the sea trials of *Olympias*. Although she cannot be cruised at 3.9 m/s (7.5 knots) experience in her is instructive and relevant. It indicates that if a trireme remains on a even keel without significant pitching, good progress under oar can be maintained for 3 or 4 hours in short waves of height up to about 0.30 m (the crests rising about 0.15m up the ship's side): in a ship built in accordance with Plan 201–12 a well-trained and determined crew should be able to row strongly and at full length in waves of this height although we have yet to demonstrate that such an effort could be sustained all day in such waves. Waves 0.3 m high would have a wavelength of about 5 m. The ship would overtake them at a relative speed of about 1 m/s (2 knots). There could be about 7 crests in the wetted length of the ship.

From Table 8.3 it appears that a trireme could maintain reasonably good progress under oar for at least the first 50 km and 3.2 hours in a tailwind of up to 5.5 m/s (10.7 knots) relative to the water, the wind arising as the ship leaves the Bosporus, as the significant height of the waves does not exceed 0.3 m. The rowing would occasionally be rendered more difficult by larger waves of heights up to those of the 3-hour waves of Table IV at the given fetch and duration. But the assistance afforded by the wind via the sails would be slight, only 12 percent of the total thrust as shown for a true wind of 6 m/s (11.7 knots) in Table 8.1.

At longer distances and durations the picture looks less rosy. The crew of a ship built in accordance with Plan 201–12 would not be able to maintain their long stroke in waves more than about 0.5 m in height (the crests then giving about the same effect, at the blade tips, as a heel of 3 degrees) because they would have to adjust the heights of their blades to the crests and troughs. With increasing wave height, oarsmen would have to adopt progressively shorter but less powerful strokes so that their rowing would become more like that employed in later galleys as described by Burlet and Zysberg and as used in oared seaboats generally (though not in Cornish racing gigs).

Most waves of height 0.5 m would keep pace with the ship; higher ones would overtake her. Because of the fore-and-aft oscillation of the water the men whose blades were in the crests would have to pull much harder than those whose blades were in the troughs (assuming the latter could reach the water) impairing uniformity and making timekeeping difficult.

I conclude that it is not possible to continue rowing powerfully enough to sustain a cruising speed of 7.5 knots in a trireme when the significant height of the waves exceeds about 0.5 m. Even in a wind as light as one of 5.5 m/s (10.7 knots) relative to the water these conditions would arise well before 150 km and 9.5 hours, and difficulties caused by waves greater than the significant height would become more serious than they would be in the first 50 km.

Further effects of waves higher than 0.5 m are considered below.

As mentioned earlier, the leather seals of the thalamian oarports would begin to be wetted when the water came up to about 0.3 m, implying a wave height of 0.6 m if their were no rolling, pitching or heaving. Possibly the thalamian oars could still be used but their power would be small. If the water came up 0.4 m (wave height about 0.8m) the thalamian oars would have to be drawn in and the power of the other oars would be severely reduced. (Of the three levels of oarsmen the thalamians are put out of action first, reducing the already limited oarpower by a third.)

As the waves rise they make it progressively harder for the blades to reach the water in the troughs and to be recovered when buried in the crests. Certain photographs of the *Olympias* in a swell, when compared with an elevation drawing of the ship, show that waves rising no more than about 0.4 m above the calm waterline were more than high enough to have this effect; the thalamian oars were out of action. Furthermore the wave height was less than twice this figure because the height to which some of the crests rose in relation to the ship was enhanced by the pitching

and heaving of the ship. These measurements discredit a statement reported on p. 40 of *The Trireme Trials 1988* that the whole crew had rowed (admittedly only a short distance) in waves of up to 1.2 m. The whole crew did row but the height of the waves was overestimated. According to a statement on p. 45 of *The Trireme Trials 1988* waves 1.0 m in height caused problems to some oarsmen (they were thranites and zygians, the thalamian oars having been drawn in). The report goes on to describe the conditions as "very difficult…when three big waves came together they seriously disrupted the stroke and it appeared that these conditions were about on the limit for rowing at two levels". The occasion was that on which the photographs referred to were taken and it would seem that the wave height given in that report was an overestimate.

According to Table 8.3 the significant height of the waves raised by a 5.5 m/s (10.7 knot) wind relative to the water would reach 0.65 m at 150 km and 9.5 hours; and I propose that this rules out any hope of a strong rowing performance in such a wind beyond this distance and duration. Table 8.4 shows that occasional disruption of the rowing by such waves would set in much sooner and of course it would become much more frequent and more severe as the voyage progressed and the waves grew higher.

As already mentioned, the 3-hour wave raised by a 5.5 m/s (10.7 knot) wind relative to the water at 200 km and 12.6 hours has a height of about 1.3 m. It would overtake the ship at a relative speed of about 1.4 m/s. Rowing would become impossible. The thalamians, of course, would be completely out of action. Although the sills of the zygian oarports are 1.0 m above the mean water level, and so a wave of height 1.3 m rising 0.65 above the calm waterline would not reach them if the ship remained on a even keel and did not heave or pitch severely, such a wave would make it very difficult for the zygian and thranite oarsmen to reach the water in the troughs and impossible for them to recover their blades if they were buried in the crests. The reason for this is that although the thranites, zygians and thalamians sit at different heights the height above calm water to which they can lift their blades is little if any higher for the upper two levels than it is for the thalamians. This is because they all have to reach calm water with their blades without raising their hands too high and therefore they all have about the same scope for lowering their oarlooms to their thighs at the recovery. Finally, a pitch amplitude of 1 degree either side of the horizontal would alternately raise and lower the foremost and sternmost zygian oarports by about 0.22 m.

In practice the waves will not be regular; also the ship will probably roll, pitch and heave. And of course, oarsmen who become seasick will contribute little propulsive power.

Tables 8.3 and 8.4 show that even in a wind for which W is only 4.5 m/s (8.7 knots) and V = 5.0 m/s (9.7 knots) affording, as shown in Table 8.1, very little thrust from the sails, the significant wave height of the fully-developed sea is 0.49 m and there will be a number of waves between this height and 0.87 m, the height of the "3-hour" wave.

There is a further point. Oarsmen cannot give of their best if they are overheated. During the "sailing" season of antiquity the climate in the Black Sea was probably as hot as it is now. That means the ship would have to be well-ventilated in order that the men's sweat could cool them by evaporating. Otherwise it would drip off uselessly. A tailwind of only 1.6 m/s (3.1 knots) relative to the ship (true wind, 6.0 m/s (11.7 knots)) would scarcely be enough, but a stronger one would certainly make the sea too rough for fast rowing. In a calm, the ship would be ventilated by her own motion through the air at 4.4 m/s (8.5 knots).

Commonsense suggests that assistance from the wind would have been accepted if it blew at a suitable velocity for a fairly short time, not long enough to raise hampering waves, and if on the quarter, not strongly enough to cause excessive heel. But it would be absurd to assume that any ancient trierarch or *kubernetes* would have set out knowing that he needed to rely on such an unpredictable phenomenon. If the wind continued to blow, the oarsmen would eventually have to give up and perhaps the ship would have to find shelter.

I mentioned in the Introduction that quite apart from the arguments presented here, there is good reason to think that assistance from the wind was unnecessary. This does not exclude the possibility of sail assistance in places where the fetch or duration of the wind were short enough to preclude the generation of hampering waves or where low speed was acceptable. But I regard it as certain that ancient Greek oarsmen making fast passages in their triremes between Byzantium and Heraclea did so under oar in smooth seas, or seas in the lower range of "slight" *i.e.* waves no higher than 0.3 m. They needed no help from the sails and they expected none.

It appears from the *Black Sea Pilot* that at the present time there are days with suitably calm weather particularly during the spring and autumn. The prevailing wind, however, is from the north-east, as was probably the case in antiquity.

A trireme was unsafe in even moderately heavy weather. No wonder that larger ships with longer oars permitting higher freeboard and higher oarports were eventually developed, though at a cost in speed and agility under oar.

4. Conclusion

Given all the foregoing, it seems necessary to believe that when Xenophon said "under oar" that was precisely what he meant. The high cruising speed implied by his account is the reason why a wind gentle enough not to hamper the oarsmen by raising waves or heeling the ship would also give hardly any propulsion, and why the oarsmen would overheat. Stronger winds would be objectionable unless the wind blew for only a short time. While sail-assistance during a short-lived blow was acceptable, a good oarcrew in a fast ship neither needed nor expected

it. In the Black Sea the fastest passages were made under oar in calm weather.

Acknowledgements

I am much indebted to D. J. T. Carter who read and commented on an earlier draft of this paper. Any errors, however, are entirely my responsibility.

Bibliography

The Black Sea Pilot. (Admiralty Sailing Directions) London, HMSO.

Bondioli, M., Burlet, R., and Zysberg, A. (1995) Oar mechanics and oar power in medieval and later galleys. In Gardiner, R. and Morrison, J. S. (eds), *Conway's History of the Ship. The Age of the Galley*. London, Conway Maritime Press, 172–205.

Burlet, R., Carriere, J., and Zysberg, A. (1986) Mais comment pouvait-on ramer sur les galères du Roi-Soleil? *Histoire et Mesure* I-314, 147–20.

Burlet, R. and Zysberg, A. (1986) Le travail de la rame sur le galères de France vers la fin du XVII siècle. *Neptunia* 164.

Carter, D. J. T. (1982) Prediction of the Wave Height and Period for a Constant Wind Velocity using the JONSWAP Results. *Ocean Engineering* 9, No. 1, 17–33.

Carter, D. J. T. (1996) Personal communications.

Coates, J. F., Platis, S. K. and Shaw, J. T. (1990) *The Trireme Trials 1988. Report on the Anglo-Hellenic Sea-Trials of Olympias*. Oxford, Oxbow Books.

Encyclopaedia Britannica, current edition (2009).

Frost, H. (1973) First season of excavation on the Punic wreck in Sicily. *International Journal of Nautical Archaeology* 2.1, 33–49.

Frost, H. (1974a) The Punic Wreck in Sicily. *International Journal of Nautical Archaeology* 3.1, 35–54.

Frost, H. (1974b) The third campaign of excavation on the Punic ship, Marsala, Sicily. *The Mariners Mirror* 60.3, 265–6.

Greenhill, B. and Allington, P. (1993) 'Sail-Assist and the Steamship. In Gardiner, R. and Greenhill, B. (eds), Conway's *History of the Ship. The Advent of Steam*. London, Conway Maritime Press, 146–55.

Morrison, J. S. and Coates, J. F. (1986) *The Athenian Trireme. The History and Reconstruction of an Ancient Greek Warship*. 1st ed. Cambridge, Cambridge University Press.

Pryor, J. H. (1995) The geographical conditions of galley navigation in the Mediterranean. In Gardiner, R. and Morrison, J. S. (eds), *Conway's History of the Ship, The Age of the Galley*. London, Conway Maritime Press, 206–16.

Shaw, J. T. (1993a) Rowing in Ships and Boats. *Transactions of the Royal Institution of Naval Architects* 135B, 211–224.

Shaw, J. T. (ed.) (1993b) *The Trireme Project. Operational Experience 1987–90. Lessons Learnt*. Oxford, Oxbow Books.

Shaw, J. T. (1994) *The 1994 Trireme Trials 1994. Research Results and Discussion* Watlington, The Trireme Trust.

See also chapters by Coates, by Morrison, and by Shaw in Gardiner, R. and Morrison, J. S. (eds) (1995) *Conway's History of the Ship, The Age of the Galley*. London, Conway Maritime Press.

9. Towards a Revised Design of a Greek Trireme of the Fourth Century BC: advantages of a long stroke

Timothy Shaw

Summary

Experimental data from the sea trials of *Olympias* are put into a simple mathematical model. The length of the stroke available to the oarsmen in *Olympias* is too short to allow the ship to cruise at 7 to 8 knots under oar and at a sustainable rate of striking. The changes proposed in Ch. 12 of *The Trireme Project* would increase the available length but it would still be too short. A satisfactory length could be obtained by adopting the further changes proposed in *The 1994 Trireme Trials* and in Plan 201–12, mainly the skewing of the rig by 18.4 degrees (the angle whose tangent in 1/3.)

1. Introduction

In my two papers above, I sought to show that Xenophon's statement that a trireme could make Heraclea from Byzantium in "a long day under oar" entails (a) a cruising speed of 7 to 8 knots and (b) that the passage could be made with no help from the wind. As this could not be done in *Olympias* various changes to her design are needed. I think that it is generally agreed that the stroke available to oarsmen in the *Olympias* has been too short. A longer stroke would be available in the revised design (here called *Mark IIa*) described by John Coates in Ch. 12 of *The Trireme Project* (Shaw 1993b, 71–4) but there are reasons for thinking an even longer stroke is required. A way of obtaining such a stroke without increasing the *interscalmium* beyond 0.98 m, namely by skewing the oar-rig, was suggested by me in *The 1994 Trireme Trials* (a slightly edited version of this Report is reproduced above, pp. 43–9) and was adopted by John Coates in his plan 210–12 (see the preceding paper, Fig. 8.1). I call this *Mark IIb*. An alternative, that of increasing the *interscalmium* by enough to eliminate the need for skewing the rig, is dismissed on the grounds that it would make the ship too weak structurally, and perhaps too long for the ancient slipways, also its greater wetted hull area would cause increased resistance. These points may need further attention.

In this note I begin by showing how far the distance advanced by the ship during the pull is increased by rowing a longer stroke with the given oars. I consider the thranite oars of three ships: *Olympias*, and the hypothetical improved designs I am calling Mark IIa and Mark IIb. In order to reduce the number of tables I consider for each ship only those thranite (top level) oars that were 9½ cubits long. The reader may work out the arithmetic for the zygian and thalamian oars and for the few in each level that were 9 cubits long.

2. Discussion

The first step is to list the dimensions of the oars both along their length and as seen in plan assuming them to be thranite oars inclined at 30 degrees to the horizontal. The dimensions in plan (*i.e.* in horizontal projection) are shown in brackets. It will be recalled that the oars in *Olympias* were made in accordance with a cubit of 0.444 m whereas those of the other two ships would conform to a cubit of 0.49 m. The inboard length of *Olympias*' oars was not closely fixed: it was to a slight extent under the control of the rowers. Those who were allotted some new light oars made of spruce seemed to prefer to use about 3 ft 7 ins to 3 ft 8 ins inboard, say 1,105 m. This dimension will be assumed correct for *Olympias* in what follows. It gives an outboard:inboard length ratio of 2.817.

I assume that the outboard and inboard lengths of the 9½ cubit oars in *Marks IIa* and *IIb* would be 7 cubits and 2½ cubits exactly, giving an outboard:inboard ratio of 2.80. The ratio cannot be much less than this if the ships are to be fast. 2½ cubits of 0.49 m are equal to 4 ft 0.2 ins. This length is convenient if the rig is skewed as in *Mark IIb* (Table 9.1).

The widths and details of the shapes of the blades need not be specified here but it is important to realise that they must be such as will enable the blades to absorb the required power. This may entail having different blade widths for the three different ships.

Next, I list the lengths of the chords of the horizontal

Table 9.1. Main dimensions of oars (those in brackets refer to the horizontal projection).

	Olympias	*Mark IIa*	*Mark IIb*
Length overall, m	4.218 (3.653)	4.655 (4.031)	4.655 (4.031)
Length outboard, m	3.113 (2.696)	3.430 (2.970)	3.430 (2.970)
Length of blade, m	0.550 (0.476)	0.550 (0.476)	0.550 (0.476)
Length inboard, m	1.105 (0.957)	1.225 (1.061)	1.225 (1.061)
Length between thole and neck, m	2.563 (2.220)	2.880 (2.494)	2.880 (2.494)

Table 9.2. Lengths and arcs of the pull.

	Olympias	*Mark IIa*	*Mark IIb*
Interscalmium, m	0.89	0.98	0.98
Chord between deadpoints, m	0.89	0.98	1.10
Effective chord, m	0.78	0.87	0.99
Inboard length in plan, m	0.957	1.061	1.061
Effective angular sweep, degrees (radians)	48.1 (0.839)	48.4 (0.845)	55.6 (0.971)
Ratio of effective chords	0.90	1.00	1.14
Ratio of effective angular sweep	0.99	1.00	1.15

projections of the arcs described by the butt-ends of the oars during the pull (*i.e.* between the deadpoints) and the effective length of the pull (*i.e.* the chord between deadpoints minus the unavoidable end-losses), and I give the angular sweeps the latter entail. For *Olympias* and *Mark IIa* the total length of the pull between deadpoints is at most that of the *interscalmium*, respectively 0.89 m and 0.98 m., and this assumes that just before the catch the clearance between one man's knuckles and the back of the next man aft is only 0.15 m (six inches). This may be impractically tight but I don't want to be accused of making the effective stroke in *Olympias* and *Mark IIa* shorter than it conceivably could be. In *Mark IIb* the *interscalmium* is still 0.98 m but owing to the skewed rig the men can reach up to 1.1 m between deadpoints. This is limited by their physique, it being assumed that men who are only 1.68 m tall can reach this far if trained from boyhood on fixed thwarts. I take it that the end losses are the same in all cases and I assess them as 0.11 m. The effective angular sweep is twice the angle whose sine is half the effective chord divided by the inboard length in plan. Thus we find the results tabulated in Table 9.2.

The last line emphasises the advantage in angular sweep gained by *Mark IIb*. I should add that the effective sweep angle given for *Olympias* has been attained only when the crew were making an exceptional effort. The gain in effective sweep angle that the increased effective chord available in *Mark IIa* might be expected to give (as compared with *Olympias*) is largely neutralised by the increased inboard length of the oars. I regard the swept angle of 65 degrees for *Mark IIa* implied on p. 72 of *The Trireme Project* as unattainable even though it includes the end losses. It does not allow enough clearance between oarhandles and men's backs at the catch.

The swept angle is very important as will be seen.

Next, I need to explain how the instantaneous turning point of the oar (in relation to undisturbed water) shifts up and down the shaft during the pull.

In (*e.g.*) Bourne (1925) and Sayer (1991) diagrams are given to show this shift for sliding-seat rowing but it is clear that the extent of it depends very much on the oarsman. It is not possible to quote one equation to cover all cases and so a more-or-less plausible selection must be made. I shall assume that in competent fixed-seat rowing, using oars carefully matched to the men's capability and to the ship, the turning point at the effective catch and finish is at the neck of the blade (*i.e.* 0.55 m from the tip), that at mid stroke (considered geometrically not time-wise) it is twice as far as that from the tip, and that the variation in between is that of a sine curve. These distances, as seen in plan with the blade fully immersed making an angle of 30 degrees to the horizontal, are 0.476m and 0.953 m.

To create an expression for this movement I define:

d as the distance in metres between the turning point and the tip (measured in plan)

A as the angle of attack at the effective catch

B as the effective swept angle

C as the angle (somewhere between A and A + B) adopted by the oar at any given instant during the effective pull

The angles are in plan and in degrees. Then:

$$d = 0.953 \sin [120(C - A)/B + 30 \text{ deg.}]$$

Then where L is the outboard length of the oar in plan, we see that p the distance in plan between the thole and the instantaneous turning point is given by:

$$p = L - d.$$

This is made use of later.

We already know B. It is now necessary to set values for A. As shown by video recording, the way people rowed in *Olympias* indicates that in her the stroke was roughly symmetrical about an athwartships line enabling me to put, with little error, $A = 180 - A - B$. Since angle B is 48.1 degrees this means that angle A is close to 66 degrees. John Coates did not intend this result; it arose because most of the rowers were too tall. He intended that much more of the stroke should have been cast "in front" of the athwartships line. We intend to achieve this in *Marks IIa* and/or *IIb*. It is necessary here to discuss how far this should be taken.

Where J is the inboard length of an oar in plan, V is the ship's velocity, p and A have the meanings given above, and Q is the angle of skew of the seats and stretchers relative to the keel, then the velocity v of an oarsman's shoulders required at the catch, relative to the ship, is given by:

$$v = J(V/p)\sin A \sin (A + Q)$$

The value of v is limited by the oarsman's physical ability and the available time since the deadpoint. In turn this prescribes the best angle for the catch (A), given the required speed of the ship V, the valueof Q and the dimensions of the oars.

In order to obtain a reasonable value for v, I examine the case of the Oxford Etonian VIII of 1870, record-setters for fixed-seat rowing at Henley Royal Regatta, England. Their time for the course shows that their average speed V was 5.00 m/s (9.7 knots) if the adverse stream had its normal value of 0.17 m/s (0.33 knots). Their oars were 12 ft long overall (3.66 m) and 3 ft 5 ins. long inboard (1.04 m). The blades were 3 ft 3ins long (0.991 m), *i.e.* the neck was 5 ft 4 inches (1.63 m) from the thole. The inclination of the oars to the horizontal was small and it can be ignored. From a statement in Cook (1919), I assume the men's length of stroke at the butt was 4 ft 0 ins. (1.22 m). The swept angle between deadpoints was therefore 71.7 degrees. Data from Bourne (1925) that I collected in Shaw (1993ba) show a stroke length of 4 ft 0 ins (1.22 m) but the inboard length is given as 3 ft 6 ins. (1.07 m) and drawn (to a small scale) as 3 ft 7½ ins. (1.10 m). Accordingly the angular sweep is shown as 67 degrees; the angle of attack at the catch (A) is shown as 43 degrees. Making appropriate corrections and taking end losses into account we find that angle A for the Oxford Etonian crew may have been as little as 41 degrees, and this may have been partly responsible for their high speed.

In an eight the skew angle Q is zero. I assume that in a record-setting crew the men rowed skilfully, immersing their blades fully but not overburying them: *i.e.* p at the catch = 5 ft 4 ins (1.63 m).

The speed of a sliding-seat eight fluctuates considerably so that it would be quite unfair to assume the speed at the catch was the same as the mean. Edwards (1963) gave a graph obtained from a slow-motion film and an accelerometer showing that the speed dipped sharply at the catch, so that when the blades were just covered it was only 17.0 fps (5.18 m/s (10 knots)) and it subsequently fell further to 15.5 fps (4.72 m/s (9.2 knots)) although the average speed over the whole pull and run was as much as 18.5 fps, (5.64 m/s (11 knots)). In a fixed-seat eight the dip would presumably be rather less as a smaller proportion of each man's mass would be in accelerated motion relative to the boat at the catch. I shall assume the dip for the Oxford Etonian crew of 1870 amounted to 0.3 m/s (0.58 knots) so that the speed V to be considered in

the calculation below is not the target speed of 5.00 m/s (9.7 knots) in a 7 minute sprint but 4.70 m/s (9.1 knots). Better information on this point would be welcome. As for the triremes, their mass in relation to that of the men is so great that the dip can be ignored. (A man standing on the canopy of *Olympias* can, however, sense it though his feet.)

Stating the distances in metres we find that:

$$v = (JV/p)\sin^2 A = (1.04 \times 4.70/1.63)\sin^2 41 = 1.29 \text{ m/s}$$
$$(2.5 \text{ knots}).$$

This was the probable speed of movement of the Oxford Etonians' shoulders at the catch if they obtained it correctly with straight arms as they almost certainly did. I shall assume that a well-trained trireme crew could attain this shoulder speed for the catch, in a sprint lasting about 7 minutes. (The Oxford Etonians' record time in 1870 was 7 min. 17 seconds.)

One reason for the limitation of *Olympias'* speed can now be seen. If the rowers' shoulder speed v is not to exceed 1.29 m/s (2.5 knots) and the angle A is about 66 degrees the formula given restricts *Olympias'* speed V to about 7 knots (3.6 m/s) irrespective of the number of levels at work. This might be called her normal top speed. It has been demonstrated in rows of ¾ and 1 mile. As disclosed by the sea trials, however, any higher speed than this calls for exceptional efforts resulting in rapid exhaustion even though the mean effective power exerted may seem to be within the crew's capacity.

For *Marks IIa and IIb* we may set V the top speed in a 7 minute sprint as 5.00 m/s (9.7 knots) (by equating power available to power required) and this is also the speed at the catch as explained above. I shall assume that the men's shoulder speed at the catch was 1.29 m/s (2.5 knots). Then a cruising speed of 3.86 m/s (7.5 knots) entails a shoulder speed of 1.00 m/s (2 knots). In *Olympias* this would correspond to a speed of about 2.8 m/s or 5.4 knots. Reference to the logs of *Olympias* shows that she could reach this speed when cruising.

Now to calculate angle A for *Marks IIa* and *IIb*.

For *Mark IIa* Q is about zero but for *Mark IIb* as currently envisaged it is 18.4 degrees. We may tabulate the calculation for thranite oars (Table 9.3).

These angles A apply to the zygians and thalamians also.

Warning is given that these values of A are subject to some uncertainty. However, they are not likely to be far wrong. I can proceed to work out the values of p at all angles C and hence use the values of A and B to obtain the distances advanced by the ships during the pulls of different lengths.

Remembering that d = 0.953 sin [120(C – A)/B + 30] and that:

$$p = L - d$$

I obtain various lengths and angles as shown in Table 9.4.

While this may seem a long way round to a simple answer the formula enables me to find p (*i.e.* L – d) at any permitted value of C and this is useful as will now be shown.

Table 9.3. To find Angle A

	Mark IIa	**Mark IIb**
J, m	1.061	1.061
V, m/s	5.00	5.00
p, m	2.494	2.494
v, m/s	1.29	1.29
Q, degrees	nil	18.4
Accordingly,		
sin A sin (A + Q)	0.6065	0.6065
A degrees (in plan)	51.1	43.4
I repeat:		
B degrees	48.4	55.6
A + B degrees	99.5	99.0

Table 9.4. Various lengths and angles

	Olympias	**Mark IIa**	**Mark IIb**
Length L in plan, m	2.696	2.970	2.970
Angle A degrees	65.95	51.1	43.4
Angle B degrees	48.1	48.4	55.6
d when C = A degrees, m	0.4765	0.4765	0.4765
d when C = A + B/2 deg.	0.953	0.953	0.953
d when C = A + B deg.	0.4765	0.4765	0.4765
and L − d (m) when C = A	2.220	2.494	2.494
L − d (m) when C = A + B/2	1.743	2.017	2.017
L − d (m) when C = A + B	2.220	2.494	2.494

Table 9.5. The advance and the mean ideal efficiency

	Olympias	**Mark IIa**	**Mark IIb**
Total advance during pull, S m	1.654	1.978	2.362
Ratio	0.836	1.000	1.194
Mean ideal efficiency (oarcrew of 170)	0.756	0.780	0.780

A sufficiently accurate value for the differential advance ds of the ship per differential angle dC of the angular sweep of the oar is given by:

$$ds = [(L − d).dC]/\sin C$$

A simple computer programme sums ds between the limits C = A and C = A + B and thereby reveals the total advance during the effective pull; if desired the advance at any intermediate angle can be obtained. Fig. 9.1 illustrates this. The step dC is given the value 0.01 degrees.

Here I need to mention q, the distance between the instantaneous turning point and the centre of pressure.

The mean value of the ratio p/(p + q), the mean ideal efficiency of the oars, is also tabulated. This is the efficiency that oars lacking inertia and hysteresis but having the given dimensions would exhibit if skilfully used. It is quite easily obtained by analytical methods (see Appendix). The results are shown in Table 9.5:

The mean ideal efficiency is affected by, amongst other things, the number of oarsmen in action, n, and I need to discuss this here. The thrust per oar normal to the blade at the centre of pressure of the blade is equal to:

$$(a/b)P \sin (C + Q) \text{ and to } k(q/p)^2 V^2 \sin^2 C$$

The first of these expressions is derived by considering the handle force P, assuming no friction losses at the thole; a/b is the reciprocal of the effective gearing. The second expression represents the resistance offered by the water to the blade.

The second expression is of course an approximation. k is a coefficient of proportionality and q is the distance between the instantaneous turning point and the centre of pressure. For given k, V and angles C and Q the thrust per oar varies in inverse proportion to n. Hence q/p is inversely proportional to the square root of n and in particular, if n changes from 170 to 116, q/p increases by a factor of 1.21.

Since the mean ideal efficiency E is related to q/p by the expression:

$$1/E = 1 + q/p$$

it follows that if P, V and the angles are kept constant but three levels of oarsmen are reduced to two, the mean ideal efficiency of the oars of the *Olympias*, initially 0.756, becomes 0.719. This result is required later.

If I am justified in assuming the check to hullspeed at the catch and the corresponding rise at the recovery can be neglected in a trireme, I can say with little error that when

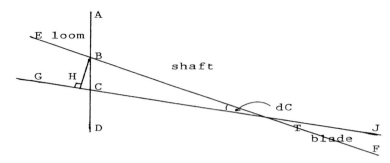

Figure 9.1. Diagram to calculate the advance of the tholepin (i.e. of the ship) per differential angle of sweep of an oar knowing the position of the instantaneous turning point relative to undisturbed water. The diagram gives a plan view of the situation at some stage during the pull. ABCD is the line of advance of the tholepin. EBTF and GHCTJ are two successive positions of the oar, BC (called ds in the main text) being the differential advance of the tholepin, greatly exaggerated for clarity. T is the turning point. The angle BTC (called dC in the main text) represents the differential swept angle, greatly exaggerated. The distance BT is called p in the main text. The instantaneous angle of attack DCT is called C in the main text. As dC tends to zero, BH tends to p.dC, where dC is in radians, and so ds tends to p.dC/sin C, i.e. (L – d).dC/sin C (Drawing: J. T. Shaw).

Table 9.6. Duration of the effective pull

		Olympias	*Mark IIa*	*Mark IIb*
Duration of effective pull, sec.	at 7.5 knots	0.428	0.512	0.612
	at 8.2 knots	0.392	0.469	0.560
	at 9.7 knots	–	0.396	0.472

the ship's speed is the same at the finish of one stroke as it is at the finish of the next one, the mean speed during the effective pull is the same as it is during the rest of the time, namely the run, including the entry and extraction of the blade.

Then if I postulate a mean speed I can use the values of S tabulated above to specify the duration of the pull. I select three speeds, 7.5 knots, 3.86 m/s, about the speed at which a trireme would have to be rowed in order to reach Heraclea from Byzantium in "a long day", 8.2 knots (4.22 m/s) which *Olympias* has attained for very short periods, and 9.7 knots (5.00 m/s) which should be attained by *Mark IIb* if not by *Mark IIa* (Table 9.6).

To proceed further I note from experiments carried out by and for The Trireme Trust that:

the mean effective power W watts required to drive *Olympias* at speed V m/s with rudders partly raised to minimise their resistance is given by:

$$W = 155 \, V^3 + 4.13 \, V^5$$

and I postulate that the power required by *Marks IIa* and *IIb* would be 8% greater than this because of their greater length and displacement.

In what follows I assume that during the trials about to be described the exceptionally-determined crew of the *Olympias* did attain the stroke length and angular sweep given in Table 9.2.

It is the case that:

$$W = nPLrE/60$$

where n = number of rowers in action
P = a rower's mean pull in newtons assumed to act at the butt
L = the effective length of the pull measured at the butt, in metres
r = the rate of striking in spm
E = the mean ideal efficiency.

To obtain the magnitude of a good rower's mean pull I refer to a trial in which the 116 rowers in the two upper levels of *Olympias* sprinted for ¾ nautical mile. Their speed was 6.8 knots – 3.50 m/s – and the mean effective power required with rudders down and in a tailwind of 4 to 5 knots absolute was calculated to be 12100 watts (Shaw 1993b, 43). The rate of striking varied between 38 and 39.5 spm. Taking the mean stroke rate as 38.75 spm and the mean ideal efficiency (calculated above) as 0.719, I find that the mean pull P comes to:

12100 × 60/(116 × 0.78 × 38.75 × 0.719) = 288 newtons

which is 64.7 1bf. I shall assume that young adult oarsmen in ancient Greece could pull this hard. This information relates to a sprint lasting about 6½ minutes. In order to apply it to other durations I shall assume that the mean pull varies directly as the rate of striking. (This is in accordance with oarsmen's common experience.)

This entails that Mean P = 7.43 r

I now test these findings against the result of four short sprint trials of *Olympias* using all three levels of oars but in which (according to *The Trireme Project*, p. 43) probably only

Table 9.7. Rates of striking, etc, required at 7.5 knots and 9.7 knots.

	Mark IIa		Mark IIb	
Speed, knots	7.5	9.7	7.5	9.7
Speed, m/s	3.86	5.00	3.86	5.00
Watts	13460	34860	13460	34860
L, m	0.87	0.87	0.99	0.99
E	0.780	0.780	0.780	0.780
Therefore:				
Pr	7001	18130	6152	15930
therefore r^2	942	2440	828	2144
therefore r spm	30.7	49.4	28.8	46.3
therefore P newtons	228	367	214	344
P in pounds force	51.3	82.5	48.1	77.3
And rhythm factor	3.82	3.07	3.40	2.75
Duration of run, sec	1.44	0.819	1.47	0.824

about 130 rowers were effective as most of the thalamians still had unsatisfactory oars. E now becomes 0.730.

Given that the mean stroke rate overall was about 44.5 spm the theory indicates that the effective power amounted to:

$$130 \times 0.78 \times 7.43 \times 44.5^2 \times 0.730/60 = 18152 \text{ watts.}$$

With rudders partly raised and negligible breeze this indicates a speed of 4.285 m/s or 8.32 knots. The mean speed sustained for about 45 seconds in each of the first three runs was 8.2 knots, and in the fourth run it was 8.3 knots. Agreement between experiment and theory appears to be good and gives me confidence to continue.

By the method just illustrated I now obtain the rates of striking and the mean pulls *etc.* required in *Marks IIa* and *IIb* for a cruising speed of 7.5 knots and a sprint speed of 9.7 knots as under. I assume n = 170, E = 0.780, P = 7.43 r as already shown (Table 9.7).

It should be recalled that the data for *Mark IIa* have been obtained on the assumption favourable to that design that clearance of as little as 0.15m between a man's knuckles and the back of the man next aft, just before the catch, is adequate, on the one hand during cruising for hours on end, and on the other during a flat out sprint. Both propositions are doubtful and if they are not accepted the case for *Mark IIb*, already strong, is made stronger still. By permitting a longer stroke *Mark IIb* allows of a lower rate of striking, a lighter pull, and a more normal (for fixed-seat rowing) rhythm at both cruise and sprint conditions.

The last remark may need further explanation. It is because the stroke in *Mark IIa* is shorter than in *Mark IIb* that *Mark IIa* requires not only higher rates of striking and stronger pulls but also higher rhythm factors. High rhythm factors feel artificial; they are resorted to in training in order to counter the tendency of unfit or inexperienced crews to go to the opposite extreme. In fixed-seat rowing the rhythm factors tend to be lower than on long slides (Bourne 1925). The Oxford Olympic VIII of 1960 exhibited rhythm factors in the region of 2.7 when rowing at about 35 spm even though they were on long slides (Edwards 1963). This puts the factors given above into perspective.

3. Conclusion

A case has been made for canting or skewing the rig in a Mark II trireme by an angle whose tangent is about 1/3, in order to lengthen the available stroke. Such a design of trireme can reasonably be expected to achieve a performance under oar consistent with Xenophon's statement in the *Anabasis* (6.4.2); and if so, there would be implications for the design of other oared longships of classical antiquity.

Appendix: Calculation of the mean ideal efficiency of oars

The expression given in this paper for the variation of the position of the instantaneous turning point has the effect that the distance of that point from the tip varies as a sine, from sine 30 deg. to sin 90 deg. to sin 150 deg., *i.e.* as (some constant) times a variable that varies as a sine from 0.5 to 1.0 and back to 0.5.

Bibliography

Bourne, G. C. (1925) *A Textbook of Oarsmanship*. Oxford, Oxford University Press.

Coates, J. F., Platis, S. K. and Shaw, J. T. (eds) (1990) *The Trireme Trials 1988. Report on the Anglo-Hellenic Sea Trials of* Olympias. Oxford, Oxbow Books.

Coates, J. F. (1994) 'The Naval Architecture of European Oared Ships', *Transactions of the Royal Institution of Naval Architects* 136B, 175.

Edwards, H. R. A. (1963) *The Way of a Man with a Blade*. London, Routledge and Keegan Paul.

Sayer, Bill. (1991) *Rowing and Sculling: the Complete Manual*. London, Hale.

Shaw, J. T. (1993a) Rowing in Ships and Boats. *Transactions of the Royal Institution of Naval Architects* 136B, 211.

Shaw, J. T. (ed.) (1993b) *The Trireme Project. Operational Experience 1987–90. Lessons Learnt*. Oxford, Oxbow Books.

Shaw, J. T. (1994) *The 1994 Trireme Trials. Research Results and Discussion* (Watlington).

Sherwood, W. E. (1900) *Oxford Rowing* (Oxford).

10. The Proposed Design of any Second Reconstruction

John Coates

Introduction

In his three papers published in this volume (pp. 63–7, 68–75, 76–81), Timothy Shaw has demonstrated by close argument with a sufficiency of physical evidence that:

i)   Xenophon's account that triremes could row the 129 sea miles from Byzantium to Heraclea in 'a long day' should be accepted as being true, provided that the sea was smooth or slight.

ii) The passage was made under oar because significant sail assistance at a ship speed of 7 knots or more would require wind speeds high enough to raise waves and swell too great for rowing or for triremes' hulls to survive without structural damage.

iii) Xenophon's evidence therefore demands that a trireme with a moderately good oarcrew could maintain 7–8 knots for many hours on end and that that ability is a necessary criterion of the authenticity of any reconstruction.

iv) Attainable oar power depends greatly upon length of stroke.

v)   To enable a moderately good oarcrew to maintain 7–8 knots in a trireme it must be possible for them to row with the longest physically practicable oar stroke.

Of these five conclusions, iii) provides a necessary and important (but not sufficient) test of the authenticity of any reconstruction and v) indicates the main means by which that test may be passed.

Thirty-odd other lessons or conclusions from the sea trials with *Olympias* have previously been published (Shaw 1993), and they are also listed in the Annex. All but a few remain valid and it is hard to imagine how they or the five conclusions above could have been learnt or deduced except from results of sea trials with an actual reconstruction built in all respects material to performance according to available evidence about triremes. It has to be acknowledged therefore that we owe our present understanding about triremes to that ship and to the generosity of the Greek people who made her building and testing at sea possible.

The aims of the trireme project and in testing any future reconstruction of a trireme (Shaw 1993) are:

i)   To achieve attested performance under oar.

ii)   To simulate and study manoeuvring and battle tactics by computer simulation of ship movements.

iii) To explore the effects of being 'heavy in the water.'

iv)   To study the kinematics and structural mechanisms of damage by ramming, and then apply Aim 2 to find the required tactics.

v)   To study hauling triremes out of the water and launching them.

vi)   To establish sailing characteristics.

vii) To gather more experience in making sea passages in oared ships.

viii) To continue investigation of *hypozomata*.

The main proposed changes from the design of *Olympias*

To pursue the above aims, the design will take into account the sixteen lessons from *Olympias* which call for changes. The main features of *Olympias* were vindicated by the sea trials and most of the changes would be better described as adjustments which, though they would not appear to be immediately obvious, would nevertheless be significant improvements. Two changes however are more apparent but even so may not be obvious to many, except by direct comparison with *Olympias* (Fig. 10.1). Together they would enable a large increase in oar power to be achieved, expected to be sufficient to pass the test of conclusion v) above and so justify a second reconstruction built otherwise on the same general lines as *Olympias*.

The first main change in the design of any second reconstruction would be to increase the spacing of the beams, clearly shown by trial to be needed for powerful rowing. Since 1989 and 1990 (that is, after *Olympias* was built) that increase is also required to accord with new archaeological evidence about the length of the cubit used in 5th and 4th century BC building in Attica (Steinhauer

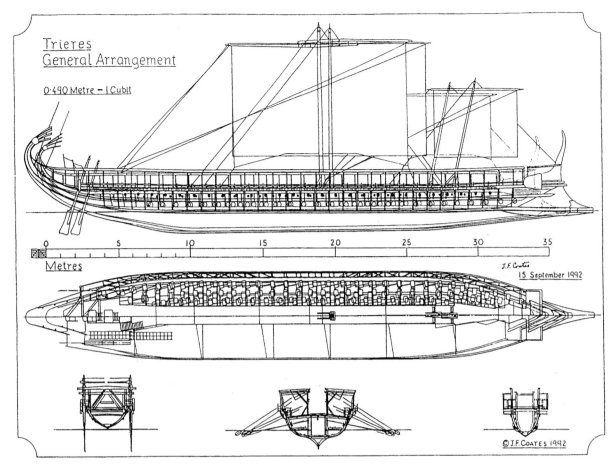

Figure 10.1. General arrangement drawings of Olympias *and of the proposed second reconstruction superimposed (Drawing: John Coates).*

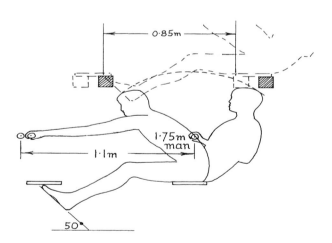

Figure 10.2. Position of ship beams relative to thalamians (Drawing: John Coates).

1989; Dekoulakou-Sideris 1990). The new information makes it virtually certain that the cubit to which triremes would have been built was about 0.49 metre long, not the 0.444 metre cubit, previously taken to have been the Attic cubit, and to which *Olympias* was built. Following Vitruvius (*Dr Arch.* 1.2.4), the two-cubit spacing of thole

pins would therefore be increased from 0.888 m. to 0.980 m. adding on that account 92 mm to the length of oar stroke. It would in turn also increase the length of the ship from 36.8 m to about 40 m (but see now Rankov, pp. 225–30). That greater spacing however allows the heads of thalamians to clear the beams by raising them (and the whole of the crew and structure above them) by an amount small enough not to reduce the ship's stability unduly (Fig. 10.2). Freeing the thalamians, provided of course that they are not too tall, also frees the whole crew, which had to keep their oars in mesh with them, from the restricted length of stroke which had to be endured by all oarcrew in *Olympias*. Thus the 10% increase in beam spacing would enable a worthwhile increase in stroke length to be obtained not only by the thalamians themselves but by the whole crew.

The second of the bigger changes, whose great advantage could not have been realised without carrying out the first one, would be to set the whole oarcrew facing somewhat outboard, in other words skewed or canted, generally by about 18° from the true fore and aft direction, as discussed by Shaw (pp. 76–81) and drawn in Fig. 10.3. That skew is necessary to enable butts of oars to pass outboard of the rower next aft and so allow the stroke to be as long as

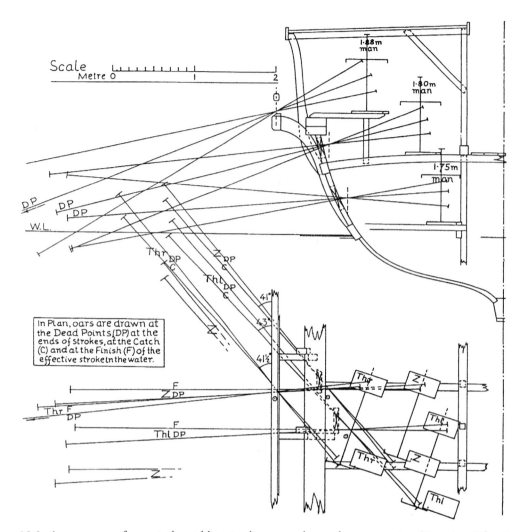

Scale
Metre 0 ⎯⎯⎯ 1 ⎯⎯⎯ 2

In Plan, oars are drawn at
the Dead Points (DP) at the
ends of strokes, at the Catch
(C) and at the Finish (F) of the
effective stroke in the water.

Figure 10.3. Arrangement of one triad amidships in the proposed second reconstruction (Drawing: John Coates).

is physically possible from a fixed seat at any of the three levels throughout the ship, given that the thalamians are released from restriction by the beams. The length designed for is a total stroke between dead points of 1.1 m at the butt, a gain for the whole oarcrew of at least 25% on the greatest possible stroke in *Olympias,* and for the thalamians the ability to be as effective as the others at all speeds.

The proposed oarsystem

If the chords of the arcs swept out by the oar handles are in plan to remain perpendicular to edges of seats, skewing the seats to move stretchers outboard will necessarily swing the arcs swept out by the oars forward into the positions shown in Fig. 10.3, where the arcs lie almost entirely forward of athwartships. Oars working over such a large part of their time in the water so far from athwartships may seem to make them less effective in propelling the ship forward, but this is not so, as common rowing practice would suggest and Shaw's theoretical analysis shows (Shaw 1993b). There are also advantages. First, the speed of the

oar handles needed to enter the water cleanly and to start effective strokes is smaller so that the effective stroke can start more quickly; second, there is a faster flow of water past the blade from the tip to the neck, mainly during the first part of the stroke, helping to reduce the extent of stalling and therefore the effectiveness of the blade in developing lift as well as reducing the amount of slip in the water (particularly if the blades are relatively wide and short as it is intended that they will be); third, fresh, stationary water will be pulled by the blades outboard into the oar race, reducing its increase in velocity towards the stern and thus helping to equalise the work done by oarcrew over the whole length of the oarsystem. It is not possible to put figures to these advantageous factors but they may be expected to compensate for any loss of forward thrust owing to the generally forward inclination of oars while in the water.

The arcs of oars, shown in Fig. 10.3, have been placed to minimize interference between blades in the water, particularly at the finish, and any crossing of shafts in the plan view occurs too far inboard to be able to cause

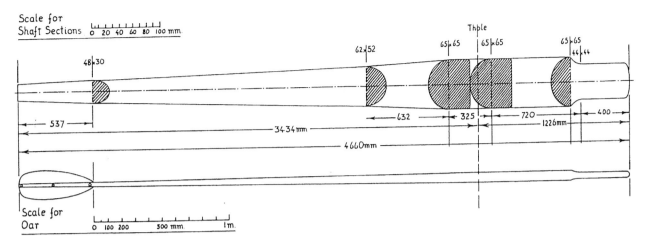

Figure 10.4. Proposed oar (Drawing: John Coates).

collisions. The placing of tholes and oarports has not only to be satisfactory from those two aspects but also to accord with the generally accepted interpretation of the Lenormant relief and with a feasible arrangement of framing and beams within the ship. As will be mentioned, thranite blades have been separated laterally from the others as far as possible at the finish. The need to avoid undue interference between oars hindering their extraction from the water, particularly by thalamians, was evident in rowing *Olympias*.

i) Oars

It is proposed that oars at all three levels shall be of the same design and be identical to the experimental spruce oars which were tested in *Olympias*. In a future reconstruction they would be made to the longer cubit and the oar rig would be designed for the 9-cubit oars to be worked with a crude gearing (length outboard/length inboard) of 2.8. That the oars on all levels should be the same may not seem to respond to the evidence from the naval inscriptions of the inspector who somehow distinguished between thranite and zygian oars; the difference could have been in their identification marking. Even differences in wear patterns from use may yet offer an explanation of this piece of evidence. In the meantime it seems sensible to use the best kind of oar which could have been adopted in triremes.

The proposed design of oar is shown in Fig. 10.4. It is as light as practicable if made of solid selected spruce and the diameters of the shaft are determined by the need to limit deflection when pulled hard. The calculated deflection of the blade will be about 200 mm for a pull of 45 kg. f. on the handle. The blade area, 0.078 m², is the minimum at present judged to be effective, reducing oar mass without causing too much loss by slip in the water. Lightness of oars is most important in view of the high rates of striking in a fast fixed-seat ship, lightness being

necessary to minimize mass inertia losses. There may be some advantage to be had from spooning the blades, in view of working oars so far forward of athwartships. If they were spooned, they should be given squarer tips to gain the greatest benefit. On blade shape, it should be noted that there is little guidance to be had from ancient ship representations which show a number of shapes on one-man oars whose blades may be interpreted as being attached to shafts. Monoxylous oars with narrow blades are associated in ship representations with polyremes in which the angular oar arcs are likely to have been smaller and the stroke deeper in the water.

The main object of skewing the seats is to enable butts to pass the next rower aft, but that cannot be simply achieved where the hull tapers in the bow, as will be clear from the plan view of the forward third of the oarsystem in Fig. 10.5. However, we know that of the 30 spare oars carried by triremes (*IG* 2² 1606.43), three were short ones, 9 cubits long, indicating (assuming an equal failure rate for long and short oars) that about 10% of the 170 oars in the oarsystem were also short. Aristotle and Michael of Ephesus refer to oars amidships being long (Aristotle *On the parts of animals*, 687b.18; Michael of Ephesus *Commentaries on Aristotle*, 22.118.15) and Galen states that all the oars extend an equal distance and likens them to the fingers of the hand where on one side there is the little finger (Galen *On the Use of Parts of the Body* 1.24). These references indicate that about 10% of oars were short (9 cubits long), that they nevertheless extended from the ship by the same distance as the long oars, and that they were at one end of the ship. In Fig. 10.5 short oars are shown in the bows where their short looms either enable the butts to pass the next rower aft even though that person is sitting further outboard, or the butts do not reach the next rower aft in sweeping out the same arcs as elsewhere in the system. This problem does not arise in the stern where 9-cubit oars can be worked.

If the short oars are to extend by the same distance

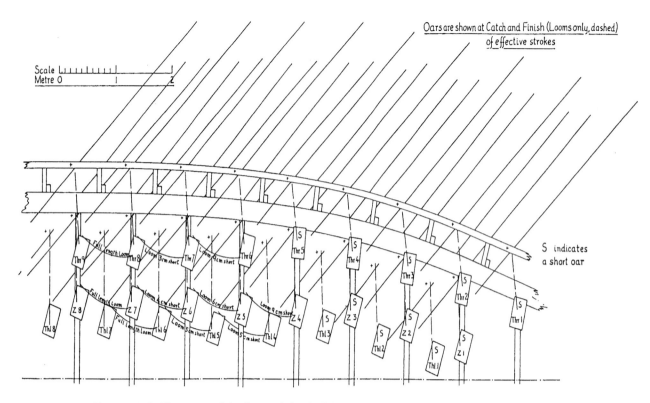

Figure 10.5. Plan view of the forward third of the proposed oarsystem (Drawing: John Coates).

from the ship as the long ones, their gearing is going to be indeed high. If that of the long oars is to be 2.8, then the gearing of the short oars will be 3.5, which is probably near to the maximum practicable. If that does prove to be too high, the blade areas of those oars could be reduced to compensate for their higher gearing. Alternatively, as the position of the oar at the thole is not definitely fixed by a button, it would be possible for short oars, as may be seen from Fig. 10.5, to be worked a few centimetres further inboard.

ii) Tholes

The evidence as to whether oars in triremes were forward or aft of their tholes has been published before (Coates 1993), and it is heavily if not conclusively in favour of the oars being forward of their tholes, as they invariably are in the Mediterranean today. The advantage of that position is that, in the event of 'catching a crab' or of losing control of the oar when stopping the forward motion of the ship by holding her up, the oar is not jammed between the internal thole and the after edge of the oarport, which would make extraction difficult if not impossible. The disadvantage is that whatever binding is used to hold the oar to the thole it must do so without stretching with use; if it does stretch valuable oar motion is lost, particularly to oars working through oarports. In *Olympias* we have had a lot of trouble from this cause: leather loops, seemingly attested in Homer, stretched far too much: rope grommets

were better but still not satisfactory. In 1994, however, we rather belatedly learnt how Greek fishermen do it today. The essence of the method is to use a lanyard (it could be a leather strap better to accord with Homer) tied round oar and thole by a knot which does not slip and, equally important, when the lanyard has stretched after use it can be retied easily to make it tight again. It is proposed to use lanyards with this knot in future, and in view of the importance of this detail to the oarsystem and its performance, how to tie this knot is described elsewhere in this volume (pp. 43–4 with Fig. 3.1). It is proposed that oars should continue to be forward of tholes.

In *Olympias* oars were never feathered and we think on balance that they should not be in future. It is much more important that blades be kept vertical in the water which calls for a D-shaped section in the shaft at the thole; if the flat of the D is against the thole and the thole is vertical and the lanyard is holding the shaft close to the thole, the blade should never be far from the vertical. The carling or rail on which oars rest should be shaped so that the oar rubs on a ridge (sheathed with copper) in the same plane as the thole and sloping down from it so that at the catch oars will lie with their blades vertical. In that way the tendency of shafts to roll on the carling during the stroke will be reduced, together with wear. It will nevertheless be necessary (and the responsibility of every rower) to keep lanyards tight, and the oar carling or rail, and the thole, greased.

iii) The stature of oarcrew

As experience in *Olympias* amply showed, the taller, long-limbed rowers of the sliding-seat eights of today cannot work properly in a fixed-seat trireme. Before settling the exact heights of seats, beams and canopy of any future reconstruction, it will be necessary to decide the limiting statures of each of the three levels of oarcrew for that reconstruction. Figs 10.2, 10.3 and 10.5 have been drawn for the following statures of oarcrew:

Level	Approximate stature	Principal limitation
Thranite	1.88 m. (6' 2")	Height of canopy
Zygian	1.80 m. (5' 11")	Maximum leg length, seat to stretcher; beam spacing
Thalamian	1.75 m. (5' 9")	Height of beams and all structure and oarcrew above them, affecting ship stability and vertical angles of oars in the top two levels

Raising the canopy to accommodate thranites taller than 1.88 m would have relatively little effect on the ship. The stricter limitation on the leg length of zygians is imposed by the beam spacing, 0.980 m. The sitting height of thalamians directly affects ship stability; a 1 cm. increase would raise the ship's centre of gravity (G) by about 0.5 cm. *Olympias* had a metacentric height (GM) of about 0.9 m on trial with dry bilges, which may appear to be more than ample, but it was not enough to prevent small lateral movements of other ship's crew from being in practice noticeable to the oarcrew. In any case, the presence of an otherwise quite tolerable amount of bilge water would reduce effective GM by about 0.2 m (see pp. 182–4), and as also about a third of the mass of a trireme is oarcrew, able to roll on their seats in response to ship movement, they can raise the ship's effective centre of gravity and so further reduce the effective GM by between 0.1 and 0.2 m. By those causes the ship's GM and hence stiffness in roll could and at times probably was reduced by 30% to 40% below the more theoretical GM of 0.9m. Most oarcrews of *Olympias* did not seem to think that she was by any means unduly stiff in roll.

In any second reconstruction, to enable the thalamians' heads to clear the beams, these and everything and everybody above them, about half the whole mass of the ship and crew taken together, would have to be raised by about 15 cm, which would raise G and so reduce GM by say 7 cm. Thus a second ship would have to be about 10% less stiff in roll than *Olympias*, probably an acceptable price to be paid for freeing the thalamians from the beams and thereby increasing achievable power and speeds by the proposed oarsystem. Lateral movement by non-rowers would, however, in consequence have to be somewhat more firmly restricted.

iv) Coping with waves

Having their tholes only 0.45 m. above the waterline, thalamians will be in difficulties when rowing in waves higher than about 0.7 m, trough to crest (though in *Olympias* they did on occasion cope with such waves). The vertical clearances in the proposed oarsystem, however, allow more generous movements for rowing in waves than is the case in *Olympias*. Fig. 10.3 shows that blades can clear waves on otherwise level water of about a maximum height of about a metre, but in practice the maximum for the two upper levels and for any length of time is more likely to be about 0.8 m. The long strokes necessary for high power cannot be made in rough water, as every seaman who has rowed a seaboat knows, though in calmer conditions and when speed was needed longer strokes were used at sea, even though such a style with narrow blades would not be as efficient as it otherwise could be. Latter-day sea oars have for centuries been monoxylous and narrow bladed for good reasons, practical as regards use and strength in common conditions at sea and in harbours, as well as economic. As waves get rougher, so stroke length has to be shortened and the blade moved more quickly down and up to be sure of making the stroke as effective as possible in lumpy water, and, most important, to be as sure as possible of being able to extract the blade on time. In such conditions narrow blades should actually be more efficient than wide blades because the water is flowing more across than along them, raising their aspect ratio. Further, in rough water the immersed area of the blade must be variable and that can be achieved with long narrow blades (McKee 1983). Shortening the stroke necessarily reduces attainable power and is a factor limiting the effectiveness of oars in rough water, a no doubt compelling factor in determining the safety of trireme deployments. It is interesting that in modern times wide blades took so long to be adopted in river rowing.

The hull

Olympias was built according to available archaeological evidence on ancient Mediterranean ship construction and the hull has been indicated by trial to be sufficiently robust to have a service life generally not inconsistent with literary evidence. The lives of individual hulls almost certainly depended greatly upon the quality of build and the operational circumstances they encountered. This has always been true of wooden ships.

i) Hull planking tenons

Olympias however soon developed a hog (the ends of the hull dropping relative to the middle). Hog has been a chronic tendency in wooden ships for millennia (Coates 1985); in *Olympias* it was due not to any lack of strength but to the tenons joining the planks together (Fig. 10.6) working in their mortices in the fore-and-aft direction allowing adjacent planks to slide a little. In long and

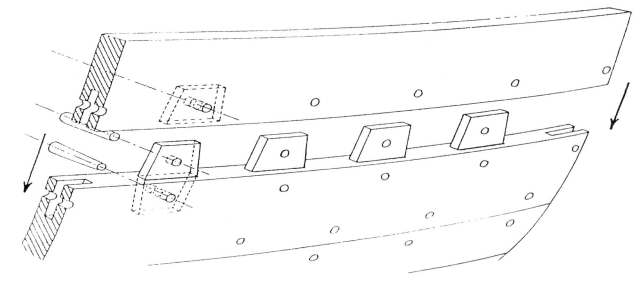

Figure 10.6. Hull planking tenons (Drawing: John Coates).

slender hulls, like those of triremes, hull bending moments and therefore shear forces are large (indeed they impose practical limits on the overall proportions of long ships of all kinds). Thus the principal purpose of planking tenons in ancient Mediterranean warships was to carry hull shear forces between planks, to do which without crushing called for a tight fit in the longitudinal direction (for a stress analysis, see Morrison 1996, 347–8). In *Olympias*, the average longitudinal play in the tenons, measured while the hull was being built, corresponded closely to the 10 cm or so hog which developed in service, measured over the length of the hull.

Obtaining a tight and simultaneous fit of the numerous tenons joining one plank to the one below calls for much accuracy and skill, and to help in that task it is proposed that in a second reconstruction the tenons should be tapered as shown in Fig. 10.6 (as has been found to have been done in many, but by no means all, ancient wrecks) and sized to an interference fit in the mortices as cut, so that, when a plank is driven down on to the one below to close the seam, a crush fit will be obtained. Interferences, tapers and cutting techniques will have to be decided by preliminary experimental development and testing before building is undertaken. This detail is discussed first among the changes to the hull because it lies at the heart of its soundness. In addition, it is proposed that the side planking between the lower and middle wales be thickened to 60 mm (3 Athenian inches) in order that the tenons in the whole of the side planking can be made thicker than in *Olympias*, to increase their shear carrying capacity with less risk of crushing the tenons and so developing hog in the hull. It is proposed in addition to build the hull with a small sag (the opposite of hog) because in practice some hog, say of 5 to 10 cm, is nevertheless bound to occur in time through unavoidable imperfections.

ii) Dimensions and shape of hull

A new reconstruction would be just short of 40 m long overall to house 30 *interscalmia* of 0.980 m each, the bow and stern being the same as in *Olympias* (giving a length of 36.8 m (as in *Olympias*) + 30 (0.980–0.888) m = 39.6 m). It is proposed to separate the tracks of thranite blades in the water as far as possible from the others by reducing the clearance between the ship and the pillars of the ancient Munychia shipsheds in Piraeus to 7 cm by increasing the breadth overall (*i.e.* over the outriggers) from 5.45 m to 5.60 m while keeping the breadth on the waterline, the dominant determinant of stability, the same as in *Olympias*. The new hull would therefore have a slightly greater flare above water and the sides would be made a little flatter. It is proposed to reduce the depth of the bottom curve of the 'wineglass' section of the ship, reducing draft by about 10 cm, which may increase leeway a little when the ship is sailing into the wind, but it would reduce hull wetted area and therefore the ship's resistance through skin friction.

iii) Ship displacement

The displacement of the ship may be expected, by these changes in dimensions and other adjustments to timber sizes in following the 10% larger cubit, to increase by less than 10%, and her resistance by slightly less proportionately. Many internal timbers could be reduced in scantlings by half an (Athenian) inch (which will be 10% larger than that to which *Olympias* was built). Timbers would again be assumed to have been sized in Athenian inches and easy fractions of inches. Such timbers would be on average about 5% lighter (and no more numerous), offsetting the 20% increase in planking mass (owing to a 10% increase in thickness and in length). Thus the shell would increase by 1 tonne, from 7 to 8 tonnes; framing, beams etc. would decrease by 1 tonne, from 6 to 5 tonnes; other timbers, decks and furniture would probably increase by about 1 tonne. The net result would be an increase in light ship mass of about 2 tonnes, or 5%. Closer estimates will have to await detailed design calculations which would be part of the early programme of any reconstruction project.

iv) Ship resistance

Resistance is made up of two main components, skin friction and wavemaking. The first depends upon the wetted area of the hull and its smoothness, and varies approximately with the square of the ship's speed. The second depends upon the length of the ship, upon the slenderness of its hull form, and upon speed in a more complicated way. Displacement is not itself intrinsically connected with resistance, but it is necessarily connected with wetted area, length and slenderness which are. For a hull like that of *Olympias*, skin resistance is dominant at speeds up to about 6 knots, above which wavemaking resistance increases more rapidly, becoming about equal to the other at about 9 knots, and more dominant at speeds above that again. Speed-power curves for *Olympias* have been derived from tank tests of a model of the hull (Grekoussis and Loukakis 1985); curves of resistance against speed have already been published (Shaw 1993c). The resistance of the proposed second reconstruction may be expected to be about 7% higher than that of *Olympias* at lower speeds, reflecting the net increase in wetted area, but only about 5% greater at sprint speeds owing to the beneficial effect of greater length upon wavemaking.

v) Attainable speeds under oar

Shaw (above p. 81, Table 9.7) has derived figures for mean handle pull, striking rate and effective stroke length, and effective oar power attainable by a moderately good crew working in the proposed oarsystem (called by him Mark IIb). Together with the expected power-speed curves for a proposed future reconstruction, these figures imply an attainable short sprint speed of 9.7 knots and a cruising speed sustainable for some hours of 7.5 knots. Shaw has shown that the achievement of such a performance under oar is a necessary test of authenticity of any reconstruction of a trireme. It is certainly a searching test, as his paper and the performance obtained in *Olympias* show, but it should be passed by the reconstruction proposed here. 10 knots is probably about as fast as any kind of craft today could be rowed from fixed seats: in 1870, the Oxford Etonian crew achieved a mean speed for about 7 minutes over the course at Henley of 9.7 knots in a fixed-seat eight.

vi) Sailing

The performance of *Olympias* has not yet been by any means fully tested, owing largely to the overriding importance felt to use the limited time for trials to gain as much information as possible about the oarsystem, but also to the expectations of the volunteer oarcrews to row the ship rather than to act as sailing ballast, to scarce opportunities, to some lack of confidence by those responsible for the ship, and to the omission of stopping in the planking seams above the lower wale, causing minor leakage when heeling to a wind. As Owain Roberts, sailing master in 1990, reported, 'The results obtained in 1990 must represent the bottom end of her sailing ability.' (Roberts 1993, 37). Within those limits, however, the rig and helm proved handy and responsive to changes in the wind.

It was nevertheless clear that *Olympias'* sailing ability, if not yet fully tested, was potentially considerable and in accordance with such few records as exist of passages under sail by warships in the ancient Mediterranean and with the established belief that oared ships by choice made passages under sail whenever conditions allowed. That ability must have been an important factor in the deployment of squadrons of triremes and therefore the exercise of sea power with them. In view of its operational importance, and despite the small attention yet given to it in the Trireme Project, for reasons already mentioned, sailing ability needs to be properly explored with any second reconstruction if any full understanding of the naval use of triremes in history is to be gained.

Some relatively minor changes in the masting and rig are proposed, as indicated by three of the lessons listed in the Annex, together with making the hull above the upright waterline and the *askomata* watertight.

Investigations needed before building

i) Tenons

The exact shape of tenons, the fit in the mortices, the method of marking and cutting, lubrication, and method of assembling plank seams need to be developed, and the resulting joints tested under shear loading so that building can proceed without unnecessary delays and with confidence about the stiffness of the hull in hog.

ii) Oar rig

A full-scale mock-up should be built to test body and oar movements as well as clearances. It would be desirable that oars could be worked in water from the mock-up.

iii) Hypozoma

The rig with dead eyes already proposed (Coates and Shaw 1993), and the method of tightening and maintaining tension should be developed.

iv) Rudders

Tackles to raise and lower the rudders while the ship is underway should be developed.

Conclusion

This outline of the main modifications in any second reconstruction of a trireme is based on the lessons learnt from *Olympias,* which has played a vital part in the practical study of ancient Mediterranean oared warships. The proposed second trireme reconstruction must be considered to be yet subject to i) any further modifications which may be shown to be necessary in the course of the detailed design to define a second ship for building, and to ii) the possible adoption of materials other than wood in which to build the hull. This paper shows, however, that a proposed second reconstruction incorporating the features described can be expected with some confidence to achieve the level of performance of a trireme under oar and under sail required if it is to be considered authentic.

Annex: Summary of lessons learned from the sea trials in *Olympias*
(reproduced from Coates and Morrison 1993)

1. Oarsystem

1. Oars of equal length are workable together from three levels simultaneously and after only a relatively short period of training.
2. Damage to oar blades by clashing together was minor and avoidable.
3. An *interscalmium* of two cubits of 0.444 m. (*i.e.* 0.888m.) is too short to enable maximum power to be reached.
4. The position of the hull beams in *Olympias* caused the thalamians' stroke to be too restricted for high-powered rowing. Given a longer *interscalmium* of 0.98 m, now thought to be correct, that restriction could be avoided in any further reconstruction.
5. The oar gearing required in fast triremes is a high one, about 2.8 (i.e. the ratio of the length from the centre of pressure of the blade to the thole to that from the thole to the mid-handle).
6. Oar straps of tanned leather stretched in use (oars being forward of their thole), causing too much lost motion in oars, particularly those working through oarports. If straps are to be of leather (as attested) they must be of rawhide, a material hard and unyielding provided it is dry, true of most circumstances in ships in the Mediterranean but certainly not in open oared craft in northern European waters where oars have usually been worked aft of the thole (but see now above, pp. 43–4).
7. Sustained lubrication of oars and *askomata* is essential for higher powered rowing.
8. An oar blade area of 0.08 m² is sufficient, owing to the high gearing of the oars.
9. Oars must be as light as they can be made without becoming too flexible if high powers and rates of striking are to be reached, irrespective of consequent fragility and risk of damage in battle.
10. The longest attainable oarstroke is necessary to develop the maximum power.
11. Maximum power is achieved at a striking rate of about 45 strokes per minute.

12. Modifications to the oar rig in *Olympias* that are needed to enable the required power to be reached in a sprint (raising maximum power by 25–30% and speed to 9.5–9.7 knots) have been established clearly enough to make building and testing a modified ship a worthwhile experiment.
13. The same modifications are expected to enable the ship with a good oarcrew to maintain 7 knots all day continuously, as attested.
14. If going astern by pulling were acceptable practice, it would require additional footstretchers, and some modification to the spatial relationship of seats and tholes might be called for.
15. Cushions on the seats of oarcrew are necessary for repeated sustained periods at the oar, not merely a comfort.
16. Oarcrew must be protected from the sun.
17. Ventilation for the lower oarcrew is barely adequate in *Olympias*.
18. In hot weather each member of the oarcrew needs about one litre of water per hour while working hard. Dehydration is a real danger for oarcrew: the need, on the other hand, to urinate is minor.

2. Ship

1. Oarports near the waterline of the ship when loaded with crew are safe if provided, as attested, with *askomata* to prevent entry of water.
2. A hull constructed with the same arrangement of timbers and broadly similar scantlings as were found in the Marsala ship is satisfactory for a trireme.
3. If hogging is to be prevented the plank tenons must fit tightly in the longitudinal direction. This has been indicated to be a critical aspect of the construction of long ships built in the ancient Mediterranean manner.
4. Side winds do not cause the ship to heel over enough to affect oar performance, except when also under sail.
5. No undue vertical oscillations of the ship are developed under oar.
6. The ship is easily steered and turned under both oar and sail, rudders being effective and light to handle.
7. As attested by Thucydides (1.45–54), no ballast is required for stability or to bring the ship to her correct waterline for rowing when fully loaded.
8. The resistance or drag of the quarter rudders when fully immersed is high, strongly indicating that in antiquity it would have been the practice to have as little of blade and stock immersed as expected demands for manoeuvrability allowed, rudders being readily adjusted to suit circumstances.
9. Quarter rudders become uncontrollable in their normal position at astern speeds above about three knots. For use astern above that speed, they would have to be able to be reversed (but see now above, pp. 54–5).
10. The torsional stiffness of the open hull (undecked) is adequate owing to the cross-bracing fitted between the hull beams which are also clamped by lodging knees (which are horizontal). Without such bracing the torsional stiffness would have been much lower, leading to resonance in torsion with oar strokes at higher rates of striking.

11. The height of the centre of gravity of *Olympias* has been established by experiment, the only way to do so accurately. The metacentric height when fully manned is between 0.88 m and 1.1 m depending upon the load and disposition of variable and moveable weights.

3. Sail

1. The ancient Mediterranean rig, of which there has been no practical knowledge in a long ship, has proved to be effective, handy and weatherly, enabling the ship to make way pointing 60° into the apparent wind with only 7° to 10° of leeway.
2. The area of the main sail, 95 m², could be increased a little by lengthening the main yard.
3. Spars were unnecessarily heavy.
4. The mainmast tabernacle is not secured to beams and floors strongly enough to give confidence of its safety in supporting an unstayed mast.

4. Navigation

1. The main means of propulsion over long distances, as a usual practice, has been shown to have been by sail, oars being used generally only when necessary on account of urgency, safety or the need to come into or clear the land.
2. On passage, oars can usefully supplement sails (motor-sailing, as it were) but only in light breezes astern or on the quarter, raising the speed under sail from about 4 to 6 or more knots, without drawing on the physical reserves of the oarcrew to any significant extent. Such combined use of sail and oar has been found to be less useful in beam winds owing to interference in working oars due to heel of the ship. However, if the beam wind is steady, and not too severe, its heeling effect can be offset by stationing spare crew members on the windward side of the canopy.
3. The capacity of an oared ship to reach shelter, to claw round a headland or to keep clear of a lee shore under oar and against head winds has been tested. This is a most important factor in making navigational judgements and in keeping in mind reserve courses of action on passage in this type of craft. *Olympias* has made good 3

knots against a head wind gusting to 25 knots and in waves of up to one metre in height for 70 minutes. The oarcrew had by then become exhausted, a reminder of a state of affairs which, for thousands of years, captains of oared ships had to keep in mind constantly irrespective of whether their oarcrews were of free men, convicts or slaves.
4. The wind resistance of the ship in a head wind has been found to be 1/30 of the water resistance of the hull at the same fluid speeds past the ship. In beam winds the ship drifted at 1/26 knot sideways per one knot of wind speed.

Bibliography

Coates, J. F. (1985) Hogging or 'breaking' of frame-built wooden ships. *The Mariner's Mirror* 71.4, 437–442.

Coates, J. F. and Morrison, J. S. (1993) Summary of lessons learned. In Shaw 1993, 108–9.

Coates, J. F. and Shaw, J. T. (1993) Speculations on fitting *hypozomata*. In Shaw 1993, 82–6.

Coates, J. F., Platis, S. K. and Shaw, J. T (1990) *The Trireme Trials 1988*. Oxford, Oxbow Books.

Dekoulakou-Sideris, I. (1990) A metrological relief from Salamis. *American Journal of Archaeology* 94, 445–51.

Grekoussis, G. and Loukakis, T. (1985) *Athenian Trireme: Calm Water Tests without Ram* (National Technical University of Athens Report No. NAL 06–F-1985). Athens, National Technical University of Athens.

McKee, E. (1983) *Working Boats of Britain, their Shape and Purpose*. London, Conway Maritime Press.

Morrison, J. S. (1996) *Greek and Roman Oared Warships* (Oxbow Monograph 62). Oxford, Oxbow Books.

Roberts, O. T. P. (1993) The sailing rig of *Olympias*. In Shaw 1993, 29–38.

Shaw, J. T. (ed.) (1993a) *The Trireme Project: Operational Experience 1987–90: Lessons Learnt* (Oxbow Monograph 31). Oxford, Oxbow Books.

Shaw, J. T. (1993b) Rowing in ships and boats. *Transactions of the Royal Institution of Naval Architects, 1993*.

Shaw, J. T. (1993c) The resistance/speed curve of *Olympias*, with a section on rudder resistance by Ian McCallum. In Shaw 1993, 45–7.

Steinhauer, G. (1989) Communication in *Hellenike Archaeologike Hetaireia*, 20 April 1989.

Part 3

Critiques of *Olympias*: For and Against

11. As Seen by a Passer-by

René Burlet (translated by H. K. Boller)

I got to know John Coates by a round-about route, as it were, after the *Olympias* trials had been concluded. It was over a question of water consumption. The *Olympias* rowers drank as much water as those in the 18th-century galleys and the sugar-cane harvesters of the 20th century. Moreover, it seems more than likely that their Athenian predecessors drank a similar amount, and that the question of water supply on triremes arose at an early stage. This reflects an essential fact: that the 'human engine' has remained the same over the centuries. The water question led to a long correspondence with John, and we later rowed together on an astonishing series of craft.

I thus stand outside the *Olympias* project – my preferred galleys being those of Venice in the 15th century, or the Royal galleys of the 17th or 18th centuries. These periods are of interest because they have left behind valuable written evidence for the functioning of the human engine. The *Olympias* trireme has had several factors in its favour which have not, in my opinion, been sufficiently recognised hitherto, and this I shall now attempt to put right. As in every undertaking, there were also negative factors which should not be ignored. To an observer like myself, this project has been based on a realistic hypothesis, which all those previously attempted have not. The hypothesis has been probed and tested, which is probably the strongest possible argument in its favour. In spite of a number of unavoidable problems, the thing has worked. We are well aware that some trireme reconstructions, even though they were produced by talented engineers, have turned out to be fiascos. The fact that *Olympias* is workable is indisputable, and thus a number of aspects of the design have been verified.

The hull was constructed 'shell first' with mortise-and-tenon joints, as in antiquity. This is familiar to the 'archaeologist-diver' but has never, to the best of my knowledge, been applied in the 20th century in a hull of this size. This allowed the construction of a hull with a low displacement, a feature well-suited to propulsion by oars.

Professor John Morrison wisely consulted a professional naval architect about the hull, and its lightness in conjunction with the form designed by John Coates has resulted in a very manoeuvrable vessel, a feature essential in a ship armed with a ram. It is certain, however, that the Athenians did not possess John Coates' knowledge of hydrodynamics, and from this point of view *Olympias* may well be a 'super-trireme.'

The system of lateral rudders has proved effective, although it was already known to function reasonably well because it is still in use in Indonesia today. It was, however, interesting to discover that with only one such rudder in the water, there was a speed gain in *Olympias* of 9%.

Another very strong point in the project's favour is the discovery of the need for 'cooling' of the rowers, which is vital for a group of men working under difficult conditions. I have no idea whether the ancient Greek authors make reference to it, but if they did not this may imply that solutions had already been found in antiquity.

The problem of stroke rate and how to maintain it is another important question which appears to have been resolved in the course of the trials. The problem is completely different in the galleys known to me, since their longitudinal curvature allowed the oarsman at the end of each oar to see his counterpart on the sternmost bench who set the pace, allowing a sort of visually-maintained togetherness. In fact, as it would appear, rowers can successfully follow the stroke using a variety of movement indicators (knocking of oars on thole pins, grinding noises, *etc.*). The fact that the trireme was noisy as a result of the clashing of oars is not surprising. The inability of galleys rowed 'alla zenzile' (*i.e.* three men / three oars per bench) to proceed quietly was one of the well-known drawbacks of the system. The consumption of oars was amazing – Venice ordered them by the thousand.

One of the most interesting questions raised was that of the work done by the thalamians. Their effectiveness was in doubt at speeds above 6 knots, something which, with hindsight, could perhaps have been foreseen, but no one had hitherto seen a thalamian in action and it was all a matter of conjecture. I am not here going to dwell on the fact that the thalamians were badly positioned (John is still convinced that I think he is a torturer). To ask someone to row with a clearance of 70–75 cm between two beams remains in my view the biggest problem in the positioning of the rowers, and the change to a slightly longer cubit will not significantly affect this.

People cannot work comfortably except within limits within which they judge themselves to be safe – which was not the case in *Olympias* given the risk of collision with a beam both in front and behind. Thalamians will row normally as long as they are sure that they will not injure themselves. This point needs to be stressed. The existing conditions led to astonishing body movements, shown perfectly in the stroke diagrams: compensatory movements are clearly visible. The rowers wanted to work but were prevented by the beams, and so they did something else, making disjointed movements in a vertical plane, which was the only one in which they could operate without risk. Generally speaking, the design of *Olympias* took a very optimistic view of the capacity of the human engine and the movements it was capable of sustaining.

Apart from this problem, and in spite of it, we now know how a trireme works and how it manoeuvres, and we have credible performance figures to prove it. The fact that *Olympias* was able to move and manoeuvre under both oar and sail with a relatively untrained crew remains in my view the most tangible proof of the success of the operation.

The real problem confronting *Olympias* is of a different nature – it is a conceptual one. As I mentioned above, on the one hand the originators of the *Olympias* took a very optimistic view of the human engine and its capabilities, whilst on the other they appear to have had little knowledge of what happened on later galleys and how the *comites* and skippers actually managed their oarsmen. Let us not forget that often, and for long periods, the rowers under their command were free men: at the battle of Lepanto in 1571, the majority of the Venetian galleys were 'free.'

The human engine is not very reliable, and produces very little power, which decreases rapidly with the period of exertion. When Napoleon first decided to invade England, there was great deal of rowing activity at Boulogne. Forfait, a naval engineer of note, has left us definitive writings on the subject, based on rowing exercises in a wide range of boats. In summary, his findings are as follows: that a well-operated galley can manage one hour at four knots, and then two to two-and-a half hours at two to two-and-a-half knots, after which the crew blows up unless it has a rest. Under these conditions, incidentally, Dover would still have been a long way off.

The Comite Réal Masse (the younger), who was commander of a French flagship and well placed professionally to know what to expect from a crew of oarsmen, says exactly the same at the beginning of the 18th century. Moreover, it is not so much speed which concerns us here. *Olympias*, with her low displacement, can easily reach 7 knots, and no doubt more on short runs, but it seems illusory to believe her to be capable of sustaining this for hours on end. Besides, little purpose would have been served by her doing so. In practice, a trireme, a galley, a felucca or a brigantine, all of them equipped with fixed rowing systems, would have travelled under sail as often as possible. This is the paradox of this type of oared vessel, which sails as often as it can because those in command are perfectly aware of the capabilities of the human engine whose power must be conserved. Let me add that *Olympias*, with a good set of sails, would surely travel faster than 7 knots.

Many of the trials staff of *Olympias* had been competitive rowers or had coached others in the sport. They were used to rowing the equivalent of a 100-metre sprint, whilst the *Olympias* rowers had to run a Marathon, and these are different types of event.

On this point, the ancient sources are quite explicit. In the course of an historic passage under oar from Athens to Lesbos (184 sea miles), one trireme gained 24 hours on another which had left earlier. In the eyes of the Athenians, this was a great feat, and it will always remain so. The stakes were enormous and the second trireme had to be the best available: a lightened ship with a hand-picked, highly-motivated crew, conscious of their mission. Despite this, the average speed attained did not exceed 6 knots, if that. John Coates has a schedule which I have adapted to fit a number of different scenarios, and it has proved to be very revealing. The objective of this feat was ambitious but realistic – at the extreme limit of what trireme rowers could achieve under difficult conditions.

The second voyage for which we have an explicit reference was a 'normal' trip of 129 sea miles between Byzantium and Heraclea, which could be completed under oar in a single day. Presented in this way, it dwarfs the achievement of the Lesbos rowers. A ten-hour day would have meant an average speed of 12.9 knots, double the speed of what was considered a 'special feat.' Special conditions must be assumed to explain this away – rowing on the day of the summer solstice (what about other days?), or using oars lighter than those of *Olympias* (why not carbon-fibre oars?). All of this detracts from the realism governing the design of *Olympias*: the facts are there and must be respected. But the argument is largely irrelevant: any captain, be he Athenian, Venetian, Provençal or Catalan, who was making this trip under normal conditions would surely have made it under sail, or more precisely rowing under sail. An average of ten knots then becomes possible, as was proved by much heavier galleys later on.

Rowing under sail is an exclusive speciality of this type of vessel: when the wind drops a little the rowers join in, when it becomes stronger they stop. Passage is achieved with astonishing ease, and without tiring the oarsmen who can carry on in this manner for hours on end – there is plenty of evidence for this. It seems almost inconceivable that people who had rowed for centuries would not have discovered this trick.

With a speed of 7 knots on short trips, *Olympias* is an oar-propelled vessel worthy of note. It is a quite exceptional ship, but when powered solely by oars its average speed over long distances will be a great deal lower, as was that of all galleys. This was why the latter made use of sail.

This forced economy of the human engine remains the paradox of this kind of vessel down through the centuries. The time spent propelled solely by oars never exceeded 10–15% of the total time at sea. All ships which have used human muscle to propel them into battle offer analogies which have hitherto not been taken sufficiently into account: the common factor is the human engine. Over a thousand years, from Athens to Venice to Barcelona, this factor changed very little: the trireme is not an unusual vessel, but one of a great line of combat ships.

However, as far as I am concerned, *Olympias* will always be an indisputable success, because her creators have broken new ground and because their 'floating hypothesis' has worked. We have learnt a great deal on our way through a field of scholarship which has hitherto belonged strictly to the literary sphere. In view of the problems which are inherent in this type of undertaking, could we have expected any more?

12. Comments on *Olympias*

Edwin Gifford

Definition of the Author's Role

I have been asked to read the literature and to comment as an independent naval architect. This role is appropriate as when I first saw the mock-up at the Boat Show I was sceptical of the possibilities of the oar system rig because of the angle of the upper oar and the likelihood of clashing of the whole set. This attitude has slowly changed as I learned more about the basis of the design. At that time I knew none of the people directly concerned with the scheme and made the acquaintance of the designer, John Coates, as a result of my interest in the evolution of this detective story.

Eventually I became satisfied with every aspect of the design except the spacing of the deck beams in relationship to the thalamians' heads, which has emerged as the only major problem in the scheme and was largely brought about by an error in the value of the appropriate cubit (Morrison 1941) – I shall discuss this later in further detail.

Criticism

Rather than attempt a further resumé of the substantial body of *Olympias* literature, I have set down my reactions to the individual criticisms that have been made and concluded with my own opinion on the project as a whole.

Oar system

This is of course, the key to the design. The designer's problem is to design a vessel propelled by oars and sail that can, under oars alone, maintain the speed of seven knots defined in the literature, over a full day, with a higher sprint speed for battle assessed by the design team as 9–10 knots.

It appears virtually certain, from the evidence from literature, inscriptions and representations of triremes, that the oarsmen were arranged in groups of three, one on each of three levels, and that they were 170 in total.

The speed of 10 knots is very high for a rowing boat (similar to that of a modern racing four) and requires full efficiency from each oarsman at a rate of striking in excess of 40 strokes/minute.

As the length of the oars is defined in an ancient naval inscription, the arrangement with an outrigger as proposed in 1941 by John Morrison (1941) appears logical in that it enables each oarsman to apply full work to the oar at the necessary gearing of about 3 to 1 required for this speed, provided that:

a) the angle of the upper oar was not excessive;
b) that oar clashing did not occur;
c) that all oarsmen could apply full work at 40/45 strokes/minute with complete confidence.

In the event the trials have fully answered (a) and (b) in that the thranites were able to give their full power (just), and from the start, the crews very swiftly learnt to row without clashing. (c) produced the only real problem in that the restriction of the beams with the consequent shortness of stroke reduced the output of the thalamians in particular to such an extent that at the higher speeds their contribution was very low. Nevertheless, despite a number of crabs caught, there were no casualties!

With the increase of the cubit from 0.444m to 0.49m the distance between the beams will increase by 10% to 0.98m, which is sufficient to increase the length of stroke to one metre and to allay the fears of the thalamians head-banging. These two factors should allow them to increase their output sufficiently to raise the sprint speed over five minutes from about 8.5 knots to 9.5 knots.

The reason for the low level of the thalamians is to keep down the centre of gravity and thus maintain the stability of the slim hull. It would have been possible to raise the main beam over the heads of the thalamians, but this in turn would have raised the centre of gravity of the remaining oarsmen, which at the time of design was seen as a risk. Subsequent inclining tests on the actual hull have shown a sufficient margin in stability to enable the vertical clearance to be increased, which will give further space for the oarsmen to work without anxiety and hence with full efficiency.

Another possibility would have been to omit alternate main beams to give the thalamians greater head space, but this would have reduced the torsional stiffness of the craft, which has been shown by trials to be just sufficient.

Although both stiffness and stability are now shown to be adequate and with hindsight could perhaps have been slightly reduced, the designer could not have taken the risk of doing so with such a unique design.

Two other oar arrangements have been proposed, but neither has been supported by worked-up schemes illustrating the oar paths. Both have the objection that some of the oarsmen are obstructed which would inhibit both the length of stroke and the oarsmen's confidence, precisely the kind of faults that the thalamians had in *Olympias*. But whereas the simple increase in the spacing of the oarsmen will surely overcome the *Olympias* problem, it would seem, until proved otherwise, that these objections are fundamental to the other schemes.

Hull dimensions

The hull cross-sections and lines seem ideal for the length and width of the slipway described in the literature. They are the best compromise between speed and stability with deck crew and when under sail. This has been proved by the tank test and the behaviour of the craft itself.

It has been suggested that the hull could have been built for a shorter life and so be lighter and more flexible. Analysis of the hull stresses shows that it is on the limit for wave bending, and although the Athenians might have taken more risks than present regulations would permit, it is not clear that the small reduction of weight would have had any great effect, particularly as the sustained and sprint speeds can almost certainly be achieved by the increase in length of the "room".

In fact, despite being built to resist the forces induced by ramming, *Olympias* is quite light at a ship weight of 25 tons for 170 oars or 147 kg/oar. An approximate check on the Sutton Hoo ship gives eight tons for the maximum of 40 oars that she could carry or 200 kg/oar, which is considerably heavier, and Sutton Hoo was lightly built of 25 mm planking. The difference is, of course, due to the high density of oarsmen given by the trireme arrangement, but there is little scope for a lighter build that would hold together in a seaway, resist ramming and not be seriously leaky.

It has been suggested that longitudinal flexibility could be controlled by the *hypozoma*, but this is not the case. Whilst the truss can exert a force that, when first applied, might "set up" the hull after deflection, the high stretch of the linen rope means that this force would be soon lost and thus not be available to resist repeated hogging at sea. Indeed, the function of the *hypozoma* is not yet

fully understood and is still a subject of great interest for further research. But it would certainly not stiffen the boat torsionally, which would be needed if the hull had greater flexibility. Such torsional slackness could be a severe handicap to the oarsmen as it could result in the bow and stern oarsmen on opposite sides being simultaneously unable to clear their oars from the water on the recovery. The writer has experienced an old clinker racing eight in which it was possible for bow and stroke to catch crabs simultaneously and be unable to clear them because of the temporary twist of the slack hull. Imagine that in a trireme!

Oar weight and dimensions

My first reaction to the revised oar design was to doubt whether such sophistication existed in antiquity, but as it has been shown that such a lightweight and special shape is necessary for the high rate of striking needed for 9–10 knots, the possibility of such a design must be considered seriously. There is no doubt that the ancients had great skill in wedged trenails, as well as pegged mortice-and-tenon joints, so the attachment of blades to the shaft by such means is practical.

Hull construction methods and materials

It would of course be ideal to have used the same timbers and tools employed by the ancients, but the former are not available in sufficient sizes and quality, and cost would prevent the extensive use of hand tools.

The project team have used timber of equivalent weight and strength and have given the relative values. Their building method approximates to those of the ancients, except for the moulds used to obtain the shape needed, as the technique of forming the hull by shaping the blanks has been lost in the Mediterranean. It still exists in India and has been revived in Roskilde, but it is not vital for the purpose of this project. It could perhaps be used on another smaller scheme in the future.

My conclusion

Archaeologists more used to basing their studies mainly if not exclusively on discovered physical remains have been understandably somewhat sceptical of the authenticity of *Olympias* because no remains of a trireme have yet been discovered, probably because being unballasted they could not sink, and thus become preserved, when abandoned.

Identifiable remains of ancient Mediterranean oared ships have so far been limited to:

a) The Punic ship found by Honor Frost near Marsala in the early 1970s (Frost 1973; 1974a; 1974b).
b) The Athlit ram (Steffy 1983).
c) The ships in Lake Nemi.

(a) is not a warship for which purpose it had an insufficient number of levels of oars. She sank because she was ballasted, supporting the notion that she was a cargo carrying ship. It did however reveal how long ships were built in the ancient Mediterranean, essential information for reconstructing a trireme.

(b) is a ram and little else apart from the important timber structure inside the casting. The timber exhibited the same kind of construction as the Marsala ship, strengthening the belief that a trireme hull would have been built in the same way.

(c) are of grotesquely widened ships built on this lake as floating pleasure palaces and gardens. They show the same method of construction, but could not be taken as reliable guides for the construction of oared ships in general until corroborated by (a) and (b).

However, despite this paucity of remains, which is the total specifically for triremes, when the accumulated archaeological, epigraphical, literary and iconographical evidence is assembled, and a ship designed to accord with it, including a severe requirement for a sustained speed of 7 to 7½ knots for about 18 hours continuously, it can be seen by any one familiar with ship design that technically there was little, if any free choice in the essentials of the design of a trireme if it was to be stable, strong and very fast indeed, when fully manned and if its long and very slender open hull was to be strong.

I appreciate that it would be difficult for those unfamiliar with ship design to realise how close are these restraints and how consequently they permit only one solution (albeit with the possibility of variation in minor details) and thus increase the likelihood of authenticity.

After a long study of the extensive literature (which I recommend to some of the critics) I cannot see how the design of *Olympias* could be improved as a solution to the parameters of beam, length, number and length of oars and speeds that have been set, except for the matter of the revised cubit that was demonstrated by carrying out sea trials and referred back to the historians.

There can be no serious doubt that this project has added enormously to our knowledge of ships of that period, particularly in the organisation and practice of rowing and in operating large, fast oared ships. It is hard to see how that knowledge could have been gained in any other way and the high standard of prompt reporting of the carefully conducted sea trials of this ship has made that knowledge available to all, adding greatly to the overall value of the project.

Bibliography

Frost, H. (1973) First season of excavation on the Punic wreck in Sicily. *International Journal of Nautical Archaeology* 2.1, 33–49.

Frost, H. (1974a) The Punic wreck in Sicily. *International Journal of Nautical Archaeology* 3.1, 35–54.

Frost, H. (1974b) The third campaign of excavation on the Punic ship, Marsala, Sicily. *The Mariner's Mirror* 60.3, 265–266.

Morrison, J. S. (1941) The Greek Trireme. *The Mariner's Mirror* 27.1, 14–44.

Morrison, J. S. (1991) Ancient Greek measures of length in nautical contexts. *Antiquity* 65, 298–305.

Steffy, J. R. (1983) The Athlit Ram, a preliminary investigation of its structure, with additional notes by Patrice Pomey, L. Basch and Honor Frost. *The Mariner's Mirror* 69.3, 229–250.

13. Comments on *Olympias*

Seán McGrail

When compared with other projects in experimental boat archaeology, the Trireme project is in a class of its own in terms of its rigorous search for authenticity, its openness to criticism, and its publication record. One significant difference from some other projects is that documented aspects of 5th/4th century BC trireme performance were included in *Olympias'* design specification, whereas elsewhere performance has to be established during trials. However, discussion at the Oxford/Henley conference seems to have shown that the documentary evidence for trireme passage speeds of *c.* 7.5 knots is not as convincing as was once thought (see pp. 145–60): the high sprint speed of 9 knots that this implied need therefore no longer be considered as a 'historical requirement.' The impressive speeds under oars that *Olympias* did achieve strongly suggest that she is close to attaining passage speeds derived from a more realistic interpretation of documented voyages.

Everyone, even the strongest critic, has benefited from the Trireme Project. We have all needed *Olympias* as a focus for our criticism, with the happy result that alterations to the Mk I design can now be proposed which would make it more likely that a Mk II *Olympias* would represent a typical 5th century BC Athenian trireme. If key modifications suggested in these discussions (Morrison, Coates and Rankov 2000, 245–246, 267–273; above pp. 76–91) were to be incorporated, the shape, structure, and performance of the resulting vessel would probably be as near that of a typical 5th/4th century BC trireme as it is possible to get with the incomplete information at present available.

Bibliography

Morrison, J. S., Coates, J. F. and Rankov N. B. (2000) *The Athenian Trireme. The History and Reconstruction of an Ancient Greek Warship*. 2nd ed. Cambridge, Cambridge University Press.

14. The Reconstructed Trireme *Olympias* and Her Critics

Anthony J. Papalas

The trireme, the premier fighting galley of the fifth century BC, is a significant technological achievement of the ancient Greeks. One of these triremes has been reconstructed in our own era. John Morrison, Classical scholar and former President of Wolfson College, Cambridge, John Coates, a naval architect retired from the Ministry of Defence, and Frank Welsh, a writer and banker, pooled their talents for the purpose of its creation. Their reconstruction was based to some extent on the ideas Morrison proposed in an important study published in the *Mariner's Mirror* in 1941. His views were considerably influenced by an interpretation of the Lenormant relief, a marble plaque 52 cm wide and 39 cm high preserved in the Acropolis Museum that shows a trireme in realistic detail (Morrison 1941, 27–31). He argues (p. 28) that the artist did not bother to sculpt images of some of the oars between the wales because this was indicated by paint. (see further Morrison, Coates and Rankov 2000, 138–150).

The reconstructed trireme, the *Olympias*, was commissioned in July 1987 into the Hellenic Navy as a training ship. The multi-level oared vessel proved satisfactory in four sea trials, in 1987, 1988, 1990 and 1992 (Coates, Platis and Shaw 1990; For the history of the reconstruction, see the delightful and instructive account of Welsh 1988.). According to a shore-based geodimeter, the *Olympias* achieved a speed of 8 knots at a rate of 45 strokes per minute. The oars were almost of equal length and were manipulated simultaneously from three different heights. Oarsmen rowing only on one side achieved a turning diameter of 1.9 lengths, performing a 360-degree turn in 128 seconds (Morrison 1988). While the speed and manoeuvrability of the *Olympias* was generally in line with fifth-century performance capabilities, some questions remain unsolved and a certain degree of scepticism remains about the accuracy of the reconstruction. In this paper, I hope to place some of these questions in perspective.

In the course of the sea trials much was learned. The builders were able to solve the problem of securing the oars by copying the method of Greek fishermen who hold the oar to the thole with a lanyard of leather or rope tied with a particular knot. But a more serious problem related to the oarsmen was not adequately addressed. The thranites, the oarsmen at the top level, and the zygites, who sat on the thwart, were relatively comfortable, but the thalamians, the men at the lowest level, were cramped even though their maximum height was limited to 5 feet 9 inches (Rankov 1994, 137–8). The *Olympias'* thalamians barely squeezed into their position and would not have fitted into the lowest level of a Greek trireme.

The recruiters for the *Olympias'* oarsmen could not find enough short, strong people. The Greeks, on the other hand, had a good supply of men under 5 feet 6 inches, the average height of the ancient Greeks (Angel 1971, 85). The trireme provided small men, who were too short for hoplite service (Hanson 1989, 66; 1991, 81 n. 4.), an opportunity to contribute important military service. The hoplite carried a shield about three feet long, bore about 50 pounds of body armour, and wielded an eight-foot doubled spear. A short man, however strong, could not effectively manage such arms, nor could he hold his shield high enough to protect the man on his left, who in phalanx formation partially relied on his neighbour's shield for safety. This may well explain the deployment of the seventy Athenian triremes at Sphacteria in 425 BC (Thucydides 4.32.2). The oarsmen from the first two levels disembarked to fight the Spartans, but the thalamians, about 3,700 men, were kept aboard. Basch (1988, 187) and Morrison and Williams (1968, 269) reasonably suggest that the thalamians were kept out of the final attack on the Spartans because either the Athenians needed to keep some oarsmen in the ship or they had no weapons, or were disqualified because they were slaves. They probably did not have military equipment because they were too short to take a place in the phalanx formation but this would not exclude them from peltast service.

Thucydides (4.28.4) reports that the Athenians recruited for this expedition peltasts from Aenus, a city on the coast of Thrace. This type of light-armed soldier carrying a crescent-shaped wicker or leather pelta, hence the name peltast, originated in northern Greece. Since these men did not have to fight in hoplite formation presumably height qualifications for them was not necessary and thalamians may have qualified for peltast duty. But as we have seen Thucydides (4.32.2) is quite clear that the thalamians remained aboard. Although triremes were often used as troop transports the Sphactereia campaign is a special case. Cleon promised to settle the matter in twenty days and thus speed was necessary. (Thucydides 4.28.4.) The trireme was a good sailing vessel as trials of the Olympias has proven. The Athenians relying mainly on sails left Piraeus for Sphacteria with the decks of their triremes packed with hoplites, peltasts and archers and with some additional hoplites pulling oars at the first two levels. Such a crew would have been ineffective in a naval battle but since the Athenians did not anticipate confronting a Peloponnesian navy the quality and experience of the oarsmen was not an issue. What made this expedition especially unusual was the marine landing aspect. The oarsmen at the first two levels had to leap off their triremes and establish a beachhead. The peltasts, who probably were on the decks, joined them while the thalamians stayed on board controlling their vessel.

The thalamians were presumably the most radical element in Aristotle's (*Politics* 1291 b 21–25) 'trireme democracy.' Aristophanes (*Knights* 541 ff.) notes the ladder of promotion from oarsman, assistant at the steering oar, lookout, and finally steersman. A short thalamian would probably not be tall enough for these choice assignments. The thranites had greater physical abilities, more responsibilities, and therefore enjoyed higher pay (Thucydides 6.31.3). The inferiority of the thalamians is implied in Herodotus 8.118–119, and the humble status of this lowest level makes Aristophanes' (*Frogs* 1074–1076) joke about them comprehensible. In the *Olympias*, the thalamians were ineffectual at speeds greater than six knots. (Rankov 1994, 135).

The cramped space for the oarsmen at the thalamian level may partially explain why the *Olympias,* apparently, does not have the range of the ancient trireme. According to Xenophon (*Anabasis* 6.4.2) a trireme had the ability to cover the distance between Byzantium and Heraclea, 129 nautical miles, in a long day. If we assume a "long day" consisted of fifteen hours and that the voyage was undertaken mainly by oar rather than sail, then the *Olympias*, as an oar driven vessel, was inferior to its ancient counterpart. Shaw (1993b, 43) reports that in *Olympias* a speed of 8.5 knots was maintained for about 20 seconds, and that full pressure was sustained for only 90 seconds because rowers at this rate going beyond a minute become fatigued and accident-prone. He argues (1993d, 64) that an Athenian crew could maintain 10 knots for about a minute and (p. 58) cruise for hours at 7 knots. Shaw was particularly concerned (1993b, 41) about the minimal power contribution of the thalamians, and explained (1993d, 62) that 40 of the 54 thalamians

could not row effectively, restricted by fear of hitting their heads on a beam, or getting caught in a crab. They also had inadequate oar blades, and many of the thalamians were moreover women not robust enough for the task. Rankov (1994, 131–132) discusses some of the difficulties in the first trial. The *keleustes* was unable to herald his commands throughout the ship. Inexperienced oarsmen with ineffective rowing strokes were another concern. Rankov (1994, 144) contends that contemporary oarsmen cannot be compared with their Athenian counterparts. An ancient Greek had skill and stamina for the job acquired at an early age. Manipulating an oar in a limited patch of water is a talent comparable to shooting a basketball through a hoop, a dexterity acquired in boyhood. He notes (1994, 136) a speed in *Olympias* of 8.9 knots for a few seconds and that with modifications 10 knots would be possible. Papalas (1997, 268 n.14) was, however, wrong in stating that Morrison and Coates in *The Athenian Trireme* suggested that 11 knots could be maintained for any length of time, though Morrison in a letter to the London *Times*, 2nd October, 1975, thought a trireme using full oars could produce eleven and a half knots in short bursts, and with one tier rowing could maintain seven and a half knots for a long period. Morrison thus believed that the 120 (actually 129) nautical miles Xenophon (*Anabasis* 6.4.2) claimed a trireme covered in a long day was a 15-hour voyage during which the trireme averaged seven and a half knots. (Tilley 1997, 12 mistakenly claims Morrison stated that a trireme could maintain a speed of 12 knots to cover this distance).

Although the Greeks did not like to voyage at night, it would be possible to set out several hours before dawn from a known point in halcyon conditions. We need not, therefore, take Xenophon's 'long day' from Byzantium to Heraclea literally (see Thucydides 1.48 and possibly 8.99 for such night-time voyages). The direct route from Byzantium to Heraclea was necessitated by the hostility of the Bithynians and Thracians who denied port facilities, and this was the usual way for a trireme to cover this route and probably not, as Morrison (1993, 16) suggests, an unusual performance. Shaw (above, pp. 63–7) supports Morrison's estimate of seven to eight knots cruising speed, and concludes that a good crew could achieve the voyage in eighteen hours while a moderately good one could do it in sixteen. He also (above, pp. 68–75) dismisses the possibility of Xenophon's Bosporus to Heraclea voyage being assisted by sail.

The most serious problem in limiting the cruising capacity of the *Olympias* was the result of packing all the oarsmen, not just the thalamians, too closely together, and not providing them with ample room to make a full stroke with their oars. The situation is comparable to a golfer losing distance by taking only a half swing. The mistake was a result of Coates utilising the Attic cubit of Niessen (1892) of 0.444 metre for an *interscalmium*, the distance between two tholes or a room. This length proved too narrow. New information demonstrates that the Greeks built the trireme using a cubit of 0.490 metre. The additional space between the thole pins would add 92 mm to the length of an oar stroke (Morrison 1991; Coates, above p. 83). A trireme built to the longer cubit would be 40 metres long rather than the 36.8, but Basch (1987b, 94) appropriately points out that the preserved length of the Zea ship sheds, 37 metres long, does not determine the maximum length of the trireme. The additional room would provide the oarsmen with room to take a full stroke. With such a modification a trireme could produce bursts of speed up to 9.7 knots, and possibly an adequate cruising speed to cover the Byzantium-Heraclea route in one long day (Shaw, above pp. 62–81; Coates, above pp. 82–91).

The chief aim of the trials was to determine the *Olympias'* performance under oars. Further tests will no doubt provide information about such matters as her battle worthiness, rough sea range, out of water hauling and launching, sailing abilities, long distance capabilities, and the rigging of the *hypozomata,* ropes forming the under girdle of a trireme. Coates and Shaw (1993, 85–86) report that the tension tourniquet produced by following Apollonius of Rhodes' description of the launching of *Argo*, 'to girdle the ship strong with a well-twisted rope from within,' did not work on the *Olympias*. The authors recommend that *hypozomata* consisting of polymer be fitted with deadeyes and a double whip. One would also hope that further investigations will be made into the *diekplous*, the manoeuvre that enabled the trireme to obtain the optimum ramming angle. How effective was the ram in inflicting structural damage on a rival trireme? How did triremes disengage after ramming? Was it done by pulling – the oarsmen having turned to face what had been the bow (Tilley 1992a) – or by remaining in the same position and pushing? Shaw (1993e) notes that while the *Olympias* was not fitted with the requisite additional foot stretchers, the oarsmen were able to row astern by pulling. Furthermore, we do not yet know how effective and durable the trireme was. The *Olympias*, which made a 90-degree turn in seconds, and a 180-degree turn inside two ship lengths within a minute, would not be a 'sitting duck' in a trireme duel. Shaw (1993g, 99) draws the useful analogy of duels between the triremes and aerial dog fights of World War I and II. Expert helmsmen, like ace pilots, were needed to elude and trick the enemy. According to Thucydides (2.87), Phormio told his men before the second engagement off Naupactus 'one cannot ram an enemy ship if one does not get the enemy in sight from a considerable distance.' We must assume that the officer in command made his strategic decision when the enemy fleet was first sighted, and then kept his ships in motion with a leisurely stroke rate increased at a critical moment. If the crew maintained a high stroke rate for a minute or more before the ramming manoeuvre, it would have been too fatigued to continue operations. Shaw (1993d, 64) argues that an Athenian crew could maintain 10 knots for about a minute. At impact, however, the attacking ship needed only three to four knots; (John Haywood in Shaw

1993g, 100). Shaw (1993g, 101) cites Herodotus 1.166.2 to argue that rams were occasionally wrenched off, but in this passage Herodotus refers to pentecontors; we do not have one reference of rams wrenching off triremes during battle.

As more information is accumulated, many of the above questions will surely be answered even if controversy can never be fully excluded. Consider, for example, the present successful performance of the *Olympias*. Despite it scholars and seamen continue to disagree about the nature of the trireme and the fundamental accuracy of the reconstruction. But one of our aims should be the reduction of controversy through the provision of more accurate analysis. Hence, this study will review the discussion to date and conclude that the *Olympias* is indeed a reasonable representation of the ancient trireme.

Let us first consider the opinions of Lucien Basch, an astute student of the iconographic evidence, who believes that the *Olympias* reconstruction does not accurately reflect the pictorial data. He is particularly critical of the oar system of the *Olympias*, which is based on oars of approximately the same size. He argues that the ancient trireme was propelled by oarsmen with oars of different lengths, and diagrams this type of oar system with the thalamians working from a rather high oar port. Basch (1987b, 94–99) suggests that the dimensions of the oars of the thalamians, zygites and thranites are not mentioned in the Athenian naval inventories because they were differentiated in appearance. Basch made these observations shortly before *Olympias'* first sea trial (see also Basch 1988), but Coates and Morrison (1993, 132) note that inscriptions of the fourth century BC (*IG* 22 1604.43–44 and 1605.14) confirm that oars were of similar lengths. Coates (above pp. 82–91) also finds the results provided by the equal length of oars for the oarsmen at three levels in the *Olympias* perfectly acceptable, while Tilley (1997, 4) finds Basch inconsistent in his use of iconographic evidence.

Basch also sees less uniformity in the design of triremes than the designers of *Olympias* do. Before the battle of Artemision, Herodotus (7.194) notes a Persian squadron mistakenly took Greek triremes for Persian, and so Morrison, Coates and Rankov (2000, 156) suggest that the differences between the Greek and Persian ships 'was not such as would be obvious under such conditions.' Basch (1979, 318–19) misinterprets Morrison's remarks to mean that the triremes from the respective fleets were 'identical', and argues that it is not uncommon to fail to distinguish vessels at sea. Basch emphasizes diversity in design: 'At the risk of giving offense, I ask under what authority is it permissible to assert with certainty that the *triereis* of Ionia, including the 353 *triereis* at the Battle of Lade, were, shall we say, of the Lenormant relief type?' Torr (1894, 100) also noted the necessity of displaying national flags on ships to distinguish them from the enemy, although in his article '*Navis*' in Daremberg and Saglio (1904, 214) he saw a consistency in the design of ships among the Etrsucans, Greeks and Phoenicians evolving simultaneously.

Basch (1988, 165–71) detects in a mutilated marble plaque, the Eleusis relief of *c.* 350 BC, a more technologically advanced trireme than the one depicted on the Lenormant relief, and equates it to vessels depicted on fourth-century BC coins (cf. Morrison 1996, 187). He maintains that by the fourth century BC, ships with a *parexeiresia*, an outrigger, supported by exterior struts were being replaced by those which did not have external supports, and cites the Eleusis trireme and the trireme depicted on the L'Aquila relief as examples. Basch (1988, 176) also maintains that the Lenormant relief, which depicts struts supporting an outrigger, is an inaccurate Roman copy. He argues that if the L'Aquila relief had been found on the Acropolis the *Olympias* would have looked much different. According to Basch, the trireme went through a number of major changes in antiquity, evolving into the sort of vessel depicted in the funerary relief of Cartilius Poplicola at Ostia, a ship driven by oars coming out on the same vertical line from a giant oar box or outrigger. Triremes in the 5th century BC tended to be similar but that is not to say that a trireme that saw service at Salamis would closely resemble one in the Roman navy. After Actium, the Romans went many centuries without a major sea battle, and deployed their fleet as a deterrent (Starr 1941, 7). This fact doubtless had something to do with the type of trireme that evolved in the Roman Empire. The Romans used the vessel as an escort or a means to show the flag. Perhaps the giant outrigger in Poplicola's trireme added speed but rendered the ship less combat-worthy because it would have been a convenient ramming target for an enemy ship (for the vulnerability of outriggers, see Morrison 1993, 15). Morrison (1996, 267), contrary to Basch's criticism, is not unaware of the changes in the role and construction of the trireme. Throughout the work of Basch, there is the implication that the creators of the *Olympias* could have built a more authentic trireme if they had meticulously assessed more of the evidence. In addition to Basch's views on the length of the oars (1979, 290–7), he has reservations about the length of the hull (1990), the thickness of the tenons fixed at 12 mm, and the use of polysulphide sealant to assure the water-tightness of the hull (1987b, 105).

Scepticism is here carried too far. Although Basch argues persuasively about the evolution of the trireme, he forgets that the design of the *Olympias* was based on fifth century BC models. Basch suggests that Morrison and Coates relied too much on the Lenormant relief. They, in fact, gained much knowledge from the Talos vase, a late fifth century work of art that gives a detailed picture of the stern of a trireme. They argue that the triremes depicted on both these works of art complement each other and provide special insights. The former depicts a warship afloat and the latter renders a galley resting on a beach. Each has thalamian oar ports, and a projecting outrigger, which suggests a three-level oar system. Taken together these triremes support the present reconstruction of the *Olympias*. Basch's proposed trireme with high thalamian oar ports, oars of different lengths, awkwardly placed zygian oarsmen, and a heavy hull, seems to be nautically unsound (Coates and Morrison 1993, 136–137; Morrison, Coates and Rankov 2000, 146–150).

A. F. Tilley, a retired naval officer, questions whether the *Olympias* has any resemblance to an ancient trireme. He suggests that the concepts used to build the *Olympias* are overly complicated, and generally unscientific. He maintains that Morrison and Coates misinterpreted the Lenormant relief and argues that the Lenormant artist depicted a single row of oars, and the oblique and horizontal lines cannot be used as evidence for three-level oar system. Tilley not only concludes that to see a three-level oar system in the Lenormant relief is wishful thinking, he finds no evidence in any of the iconographic sources for three levels of oars (Tilley 1997, 1: 'But ancient literature and iconography have not yet been approached in a scientific way. The study of ancient ships seems stuck in a pre-scientific time-warp;' see also his p. 6 on the Lenormant relief).

Tilley (1976) argues that the 'tri' of the trireme actually refers to three oarsmen to a 'room,' a space produced by each bench extending across the ship. Consequently, in Tilley's trireme there are three men abreast (cf. Morrison and Williams 1968, 155 defining a 'room' as a separate space on each side of the ship). He discerns this oar system in the Siren vase, an Attic red-figure stamnos of *c.* 490 BC, which in his view depicts the port side of Odysseus' ship with seven oar ports, six oars and four oarsmen. As seen from above, the Siren vase allegedly reveals three men, each working one oar extending across the deck. The inner rower passes his oar under the arms of the outer man. Thus, in each 'room' there are two oars over one side of the ship and one over the other. It demonstrates the three-men-abreast system. He concludes that while the Siren vase ship is not a trireme, the Athenians employed this system on a larger scale for triremes. In his view, the trireme was a triple-banked galley propelled by two levels of oarsmen. The oarsman at the lower level sat in the middle and served as a sculler (Tilley 1970; 1976, 364). Tilley, who cites additional iconographic evidence to support his thesis, made extra rowlocks in a standard naval cutter and successfully utilised the Siren vase arrangement of oars men (Tilley 1976, 358–9).

Tilley further argues that around 470 BC when Cimon broadened the decks of hise triremes, he was simply making room for four oarsmen. Thus two men now replace Tilley's robust oarsman who previously wielded two oars. In this arrangement there are four men to a 'room,' one on each side at each level increasing the oarsmen from the 90 deployed on the ships that won the battle of Salamis to 120 who defeated the Persians at Eurymedon. Tilley's 90 to 120 oarsmen go against the well-documented fact that there were 170 oarsmen assignment to each trireme. This presents no problem to Tilley who argues that the *pentekontarchos*, apparently the pursuer, kept the names of 50 men on the books who had some unspecified role in supporting the trireme. Thus Tilley appends these 50 reservists to Cimon's alleged 120 oarsmen and tallies the trireme's 170 oarsmen. With such an arrangement of oarsmen there is no need for thalamians. Tilley concludes that the *Olympias* not only produced an impractical rowing system, with thalamians crouched so low beneath the benches above them that they could not be effective, but that three levels of oars men contradicts the ancient sources (Tilley 1970, 366–9). Tilley calls for a revised understanding of the terms 'bank' and 'room,' suggesting that much of the murkiness results from their inaccurate use. Furthermore, this seaman finds the data on speed confusing, varying from a projected 12 knots to 2.9 knots. He maintains that the hold of the *Olympias* with room for sixty is too large while the space below the deck of the ancient trireme was extremely confined (Tilley 1997, 12–13).

We now have much to ponder and assess. Let us review the development of the trireme and the iconographic evidence before addressing Tilley's views. There is no vase painting, likeness on coins, or sculpted artwork until the 6th century BC that suggests a three-level system of oars. According to Thucydides (1.12.4–13), the Corinthians were the first Greeks to build triremes, and Ameinocles, a Corinthian shipwright, designed four modern ships for the Corinthians some three hundred years before the end of the Peloponnesian War, *c.* 700 BC. Some scholars thus place the first triremes at the end of the eighth century BC, while others dismiss Thucydides' statement and put the appearance of the triremes about a century and a half later. Ameinocles probably had something to do with the first triremes, but it seems that they may have been too expensive and at first not sufficiently efficient to warrant the building of fleets, and so did not attract the attention of artists (Papalas 1997). Tilley (1976, 366) notes 'no practical man will suppose that the first triremes had 170 oarsmen ... A jump from 50 to 170 oarsmen is incredible.' There no doubt was an evolutionary process which was not amply recorded in the literary or iconographic evidence, but Thucydides (1.14.1) does distinguish long ships from pentecontors and triremes (see the comment of Morrison 1978, 207–208.). The side of a trireme was honeycombed with oar-holes, some of them closed with *askomata* (leather sleeves). It was clearly no easy task for an artist who was probably not a seaman and usually saw ships in harbour without the crew to accurately depict these apertures with a vertical triad of oarsmen (Morrison and Williams 1968, 169; Coates and Morrison 1993, 134). And the artists who attempted to depict the early triremes did not come from Corinth, Ionia and Western Greece, which pioneered the trireme, but rather from Athens, a state lagging behind others in adopting the trireme. Morrison catalogues ship representations from 760 BC to 480 BC, and notes that out of 158, 106 are of Attic origin. The largest non-Attic groups are seventh-century Boeotian *figulae* depicting

outlines of ships. The Corinthian evidence of the first half of the sixth century BC is too fragmentary to be useful (Morrison and Williams 1968, 73–118; Morrison 1978, 206–7).

The poet Hipponax, a native of Ephesus, in *c.* 540 BC, was the first writer to mention a trireme with a ram (Hipponax frag. 45 Diehl; Morrison and Williams 1968, 120). He ridiculed the painter Mimnes for painting a snake on the side of a many-benched trireme to look as if it was running away from the ram and towards the helmsman. It is not clear whether Mimnes was commissioned to embellish the ram of a trireme or in fact adorning a vase with a representation of this type of vessel. It is not important for our purpose. Mimnes did not know that the snake, an apotropaic, had to be facing the enemy. He had it confronting its own crew. The significance of Mimnes' trireme is that it provides proof that around 540 BC the trireme had emerged as a warship equipped with a ram. Mimnes may have made a mistake in depicting the ram because it was a recent addition to the trireme, and that in the earlier stages of this vessel it was not equipped with a trireme and did not have military functions. It gradually became a war vessel. According to Herodotus (5.99.1) in 495 BC the Ionians mustered 353 triremes against 600 Persian at the battle of Lade.

Artists like Mimnes, however, were not concerned with precise details. There was a fanciful element in their work, which intended to give a flavour of the sea. Representations of athletic events were no more accurate than those portraying naval scenes. One would think that the artist commissioned to portray athletes in action on vases, which were often awarded to a victor, would take care to depict the contests accurately. In a famous Panathenaic amphora in the British Museum (Harris 1964, pl. 3 and p. 228 n. 3), the runners are shown in an absurd posture with left arm and left leg proceeding together. Harris (1964, 87) also makes some interesting comments on the inaccuracy of Myron's famous statue, the Discobolos. The artistic interpretation of ships under oars was a more difficult task than depicting athletes in action, and it was certainly no more accurate (see the remarks of Basch 1985, 41. Tilley 1997, 2–3 takes Basch to task for later arguing that Greek artists provided photographic realism in their depiction of ships; cf. Basch 1988, 177. Basch, however, suggests this hypothesis only to dismiss it and concludes (1988, 179) that 'the certitude lies in the lack of precision and gaucheness of the sculptor representing certain elements in the Lenormant relief'). This, of course, does not mean that pictographic evidence is worthless for either athletic or maritime matters. Unfortunately, Mimnes' painting does not survive. But we do have, as noted above, significant representations of the trireme. The Lenormant relief and the Talos vase come from the fifth century BC, and both indicate a three level system of oars. Trajan's column dates to the early second century AD. The artist sculpted details about military garb, equipment, standards and ships, although in doing so he enormously magnified the people relative to the size of the ships. The admiral's flagship, with three tiers of oars, is a trireme. The iconographic evidence stretching from the fifth first century BC to the second century AD proves the three level oar system of the trireme (Morrison, Coates and Rankov 2000, xx–xxi, and the remarks of Torr 1894, 212–213; on realism, see Rossi 1971, 14–16, ill. 41).

The above survey of the development of the trireme demonstrates that the Greeks did not simply leap from a 50 oared vessel to one of 170 overnight. Furthermore, the evidence is clear that the trireme was prominent a good half century before the Persian Wars and that there is considerable evidence dealing with its tri-level oar system. Tilley's analysis of the trireme suffers from his lack of knowledge about the history of the period in which the trireme flourished. But for the sake of argument let us temporally disregard this compelling literary and iconographic evidence about a three-level system and assume the possibility of Tilley's trireme with 90 rowers arranged on two levels. It is difficult to imagine the operation of such a vessel. The man in the middle, pulling two oars each about 14 feet long, would have to possess fantastic strength to perform his task. His oar would pass under the chest of his colleague on the side, thus restricting the manipulation of his oars. Furthermore, such an oar system could not produce the manoeuvrability required to carry out a diekplous. Tilley's oarsmen spread across the deck would have interfered with the fighting personnel. At the Battle of Lade in 495 BC the Persians added an additional 40 soldiers to their deck personnel bringing the number of fighting men to 70. It would have been impossible for these soldiers, or even half that number, to fight from the deck of Tilley's trireme.

Tilley's figure of 90 oarsmen for the triremes of the Persian Wars disregards not only the register listing three classes of oars, thranite, zygian and thalamian numbering 62, 54, 54 (Morrison 1941, 24; Morrison and Williams 1968, 122 ff., 134; Morrison 1978, 204; for a critique of Tilley's trireme, see Coates 1995, 160), but the report of Herodotus (7.184.1) that ships at Salamis had 200 crew members, 170 oarsmen and 30 marines Morrison and Williams 1968, 122ff; Morrison 1978, 203). But for the moment let us assume that all of the literary and inscriptional evidence that attest to 170 oarsmen in the early decades of the 5th century are inaccurate and Tilley is right about 90 oarsmen. This leads us to one of Tilley's most ingenious arguments that the *pentekontarchos* was an officer who kept the names of 50 oarsmen on the books. What was the role of the *pentekontarchos* before this date? Furthermore, Tilley's 120 oarsmen, three to a bench, would not fit on such a deck, and this arrangement would require an impossibly long ship. It is curious that Tilley, who is calling for higher scientific standards, simply ignores evidence when it does not support his thesis. His trial with the naval cutter does not demonstrate much since it produced negligible speed in tranquil waters (Tilley 1992b, fig. 8).

Tilley's objection to the hold of the *Olympias* being too large may have some merit. According to Herodotus (8.118) after Salamis Xerxes fled to Thrace where he boarded a Phoenician trireme sailing from Eion to the Hellespont. This story is clearly apocryphal for Xerxes returned to Asia by land but it does reflect conditions on the deck of a trireme. A sudden storm endangered the ship. The helmsman advised Xerxes to get rid of his fellow Persians on deck. Accommodating the king, they jumped overboard. Herodotus (8.119) dismissed the story of Persian notables sacrificing themselves to save their master because it would have been more practical to force the 54 Phoenician at the thalamian oars to abandon ship and relinquish their place to the Persian notables.

Scholars generally interpret this passage as proof that there was little room below deck. The *Olympias,* on the other hand, has a spacious hold (Morrison, Coates and Rankov 2000, 130–131 and Tilley 1997, 14). Herodotus and his audience would have assumed that Xerxes was travelling with a large retinue, let us say 100 men, and many valuable possessions and there was room enough below the deck to accommodate a number of men and supplies along with the thalamians. Indeed the Persians deployed their triremes more than the Greeks for transporting men and supplies. We must also note that the trireme in question here was Phoenician and these vessels were generally faster than Greek triremes and possibly constructed with somewhat smaller holds. In this case Xerxes would have been taking the fastest trireme available. But it does seem that the space below the deck of the *Olympias* is somewhat too large.

Let us examine more carefully Tilley's post-Persian war trireme. Tilley's 120 oarsmen for the "Cimon model" requires four oarsmen abreast. This arrangement is an improvement over his Persian war trireme in that it replaces the dubious sculler, but it leads to another mechanical impossibility. Tilley's new trireme is even less stable than his old one. This ship of 135 feet for a beam of 8 ft could not be housed in the ship-sheds built for the Athenian triremes, and would be too clumsy to perform any of the manoeuvres required in trireme warfare (Tilley 1976, 365–366; cf. Morrison 1978, 205). Tilley, without much knowledge of the history of the 5th century BC, misunderstands the purpose of Cimon's overhauling triremes of Persian war vintage. They were about 20 years old, near the end of their life span, and clearly not as quick and agile as when the Athenians had deployed them against the Persians. Thus Cimon transformed some triremes into troop transports with fighting platforms by enlarging their beams and thus widening their decks. The purpose of this modification was not to add oarsmen but to provide space for hoplites who, at Eurymedon, fought from the decks and then pursued the enemy and won a land victory (Morrison 1993, 15; Morrison, Coates and Rankov 2000, 153–154). By widening the deck, Cimon improved the trireme's stability and enhanced its sail-carrying capacity, but reduced its ability to perform the manoeuvres necessary for ramming. There is no reason to believe that Cimon's modified the oar system of the Athenian trireme. The type of triremes the Athenians deployed at Salamis was similar to the ships Phormio and other Athenian admirals commanded some fifty years later in the Peloponnesian War.

Conclusion

Can a scientifically based reconstruction of a ship type be made when there are no physical remains? The answer is yes, if the iconographic and literary sources are adequate. In the case of the trireme these sources exist, but scholars have not entirely agreed on their adequacy and meaning. The builders of the *Olympias* by carefully analysing the evidence comprehended the trireme's physical requirements for speed, oar power, weight, displacement stability and hull strength. While the *Olympias* may not be a replica of the ancient trireme it is a reasonable facsimile.

The ancient sources report a remarkable performance level of the Greek trireme under oar. It achieved maximum efficiency with the materials and technology available to fifth-century Greek shipwrights. But the Greeks used a quality of timber no longer available in the Mediterranean. Thus in *Olympias* Douglas fir was employed for the planking, iroko for the keel, and live oak for the tenons. Basch (1987b, 104) in a spirit of antiquarianism protested about the sealing of the seams of *Olympias* with polysulphide elastomer. Furthermore, the builders used modern underwater paints, treated the timber with preservatives, and employed power hand tools. It cannot be expected that men are capable of building a modern trireme with exactly the same materials and technology used to construct the originals of the time of Themistocles, but it is reasonable to expect that they can adhere to these factors as much as possible while achieving the same high performance level. Historians like myself may not be able to judge fully the relative merits of conflicting and untested hypotheses about ships, nor fully understand the physical essentials which triremes demanded in their design according to factors of physiology and engineering. They can, however, understand the literary and iconographic evidence, and assess the results and lessons from any actual tests and trials. The *Olympias* is more than a 'floating hypothesis' (McGrail 1992). To a great extent, it has resolved the trireme puzzle! With 170 amateur oarsmen rowing at three levels, it achieved a speed of about 8 knots, and performed like its ancient Greek counterpart. With a more professional crew, trained more rigorously, the performance level should be moderately enhanced while a second reconstructed trireme with some slight modifications would improve the performance level considerably. Until other hypotheses are explored and tested by experiment, the *Olympias* should be accepted as an authentic representative of the type of ship upon which the Athenians based their fifth-century thalassocracy.

Bibliography

Angel, J. L. (1971) *The People of Lerna: analysis of a prehistoric Aegean population.* Princeton, NJ, American School of Classical Studies at Athens.

Basch, L. (1979) Roman triremes and the outriggerless Phoenician trireme. *The Mariner's Mirror* 65, 289–326.

Basch, L. (1985) Appendix A to the Thera ships as sailing vessels. *The Mariner's Mirror* 71.4, 413–15.

Basch, L. (1987a) *Le musée imaginaire de la marine antique.* Athens, Hellenic Institute for Preservation of Nautical Tradition.

Basch, L. (1987b) Review article of *The Greek Trireme of the Fifth Century B.C.: discussion of a projected reconstruction* edited by John Coates and Seàn McGrail, and *The Athenian Trireme: the history and reconstruction of an ancient Greek warship* by J. S. Morrison and J. F. Coates. *The Mariner's Mirror* 73.1, 93–105.

Basch, L. (1988) The Eleusis Museum trireme and the Greek trireme. *The Mariner's Mirror* 74.2, 163–197.

Basch, L. (1990) La galère de l'Antiquité. In *Quand voguaient les galères.* Paris, 22–23.

Coates, J. F. (1993) Carrying troops in triremes. In Shaw 1993a, 78–81.

Coates, J. F. (1995) Tilley's and Morrison's triremes – evidence and practicality. *Antiquity* 69, 159–162.

Coates, J. F. and Morrison, J. S. (1993) The sea trials of the reconstructed Athenian trireme *Olympias*: a reply to Lucien Basch. *The Mariner's Mirror* 79.2, 131–141.

Coates, J. F. and Shaw, J. T. (1993) Hauling a trireme out on a slip or a beach. In Shaw 1993a, 87–90.

Coates, J. F., Platis, S. K., and Shaw, J. T. (1990) *The Trireme Trials 1988: report on the Anglo-Hellenic sea trials of* Olympias. Oxford, Oxbow Books.

Daremberg, Ch. and Saglio, E. (1904) *Dictionnaire des antiquités grecques et romaines* Vol. IV: N–Q. Paris, Librairie Hachette et Cie.

Hanson, V. D. (1989) *The Western Way of War: infantry battle in Classical Greece.* New York, A. A. Knopf.

Hanson, V. D. (ed.) (1991) *Hoplites: the Classical Greek battle experience.* London, Routledge.

Harris, H. A. (1964) *Greek Athletes and Athletics.* London, Hutchinson.

McGrail, S. (1992) Replicas, reconstructions and floating hypotheses. *International Journal of Nautical Archaeology* 21, 353–355.

Morrison, J. S. (1941) The Greek trireme. *The Mariner's Mirror* 27.1, 14–4.

Morrison, J. S. (1978) Rowing the trireme. *The Mariner's Mirror* 64.3, 203–208.

Morrison, J. S. (1988) The second British sea trials of the reconstructed trireme, 20 July–5 August, 1988. *Antiquity* 62, 713–714.

Morrison, J. S. (1991) Ancient Greek measures of length in nautical contexts. *Antiquity* 65, 298–305.

Morrison, J. S. (1993) *Triereis*: the evidence from antiquity. In Shaw 1993a, 11–20.

Morrison, J. S. (1996) *Greek and Roman Oared warships, 399–30 BC* Oxbow Monograph 62. Oxford, Oxbow Books.

Morrison, J. S. and Williams, R. T. (1968) *Greek Oared Ships, 900–322 BC.* Cambridge, Cambridge University Press.

Morrison, J. S., Coates, J. F. and Rankov, N. B. (2000) *The Athenian Trireme: the history and reconstruction of an ancient warship.* 2nd ed. Cambridge, Cambridge University Press.

Papalas, A. J. (1997) The development of the trireme. *The Mariner's Mirror* 83.3, 259–271.

Rankov, N. B. (1994) Reconstructing the past: the operation of the trireme reconstruction *Olympias* in the light of the historical sources. *The Mariner's Mirror* 80.2, 131–46.

Rossi, L. (1971) *Trajan's Column and the Dacian Wars,* transl. J. M. C. Toynbee. Ithaca, NY, Cornell University Press.

Shaw, J. T. (1993a) *The Trireme Project: operational experience 1987–90. Lessons learnt* Oxbow Monograph 31. Oxford, Oxbow Books.

Shaw, J. T. (1993b) The voyage and speed trials of *Olympias* in 1990. In Shaw 1993a, 39–44.

Shaw, J. T. (1993c) The resistance/speed curve of *Olympias,* with a section on rudder resistance by Ian McCallum. In Shaw 1993a, 45–7.

Shaw, J. T. (1993d) Rowing *Olympias*: further lessons from the sea trials. In Shaw 1993a, 58–68.

Shaw, J. T. (1993e) 'Rowing astern' in Shaw 1993a, 69–70.

Shaw, J. T. (1993f) The meshing of oars in *Olympias* and in a 'stretched' design. In Shaw 1993a, 75–77.

Shaw, J. T. (1993g) Steering to ram: the *diekplous* and *periplous,* with a section by John Coates and John Haywood. In Shaw 1993a, 99–104.

Starr, C. G. (1941) *The Roman Imperial Navy, 31 BC–AD 324.* Ithaca, NY, Cornell University Press.

Tilley, A. F. (1970) The ship of Odysseus. *Antiquity* 44, 100–104.

Tilley, A. F. (1976) Rowing the trireme – a practical experiment in seamanship. *The Mariner's Mirror* 62.4, 357–369.

Tilley, A. F. (1992a) Rowing astern – an ancient technique revived. *International Journal of Nautical Archaeology* 21, 55–60.

Tilley, A. F. (1992b) Three men to a room – a completely different trireme. *Antiquity* 66, 599–610.

Tilley, A. F. (1997) Ancient warships – a scientific approach. In Cogar, W.B. (ed.), *New Interpretations in Naval History: selected papers from the Twelfth Naval History Symposium.* Annapolis MD, Naval Institute Press, 1ff.

Torr, C. (1894) *Ancient Ships.* Cambridge, Cambridge University Press (reissued 1964. Chicago, Argonaut).

Torr, C. (1904) '*Navis*' in Daremberg and Saglio 1904, 24–40

Welsh, F. (1988) *Building the Trireme.* London, Constable.

15. Beyond *Olympias*: an outsider's view

André Wegener Sleeswyk

1. Introduction

In discussing what we have discovered about ancient triremes since *Olympias* was designed and launched, it is useful to distinguish between what was learned from experiments in which *Olympias* was used as a tool, and what was learned from other investigations into how the ancient trireme was operated, but in which the reconstruction played no role. In addition, there are some problems associated with ancient triremes which remain unresolved. Making the distinction between these categories of problems will help us to focus on the different requirements which an ancient trireme had to fulfil, and which a modern reconstruction, such as any successor to *Olympias*, must match.

The author is an outsider in the sense that he took no part in the work of the Trireme Trust, but he has investigated a number of technical aspects of oared ships in ancient Greece. The results of these investigations, reported in a number of publications, form the basis from which the author will attempt to pinpoint problems requiring further examination. These, together with the results obtained in *Olympias*, may help to serve as a base for a programme of further experimentation, and in particular, for the design of a new trireme reconstruction.

In the view of this outsider, it appears that so far the experimental effort, which has been executed admirably, has been focused largely on the oarsystem and the organisation of the rowing. These are undoubtedly important aspects of the ship which lend themselves most readily to testing by experiment in the first stage of investigation, but other aspects have to be kept in mind as well.

The experimental results obtained so far are best discussed by those who organised the sea trials, but their manner of continuation will depends to a large extent on requirements other than those of the oarsystem. What should be avoided is for some of these to be quietly ignored, *e.g.* because they appear at first sight to be inconvenient. If some passages in the literature on triremes remain puzzling, the fact should be stated clearly and explicitly. This would

be in keeping with the scientific approach which is a declared aim of the trireme project according to Rankov (1989), and involves weighing pros and cons of proposed reconstructions against what is known from all the known literary texts and all the available iconography.

Now that the practicality of the three-level rowing system has been established beyond reasonable doubt – an important achievement – refinement or modification of that oarsystem is in order to raise the performance to an historically acceptable level. Moreover, the military function of the trireme should now receive the same careful attention which was given to the oarsystem. The ship's principal weapon was the ram. A corollary of the use of this armament is that the retardation or deceleration of the attacking ship upon ramming is a dire necessity. The unpleasant consequences for the way the crew members could fulfil their various tasks should receive more attention. In particular, deceleration influences the ship's secondary military function of acting as a platform for the marines who were part of the crew.

The military aspect of the trireme apparently received comparatively little attention when *Olympias* was designed. For instance, the gangway was considered primarily as a passageway for allowing the oarsmen to urinate regularly, and its military use received scant attention. That the effect of ramming was not tested to any extent on *Olympias* is understandable, but the outsider wonders why, for instance, no computer simulation of the effects of the act of ramming on the attacking ship has been undertaken, analogous to the computer simulations of the effects of collisions which are routinely performed in the automobile industry, and as suggested earlier by Rankov (1989, 65). The oarsystem, although investigated first, is essentially a corollary of the requirement that the ramming blow be delivered with sufficient momentum. The latter is a mechanical quantity of a magnitude which is equal to the arithmetical product of mass and velocity of the ship. The mass is something which is better discussed as a property of the hull, but in any case, the velocity has to be as high as possible if the ramming blow dealt to the enemy is to be as fierce as it can be.

A third aspect of the ship to be considered is the hull itself, its shape, principal dimensions, displacement, and the methods employed in its construction. The vessel's functions as a warship, the requirement of sufficient speed and the necessity to conform to the available archaeological and historical evidence, *e.g.* dimensions of shipsheds, allusions in the literature bearing on draught, the width of the outrigger etc., should all be taken into account in determining the design parameters of the hull, which, in their turn, influence the design of the oarsystem also. One must remember that no remains of a Greek trireme have been found to date, so the evidence is not nearly as firm as we would like it to be. Consequently, hull reconstructions are of necessity no more than floating conjectures.

2. Ramming

i) Various aims of ramming

The author has argued earlier (Sleeswyk 1996) on the basis of elementary mechanics that, depending on the relative values of the displacements of the attacking ship and the ship being rammed, the attacker could either try to hole his opponent, or, if the displacement of his ship was relatively large, to cause his victim to capsize or roll over. If the latter was the aim, the ram of the attacking ship had to be elevated above the water line. A third possible aim of ramming was to break the oars of the enemy ship. In the literature, references are found to all three modes of incapacitating the enemy. A few examples of each method are given here:

a) Holing the hull of the enemy's ship
Diodorus Siculus (13.99.4):

> 'Last of all he rammed the trireme of Pericles with a rather heavy blow and broke a great hole in the trireme ...'

Polybius (16.4.12–13):

> '... but piercing him below water produced breaches which could not be repaired.'

b) Capsizing the ship of the adversary:
Aeschylus (*Persians* 417–420):

> '... while the Hellenic galleys, not heedless of their chance, hemmed them in and battered them on every side. The hulls of our vessels rolled over and the sea was hidden from our sight, strewn as it was with wrecks and slaughtered men.'

The elevated bows of a large ship and the waterline ram of a smaller one are referred to by Polybius (16.3.8–9):

> 'Dinocrates engaged an 'eight' and himself received his adversary's blow above the waterline, since the opposing vessel had its bows elevated, but striking the enemy underneath ... he could not at first get free of her although he repeatedly tried to back out.'

c) Breaking the oars of the enemy:
Aeschylus (*Persians* 416):

> '... shattering their whole array of oars

Diodorus Siculus (13.99.3–4):

> ' ... and from others he tore away the rows of oars and rendered them useless for the fighting.'

ii) Ramming deceleration

An estimate of the retardation or deceleration of the hull when one ship rams another has been calculated by John Coates (Morrison, Coates and Rankov 2000, 221–2). He shows that if a ship is brought to rest from a speed of 10 knots in a distance of one metre by a constant force, the deceleration can be estimated at 13 m/sec2. That value is one-third more than the acceleration of gravity. If the hull weighs 50 tonnes, the force on the hull due to deceleration is 66 tonnes, which is relatively small.

Coates very properly considers the maximum deceleration upon ramming rather than the average value. But such a maximum might have been higher still when a trireme rammed a heavier adversary amidships, as is reported not infrequently in descriptions of sea-battles. The deceleration will often have been much less than this maximum value, but the design must be based on a worst case scenario.

If one considers the effect of the deceleration estimated by Coates on the oarsmen rather than on the hull, it implies that an oarsman weighing 75 kg would suddenly be subjected to a horizontal force of 100 kilograms pushing him backwards towards the prow. As will be seen, that force might have been considerably higher than this estimate, implying that crew members might be subjected to sudden, and on the human scale, truly violent forces, when their ship rammed an enemy.

An alternative way of arriving at a value for the deceleration upon ramming is based on the shape which the Athlit ram was given. The sort of damage which that type of ram was designed to inflict on the hull has been described succinctly by Steffy (1983):

> 'First of all, this ram was designed to pound the surface of an enemy hull rather than to pierce it. The ram head, in fact, seems carefully designed to prevent it from impaling a victim.'

The ram indented the hull of the enemy ship, causing the planking or the horizontal seams immediately above and below the contact area to tear by shearing, and the interconnecting tenons to break, but it did not pierce the strakes in-between. When the ram was subsequently retracted, the ragged torn seams would not close again, resulting in huge leaks if they were below the waterline.

That the design aimed at avoiding the ram being caught between the upper and lower torn seams of the rammed hull explains the purpose of the slight reduction in height of the Athlit ram immediately behind the vertical frontal

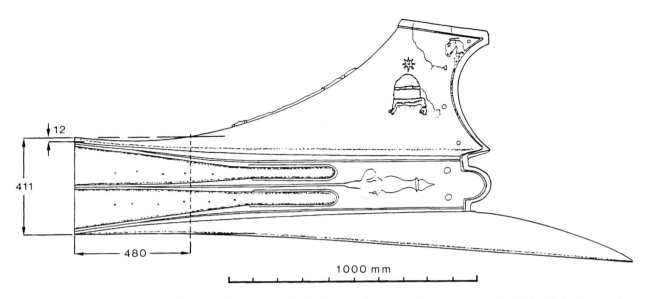

Figure 15.1. The Athlit ram, showing the point at which the curved upper surface returns to the height of the front end.

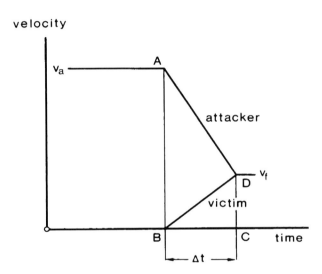

Figure 15.2. Schematic velocity/time graph of ships during ramming. Δt marks the time taken for the ram of the attacking ship to indent the hull of the ship being rammed.

area (Fig. 15.1). It is only some 48 centimetres behind that frontal area that the height regains its initial value; the maximum reduction in height occurs at about half this distance. Apparently, the design of the ram was based on a maximum indentation of 48 cm and perhaps more usually half of that. This observation allows us to estimate the deceleration upon ramming on a somewhat more quantitative basis than before.

In order to obtain this estimate, it is assumed that the hulls of the ramming and the rammed ships suffered an inelastic collision, such that after some time interval Δt during which the ram indented the enemy ship, the

two hulls were moving at the same velocity (Fig. 15.2). Additional assumptions are that the two hulls were equally heavy and that the victim was rammed amidships perpendicular to its midline. The only velocity component considered here is the one perpendicular to the midline of the victim. The potential theory of hydrodynamics predicts (Lamb 1879; Sleeswyk 1996) that the influence of the surrounding water manifests itself by the acceleration of the submerged hull of the victim taking place at a rate as if the inertia of the hull had been doubled. When the ram has come to rest relative to the victim after impact, the common velocity of the two ships would therefore have been ⅓ of the velocity of the attacking ship just before impact.

The velocity-versus-time diagram presented in Fig. 15.2 illustrates the effect of ramming on both the attacker and the victim. The velocity of the attacker decreases from v_a to v_f, while the transverse velocity of the victim increases from zero to v_f. If it is assumed that the hull is indented by the ram over a distance of 45 cm at most, and if v_a is 5 m/s (10 knots), the time interval Δt may be calculated as 0.22 s. The magnitude of the deceleration of the attacker, which is represented by the slope of the trajectory *AD* in the diagram, is then 2/3 × 5 × 1/0.22 = 15.0 m/s², *i.e.* about 1½ times the acceleration of gravity. An oarsman weighing 75 kg would be pulled forward to the prow with a force of 113 kg, somewhat more than Coates' value.

But the use of the inelastic collision model allows us to go beyond that simple estimate, and to investigate, for instance, the effect on the deceleration if the trireme rammed a heavier ship. If the ram indented the hull of a quinquereme over the same distance, the greater displacement of the adversary (about twice that of a trireme) would cause an increase of the value of the deceleration of the attacker to about 18 m/s². The horizontal force on the 75 kg oarsman would then be about 137 kg. But it might well be that the ram would not penetrate as deeply into the structure of the more heavily built ship, in which case the deceleration would be larger still. In the light of these various considerations, a moderate but realistic design estimate of the value which the maximum deceleration might attain would be 2 g, *i.e.* twice the value of the acceleration of gravity. Although that maximum deceleration would, presumably, not have been attained very often during the lifetime of a trireme, it was a contingency which should not have impaired in any way the functioning of the ship. The corresponding sudden horizontal force on the 75 kg oarsman would be 150 kg, which would be, as stated before, a truly violent force on the human scale.

iii) The effects of deceleration and measures to counteract them

Ramming, then, could have had the effect of pushing the bodies of the oarsmen and other crew members towards the prow with great force, which would be dangerous enough in itself. That danger is exemplified by the fate of the Spartan admiral Callicratidas, who, according to Xenophon (*Hellenica* 1.6.33) was flung in the sea and disappeared when his ship rammed an enemy. But even for the oarsmen who were firmly seated, the tendency of the oarlooms to be flung towards the prow upon impact would present a real danger. Obviously, the question of what safety measures might have been taken in order to obviate the ill effects of deceleration in the attacking ship needs further consideration.

The interior of the ship would have been designed in such a way that the chances of oarsmen being hurt when their ship rammed an adversary would be minimised. The interior of *Olympias* was obviously not designed to meet that requirement, but in designing any new reconstruction it would seem that this aspect ought to be given careful thought. It does not seem probable, for example, that oarsmen sat in individual seats, from which they could thrown by the ramming impact. It would have been safer if they sat astride continuous benches aligned alongships, such as those which one observes on some representations of ancient Egyptian oared ships.

Such an arrangement would suggest several obvious methods by which the oarsmen could prepare to brace themselves against deceleration upon impact. For instance, the oars might be immobilised, *e.g.* by attaching a rope fixed to the hull round the knob at the end of the oarloom (see section 3 i), as schematically indicated in Fig. 15.3, or by retracting them as suggested by Rankov (1989, 63) and fixing the handles by other means. In the solution offered in Fig. 15.3, if the oarsmen took their hands off their oars, they would slide back some 15 or 20 cm until the backs of their knees met a restraining bar fastened athwartships under their bench. They would grip the bar with their hands and press their backs against the oar of the man sitting forward of them, and await the impact.

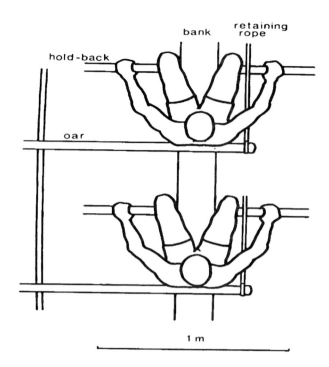

Figure 15.3. Hypothetical method by which the oarsmen in a ramming ship could brace themselves for the shock, as viewed from above.

These preparations would be entirely adequate to withstand a deceleration of 2 g, and their execution would require only a few seconds. Other measures are possible, and this example is presented as merely one of a number of options to be considered before deciding on the design.

iv) Being rammed

It was noted above (Section 2 i) that according to Aeschylus (*Persians* 418–9) the hulls of rammed ships capsized. Aeschylus continues: '... and the sea was hidden from our sight, strewn as it was with wrecks and slaughtered men', from which it may be deduced that the overturned wrecks remained afloat. This implies either that the ships did not carry sufficient ballast to sink them, or that they lost their ballast when turning turtle. The latter is neither improbable nor impossible: 19th century Norwegian fishing boats, for instance, were designed so as to loose their ballast upon capsizing, 'so that the crew had something to hang on to' (Færøyvik and Christensen 1979, 86). Even if a great hole had been made in the hull by ramming, there might have been sufficient time for the crew of the sinking ship to overwhelm the crew of the attacker (Diodorus 13.99.4). In a capsizing ship, on the other hand, the thalamians sitting under the gangway (section 3.iv) would be trapped without time to make their escape (Appian *Civil Wars* 5.107).

3. The oarsystem
i) The type of oar
For some reason which is not clear to the author, the oar

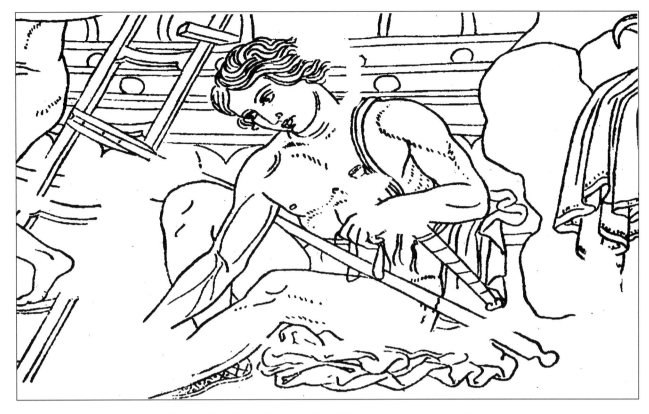

Figure 15.4. Scene from the Cista Ficoronica: Argonaut with oar.

depicted (Fig. 15.4) on the 'Cista Ficoronica' of about 300 BC (Baumeister 1888, 454) appears not to have been discussed as evidence for the oarsystem of the trireme. The square-ended, narrow blade and the knob at the end of the loom are characteristics which would seem to merit discussion. A possible use for the knob is discussed above in section (2 iii).

ii) *The* interscalmium

The term *interscalmium* as used by Vitruvius should not be taken as a heart-to-heart distance, but as the clear distance between tholepins, in analogy to the word *intercolumnium* which he uses (*e.g.* in 3.3.1) to denote the clear distance between columns, *i.e.* from column surface to column surface. The thickness of the tholepin, some 5 cm, must be added to Vitruvius' *interscalmium* in order to obtain the heart-to-heart distance.

The value of the heart-to-heart *interscalmium* depends on the unit chosen. If it is based on the common cubit of 44.4 cm, the value is 94 cm, and if on the newly proposed value of the Attic cubit, it is 103 cm. It should not be regarded as a foregone conclusion that the larger value is the better one, because it aggravates the problem of distributing the oarsmen over the length of the ship.

iii) *Length of stroke*

Since the performance of *Olympias* has fallen below that of the classical trireme as deduced from historical data,

the need to improve the effectiveness of the stroke in the reconstruction is evident. Shaw (1993b and this volume pp. 76–81) has suggested that this might be achieved by making the stroke longer. The remedy proposed by Shaw makes ingenious use of geometry, which allows the length of the stroke to be longer than the *interscalmium*. It consists of canting the oarsmen relative to the midline of the ship, so that the inboard end of each oar swings past the body of the oarsman sitting one place further aft. The necessary skewing or canting would be 18.4 degrees, 'the angle whose tangent is ⅓'.

Canting the oarsmen is at first sight an attractive possibility, but it also presents several disadvantages. Elementary mechanics would predict from the parallelogram of forces that the propulsive force component of skewed oarsmen is inevitably smaller than the force produced by the oarsmen. However, some part of the loss of propulsive force delivered by the oarsmen – somewhat less than half – may be recovered if the hull deflects the turbulence produced by the oarblades. The component propelling the ship if no such recovery took place may be calculated from the laws of mechanics. It is not much smaller than the force produced by the oarsmen; with the geometry proposed by Shaw, the alongships component of force would be $3/\sqrt{10}$ = 0.949 of that actually produced by the oarsmen. Partial recovery of the loss would probably increase that fraction to about 0.97. The losses caused by skewing may therefore be regarded as equivalent to eliminating 9 oarsmen from

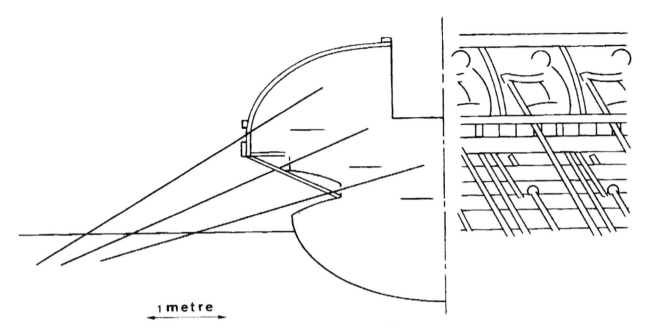

1 metre

Figure 15.5. Schematic drawing of the regular arrangement of oarsmen with oars of equal length across a trireme, as proposed by the author in 1980 (Sleeswyk 1982a), compared with a schematic rendering of the Lenormant relief.

a crew of 170 if no recovery took place, or 5 men taking partial recovery into account.

The other disadvantages are associated with deceleration of the trireme in battle and when ramming an enemy. Canting would not only have made it more difficult to brace the skewed oarsmen against the shock of ramming, but also if they suffered smaller decelerations when, after a few hours of battle, the ship had to cross at speed a sea strewn with wreckage and other flotsam which could not all be avoided by the helmsman. These unpredictable smaller shocks might have had unpleasant consequences for the oarsmen if they occurred while the looms of the oars were just passing behind their backs.

The alternative to canting the oarsmen which Shaw considers is to increase the *interscalmium*, but he rejects this suggestion on the grounds that it would make the ship structurally too weak, and that it would add to the wetted surface. As argued below, the first is probably true for *Olympias*, but there are reasons for thinking that she was rather too lightly constructed (section 4 v), in which case the objection is no longer valid. If the hull were more heavily built, it could be made longer. If in that case the beam of the ship were reduced by the same percentage by which the length were increased, both the wetted area and the displacement would remain the same. Whether a reduction of the wetted area by using a more rational cross-section is of any great consequence will be discussed in section 4 iv.

A second alternative would be to have the oarsmen pulling on sliding seats or cushions, as proposed by Hale (1996) using both technical and historical arguments. This would be compatible with the suggestions made in section 2 iii as to how the oarsmen might have prepared

themselves for deceleration upon ramming, but it seems an attractive possibility, meriting serious consideration, also because it would allow the stroke to be somewhat longer than the *interscalmium*. Thus there might be no need to increase the latter, nor to skew the oarsmen.

iv) Arrangement of the oarsmen

If the historical indications are respected, the thalamians ought to be seated underneath the *katastroma* or gangway, not next to it, as is argued in section 4 1. There would then be more space for them athwartships and no need for them to be seated half underneath the zygians, as in *Olympias*. They could be seated vis-vis the zygians in the same manner as the latter are seated relative to the thranites.

The resulting arrangement was first proposed by Torr (1904) and worked out by the author in 1980 for oars of equal length (Sleeswyk 1982a). It requires less height (Fig. 15.5) than the arrangement utilised in *Olympias*, and the details of the 1980 figure which may now seem doubtful, *e.g.* the shape of the hull and the absence of a canopy deck, are of course not essential to the seating arrangement proposed. The comparison with the schematic side view shown in the Lenormant relief emphasises the presence of an outrigger support, which ought to be present in any reconstruction.

v) Size of oarports and **askomata**

Where *Olympias* appears at first sight to deviate most from all the known iconography of the trireme hull (Basch 1987, 285–92) is in the size of the oarports, which seem to be larger than anything known from antiquity. Their large size is, of course, based on the story in Herodotus of the punishment of the *trieres* captain Scylax, whose head was thrust through a *thalamia*. The explanation given by Morrison and Williams (1968, 132) brings out the somewhat speculative nature of this interpretation: it is stated that there 'can be little doubt that 'oar-port' is the right translation for the word *thalamia*'. But, apart from the conflicting iconography, some doubt does remain, as the word is seemingly attested in this sense in this passage only. Other possible apertures in the hull or superstructure associated with the *thalamos* or hold, for instance for access or ventilation, ought also to be considered.

4. The hull

i) Length

The shipsheds at Zea appear to have been at least 44 m long according to the drawings by Dörpfeld (Morrison and Williams 1968, pl. 29). The average dry length of these slipways was 37 metres around 1900, from which it was inferred that around 35 metres was a reasonable overall length for a trireme (Morrison and Williams 1968, 285). *Olympias* was given a length of 36.8 m.

The provisional nature of this conclusion is apparent from Blackman's discussion (Morrison and Williams 1968, 182) of the effect of a change in the average dry length since antiquity. In fact, many land masses in the eastern Mediterranean have either risen or sunk by several metres relative to sea level over the past two and a half millennia. Moreover, it is not credible that the roofs of the shipsheds would have covered the wet portion of the slipway to any significant extent. Consequently, the Zea sheds may have housed ships that had a maximum length of somewhat more than 40 metres.

ii) Width

From the clear widths between the columns of the Zea shipsheds it may reasonably be inferred that the overall width of the trireme was somewhat more than 5 metres (Morrison and Williams 1968, 285), but in any case not more than about 5.4 m. If the outrigger projected 50 cm outwards, the width of the hull from gunwale to gunwale would have been 4 to 4.4 m. The outrigger cannot have projected less than about 40 cm beyond the deck, because otherwise it would have been impossible for the wounded Brasidas to fall into it (Thuc. 4.12.1). As the width of the gangway was probably about 1.2 m (see below, section 4 vii), the canopy decks would each have been 1.7 m wide at most, which may have been sufficient because these narrow decks were used in action by the marines only when boarding the enemy.

iii) Draught

According to Thucydides (2.90.6), in the second action in the Gulf of Corinth in 429 BC:

'Some of the ships they made fast to their own and proceeded to tow away empty – though they had already captured one with its crew – but some others, which were already in tow, were taken from them by the Messenians, who came to the rescue, rushed armed as they were into the sea, boarded the ships, and fought from their decks.'

The Messenians cannot have waded in full armour to a depth of water much exceeding about 1 metre to recapture their ships. The draught of these cannot have been much in excess of about 90 centimetres, as they were not aground. The ships were empty of their crews, and so were lighter by 15 tons than when fully manned. With a sinkage of 1.1 cm per ton (Morrison and Coates 1989, 20), the hulls would have been floating about 16 to 17 cm higher than with their crews on board. Thus the fully-manned ships cannot have had a draught of more than about 100–110 cm, and probably less.

iv) Shape of cross-section

The shape given to the mid-section of the hull of *Olympias* has been justified as follows by John Coates (Morrison and Coates 1989, 17):

'The normal method of ship-building in the ancient Mediterranean, as demonstrated by underwater archaeological work, required a ship of the fourth century BC to have a wine-glass shaped mid-section.

The only known example of an oared ship equipped with a ram which possessed a wine-glass shaped mid-section is the Punic wreck of Marsala. It would seem that the statement implying that this shape was customary for Greek oared ships requires the support of more evidence, the more so because the Marsala ship's ram was of a type that was definitely out-of-date in the Greek world at the time of the battle of Salamis.

Two additional arguments militate against the notion that a peaked cross-sectional shape was commonly employed for Greek oared ships:

a) The peak and its extension add considerably to the wetted surface – some 15 percent – causing a proportional increase of the resistance of the hull in the water, particularly at lower speeds. In addition, the long fin must have made the turning circle larger than it would have been without this appendage. In modern times the wine-glass shape has been typical not of a nimble oared vessel, but of a weatherly sailer. There does not appear to be any literary evidence that the trireme might be considered as such.

b) Most probably there was a continuous development of oared ships from Antiquity to the Renaissance, because Byzantium was active for a long time in Italy, parts of which continued to be claimed by the eastern Empire (see *e.g.* Nicol 1988). The galleys of the Renaissance possessed a flaring U-shaped mid-section. If that shape was not inherited from ancient Greek and Roman oared ships, its provenance would need to be explained. Conversely, the hypothesis of a wine-glass shaped cross-section for ancient Greek ships implies that there was at some time a break in the tradition of shipbuilding; the time and cause of that break would then need to be elucidated. To date, no evidence for the existence of such a break in the tradition has been presented.

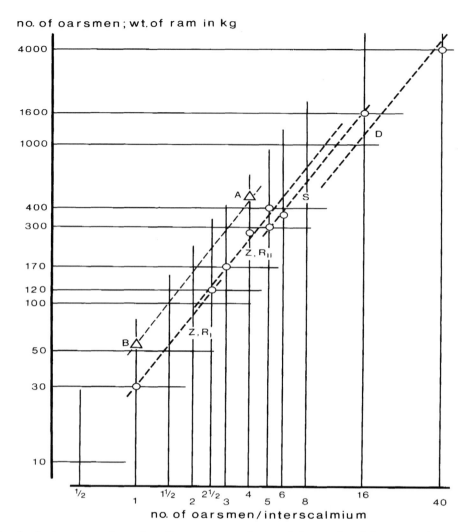

Figure 15.6. Graph plotting the total number of oarsmen in a ship, and the weight of the ram in kgs, against the number of oarsmen per interscalmium on one side of the ship. Z, S and D indicate ships rowed alla zenzile, a scaloccio and double-manned (i.e. with oarsmen on both sides of the loom) respectively. R_I and R_{II} refer to ships without outriggers and with outriggers respectively. A represents the weight of the Bremerhaven ram and B that of Athlit ram. The dashed lines are drawn at a slope of 3 to 2, in accordance with the proposed proportionality rule.

v) Weights of the hull and ram

In a paper presented in 1996 to the Sixth International Symposium on Shipbuilding in Antiquity, the author (Sleeswyk 2001) showed that, for oared ships of different sizes possessing the same hull proportions, there is a simple rule of proportionality, viz. the square of the total number of oarsmen r_t is proportional to the cube of the number of oarsmen contained in one *interscalmium* on one side of the ship r_i provided that the length of the *interscalmium* l_i remains unchanged. The latter will depend on the way the ship is rowed, *i.e. alla zenzile* ($l_i = l_z$) or *a scaloccio* ($l_i = l_s$) or double-manned, *i.e.* with men working at both sides of the loom of the oar ($l_i = l_d$).

The total number of oarsmen on board ships with hulls of the same proportions, or ships of the same lineage (i.e. employing the same oarsystem), may then be given by the formula:

$$r_t = R \times r_i^{3/2} \times (l_z/l_i) \ (1)$$

in which R is, within a narrow margin of error, equal to the number of oarsmen in a monoreme of the same lineage, which in this case is, of course, *alla zenzile*. The reader is referred to the aforementioned paper for the refinements which can be added to this formula, taking into account, for instance, the presence of an outrigger which would increase the space available for seating oarsmen. In the accompanying graph (Fig. 15.6), the logarithm of the total number of oarsmen r_t is plotted against the logarithm of r_i; according to formula (1), values for ships of the same rowing system should be situated on straight lines inclined at a slope of 3 to 2, as drawn. The data were mostly obtained from Casson (1973) and Morrison (1995). The results appear to confirm the idea that ships such as the trireme and the quadrireme, were modelled on the triacontor. Not all ancient oared ships can be regarded as derived from the triacontor, however; the data for the pentecontor, for instance, would seem to indicate that its rowing system could have been that of a *hemiolia*, for which there is no evidence.

The graph probably indicates that the simple proportionality rule given above was actually used by the ancient shipbuilders in designing their ships. Another design rule which they seem to have applied was that the weight of the bronze sheath of the ram was proportional to the number of oarsmen on board. Two such bronze rams are known, those from Bremerhaven and from Athlit, weighing 54 kgs and 465 kgs, respectively. The first obviously belonged to a monoreme, the second probably to a quadrireme or 'four' (Murray and Petsas 1986, 103–14). These weights are plotted onto the graph on that basis; it may be observed that they accord with the proposed rule surprisingly well. These findings imply that the weight of a trireme ram would have been approximately 290 kgs.

The weight of *Olympias'* bronze ram, at 203 kg, represents approximately 1/200 of the weight of the fully-manned ship, a fraction which seems to be about right. But the foregoing analysis of the historical evidence which suggests that the weight of a trireme ram was about 290 kgs, leads to an estimate of the weight of 58 tonnes for a fully manned and provisioned ship. If, furthermore, the weight of the water provision is taken as 8 tonnes (Sleeswyk and Meijer 1998), and that of the crew, including the marines, at 15 tonnes, the weight of the empty hull would be 35 tonnes, which is considerably more than *Olympias'* 25 tonnes.

That the weight of the ancient trireme may well have been more than that of *Olympias* is also suggested by what Steffy has to say on the subject (Casson and Steffy 1991, 33):

'... the very lightest militarily useful trireme would have to contain 0.75 ton of material per meter of length. Add to that the weight of crew and gear, and there is no doubt that the hull would be heavy enough for ramming. But even that weight represents a comparatively thin-skinned, lightly braced hull. A heavier frame plan and planking and wales the size of those on the Athlit ship would raise hull weight alone to around a ton per meter of length. This is by no means intended to establish hull weights for warships; my calculations are too primitive for that. It does, however, give an indication of the weights we are dealing with when discussing large oared warships. Displacement weights of more than a ton per meter of hull length are entirely realistic.'

On the basis of Steffy's observations, it would seem best to assume a weight of hull for the trireme between ¾ and 1 tonne per metre of length. If the hull was 42 m long, the weight per length for an empty hull of 35 tonnes would come to 0.83 tonnes per metre, if 37 m long, to 0.95 tonnes per metre. Both values fall within the range of Steffy's estimates.

Olympias' weight of 25 tonnes for a length of 36.8 metres is equivalent to 0.68 tonnes per metre of length. If that hull had to be able to withstand a maximum deceleration of about 2 g upon ramming an adversary without damage to itself or the crew, it would probably have had to be constructed more solidly, which would have entailed more weight.

An additional reason for supposing that the hull of a Greek trireme was more heavily built than that of *Olympias* is that the latter was not designed to carry a significant provision of water. In a recent paper by Sleeswyk and Meijer (1998), it is shown that Greek triremes, when fully provisioned, most likely carried some 8 tonnes of water-filled jugs (*kadoi*), additional weight which would have required a stronger and heavier hull.

vi) Strength of hull and hypozomata

To anyone familiar with the carrying capacity of the wooden *barque du Léman*, a type of ship supposedly derived from the Venetian galley and which clearly shows such an ancestry, it may come as a surprise that there could be any problem in giving the hull of the ancient trireme sufficient strength. Fig. 15.7, taken from Pâris' *Souvenirs de Marine IV* (Pâris 1888, no. 200), gives an outline of the hull of a *barque* of the nineteenth century, from which the similarity in shape to a galley hull is evident. It is recorded that the *Vaudaire*, another *barque* built in 1894, at 35 m in length and 50 tonnes hull displacement, could carry 140 tonnes of building stone. These ships commonly lasted for about half a century (Guex 1975).

If giving the hull sufficient strength is perceived as problematical, it seems logical to interpret the *hypozomata* which are mentioned in the classical literature as hogging trusses. Yet one may wonder whether there really was a problem and whether, in any case, *hypozomata* could have functioned as hogging trusses. The latter were often provided on Egyptian ships, as is shown in a number of depictions, but mostly for hulls which either were constructed as a patchwork of short pieces of wood or which had to operate under circumstances which were unusual for Egypt, such as at sea or carrying an exceptionally heavy load.

The diameter of 40 mm for *hypozomata* ropes which is deduced from the literature (Morrison and Williams 1968, 296) seems rather paltry in comparison to the diameter of the ropes of the hogging trusses on the Egyptian ships. For comparative purposes, the diameter should be expressed as a fraction of the length of the ship, thus giving a 'relative diameter'. As the trireme must have been similar in length to Egyptian ships, this type of comparison should not lead to gross errors, and there is no alternative approach available

The force which can be exerted by the ropes will be proportional to their cross-sectional surface area, or to the square of their diameter. The relative diameter of the ropes of *hypozomata* of 40 mm diameter on a trireme 36 to 40 m long is 1.0 to 1.1×10^{-3} of that length, and corresponding to this is the 'relative cross-sectional area', obtained by squaring the relative diameter and multiplying by $\pi/4$ to account for the circular cross-section. The total relative cross-sectional area for the four *hypozomata* ropes

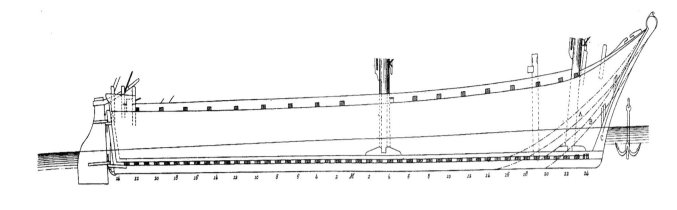

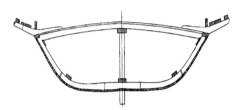

Figure 15.7. Longitudinal and transverse cross-sections of a barque du Léman, taken from Pâris 1888, no. 200.

in a trireme (in fact, two ropes fitted doubled) works out at 3.1 to 3.7 × 10⁻⁶.

We can compare this value with those determined for the hogging truss and for the roughly horizontal 'undergirdings' encompassing the hull under the gunwale of the sea-going ship of Sahure of *c.* 2500 BC (Fig. 15.8, from Landstrom 1970) (Borchardt 1913). The relative diameter of the hogging truss on that ship is 9.2 × 10⁻³, that of one of the undergirding ropes is 2.8 × 10⁻³. The corresponding relative cross-sectional areas are 66.5 ×10–6 for the hogging truss and 12.3 × 10⁻⁶ for the two undergirding ropes together.

Although both values are considerably in excess of the total relative cross-sectional area of the *hypozomata* of the Greek trireme, clearly the latter compares far better with the relative cross-sectional area of the Egyptian undergirdings than that of the hogging truss. This finding suggests that it is more plausible to interpret the *hypozomata* as undergirdings than as hogging trusses.

The above vindicates Casson's conclusion regarding the long-standing problem of the functional interpretation of the *hypozomata*, namely that they were undergirdings (Casson 1971, 91). Moreover, the provision of *cordone* parallel to the gunwale around the hull in early 17th-century Genoese galleys, allows us to postulate a historical process in which the Greek *hypozoma* is regarded as an intermediary stage in a development from Egyptian undergirdings to the Genoese *cordone*, as explained in the author's note on pp. 207–12 of this volume.

vii) Position and depth of gangway

There is one three-dimensional depiction of an ancient ship showing a central gangway, the marble hull, now in the Louvre museum, on which the statue of the Nike of Samothrace stands. The depth of the gangway in the monument is 60 cm, the width 73 cm. The hull is obviously shown on a reduced scale: if one considers the amount of room available for oarsmen's bodies, the scale of the model is at most 1:1.5 (Sleeswyk 1982b), but if the subdivision of the Greek foot into 16 inches is taken into account as well, a scale of ⅝ or 1:1.6 seems more probable. The corresponding dimensions of the gangway in the real ship would then have been: depth 96 cm, width 117 cm.

The military use of the gangway would have been at least three-fold:

a) It would have provided protection for the legs and lower bodies of the marines when they were shooting arrows and throwing javelins in battle.

b) It would have prevented these men from being flung into the water when the ship rammed an adversary. The canopy deck of *Olympias* does not offer bulwarks against which men could brace themselves sufficiently to prevent this from happening. Conceivably, the gangway could also have been partitioned by ropes athwartships during battle, to prevent the fighting men from being flung forward over any large distance upon ramming. They would have stood on the canopy deck only when preparing to board an enemy ship during an engagement.

c) It would have offered the opportunity for the javelin

Figure 15.8. Sea-going ship depicted in the tomb of Sahure, the second king of the Fifth Dynasty, 2510–2460 BC. (after Borchardt 1913, from Landström 1970).

throwers to sit on deck and brace their legs in the gangway when throwing their javelins from a seated position (Thuc. 7.68.1). Javelin-throwing is based mainly on a rapid twist of the upper body and pelvis (cf. Muybridge 1955, Pl. 48), requiring the legs to provide the necessary reactive forces. This would not have been possible if these men were seated on a flat deck. A kneeling position would then appear to be the minimum requirement, but that is not historically attested.

There does not seem to be an overriding reason to maintain *Olympias'* dangerously deep gangway, which does not serve a primarily military purpose. Having a higher gangway would remove a constraint from the arrangement of the oarsmen as well, because it would allow the thalamians to be seated not next to the gangway, as in *Olympias*, but under it, as explained in section 3 iv.

5. Conclusions

The foregoing is certainly not an exhaustive list as regards the issues which should be considered when designing a new reconstruction. Others include: the shape and solidity of the *epotides*; the amount of ballast carried in the ship; the positioning of the main beams between the thalamians; etc. Nevertheless, a number of key points have been raised here, and the conclusions reached may now be summarised. Any new reconstruction should be more heavily built than *Olympias*, displacing about 35 tonnes when empty, with a length of approximately 40 m, a hull shape resembling that of the Renaissance galleys with a flaring U-shaped cross-section, and a gangway situated at a higher level, above the heads of the thalamians. The thalamian oarports and their *askomata* are to be much smaller, in accordance with the iconography. The new design should aim at minimising the adverse effects of deceleration during ramming upon the crew. The *hypozomata* are not to be fitted as hogging trusses, but as girdling the hull under the gunwale, similar to the *cordone* in Genoese galleys of c. AD1600 and the undergirdings observed on some ancient Egyptian ships.

These points should be considered in detail from both the historical and the technical viewpoints for incorporation into the design of any successor to *Olympias*.

Acknowledgements

The author is greatly indebted to Professors F. J. A. M. Meijer and H. Th. Wallinga and to Dr. J. F. Coates for comments and discussion on a number of points raised in this paper.

Bibliography

Basch, L. (1987) *Le musée imaginaire de la marine antique*. Athens, Hellenic Institute for the Presevation of Nautical Tradition.

Baumeister, A. (1888) *Denkmäler des klassischen Alterums*, Bd. I. Munich and Leipzig, Druck und Verlag von R. Oldenbourg.

Borchardt, L. (1913) *Das Grabdenkmal des Königs Sahu-re*, Bd. II. Leipzig, J. C. Hinrichs.

Casson, L. and Steffy J. R. (eds.) (1991) *The Athlit Ram*. College Station TX, Texas A & M University Press.

Coates, J. F., Platis, S. K. and Shaw, J. T. (eds.) (1990) *The Trireme Trials 1988. Report on the Anglo-Hellenic Sea Trials of* Olympias. Oxford, Oxbow Books.

Casson, L. (1971) *Ships and Seamanship in the Ancient World*. Princeton NJ, Princeton University Press.

Færøyvik, B. and Ø. and Christensen, A. E. (eds.) (1979) *Inshore Craft of Norway*. London, Conway Maritime Press.

Gardiner, S. and Morrison, J. (1995) *The Age of the Galley. Mediterranean Oared Vessels since Pre-Classical Times*. London, Conway Maritime Press.

Hale, J. R. (1996) The Lost Technology of Ancient Greek Rowing. *Scientific American* 274, 66–71.

Lamb, H. (1879) *Treatise on the Mathematical Theory of the Motion of Fluids.*. Cambridge, Cambridge University Press.

Landström, B. (1970) *Die Schiffe der Pharaonen*. München, Gütersloh, Bertelsmann.

Morrison, J. S. (1995) Hellenistic oared warships 399–31 BC. In Gardiner and Morrison 1995, 66–77.

Morrison J. S. and Coates, J. F. (eds) (1989) *An Athenian Trireme Reconstructed. The British Sea Trials of* Olympias, *1987.* BAR International Series 486. Oxford, Archaeopress.

Morrison, J. S. and Williams, R. T. (1968) *Greek Oared Ships 900–322 BC.* Cambridge, Cambridge University Press.

Morrison, J. S. and Coates, J. F., and Rankov, N. B. (2000) *The Athenian Trireme. The History and Reconstruction of an Ancient Greek Warship.* 2nd ed. Cambridge, Cambridge University Press.

Murray, W. M. and Petsas, P. M. (1989) *Octavian's Campsite Memorial for the Actian War.* Philadelphia, The American Philosophical Society.

Muybridge, E. (1955) *The Human Figure in Motion.* New York, Dover Publications

Nicol, D. M. (1988) *Byzantium and Venice: a Study in Diplomatic and Cultural Relations.* Cambridge, Cambridge University Press.

Pâris, F.-E. (1888) *Souvenirs de Marine IV.* Paris, Gauthier-Villars.

Rankov, N. B. (1989) The scientific aims. In Morrison and Coates 1989, 61–66.

Shaw, J. T. (ed.) (1993a) *The Trireme Project. Operational Experience 1987–90. Lessons Learnt.* Oxbow Monograph 31. Oxford, Oxbow Books.

Shaw, J. T. (1993b) Rowing *Olympias:* further lessons of the sea trials. In Coates, Platis, and Shaw 1990, 58–68.

Sleeswyk, A. W. (1982a) A new reconstruction of the Attic trieres and bireme. *International Journal of Nautical Archaeology* 11.1, 35–46.

Sleeswyk, A. W. (1982b) 'The prow of the 'Nike of Samothrace' reconsidered', *International Journal of Nautical Archaeology* 11.3, 233–243.

Sleeswyk, A. W. (1996) Ramming trim of ships. In Tzalas, H. (ed.), *Tropis IV. 4th International Symposium on Ship Construction in Antiquity, Athens 1991. Proceedings.* Athens, Hellenic Institute for the Preservation of Nautical Tradition, 429–49.

Sleeswyk, A. W. (2001) The lineage of the triacontor. A verifiable hypothesis. In Tzalas, H (ed.), *Tropis VI. 6th International Symposium on Ship Construction in Antiquity, Lamia, 1996. Proceedings.* Athens, Hellenic Institute for the Preservation of Nautical Tradition, 517–527.

Sleeswyk, A. W. and Meijer, F. (1998) The water supply of the Argo and other oared ships. *The Mariner's Mirror* 84, 131–138.

Steffy, J. R. (1983) The Athlit Ram: A preliminary Investigation of its Structure. *The Mariner's Mirror* 69, 229–247.

Torr, C. (1904) 'Navis' in Ch. Daremberg and E. Saglio (eds.), *Dictionnaire des antiquités grecques et romaines.* Vol. IV: N–Q. Paris, Librairie Hachette et Cie., 24–40.

16. An Unauthentic Reconstruction

Alec Tilley

The four papers circulated by members of the Trireme Trust for consideration at their Athenian Trireme conference (see pp. 63–91) dealt mainly with performance under oars.

Timothy Shaw suggested that in an ancient trireme the whole crew rowed for 16 to 17 hours at 7 to 8 knots to cover 129 miles in a day. Some readers will consider, as I do, that 16 to 17 hours as a man's rowing day with 'no indication of haste' (Morrison, Coates and Rankov 2000, 103) is preposterously too long.

Dr Coates said in his paper that the first aim of any future reconstruction would be 'To achieve attested performance under oar'. It is difficult to believe that his trireme's crew could ever be asked to row for 16 or 17 hours. I do not believe that a rower in Dr Coates' projected ship could even go through the motions of rowing for 16 hours, irrespective of the distance covered. No doubt much the same 'trials' philosophy will be adopted as before:

> 'A test lasting one hour seems too long to be practical, but one of six minutes would be convenient and on average equivalent to the longer one, because if a man can deliver 230 watts for 6 minutes with no need to resume, he can probably deliver 160 watts for one hour and, after 30 minutes rest, do it again for another hour, and so on' (Coates, Platis and Shaw 1990, 15).

And again and again and again. It is unclear how the 30-minute rests could be fitted in, since the calculations are based on the full crew rowing. A six-minute test might convince the faithful of a 129-mile day, but would not impress the sceptic. As Dr Coates has rightly pointed out, performance alone is not a sufficient test of authenticity.

The main aim of this paper is to show that the proposed new design is, like the *Olympias*, at variance with almost all the evidence concerning ancient triremes. Unfortunately, conformity with ancient evidence is not widely accepted as a requirement where 'reconstructions' of ancient ships are concerned, and is not included among the aims of the trireme project listed in Dr Coates's conference paper (p. 82). The subject is discussed in Annex 1. The conference ought to have taken cognisance of each item of evidence, if only to discount it, but it did not.

Although my views on triremes differ fundamentally from those of the Trireme Trust, there has been some convergence in recent years, and in order to strike an early positive note that topic is covered in Annex 2.

Linguistic evidence

There are six oarsmen in nearly every cross-section of the proposed design, whereas there is evidence that the number in the name of ancient warships referred to the number of oarsmen in cross-section. Thus the eponymous *trieres*, with a name incorporating the number three, would have had three oarsmen, not six, in cross-section. The linguistic evidence (summarised in Annex 3) that supports my contention ought to have been discussed at the conference.

Iconographic evidence

The proposed new design, like the *Olympias*, has oars pivoted at three distinct levels. In that it is strikingly unlike any ship representation made before the introduction of warships named after the number six.

Professor Morrison's explanation of this discrepancy is that a trireme's oars were arranged in such a manner that ancient artists found them too difficult to attempt to draw:

> 'It seems likely that the ship had become so complicated a subject to depict, with its three banks [Anglice three levels] of oars and the problems of perspective which these, as well as the outrigger supports and deck stanchions, presented, that artists in general had been avoiding the task' (Morrison and Williams 1968, 169).

What Morrison sees as likely seems highly unlikely to me, especially in view of the ease with which modern artists and even school children draw the *Olympias*, producing representations that clearly show three levels of oars. Surely, if Athenian shipwrights could build them and the citizens row them with such success, their artists could depict them?

Dr Coates' new design is no more likely than the *Olympias* to meet the too-difficult-to-draw requirement, and it differs even more than the *Olympias* from the Lenormant Relief in that the oarsmen are skewed outboard, so that viewed from abeam their arms overlap the oarsman next aft. It is unclear whether or not the Lenormant Relief will be cited in support of the new design, but it would be prudent to carry out trials (by offering professional artists their usual fee to draw a mock-up of the new design and noting the proportion of those who refused on the grounds that the task was too difficult) before going ahead with construction.

Pseudo-evidence

To make up for the absence of three-level ships in the iconography, representations which do not show oars at three levels are often put forward as pseudo-evidence for three-level triremes, by adding supposed paint of which there is now no trace, or 'correcting' supposed artistic errors, or by assuming three-level originals of which the actual work of art is supposed to be an inaccurate copy by an ignorant artist. The technique is examined and deplored in Annex 4.

Three-level ships

There are representations dating from Hellenistic and Roman times, when warships named after the numbers six and higher were in service, which undoubtedly show oars at three levels. These have, from time to time, been put forward irrationally as evidence for three-level triremes.

Torr (1895, 466) and Dr Papalas in his conference paper (see pp. 101–8), cited three-level ships on Trajan's column as evidence for three-level triremes, so assuming what they were trying to prove.

Professor Morrison deployed the same fallacious argument in connexion with a clay model which shows oars at three levels:

> 'This model of a trieres has been included to confirm the theory, if further proof be needed, that the trieres was propelled by three banks of oars [Anglice oars at three levels]' (Morrison and Williams 1968, 180).

yet there is no reason to believe that the ship the artist had in mind had only six oarsmen in cross-section or that it was called a trireme. The model, bought in an Egyptian bazaar in the nineteenth century, and with no archaeological provenance, is described as Hellenistic. In Hellenistic times there were warships named after the number six, and higher numbers too. If representations of oars at three levels were made without difficulty in the era of the 'six' but not before, it is evidence that the three-level ships were 'sixes' or above, not triremes.

Morrison (1979, 55) seems to have accepted the logic of this, and has silently revised his assessment of the model to that of a polyreme. It shows a striking inability to distinguish opinion from evidence.

Essentially the same fallacy has recently been revived by Höckmann (1997, 196). Because they have oars at three levels, he writes of some 1st-century BC depictions of ships: 'This makes the vessels triremes ...'

Three classes of oarsmen

Before the *Olympias,* the ancient evidence that the three classes of oarsmen in a trireme sat forward, amidships and aft was generally accepted, the thranites furthest aft and the thalamians furthest forward (Morrison 1941, 20). The original arrangement in the *Olympias* could, with a measure of goodwill, be said to conform. The three classes were assigned to the three levels, the thalamians at the bottom. On either side, three rowers, one from each level, were regarded as a 'triad', the uppermost furthest aft and the lowest furthest forward. But it was found impossible to keep time with that arrangement, and the triads were reformed with the thalamians furthest aft, where they could be seen by the others of the triad. This discrepancy with the ancient evidence was never remarked upon, and the fore-and-aft evidence is no longer mentioned in Trireme Trust literature.

It was not made clear at the conference whether or not the new design is intended to conform with this evidence, but as Dr Coates said he was not aware of it, presumably the new design ignores it.

There is evidence against seating the thalamians below the other oarsmen, in the hold, where they are in the *Olympias* and where they will be in the new design. The hold is hotter and airless compared with the upper levels, so that when the thalamians alone row the *Olympias* they generally (and understandably) change places with the rowers of a higher level. But that did not happen in antiquity. When ancient thalamians rowed alone they stayed in their usual places unless intending to deceive the enemy (Polyaenus *Strat.* 5.222.4, cited in Tarn 1906). It indicates that ancient thalamians did not sit as they do in the *Olympias* and will in the new design. The Trireme Trust's views on this were not revealed at the conference.

The arrangement in the *Olympias* is sometimes justified with the assumption that the ancient Greek *thalamos* meant a ship's hold, and that the name for one group of a trireme's oarsmen was derived from it. But *thalamos* did not mean a hold, it meant a cabin, as Casson (1995, 401, citing the evidence on pp. 180–1) defines it. A *thalamegos* literally 'cabin carrier' was a vessel with a cabin, not a vessel with a hold (Casson 1995, 341–342; Höckmann 1993, 133 and fig 6.2). Modern Greeks use the word *thalamos* for a telephone kiosk, with no suggestion of anything that is, like a hold, down below.

Whatever the seating plan, the three designations, thalamian, zygian and thranite, implied a difference in rank, something like Ordinary Seaman, Able Seaman and Leading Seaman. In Dr Coates' new design, the maximum allowable stature of the oarcrew varies: The thranites can be 1.88m (6' 2") tall, but the thalamians no more than

1.75m (5' 9"). It is difficult to see how tall veterans could have been produced from short recruits, unless the recruits were less than full-grown, and that seems unlikely.

Moreover, a rank structure based on the seating plan of a three-level ship would not have been convenient in the course of changing over to the *tetreres,* a type of ship which did not have oarsmen at three levels. Better to have the arrangement, forward, midships and aft, which suits any ship.

Furthermore it would not have been sensible to put inexperienced recruits in every room, where their shortcomings, such as 'catching crabs' and getting out of time, would have impeded the more expert. Better to have them grouped separately.

The fact that the Athenian trireme used three types of oar has sometimes been put forward as evidence for oars at three levels, but Dr Coates' new design does not require different types of oar for his different levels. The question of how the oars *did* differ is addressed in Annex 5.

Early Greek warships typically had a raised fore-deck, and beneath it the only enclosed space that could be called a cabin. Locating the thranite oarsmen aft, nearest the *threnos,* the heavy beam across the ship's stern, which Morrison suggests may have given its name to the thranites (Morrison and Williams 1948, 49), and the thalamians forward, nearest the *thalamos* in the bows, gives an eminently practical arrangement that conforms with the ancient evidence, does not require recruits shorter than veterans, and is suitable for any type of ship. Had this aspect been considered at the conference, it might have been possible to reach agreement without renouncing faith in three-level triremes.

Passenger capacity

It is clear from the account by Herodotus of Persians jumping overboard from Xerxes' trireme to save the ship in heavy weather, that there was little or no room below the deck for any but the rowing crew. Morrison concludes:

' ... while there may have been a small cabin for the trierarch and an important passenger, there was no room elsewhere below decks for anyone else' (Morrison, Coates and Rankov 2000, 131).

This evidence was apparently disregarded in the design of the *Olympias,* where (I would estimate) there is room for at least 60 men. If there is any significant disagreement about it, trials could easily be carried out.

The new design seems to have the same unauthentic capacity. Below the deck there is a gangway about a metre wide running most of the length of the ship. Dr Coates insists on a gangway, citing the opinion of 'most if not all rowers in *Olympias*' that things would be impractical without it, thus seeking to overrule ancient evidence with modern opinion. The conference did not attempt to reconcile the proposed gangway with the accepted evidence of lack of space below the deck.

The only wreck so far to throw light on ancient warships' rowing arrangements, the 30-oared warship described by

Olaf Höckmann (1993, fig. 6), has 15 double-banked rooms and no gangway.

The number of places for oarsmen in a trireme

The Trireme Trust assume that in the evolution of ancient warships there was a single jump from ships with places for 50 oarsmen to those with 170. In putting that proposition, Dr Coates admits that it is 'astonishing', but hopes it is 'something that historians may one day be able to illuminate for us' (Shaw 1993, 23). Illumination day did not arrive in time for the conference. I think Dr Coates' proposition is incredible rather than just astonishing and that no evidence will ever be discovered to explain it.

The Decree of Themistocles, mobilising the Athenian navy in 480 BC, ordered 100 oarsmen to each trireme. My hypothesis that pre-Cimon Athenian triremes had places for 90 oarsmen accords with it well. To conscript ten extra men to allow for evasion and unfitness was prudent. But it is difficult to reconcile Dr Coates' notion of a trireme with seating for 170 oarsmen with the decree. Even if it is assumed that no more than 100 oarsmen per trireme were available, it is hard to see why the Athenians should have built, only shortly before the decree, a great many more triremes than they could fully man.

It is not just a question of evolution. It is unlikely that at any one time an admiral had at his disposal nothing between a 50 and a 170. It would have been extravagant to send a 170 to hunt down a 50. Cost-effectiveness requires a finer graduation.

When they were used as transports, triremes retained 60 oars. Professor Morrison has calculated that the troop-carryings triremes that sailed from Corcyra on the expedition to Sicily each took about 72 soldiers as passengers (Morrison and Williams 1968, 248), basing his calculation on the overall numbers, not on the details of the ships. Seventy-two is far too few for a vessel like the *Olympias*. With seating for 170 but only 60 oarsmen, the *Olympias* would have 110 oarsmen's places available for soldiers. In addition, like an ancient trireme, it could go to sea with at least a further 14 soldiers on deck, making 124 in all. The gangway of the *Olympias* and of the new design have room for many more men. Clearly, the *Olympias* and the new design seat too many oarsmen (and have far too much space below the deck) to resemble an ancient trireme. The Trireme Trust has always refused to address this discrepancy, and did not do so at the conference.

The Weight of an Athenian trireme

An Athenian decree required 140 men to get a trireme up a slipway and 120 to get her down. Those figures suggest that the trireme was lifted rather than dragged. Coates and Shaw calculate that if the trireme had been dragged, it would have taken three times as many men to drag it up as to drag it down a likely slipway, the numbers for the weight of the *Olympias* being 110 and 37 respectively (the figure that should be 37, as cited here, was confusingly misprinted '48' in the reference) (Shaw 1993, 87). But Coates and Shaw make the astonishing assertion that the ratio three-to-one fits the decreed 140 and 120 'fairly well'. It is surely essential for the Trust to dissociate itself from Coates-and-Shaw mathematics if its estimates and calculations are to be respected, but it did not do so at the conference. Looked at rationally, the evidence suggests that it ought to be possible for 140 men to lift the new design and walk her up a one-in-ten hill.

Professor Casson (1995, 89) likened an ancient warship to 'an overgrown racing shell' and drew attention to the evidence that triremes were 'drawn up by their crews on the beach at night' and hauled overland more than two miles in a day. To put the *Olympias* ashore requires heavy machinery and the expense that goes with it. She has therefore been kept afloat, and shipworms have eaten enough of her to put her out of service. Ancient triremes spent most of their lives ashore, carried there by their crews. That is why so many of them lasted a remarkably long time.

By allowing a lift of only 50 kilos a man, Coates and Shaw have persuaded themselves that an ancient trireme could not have been lifted even by 140 men, but the estimate of 50 kilos is ridiculously low. Almost any man fit for military service today can carry twice that on his shoulders, and strong men manage 300 kilos. Men who regularly rowed some 17 hours a day, and covered 129 miles 'with no indication of haste' (Morrison, Coates and Rankov 2000, 103) were probably quite strong. Trials would help to resolve the matter.

If the estimate of 50 kilos *is* accepted and made a requirement, it will be difficult to recruit rowers for the new design, let alone approach the performance of a trireme. People puny enough to match the Coates-and-Shaw estimate are not likely to be interested in a hearty occupation like rowing.

The height of an Athenian trireme

The largest ship in Anthony's fleet at Actium was a *dekeres*, a polyreme named after the number ten, and its height of ten feet above the water was considered remarkably imposing (Tarn 1905, 171). The deck of Dr Coates' new design is nearly as high. One would expect a trireme to be a good deal lower. An examination of rowing arrangements confirms it.

In the *Olympias* it was found that 'Even though the biggest and strongest rowers occupied the thranite [uppermost] level they still found it very hard work. The steep angle of the oar made pulling it awkward. At the finish hands were high, making it difficult to apply the downward force necessary to recover the blade' (Morrison and Coates 1989, 40).

Figures 14 and 15 in the same trials report (Morrison and Coates 1989, 33) add weight to those words. To my mind, no one could row efficiently like that, still less keep it up for a 16 or 17 hour day. In the new design, it

appears that the uppermost rowers will be higher still, and the angle of the oars correspondingly steeper. I conclude that the new design is too high.

In a study of early modern galleys, Dr Coates (1993, 4) points out that the shaft length of their oars must generally have been proportional to the height of the thole above water: 'length of oar and freeboard were critically related'. The opposite is true of the new design, where the oars are of the same length at all levels. The discrepancy suggests that it is a fundamental error to have rowers at markedly different levels if the oars in nearly every room are to be all of the same length. In early modern galleys the importance of avoiding too steep an angle was apparently considered so important that 'longer oars were supplied temporarily to newly-built galleys for use at each end of their oar systems until the hulls had hogged sufficiently to allow regular oars to work properly'. There is a clear implication that oars at too steep an angle will not work properly.

In early modern galleys the slope of the oars on the working stroke 'appears to have lain for centuries within a narrow range around 15°' (Coates 1993, 4). To achieve that, the shortest oars of their six-man-cross-section galleys were more than twice as long as the Athenian trireme lengths. In the new design, the slope of the uppermost oars is more than twice as steep: about 32°. The oars at the middle level are also too steep at about 22°. Clearly, the new design is unsuited to the oar lengths used in Athenian triremes.

Towing

In the opinion of at least one member of the Trireme Trust, an ancient trireme would not have been able to tow a bulky cargo vessel for a usefully-long period 'even in a calm' (Roberts 1995, 314). It is clear from the context that Roberts had in mind lack of oar-power or endurance, not for example very weak tow ropes, because he adds that Demosthenes' account (cited in Morrison and Williams 1968, 245) of triremes towing grain ships for 50 miles 'shows no experience of the stamina needed to row a galley'. The Trust should, I think, dissociate itself from Roberts' opinion, though it did not do so at the conference. If lack of oar power for towing is accepted as a requirement for the new design, it will make it harder to come anywhere near the 129 miles a day normally expected of triremes.

Lack of evidence for three levels

In his second paper Shaw asserts that 'there is massive evidence ... that an ancient trireme's hull and the main principles of her oarsystem were very like those of the *Olympias* and Plan 201–12' [the new design] (p. 68), but he does not say what it is. Morrison wrote: 'The written evidence for this type [the trireme] suggests that it was rowed by oarsmen at three levels' and also omitted to specify it (Morrison and Williams 1968, 169). In his paper for the conference (pp. 101–8), Dr Papalas made a similar evidence-free assertion. The great bulk of the literature advocating three-level triremes consists of explanations for the lack of evidence (three-level ships were too difficult to draw); or beating down the evidence (philosophers were inexact); or concocting pseudo-evidence by adding imaginary rows of oars to monuments that show less than three (my Annex 4); or fallaciously advancing Hellenistic and Roman depictions of three-level ships as evidence of three-level triremes; or counting on evidence which historians may one day be able to discover (Shaw 1993, 23).

There remains the argument that:

'A passage in the Frogs of Aristophanes (405 BC) implies that the thalamite oarsman sits behind and below at least one of the other two, since it speaks of someone "making wind in the face of the thalamite"' Morrison 1941, 20).

Morrison's inference rests on the assumption that the incident occurs while the oarsmen are aboard ship in their rowing positions, but it is more likely to have happened on shore. It is associated with a call for rations, and a trireme's crew rarely ate onboard (Morrison and Williams 1968, 269). In any case, there is no suggestion in Aristophanes that the disagreeable habit was indulged in only by the zygian oarsmen. Even if it is insisted that the practice took place onboard a trireme, the superior classes of oarsmen could have annoyed the thalamians (who sat furthest forward in the ship according to the once-accepted evidence) on their way forward to the heads.

The way ahead

I suggest that instead of building a new three-level, six-banked ship, the Trireme Trust should first study the 25-benched, double-banked pentekontor. Almost everyone believes in such a pentekontor – very few supporters of a later, two-level pentekontor (with either 50 or 100 oars) dispute a preceding, double-banked version.

The advantage of such an approach is that with the basic configuration not in dispute, one could concentrate on aspects other than how to arrange the oars. Two of the most important factors that would have affected the performance of any oared warship are:

1. How much was sacrificed in the interests of performance? What was the compromise between speed and seaworthiness?
2. Did the oarsmen's cushions provide the equivalent of a sliding seat?

By contrast, it is difficult in the trireme controversy, by long tradition acerbic, to get beyond disputing the number of banks, levels and oarsmen.

It would be interesting to see how much agreement could be reached on the fastest possible 25-benched pentekontor. How light and narrow could it be without being impossibly unseaworthy? I leave open the question of what degree of 'reconstruction' would be needed

– calculation, tank-testing of a model, mock-ups or a full-sized floating vessel. If no agreement could be reached, in respect of a pentekontor, on the two questions posed above, it would at least suggest that similar efforts in respect of a trireme would continue to be fruitless.

But given an agreed pentekontor hull, (whether the 'hull' existed in a computer, as a scale model or as a full-sized floating vessel) it would take little extra effort to assess the effect of adding an outrigger and rowing 30 benches, triple-banked, Siren-Vase-fashion. That is the sort of ship I have put forward as a pre-Cimon trireme, but it is important to emphasise that there need be no consensus on what to call it. Casson calls the arrangement *moneres* on the grounds that all the oarsmen are at one level, and Morrison used to call it *hemiolia*, on the grounds that there are one-and-a-half oarsmen each bench each side. Believers in six-banked triremes need have no difficulty in accepting a three-banked ship (provided it is not a trireme) on the evolutionary road between two banks and six. At the conference Dr Coates said that he had no objection to the idea that the Siren Vase shows a vessel with three oarsmen to a bench, and no one expressed dissent.

A small modification, such as Cimon's widening of the triremes that fought at Salamis, would allow the ship to be rowed with four men to a bench, the extra oarsman having his own oar. Dr Coates'asserts that such a ship would not have retained the designation (trireme) that was appropriate when it was built, and would not have been as fast as his new 170-oared design, but neither of those assertions (which I dispute in my Annex 6) are relevant provided the vessel I have in mind is not called a trireme. It could be a bireme to some, and a *moneres* to those, like Casson, who go by the number of levels, irrespective of oarsmen.

Another small modification to the ship, and perhaps different oars, and one would have a ship with two two-man oars on each bench, which I would call a *tetreres* and others could again call a bireme – or yet another *moneres*.

Waiting for wrecks

It is sometimes suggested that we are all wasting our time discussing ancient warships while there are so few remains, and that we should wait for more wrecks to be excavated. An argument against that point of view is at Annex 8.

A riddle

To close this paper, I ask a riddle:

Twenty, Thirty, Fifty, One-hundred-and-seventy.
What is the missing number?
What has it to do with ancient ships?

Annex 1

Differing attitudes to ancient evidence

The idea that an attempted reconstruction should follow the ancient evidence is axiomatic in many fields, but not in the study of ancient ships. Lucien Basch considered that:

> 'In the case of every ship representation, whether painted or carved, irrespective of whatever period it may be referring to ... error is always to be assumed unless the contrary is proved' [italics in the original] (Basch in Gilmer 1985, 413).

Since it is impossible to prove that an ancient representation of a ship is not in error, M. Basch invites us into a looking-glass world where the more closely a hypothesis agrees with iconographic evidence, and the more iconographic evidence there is, the stronger the presumption that the hypothesis is wrong. This paper is based on the opposite assumption – that there is merit in a hypothesis which conforms with ancient representations, even though there is no proof of their accuracy.

Dr Coates (1995) shows a similar disdain for evidence. In disputing the arrangements of oars put forward in Tilley (1992), he does not deny that they conform with the ancient written and iconographic evidence, but claims only that they fail to accord with 'generally accepted interpretations of ancient evidence'.

An examination of the so-called Vienna fragment of an Attic red-figure cup (Morrison and Williams 1968, 176, clas. 3 and plate 26b; Morrison, Coates and Rankov 2000, 149, fig. 43) will show the important distinction between interpretation and evidence, and the way in which Dr Coates 'improves' ancient evidence that does not suit his notions. His interpretation (perhaps one of the 'generally accepted interpretations' he alludes to) is of oars arranged as in the *Olympias*. The *Olympias*'s uppermost level of oars is suggested to him by a line of thole pins which through 'rough drawing' (Morrison, Coates and Rankov 2000, 148) the artist has neglected to depict. He interprets the lower-level oarport as a large, circular, *Olympias*-type oarport, transmuted by the same 'rough drawing' into the equal-sized, semi-circular oarport that we can actually see. Thus the interpretation is amazingly like the *Olympias* and thus the study of iconography is reduced from science to crystal gazing.

If on the other hand one works directly from the evidence, ignoring interpretation, one can see three equal-sized, semi-circular oarports, arranged in a way that is suitable for rowing triple-banked (Tilley 1992, figs 6, 7 and 8). Arguments based on evidence and arguments based on interpretation are very different things, as different as astronomy from astrology, and often reach diametrically opposite conclusions.

Professor Morrison has extended the doctrine of artistic error to cover ancient literature. Because the arrangement in the *Oympias* does not agree with the evidence of 'Aristotle' and Galen, he concludes:

> 'We may suppose that 'Aristotle' and Galen were guilty of unwise generalisation, a fault of philosophers' (Morrison in Shaw 1993, 19)

Freed from the constraints of iconographic evidence by M. Basch's doctrine and from the constraints of written evidence by Professor Morrison's, every hypothesis is invincible, and one writer very rarely convinces another. If, on the other hand, one accepts the limited aim (one that is almost universally adopted in scientific fields) of finding hypotheses that conform with the evidence, consensus becomes a distinct possibility.

Annex 2

Convergence

A good deal of this paper is diametrically opposed to the published views of Professor Morrison and other members of the Trireme Trust; but since the publication of *Greek Oared Ships* in 1968, I am glad to see that our views have converged in quite a number of ways, and I hope may continue to converge in future.

First, Professor Morrison came to agree that the well known eighth-century wall relief from the Palace of Sennacherib, showing Phoenician warships with oars at two levels, is a trireme, an opinion I have long maintained and he has long resisted. I see it as a triple-banked trireme, fully manned, whereas Professor Morrison sees it as a three-level ship with the uppermost level unmanned, but his new opinion is still important.

In *Greek Oared Ships*, his mistranslation had made it appear that Thucydides described the Corinthians as the first absolutely to build triremes, rather than the first of the Greeks. Moreover, by suggesting that when Thucydides wrote *naus* he did not mean *trieres*, and later by supposing that Thucydides had his dates wrong, he was able to put forward a later date for the invention of triremes, which would have invalidated my own identification of two-level ships as triremes.

The important innovation, though, was that Professor Morrison no longer militated against the opinion generally held outside the trireme controversy, that triremes were invented by Phoenicians in the eighth century. That gives us a common and early starting point from which to begin the search for triremes in iconography, and lengthens the period for which the lack of three-level representations has to be explained.

Next, the Trireme Trust's new design no longer has differently shaped oars at different levels. That nullifies the argument that the Athenian trireme's three types of oar indicated oars at three levels. (Annex 6 gives my views on the three types of oar).

The idea of thirty rooms for the new design is contained in Dr Coates's paper on page 88, though at the conference Dr Coates said that he was not aware of this aspect. I have always maintained that thirty rooms is the right number for a trireme. The *Olympias* had thirty-one. Apart from a small but useful easing of the problem of conforming with the length of the ship-sheds, a thirty-roomed design discards the earlier idea that the numbers and types of oar in the naval lists should dictate the configuration of a trireme reconstruction.

At the conference, Dr Coates said that he had no objection to the idea that the Siren Vase shows a vessel with three oarsmen on each bench, and no one at the conference dissented. This is an important development, as no member of the Trireme Trust has publicly accepted any form of triple-banked ship until now, and some members have published lampoons of the idea. If one took notice of the linguistic evidence in Annex 3 (which the Trireme Trust do not) it would be hard to avoid the conclusion that Athenian triremes originally had three oarsmen in cross-section.

Finally, the idea that ancient oarsmen turned round to face the bow in order to pull their ships astern (Tilley and Fenwick 1973), long resisted by Morrison and Coates, has been publicly accepted by Shaw (1993, 69–70), and privately by Dr Coates on behalf of the Trireme Trust. This will be of some value in the operating of the new design. But its greatest significance is that it upgrades the assessment of at least six ancient representations of ships, from erroneous or whimsical to accurate and knowledgeable. Differing ideas as to the merit of ancient ship representations are perhaps the greatest of the many obstacles to reaching consensus in ancient ships disputes.

Annex 3

Linguistic evidence

The written and linguistic evidence suggests that ancient Greeks and Romans used the same nomenclature as current English, Italian, Greek and other European languages, in that the number in the name of a rowing system or oared ship indicated the number of men in cross-section: to them a bireme meant a double-banked boat, a trireme was originally triple banked and so on.

Everyone agrees that when the Greeks described ships such as pentekontors they counted the oarsmen on both sides, yet advocates of six-banked triremes choose to assume that when they described a ship by its cross-section, they counted the oarsmen on only one side. The discrepancy is generally ignored, and it ought not to be. Linguistic questions such as this have general, not only nautical, implications. Would Dr Coates be able to persuade us to describe a cow as bipedal on the grounds that it has two legs on either side? Who would dare argue that ancient tridents had six prongs or that quadrigas were pulled by eight horses?

Consider single-banked rowing. If the ancient trireme, named after the number three, had six oarsmen in cross-section, then boats with a single line of oarsmen would have been named for the number 'a half' – zero decimal five. But there is no such rowing word in ancient Greek or Latin. The lowest number used to described a rowing

system is 'one': which suggests that the ancients used the same nomenclature as we do. It should be remembered that the Greek language is far older than complicated rowing systems. For many centuries, ancient Greek seamen, like the seamen of my youth, had only to distinguish a system with one man per bench from a system with two. In that simple era, before oars at different levels had been thought of, it is surely very unlikely that they would have called a boat with two men on a bench after the number 'one' on the grounds that they were, like all other oarsmen of the time, all at the same level; nor would they, I assert, have called a boat with a single line of oarsmen a 'halfer', on the grounds that there was half an oarsman on each bench either side. I would be glad to know if there is any modern language that does use the system I disparage.

Advocates of three-level triremes always treat the ancient Greek *dikrotos* as though it meant 'four-banked' or 'two level', which they often confusingly miscall 'double banked'; whereas the modern Greek *diplokopos* means 'double banked'. Similarly, they translate the Latin *ordo* as though it implied a row of oarsmen on each side, whereas the Italian *doppio ordine di reme* refers to double-banked, not four-banked, boats.

A Latin poet, Manilius, wrote about a man swimming:

'nunc alterna ferens in lentos bracchia tractus ... nunc aequore mersas/ diducet palmas furtiva biremis in ipso' (Astronomicon 5.423–6)

which Goold translates:

'Now lifting one arm after the other to make slow sweeps ... now like a hidden bireme he will draw apart his arms beneath the water'.

The first swimming action is the crawl and the second is the breast stroke. Assuming that a Roman of the time had only the two arms considered normal today, the man's arms swimming breast stroke were like the oars of a double-banked boat. They would have given Manilius no impression of a vessel with oars at two levels. At the conference it was pointed out that Manilius was only a minor poet, and that a swimmer has legs as well as arms, but neither observation seems to me to reduce the importance of the quotation as evidence for double-banked (as opposed to two-level) biremes.

The Greek word *dieres*, combining the ideas of 'two' and 'rowing', is absent from literature until the Roman period. If it was applied by the ancient Greeks to two-level ships, the absence is extraordinary, because:

'The development of a ship of *two* [my italics] levels of oarsmen emerges clearly from the ship representations of the period 700–480 BC' (Morrison and Williams 1968, 155).

Modern writers, for example Morrison and Coates (1986, 32) understandably think these ships are remarkable and ancient writers would have thought so too. If on the other hand the word *dieres* meant 'double banked', the commonplace arrangement of a port oarsman and a starboard on every bench, then its absence is not surprising. That simple arrangement would have been assumed unless the ship-type name implied something more complicated. Morrison meets the difficulty with a curt but unenforceable command:

> ' ... it must be assumed that the term pentekontor ... covered the two-level type' (Morrison and Williams 1968, 155)

Consider the number 'three' applied to rowing. There was a small Greek merchant vessel called a *phaselos,* which could be converted in an emergency into an auxiliary warship called a *phaselos trieretikos.* The word *trieretikos,* like the Greek and Latin words for trireme, implies a three-fold rowing system. No one supposes that a *phaselos trieretikos* could have had six banks of oars (Casson 1995, 168). It could well have had three, the conversion consisting of adding a third bank of oars and oarsmen down the middle line of an originally double-banked *phaselos*, as I did with a naval cutter (Tilley 1971).

Now consider 'four'. There was an oared ship named *tetreres* after the number four. It is accepted that the *tetreres* was the first warship to use more than one man to each oar. The new system is likely to have been introduced in its simplest possible form. As Morrison wrote:

> 'The *tetreres* could then have had four men to each 'room' ... rowing two men to each of two oars. (Morrison and Williams 1968, 291).

He meant *eight* men rowing, with two men to each of *four* oars, but that is improbably complicated for a first attempt at a new system. He was, I think, wrong in what he meant but right in what he wrote.

That is confirmed by remarks of Paulinus of Nola, cited by Casson (1995, 148). An ordinary merchant ship, too small to have had eight banks of oarsmen, was referred to as a quadrireme. The oar arrangement I suggest for a 'four', two two-man oars to each bench, would suit a nondescript merchantman very well.

Now consider the number five. Alexander the Great was criticised for ostentation because his barge (*keles*) was rowed in a manner designated by the number five (Ephippos in Athenaeus 8.38, cited by Torr 1894, 109). Nobody believes that it had ten banks of oars. A *keletes* was something less than a ship. It could well have had five.

The idea that the number in the name was the number in cross-section is new only in respect of the lower numbers. Admiral Rodgers, USN considered that the monstrous ship called a forty had forty oarsmen to a 'room', regarding as preposterous the eighty men that the three-level trireme hypothesis requires (Rodgers 1937, 256). Needless to say, I agree.

Annex 4

Pseudo-evidence

Several representations that do not show oars at three levels

have been 'improved', by members of the Trireme Trust, with imaginary additions or distortions and presented as pseudo-evidence in favour of three-level triremes.

The sherd known as the Vienna fragment (see Annex 1) is not very impressive in itself, but it illustrates the use of pseudo-evidence most clearly. The rowing arrangement that the artist has actually shown consists of three semi-circular oar-ports at two levels. Morrison and Coates see it as a representation of a warship with *three* levels of oars, just like the *Olympias*. The *Olympias*'s uppermost row of oars is suggested to them by a line of thole pins which through 'rough drawing' the artist has entirely neglected to depict. They interpret the lower-level oarport as a large, circular, *Olympias*-type oarport, transmuted by the same 'rough drawing' into the equal-sized, semi-circular oarport that we can actually see.

The Dal Pozzo drawing (Morrison, Coates and Rankov 2000, 13, fig. 11) was made in the seventeenth century AD. It shows a ship with oars at two levels. It is used by Morrison and Coates as evidence that triremes had oars at *three* levels, by first imagining that it is a copy made by an ignorant artist of a three-level original and then assuming that the imaginary three-level original was a trireme.

In the well-known Lenormant relief (Morrison and Williams 1968, 170–3, clas. 1 and pls 23a; 24; Morrison, Coates and Rankov 2000, 16, fig. 13), what the sculptor has actually shown is a single row of oars and oarsmen. The other oblique and horizontal lines resemble the side of the sixteenth-century galeasse from the Battle of Lepanto depicted in an engraving of 1573 by Fernando Bertelli in the Museo Storico Navale in Venice (see Gardiner and Morrison 1995, 161, bottom right).

To transform what we actually see into something resembling the *Olympias,* Morrison assumed ancient paint (of which there is now no trace) to run the oblique features across the horizontal ones so that they could be interpreted as a second and third level of oars. The undisputed oars do cross the horizontal wales. The oblique features do not.

Basch rightly pointed out that even with the addition of ancient paint, the oblique features would not form straight lines. He therefore proposed an ancient original of which the Lenormant relief is an inaccurate copy by an ignorant artist. That is just what Morrison and Coates proposed for the Dal Pozzo drawing.

It has been remarked that the oars could not have been parallel to each other at the point in the stroke shown on the Lenormant relief. One is asked to presume that the Lenormant sculptor really saw oars as in Morrison, Coates and Rankov 2000, 281, fig. 83, but carved what he actually did carve 'for the sake of art' (Shaw 1993, 1).

Morrison and Coates observed that there is not enough space between the wales on the actual sculpture for oarports as large as the lowest ones of the *Olympias* (Morrison, Coates and Rankov 200, 280). We are asked to assume, and mentally correct, an error on the part of the sculptor, not in the design of the *Olympias*.

In the new design, the oarsmen are skewed, so that at

the beginning of the stroke each rower's arms, viewed from abeam, will overlap the body of the rower next aft. Even the most imaginative application of supposed ancient paint that has subsequently perished will surely not be able to transform the Lenormant relief into something resembling this new design.

At the conference, Dr Coates perceived a waterline located in such a way as to make the ship on the Lenormant relief unlike Bertelli's Lepanto galeasse. I cannot see a waterline on the Lenormant relief. Perhaps, like the supposed two lower levels of oars, it was depicted in ancient paint of which there is now no trace.

Finally it should be noted that there is no evidence that the Lenormant relief pre-dates polyremes, so that if it *did* have oars at three levels, it could have been a six. Lucien Basch thinks it is Roman.

The Trireme Trust's approach to iconography allows rows of oars to be subtracted as well as added. A sixth-century vase painting (Greenhill and Morrison 1995, fig. 179) shows a ship that appears to have been built for around 100 oars, half of them rowed over the top wale and half through the empty oarports. But that would conflict with the Trireme Trust's doctrine that the two-level ships portrayed in the trireme era must be 13-roomed, 50-oared, two-level pentekontors (despite the fact that no ancient author mentions them). As Morrison sees it:

> 'The oars however have been carelessly shown as coming quite unrealistically over the topwale and leaving the oarports unmanned' (Morrison in Greenhill and Morrison 1995, 148).

Those heroic efforts to make evidence fit theory transform several monuments into ships exactly like the *Olympias*; but in science, theory must be adjusted to suit evidence. If we allow ourselves to argue from supposed ancient paint of which there is now no trace, or from supposed originals of which the actual monuments are supposed to be erroneous copies, then we will be able to find ample evidence for the proposition that ancient pigs had wings.

Annex 5

How did the oars differ?

Athenian inscriptions show that an Athenian trireme had three types of oar, in addition to the spares. In the *Olympias* a different type of oar was supplied for each level, but for the new design it is considered that one type of oar will suit all. Thus the question of how the oars differed remains a minor mystery. Dr Coates has cautiously suggested that the difference in the oars may have been only a question of marking or of wear pattern. Though one of those might be the right explanation, I think there are two scraps of evidence against them: first, an oar put forward as a thranite oar was rejected as such by the dockyard, but accepted as a zygian. This suggests to me that a thranite oar was more valuable than a zygian. Second, it appears (admittedly from evidence of a later date) that thranite

oars alone were balanced with lead in the handles. Those two factors suggest an answer based on twentieth-century Royal Naval practice.

A naval gig was the captain's particular boat, and the crew of the captain's gig were selected oarsmen. Gigs' oars were narrow in the loom (hence light) with broad, spoon-shaped blades and (unlike other naval oars) balanced with lead. A gig's crew needed the skill to feather their oars, or the broad blades would have been a hindrance when going against a strong wind. The oar was made in one piece, so that the broad blade was extravagant in timber as well as in the skill and time required to make one. Officers were taught that the width of blade should be measured to forestall rascally contractors.

A naval whaler was the sea boat used for general purposes and rowed by sailors of the seaman branch. The oars were thicker than a gig's and had narrower blades, not spoon-shaped.

A naval cutter was a bigger boat, often rowed by libertymen not necessarily of the seaman branch and not necessarily quite sober. The oars were thick in the loom and the blades were narrow.

Slim, light oars are essential for a good performance. In naval regattas, the oars were shaved down to the limit allowed by the rules. It may seem slightly contrary to common sense that the best oarsmen, who could be expected to pull the strongest, used the slimmest and hence weakest oars, but it is so. Oars are broken more by some error or clumsiness than by a fair strain. In regattas, oars were often broken and spares (limited by the rules to one or two) were carried. Crews practised the drill whereby the cox tossed a spare oar to an oarsman, over the heads of the others.

If the thranites used oars like a gig's, the zygians like a whaler's and the thalamians like a cutter's, it would suit what evidence we have. The oar he carried would mark a sailor's rank when ashore. Spare oars had to be different enough to thwart would-be tricksters' claims for pay. Only a man with a thranite oar could draw a thranite's extra pay.

Annex 6

A reply to Dr Coates

In an Annex produced for the conference but printed in this volume, Dr Coates began by deftly demolishing a hypothesis which no one has ever advocated – a trireme of 40 rooms. He went on to ask why the 'post-Cimon' triremes I advocate should have been called a *trieres* when they could be rowed with four oarsmen abreast. The answer is that they retained the name because they were built for three oarsmen abreast, and famously fought triple-banked at Salamis, acquiring the capacity for four oarsmen abreast only when Cimon widened the Salamis fleet.

Even then, they were not always rowed with four banks of oarsmen. Some admirals preferred to keep them triple banked, ancient fleets being limited by the number of oarsmen available. In defensive operations, Alcibiades manned about 100 ships, presumably triple banked. When Konon replaced him as admiral at Samos, he adopted an aggressive strategy requiring high-performance ships, presumably four-banked, and so could man only about 70 (Xenophon *Hellenica*, 1.5.19).

Dr Wallinga wrote in his paper for the conference, citing Xenophon *Hellenica* 1.6.19:

> 'To this end Konon chose the two fastest ships – *tas arista pleousas* – in his squadron and took the best rowers from all his ships to man them. Here the term *tas arista pleousas* cannot have what in my view is its usual meaning – that the ships had very large or full crews – because Xenophon gives them this title before they were manned' (see p. 152).

I suggest that *tas arista pleousas* means that the chosen ships were fitted for very large or full crews, confirming my hypothesis that some triremes of the time, having been widened by Cimon, could take four oarsmen on each bench; while other (unmodified) triremes remained suitable only for the three oarsmen per bench that their name implies. At the conference Dr Wallinga opposed this suggestion.

In criticising the characteristics of four-banked ships Dr Coates goes badly astray, asserting:

> 'If the oarcrew were on one level the hull could not be any narrower [than a 170]...'

Since he goes on to discuss performance, I presume he means 'narrower at the water line' rather than narrower overall. But the ship I envisage had an outrigger, and closely resembles the Nike of Samothrace ship. The rowing arrangements relate to the waterline width no more than the width of the flight deck relates to the waterline width of an aircraft carrier. The waterline width of Dr Coates' new design seems from his fig. 10.1 (p. 83) to be a little under 4 metres, while I suppose that of a trireme to have been considerably less.

The new design has one room less than the *Olympias* and (as I have always suggested for triremes) has 30 rooms – a small but not insignificant convergence. Nevertheless, I think most triremes were rather shorter than the 40 metres Dr Coates specifies. As we can see from the Nike of Samothrace ship, the backs of the foremost oarsmen can be nearly level with the stem post.

Some of Dr Coates' criticism I cannot understand: 'If there were two levels with four men to a 'room' ... the hull could be narrower only if the hypozoma were not present, thus ignoring evidence ...' Drawings would perhaps help to clarify this.

In discussing stability, I suspect Dr Coates is harking back to the lampoon he published in *Antiquity* (Coates 1995, 160), ascribing to me the notion of a trireme with 'two superimposed levels of oarsmen'. Otherwise he has no way of knowing the difference in height (which I think could be very slight) between the two levels. In any case, the question of stability is more difficult than he supposes,

and cannot be calculated from the shape of the ship alone. The distribution of weight is an important factor (Gilmer 1975, 68).

The sentence 'This [Tilley's] proposed ship cannot therefore not be expected to be quite as fast in sprint as '170', but slower at lower oar powers' is incomprehensible to me, but perhaps misprinted. In any case it rests on the false assumption that an oarsman in his design would produce as much power as one in mine. But my oarsmen gain the benefit of a sliding seat (Hale 1996), which makes a big difference, while the upper two levels of his oarsmen are not able to row efficiently, even by the standards of fixed-seat rowing, because their oars are at too steep an angle.

The weight of the ship I propose is an important factor in relation to its performance, and the 'calculations' that Dr Coates makes about it are no more than guess-work. Any ship's weight must depend a great deal on how strongly it is built. I agree with Casson (1995, 89) that an Athenian high-performance trireme (there may well have been other kinds) was ' ... like an overgrown racing shell', and ' ... light enough to be drawn up by their crews on the beach at night' and hauled overland more than two miles in a day. By contrast, 'the need to beach to escape bad weather and overnight was <u>not</u> [original underlining] agreed' as a requirement for the *Olympias* (Coates and McGrail 1984, 87), though it is not clear why not.

Finally, I envisage a trireme with the 'rocker or sprung keel shape' advocated by Professor Gillmer (Coates and McGrail 1984, 114–23) and rejected in Dr Coates' *Olympias* and in his new design, which allows a lighter hull for a given strength, as well as conforming with the iconography.

Annex 7

Some comments on Dr Papalas' paper

Dr Papalas considers that the speed of the *Olympias* under oar was:

> ' ... generally in line with fifth century performance capabilities ... ' (see p. 101).

I suggest the opposite. The best speed that the *Olympias* has been able to sustain for not quite five minutes is 7.1 knots (Shaw 1993, 42), appreciably less than the 7.5 knots that ancient triremes kept up for *seventeen hours* to cover 129 miles in a day according to Morrison, Coates and Rankov (2000, 103–4). It seems a vast discrepancy to me. Moreover, when Dr Papalas says that

> ' ... the multi-level oared vessel proved satisfactory in four sea trials ...' (see p. 101)

he does not mention one important finding of the rowing trials:

'The thalamian [lowest] level was not worth its place in the ship' (Coates, Platis and Shaw 1990, 77).

That seems *un*satisfactory to me. It might well have been acceptable in an 18th-century French galley, more valued as a prison hulk than as a warship, but in the Athenian navy a trireme was judged principally by its performance under oars, and the number of oarsmen available limited the size of the fleet.

Dr Papalas considers that the Lenormant relief shows a trireme in realistic detail, but does not tell us why he thinks the ship depicted is a trireme. As he says, Morrison's views on triremes were ' ... considerably influenced by an *interpretation* [my emphasis] of the Lenormant relief ...', the interpretation being very unlike the relief itself. See Annex 4 to this paper. Similarly, a ship depicted on Trajan's column is said by Dr Papalas to be a trireme (pp. 105–6), but he gives no evidence to support his contention.

In criticising my ideas on triremes, Dr Papalas conflates the two different systems of triple-banked rowing that I have put forward (Tilley 1970; 1971; 1976; 1992; 1997; 2004; Tilley and Fenwick 1973): a two-level system, and the system shown on the Siren Vase (Morrison and Williams 1968, 114, arch. 94 and pl. 21e). Then he asserts that 'this ship of 135 feet for a beam of 8 ft could not be housed in the ship-sheds built for the Athenian triremes' (p. 106). I cannot understand the length or the beam he cites. Neither figure has anything to do with me. I have always had in mind a trireme slightly shorter than most reconstructions; one of 30 rooms, as now proposed by the Trireme Trust, as opposed to the 31 rooms of the *Olympias*. Moreover Dr Papalas seems not to perceive any difficulty in fitting the 40-metre length of the Trireme Trust's proposed new trireme into the same ship-sheds.

Dr Papalas (p. 106) asserts that the evidence for a trireme with three tiers of oarsmen is substantial, but does not tell us what it is. He says that 'Tilley ... ignores evidence when it does not support his thesis' but does not say what I have ignored. He thinks that a man pulling a pair of oars each 14 feet long would require 'fantastic strength' but the opinion, true or false, is irrelevant. There is no evidence as to the length of the oars used in two-level ships. He refers to 'Tilley's oarsmen spread across the deck', but I do not envisage any oarsmen at all on deck. He suggests that the oar system shown on the Siren Vase would not work well, seeking to beat down from the armchair conclusions based on trials.

I must agree with him that my trials of the Siren Vase oar system (Tilley 1971) were extremely sketchy, and did not meet scientific standards. The deficiency was the result of lack of time and resources. Neither Dr Papalas' assertion that the system would not work, nor Dr Coates' recently expressed opinion that it would, is of much value. The crying need is for triple-banked rowing to be evaluated thoroughly by trials.

Annex 8
Against waiting for wrecks

It is sometimes suggested that we are all wasting our time discussing ancient warships while there are so few remains, and that no solution to the trireme problem based on ancient written and iconographic evidence (as solutions have to be at present) will ever be agreed upon, and that we should therefore wait until archaeology gives the answer. It is on that basis that editorial policy does not allow the idea that triremes had six oarsmen in cross-section to be questioned in *The International Journal of Nautical Archaeology*. But archaeology will not solve the problem.

Imagine that an ancient Mediterranean warship wreck is found, perfectly preserved, with the remains of three oarsmen on each bench, oars clutched in their skeletal hands, in a rowing arrangement exactly like my decoding of the Siren Vase. Suppose that the wreck's dimensions are exactly those of the Samothrace ship. Will people who at present support three-level triremes concede that it supports the idea of triple-banked triremes? Certainly not. Even those of them who at present believe that the Siren Vase ship was rowed three men to a bench (and they include Casson and Coates, and once included Morrison) do not waver in their faith in three-level triremes. To describe the Siren Vase system they use the word *moneres,* because all the oarsmen are at one level (Casson); or used the word *hemiolia* because on each bench there are one-and-a-half oarsmen each side (Morrison). We might discover that the bottom of the Bay of Salamis was littered with triple-banked warships, without faith in six-banked triremes being in the slightest degreee shaken.

Or imagine (as is slightly less unlikely) the discovery of a Hellenistic or Roman wreck with oars at three levels. The same woolly-mindedness that allows advocates of three-level triremes to use Roman and Hellenistic three-level representations as evidence for three-level triremes, would allow three-level wrecks to be used for the same purpose.

Yet again, postulate the discovery of a wreck with clear evidence of oars at one or two levels, and above that the jumbled remains of upperworks. What could be easier than to postulate a lost line of thole pins to make pseudo-evidence for a three-level trireme? It would be much easier and less unconvincing to add imaginary thole-pins to an actual wreck than to add (as Morrison and Coates do), an imaginary third level to a representation such as the Vienna fragment which clearly never had it.

It seems to me highly desirable to adopt reason and logic in the study of ancient warships, *before* ancient warship wrecks are discovered.

Bibliography

Casson, L. (1995) *Ships and Seamanship in the Ancient World.* Baltimore, Johns Hopkins University Press.

Coates, J. F. (1993) The naval architecture of European oared ships. *Royal Institution of Naval Architects Record of Spring Meeting.* London, Royal Institution of Naval Architects, 1–9.

Coates, J. F. (1995) Tilley's and Morrison's triremes. *Antiquity* 69 (1995), 159–62.

Coates, J. F. and McGrail, S. (eds) (1984) *The Greek trireme of the 5th Century B.C.* Greenwich, Trustees of the National Maritime Museum.

Coates, J. F., Platis, S. K and Shaw, J. T. (ed.) (1990) *The Trireme Trials 1988. Report on the Sea Trials of* Olympias. Oxford, Oxbow Books.

Gardiner, R. and Morrison, J. S. (eds) (1995) *The Age of the Galley. Mediterranean Oared Vessels since Pre-Classical Times.* London, Conway Maritime Press.

Gillmer, T. C. (1975) *Modern Ship Design.* Annapolis, Naval Institute Press.

Gillmer, T. C. (1984) An alternative reconstruction. In Coates and McGrail 1984, 114–23.

Gillmer, T. C. (1985) The Thera ships as sailing vessels. *The Mariner's Mirror* 71.4, 401–16.

Greenhill, B. and Morrison, J. S. (1995) *The Archaeology of Boats and Ships.* London, Conway Maritime Press.

Hale, J. R. (1996) The lost technology of ancient Greek rowing. *Scientific American* (May), 66–71.

Harden, D. (1962) *The Phoenicians.* London, Thames and Hudson.

Höckmann, O. (1993) Late Roman Rhine vessels from Mainz, Germany. *International Journal of Nautical Archaeology* 22, 125–35.

Höckmann, O. (1997) The Liburnian: some observations and insights. *International Journal of Nautical Archaeology* 26, 192–216.

Morrison, J. S. (1941) The Greek trireme. *The Mariner's Mirror* 27, 14–44.

Morrison, J. S. (1979) 'The first triremes', *The Mariner's Mirror* 65, 53–63.

Morrison, J. S. and Coates, J. F. (eds) (1989) *An Athenian Trireme Reconstructed. The British Sea Trials of* Olympias*, 1987.* BAR International Series 486. Oxford, Archaeopress.

Morrison, J. S. and Williams, R. T. (1968) *Greek Oared Ships 900–322 B.C.* Cambridge, Cambridge University Press.

Morrison, J. S., Coates, J. F., and Rankov, N. B. (2000) *The Athenian Trireme. The History and Reconstruction of an Ancient Greek Warship.* 2nd ed. Cambridge, Cambridge University Press.

Roberts, O. (1995) An explanation of ancient windward sailing. *International Journal of Nautical Archaeology* 24, 307–15.

Rodgers, W. L. (1937) *Greek and Roman Naval Warfare.* Annapolis MD, United States Naval Institute.

Shaw, T. (ed.) (1993) *The Trireme Project. Operational Experience 1987–90. Lessons Learnt.* Oxford, Oxbow Books.

Torr, C. (1894) *Ancient Ships.* Cambridge, Cambridge University Press.

Torr, C. (1905) Triremes. *Classical Review* 19, 466.

Tarn, W. W. (1905) The Greek warship. *Journal of Hellenic Studies* 25 (1905), 154–95.

Tarn, W. W. (1906) Thranite, zugite, and thalamite. *Classical Review* 20 (1906), 75–7.

Tilley, A. F. (1970) The ship of Odysseus. *Antiquity* 44, 100–104.

Tilley, A. F. (1971) 'An experiment under oars', *Antiquity* 45, plates 10 and11.

Tilley, A. F. (1976) Rowing the trireme – a practical experiment in seamanship. *The Mariner's Mirror* 62.4, 357–369.

Tilley, A. F. (1992) Three men to a room – a completely different trireme. *Antiquity* 66, 599–61

Tilley, A. F. (1997) Ancient warships – a scientific approach. In Cogar, W.B. (ed.), *New Interpretations in Naval History: selected papers from the Twelfth Naval History Symposium.* Annapolis MD, Naval Institute Press, 1ff.

Tilley, A. F. (2004) *Seafaring in the Ancient Mediterranean. New Thoughts on Triremes and Other Ancient Ships.* BAR International Series 1268. Oxford, Archaeopress.

Tilley, A. F. and Fenwick, V. H. (1973) Rowing in the ancient Mediterranean: a new aspect. *The Mariner's Mirror* 59, 96–9.

Part 4

The Operation and Performance
of Ancient Triremes

17. On Slipping and Launching Triremes from the Piraeus Shipsheds and from Beaches

John Coates

It may safely be assumed that the shipsheds in Zea harbour in the Piraeus were built to house Athenian triremes of the fourth-century BC, a period when it is probable that the design of the trireme had matured and become largely standardised. It may also be assumed that for decades before that time triremes had been beached as a routine for drying out, repair and storage ashore before the Piraeus sheds were built. The sheds would therefore have been built to use much the same procedure as had been established for hauling up on to and launching from beaches. Because some aspects of the sheds are known by excavation, launching and slipping in the Piraeus sheds will be considered in this paper first, before discussing beaching triremes.

The Piraeus shipsheds

In view of the considerable cost of the sheds and slipways (probably more than that of the ships themselves) and the restricted space available in Zea harbour, it seems likely that they were built no larger nor any more elaborately than was necessary for their purpose. Nevertheless, there can be little doubt that the shipsheds were as necessary to sustaining the power of Athens as the ships they housed; they were the essential means not only to keep unsheathed hulls of the warships out of the water as far as possible, in order to keep them clean and free of *teredo* worms, but also to protect the ships from sun and rain to extend their lives. The cost of the sheds must have been considered to be an economic investment. Later in the fourth century some of them housed quadriremes.

Until the recent, ongoing work of the Greek-Danish Zea Harbour Project, our knowledge of these sheds came mainly from the hurried rescue excavation carried out in 1885 by Iakob Dragatsis (Dragatsis 1886) and whose findings were drawn by Dörpfeld. In the short time at their disposal those 19th-century excavators did remarkably well, but there are gaps in their evidence which have raised a number of questions which have remained with us in the absence of excavations of shipsheds in Zea since 1885, although some are now being answered.

In designing *Olympias* to accord with the evidence available at the time of her construction and to be operationally workable, the demands of space for the oarsystem and of waterline breadth for adequate stability afloat called for her overall breadth to be little short of the breadth between the columns of the sheds as revealed by Dragatsis. The recent underwater surveys of some Zea slips have established the total length of at least one slipway to be in excess 50 metres, and it has been suggested that some at least may have been as much 90 m long; in other words, they may have housed two triremes, one behind the other (see now Lovén 2011). This does not alter the considerations and arguments of this paper apart from indicating that triremes could have been longer than *Olympias'* length of 36.8 metres, and perhaps as long as 40 metres or more overall.

Though not without her shortcomings, *Olympias* has proved herself by trial to be as seaworthy as her proportions allow and has given good indications of being very close to the original. Blackman (1987) has already considered some questions about these sheds and slipways: the number of men needed to haul ships up the slips; the friction between keel and groundways and lubrication; coatings for bottom planking; the use of timber on stone slips; the length of the slips and the operations carried out on ships in the sheds. It is therefore appropriate now to consider in more detail how such a ship could have been manipulated in a Zea shed.

The essential operational questions are:

i) As triremes, not having flat bottoms, would have been unstable when supported on their keel out of the water, how were they supported laterally in the sheds?

ii) At what point did triremes become stable as they entered the water from the slip?

iii) How far below the water level must the slips have extended?

iv) How could the ships have been hauled up and down the slips?

The writer has reviewed the hazards of launching ships and some of those affecting triremes in particular (Coates 1993). In this paper, further work by William Penney (1987) as well as by the writer on the mechanics of launching (and equally, of hauling up) *Olympias* on a reconstructed slipway is reported. This work, by hydrostatic and structural calculation with some corroboration by ⅟₂₅th scale model experiments (Annex 1), has first re-examined the lateral support of the ship while being moved on the slip and some details of moving the ship, then the point during launch or hauling up when the bow lifts from the slip, then the point at which the ship is neutrally stable, and finally where the after end of the keel would leave the bottom of the slip as the ship floats free. The hull lines of *Olympias* at displacement stations Nos. 1 to 23 spaced 1.6155 m apart (1 Station is near the tip of the ram) are shown in Fig. 17.1. Her relevant numerical particulars, and those of the shed and slipway are given in Annex 2.

Lateral support in the shed

To keep the ship upright when out of the water, the hull shape of a trireme makes some form of lateral support essential. It could be provided by a sliding cradle (or two cradles) under the hull, or by sliding supports on each side, or by the pillars of the shed. In launching, support is needed until enough of the ship is in the water to give her at least neutral stability. The support must also allow the ship to hinge about the after end of the flat keel (called the after cut-up, or ACU) as the bow lifts; it must therefore extend aft as far as the position of the ACU at the point of travel at which the ship has neutral stability.

The length of a trireme would call for a cradle (or the extent of two cradles) to be at least 15m long to provide sufficient vertical support longitudinally. There is no mention of such things in the literature which, if they existed, is strange because they would have been large and important. While it is possible that triremes were floated onto and off wheeled trolleys functioning like cradles at each end of the Corinth *diolkos*, the extra height and length of underwater slip needed, the depth of water and the rocky bottom of the Piraeus harbours make the use of such vehicles there most improbable, and handling a cradle, even if contrived to float at a suitable waterline, under a hull while afloat would be a cumbersome manoeuvre to manage for a ship as long as a trireme. A cradle would have to have timbers passing under the keel, raising the necessary height of the roof of the shed. It would also add substantially to the mass to be hauled up and down the slip. Support of *triereis* by cradles is not therefore an attractive hypothesis even though it is the normal method employed today with generally shorter ships on slips usually in the open.

The writer previously advocated the use of sliding supports on each side of the ship, placed at the ACU. These could have slid on timber rails set near the edges of the masonry slips; they would have to be rigged soon after the ship made contact with the slip. However, the complexity of handling such supports, ensuring their safety, and the need for two additional timber groundways for them to slide on, as well as their interference with the wooden decking which must have existed between the stone slips, have persuaded the writer to think that the ships were supported laterally more simply (and cheaply) by the stone pillars of the sheds themselves, which can be calculated to be capable of safely withstanding the forces required, provided that the clearance with the ship is not too great. Stone pillars of the dimensions given by Dragatsis with lateral connection at the roof which they support can each withstand horizontal forces at the level of the main rail of *Olympias* up to safe lower limits of 1 tonne in the case of the roof ridge pillars 8.3 m high, and of 0.67 tonne in the case of the shorter roof valley pillars 5.5 m high. These limits neglect the stabilising effect of any thrust in them from the weight of roof bearing upon them (being a timber structure, the roof could bear unequally upon its supporting pillars, particularly the ridge pillars). These limiting loads are those needed to cause uncemented joints between drums nearest to the ship's rail to open and form a hinge in the pillar. The lateral force required from the roof structure is in both cases only 0.2 tonne. Friction between pillar drums would be sufficient to prevent sliding except possibly in the case of any short, and so light, drums under the capital which may have to be pinned to ensure against sliding under the lateral roof force.

The total lateral force needed by *Olympias* when her keel is assumed to be on a notional knife-edge on the slip at the middle line varies with the clearance between her outrigger rail and the pillars. If that were 10 cm, a quite practicable clearance, the total force would be 0.7 tonne, a force which the eight tall pillars or the 12 short pillars next to the parallel length of the outrigger could most safely provide, even if owing to lack of alignment or ship deformation only a few of them are actually in contact with the ship. That lateral support was indeed provided by the pillars of the sheds is suggested by the relative constancy of the breadth between the columns of the sheds excavated by Dragatsis. That breadth varied from 6.47 m to 6.54 m, a range of only 7 cm, whereas the breadths of the stone slips varied one-and-a-half times as much. It may also be significant that the lateral strength of the ridge pillars, spaced further apart than the valley pillars, is the same per unit-length of slip as that of the valley pillars; they were equally capable of supporting the ships whichever way they leaned as they moved up or down the slips.

The outrigger rail would probably have rubbed on softwood pads set into the pillars rather than on the stone of the pillars themselves. As it would have been the breadth over the outrigger rails which would have had to have been a standard dimension to allow pillars to support the ships when being moved on the slips, likely variations in breadth of the hulls proper could have easily been compensated for when setting the overhangs of outriggers so that the overall breadth conformed to a standard specified dimension so that the required clearance with the shed

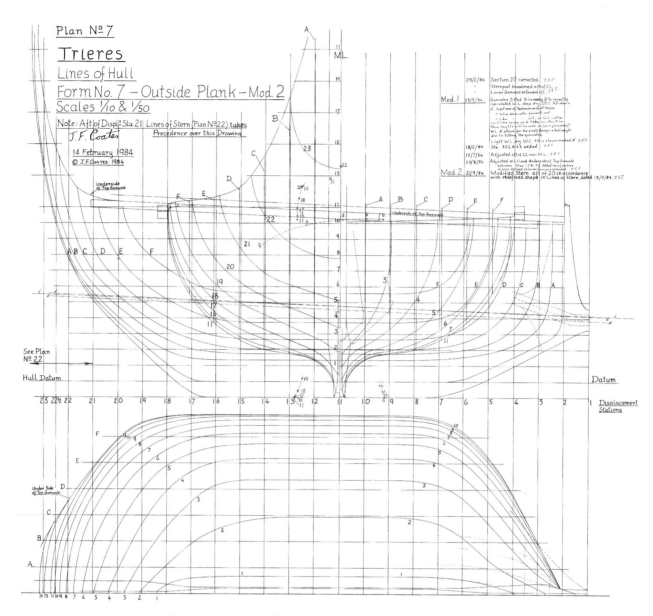

Figure 17.1. Lines of hull of Olympias *(Drawing: John Coates).*

pillars was obtained with an acceptable accuracy. In the case of *Olympias* the pads on the pillars should protrude from the stone by about 25 cm, but less for any second, refined reconstruction of a trireme.

Support by pillars would give a clear space at slip level between ship and pillars for men heaving on ropes to haul the ship up the slip; they would certainly need that space to be unobstructed. Lastly, when the ship was secured in the housed position, she could be wedged upright on shores, leaving the whole of the bottom clear for access for repairs, tightening tenon pegs, scraping, rubbing down, caulking and recoating, all of which operations would have been important for her good future performance. All things considered, and given the known existence and details of the stone pillars, their use to support the ship when being launched or slipped seems simplest and most likely.

Moving the ship on the slip

As already proposed by the writer (Coates 1993; 1997), a coefficient of friction of about 0.2, both static and dynamic, may be assumed to have been reliably attainable; lower values may be attainable in favourable circumstances but could not be relied upon in day-to-day practice. The hauling teams on each side of the ship, 70 men in each, pulling on each side of a rope in pairs could provide the required pull of 7.5 tonnes in heaves to haul the ship up the slip. Secure footholds would have been essential and this demands with some certainty that the 2.5 m wide rocky-bottomed spaces between the masonry slips were boarded over firmly and provided with cross battens to make footholds. If unobstructed there would be just enough space for such teams to work. They would mostly stay in the same place as the ship is hauled up the slip, each man at his foothold, coming forward on the rope after each heave. The hauling force would be about 4 to 5 tonnes to start the ship up the slip (see below) and until, at the point called bow lift when launching, the flat keel settles on the slip. During further travel up the slip the hauling force will rise to 7.5 tonnes when the hull is clear of the water and the whole mass of the ship is supported on the groundway. At the housed position the hauling force needed would be increased, owing to the unavoidable obliquity of the pull to the leading blocks (see below), by 12% to 8.4 tonnes, or 60 kg f. per man.

The force needed to move the ship down the slip with the same coefficient of friction would be only 2.5 tonnes, which could be provided by 50 men pulling on ropes secured to some convenient points near the stern. A small party on a check rope round a bollard at the head of the slip to control any motion between heaves would be needed in both cases, but particularly during the later stages of launching when the force needed to move the ship will become small.

Bow lift

In considering launching (or, in reverse, hauling up), the longitudinal equilibrium of the ship as she enters (or leaves) the water is determined by her mass, position of her longitudinal centre of gravity, her buoyancy, the longitudinal position of the centre of buoyancy, and the longitudinal position of the ACU. In *Olympias* the bow starts to lift to the increasing buoyancy, hinging at the ACU, (16 Station, Annex 2); the hinge point moves aft a little as she rolls on the upcurving after keel. The bow will lift off the groundway when the moment of the ship's mass about 16 Station is equalled by the moment of the buoyancy about the same point. William Penney (1987) has shown that equality between them occurs when ACU at 16 Station is 6.5 m from the point where the groundway's sliding surface enters the water (GEW). In the $\frac{1}{25}$ scale model bow lift occurred at the same point, in scale; its position will of course be sensitive to the actual mass of the ship when launched.

The upthrust acting at the hinge point when the bow lifts will be about 15 tonnes, a concentrated force which could cause lubrication to break down and the ship to stick on the ways. Lubrication in that region of the groundway is therefore particularly important and it may be advisable for the groundway to be of softwood to spread the length crushed and so reduce the pressure on the lubricant to a value under which it will remain effective. The well-rounded curve of the keel at the ACU is helpful for that purpose. Greasing that part of the groundway before a launch would be possible because it lies under the ram when the ship is in the housed position. The lower 11 m of the groundway need to be able to withstand the load which diminishes to something less than 10 tonnes at the bottom end of the groundway.

At bow lift the sagging bending moment on the hull is at its maximum during launch. Owing to the ACU being so far from the stern, this bending moment is fortunately only about 22 tonne m, whereas if the ACU were further aft it would be greater. This is a point of importance from the point of view of the working of the hull in service owing to unavoidable, if small, looseness of plank tenons in their mortices, allowing hull planks to slide upon each other and so inducing onset of leakage. For most of the time afloat, the hull will experience hogging bending so any significant reversal of bending, by sagging, would tend to induce plank sliding and hence leakage.

As the bow lifts it will be less constrained by the groundway, so the bow of the ship may have to be prevented from being blown sideways should a side wind be blowing. In such winds, it would for that reason be prudent to keep the ship's travel under firm control.

The point of neutral stability

The ship will continue to need lateral support as she travels down the slip until she has acquired neutral stability at least. If she is supported by pillars, these must extend far enough to support the after end of the outriggers, or some extensions if necessary, until she can stand up by herself. Like the point of bowlift, the point of neutral stability will move on the slip with the height of the mean water level and also with the tide. The mean water level at Piraeus in the fourth-century BC is not known but now appears to have been *c.* 2 m below the level in AD 1885. The tidal range is now between 10 and 28 cm. Hydrostatic calculation gives the ship neutral stability when supported at the ACU when the draft at ACU is 0.48 m, while the model indicated that point to be when the draft is 0.57 m. The upthrust on ACU is about 10.5 tonnes. The point of neutral stability naturally varies according to where the ground support is applied to the ship, and experiments with the model show how it moves along the rising after keel as the depth of immersion of the pivoting point varies. The results from the model have been converted into metres in the ship.

The positions of the ship along the slip at those drafts naturally depend upon the slope of the slip underwater. If the slope were to continue underwater at, say, 1 in 10, those positions would be 4.8 and 5.7 m from where the groundway entered the water (GEW), but if the slope were to increase below water the sloping after keel might cause the ship never to touch any underwater part of the slipway. No underwater slip would then be necessary.

Bringing a *trieres* in to the slip

We have thus far discussed and arrived at some critical features of the shed and slip needed for launching and hauling a trireme up the slip which conform to the available archaeological evidence. There is also the need to be able, as a practised routine, to bring the ship afloat stern first to the slip before hauling her up the slip. Harry Tzalas (1993) has usefully considered the important matter of manoeuvring triremes in Zea harbour and how they may have been lined up to enter sheds. Ships would then have to be guided more exactly on to the groundways. One has to allow for side winds blowing the ship off-centre to some extent and it must be expected that there were guides in some form to funnel the stern, as hauling began, on to the centreline of the slip and so on to the groundway.

Once again it is found that the shape of the stern of a trireme helps the alignment to occur. As soon as the ship has been hauled, floating, far enough for the after end of the outrigger, which is strongly supported by the *threnos* beam across the hull, to be past the first pillar of the shed, the ship can be allowed to rub if necessary against the pillar to bring the ship nearer the centreline of the slip as she is pulled aft. The next guide could be at the end of the groundway in the form of stout timbers sloping up from each side of the groundway at about 30° to a height of 0.5 m (or 1 cubit) above the stone slip. These would catch the sloping keel of the ship, which would be constrained as the ship is hauled in to slide down whichever timber it was rubbing upon towards the middle until the keel landed on the groundway itself, 0.23 m below the water (when at its assumed mean level). At that point the stern would be held by mooring lines, possibly secured to some pillars or bollards, and some bow lines would be rigged and heaved upon as necessary to align the ship more accurately for hauling up the slip.

To prepare for hauling, two 40 mm diameter ropes each two ship-lengths long with bights at one end could be looped over the ram and led back up the slip on each side through leading blocks. It is proposed that hauling ropes are secured to the ram so that it should be near hauling height and be attached to the ship as far forward as possible to reduce its obliquity near the end of the haul up the slip. The hauling ropes could have been discarded *hypozomata*; the diameter of 40 mm is more than is necessary as regards strength but it would give a good hand-grip for the haulers.

The roof

The roof structure (Coulton 1977, 154–7) would probably have consisted of timber rafters laid on and secured to timber ridge beams spanning the ridge pillars and to stone architraves spanning the valley pillars. The weight of such stone architraves would significantly increase the strength of the valley pillars to resist forces needed to support ships on the slips laterally. Rafters would probably have coincided with each valley pillar and tile battens would have spanned the spaces between rafters. The rafters at mid-span must be more than 6.40 m above the sliding surface of the groundway to allow the tip of the *aphlaston* to pass under them safely. The area of roof over two slips with a common valley would have been about 570 m² , so in heavy rain, falling for example at 30

mm per hour, the flow to be cleared by the valley gutter would have been considerable, about 0.3 m³/minute; there would have to be a generous gutter (lead-lined?) on top of the architrave to avoid overflowing into the shed near the seaward end. In heavy rain, heavy falls of rainwater would have spouted from these gutters into the harbour. The design of the roof does not however bear on the main subject of this paper.

What size of trireme?

So far what has been considered has been launching and hauling out *Olympias*. However, as has been made well-known from the results of the lengthy sea trials of that ship, it has been found beyond reasonable doubt that *triereis* were built to a longer cubit than the so-called Attic cubit of 0.444 m to which *Olympias* was built; they were much more likely to have been built to the cubit of 0.490 m (see Coates, pp. 82–91 above) and so triremes would probably have been about 40 m long overall, 3 m longer than *Olympias*. It would therefore be natural to ask whether the shed and slipway discussed above could accommodate a 40 m ship. Breadth, height, shape of stern and length would be so little different from *Olympias* as to need no changes to the shed or the slip.

Conclusions on the Piraeus shipsheds

This discussion about working the Piraeus sheds and slipways to house triremes leads to the following particulars for a practicable shipshed which would be consistent with the findings of Dragatsis and Dörpfeld, and of the Greek-Danish Zea Harbour Project:

i)   the bottom end of the groundway should have vee-timbers to guide the rising after keel on to the centre of the groundway;

ii) the bottom 12 m of the groundway should be capable of carrying a concentrated load of 15 tonnes at the top of that length, diminishing to 10 tonnes at the end of the groundway;

iii) the space on either side of the stone slip would have to be boarded over and firmly secured to transmit a hauling force of 4 tonnes on each side, and have cross-battens to provide firm footholds for hauling teams of 35 pairs of men;

iv) hauling ropes could be discarded *hypozomata*;

v)   pillars should have greased softwood rubbing blocks set into them at the height of the main outrigger rails of the trireme, and equidistant horizontally from the middle line of the groundway 0.10 m more than half the overall breadth of the ship, the blocks on the two seaward-end pillars being rounded to receive the stern-end of the rails and to extend over the range of their heights when the ship is afloat at all states of the tide;

vi) the underside of the roof structure at the middle line of the groundway throughout its length must be clear of the *aphlaston* of the ship.

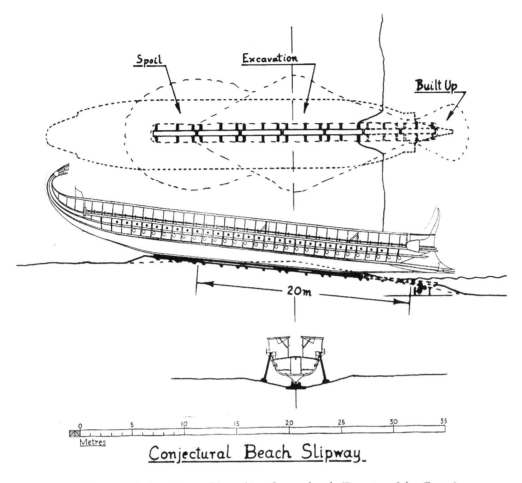

Figure 17.2. Slipping and launching from a beach (Drawing: John Coates).

Beaching

The writer has previously discussed problems raised by hauling a trireme up a Mediterranean beach (Coates 1993; also, with Timothy Shaw, in Coates and Shaw 1993). As the force needed to pull a heavy mass up a slope on greased timber is so much less than that needed to do it directly on pebbles, it must be virtually certain that a ship would have been hauled up a beach on greased timbers, just as in the ship sheds. On a beach there is an additional reason for reducing the hauling force required as far as possible, namely the less secure footholds provided by pebbles instead of purpose-made timber footholds proposed in the shed. The figures for coefficients of friction between timber and greased timber (0.2) and between timber on stone (0.4 to 0.5, *i.e.* more than double) are so compelling that the supposition that some form of timber ways were used on beaches even though no such items are recognisably included in the naval inventories.

Also, to keep the hauling force within practically achievable limits, it is not likely that ships were hauled up slopes of more than 1 in 10. However, Mediterranean beaches are, and presumably have been for some time, steeper than that, typically more like 1 in 5 (Fig. 17.2).

They are commonly storm banks of pebbles thrown as high as they can be in extreme weather and below water there is often a plateau 1.5 to 2 m deep, being the limit of the reach of more common wave action. The 1 in 5 slope is not often long enough to support the length of a trireme, so it would have been necessary to excavate a slipway to reduce the slope and increase the length of support. A slope of 1 in 10 could alternatively have been obtained by hauling out at an acute angle to the shoreline, but that course would have generated more problems than it solved. Each ship would need a greater length of beach, not always available, be exposed to wave damage (as indeed Julius Caesar's triremes were in Kent in 55 BC), and a beached fleet would need a longer defensive perimeter.

Beaching triremes must, by these arguments, have been appreciably larger operations than beaching smaller types of warships and merchant ships: this point has not however come down to us in the literature (but as always, absence of evidence is not proof of absence). It must surely be the case that while beaching warships smaller (particularly if shorter) than triremes could have been practicable fairly frequently, and even overnight, it is hard to see that triremes would have been beached except from necessity.

That would have been an operational and material penalty bearing upon the very decision to develop the larger and more powerful type in view of the increased risks and costs involved.

It would, it is proposed, be possible, having formed a slipway as indicated in Fig. 17.2, to make a groundway of poles acting as sleepers on the pebbles across the slipway, with portable lengths of greased planks laid over them to form a groundway for the keel. Some form of bolsters would also be needed to provide a guide for the keel. As previously considered by the writer, triremes would have been both launched and hauled out upright, supported laterally by portable shores (the *parastatai*) during the process (Coates 1993). This hypothesis was supported by the experiment with the model (Annex 1) adapted to simulate launching from a beach. With the keel at a slope of 1 in 10, bow down and the hull resting on one bilge at an angle of 30° heel, the model showed that as the water level in the trough was raised, to simulate launching a ship leaning on one bilge, the water on the downside of the ship rose almost to the topwale of the hull before the ship righted herself shortly before becoming stable upright and then floating off the beach. Launching (or equally, hauling out) on one bilge would therefore result in flooding the ship through both thalamian oarports, whose *askomata* would certainly not reliably withstand the water pressure imposed, and zygian oarports, unless the ship was equipped with well-fitting blanks to plug the oarports. About 15 to 20 oarports would have had to be so equipped if triremes were beached when leaning on one bilge. There is no mention of such items in the inventories, but it could be that, because they must be a good fit in each port, they were singular to each one and therefore numbered and kept in the ship at all times, not in the main storehouse, and therefore do not appear in the naval lists. This method calls for a second groundway for the bilge to slide on and a stout bilge rubbing strake to be incorporated into the planking of the ship. The weight of the ship would be about equally shared between keel and bilge and it would be desirable, if not essential, for the hull to have a good length of parallel middle body to spread the load on the bilge as far as practicable fore and aft.

Alternatively, to keep the ship upright while being moved up or down groundways on a beach as suggested in Fig. 17.2, the technique of 'walking shores' would have had to be used, by which the heel of one of each pair of shores would be brought forward between each heave on the hauling ropes to be in a position to support the ship during and after the next heave. During that heave, the shore just brought forward would take the load while the other shore of the pair would trail on the ground if, as is likely, its head is secured to a suitably strong point in the hull, freeing it to be brought forward in its turn. The naval lists (*IG* 2² 1611.38) indicate that two *parastatai* were carried in each ship, and if that indication is correct the practice must have been to keep the ship leaning over

to one side sufficiently far to make sure that she would never fall over on to the other bilge, which would be very damaging. On the other hand, if that angle were excessive, so would be the thrust in the walking shores (*e.g.* if the ship were to lean over by 10° the required thrust in the supporting shore would be 3 tonnes); perhaps some auxiliary shores (not mentioned in the naval lists) were also manned and kept in place on the other side of the ship as a precaution to prevent such a disaster to the beaching operation. Walking shores call for skill and co-ordination in their safe use.

As the stern is pulled out of the water, the ship will quickly become unstable upright, as already described in connection with the shipsheds, and the ship must either be kept upright or allowed to lean over on to one bilge. Both procedures have their difficulties and dangers. Hauling ropes could have been rigged as proposed for the sheds, but probably without the benefit of leading blocks. The spare *hypozomata* carried in triremes could have been used for hauling out on to a beach when that became necessary.

As one of the main objects of hauling out would have been to dry out the hull, tighten tenon pegs, clean, stop and re-coat the bottom, the whole bottom would have had to be made accessible on both sides of the ship, only possible if the ship was upright. The crew of a trireme could however raise the unloaded ship upright if she had been hauled out on one bilge by the combination of their weight pulling down on the high side and a smaller number lifting and then pushing up on the low side. When upright, shores would have been set up (Homer *Odyssey* 2.153 describes an earlier and smaller type of ship supported, when ashore in a trench, by piles of stones confirming also that their bottoms were not then flat).

It is clear from these considerations taken together that beaching a trireme is no light operation and that it is unlikely that triremes were any heavier than *Olympias*.

Acknowledgements

The writer is indebted to William Penney for permission to make use of his unpublished launching calculations, to David Blackman for his great knowledge of ancient Mediterranean shipsheds, and to Norman Gundry for permission to use his ship model for the experiments described in Annex 1.

Annex 1

Experiments with ⅟₂₅th scale model of Olympias

The object was to find:

i) the immersions of points of support from the ground, bearing on various positions on the after keel, at which the ship was neutrally stable;
ii) the height above water of the ACU when the bow lifts from a 1 in 10 slipway;
iii) the upthrusts at the ACU at various points of travel while pivoting about ACU.

The model, made in 1983 to demonstrate the appearance of the reconstructed trireme, was shaped to an earlier proposed hull form of which that of *Olympias* is a not very different development, except that the keel in *Olympias* is deeper by 0.2 metre (8 mm in the model). Its main dimensions and displacement volume are close to those of *Olympias* on ⅟₂₅th scale. It was therefore thought that some hydrostatic experiments could provide some useful indications about some critical stages of launching and slipping *Olympias* to corroborate William Penney's calculations and also to explore conditions for neutral stability.

The experiments were made by a rig where the model was in a trough containing adjustable levels of water and a pivot point (attached to a brick on the bottom of the trough) to engage with the keel as desired. The model was heavier than its scaled displacement, so, by means of a calculated weight and a lever, a constant upward force was applied to the model at a calculated point, to make the effective mass and effective position of the model's centre of gravity correct to the scale of the model. The displacement was also corrected to allow for the use of fresh water in the trough for floating the model. The upthrusts at ACU were measured by applying an vertical upward force above the ACU by means of weights in a balance set on a stool over the trough. To obtain approximate measures of the thrust of the ship on pillars, vertical battens were placed on either side of the model in the plane of the pivot and the correct distance apart to simulate pillars with rubbing pads. Measurements of the model's draft were taken fore and aft.

To simulate the ship's travel down the slip without moving the ship, the model was placed with its ACU (16 Station) on the pivot and its forward keel supported at the slope of the slip. Water was added to the trough in stages and the height of waterline relative to pivot, drafts, upthrust at ACU, and weight on one outrigger needed to cause the model to roll from one 'pillar' to the other, measured at each stage.

The model bow lifted at the same travel as calculated, after allowing for the shallower keel of the model. The measured upthrusts at ACU were about 8% higher than calculated (at bow lift only) but followed a reasonable curve to zero at the point where the model floated free. Measurements of force on pillars were more difficult because as it diminished to zero as the ship moved to the upright position, the starting value was not easy to identify; readings were plainly too low, but though the measurements are unreliable, the manner of variation with travel is clear.

To find where ship stability becomes neutral as the position of support from the groundway is moved along the after keel and the immersion of the support to give neutral stability, the pivot was moved under the ship, its longitudinal position noted, and then the water level adjusted until the model appeared neutrally stable when upright. The points and their immersions are laborious to calculate with any accuracy so the model determination is useful; immersion of ACU at neutral stability was calculated to be 0.48 m while the model indicated (full scale equivalent) 0.57 m. These points are critical to the position of the ship where support from the seaward-end pillars becomes necessary.

Annex 2

Some particulars of Olympias

Length overall: 36.8 m.

Breadth overall: 5.45 m.

Height overall (from underside of keel to top of *aphlaston*): 6.40 m.

Height of outrigger rail above keel: 2.43 m.

Displacement stations nos 1 to 23: spaced 1.6155 m apart (1 Station is near tip of ram).

At launching and slipping:

> mass, W: 25.0 tonnes.
> mean draft: 0.89 m.
> draft at 16 Station: 0.95 m.
> longitudinal centre of gravity aft of 11 Station: 1.87 m.
> vertical centre of gravity above underside of keel, KG: 1.58 m.

After cut up (ACU) is at 16 Station.

Hull lines of ship, with displacement stations: Fig. 17.1.

Bibliography

Coates, J. F. (1993) Long ships, slipways and beaches. *Tropis V*, 103–18.

Coates, J. F. (1997) Some comments on the article on shipworm in (and beaching of) ancient Mediterranean warships in *IJNA* 25. *International Journal of Nautical Archaeology* 26, 82–83.

Coates, J. F. and Shaw, J. T. (1993) Hauling a trireme up a slipway and up a beach. In Shaw 1993, 87–90.

Coulton, J. J. (1977) *Greek Architects at Work; Problems of Structure and Design*. Oxford, London, Elek.

Blackman, D. J. (1987) Triremes and shipsheds. *Tropis II*, 35–52.

Dragatsis, I. Ch. (1886) Report of the excavations in Piraeus. *Praktika tes en Athenais Arkhaiologikes Etairias tou etous 1885*, 63–8.

Lovén, B. (2011) *The Ancient Harbours of the Piraeus. Volume I.1 – The Zea Shipsheds and Slipways: Archaeology and Topography*. Athens, Danish Institute at Athens.

Penney, P. W. (1987) Greek *trieres* – launching calculations. Unpublished.

Shaw, J. T. (1993) *The Trireme Project. Operational Experience 1987–90. Lessons Learnt*. Oxford, Oxbow.

Tzalas, H. E. (1993) Were the "pyramidal stone weights" of Zea used as anchors? *Tropis V*, 429–454.

18. *Olympias* Under Sail, and other Performance Matters: a practical seaman's perspective

Douglas Lindsay

While acting as Sailing Master on *Olympias* in 1992, '93 and '94, I studied the question of "motor sailing" closely, comparing the results on *Olympias* with a great deal of experience of operating large sailing ships under sail and engine. As a matter of semantics I prefer the term "combined sailing" for what is done on *Olympias,* as "motor sailing" implies a level of relentless mechanical impetus which cannot be achieved by human power. Of most significance to this topic, and the allied one of rowing crew endurance, was the six-day sea voyage undertaken during the '92 trials (see pp. 14–15).

There are two preliminary observations: the first, that *Olympias* has proved to be an excellent sailing boat, fast and responsive but well-mannered and directionally stable. While one might reasonably expect a long thin hull with relatively small wetted surface area to be so, *Olympias* exceeded my expectations. And the second, that the ship proved, within limitations, to be tough and seaworthy and capable of living in a seaway without visible distress.

Combined sailing

Timothy Shaw has given a great deal of closely studied detail about the technicalities of combined sailing (pp. 68–75) and there is no point in re-treading his ground. As a generalisation my conclusion is that there is a limited speed range over which using oars and sails together can bring the benefit of higher sustained speeds. Equally, the conclusions differ with whether the ship is close-hauled or running before the wind, as the mechanics of the action of wind over the sails differ. The basic principle is that sails work as aerofoil sections, attempting to move into the partial vacuum created by their shape and hence pulling the vessel they are attached to with them.

When running before the wind, the sails act as a barrier impeding the free flow of the wind, creating a partial vacuum all over their forward (lee) sides as described above. It follows that in light breezes even minimum oar speed will outpace the wind and cause the sails to hang slack, contributing nothing. My estimate of this minimum is about three knots. And above a certain speed the contribution of the oars fades away rapidly, the oarsmen having to work excessively hard just to keep up with the vessel's wind-driven speed through the water. They will tire rapidly for minimal contribution, and above perhaps nine knots or so it will become actively dangerous to use oars. When under oars alone the vessel's speed fluctuates with each stroke, and is geared to the drive from the oars. Under sail (assuming constant wind) the vessel is driven relentlessly through the water. At the catch, oarsmen will find their oar blades 'snatched' by the water rushing past the hull, with all the pressure on the front side of the oarblade, and my guess is that they would find their looms driven into their bodies before they can react to the pressure on their oars. While it would be interesting to experiment to establish just where that upper safety limit lies, we had better have ambulances standing by when we do it. My own estimate is that seven knots or so represents the upper limit of comfortably safe and useful combined sailing.

Due to a certain nervousness *Olympias* has only briefly been tested close-hauled, an omission which it is hoped will be rectified if and when a Mark II trireme becomes available. But working from general principles and accepting the limitations, discussed by Shaw (pp. 68–75), of heel on use of oars and the dangers of putting thalamian oarports under, a few conclusions can be drawn. The benefits of applying extra power to a vessel when close-hauled come from the extra acceleration of the wind-flow across the fore face of its sail(s). This produces increased lift on the leeward side of the aerofoil section to produce two effects: one, it allows a sail to point closer to the wind (typically, an extra point is gained and nothing has been observed to suggest *Olympias* would be different), and two, it provides a modicum of greater speed through the water. The combined effects reduce leeway and give a significantly better course-made-good.

In the case of *Olympias,* the benefits of "combined sailing" close-hauled could be gained from perhaps one knot of boat speed upwards, the impetus of the oars causing wind to flow across the face of the sails allowing them to draw and contribute back to the vessel's overall drive. Thereafter the benefits are the classic ones, enabling the boat to weather points not layable under sail alone and to make good passages which – at the least – would have taken longer under either propulsive system on its own. The upper limits of benefit are set by the vessel's heel, a subject Shaw has devoted some consideration to. In practice five knots will be the absolute maximum before heel renders the oars impotent, watertight integrity is threatened by approaching submergence of the thalamian oarports, and rising seas make the operation of oars too difficult to persist with.

In 1992 a brief close-hauled sail took place. With wind on the starboard bow blowing between 10 and 15 knots, the boat (that is, the fore-sail) was set and, with three banks of oars pulling a speed of 3.8 knots was achieved, compared with 2.8 knots on easy pressure before setting the sail. With main sail set as well heel increased to 4° and rowing became very difficult on the leeward, or lower, side so it was stopped. After persuading the main sail to fill properly by rigging a bowline, a gust up to about 20 knots caused *Olympias* to surge up to 4.6 knots boat speed, and to heel to about 7°. At this the thalamian oarports were still clear of the water but it was felt prudent to take in the sails and progress resumed under oars only. During this brief period the ship laid about 60° to the wind and made perhaps 15° of leeway.

One therefore has to conclude that "combined sailing" could be a very useful close-hauled operation in light winds, but that any form of progress to windward would become impossible at altogether lower speeds than would be the case with a fully watertight hull driven by wind alone. The accounts from the ancients seem to suggest that only occasionally were attempts made to force a passage to windward; in adverse weather the vessels were hauled up on the beach and everyone waited patiently until conditions were more favourable.

A minor point to consider is that the ability of a square-rigged vessel to point to windward is not limited by its yards *per se*, but by how far round they can be braced. In modern-era square-riggers, designed above all to go down-wind, rotation of the yards has been severely restricted by the plethora of shrouds and fittings needed to keep the masts up. The evidence from ancient Greek times seems to indicate that the masts and yards of triremes were light, unstayed things; the heavy spars and shrouds of *Olympias* were not the original design, but added during construction to allay modern nervousness. It is to be hoped that in a Mark II trireme we would have the courage of our convictions to build the spars light and stayless; this way the yards might be braced right round through 90° and the Mark II trireme would point as close to the wind as any modern yacht.

Olympias as a sailing craft

There has been some discussion about the sailing abilities of triremes. Observation on *Olympias* suggests that the design lends itself to sailing very well. On the last day of the voyage in 1992, sailing downwind from Salamina towards our base at Poros, *Olympias* surged up to 10.8 knots with the wind 25 knots fine on the port quarter and both sails drawing well. This was by no means the vessel's maximum possible speed and it would certainly be capable of around 12 knots, which corresponds with $\sqrt{L}$, but I had a feeling that the ship might do more than that (the maximum hull speed of any displacement craft is derived by the formula: square root of the wetted length; this, however is subject to some extending on extreme craft and it may be argued that *Olympias* with its exceptional length/breadth ratio and small wetted surface area, has the capacity to exceed the formula). Running before the wind in the Saronic Gulf, with short choppy seas, *Olympias* was entirely comfortable and my own speculation is that short seas will not trouble it; long oceanic sea or swell would be quite a different matter.

Equally, the vessel ghosts very well – perhaps a less important attribute with banks of oars available but the lightest puff of wind would see the vessel slip through the water at a knot or two. Under sail, the ship remains stable directionally and even at maximum speeds has no steering vices when running free. Brief experience close-hauled produced extreme weather helm and the ship was almost unmanageable. It is almost certain that this could be countered by brailing up the lee side of the mainsail, but unfortunately it has never been possible to sail the boat close-hauled for long enough to test this. This problem was anticipated by Owain Roberts (1993) when he first designed and described the rig, and his preferred control method of tightening the central brails remains an interesting hypothesis to be tested when a trireme can be sailed close-hauled.

During trials in 1992 we deliberately tried *Olympias* under boat sail only, to test the view that this was all that was carried into battle as a means of escape if the oar crew were incapacitated. Running free before 12 knots of wind, *Olympias* managed 3.4 knots and sailed perfectly well. Close-hauled would have been much more problematic, however, and to escape by boat sail alone would require a safe haven to leeward of the battlefield.

Seakeeping qualities

Always allowing for the limitations imposed by oars, *Olympias* proved to be a good sea boat. On several occasions during the 1992 voyage she was caught out in rough weather, and had little difficulty with it. As might be expected from a long thin hull the vessel rolled heavily when across any significant sea or swell, and this of course made rowing very difficult to impossible. But head or stern to weather, in short steep seas with breaking crests, the ship rode well.

A conspicuous feature of *Olympias*' design is the amount of wind-drag her honeycomb structure creates. The inside of the hull catches the wind to a substantial degree, so much so that nearly two knots of leeway could be observed when the vessel lay-to across the wind. This contributed significantly to the extra work required of the oarcrew when pulling to windward, which was a tiring and dispiriting process. It seems unlikely that any of the record passages of antiquity called for pulling to windward or they would have been much less remarkable, even without taking into account the difficulties of pulling on an oar in a choppy sea. *Olympias'* high scalloped stern was also a major air brake when pulling to windward and I have questioned whether, *in extremis*, the ancients might not have turned their craft stern-to the weather and sheltered behind it.

Crew endurance

As a contribution to the on-going debate about crew endurance, a day of the 1992 voyage might be illuminating (see p. 15). On the second day, with nine days' training behind them, the crew took the boat from Aegina to the Eastern entrance to the Corinth Canal, a distance of 27.15 nautical miles. Apart from the brief period when sailing close-hauled was tried, as described earlier, the whole passage was under oars and was into the wind which blew from 10 knots upwards. The first two-thirds of the passage was under two banks of oars, with a crew rotation of 40 minutes rowing and 20 minutes out. *Olympias* was slowly forced off to leeward and by early afternoon, with the Meltemi blowing up to 25 knots direct from our destination, the ship was struggling. Speeds were consistently below 3 knots. For a period from 15:31 hrs to 16:19 hrs, the thalamian oars were also used and the whole crew were rowing at full pressure for very little if any forward progress. By 16:19 hrs the thalamian oars had to be shipped in again as choppy sea had rendered them unusable. During this period a serious problem arose with oars getting caught by the short steep seas, with crabs, oars stuck submerged, and oarclashes making consistent rowing impossible and equally meaning that the oarsmen were unable to pull full power on their oars. Just when it is needed most full power becomes impossible.

Because of the difficulties with rotation, and the need to keep the vessel off lee shore islands, many of the oarsmen rowed without a break at full pressure from 14:13 hrs until 16:47 hrs, when a tug took *Olympias* in tow – this effort after having done 40 minutes of each hour for seven hours already. The voyage recorder noted "crew tiring" and "poor timing" by 16:00 hrs. Despite this there did not appear to be any serious problems with overheating among the crew, nor of thirst, partly due no doubt to the strong (and fairly cool) wind blowing through the boat. And although more than a little weary, the oarcrew found the energy to row another 21 minutes from the north side of the Corinth Canal to Corinth harbour, after being towed through the canal and having 1hr 25 minutes rest.

Based on experiences like these, it seems probable that toughened professional crew, oarsmen from childhood, and accustomed to living and working in fairly high temperatures, could row for a long day without undue distress.

Bibliography

Roberts, O. T. P. (1993) Rigging the *Olympias* – a reconstructed trireme. In Shaw 1993, 29–38.

Shaw, J. T. (1993) The Trireme Project. Operational Experience 1987–90. Lessons Learnt. Oxford, Oxbow.

19. On the Speed of Ancient Oared Ships: the crossing of L. Aemilius Paullus from Brindisi to Corfu in 168 BC

Boris Rankov

One of the most contentious issues about the proposed modifications to the *Olympias* design is the performance to be expected of a reconstructed *trieres* under oar (see Shaw, above pp. 63–7; Wallinga, below, pp. 152–4; Whitehead, below pp. 155–60; also Coates, pp. 161–4, Rossiter and Whipp, pp. 165–8). In *The Athenian Trireme*, John Morrison attempted to provide some figures for maximum cruising speeds derived from a variety of literary sources. His conclusion, that 7 to 8 or even 8.6 knots should be attainable, was based on recorded voyages where, even if the distance covered could be established with reasonable precision, the exact time-frame could not (Morrison, Coates and Rankov 2000, 94–106, esp. 103–4, 264–6). This paper considers what is probably the only voyage from antiquity which provides us with both a measurable distance and a precise time for the crossing undertaken, albeit by a Roman rather than a Greek fleet. The significance of the voyage was first recognised by Ernst Assmann (1888, 1622–3; cf. Schmidt 1893) in the late 19th century, but he did not explain its importance in detail and it has not been emphasised in more recent scholarship.

The crossing from Brundisium to Corcyra by L. Aemilius Paullus in 168 BC

In the summer of 167 BC, L. Aemilius Paullus, twice consul, celebrated a triumph for his victory over the forces of Perseus, the king of Macedonia, at the battle of Pydna a year earlier. The celebrations were marred by the deaths of his two younger sons, one five days before the triumph and the other three days after. A few days later, he addressed an assembly of the Roman people in which, despite his grief, he recounted to them how he had won his victory, describing in detail his movements in the whirlwind final campaign (Diodorus Siculus 31.11; Livy 45.40–1; Plutarch *Aemilius Paullus* 36; Appian *Macedonian Wars* 19). In the version given by the Roman historian Livy (45.41.3), Paullus begins as follows:

'Having set off from Italy – I moved the fleet out from Brundisium at sunrise – I put in at Corcyra at the ninth hour of the day, together with all my ships.'

Livy does not make it clear whether the voyage was under oar, under sail or both, nor does he specify what types of ships were involved. It will be argued later in the paper that the passage is most likely to have been made under oar rather than under sail. We can be more or less certain, however, that a consular fleet such as this will have consisted of quinqueremes, the standard Roman capital ship of the period. In 171 BC, the praetor in charge of the fleet sent out from Rome to operate against Macedonia, C. Lucretius Gallus, had 40 quinqueremes under his command, and when he sent ahead his brother – a mere legate – to collect allied ships, he supplied him with one of these quinqueremes (Livy 42.48.6–10). Similarly, in 170 BC, the eight (or eighteen) fully fitted-out ships (*naves ornatas*) sent across the Adriatic from Brundisium with 2,000 troops aboard to join the forces of C. Furius, the legate at Issa, were almost certainly quinqueremes (43.49.5; cf. Morrison and Coates 1996, 110). Paullus himself, as the consul, may have used an *hexeres* ('six') of similar or very marginally better performance as his flagship (cf. Polybius 1.26.11; Livy 29.9.8; Coates, in Morrison and Coates 1996, 345 Appendix D estimates the cruising speed of a Roman *hexeres* at 7.1 knots, compared with 7.0 knots for a quinquereme of the same period), but the speed of the fleet would of course have been determined by the main body of ships. The quinquereme was a larger vessel than a trireme, with two men to an oar at the top (thranite) level, two to an oar at the middle (zygian) level, and one man to an oar at the lowest (thalamian) level, compared to the single man to an oar at each of the three levels of a trireme. It was thus powered by 282 or 300 rowers, compared to a trireme's 170. Although, its flat-out speed in battle would have been significantly less than that of a trireme of the fourth century BC, the difference in cruising speed under oar would have been perhaps only half a knot (Morrison and Coates 1996, 296–303, 345 Appendix D).

The average speed achieved by Aemilius Paullus in his crossing from Brundisium (Brindisi on the Adriatic coast of Italy) to Corcyra (Corfu) should thus have been broadly comparable with what a trireme could have attained in similar conditions, and certainly no higher.

The reliability of the historical data: Livy, Diodorus and Polybius

What makes this voyage special are both the unusual reliability of the historical data and the possibility of calculating the average speed within narrow, known parameters. The source most often cited for Paullus' speech, Livy, was a great stylist and story-teller but is not regarded as particularly reliable by modern standards, especially on military matters. He was also writing the relevant section of his history at the end of the first century BC, about 150 years after the event. He does, however, have the advantage for the modern historian that in the later parts of his work he is frequently quoting (without acknowledgement) from passages of the Greek historian Polybius which are now lost. Indeed, at times he seems to have been translating word-for-word in a manner which we should now regard as plagiarism.

This is almost certainly what is happening in the passage in question. We know from comparisons with the surviving fragments of Polybius' Books 29–30 that in his own Book 45 Livy was using Polybius extensively. The speech is also recorded by other writers, in abbreviated form by Plutarch (*Life of Aemilius Paulus* 36) and Appian (*Macedonian Wars* 19), both of them writing in the first half of the second century AD, and in detail by Diodorus Siculus (31.11.1), who was writing about 20 years before Livy. Diodorus' version, in Greek, is very close indeed to Livy's:

> 'For he said that when he intended to transport his forces across from Italy to Greece, he saw the sunrise and then, having made the crossing, sailed into Corfu at the ninth hour, not having left anyone behind.'

It is clear that both of them are following a common source – who can only be Polybius – very closely (see De Sanctis 1923, 371). In other words, it is reasonable to assume that Livy is giving us more or less a direct translation from Polybius, and that Diodorus' Greek may be very similar to what Polybius himself had written.

Now, Polybius was writing much closer to the events in question than either Diodorus or Livy; his Book 30 was composed sometime between 150 and 130 BC, perhaps only a quarter of a century after Paullus' speech. Much more importantly, Polybius knew Aemilius Paullus and his family intimately. He had been hipparch of the Achaean confederation and had been taken to Italy as a hostage in the aftermath of the battle of Pydna. There he became friend and tutor to Paullus' two surviving sons, Scipio Aemilianus and Q. Fabius Maximus Aemilianus, and the family inevitably figure very prominently in his history of the rise of Rome (Walbank 1972). There is every possibility, therefore, that Polybius had access to a text of the speech which is reflected in Diodorus and Livy, and he would at any rate have known the details of its contents either from Paullus himself or from his two sons (who, moreover, probably accompanied Paullus on the crossing in question).

This is about as strong as ancient literary evidence can be, and there is no reason to doubt it either generally or in detail. We can be absolutely certain, therefore, that Aemilius Paullus claimed, in public and before an audience which would certainly have included some of his own troops, to have made a crossing between Brindisi and Corfu in nine (Roman) hours.

The distance from Brundisium to Corcyra

One of areas where there is some uncertainty is the actual distance covered in the crossing. Fortunately, the outer parameters can be determined very precisely, and we only have a choice between three well-defined possibilities. The first commentator to use the Livy text for this purpose, Ernst Assmann (1888, 1623; corrected in Assmann 1923, 1054 on the basis of Schmidt 1893, 83), evidently calculated the passage to be from Brindisi to the 'northern end' of the island of Corfu, by which he seems to have meant the north-western tip closest to Italy. He thus made the distance about 170 km (= 92 nautical miles), although he also noted that Livy could have been referring to the actual city of Corcyra, in which case the distance would have been 216 km (= 117 nautical miles).

The figure of around 90 nautical miles has been followed by Casson (1971, 292 with n. 94; cf. How and Wells 1912, 184; Köster 1923, 180; Rodgers 1937, 53 n. 57; Möhler 1948, 54 n. 26) but has the problem that the texts of both Diodorus (*katapleusai ... eis Kerkyran*) and Livy (*Corcyram tenui*) imply that Paullus and his fleet came into land at this point rather than simply reached the island. There was, however, no obvious place for the fleet to come ashore in the north-western part of the island, since we know of no settlements there in antiquity where it could easily find water or supplies. Corcyra had, moreover, been a Roman-controlled island since 229 BC (Polybius 2.11), so there was no military reason to avoid the main ports.

A much more likely proposition is that Paullus put in further along the northern coast at Kassiope, the only other port on the island apart from Corcyra itself. This town lay 104 nautical miles from Brundisium, at the island's north-eastern corner, just before the entrance to the straits which lie between the island and the mainland of Epirus (we can discount the possibility that the fleet would have taken a route down the relatively inhospitable and sparsely inhabited western side of the island, which is dangerously exposed in summer to the prevalent north-westerly winds). Kassiope is a strong candidate not just because it was closer to Brundisium than the city of Corcyra (which bore the same name as the island) but because it seems in the Roman period to have been the usual stopping-off point for crossings between Italy and Greece and vice versa. This is indicated by the early first-century AD geographer Strabo (7.7.5.21 (324)), who measures the sea-crossing from Corfu to the Adriatic coast of Italy between Kassiope and Brundisium; he gives the distance as 1700 stades (170 nautical miles), which is clearly incorrect, but if the number was written in the original manuscript in numerals this could very easily have been corrupted from 1070 stades (107 miles), which would be very close to the real figure of 104 nautical miles. When Cicero was on his way back from Cilicia in November, 50 BC, he was detained by winds at Corcyra city, but then moved on the 120 stades (= 12 nautical miles) to Kassiope, where he was detained again before tackling the crossing to Brundisium via Capo d'Otranto (Hydrous) (Cicero *Letters to his Friends* 16.9.1–2). Nero also stopped here on his way to Greece in AD 67 and sacrificed at the local shrine of Zeus Kassios (Suetonius *Nero* 22.3), and in the mid 2nd century AD, Aulus Gellius (*Attic Nights* 19.1) described crossing from Kassiope to Brundisium on his way back to from Athens to Rome. Today, the annual sailing 'Regata Internazionale 'Brindisi-Kerkyra'' instituted in 1986 is raced from Brindisi to Kassiopi and takes place in early June, at almost the same time of year as Paullus' crossing. The record time was set on 9th June, 2005 by the yacht *Pegaso*, which covered the 104 miles in 8 hours 7 minutes 6 seconds; conditions were exceptional, however, and the race had been postponed from the previous day because of strong winds. The previous record, set in 1994, was 13 hours 50 minutes 35 seconds, while times over 20 hours are the norm, and the slowest successful crossing in the race took place in 1999 in precisely 37 hours 30 minutes (see http://www.brindisi-corfu.it). It is easy to see why Kassiope (which is not mentioned in any source earlier than the Roman period; see Philippson and Kirsten 1958, 430) should have been chosen as the point of arrival and departure for Italy, since it avoided the necessity of having to negotiate the straits north of Corcyra, where a ship might be delayed by unpredictable winds and currents, on the same day as making the crossing itself.

The third possibility is that Paullus carried on to the city of Corcyra itself, and indeed this is the most natural interpretation of the texts of Livy, Diodorus, and presumably Polybius. A possible objection to this, however, may be the distance which would then have been covered – 117 nautical miles in nine Roman hours – and the average speed which that would imply (see below).

The distance covered by Paullus was thus either 92 nautical miles as a minimum, 104 miles to Kassiope, or 117 miles to Corcyra city as a maximum.

The time taken for the crossing

The texts in question are unique in that they give the time taken for the voyage with extreme precision – from sunrise to the ninth hour of the day. The Roman day was divided into 12 hours of daylight and 12 hours of night (see Mau 1886, 253ff; Bilfinger 1882; id. 1888); Carcopino

1941, 161–168, esp. 167–168; Sontheimer 1979). Thus the length of each hour varied with the seasons and with the actual length of day and night. In order to determine how long the nine hours in question were in standard modern hours, we need also to know the precise date of the crossing. By a fortunate coincidence, we are able to identify this date.

In the speech recorded by Diodorus (31.11.1) and Livy (45.41.3–5), Paullus pointed out that it took him less than a month to put an end to a four-year war against Perseus of Macedonia, and gave a detailed account of his movements from leaving Brundisium until his crowning victory at Pydna. He took a day to get to Corcyra, four or five more days to Delphi, arrived at the camp of the Roman army five days later, and won the battle fifteen days after that, a total of either 25 or 26 days, depending on how one reads the sources. Livy seems to imply that the crossing was 26 days before the battle (after the crossing, five days from Corcyra to Delphi, five days from Delphi to the army's camp, and then 15 days until the war was ended at Pydna), but Diodorus only 25 (four days from Corfu to Delphi, five days to joining the army, and then fifteen days to the battle). Livy's fifth day (*quinto die*) after the crossing may, however, have been counted inclusively in the usual Roman fashion. This would accord better with Diodorus' four days (τεταρταῖον) from Corcyra. It could even be argued that his fifth day (*quinto die*) from Delphi should also be counted inclusively, making the crossing 24 days before the battle. It is Diodorus, however, who is the more likely both to have understood and to have accurately represented Polybius' Greek, so 25 days is arguably the most plausible interpretation. The battle itself is dated by Livy (44.37.8) to 4th September, but the Roman calendar at this period was in disarray and out of line with the seasons; it remained so until Caesar corrected it in 46 BC (which had 445 days) and then introduced the Julian calendar (Suetonius *Caesar* 40; Plutarch *Caesar* 59; Dio 43.26; Censorinus *On the Birthday* 20.8; Macrobius *Saturnalia* 1.14.2–3). We would not in fact know the 'real' date of Pydna were it not recorded by Livy and the other sources that it was fought on the day after a lunar eclipse (Polybius 29.17 (frag.); Livy 44.37.8; Plutarch *Life of Aemilius Paullus* 17.7; Zonaras 9.23 with Dio 20.66.3; Justin 33.1.7). Since the eclipse can be dated to 21st June, 168 BC (Walbank 1979, 386 citing Ginzel 1899, 191–2; id. 1911, 540, Tafel ii.2), the battle can be fixed precisely to 22nd June, 168 BC, making the Roman calendar some 68 days in advance of the seasons at this date. Counting back 25 or 26 days from the battle, this would put the real date of the crossing on 28th (cf. Meloni 1953, 359; Walbank 1979, 378) or 29th May.

We are now in a position to determine the length of the day, and therefore the length of the nine Roman hours in question. Since sunrise on the 29th May is less than a minute earlier, and sunset less than a minute later than on the 28th; this difference is ignored in the following calculations, which are based on the times given by the tables in Brown and Cockcroft (1987, 119) covering 27th to 29th May. There is a small complication, however. The sunrise was of course observed at Brundisium, while the ninth hour would have been judged from the position of the sun in the sky at the point of arrival. Thus we will need to make minor adjustments both for the actual length of day at each of the three possible arrival points, and for how much earlier the sun had risen at Brundisium than locally.

The north-western tip of Corfu (39° 48' N and 19° 34' E), the harbour at Kassiope (39° 47' N and 19° 52' E), and the city of Corcyra (39° 38' N and 19° 52' E) all lie at more or less the same latitude, so their sunrise and sunset occur at the same Local Mean Time (LMT) to within 30 seconds, which is usually less than variations resulting from the relative heights above sea-level of the observer and his horizon. On May 28th or 29th these would be at approximately 4.36 a.m. and 19.19 p.m. LMT respectively. The local length of day on these dates is therefore 14 hours and 23 minutes, each Roman hour would be 71 minutes and 55 seconds long, and the ninth hour would fall between 14.35 p.m. and 15.23 p.m. LMT.

Brindisi (40° 38' N and 17° 58' E) lies 1° 36' west of the north-western tip of Corfu, and 1° 54' west of Kassiope and Corcyra city which share the same longitude. This means that Brindisi Mean Time (BMT) is about 6 minutes earlier than LMT at the north-western tip, and about 8 minutes earlier than LMT at Kassiope and Corcyra city. Thus, on 28th and 29th May, the Roman ninth hour would fall between 14.29 p.m. and 15.17 BMT at the former place and 14.27 p.m. and 15.15 p.m. at the latter two places. Since sunrise at Brindisi was at approximately 4.33 a.m. BMT, the crossing would have taken between 9 hours 56 minutes and 10 hours 44 minutes to the north-western tip of the island and between and between 9 hours 54 minutes and 10 hours 42 minutes either to Kassiope or to Corcyra city.

Average speed over the sea-bed

From this it follows that Paullus' average speed would have been between 8.6 knots and 9.3 knots if the crossing comprised the 92 nautical miles to the north-western tip of Corfu, between 9.7 knots and 10.5 knots if it comprised the 104 nautical miles to Kassiope, and between 10.9 knots and 11.8 knots if it comprised the 117 nautical miles to Corcyra city.

We can perhaps dismiss the higher of each of these figures – Paullus would surely have claimed the beginning of the ninth hour as the end of the eighth if he could do so. We might also allow for a little exaggeration on Paullus' part, or take the ninth hour as approximate, since the Romans tended to think in quarters of a day as well as in hours (as judged by the height of the sun above the horizon). Nevertheless, the speech clearly implied that the sun was still well above the horizon when the fleet came into harbour. If we were to extend our estimate of the time taken by a whole Roman hour, and bring it up, say, to 12 of our hours, this would still produce average speeds of 7.7 knots, 8.7 knots, and 9.8 knots respectively.

Sail or oars?

Even the most conservative of the speed estimates offered here would represent an impressive performance by Paullus' fleet. Our lowest estimate – 7.7 knots – based on the most generous possible interpretation of our texts, would have been good enough to win the modern 'Brindisi-Corfu' race in all but the record-breaking year. The estimate which accords best with our historical data – 9.7 knots between Brundisium and Kassiope – is two knots higher and would have put Paullus's fleet fifth even in the record-breaking year when sailing conditions were extreme. It is hard to believe that a whole fleet of quinqueremes under sail could have outperformed modern 40' racing yachts.

Moreover, it has been noted by Shaw elsewhere in this volume (pp. 68–71) that *Olympias'* speed under sail was under half the true wind speed, astern or on the beam. If this is any indication of how a quinquereme might have performed, then the estimated speeds would have required true wind-speeds of at least 16 to 20 knots (8.2 m/s to 10.3 m/s). As explained in Shaw's paper (pp. 68–75), such north-westerly winds blowing steadily astern, with a fetch along the whole west coast of the Adriatic, would be likely to produce waves damaging and at some stage dangerous to long, narrow, wooden, oared warships. He calculates that a true windspeed of 8.5 m/s (just over 16 knots) with a fetch of 200 km and a duration of 12.6 hours, would produce waves of a significant height (*i.e.* average roughness) of 1.4 m with wavelength of about 28 m, and three-hour waves of 2.5 m height with about 34 m wavelength. This accords broadly with the conditions implied by our estimated speeds for Paullus' fleet if achieved under sail (*i.e.* winds of at least 8.2 m/s). Wave heights and wavelengths like this would be almost as dangerous to a 45-metre quinquereme of 1.5 m draft as they would be to a 40-metre trireme of 1.1 m draft (see Morrison and Coates 1996, 345 Appendix D). It is hard to believe that any quinquereme commander would set out if such conditions were threatening.

These considerations suggest that the average speeds indicated could only have been achieved under oar.

Speed through the water: the effect of the wind

The speed estimates produced above represent speed over the sea-bed. In order to obtain estimates of speed through the water, which is the true reflection of a ship's performance, we must take into account the likely effects of wind and currents.

The predominant local wind in the Adriatic in summer is the Maestrale from the north-west, and it is fairly safe to assume that it was blowing and provided Paullus with more or less a direct tailwind all the way from Brindisi to Corfu. Although the speed of the voyage makes this very likely, as has already been noted it cannot have been particularly strong for the voyage to have taken place at all. Moderate winds would in any case have been the norm at this time of year: the eighth edition of the Mediterranean

Pilot (1957, 36, 44, 50) tabulates mean wind speed at Brindisi as 9 knots (4.6 m/s) at 0800 and 8 knots (4.1 m/s) at 1900 in May, and 9 knots at 0800 and 7 knots (3.6 m/s) at 1900 in June; for Kérkira (Corfu city) it tabulates 3 knots (1.5 m/s) at 0800 and 6 knots (3.1 m/s) at 1400 in both May and June.

It is reasonable to postulate, therefore, that Paullus would have had favourable winds of perhaps 9 knots on his morning run down the south-eastern coast of Italy from Brindisi to Capo d'Otranto, and would still have been benefiting from favourable winds of around 6 knots in the afternoon as he approached Corfu. Tailwinds of these speeds, which rate as no more than Force 3, Gentle Breeze, would have been ideal for fast, comfortable rowing, providing both moderate extra propulsion and cooling for the oarsmen. Conditions of slightly stronger wind would still have been rowable, up to a little under 11 knots (5.5. m/s), that is bordering on Force 4, Moderate Breeze (see Shaw, above pp. 73–5; since the lowest (thalamian) level of oars in a quinquereme would be at almost exactly the same height above the water as in a trireme, Shaw's calculations and arguments are directly applicable here). Anything more would at some stage of the crossing not have been rowable by the thalamian oarsmen.

As we shall see, Paullus would also have benefited from favourable currents both between Brindisi and Capo d'Otranto and possibly also as he approached Corfu. These too would have been propelling the fleet and so would have reduced the effect attributable to the wind. We may, however, make an estimate of that effect in normal conditions as being the equivalent of a 6-knot tailwind over still water throughout, and perhaps of a 9-knot tailwind throughout if conditions were fresher than normal but still rowable.

Tests carried out on the *Olympias* trireme reconstruction in order to calculate her wind resistance showed that she drifted at around 0.16 times the true wind speed (Coates, Platis and Shaw 1990, 32). The wind resistance of a quinquereme, which would have been about 1.4 m broader overall and about 0.4 m higher from waterline to deck, would have been greater, but so would the resistance through the water of her hull, which would have been about 0.4 m deeper, 1.6 m broader at the waterline, and 5 m longer overall (Morrison and Coates 1996, 345 Appendix D). If we assume that a quinquereme would have drifted at roughly the same rate as *Olympias*, then a constant 6-knot wind would have caused it to drift at around 1 knot, and a 9-knot wind at around 1.5 knots. In other words, we can assume that the wind contributed between 1 and 1½ knots of speed to Paullus' fleet throughout.

Speed through the water: the effect of the currents

The currents which Paullus would have encountered would also have contributed significantly to his average speed over the sea-bed. The general pattern of currents in the Adriatic is a counter-clockwise circulation, running north-westwards up the coasts of Albania, Montenegro and Croatia, and then south-eastwards along the cost of Italy (Pryor 1995, esp. 212 and the map on 206). Over the first 40 nautical miles of his voyage, Paullus would have been able to make use of a favourable current between Brindisi and Capo d'Otranto, where with a good north-westerly wind it can reach a speed of 3 knots close to the coast. In the central part of his voyage across the entrance to the Adriatic (around 34 nautical miles), he would probably have encountered an opposing current of about ¾ to 1 knot flowing westwards, but as he approached the small islands north-west of Corfu he might, if the wind was right, have been able to pick up an eastward-flowing current of about 1 knot. If he proceeded as far as Corfu city, the underlying current in the straits between the island and the mainland runs northward at about 0.5 knot, but with north-westerly winds there is often a south-running surface current of about 1.5 to 2 knots (Mediterranean Pilot 1957, 11, 13, 15–16: 3-knot current down the south-east coast of Italy; 13: ¾- to 1-knot westward current at entrance to Adriatic; 14: 1-knot eastward current north-west of Corfu; 10–11, 164: 1.5- to 2-knot southward surface current in the Straits of Corfu). These would represent the most favourable conditions of current which Paullus is likely to have encountered, and they are assumed for the calculations below. If Paullus in reality met with less favourable currents, then our estimates of the raw speed of his ships would have to be adjusted upwards.

Raw speed

On the basis of the above figures, wind and current would add 4 knots to the fleet's speed for the first 40 nautical miles (assuming a drift of 1 knot attributable to the wind and a current of 3 knots), ¼ knot for the middle section of 34 nautical miles (assuming 1 knot attributable to the wind but an opposing current of ¾ knot), then 2 knots for the next 18 miles to the north-western tip of the island and the following 12 miles to Kassiope (assuming 1 knot attributable to the wind and a 1-knot current), and 3 knots for the final 13 miles to Corcyra city (assuming 1 knot for the wind and 2 knots for the current). If one assumes a fresher but just about rowable wind, then one can add 0.5 knots to each of these figures.

From this, one can calculate Paullus' average raw speed. As we saw above, his average speed over the sea-bed can be estimated at between 7.7 and 8.6 knots for a 92-mile voyage, 8.6 to 9.7 knots for a 104-mile voyage, or 9.8 to 10.9 knots for a 117-mile voyage. Taking the effects of wind and current into account, these imply raw speeds of 5.8 to 6.7 knots, 6.7 to 7.8 knots, and 7.8 to 8.8 knots respectively (see the table in the Appendix to this paper, from which these figures have been extrapolated). If we were to assume a fresher wind throughout, then the raw speed figures would be about half a knot less, *i.e.* 5.3 to 6.2 knots, 6.2 to 7.3 knots, and 7.3 to 8.3 knots.

Thus the most generous interpretation of all our data (12-hour voyage to the north-western tip of Corfu) gives an average raw speed of around 5¼ to 5¾ knots, while a slightly stricter reading (10 hours 42 minutes to the same point) gives 6¼ to 6¾ knots. Taking the voyage to a more plausible destination at Kassiope results in 6¼ to 6¾ knots again (12-hour voyage) or 7¼ to 7¾ knots (10 hours 42 minutes). If Paullus really did sail to Corcyra city, then it is possible that he could have done so at 7¼ to 7¾ knots (12 hours), while the interpretation which is most easily reconciled with our texts gives 8¼ to 8¾ knots (10 hours 42 minutes).

Conclusion: the speed of ancient oared ships and the revised trireme design

This is of course a broad range of speeds. Only the interpretation which stretches the evidence furthest comes close to agreeing with the 5 knots cruising speed suggested for triremes under oar in the two following papers (Wallinga, below pp. 152–4); Whitehead, below, pp. 155–60). It should be noted, however, that these calculations have assumed both optimal conditions of wind and current and that the oarcrews took no breaks at all. While such crews would undoubtedly have been inured to long periods of physical work at the oar with little or no interruption in a way which can hardly be imagined today, this is still an extreme requirement. In addition, the figures relate to a whole fleet moving together, and therefore reflect the speed of the slowest of its vessels. The fleet also almost certainly consisted of quinqueremes, whose cruising speed would have been perhaps a ½ knot slower than a 4th-century trireme. Even this interpretation therefore suggests that the 5-knot estimate for triremes is definitely too low

The more reasonable interpretations based on a voyage to Kassiope, and even perhaps to Corcyra city, accord

very well with Shaw's estimate of 7¼ knots for a trireme, based on the passage from Byzantium to Heraclea in Xenophon *Anabasis* 6.4.2 (Shaw, above pp. 63–7), with John Morrison's low-end estimate of 7 to 8 knots for a trireme based on this and other texts (Morrison, Coates and Rankov 2000, 94–106 (esp. 103–4), 264–6), and with John Coates' estimate of 7.0 knots for a Roman quinquereme of 100 BC based on his hypothetical reconstruction of the hull and oarsystem (Morrison and Coates 1996, 345 Appendix D). The figure of 8¼ to 8¾, knots which accords most closely with Diodorus and Livy, may even support Morrison's top estimate of 8.6 knots; this does seem to be extreme for a fleet of quinqueremes, but it is difficult for historiographical reasons to rule it out altogether.

It is my conclusion that the voyage of L. Aemilius Paullus from Brundisum to Corcyra in 168 BC was most likely undertaken at an average raw speed through the water of around 7 knots. Given that this was clearly a performance exceptional enough for Paullus to have boasted about it, we may take this as representing the maximum cruising speed of a quinquereme. That implies that the maximum cruising speed of a trireme, which will have been perhaps ½ knot higher (Morrison and Coates 1996, 345 Appendix D), would have been around 7½ knots. That in turn supports the contention that the *Olympias* reconstruction, even allowing for any shortcomings in the oarcrew, has underperformed to at least some extent. It consequently offers further evidence in favour of modifying her design either by a simple lengthening of the *interscalmium* (cf. Rankov, below pp. 225–30) or along the lines indicated earlier in this volume by Timothy Shaw and John Coates (above pp. 76–91).

Appendix

The Voyage of L. Aemilius Paullus from Brindisi to Corfu: table of raw speed vs average speed over the seabed

Raw Speed	*5 kts*	*6 kts*	*7 kts*	*8 kts*	*9 kts*
Stage 1	4.44 hours	4.00hours	3.64 hours	3.33 hours	3.08 hours
Stage 2	6.48 hours	5.44 hours	4.69 hours	4.12 hours	3.68 hours
Stage 3	2.57 hours	2.25 hours	2.00 hours	1.8 hours	1.64 hours
Av. Speed Brindisi–NW Corfu	13.50 hours = **6.82 kts**	11.69 hours = **7.87 kts**	10.33 hours = **8.91 kts**	9.25 hours = **9.95 kts**	8.4 hours = **10.95 kts**
Stage 4	1.71 hours	1.50 hours	1.33 hours	1.2 hours	1.09 hours
Av. Speed Brindisi–Kassiopi	15.21 hours = **6.84 kts**	13.19 hours = **7.88 kts**	11.66 hours = **8.92 kts**	10.45 hours = **9.95 knots**	9.49 hours = **10.96 kts**
Stage 5	1.63 hours	1.44 hours	1.3 hours	1.18 hours	1.08 hours
Av. Speed Brindisi–Corfu city	16.84 hours = **6.95 kts**	14.63 hours = **7.98 kts**	12.96 hours = **9.02 kts**	11.63 hours = **10.06 kts**	10.57 hours = **11.07 kts**

Stage 1: Brindisi-Capo d'Otranto: 40 NM, current +3 kts, wind effect +1kt

Stage 2: Capo d'Otranto-approach to Corfu: 34 NM, current -¾ kt, wind effect +1 kt

Stage 3: Approach to Corfu-NW tip of island: 18 NM, current +1kt, wind effect +1kt

Stage 4: NW tip of island-Kassiopi: 12 NM, current +1kt, wind effect +1kt

Stage 5: Kassiopi-Corfu city: 13 NM, current +2kts, wind effect +1 kt

Brindisi-NW Corfu (92 NM) = Stage 1 + Stage 2 + Stage 3

Brindisi-Kassiopi (104 NM) = Stage 1 + Stage 2 + Stage 3 + Stage 4

Brindisi-Corfu city (117 NM) = Stage 1 + Stage 2 + Stage 3 + Stage 4 + Stage 5

Bibliography

Assmann, E. (1888) Seewesen. In Baumeister (1888), 1593–1639.

Assmann, E. (1923) Segel. In Pauly, A., Wissowa, G. and Kroll, W. (eds) *Realencyclopädie der Altertumswisseschaft.* Bd II A. Stuttgart, Alfred Druckenmüller Verlag, 1049–54.

Baumeister, A. (1888) *Denkmäler des klassischen Altertums.* Bd III. München/Leipzig, Druck und Verlag von R. Oldenbourg.

Bilfinger, G. (1882) *Die antike Stundenangaben.* Stuttgart, W. Kohlhammer.

Bilfinger, G. (1888) *Der bürgerliche Tag. Untersuchungen über den Beginn des Kalendertages.* Stuttgart, W. Kohlhammer.

Brown, T. N. and Cockcroft, A. N. (eds) (1987) *Brown's Nautical Almanac 1988* Glasgow, James Brown and Son.

Bursian, C. (1893) *Jahresbericht über die Fortschritte der classischen Alterthumswissenschaft* (ed. I. v. Müller) Zwanzigster Jahrgang. Bd 73 (1892). Berlin, S. Calvary and Company.

Casson, L. (1971) *Ships and Seamanship in the Ancient World.* Princeton, NJ, Princeton University Press.

Coates, J. F., Platis, S. K. and Shaw, J. T. (1990) *The Trireme Trials 1988. Report on the Anglo-Hellenic Sea Trials of Olympias.* Oxford, Oxbow Books.

De Sanctis, G. (1923) *Storia dei Romani* IV.1. Torino, Fratelli Bocca.

Carcopino (1941) *Daily Life in Ancient Rome.* London, Routledge.

Gardiner, R. and Morrison, J. S. (eds) (1995) *The Age of the Galley.* London, Conway Maritime Press.

Ginzel, F. K. (1899) *Spezieller Kanon der Sonnen- und Mondfinsternisse für das Ländergebiet der klassischen Altertumswissenschaft und den Zeitraum von 900 vor Chr. bis 600 nach Chr.* Berlin, Mayer and Müller.

Ginzel, F. K. (1911) *Handbuch der mathematischen und technischen Chronologie.* Bd II. Leipzig, J. C. Hinrichs.

How, W. W. and Wells, J. (1912) *A Commentary on Herodotus* Vol. II (Books V–IX). Oxford, Oxford University Press.

Köster, A. (1923) *Das Antike Seewesen.* Berlin, Schoetz and Parrhysius.

Mau, A. (1886) *Privatleben der Römer* (J. Marquardt and Th. Mommsen, *Handbuch der römischen Alterthümer* VII.1.2). 2nd ed. Leipzig, Verlag von S. Hirzel.

The Mediterranean Pilot (1957) Vol. III. 8th ed. London, Hydrographer of the Navy.

Meloni. P. (1953) *Perseo e la fine della monarchia macedone.* Cagliari, Università di Cagliari.

Möhler, S. (1948) Sails and oars in the *Aeneid. Transactions of the American Philological Association* 79, 46–62.

Morrison, J. S. and Coates, J. F. (1996) *Greek and Roman Oared Warships 399–30 BC.* Oxford, Oxbow Books.

Morrison, J. S., Coates, J. F. and Rankov, N. B. (2000) *The Athenian Trireme. The History and Reconstruction of an Ancient Greek Warship.* 2nd ed. Cambridge, Cambridge University Press.

Philippson, A. and Kirsten, E. (1958) *Die Griechischen Landschaften.* Bd 2.2. Frankfurt-am Main, Klostermann.

Pryor, J. H. (1995) The geographical conditions of galley navigation in the Mediterranean. In Gardiner, R. and Morrison, J. S. (1995), 206–16.

Rodgers, W. L. (1937) *Greek and Roman Naval Warfare.* Annapolis, MD, The United States Naval Institute.

Schmidt, M. (1893) Bericht über Mass und Gewicht, Naturgeschichte und Technik, Handel und Verkehr. In Bursian (1893), 34–113.

Sontheimer, W. (1979) *Der Kleine Pauly* Vol. 5. München, Deutscher Taschenbuch Verlag, 496–497 s.v. Tageszeiten.

Walbank, F. W. (1972) *Polybius.* Berkeley, Los Angeles, London, University of California Press.

Walbank, F. W. (1979) *A Historical Commentary on Polybius Vol. III Commentary on Books XIX–XL.* Oxford, Oxford University Press.

20. Xenophon on the Speed of Triremes

Herman Wallinga

In the discussions of the Trireme Trust, Xenophon's statement in the *Anabasis* (6.4.2) that it took a trireme a long day under oar to go from Byzantium to Heraclea Pontica (mod. Eregli) is a truly fundamental datum. The ability of a reconstructed trireme to maintain a speed of seven to eight knots for some 16 to 18.5 hours implied in Xenophon's affirmation is declared to be 'a necessary criterion of the authenticity of any reconstruction' (Coates, above p. 82; cf. Shaw, above p. 67). The only reconstruction realised so far has not come up to this standard: 'It is acknowledged that *Olympias* is incapable of cruising all day at 7 to 8 knots under oar' (Shaw, above p. 68). Proposals have therefore been submitted to ensure that any second, improved, reconstruction would pass this test (Coates, above pp. 82–91).

This implicit trust in the isolated testimony of a writer not especially known for intimate association with maritime matters is surprising, the more so since at least one ancient reader of the *Anabasis* vented his disbelief and convinced others, so that they broadcast his doubts. Xenophon must not in any way be taken for a naval expert. He never held any Athenian command, let alone a naval one, and a crass example of his lack of interest in naval matters is noticed by Gauthier (1976, 62). To this ancient reader I shall turn in a moment, but let me first say something about my personal reasons for surprise. I have never had any doubt that *Olympias* – whatever the possible (in fact unavoidable) anachronisms in the details of her construction – represented a very high standard of ship in the class of ancient triremes. In my view, the scaling up of what I considered a very well-constructed model (the one presented by Morrison 1941) would have resulted in a ship roughly as good as its ancient prototype, and this would certainly be true of a version much improved by the involvement of a modern shipbuilder of great experience. Moreover, my reading of the sources on naval warfare in the 5th and 4th centuries BC and on the use of the trireme leads me to think that speed, though important, was never paramount in the consideration of naval authorities.

When, for instance, on the eve of the Peloponnesian War, Pericles lectured his compatriots about Athenian naval superiority (Thucydides 1.142f, esp. 143.1), he did not even mention the superior quality of the Athenian ships as such, nor of their rowers, but stressed the availability in Athens of experienced crews and especially of 'more and better steersmen and deck-personnel' (no need to hire them abroad). What is even more telling is the fact that speed is not in evidence as an attribute of any category of ship in the Athenian naval yards: ships are invariably categorised as 'new' or 'old', or (later) 'first,' 'second' and 'third' (as in Demosthenes), and also as *exairetoi* ('set apart'; see Morrison and Williams 1968, 248), designations that have nothing to do with speed.

I have no doubt that the reason is that, in view of the co-ordinated movements required by their favoured battle tactics of *diekplous* and ramming, *equal* speed of all the ships – *i.e.* uniformity of build – was the chief aim of the Athenian builders. That is not to say that there were no individual differences in speed between ships, but it is very seldom indeed that this is apparent. The only clear case known to me for the Athenian navy is in Xenophon *Hellenica* 1.6.19. In the situation there described, the admiral Konon was planning to break the blockade of Mytilene by the Spartans (who had faster ships). To this end, Konon chose the two fastest ships – *tas arista pleousas* – in his squadron and took the best rowers from all his ships to man them. Here, the term *tas arista pleousas* cannot have what in my view is its usual meaning – that the ships had very large or full crews – because Xenophon gives them this title before they were manned.

In this context, and compared with the modest estimates in older studies such as those of Köster (1923, 125: 5 knots 'and more, but less as a rule') and Casson (1964, 31: 7 knots top speed; both Köster and Casson were probably using information about early-modern galleys derived from Louis XIV's captain, Barras de la Penne), the speeds realised in the sea trials of *Olympias* appear to indicate that my prediction concerning the quality of the ship has been fully borne out. But then what to think of Xenophon's testimony?

A firm belief in its trustworthiness was in all probability already held by Morrison in *Greek Oared Ships* where, however, he does not get to the bottom of the matter and merely specifies the speeds implied as a result of different assumptions concerning the length of a long day, allowing for speeds of between 'less than eight' and 'between eleven and twelve knots' (Morrison and Williams 1968, 309). In the chapter on 'The speed of *triereis*' in *The Athenian Trireme* on the other hand, he endeavoured to bolster Xenophon's authority by working out the speed implied in Thucydides' (8.101) account of the Spartan admiral Mindaros' dash from Chios to the Hellespont in the autumn of 411 BC, putting it at 6.9 knots for 'two continuous periods of 9 hours' pulling and an overall distance of 124 sea miles' (Morrison, Coates and Rankov 2000, 104–5, referring back to p. 97), seemingly a reasonable correspondence with Xenophon. But Morrison's distances here cannot be accepted. He unnecessarily makes the Spartan fleet of some 73 triremes painstakingly hug the coast of Asia Minor between Arginusae and Harmatos (north of Lesbian Methymna), whereas a much shorter route along the northeast coast of Lesbos was available. With this route, his 'overall distance of 124 sea miles' is reduced to no more than some 95 and the ships' speed to upwards of 5 knots, still pretty good in my opinion (see now Wallinga 2005, 75 n. 15, and chapter 7 regarding the quality of triremes in general).

Xenophon's testimony therefore remains an isolated case, and for this reason it deserves to be approached with due caution. It is, moreover, from a very special passage, not simply a passing reference in the succession of local depictions that is so typical of Xenophon's great story. In Lendle's recent commentary on the work (1995, 385), the account of Kalpes Limen, the place indirectly specified in the passage under discussion (6.4.1–6), is characterised as the only detailed *ekphrasis* ('formal description') of a locality in the entire *Anabasis*, meriting notice because it highlights features which would be vital in the context of the foundation of a colony. Xenophon (*Anabasis* 5.6.15), to wit, had toyed with the idea of settling the rest of the returning Ten Thousand on the shores of the Black Sea, in this way 'adding territory and power to the Greek world.' Since the prospective colony, originally projected anywhere between Heraclea and Byzantium and only in the last instance at Kalpes Limen, would be surrounded by barbarian territory on the landward side, its sea link with that Greek world was a most important aspect of its position. This link is in fact the very first feature of its location that Xenophon mentions: in his catalogue of facilities, it precedes other, more immediately important, features of the site like position, capacity, water supply, *etc.*

In the context of his colonising project, Xenophon's *ekphrasis* cannot be denied a certain propagandistic intention. The Ten Thousand had to be persuaded not only that the colony was a basically sensible proposition, but even more importantly that it would be viable in the sense that, if its Thracian neighbours – victims-to-be of Greek land snatching – started hostilities, Greek allies would not be too far away. Even if Xenophon did not fraudulently minimise the distance of his colony from the Greek world, he may reasonably be supposed to have welcomed the low estimate of that distance when some informant let it slip, and refrained from verifying it.

Now, this low estimate is precisely what appears to have provoked the protest of the ancient reader I referred to at the beginning. As Morrison noted in *Athenian Trireme* (Morrison, Coates and Rankov 2000, 103 n. 4; cf. Shaw, above p. 63), there are two manuscript readings here, one measuring Xenophon's voyage as a long day's, the other making it last a very long day (*hemeras mala makras plous*). This second variant is preserved in two manuscripts of a class once know as *deteriores* (thus the Oxford edition), but nowadays of a much better reputation. Nevertheless, 'a very long day' cannot be considered equivalent to 'a long day' as a reading. No serious author would have used the expression in a straightforward account of the geography of a region. I have certainly never seen a parallel, and no recent edition prints it. I have no doubt therefore that 'a very long day' originated in some marginal comment, noted down by someone – most likely a Byzantine reader – who was certain that the feat implied in Xenophon's *ekphrasis* was too good to be true, his sarcastic *mala* ('very') in fact meaning 'impossible' (a judgement which may well be based on Athenian literary tradition lost to us). When his exemplar of the *Anabasis* was then copied, the copyists accepted his judgement and took the marginal note as a correction and incorporated it in the text, as often happened in ancient book production, to be multiplied in further copying.

In fine, nothing much can be based on Xenophon's statement. It is not confirmed by other reliable testimonies concerning the trireme's speed and its origin and intent are too dubious for it to merit credence all by itself. In contrast, Thucydides' account of Mindaros' dash is an incomparably superior testimony, not only because of its author's far greater competence in maritime matters, but also because of the greater precision of its chronology. Making Mindaros start from Arginusae while it was still fully dark and arrive before midnight – in modern terms travelling from *c.* 4.00 to *c.* 23.00 hours with a one-to-two-hour break for a quick early meal – gives him some 17 to 18 hours to reach the Dardanelles. In other words, his speed over the 95 sea miles was between 5.25 and 5.53 knots. Compared with the performance of Louis XIV's galleys – 5 knots per hour for the first hour; during the second only four and a half; after that 'they dropped down to two or slower' (Casson 1964, 121) – this is a magnificent exploit which was, as I understand it, not surpassed by *Olympias*. To my mind, it is a far better 'criterion of the authenticity of any reconstruction' of the ancient trireme than Xenophon's pious fraud.

Bibliography

Casson, L. (1964) *Illustrated History of Ships and Boats.* New York, Doubleday and Company Inc.

Gautier, Ph. (1976) *Un commentaire historique des Poroi de Xenophon.* Genève, Droz.

Köster, A. (1923) *Das Antike Seewesen.* Berlin, Schoetz und Parrhysius.

Lendle, O. (1995) *Kommentar zu Xenophon's Anabasis (Bücher 1–7).* Darmstadt, Wissenschaftliche Buchgesellschaft.

Wallinga, H. T. (2005) *Xerxes' Greek Adventure. The naval perspective* Leiden, Boston, Brill.

Used Elsewhere

Morrison, J. S. (1941) The Greek trireme. *The Mariner's Mirror* 27.1, 14–44.

Morrison, J. S. and Williams, R. T. (1968) *Greek Oared Ships, 900–322 B.C.* Cambridge, Cambridge University Press.

Morrison, J. S., Coates, J. F. and Rankov, N. B. (2000) *The Athenian Trireme: the history and reconstruction of an ancient warship.* 2nd ed., Cambridge, Cambridge University Press.

21. *Triereis* Under Oar and Sail

Ian Whitehead

Introduction

The purpose of this paper is to examine the ancient evidence concerning passage making and performance under both sail and oar of *triereis*.

Xenophon's statement (*Anabasis* 6.4.2) that the sea passage from Byzantium to Heraclea was "a long (or in one version "a very long") day's journey for a trireme with oars" has been regarded as the clearest evidence provided for the speed of a trireme under oar (Morrison, Coates and Rankov 2000, 102–3; Shaw, above pp. 63–7) and as such is considered here in some detail. Similarly Xenophon's account of Iphicrates' *periplous* of the Peloponnese is also looked at closely since this has been taken by Morrison (Morrison, Coates and Rankov 2000, 97, 102–3; cf. Xen. *Hell.* 6.2.11–14; 6.2.27–32) to show that a *trieres* in a hurry travelled under oar rather than under sail. Other voyages undertaken by *triereis* are considered in an attempt to establish how a *trieres* might use her sails and oars to best effect both under normal circumstances and when she was in a hurry. Finally I have included a study of the actions of *triereis* breaking off from battle, since there is an undoubted connection between flight and the use of sails.

Byzantium to Heraclea

Scholarly debate over the "long day's journey for a trireme with oars" has concentrated on whether or not it was physically possible for a trireme to be rowed all the way from Byzantium to Heraclea in a day and on exactly how many hours a long, or a very long, day lasts (Morrison 1991; Shaw, above pp. 63–7 and 68–75). It has been assumed that, whatever the arguments, Xenophon's account describes a journey completed entirely under oar. However the language which Xenophon uses (καὶ τριήρει μέν ἐστιν εἰς Ἡράκλειαν ἐκ Βυζαντίου κώπαις ἡμέρας μακρᾶς πλοῦς) does not rule out the use of sail. The dative κώπαις suggests that the oars are the means by which the journey is completed in a long day but it does not prove that the ship is rowed throughout the day. Oars are obviously important or there would be no reason for Xenophon to mention them but it is not possible to tell from the language employed if they were used for the entire voyage.

Xenophon (*Hellenica* 6.2.27), in describing another sea voyage, Iphicrates' *periplous,* writes "but by making his journey with the oar (τῇ δὲ κώπῃ τὸν πλοῦν ποιούμενος) he kept his men in better condition of body and caused the ships to sail better." Again he uses the dative case but we know from his own account that this voyage was completed mostly, but not entirely, under oar. When Thucydides writes about triremes under oar he uses the verb χράομαι "use", which takes the dative case, with κώπαις. Hermocrates of Syracuse talks of attacking the tired Athenians as they approached Southern Italy, "if they used their oars" (Thucydides 6.34). It would be rash to assume that Xenophon, in writing about the distance between Byzantium and Heraclea as "a long day's journey for a trireme with oars" necessarily intended his readers to understand that the ship had to be rowed all the way.

Thucydides sometimes measures distance by relating it to the time taken for a ship to complete a particular passage. Amphipolis is said to be about half a day's voyage from Thasos (Thucydides 4.104). No type of ship or conditions are specified. In the context of the events taking place, the attempt to relieve Amphipolis, one might perhaps guess that Thucydides meant half a day's voyage for a *trieres* but one can not be sure. From Abdera to the River Ister is described as a voyage of four days and four nights for a merchant ship if the shortest course is taken and the wind is always from astern (Thucydides 2.97). Since almost seventy miles of this journey have to be made against the strong currents of the Hellespont and the Bosphorus the following wind is specified because it is important. A ship relying on sail to pass through the Hellespont and the Bosphorus would undoubtedly be delayed by adverse conditions (Severin 1985,132; Tim Severin, writing about the last age of sail, says that small ships were towed up the Bosphorus by gangs of men working from a tow path), and so the description would be worthless without specifying the following wind and the shortest course. The size of Sicily is defined by describing the journey round the island as a voyage for a merchant ship of not much less than eight days (Thucydides 6.1). This historiographical practice is continued by Thucydides' immediate successor Xenophon and also by later writers (see Casson 1971, 287; cf. Diodorus Siculus 5.16.1; 3.34.7. Procopius *Bell. Goth.* 3.18.4. Strabo 10.475).

Xenophon's statement concerning the journey time for a *trieres* from Byzantium to Heraclea seems to be in this tradition. He is providing a measure of distance but there are two difficulties in using this as a bald statement of the endurance and speed characteristics of a *trieres* using oars alone.

The first difficulty is that the statement is followed in the *Anabasis* (6.4.3–6) by a long description of the virtues of Calpe Harbour, which is at the mid-point between the two cities. The import of the passage is that in many cases *triereis* and their crews would find it too great a distance in one day and, since the natives along the coast were anything but friendly, they might be better breaking their journey at Calpe.

The second difficulty is that the language Xenophon uses does not rule out the use of sail. Having oars may be just one of the conditions which enables the distance to be represented as being equivalent to one day's journey: without oars it would under most conditions have taken two days. When Xenophon (*Hellenica* 6.2.27) describes Iphicrates' *periplous* of 372 BC, he uses a similar construction and we know that sails were used on that voyage.

If one looks at the nature of the voyage from Byzantium to Heraclea one can see that whether or not a ship had oars would, under typical summer weather conditions, make a difference to the number of days taken for the trip. Shaw (above, pp. 63–7) has shown in his very thorough analysis of this journey that a *trieres* making between 7 and 8 knots would cover the 129 nautical miles of the journey in between 16 and 18 hours. Unless there was a southerly wind blowing, a ship without oars could not begin her journey north against the 1.5–2 knot current (Shaw, above pp. 63–4) of the Bosphorus. A merchantman trying to make the trip would be extremely fortunate to catch a southerly blowing early in the morning: a calm would be the most commonly encountered condition in the early morning. Any ship without oars would therefore have to wait for a suitable breeze to pick up in the afternoon to make progress against the current. Thus the journey from Byzantium to Heraclea would be certain to take more than one day.

In the case of the a *trieres* attempting the journey, the typical morning calm would be no bar to her progress since the sixteen miles up the Bosphorus could be tackled under oar with a fresh crew. This is perhaps why Xenophon used a dative of instrument in specifying the use of the oars. Once into the Black Sea she would use sail or oars according to the conditions. It would be most likely for the crew to need to row for eight to ten hours then sail for four to six hours followed by perhaps another four hours under oar. Shaw seems to quickly dismiss the use of sails without oars (Shaw, above pp. 69–73, and conclusion p. 75) on the grounds that the wind speeds required would raise waves which were too big for safe operation of a *trieres* unless the wind blew for only a short time. But this is precisely the summer pattern of fine weather both in the Black Sea and the Eastern Mediterranean (Shaw, above pp. 64–5, summarising the Admiralty Black Sea Pilot; Denham 1979, xxiv–vi) with the afternoon breeze expected to last four to six hours at wind strengths of Force 3–5. Any *trieres* design must surely be able to withstand winds of Force 3–5 for a few hours or to my mind it would not satisfy the historical evidence. Otherwise we would surely hear in our sources of *triereis* seeking shelter on most afternoons throughout the summer!

It appears that "a long day's journey from Byzantium to Heraclea for a trieres with oars" can not be taken as a bald statement of the endurance and speed characteristics of a *trieres* under oar. Other evidence must be considered to illuminate the passage making qualities of *triereis*.

The *periplous* of Iphicrates

In 373 BC Iphicrates replaced Timotheus as general after Timotheus had been deposed by the people of Athens for not setting out on the mission with which he had been charged. Iphicrates quickly manned his ships and, early in 372 BC, began his voyage around the Peloponnese to bring assistance to the Corcyraeans. Xenophon admiringly describes how Iphicrates not only succeeded in training his men during the voyage but also completed his *periplous* in good time (*Hellenica* 6.2.11–14; 6.2 27–32). Early on in his account Xenophon tells us about some of the measures which Iphicrates adopted: "As for Iphicrates, when he began his voyage around the Peloponnesus he went on with all needful preparations for a naval battle as he sailed; for at the outset he had left his large sails behind him at Athens, since he expected to fight, and now, further, he made but slight use of his *smaller sails*, (τοῖς ἀκατείοις) even if the wind was favourable; by making his journey then, with the oar, *he kept his men in better condition of body and caused the ships to go faster*" (ἄμεινόν τε τὰ σώματα ἔχειν τοὺς ἄνδρας καὶ ἄμεινον τὰς ναῦς πλεῖν ἐποίει) (*Hellenica* 6.2.27. trans. Carleton L. Brownson. Loeb Classical Library). Morrison (Morrison, Coates and Rankov 2000, 97) translates the last phrase as "he both improved the fitness of his men and achieved a higher speed for his ships." Warner's Penguin translation is "he kept them (the men) in better physical shape and got more speed out of the ships."

Brownson's translation of this passage allows three possibilities concerning the speed of Iphicrates' ships under sail and oar. Firstly it could mean that since the men were kept fitter the ships were faster under oar than they would have been had Iphicrates used his sails more. A long voyage made mostly under sail would inevitably cause rowers to lose condition, which would reduce the speed attainable under oar. The second, and perhaps the most natural interpretation, is that the ships were faster under oar than when they were using their small sails. The third possibility, which is Morrison's view, is that the ships were faster under oar than they would have been even if they had used both their big and their small sails (Morrison, Coates and Rankov 2000, 97 and 103; it is not clear to me whether the ἀκάτειον was used in conjunction with the big sail in addition to serving as a substitute for it: Casson 1971, 264–7 believes the ἀκάτειον was used on its own, while Morrison, Coates and Rankov 2000, 175–6 think the two sails were used together).

Morrison was led by this conclusion to suggest an amendment to one of the historical requirements put forward for the reconstruction of the *trieres*. "(9) To carry sail well enough for oars to be used on passage only in insufficient or contrary winds" (Coates and McGrail 1984, 91) he thinks should be adjusted by the addition of "or when the ship was in a hurry" (Morrison, Coates and Rankov 2000, 103 n. 3). All voyages undertaken in haste which we hear of in our sources are thereafter assumed to have been completed under oar, "since that was faster" (Morrison, Coates and Rankov 2000, 105).

However when we look at Xenophon's account of the *periplous* in its entirety it is clear that speed is not uppermost in his mind. The big sails are left behind, not to make the passage faster but because Iphicrates expected to fight (*Hellenica* 6.2.27). The exercises which he puts his ships through are to prepare his men for battle (*Hellenica* 6.2.28; 6.3.30). The emphasis is not on speed but on practice and preparation for a naval action.

If we adhere to a more literal translation of the last few words of the first sentence describing Iphicrates' *periplous* a picture emerges which is more in keeping with the rest of the account: "... he kept his men in better condition of body and *caused the ships to sail better*." The voyage under oar, by keeping the men fitter, made the all round performance of the ships better (for the present writer's hypothesis on the "better sailing" ship, see Whitehead 1993). The double use of ἄμεινον makes it unlikely that Xenophon means "better" when describing the condition of the men's bodies and "faster" when describing the performance of the ships. It is more probable that he is using ἄμεινον in this way for emphasis, highlighting the connection between the better condition of the men and the better sailing characteristics of the ships. We can probably still safely assume that the ships were faster under oar at the end of the voyage than they would have been had Iphicrates used his sails more, although that is not what Xenophon is telling us. The better sailing qualities acquired by Iphicrates' ships during the *periplous* are needed to enable his hastily recruited sailors to hold their own in battle against the well trained crews of the enemy (*Hellenica* 6.2.12 and 32; when Iphicrates' men go into action they do so with great success). Moreover, since it has been shown elsewhere (Whitehead 1993) that "better

sailing" is not synonymous with "faster", we are not able to draw conclusions concerning the relative speed of *triereis* under sail or oar. Other parts of Xenophon's account do provide evidence about the speed which Iphicrates' fleet was able to maintain.

The various training exercises which Iphicrates made his fleet perform must have increased the length of the voyage. For example, drawing the head of the column away from the land and making the ships race to the shore when landing for meals would have made the journey longer (*Hellenica* 6.2.28). Switching from sailing in column to sailing in line abreast and practising the battle manoeuvres would also have inevitably increased the distance run (*Hellenica* 6.2.30). Nevertheless it seems that these exercises did not make the journey any slower than it would otherwise have been (*Hellenica* 6.2.32). Since Xenophon (*Hellenica* 6.2.27) includes leaving the large sails behind in his account of Iphicrates' battle preparations, we must surely conclude that the voyage took no longer than it would have done if the ships had all their sails aboard and had been free to use them. Does this then indicate that Morrison was right to infer that passage under oar was faster than passage under sail? Another piece of evidence from Xenophon's description of the *periplous* provides a possible explanation for why the voyage was no slower than it would otherwise have been.

Iphicrates trained his ships in the various battle manoeuvres by day (*Hellenica* 6.2.30). At the end of the day the ships put into land for the men to have their dinner. It was normal practice for the sailors to sleep on land where they had stopped to dine (Thucydides 8.101; cf. Demosthenes [1213] *Against Polycles* 22, where Apollodorus complains that he and his crew had to spend the night anchored at sea off Stryme, without food and unable to sleep), and Xenophon (Hellenica 6.2.29) tells us something of the precautions which Iphicrates takes to guard against an attack when his force is spending the night ashore. Frequently however, Iphicrates does not allow his troops to sleep on land but pushes on through the night:

> But often, if the weather was good, he would put to sea again after dinner; and if there was a favourable breeze they ran before it and rested at the same time, but if it was necessary to row he rested the sailors by turns.

The rowers would have been tired by the end of the day so it made good sense to sail when it was possible and give all the men a rest. However even when he could not sail Iphicrates still put to sea since it was important for him to complete the voyage in good time. These extra sessions on the water, executed partly under sail and partly under reduced oarpower, are surely the reason why the *periplous* took no longer than it would otherwise have done. The extra sessions were necessary because the manoeuvres had slowed the fleet, and perhaps also because the distance run under sail was less than it would have been if the big sails had been aboard.

The number of unknowns: the increased distance

run, the time taken for manoeuvres, and the additional time on the water under sail or reduced oarpower make it impossible for us to determine from Xenophon's account of this voyage whether or not passage under oar was faster than passage under sail. A consideration of other source material and an assessment of the practical constraints affecting the operation of *triereis* in the Eastern Mediterranean may provide clues as to how a *trieres* went about making a fast passage.

Passage making

Summer weather in the Eastern Mediterranean is characterised by a daily cycle of sea and land breezes separated by periods of calm. Trying to proceed under sail during a calm, or with an unfavourable wind would not be conducive to fast passage making. If on the other hand a *trieres* attempted to complete a long passage entirely under oar even when the wind was favourable, her crew would become too tired to row efficiently and her speed would be bound to drop. Moreover rowing with a tail wind reduces the cooling effect of the breeze which makes it a particularly endurance-sapping activity. Common sense demands that a *trieres* in a hurry was rowed in periods of calm, when the wind was favourable but very light, and when the wind was contrary; and sailed when the wind was favourable and strong enough to maintain a satisfactory average distance run. In reality all sorts of other factors would come into play. For example, a tired crew would benefit from sailing with a favourable light breeze in order to allow the rowers to regain their strength, in circumstances where a fresh crew might row on until the wind had strengthened sufficiently for there to be no drop in average speed when switching from oar to sail power. The evidence of our sources appears to support these assertions.

Xenophon (*Hellenica* 2.3.31) relates how Critias attacked Theramenes in a speech, telling him that he should not turn around if he is hampered in his course, but should work hard, as a sailor would, until a favourable breeze arises. Apollonius Rhodius, who had lived in Rhodes and Alexandria, although ostensibly writing about a mythical voyage in the distant past, sometimes provides anachronistic nautical detail which can be useful when one is trying to understand maritime practices of a later date (for example, his description of the fitting of a *hypozoma* to *Argo* seems more likely to relate to the larger warships of the third century BC, *triereis*, *tetrereis*, and *pentereis*, than to a Bronze Age *pentekontor*)

We find that Apollonius' Argonauts row when there is a calm but sail when the breeze is favourable (*Argonautica* 1.600 and 607, 2.660). In Thucydides (6.34), Hermocrates of Syracuse suggests attacking the Athenian fleet if it makes the crossing from Corcyra to Italy under oar and the sailors are tired out from rowing. Since this is a crossing of perhaps 70–80 nautical miles this provides a useful reference for what length of passage under oar would tire out the crew of a *trieres*. When approaching enemy-held

waters a sensible commander would surely have used his sails if the wind was favourable, in order to preserve the strength of his rowers. Hermocrates goes on to say that if it did not seem wise to attack, the Syracusans could retire to Tarentum. One presumes that he would not recommend an attack if the Athenians came up under sail with their oarsmen still fresh.

Strong contrary winds (Apollonius Rhodius *Argonautica* 1.586; 2.528; Herodotus 7.168), or a storm (Thucydides 4.3.1; 8.99), might prevent a ship setting out or cause it to seek shelter. When he is not seeking to train his men Iphicrates sails when the wind is favourable and proceeds under oar if it is not. Since the oarsmen have worked hard all day they row in shifts to enable them to get some rest (Xenophon *Hellenica* 6.2.29). A non-stop voyage from Piraeus to Mytilene also requires the rowers to operate in shifts. Thucydides (3.49) tells us that the ship was lucky not to be hampered by contrary winds, but during a non-stop passage of this length, 184 nautical miles (Morrison, Coates and Rankov 2000, 95), the rowers might easily have become exhausted if they had rowed all together, even allowing for the possibility of a favourable wind and some of the passage being completed under sail. Thucydides does not mention sailing in his account of the voyage but that does not rule out the use of sails. He describes the extraordinary measures taken to ensure maximum distance run when the ship is under oar, but since it is unlikely that any such extraordinary measures were required in order to sail most efficiently, he would have no reason to write about those parts of the voyage completed under sail.

Long voyages undertaken in a hurry seem to warrant using the oarsmen in shifts. Although the two voyages mentioned above are certainly both exceptional in their different ways, it appears that rowing in shifts was quite normal practice (Morrison and Williams 1968, 309–10). Polyainos (5.22.4) relates a story of the Athenian general Diotimus, a contemporary of Iphicrates (Xenophon *Hellenica* 5.1.18–24), who landed a number of men from his ships by night to set an ambush for the enemy. At dawn he had his ships stationed offshore at the place of ambush, with troops on deck ready for action. He ordered those rowers left on board to pull in turn the thalamian, the zygian, and then the thranite oars. The ships attempted a landing and were attacked by the enemy, who were then taken in the rear by the ambushing force. There would have been no point in rowing each level in turn if it had not been normal practice since it would only have made the enemy suspicious. Although there is no evidence in the cases of Iphicrates' *periplous* and the dash to Mytilene of how the oarsmen were organised to row and rest in turn, the Polyainos passage suggests that it was usual for *triereis* to be rowed in turn by each of the three levels. The rowing of undermanned ships *monokrotos* and *dikrotos*, with one and two levels, at Aegospotami suggests that the sailors were familiar with the practice. In such a dire emergency and with no time to think they would have been unlikely to attempt anything unusual (Xenophon *Hellenica* 2.1.28). At

Sphakteria the thalamians are left aboard the ships when the Athenians make a landing on the island (Thucydides 4.32). The way that our sources sometimes distinguish between rowers by referring to their different levels may reflect the operational reality of rowing, resting, and (bearing in mind Aigospotami) eating in shifts (Thucydides 6.31; Aristophanes *Acharnians* 162; although both these cases seem to be concerned with differences in pay).

On another occasion, when a short voyage was undertaken without any need for haste, the oarsmen were handled differently. The Spartan admiral (*nauarch*) Teleutias sailed from Aigina with a fleet to attack the Piraeus. Since he had all night to complete his journey, and it seems wished to make his attack at dawn, he ordered his men to row for a while, and then to rest, and continued to alternate rest and rowing through the night. When he was a thousand metres or so from the entrance to the harbour he halted the fleet and let the men rest until daybreak. Then, as day was dawning, he led the assault on the Piraeus (Xenophon *Hellenica* 5.1.18–24). Teleutias's method of handling his oarsmen was probably a more agreeable way of making a passage than rowing in shifts. It allowed all the oarsmen to rest together and they may even have found it easier to sleep without the noise of the ship being rowed (Morrison and Williams 1968, 311; cf. Aristotle *Meteorologica* 2.9. (369b 10); Euripides *Iphigenia in Tauris* 407, 1133).

In the virtually tideless Mediterranean a ship that was not under way would only drift with the wind, so during the frequent calms no ground would be lost if all the rowers rested at the same time. Teleutias was able to allow his men to rest like this, probably taking advantage of the calm which usually descends on the Saronic Gulf at night in summer. During a daytime passage an astute commander might prefer to rest and then row his men all together through a hot, windless morning in the expectation of help from a favourable breeze in the afternoon. In good weather the afternoon breeze starts about the same time each day and dies away towards dusk. Although its direction and strength may vary depending on the locality, a good *kubernetes* would be well aware of these differences and would know whether or not the wind was likely to be favourable.

Triereis on passage used their oars during period of calm or to make progress against contrary winds. Long voyages undertaken in haste required the oarsmen to operate in shifts and it appears that it was not unusual to see a *trieres* being rowed by each level in turn. As an alternative the crew might be ordered to row and then allowed to rest all together if a ship was in no particular hurry. When the wind was favourable a *trieres* would proceed under sail although a strong contrary wind or a storm might prevent her from setting out or cause her to seek shelter.

Triereis in flight

Other evidence concerned with the performance of *triereis* under sail and oar, not connected with passage making

but, in part at least, associated with haste, is provided by accounts of *triereis* in flight. Manoeuvrability, speed of turn, ability to go directly upwind, and to go astern, were vital leading up to and during a sea fight, but once the decision had been made to flee, getting clear of the battle was the only requirement.

When the Greeks at Salamis heard of the capture of the Athenian acropolis some of their commanders hurried aboard their ships and hoisted the sails to flee (Herodotus 8.56). Following his account of Salamis Herodotus repeats a slanderous Athenian story concerning the alleged flight of Adeimantus and the Corinthians prior to the battle. This tale has Adeimantus and the rest of the Corinthian fleet hoisting their sails to make good their escape (Herodotus 8.94). Although the story is probably false, for it to have had any credibility at all, ships in flight must normally have used their sails. At Lade the Samian ships which turned away before battle had been joined also hoisted their sails (Herodotus 6.14). In all of these cases the ships had not sustained any damage, and therefore would have had their full oar power available, and yet they chose to hoist sail. Since the hoisting of sail served, rather like the striking of colours in a later era, to signal that a ship was not going to take any further part in the battle it is not safe to draw conclusions as to the relative speeds under sail or oar. However the sails must have driven the ships well enough to take them out of the battle line since otherwise they surely would have fled under oar without bothering to waste time by hoisting sail.

Speed under sail must have varied according to which sails were being used. A ship using its big sail, or perhaps even both sails, would sail faster than one which was just using its ἀκάτειον. However in the three cases mentioned above it is not possible to determine which sails were hoisted. Herodotus just uses the generic name *histia* and gives no clues as to which sails he means. Thucydides (7.24) only refers to sails once in his entire work and then only to remark on the capture of the sails of forty *triereis* from the forts at Plemmyrium. This does at least tell us that, by 413 BC, ships going into action were leaving sails on shore. We never hear of *triereis* making use of their sails; a case perhaps of the commonplace not warranting a mention. In 410 BC Alcibiades ordered forty ships under Thrasybulus and Theramenes to remove their big sails (τὰ μεγάλα ἱστία) and follow him to Parium (Xen. *Hell*. 1.1.13. cf. Lysander leaving his big sails ashore before Aigospotami. Xen. *Hell*. 2.1.29). Therefore we can be sure that by this date the smaller sail, the *akateion*, was being carried into battle since there would be no point in describing a sail left ashore as big unless it was to distinguish it from another of a different size which remained on board. Xenophon's account of Iphicrates' *periplous* in 372 BC is the earliest reference to the *akateion* sail by name but its use must have been well established by then. Although we can not be sure that the *akateion* was carried into battle in the early part of the fifth century BC we know that it was by the end of the century. Since the only evidence I have

---

quoted concerning the hoisting of sails for flight refers to actions from the early part of the fifth century BC we must consider later evidence to determine whether or not the *akateion* was used in this way.

Epicurus the philosopher, who set up a school at Athens in 306 BC, when he was 35, uses the phrase "hoist the *akatia*" (ἐπαραμένους τὰ ἀκάτια) metaphorically to indicate flight (Epicurus Frag. 163. ed. Usener from Plutarch *Moralia* 1094D; at *Moralia* 15D Plutarch uses the phrase "to hoist the Epicurean *akateion*" in connection with flight). Epicurus' association of the *akateion* with flight suggests that in his time it was hoisted by *triereis* (and perhaps *tetrereis* too) wishing to break off from an engagement. It seems that even if a ship had left its big sail ashore it still fled under its *akateion*. This implies that, even with the reduced sail area provided by the *akateion*, sufficient driving force was generated to take a ship out of the battle line.

The evidence for flight under sail suggests that when the manoeuvrability needed to press home or avoid ramming attacks was not required ships would hoist sail to take them out of the battle line. Although it is not clear when the practice began of using the *akateion* as a battle sail when a ship needed to flee, it is certain that the *akateion* was used in this way by the end of the fifth century BC. Even under *akateion* alone a ship was fast enough to break away from the battle.

Conclusions

It does not seem safe to take Xenophon's phrase, "It is a long day's journey from Byzantium to Heraclea for a trireme with oars" as a bald statement of the endurance and speed characteristics of a *trieres* under oar. The context of the passage suggests that, for many triereis, the journey would have taken more than a day. It may also be that "with oars" was included to indicate that oars will have had to be used to pass through the Bosphorus and therefore it is quite possible, given a similar use of the term by the same writer when we know that sails were indeed involved, that we could be talking about use of both sails and oars in covering this distance.

It is not possible from Xenophon's account of Iphicrates' *periplous* to determine whether or not passage under oar was faster than passage under sail. Speeds under oar and under sail would have differed with changes in wind strength, wind direction and sea state. Therefore it can not be definitively stated whether it was faster to voyage under oar than sail or vice versa. Ships in a hurry to complete long passages seem to have used their rowers in shifts. Other evidence suggests that if there was no need

for speed the oarsmen could be used, and allowed to rest, all together. *Triereis* fleeing from battle hoisted sail and, even under *akateion* alone, were swift enough to break clear of the fight.

The evidence of our sources, together with a consideration of prevailing conditions in the Eastern Mediterranean, point to the fastest passages being made under sail and oar, the exact combination of the two being dependent on the length of the voyage and the weather at the time.

Implications for a second reconstruction

The points raised above may have implications for any future reconstruction. Historical requirement (9) should in my view remain "To carry sail well enough for oars to be used only in insufficient or contrary winds" It also seems to me that it is not safe to demand that any reconstruction should be capable of being rowed by a crew of average strength and endurance from Byzantium to Heraclea in "a long day". The context of Xenophon's statement suggests that this was probably beyond many ancient *triereis* and their crews. Moreover since I hope I have demonstrated that it is likely that a *trieres* could be expected to complete some of the journey under sail we should not be demanding that our crews are able to row for 16–18 hours at between 7 and 8 knots. In my view, in line with Hermocrates of Syracuse's statement of the length of crossing using oars, about 70–80 miles, which would cause a crew to arrive tired, a *trieres* reconstruction which can maintain a speed of 7–8 knots under oar for ten hours a day would adequately fit the historical evidence.

Bibliography

Casson, L. (1971) *Ships and Seamanship in the Ancient World.* Princeton NJ, Princeton University Press.

Denham, H. M. (1979) *The Aegean: a sea-guide to its coasts and islands.* 4th ed., London, John Murray.

Morrison, J. S. (1991) Ancient Greek measures of length in nautical contexts. *Antiquity* 65, 298–305.

Morrison, J. S. and Williams, R .T. (1968) *Greek Oared Ships, 900–322 B.C.* Cambridge, Cambridge University Press.

Morrison, J. S., Coates, J. F. and Rankov, N. B. (2000) *The Athenian Trireme: the history and reconstruction of an ancient warship.* 2nd ed. Cambridge, Cambridge University Press.

Severin, T. (1985) *The Jason Voyage: the quest for the Golden Fleece.* London, Hutchinson.

Shaw, T. (ed.) (1993a) *The Trireme Project. Operational Experience 1987–90. Lessons Learnt.* Oxbow Monograph 31. Oxford, Oxbow Books.

Whitehead, I. (1993) What Constitutes a "Better Sailing" Ship? In Shaw 1993a, 91–4.

22. Human Mechanical Power Sustainable in Rowing a Ship for Long Periods of Time

John Coates

The topic of the cruising speed of the ancient trireme has come to the fore in the course of the sea trials of *Olympias* (see also the papers in this part of the volume by Rankov (pp. 145–51), Rossiter and Whipp (pp. 165–8), Wallinga (pp. 152–4) and Whitehead (pp. 155–60). The project has in particular been concerned to explore the likely performance of triremes under oar and the accounts by Thucydides and Xenophon which imply respectively average sustained speeds of over 6 knots for about 30 hours and during 'a long day', which might have been up to as much as 20 hours in summer (Thuc. 3.49; Xen. *Anabasis* 6.4.2.).

The *Olympias* reconstruction has a hull the sizes of whose timbers and planking and method of construction are based upon those of the 3rd-century BC Punic oared ship of similar size found near Marsala, Sicily. The hull structure of the trireme reconstruction is highly stressed and is therefore likely to be of about the smallest practicable weight. The hull is as small as can accommodate the recorded number of oarcrew, 170, and 30 other complement. The breadth of the hull is limited by the clear width of the shipsheds of the Piraeus and is no greater on the waterline than is needed to provide adequate stability. The effective power required to propel the ship at various speeds, displacing 43 tonnes fully manned, is therefore likely to be near the minimum for a trireme which accords with the evidence, and for *Olympias* it has been determined with some certainty for calm water and wind condition by towing tests of a model and by towing the ship herself.

The effective power applied by an oarcrew in propelling the ship may be considered to be the net mechanical power developed physically by the crew multiplied by the efficiency with which that power is converted into effective propulsive power. That efficiency of rowing has been studied by Timothy Shaw in the context of *Olympias* and he has calculated that it probably lies between 53% and 55% in calm water and wind conditions.

The net mechanical power able to be developed by a person aerobically is given by the rate of energy output of the person multiplied by the efficiency with which it is converted into mechanical power. That efficiency, in effect the thermal efficiency of the person as a heat engine, varies with the rate of energy output between 25% at 40 watts (w) to 22% at about 200w.

The power developed, whether mechanical or the rate of energy output (*i.e.* gross power) varies with the rate of oxygen absorption. A curve for measured mechanical power against oxygen absorption is given by Wyndham *et al.* (1959, reproduced in Scherrer *et al.* 1981, 12). The sustainable rate of energy output, or gross power, varies also with the period of time over which it is sustained, the maximum aerobic rate of oxygen absorption (MAO) of which the individual is capable, as well as a number of other physiological factors, such as body weight and constitution, state of physical training, ambient temperature, humidity and ventilation. The gross power of a crew can vary greatly, and that variation raises the question of what gross power would the sort of trireme oarcrews manning the ships referred to by Thucydides and Xenophon have been capable, and hence of whether the reconstruction has the right power-speed requirements. Conversely, if it can be accepted that the effective power required to propel a trireme at various speeds accords with that required by *Olympias*, and that the efficiencies of rowing and the thermal efficiency quoted are correct, the quality of those oarcrews may be estimated. Either way, sustainable gross power needs to be investigated if these reported performances are to be related to physical realities. Neither question need cast doubt upon the correctness of Thucydides or Xenophon.

There are few data in this field. One source is *Précis de Physiologie du Travail* by J Scherrer *et al.* (1981). This source has been quoted by Burlet to give three figures for sustainable mechanical power for 'an ordinary man' (Burlet, Carrière and Zysberg 1986, 198):

- 140 w for 10 hours
- 170 w for 4 hours
- 200 w for 1 hour.

However, Monod in *Précis de Physiologie du Travail* gives the following figures for sustainable gross power for 'well trained athletes and extreme performances' for maximum possible durations (Monod 1981, 130 and table 3-VI):

- 700 w for 10 hours
- 850 w for 4 hours
- 1000 w for 1 hour

These figures were derived from measured mechanical powers and then increased to give gross power by assuming a physical thermal efficiency of 20%. It will be seen that these figures are indeed five times those quoted by Burlet but refer to the mechanical powers able to be sustained by well trained athletes, and not by ordinary men as stated by Burlet.

Monod then discusses maximum tolerable (as distinct from maximum possible) and sustainable gross powers. These are difficult to determine, he says, but recommends that in the meantime a few points should be taken into account:

- More than 50% of (maximum?) aerobic power cannot be developed habitually.
- An energy output of no more than 8,400 kJ/day for professional physical work over many years; this corresponds to a gross power of 90w sustained over an 8 hour day and applies to a well-built adult man.
- The time for which gross power exceeds 280w should be limited, to limit the total energy output/day to 8,400 kJ/day.

Monod (1981, 133 fig. 3–18) gives values for thermal efficiency vs. mechanical power, thus:

Mechanical power w	Thermal efficiency %
40	25
80	24
120	23.3
160	22.8
200	22.4

These data were quoted from Galletti (1959), derived from cyclists whose mechanical power and oxygen consumption were measured. However, E. R. Nadel and S. R. Bussolari, in *The Daedalus Project* about the man-powered flight lasting nearly 4 hours by a cyclist named Kanellopoulos, found thermal efficiencies in volunteers for that project ranging from 18.0% to 33.7%, and they state that the reason for the variation is not clear (Nadel and Bussolari 1988).

The maximum duration of exercise as a function of power developed is given by Monod (1981, 129 fig. 3–16) in the form of curves of the percentage of maximum oxygen absorption at various sustained levels of exercise against the time for which that level could be sustained, for well trained and untrained people, after Astrand and Rodahl (1972). The curves pass through the points shown in Table 22.1

On the assumption, neglecting base metabolism, that

Table 22.1

Maximum duration hours		% of maximum aerobic oxygen absorption while exercising at a given level	
Well trained	Not trained	Well trained	Not trained
0.25	0.1	100	100
1.0		88	
	1.0		50
2.5		76	
	2.5		34
4.0		69	
	4.0		29
5.8		59	
	5.8		26
8.0		51	
	8.0		23

the mechanical power produced over these periods is proportional to oxygen absorption, these curves show the importance of training in sustaining high levels of power for prolonged periods.

Maximum aerobic oxygen absorption, and, it must be assumed, the associated maximum short-term mechanical power output, varies from about 4.5 l O_2/min for fit young men (no doubt exceeded by exceptional athletes) to 3 l O_2/min for ordinary young men and 2 l O_2/min for women; it reduces to about ¾ of all those figures by the age of 60 years (Monod 1981, 121).

Thus, for a period of 4 hours, the mechanical power capable of being produced by a well trained crew of fit young men would be (69/29) × (4.5/3) = 3.5 times the power produced by a crew of otherwise similar ordinary and untrained young men. As ship speed is closely proportional to the cube root of the effective power, the first crew would maintain 1.5 times the speed of the second, both for 4 hours.

A paper by W. V. Macfarlane considered cane cutters in Queensland working 9.5 hours a day to their physiological limit in dry bulb temperatures rarely greater than 35°C (Macfarlane 1981). In 8 hours they produced 13,400 kJ of work energy output (compared with the output quoted by Monod, 8,440 kJ/8 hours), which gives a mean gross power of 465 w, and therefore, at a conservatively assumed thermal efficiency of 20%, a mean mechanical power of 93 w. They drank 7.1l of water while working, and lost 2.6 kg of weight and 0.54l of urine; daily (in 24 hours) they excreted about 9l of sweat and absorbed 9.6l of water. When not working they slept, apart from time to eat. Macfarlane (1981, 284) considers that capacity for work for a duration of 6 hours corresponds to 50% of maximum oxygen consumption (compare with 59% for well trained men in the curves produced by Monod (1981) after Astrand and Rodahl (1972), summarised in my table above). Monod gives a maximum level of gross power of 700 w for 8 hours/day, presumably in temperate conditions. The difference (34%) may be the effect of the high temperature in which Macfarlane's labourers produced 465 w.

Kanellopoulos (Daedalus Project), a carefully chosen and trained athlete, developed nearly 200 w of mechanical power for nearly 4 hours, during which he drank almost 4 l of water-electrolyte drink, and could have continued for at least another two hours.

From Thucydides' account of the famous non-stop passage by a trireme from Athens to Mytilene, it may be estimated that an overall average speed of about 6.2 knots was achieved for a duration of just under 30 hours. The ship met no contrary winds and as the prevailing diurnal wind, the *meltemi*, is northerly and therefore a head wind broad on the port bow, sails could not have been used anyway, so the passage may be assumed to have been made under oars. Thucydides says of the oarcrew that some slept and others pulled (rowed), turn and turn about. The effective propulsive power required by *Olympias* at 6.2 knots with one rudder only half immersed, a clean bottom and in calm conditions is 6.2 kw. If, in pulling turn and turn about ⅔ of the crew rowed, each man would have had to develop on average 55 w effective power, or 110 w mechanical power (at a conservative figure for propulsive efficiency of 50%). Allowing an increase of 20% in required power to overcome the effects of waves in the open sea in such conditions, the required mechanical power becomes 132 w/man.

The question now arises as to the best length of the 'turns'. Sustainable power falls progressively with the time for which it is developed (Monod 1981, 129 fig. 3–16). On the other hand, recovery during rest and sleep would presumably increase according to some function of the time resting and sleeping. The first few hours of sleep are termed paradoxal and are understood to be the most valuable. Paradoxal sleep lasts for about two hours, so it seems at first sight (but this needs to be investigated) that a regime of 2 hours rest and sleeping, being the shortest of high value in achieving recovery, and therefore 4 hours rowing may be the best means for an oarcrew to maintain the highest power for many hours on end.

If men rowed in turns for 4 hours and slept for 2 hours, the curves from Monod show that they could have maintained 69% of their maximum aerobic output for 4 hours. If they were trained oarsmen, their MAO may, even in ancient Athens, be assumed to have been at least 3.1 lO$_2$/min corresponding (Monod 1981, 120 fig. 3–8) to a mechanical power of 250 w, so, as 69% of that is 172 w, it seems that the average speed could have been maintained by ⅔ of the crew at a time with a margin of 40w/man to spare. However, that takes no account of the effects of ambient temperature, which, if 34% as derived above (Macfarlane 1981) for high temperatures up to 35°C, would reduce the 172 w to 114 w. As however about half the passage would have been carried out at night and in the cooler conditions at the end and start of the day, that figure could be reduced by say half, to 17%, making the average mechanical output 172 × 0.83 = 142 w, 10 w more

than the estimated required average of 132 w. If the oarcrew were the physiological equivalents of Macfarlane's sugarcane cutters in the same hot conditions and capable of 13,400 kJ/8 hours compared with 8,400 kJ/8 hours quoted for professional labour by Monod, they could have developed about 9% less power in the heat of the day for the 4 hour period, *i.e.* about 160w, well sufficient for 6.2 knots. If however the oarcrew had an MAO of 3.1 lO$_2$/min but were not trained, they could, by the same curve, develop only 29% of 250 w, *i.e.* 72 w of mechanical power, insufficient for 6.2 knots by the above assumptions, but only enough for 5.1 knots. If of MAO of 4 lO$_2$/min but untrained they could have developed 4/3 × 72 w = 96 w, sufficient for 5.6 knots, showing the importance of training to sustained performance (as is also clear in the same curve).

The conclusion from the use of the data in Monod and Macfarlane, which omit verification of the physiological practicality of a regime of 4 hours' rowing and two hours' rest (sleep), must be that Thucydides' account is credible for an oarcrew of men below about 30 years of age and capable of a fairly commonly achieved MAO of 3.1 l O$_2$/min provided that they were physically trained (or habituated to sustained physical work). Training is the critical factor.

The 129 sea miles between Byzantium and Heraclea, which Xenophon states to be a long day's voyage for a trireme under oar, could have been performed if the same assumptions above were valid (including a 20% allowance for extra power required to cope with sea conditions but neglecting the currents examined by Shaw on pp. 63–5 above) in 20 hours continuously.

Whether the 4 hour/2 hour work/rest regime suggested here is physiologically the best is unresolved and needs to be investigated. It is likely that long experience in rowing ships would have led the ancients to adopt a practice which would have been near the optimum.

Rest periods of about two hours seem sufficient, according to Monod and Sanchez (1981, 154, 156) for digestion of food if taken, as it would have been, immediately after a four-hour period of rowing. In a 4/2 hour regime, there would be a necessary pause in rowing every 2 hours when some food and water could be taken by those remaining at their oars for another two hours and by those having just woken up, maintaining the optimum 2-hour period between intakes of food (Monod and Sanchez 1981). Thucydides wrote that the crew made such haste that they pulled and ate at the same time barley bread mixed with wine and olive oil, a suitable food rich in carbohydrates to supply energy relatively quickly. A two-hour rest period would have been sufficient nearly to complete the most valuable paradoxal phase of a sleeping period, but may not have been sufficient for other aspects of recovery. During a 30-hour passage with the crew rotating in a 4/2 hour regime there would have been five complete rotations, giving each third of the crew a total of 10 hours rest and sleep, and 20 hours rowing.

It looks, by these data and assumptions, and provided

that recovery in 2 hours was sufficient for repeating rowing performance for successive periods of 4 hours, that if a modern scratch crew of young, fit, but untrained men with MAOs of 3.1 l O_2/min, with ⅔ rowing, could maintain 5.1 knots in a Mark IIb trireme reconstruction (see Shaw, pp. 76–81 above) with a smooth bottom for 4 hours in calm conditions, they would indirectly have established the feasibility of the non-stop passage to Mytilene by trained oarsmen with an MAO of 3.1 l O_2/min of the non-stop passage to Mytilene as described by Thucydides and a 20-hour interpretation of Xenophon's 'long day' to make the passage from Byzantium to Heraclea. It seems that the maximum speed achieved in *Olympias* in a short sprint was about 8.5 knots instead of the hoped-for 9.7 knots, a shortfall of 12% in speed and about 33% in power. If that shortfall was due entirely to the oar rig of *Olympias* (though her crews on sea trials were by no means all trained nor all-male), the above feasibility would be established if an average speed of 4.5 knots could be achieved in *Olympias* by such a modern crew. The corresponding speed for a trained crew of men with MAOs of 3.1 l O_2/min would be $4.5 \times (69/29)^{1/3} = 6.0$ knots.

Bibliography

Astrand, P. O. and Rodahl, K. (1972) *Manuel de physiologie de l'exercice musculaire*, French transl. of *Manual of the Physiology of Muscular Exercise*. Paris, Masson et Cie.

Burlet, R., Carrière, J. and Zysberg, A. (1986) Mais comment pouvait-on ramer sur les galères du Roi-Soleil? *Histoire et Mesure* 1.3/4,147–208.

Galletti, P. M. (1959) Les échanges respiratoires pendant l'exercice musculaire. *Helvetica Physiologica et Pharmacologica Acta* 17, 34–61.

Macfarlane, W. V. (1981) Vie et travail dans les climats chauds. In Scerrer *et al.* 1981, 265–289.

Monod, H. (1981) Défense énergétique chez l'homme. In Scherrer *et al.* 1981, 107–138.

Monod, H. and Sanchez, J. (1981) Besoins énergétiques de l'homme au travail. In Scherrer *et al.* 1981, 139–158.

Nadel, E. R. and Bussolari, S. R. (1988) The Daedalus Project: Physiological Problems and Solutions. *American Scientist* (July–August), 351–360.

Scherrer, J. *et al.* (1981) *Précis de physiologie du travail, notions d'ergonomie.* 2nd ed. Paris, Masson et Cie.

Wyndham, C. H., Strydom, N. B., Maritz, J. S., Morrison, J. F., Peter, J., and Potgeiter, Z. U. (1959) Maximum oxygen intake and maximum heart rate during strenuous work. *Journal of Applied Physiology* 14, 927–936.

23. Paleo-bioenergetics: clues to the maximum sustainable speed of a trireme under oar

Harry Rossiter and Brian Whipp

Introduction

The major impediment to establishing plausible estimates for the metabolic demands, or limits, of sustained high-energy activities for ancient cultures is the lack of information regarding the actual work rates undertaken. As much of the discussion at the Oxford/Henley conference in 1998 was directed towards the literary evidence for the maximum sustainable speed of the ancient *trieres,* the human limitations to the production of power for movement of the warship are highly relevant. Statements by Xenophon (*Anabasis* 6.4.2) and Thucydides (3.49), for example, provide literary examples of the speed of the *trieres* under oar (although there is considerable debate about the validity of such statements). It is therefore salient to consider the physiological limitations of the 'human engine.'

Our understanding of the bioenergetics of sustained muscular work provides the potential for calculating the maximum sustainable power output by the oarsmen for the considerable speeds and distances required by the literary evidence (*e.g.* ~7 knots for ~18 hours, based on Thucydides 3.49; 8.101; Xenophon *Anabasis* 6.4.2). These estimates can be used to support or refute the plausibility of the literary evidence and consequently the justification for the *Olympias* reconstruction. Furthermore, plausible extimates for the maximum sustainable power output (in watts) may be applied to the relevant range of movement and mechanical efficiency of the *Olympias* or with respect to an, as yet unreconstructed, theoretical Mk II ship. The physiological and bio-energetic limitations to long duration exercise (such as oxygen delivery, substrate provision to the working muscle, as well as fluid and thermoregulatory balance, for example) may provide a window into better understanding the plausible maximum speeds of ancient *triereis.* Direct measurement of the relevant physiological variables, both in the laboratory and from *Olympias* herself, would provide experimental support for these theoretical calculations.

The basis of exercise bio-energetics

Skeletal muscle may be considered to be a machine that is fuelled by the chemical energy of substrates derived from ingested food and stored as carbohydrates and lipids in the body. Protein is also a viable energy source but is not used to fuel energy requirements to any appreciable extent, except under extreme conditions such as starvation. Energy for muscular contraction is obtained predominantly by the oxidation of the substrate (carbohydrate or lipid). The free energy of these substrates (*i.e.* that fraction of the total chemical energy that is capable of doing work) is not directly used for muscle contraction as it must first be stored as the bond energy of the muscles' "high-energy" phosphate pool (adenosine triphosphate (ATP) and creatine phosphate (PCr)). Exercise requires an acceleration of "high-energy" phosphate bond utilisation with their concentration being replenished through an increased oxygen (O_2) utilisation rate; this occurs with a simultaneous increase in the removal of carbon dioxide (CO_2), the major catabolic end-product of exercise.

In the simplest case, carbohydrate is metabolised (with sufficient O_2 supply) such that each glycosyl unit provides the muscle cell with 37 ATP molecules at a cost of 6 O_2 molecules utilised. Here the amount O_2 consumed and the CO_2 produced are equal and thus the respiratory quotient (RQ) in the muscle is 1.0. When the metabolite is purely lipid, 130 ATP molecules are produced for the consumption of 23 O_2 molecules, resulting in an RQ of 0.71. These processes are termed aerobic metabolism. As work rate increases during exercise, the fuel mixture derives proportionally more from carbohydrate than from lipid. This is reflected in the muscle RQ, which can be measured under appropriate circumstances from pulmonary gas exchange as the respiratory exchange ratio (RER: the rates of carbon dioxide output divided by oxygen uptake; $\dot{V}CO_2/\dot{V}O_2$). This allows the proportional utilisation of carbohydrate and lipid to be determined, *i.e.* percentage carbohydrate utilisation = $(RQ - 0.7)/(0.3)$. The "average western diet" produces a resting RER of approximately

0.8 indicating that about 33% of the energy utilisation is derived from carbohydrate metabolism. This is significant to the present consideration of very long duration exercise, as the stores of carbohydrate (glycogen and glucose) may become limiting.

Under conditions in which aerobic metabolism is inadequate for the demands of "high energy" phosphate production an alternate mechanism is utilised without the immediate use of O_2, but which results in lactate production; this is termed anaerobic glycolysis. The substrate 'cost' for the production of energy from this reaction, however, is expensive compared to the complete oxidative breakdown of glycogen. The net gain in ATP is only 3 from each glycosyl unit anaerobically as opposed to 37 aerobically. For the same work rate, therefore, this pathway causes glycogen (and glucose) to be used at a considerably faster rate than in the totally aerobic state. Moreover, the two protons formed from each glucose molecule (or glucosyl unit) in association with these lactate molecules cause a disturbance of the acid-base balance in the cell and blood and accelerating the fatigue process.

Bio-energetic considerations for long-duration trireme rowing

The main issue in the consideration of very long duration exercise, such as concerns us here, is that energy provision that includes some energy derived from anaerobic glycolysis, is not sufficiently sustainable. The increased rate of carbohydrate utilisation, that is a necessary consequence of anaerobic glycolysis, will cause the exercising athletes to become more rapidly glycogen depleted. The "standard" human stores about 400 g of glycogen in his/her muscles and a further 50 g in the liver (the liver can also produce glucose but at a slow rate compared to the rates of muscular consumption). Even with access to modern-day sports drinks and glucose-feeding régimes, it is difficult (if not impossible) for the athlete to ingest and utilise the amounts of glycogen during exercise that are required to sustain anaerobic metabolism for very long durations. Thus, as muscle and liver glycogen stores are depleted, the athlete is either forced to lower the rate of power production or he/she exhausts. The importance of muscle glycogen in work tolerance is well described and there is a strong positive correlation between the tolerable duration of high-intensity exercise and muscle glycogen content prior to the exercise. Homeostasis of blood glucose is also necessary for the maintenance of normal cerebral function.

The description, by Casson (1964, 121) of Louis XIV's galleys being able to "sustain five knots per hour (*sic*) for the first hour, during the second hour only four and a half; after that 'they dropped down to two knots or slower'" (as cited by Wallinga, above p. 153), is a likely reflection of an early metabolic acidosis and consequent effects on glycogen depletion and performance. Once the finite glycogen stores are near depletion, energy production must slow appreciably (*e.g.* Newsholme *et al.* 1992), as the combined rates of delivery of blood borne lipids, glucose, and intramuscular lipids are insufficient to meet the ATP demands of high-intensity excercise.

It is reasonable to deduce, therefore, that any long duration exercise by the anicent oarsmen would need to be undertaken at a rate that did not deplete the muscle glycogen store prior to completion of the task. The physiological parameter demarking the threshold for anaerobic glycolysis is termed the anaerobic (or lactate) threshold. In "standard" man the anaerobic threshold occurs at an average of about 50% of the maximum aerobic capacity (~50% $\dot{V}O_2$max), at which point obligatory anaerobiosis occurs. Thus, élite endurance athletes may have an anaerobic threshold at a much higher value (80% or more) of $\dot{V}O_2$max. For a group of modern-day (junior international) sliding-seat oarsmen (Steinacker *et al.* 1993) the lactate threshold occurred between ~30 to 35 ml O_2 per minute, per kg of body weight. This value may be applied in relation to the shorter, slighter statures that we would expect of the ancient Athenians (168 cm in height and 67 kg in weight). This gives us an estimated lactate threshold of ~2 to 2.3 l/min of $\dot{V}O_2$. Of this, ~300 ml/min is required for basal metabolism and ~400 ml/min for the 'internal' power required to move the oarsman's body against gravity as he rows (body-swing). The remainder is available for external power production that can be distributed to the task in hand. Available estimates for modern-day sliding-seat rowing (*e.g.* Di Prampero *et al.* 1968; Steinacker *et al.* 1993) suggest that an oxygen cost of ~14 ml O_2/min per watt power-output is a reasonable expectation. In this theoretical consideration, therefore (using modern values from sliding-seat rowing), the available power output for sustained exercise would be ~95–115W (*i.e.* from 1.3 to 1.6 l/min at a cost of 14 ml O_2.min^{-1}.W^{-1}). Interestingly, this value is close to the estimated power requirement to propel the *Olympias* at speeds appropriate for the ancient literature (with the whole crew rowing and only one rudder half-immersed in the water: 115W; cf. Shaw 1993, 58–68).

However, the total muscle mass utilised for the exercise has a significant impact on the total $\dot{V}O_2$ available for the task. During modern-day sliding-seat rowing the predominant power-generation comes from the large muscles of the legs. While these muscles are used in fixed-seat rowing, their application is more of stabilisation than of oar-applied power-production, and there is little flexion and extension of the legs during the stroke. In our laboratories we have measured the maximum attainable $\dot{V}O_2$ during fixed-seat rowing (with an effective stroke length of 73 cm and rating of 36 spm, *i.e.* to mimic the conditions in *Olympias*) and found it to be only ~65% of that attained during sliding-seat rowing. However, to its advantage, fixed-seat rowing appears to have a lower O_2-cost than sliding-seat, at about 10–12 ml O_2/min per watt power-output. This improvement in oxidative efficiency, however, does not make up for the considerable limitation of the reduced available exercising muscle mass.

These vital considerations reduce the plausible sustainable limits for external power generation to only ~80 W at best. It is of interest, therefore, that of the estimated 115 W per man required to sustain ~7.2 knots in *Olympias*, only 62 W is for propulsive movement; the remaining 53 W was lost in oar slippage and in non-propulsive oar movement (cf. Shaw 1993, 58–68). This would suggest that mechanical improvements in the oar weight or oar system design in *Olympias* may provide a profitable avenue for improving the sustainable ship speed. These two aspects of mechanical-efficiency may be improved with the canted-rig and longer stroke allowed by the proposals in a Mk IIb vessel (see above pp. 76–91). However, in our laboratory experiments using a stroke length of 99 cm and 'free rating' (resulting in 28 spm) the O_2-cost was essentially unaffected by the increased stroke length. This suggests that improvements in efficiency in a Mk II vessel may be more profitably explored through mechanical, not physiological, advances.

Further physiological aspects for sustained exercise

For very long duration exercise, not only must the athletes maintain a power output below the threshold for anaerobic glycolysis, but also one that utilises carbohydrate at a rate that will not deplete the stores before the task is completed. In order that the glycogen not be depleted before the end of a continuous row, it must be 'eked-out' for the ~18 hour duration (assuming continuous exercise, and that no carbohydrate is ingested during this time). This would require that the oarsmen exercise with an average RER of ~0.74. Previous laboratory investigations of sustained exercise have demonstrated that: 1) RER increases with increasing work rate (*e.g.* Wasserman *et al.* 1999); and 2) work rates below the threshold for anaerobic glycolysis manifest RER values close to the resting value of 0.8 (*e.g.* Wasserman *et al.* 1999; Watt *et al.* 2002). Thus, it may be that it is not enough for the trireme oarsmen simply to exercise below the lactate threshold; they may have to maintain a still lower value of $\dot{V}O_2$ in order to maintain blood and muscle glucose for the required duration. However, this aspect is hard to quantify, even in theory, as it will be significantly affected by the oarsmen's diet. The evidence that the ancient crews, on occasion, rested and rowed in turns, provides an interesting challenge for physiologists concerned with nutritional aspects of optimising prolonged activity strategies. However, it seems likely that the increased carbohydrate utilisation rate during the exercise period could not be overcome by the opportunity for partially replenishing these stores during the rest phase. These issues, however, remain to be addressed. Naturally, stresses to other physiological control systems such as thermoregulatory (mid-day ambient temperature of ~35°C), and fluid and electrolyte balance (the rowers in the *Olympias* sweated 3–4 litres/day) would also conspire to constrain the sustainable speed of the vessel.

Considerations and limitations

The relevance of applying aspects of efficiency from modern-day sliding-seat rowing to trireme propulsion are, of course, open to criticism. Further measures of fixed-seat rowing using the body positioning based on the experience from *Olympias* would be of benefit. Also, comparisons with modern-day fixed-seat rowing, such as racing gigs, would provide an insight into the likely technological limitations of the ancient Athenians. Once the limits of wholly-aerobic power production are determined for fixed-seat rowing, the maximum sustainable power output can be determined with greater accuracy. This would provide us with a means of assessing the plausibility of Xenophon's statement concerning "a long day". If we find that even a Mk II trireme would not be likely to produce the speeds expected by the designers, due to the limits of aerobic human performance, then we may conclude that Xenophon's statement that 'the passage from Byzantium to Heraclea was a long day's journey for a *trieres* with oars' was fanciful or even propaganda – assuming, of course, that there was not some 'hyper-efficient' mechanical design of the original vessel-human interface of which we are unaware.

The height and weight of the oarsmen is a significant concern with respect to establishing the relevant physiological variables. We have used the value of 168 cm for the height of the average Athenian in the current calculations, but further investigation as to whether the *trieres* oarsmen were of average stature would prove profitable. It could be inferred from the *Olympias* experience or plans for a Mk II ship that there may have been a maximum height for the oarsmen, due to constraints of rowing in the available confined space. Similarly, there is evidence from the stadium at Corinth that some ancient Greek athletes may have been considerably taller than this 168 cm estimate. A description of the starting blocks of the ancient runners provides us with indicators of their stature: "Each man has a pair of holes cut in the stone slab, left foot in front of right, twenty-five inches apart – uncomfortable for a runner less than six feet tall." (183 cm) (Harris 1974). Likewise the First Cohort of a Roman legion had a minimum recruitment height of 5 foot 9 inches to 5 foot 11 inches (180 cm). Plausible metabolic estimates have recently been made for both laden and unladen sustained marching speeds of ancient Roman legionaries; speeds which were sustained for five summer hours (Whipp *et al.* 1998). The dramatic similarity between the metabolic costs for the laden-speeds compared to speeds employed for unladen marching suggest that the ancient Roman ergonomic advisors to the military had a significant knowledge of the metabolic demands and costs of sustained activity. If the Athenians also understood the implications of very long duration exercise it could be that they were able to perform with this in mind and that the oarsmen recruited would be of larger-than-average stature. It may even be the case that the mixture of 'bread and olive-oil' that was ingested during these very long duration bouts of exercise would be particularly well suited to this type of exertion.

It is interesting that the values estimated for the $\dot{V}O_2$ requirement (~1.5–2.1 l/min) discussed above are similar to those that have been judged as being "probably about the maximum sustained output of which the human frame is capable" (Lloyd 1966). This comment was made with respect to an élite performer in the six-day 'go as you please' contests during the latter half of the 19th century, in which the performers were required to cover as much distance as possible in six days under their own power (*i.e.* walk or run). The best of these men would cover more than 600 miles at an estimated average $\dot{V}O_2$ of ~2 l/min.

Conclusion

It is clear from the sea trials that crews of *Olympias* could not sustain boat-speeds required by Xenophon's '(very) long day.' While it is also clear that great strides were made with practice and improving the technique of *trieres* rowing, paleo-bioenergetic considerations can give plausible estimates for the limitations to sustained exercise. The maximum plausible estimates consider that the ancient oarsmen would have to exercise below their lactate threshold and at rates which produced average RER values no greater than ~0.74. We conclude that a maximum estimate of ~80 W per oarsmen would be available for external power production. It seems likely that, if the ancient Athenians had knowledge and/or technologies to improve the mechanical efficiency of the rowing stroke compared to that measured in *Olympias*, then there would be metabolic scope for sustaining the required speeds for a '(very) long day.' However, the degree of mechanical advancement above those provided by *Olympias* would not be trivial and the rowers would have to have been highly fit athletes, even by modern-day standards. Further experiments are required to refine and extend these suggestions and provide evidence for the plausible metabolic limits of the 'human engine' of the ancient *trieres*.

Acknowledgements

The authors would like to thank Timothy Shaw for introducing us to this issue. His considerable and detailed accounts of the sea trials of *Olympias* were invaluable to our bio-energetic consideration. We also thank Dr John Kowalchuk of the University of Western Ontario, Canada for his time and assistance in making the metabolic measurements during fixed-seat rowing. HBR is an International Fellow of the Wellcome Trust (UK) (#064898).

Bibliography

Casson, L. (1964) *Illustrated History of Ships and Boats.* New York, Doubleday and Company Inc.

Harris, H. A. (1974) *Greek Athletes and Athletics.* London, Hutchinson.

Lloyd, B. B. (1966) The energetics of running: an analysis of world records *The Advancement of Science (London)* 22 (103), 515–530.

Morrison, J. S. and Coates, J. F. (eds) (1989) *An Athenian Trireme Reconstructed. The British sea trials of Olympias, 1987.* BAR International Series, 486. Oxford, Archaeopress.

Morrison, J. S., Coates, J. F. and Rankov, N. B. (2000) *The Athenian Trireme: the history and reconstruction of an ancient warship.* 2nd ed. Cambridge, Cambridge University Press.

Newsholme, E. A., Blomstrand, E. and Ekblom B. (1992) *British Medical Bulletin* 48 (3), 477–95.

Di Prampero, P. E., Cortili, G., Celentano, F. and Cerretelli, P. (1971) Physiological aspects of rowing. *Journal of Applied Physiology* 31 (6), 853–7.

Shaw, T. (ed.) (1993a) *The Trireme Project. Operational Experience 1987–90. Lessons Learnt.* Oxbow Monograph 31. Oxford, Oxbow Books.

Shaw, T. (ed.) (1993b) Rowing *Olympias*: further lessons of the sea trials. In Shaw 1993, 58–68.

Steinacker, J. M., Both, M. and Whipp, B. J. (1993) Pulmonary mechanics and entrainment of respiration and stroke rate during rowing. *International Journal of Sports Medicine* 14 (Suppl. 1), S15–S19.

Wasserman, K., Hansen, J. E., Sue D. Y., Casaburi, R. and Whipp B. J. (1999) *Principles of Exercise Testing and Interpretation.* 3rd ed. Philadelphia, London, Lippincott Williams and Wilkins.

Watt, M. J., Heigenhauser, G. J. F., Dyck, D. J. and Spriet, L. L. (2002) Intramuscular triacylglycerol, glycogen and acetyl group metabolism during 4 h of moderate exercise in man. *Journal of Physiology* 541, 969–78.

Whipp, B. J., Ward, S. A. and Hassall, M. W. C. (1998) Paleo-bioenergetics: the metabolic rate of marching Roman legionaries. *British Journal of Sports Medicine* 32, 261–2.

Part 5

Aspects of Trireme Construction and Maintenance

24. Uniformity or Multiplicity?
On Vitruvius' *interscalmium*

Ronald Bockius

This is an updated version of a paper previously published in German as Bockius 2000.

As is well known, reconstructions of ancient warships are characterized by a lack of physical evidence. Our understanding is limited by the fact that we have no significant remains of either Greek or Roman galleys, and essential data like dimensions, form, interior arrangements and technical equipment have to be deduced entirely from the interpretation of literary and iconographic evidence. Several surviving merchant wrecks, mostly Roman, have helped us to understand shipbuilding techniques and provided information on the materials and tools used in antiquity, but fully to understand something as complex as the oar mechanics of multiple-banked galleys, propelled by the co-ordinated efforts of massive crews squeezed into narrow wooden hulls would require access to actual warship wrecks. Since no such wrecks have yet been discovered – apart from a few light, single-banked military vessels (see below), and the Punic Marsala ships (Frost 1981) whose propulsion systems have attracted very little attention – reconstructions have to rely on clues from illustrations of warships and incidental references in Greek and Roman writers or fragmentary inscriptions. The remains of ancient ship sheds are important for estimating the maximum length and beam of certain warship types, but completely different kinds of data are required to comprehend the interiors of ships with oars operated by one or more men and arranged on two or three levels.

These are the problems which have exercised generations of humanist scholars attempting to understand the trireme mystery. The latter appeared to have been solved when John Morrison's and John Coates' reconstruction of an Athenian trireme (Morrison, Coates and Rankov 2000), the *Olympias*, was launched in 1987 and subsequently trialled over several years to test her performance under oar and sail (Morrison and Coates 1989; Coates, Platis and Shaw 1990; Whitehead *et al.* 1990; Shaw 1993a; Morrison, Coates and Rankov 2000). It was confidently expected that

these trials would not only illuminate the ship's capabilities and operation, but also produce performance figures in line with the historical data.

Neither the creators of *Olympias* nor those who conducted the trials have been entirely satisfied with the results. In particular, it has been felt that her speed under oar did not match what she was thought to be capable of hydrodynamically (Whitehead *et al.* 1989; 1990, 292–4; Coates *et al.* 1990; Coates 1993a). In the course of the trials, it soon became evident that some of the details of the reconstruction had to be modified (*e.g.* the shape and size of the oar blades), and performance was certainly not enhanced by the inexperience of her oar crews in fixed-seat rowing, nor by their being, on average, physically too large for the ship (*e.g.* Whitehead *et al.* 1989, 28, 32–45, fig. 27; Weiskittel 1989; Coates *et al.* 1990, 68; Shaw 1993b). In particular, one of the most fundamental aspects of *Olympias'* design, the distance between her thole-pins, has been called into question. Thus, the current proposal for a Mark II reconstruction is driven by a perception that the room provided for each of *Olympias'* oarsmen was too short (Coates 1993b; Coates and Morrison 1993, 108; Morrison 1993; Coates, above pp. 82–3, 138).

Olympias was designed on the basis of several disparate pieces of historical and archaeological evidence interpreted in the light of the experience and practical knowledge of a distinguished naval architect, John Coates. The ship's overall dimensions and the spacing of the interior structures were derived from two items of evidence in particular: the remains of the ship sheds of the Athenian naval base at Zea, and the implication in a passage of the Roman architect Vitruvius that the distance between the thole-pins of ancient war ships was two cubits (*De architectura* 1.2.4: *navibus interscalmio quae* διπηχυαϊα *dicitur*). Vitruvius' *interscalmium* was originally interpreted by John Morrison as a distance of two Attic cubits, *i.e.* approx. 89 cms (the same distance, incidentally, as two Roman cubits, the equivalent of three *pedes monetales*). This figure not only determines the distribution of fittings,

Figure 24.1. Reconstruction of an Athenian trireme. Perspective view of the middle (zygians) and upper level (thranites) of the oarcrew (after Morrison and Coates 1990, 235, fig. 66).

oarsmen, *etc.*, but also influences the proportions and overall length of the ship (Morrison and Coates 1989; Morrison, Coates and Rankov, 2000).

Although each oarsman in *Olympias* has 89 cms room fore-and-aft (Fig. 24.1), one component of her inner structure limits considerably the use which can be made of that room. The cross-beams (*zyga*) of the ship, on which the middle level of rowers (*zygitai*) sit, reduce the freedom of movement of the thalamians seated in the lowest level below the zygians (Fig. 24.2). The limitation of the reach of the thalamians, and therefore of their stroke-length and so that of the crew as a whole, undoubtedly affected *Olympias'* performance. So, too, did the use of individual rowers whose size made it impossible for them to obtain full reach without hitting the back of the rower immediately astern. Because of these limitations, the interpretation of Vitruvius' reference has now been revised. On the new hypothesis, based on a metrological relief found on Salamis in 1985 but not published until 1990, the two-cubit *interscalmium* of an Athenian trireme would have been approx. 98 cm long (Morrison 1991; 1993, 11–13, 18–19 n. 3; Morrison, Coates and Rankov 2000, 245–6, 268–9; Coates, above, pp. 83, 138).

A room of about 98 cm would certainly alleviate the rowing problems mentioned, but would also have other implications. It will be obvious that a reconstruction based on an increased room of just under 1 m will produce a hull which is almost 10% longer than the *Olympias* design (Coates 1996, 288–9, figs 55–56, 345 app. D; Morrison, Coates and Rankov 2000, 269; Coates, above pp. 83, 88, 138). A ship of approximately 40 m would still fit within

the Zea ship sheds, and in fact, we do not know whether triremes were the same length as the buildings which housed them. The ships themselves may well have been significantly shorter than the sheds.

Two further questions must be raised concerning the interpretation of Vitruvius' term. Firstly, should we take his two-cubit *interscalmium* to be a fixed standard or norm without any deviation, or as an average to be taken only as a guideline? Secondly, can we definitely exclude the possibility that a room of about 89 cm is too short to be viable for the oarsmen of three-banked warships?

The linguistic and metrological data are too vague to answer these complex questions definitively. It may help, therefore, to bring some comparative archaeological data to bear. A number of Roman wrecks excavated at Mainz (Rhineland-Palatinate) and at Oberstimm near Ingolstadt (Bavaria) provide such data and are considered here. At these sites, situated on the Rhine and Danube rivers respectively, the remains of several large vessels have come to light which reveal how oarsmen were arranged in ships of the Roman period. Although the vessels are characterized by a single-banked oarsystem, they represent the only opportunity offered to date to study ancient oar propulsion in any detail, since they preserve evidence of their internal furniture and mechanical fittings. In these ships at least, rooms of both 89 and 98 cm were employed, and there was no strict standardization of the oarsmen's room. Moreover, investigation of other ancient and medieval wrecks suggests that oarsmen frequently had less than 98 cm room at their disposal, and sometimes even less than 89 cm.

Figure 24.2. Reconstruction of an Athenian trireme. Longitudinal section on the port side showing the room of the oarsmen and the sweep of the upper parts of their bodies at the beginning and end of a long oarstroke. The hatched beams at the level of the thalamians' heads are 10% closer together than the interscalmium of 88.8 cms (drawing modified after J. F. Coates in Morrison and Coates 1989, 23, fig. 10).

The late Roman shipwrecks of the 4th century AD found in Mainz

In the winter of 1981/82, the remains of five ships were discovered near the ancient waterfront outside the Roman city walls of Mogontiacum (Mainz). The vessels were built in the Romano-Celtic tradition of planks nailed to frames and nearly all the constructional elements were of oak. Other features, like massive frames with mast steps and caulking, were also typical of this tradition. Two different ship types were identified (Höckmann 1988; 1991; 1993), but only the four wrecks (nos 1, 2, 4 and 5) of type Mainz I are relevant to our present discussion. According to Olaf Höckmann's most recent reconstruction of the principal dimensions, the type I ships were extraordinarily narrow, with a beam of *c.* 2.7 m, length of *c.* 21 m, and depth of 0.9 m (Pferdehirt 1995, 7–24; figs 17 and 22; pl. 1). However, further investigations have shown that only the length of wreck 5 (formerly no. 9) can be safely reconstructed. As revised analyses of both the ship's timbers and the photogrammetric documentation have proved, ship no. 5 was originally some 17.5 m long (Bockius 2006, 177–187 App. 8). The hull measurements and several structural elements of wrecks 1 and 5 indicate a crew of 24 or 26 oarsmen. The volumetric coefficients of the hulls and the number of oarsmen they accommodated suggest that the main design requirement of these craft was speed under oars.

Mainz wreck 4 is a fragment of a long but slender vessel with parts of the ship's port side preserved. Internally, between the chine and the topwale, the side frames and the upper surfaces of the floor timbers are enclosed by three wide boards nailed to the ribs (Fig. 24.3). The thole-pins are missing, but an opening in the preserved ship's side suggests that a horizontal timber protruded on both sides of the hull, presumably as an attachment for two side-rudders. A curved, wooden, fore-and-aft reinforcement for such a cross-beam was also recorded. It follows that wreck 4 represents the after part of a ship.

The upper edge of the first (*i.e.* the uppermost) board nailed inside the hull lies 12 to 15 cm below the topwale. Eight deep slots, 20–24 cm long and 3 cm deep, were cut into this edge for the insertion of board-like transoms, which without doubt acted as thwarts. The distances between the slots, each measured from central point to central point, are 84, 86, 87, 89 and 92 cm respectively. Since the removable tholes have been lost, we do not know whether these distances correspond to the original distances between the thole-pins. Nevertheless, it is obvious that the distribution of thwarts would have determined the fore-and-aft room available for each rower. Consequently, we can assume that the values of 84 to 92 cm represent the

scarboard

Figure 24.3. Photogrammetrical plan of late Roman wreck no. 4 from Mainz, Löhrstraße (after Böhler, Fachhochschule Mainz, Vermessungswesen). Hull interior of the wreck in an approximately upright position, elevation (above) and plan (below).

metrical range of the ship's *interscalmia*. Her rooms were obviously shorter than 98 cm, and most seem to have been even shorter than the equivalent of 2 Roman cubits, *i.e.* 89 cm. All the measurements of the Mainz wrecks were taken either from photogrammetrical plans or full-scale drawings of the wet wood, and the assumed error is less than ±1 cm.

The arrangement of oblong recesses for thwarts in the uppermost board corresponds to the distribution of squarer slots cut into the upper edge of the second board, situated about 30 cm below the first (Fig. 24.3). Each of the square slots is positioned 70 to 80 cm aft of its corresponding thwart recess. Their height and longitudinal positioning within the hull indicates that the slots in the second board served as fastenings for some kind of foot stretchers, presumably simple joists with one side chamfered bow-wards towards its corresponding thwart. Further slots in the third board situated low in the hull are irregularly distributed. In view of their position, it is most likely that they carried cross-beams for the lower gangboards, as indicated by fragments found in wrecks 1 and 5.

Mainz wreck 1 (Figs 24.4, 24.5 and 24.6) had the same type of steering installation as wreck 4. This wreck too must represent the after part of a ship. The topwale is well preserved as a single piece of wood over a distance of 2.5 m. It was made of oak and its upper surface was chiselled into segments with alternately square and rounded sections. This timber enclosed the upper edge of the ship's side, which is made up of the sheer strake (with a separate rubbing strake on its outer surface), the heads

of the side frames, and a wale nailed to the latter from the inside. The whole construction is about 16 cm across. The rounded D-shaped blocks in the topwale are each 35 to 40 cm long with a single hole drilled into it (one hole still contains the lower plug-end of a wooden thole-pin). All the existing holes are asymmetrically positioned in the blocks, so that the mid-axis of an oarshaft 6 cms in diameter resting directly forward of the thole-pin would mark the exact centre of the block. The three holes preserved allow calculation of two of the *interscalmia* at the stern of the boat. Here, the distance between thole-pins was 95 and 96 cm, *i.e.* closer to the value of 98 cm suggested by John Morrison for the trireme than to the 89 cm which is the equivalent of 2 Roman cubits.

In wreck 1, a board is located 20 cm below the tholes. Its upper edge shows several recesses of the kind already described for wreck 4. The slots, which originally carried thwarts, are 12 to 20 cm long and 3 to 4 cm deep. Their regular distribution corresponds to the 95/96 cm distance between the tholes. There is, however, one unusual feature: the distance measured from the centre of each slot to the bow-ward edge of the corresponding thole-pin is at least 60 cm in each case. If one considers that each recess is a maximum of 20 cm long, then the after edge of each thwart must have been not less than 50 cm away from the nearest oar pivot. This is significantly more than is normal in traditional working boats of the modern era (see McKee 1983, p. 136). The extraordinarily long distance between the tholes and the thwarts must have considerably reduced the efficiency of oar propulsion in this vessel, by moving

Ronald Bockius

Figure 24.4. Mainz, Löhrstraße. Site of late Roman wreck no. 1 (photograph by Landesamt für Denkmalpflege, Abteilung Archäologische Denkmalpflege, Mainz).

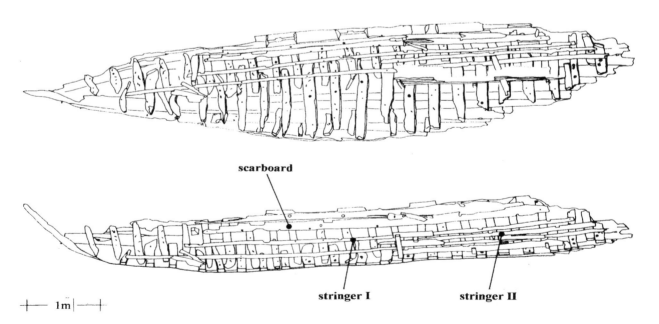

Figure 24.5. Photogrammetrical plan of late Roman wreck no. 1 from Mainz, Löhrstraße (after Böhler, Fachhochschule Mainz, Vermessungswesen). Hull interior of the wreck in an approximately upright position, plan (above) and elevation (below).

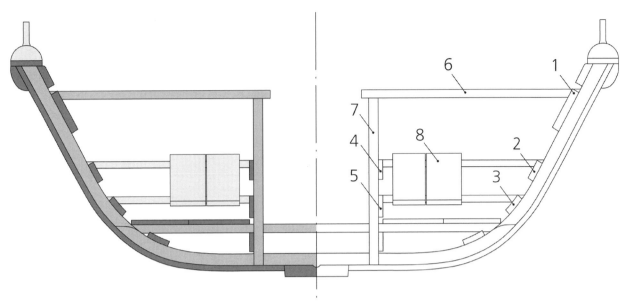

Figure 24.6. Mainz, type I. Hull interior reconstructed from wrecks nos. 1 and 5 (formerly no. 9). 1 scarboard with slots for thwarts (6); 2–3 stringers with slots for foot-stretcher (8) crosspieces; 4–5 longitudinal stringers stiffening the thwart stanchions (7), with slots for foot-stretcher crosspieces corresponding to those in the side-stringers.

much of the arc of the oar-stroke aft of vertical to the side of the ship. Since it is hard to believe that the thwarts could have been wider than 20 cm, or that the ancient shipwrights deliberately designed an inferior oarsystem, one must assume that ship 1 was intended to be rowed with short, powerful strokes, such as are normally used in rough water.

The Roman ships (*c.* AD 106) found at Oberstimm, near Ingolstadt (Bavaria)

In 1986, two wrecks were found close to the Roman fort at Oberstimm near the Danube (Höckmann 1987; 1989; 1995, 84–7; Bockius 2002). The complete excavation and salvage of these unusually well-preserved boats was carried out in 1994 by the Museum für Antike Schiffahrt, Mainz in co-operation with other German archaeological units (Hüssen *et al.* 1994; 1995; Kremer 1997). Both the wrecks were raised from the mud and have been treated in the laboratories of the Mainz museum. They are now exhibited in a museum near the site.

The Oberstimm boats have carvel-built hulls, constructed shell-first with mortise and tenon joints. The presence of keelsons and the use of pine for the strakes and oak for keels and frames (as well as the thwarts) are all typical of ancient Mediterranean construction (*e.g.* Casson 1994, 26–35; Marsden 1996). In contrast to the Mainz ships, which to date remain unique, those found at Oberstimm can be compared to a boat discovered in Vechten in the Netherlands (see below). The military purpose of both the Mainz ships and the Oberstimm boats is deduced from the fact that they were found in the vicinity of Roman military

installations, but a clearer indication of their function is given by their proportions and oarsystems. The Oberstimm boats are single-banked craft, 15 to 16 m long and 2.6 m broad, and were evidently rowed by crews of 18 or 20 men (Bockius 2002a).

As with the Mainz ships, the oarsystems of the Oberstimm wrecks have been preserved in sufficient detail to provide measurements for analysis. The keelsons found in both Oberstimm wrecks each show not only a mast step but also a series of holes distributed over their whole length. These holes originally held vertical stanchions to carry thwarts above the keel. Of the thwarts themselves, two are partially preserved in wreck 1, and others are indicated in both boats by elongated slots found in the upper edges of the wales below the sheer-strakes (though the latter are missing in wreck 2). The stanchions and slots for the thwarts lie on the same transverse axes of the ships. A sheer-strake is preserved in wreck 1 over a distance of 9.5 m, and acted both as a topwale and rubbing strip. Slit-like openings were discovered in its upper edge, some containing the remains of thole-pins with a circular section 3 cm in diameter in their upper portions, and with broadened bases.

The thwart slots found in the wale of wreck 1 (Fig. 24.8) are separated by distances of between 84 and 99 cms. The shortest room, of 84 cm, is located in the stern of the boat. The aftermost slot, however, differs in shape from the others, so that it is not certain whether it can be identified as having supported a thwart. If the room of 84 cms is included, the mathematical average of the rooms is *c.* 95 cm; without the short room, the average is *c.* 97 cms. The *interscalmia* of boat 1 measured between the thole-pins varies between 95 or 96 cm and, in a single

Figure 24.7. Oberstimm near Ingolstadt (Bavaria), wrecks no. 1 (partly covered) and no. 2 (photograph by Mittermüller, Bayerisches Landesamt für Denkmalpflege, Ingolstadt).

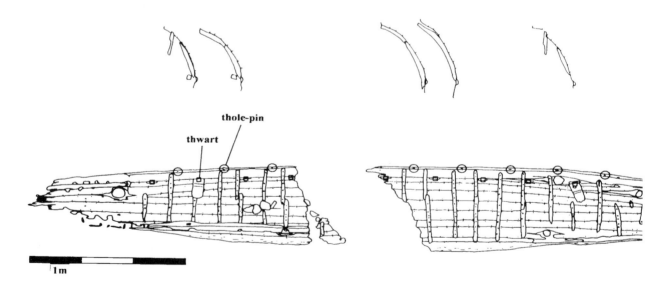

Figure 24.8. Oberstimm near Ingolstadt (Bavaria), wreck 1. Plan and cross-sections made during excavation (after H. Schaaff, Römisch-Germanisches Zentralmuseum Mainz).

instance, 99 cm. The average is 96.5 cm which corresponds closely to the average distance between the thwarts. Thus, Oberstimm wreck 1 and Mainz wreck 1 have more or less identical *interscalmia*. Furthermore, the vertical distance between the tholes and the level of the thwarts is *c.* 22 cm in both wrecks.

In Oberstimm wreck 2, the distribution of slots for the thwarts indicates only a slightly shorter *interscalmium* than in wreck 1. The slots are set at distances of between 94 and 96 (average 95) cm apart. A similar spread is shown in the distances between three holes for thwart-stanchions which were cut into in the keelson 93.5 cm apart.

Other oared vessels of the Roman period

Five other Roman wrecks provide evidence for *interscalmia*. As with the German wrecks, a military character can be assumed for the Vechten boat, discovered in the Netherlands in 1893 (Ellmers 1972, 293; De Weerd 1988, 184–94, figs 109–12; Höckmann 1994). Excavation records give a distance of *c.* 92 cm between the thwarts. This corresponds to the rooms in Mainz wreck 4.

A personal communication by the late Professor J.R. Steffy of the Institute for Nautical Archaeology at Texas A and M University indicates that the *interscalmia* measured at two places on the Herculaneum wreck which was buried by the eruption of Mount Vesuvius in AD 79 (Steffy 1994, 67–71) are 92 and 112.5 cms respectively. The small size of the vessel, however, thought to have been only 9 m long, makes a military function unlikely.

The same is true of wreck 2 found at Yverdon near the lake of Neuchatel in Switzerland. Slots found in the inner surfaces of the ship's sides indicate the existence of thwarts which were between 104 to 110 cm apart (Arnold 1992, 21–45, esp. 39 with table). The relatively heavy construction of the Yverdon boat excludes a military purpose because the narrow beam of 1.2 m would not have allowed two men to row abreast.

A non-military function is also assumed for an early 2nd-century wreck, nave F, found in Pisa, Italy. This boat has a unique oar system, with four oarsmen arranged in single file and tholes separated by two rooms of 112 cm each (Bockius 2002b; 2007, 73 fig. 82). By contrast, Pisa nave C bears the features of a small naval vessel. Dated to the beginning of the 1st century AD, the wreck is notable for its completely preserved oar system. The oars were worked through six oblong oar ports, which were originally enclosed by leather sleeves (*askomata*). The ship's bow resembles depictions of Hellenistic and early Roman war galleys, and includes a cutwater sheathed with iron plates. According to a preliminary publication (Bonino 2006), the thwarts and oar ports of Pisa C were positioned somewhat more than 1 m apart.

The implications of the Roman evidence

The data cited suggest that the *interscalmia* of the ships of the Roman fleets on the Rhine and Danube were normally between 94 and 96 cm, although occasionally shorter examples are found. In craft which are believed to have been working boats or cargo vessels much longer rooms are attested, although the 'military' *interscalmium* of 92 cm recorded for the Herculaneum wreck shows that it was also used by civilian oarsmen. It does not appear from this evidence at least that Roman military vessels were ever built to a standard *interscalmium* of as little two Roman cubits (*i.e.* 89 cm). Vitruvius, of course, chose to use a Greek word to describe the two-cubit *interscalmium*, so that it may in any case be wrong to interpret it in terms of Roman cubits. Furthermore, it is unclear whether the rooms of single- and multiple-banked units were comparable.

In fact, some of the Roman evidence fits very well with the longer Greek cubit suggested by John Morrison. An investigation of the metrological relief from Salamis which Morrison used to postulate a 98 cm *interscalmium* has indicated that it actually records a cubit of 48.38 cm ±0.2% rather than the 49 cm originally reported (Rottländer 1992). This gives a two-cubit *interscalmium* of 96.76 cm, which is close to those measured in Oberstimm wreck 2 (94 to 96 cm) and Mainz wreck 1 (95 and 96 cm). This may of course be coincidental.

The only clear deduction which can be made from Vitruvius' text seems to be that there was some sort of standard employed in the arrangement of oars in warships. This is implied in his use of the *interscalmium, quae διπηχυαϊα dicitur* in the context of a discussion of *symmetria* (*De architectura* 1.2.4). But the archaeological evidence raises doubts as to whether the standard was closely adhered to in practice. It is even possible that irregularities within the same ship, whether intentional or accidental, were used to accommodate oarsmen of differing statures, though such irregularities appear to have been greater in boats intended for civilian use than in warships.

On the other hand, the rooms of Mainz wreck 4 (84 to 92 cm) and Vechten (*c.* 92 cm), and, probably, one of the *interscalmia* of Oberstimm wreck 1 (84 cm) come close to the equivalent of 2 Roman cubits (*c.* 89 cm). Since variations are recorded in all the better-preserved wrecks, whether of military or of civilian vessels, any single measurement cannot tell us anything about a ship's average room. And since complete precision was not demanded in ancient shipbuilding and ancient measuring instruments were evidently not calibrated with absolute exactitude (Bockius 1996, 524–7, tab. 4), the *interscalmium* question cannot be answered by ship archaeology alone. Nevertheless, a survey of surviving wrecks can throw light on shipbuilding practice and reveal how much room was needed by ancient oarsmen.

Oared boats and ships from the Migration Period to the Middle Ages

A fairly large number of Germanic and Slav oared boats and ships have survived, mostly from the post-Roman period. Surveys of the distances between features such as oarports and rowlocks give us some idea about the room available

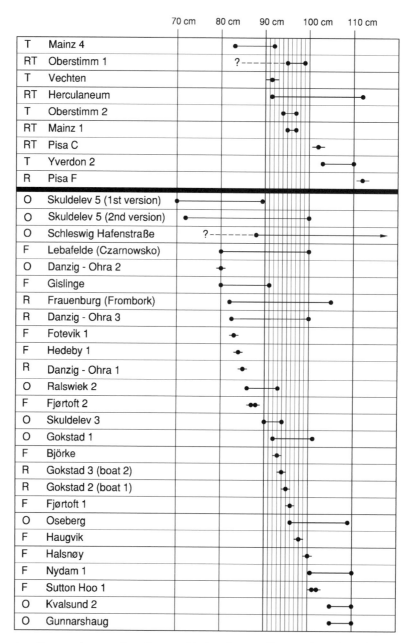

Figure 24.9. Table showing distances between installations (tholes, thwarts, floor timbers) found on wrecks dated to the Roman period (vessels built in the Mediterranean or Romano-Celtic tradition: upper group), and to the Migration Period and Middle Ages (vessels built in the Nordic tradition: lower group). Measurements are taken from centre to centre of the elements indicated: O = oarports; R = rowlocks or thole-pins; T = thwarts; F = frames. The Baltic and Scandinavian wrecks are those on the list published by Crumlin-Pedersen 1997, 110–111, Tab. 5.1 with additions.

to Dark-age and Medieval oarsmen. In some wrecks, the complete oarsystem has survived. In these cases, the entire arrangement of tholes and thwarts and their relationship to each other can be studied. Even where the upper parts of a hull have been destroyed, the distances between the floor timbers of the midship section can still indicate fore-and-aft room, because the position of the thwarts usually corresponded to that of the ribs. Although not all records of Baltic and Scandinavian clinker vessels allow exact measurement, the present writer has attempted to

compile a general synopsis. The number of measurements available allows us to even out errors caused by scaling of plans, by inaccurate reconstruction, or by generalising statements published in papers or books.

As shown in Fig. 24.8, the range of rooms recorded in post-Roman boats and ships is distinctly greater than that of the *interscalmia* of Roman wrecks. At the lower end of the range, one or more rooms were shorter than 89 cm in half the vessels surveyed. Astonishingly, a few Slav and Viking ships were provided with rooms of 80 cms or less. In

Skuldelev 5 as originally fitted out (though the arrangement was later modified), the oarcrew had an average room of only 78 cm fore-and-aft, and some individuals apparently had only 70 cms in which to take a stroke (Olsen and Crumlin-Pedersen 1968, 140–2). Skuldelev 5 thus provides evidence of just how small a room could be considered viable. Seen in this light, an *interscalmium* of 89 cm would seem to be more than adequate for normal purposes, and a room of 98 cm almost luxurious.

Conclusions: the absence of uniformity and the importance of weight:power ratio

The two-dimensional arrangement of oarsmen in the single-banked vessels considered in this paper would have differed considerably from the relatively complex arrangement in multiple-banked ships with their three-dimensional distribution of men and fittings. Nevertheless, our observations of single-banked ships suggest that the provision of generous rooms was seen as of relatively minor importance for generating speed under oar, compared to packing in the largest possible number of rowers and keeping overall displacement to a minimum. This should be equally true for multiple-banked units like the Athenian trireme. If so, the designers of ancient warships will have been keen to keep a good ratio between the mass to be accelerated and the number of oars generating the power. A further comparison may help to elucidate this.

Fully equipped and manned, a late Roman ship of Mainz I type displaces some 6.8 tonnes (Marsden 1993 makes it more). Thus the 24 or 26 oarsmen each moves 260 kg or 280 kg respectively. The 18 or 20 crew of the Oberstimm boats displacing 4.8 and 5 tonnes each moves a similar weight of vessel – 250/275 kg. In *Olympias*, each oarsman moves 235 to 265 kg of the ship's weight (based on the data in Coates 1989, 20 and 67; Whitehead *et al.* 1989, 26–27). In a Mark II reconstruction, with overall length increased by 10%, each rower would still be moving less than 300 kg (Coates 1996, 345 App D). According to these figures, a man-to-weight ratio of at most 300 kg appears to have been normal for fast oared ships in antiquity. Speed, of course, does not depend only on this ratio, but other aspects (lines, coefficients etc.) being equal, and given the limited efficiency of oar power, ancient warship designers are likely to have sought to save weight wherever possible.

The significance of a good weight:power ratio can be demonstrated by two contrasting examples. The displacements of the Nydam I and Oseberg ships as calculated by Timmermann (1956, 403–7, 607–10) and the distribution of rowlocks in Nydam ship B as reconstructed by Johannessen (Shetelig 1930, Plates I–II) suggest the following ratios: 295 kg per oarsman in Nydam I and 335 kg in the Oseberg ship. The first was a narrow ship rowed by a large number of oarsmen, while the second could be propelled either by oar or by sail. The performance of the Oseberg ship will have been similar to that of Oberstimm 2, since they have nearly identical proportions (Oseberg/Oberstimm 2: CWP 0.548/0.576; CM 0.559/0.576; CB 0.295/0.297; CV 0.528/0.516; LWL:D1/3 9.175/9.163). Clearly, the designs of all three of these vessels was geared towards saving weight, and we can guess that this was determined by the need to rely largely on oars. An opposite tendency is reflected in the Gokstad ship (Timmermann 1956, 602–7). Once her sail was shortened, each oarsman had to accelerate a mass of at least 900 kg.

For these reasons, the present writer is sceptical as to whether one should seek to optimise the speed of the Mark II trireme by giving her a longer *interscalmium* than *Olympias*. Our archaeological evidence indicates a considerable range for distances between tholes. Archaeologically, it would be acceptable to choose any of the *interscalmia* attested in the surviving wrecks of ancient military vessels. The interpretation of Vitruvius' reference allows of wide variation. Neither an 89 cm nor a 98 cm *interscalmium* can be regarded as a norm.

Bibliography

Arnold, B. (1992) *Batellerie gallo-romaine sur le lac de Neuchâtel 2*. Archéologie Neuchateloise 13. Saint-Blaise, Neuchâtel, Editions du Ruau.

Bockius, R. (1996) Zur Rekonstruktion des römischen Plattbodenschiffes aus Woerden. *Jahrbuch des Römisch-Germanischen Zentralmuseums Mainz* 43, 511–530.

Bockius, R. (2000) Gleichmaß oder Vielfalt? Zum *interscalmium* bei Vitruv (*De architectura* I 2,21 f.). In *Studia Antiquaria. Festschrift für Niels Bantelmann zum 60. Geburtstag.* Universitätsforschungen zur prähistorischen Archäologie. Institut für Vor- und Frühgeschichte der Universität Mainz 63. Bonn, R. Habelt, 111–125.

Bockius, R. (2002a) *Die römerzeitliche Schiffsfunde von Oberstimm in Bayern.* Römisch-Germanisches Zentralmuseum, Forschungsinstitut für Vor- und Frühgeschichte. Monographien 50. Mainz, Verlag des Römisch-Germanischen Zentralmuseums.

Bockius, R. (2002b) On the reconstruction of Pisa, nave F, by the Museum für Antike Schiffahrt, Mainz. In *The Ancient Ships of Pisa. A European laboratory for research and preservation.* "Culture 2000" programme. Brussels, 23–29, 101–104.

Bockius, R. (2006) *Die spätrömischen Schiffswracks aus Mainz. Schiffsarchäologisch-technikgeschichtliche Untersuchung spätantiker Schiffsfunde vom nördlichen Oberrhein.* Römisch-Germanisches Zentralmuseum, Forschungsinstitut für Vor- und Frühgeschichte. Monographien 67. Mainz, Verlag des Römisch-Germanischen Zentralmuseums.

Bockius, R. (2007) *Schifffahrt und Schiffbau in der Antike.* Stuttgart, Konrad Theiss Verlag.

Bonino, M. (2006) Il Gabbiano. Una barca a remi di età Augustea. In A. Camilli, A. De Laurenzi and E. Setari (eds), *Alkedo. Navi e commerci della Pisa romana.* Cantiere delle Navi Antiche di Pisa dal 18 luglio 2006. Pisa, 21–24.

Casson, L. (1994) *Ships and Seafaring in Ancient Times.* Austin TX, University of Texas Press.

Coates, J. F. (1989) The reconstruction. In Morrison and Coates 1989, 16–25, 67.

Coates, J. F. (1993a) The sea trials, the validity of the reconstruction in retrospect, and aims for the future. In Shaw 1993a, 110–111.

Coates, J. F. (1993b) Development of the design. In Shaw 1993a, 71–74.

Coates, J. F. (1996) Reconstructing the ships. In Morrison 1996, 279–348.

Coates, J. F. and Morrison, J. S. (1993) Summary of lessons learned. In Shaw 1993a, 108–109.

Coates, J. F., Platis, S. K. and Shaw, J. T. (eds) (1990) *The Trireme Trials 1988. Report on the Anglo-Hellenic Sea Trials of* Olympias. Oxford, Oxbow Books.

Crumlin-Pedersen, O. (1997) *Viking-Age Ships and Shipbuilding in Hedeby/Haithabu and Schleswig.* Ships and Boats of the North 2. Roskilde, Viking Ship Museum.

De Weerd, M.D. (1988) *Schepen voor Zwammerdam.* Amsterdam, Academisch Proefschrift Universiteit Amsterdam.

Ellmers, D. (1972) *Frühmittelalterliche Handelsschiffahrt in Mittel- und Nordeuropa.* Offa-Bücher 28. Neumünster, K. Wachholz.

Frost, H. *et al.* (1981) Lilybaeum (Marsala). The Punic ship: final excavation report. *Notizie degli Scavi di Antichità, Serie 8, Supplement 30.*

Höckmann, O. (1987) Roman Danube vessels from Oberstimm, Germany. In H. Tzalas (ed.) *Tropis II. 2nd International Symposium on Ship Construction in Antiquity, Delphi, 1987. Proceedings.* Delphi, Hellenic Institute for the Preservation of Nautical Tradition, 215–224.

Höckmann, O. (1988) Late Roman river craft from Mainz, Germany. In O. Lixa Filgueiras (ed.), *Local Boats. Fourth International Symposium on Boat and Ship Archaeology, Porto, 1985,* British Archaeological Reports, International Series, 438/1. Oxford, Archaeopress, 23–34.

Höckmann, O. (1989) Römische Schiffsfunde westlich des Kastells Oberstimm. *Berichte der Römisch-Germanischen Kommission* 70, 321–350.

Höckmann, O. (1991) Römische Schiffsfunde in Mainz. In (U. Löber (ed.), *2000 Jahre Rheinschiffahrt.* Veröffentlichung des Landesmuseums Koblenz, Band 40. Koblenz, Landesmuseum Koblenz, 49–64.

Höckmann, O. (1993) Late Roman vessels from Mainz, Germany. *International Journal of Nautical Archaeology* 22, 125–135.

Höckmann, O. (1994) Der erste römische Schiffsfund am Rhein. *Das Logbuch* 30, 201–207.

Höckmann, O. (1995) Antike Schiffsfunde aus der Donau. In Deutsche Gesellschaft zur Förderung der Unterwasserarchäologie e.V., *In Poseidons Reich. Archäologie unter Wasser.* Zaberns Bildbände zur Archäologie 23. Mainz, Verlag Philipp von Zabern, 82–90.

Hüssen, C.-M., K. H. Rieder, K. H. and Schaaff, H. (1994) Die Römerschiffe in Oberstimm – Ausgrabung und Bergung. *Das archäologische Jahr in Bayern 1994,* 112–116.

Hüssen, C.-M., K. H. Rieder, K. H. and Schaaff, H. (1995) Römerschiffe an der Donau. *Archäologie in Deutschland* 1995/I, 6–10.

Kremer, A. (1997) Die Bergung der Römerschiffe von Oberstimm. *Arbeitsblätter für Restauratoren* 30, 325–328.

Marsden, P. (1993) A hydrostatic study of a reconstruction of Mainz Roman ship 9. *International Journal of Nautical Archaeology* 22, 137–141.

Marsden, P. (1996) Classical Mediterranean shipbuilding outside the Mediterranean. In H. Tzalas (ed.), *Tropi IV. 4th International Symposium on Ship Construction in Antiquity, Athens 1996. Proceedings.* Athens, Hellenic Institute for the Preservation of Nautical Tradition, 297–310.

McKee, E. (1983) *Working Boats of Britain. Their Shape and Purpose.* London, Conway Maritime Press.

Morel, J.-M. (1987) Frührömische Schiffshäuser in Haltern, Hofestatt. *Ausgrabungen und Funde in Westfalen-Lippe* 5, 221–249.

Morel, J.-M. (1988) *De Vroeg-Romeinse Versterking te Velsen 1. Fort en Haven.* Amsterdam, Academisch Proefschrift Universiteit Amsterdam.

Morrison, J. (1991) Ancient Greek measures of length in nautical contexts. *Antiquity* 65, 298–305.

Morrison, J. S. (1993) Triereis: the evidence from Antiquity. In Shaw 1993a, 11–20.

Morrison, J. S. (1996) *Greek and Roman Oared warships, 399–30 BC* Oxbow Monograph 62. Oxford, Oxbow Books.

Morrison, J. S. and Coates, J. F. (eds) (1989) *An Athenian Trireme Reconstructed. The British sea trials of Olympias, 1987.* BAR, International Series, 486. Oxford, Archaeopress.

Morrison, J. S. and Coates, J. F. (1990) *Die athenische Triere. Geschichte und Rekonstruktion eines Kriegsschiffs der griechischen Antike.* Kulturgeschichte der Antiken Welt 44. Mainz, Verlag Philipp von Zabern.

Morrison, J. S., Coates, J. F. and Rankov, N. B. (2000) *The Athenian Trireme: the history and reconstruction of an ancient warship* 2nd ed. Cambridge, Cambridge University Press.

Olsen, O. and Crumlin-Pedersen, O. (1968) The Skuldelev ships (II). A report of the final underwater excavation in 1959 and the salvaging operation in 1962. *Acta Archaeologica (Kobenhavn)* 38, 1967, 73–174.

Pferdehirt, B. (1995) *Das Museum für Antike Schiffahrt I.* Mainz, Verlag des Römisch-germanischen Zentralmuseums.

Rottländer, R.C.A. (1992) Eine neu aufgefundene antike Maßeinheit auf dem metrologischen Relief von Salamis. *Jahreshefte des Österreichischen Archäologischen Instituts in Wien* 61, 63–68.

Shaw, T. (ed.) (1993a) *The Trireme Project. Operational Experience 1987–90. Lessons Learnt.* Oxbow Monograph 31. Oxford, Oxbow Books.

Shaw, T. (1993b) Rowing *Olympias*: Further Lessons of the Sea Trials. In Shaw 1993a, 58–68.

Shetelig, H. (1930) Das Nydamschiff. *Acta Archaeologica (Kobenhavn)* 1, 1–30.

Steffy, J. R. (1994) *Wooden Ship Building and the Interpretation of Shipwrecks.* College Station TX, Texas A & M University Press.

Timmermann, G. (1956) Vom Einbaum zum Wikingerschiff. *Schiff und Hafen* 1956/V, 403–412; 1956/VII, 602–612.

Weiskittel, S.F. (1989) How to row a trieres. In Morrison and Coates 1989, 98–108.

Whitehead, I, Coates, J. and Roberts, O. (1989) The sea trials of Olympias at Poros: August 1987. In Morrison and Coates 1989, 26–60.

Whitehead, I., Coates, J. and Roberts, O and Morrison, J. (1990) Die Probefahrten der Olympias von Poros aus, August 1987. In Morrison and Coates 1990, 252–294.

25. The Effect of Bilge Water on Displacement, Vertical Centre of Gravity and Metacentric Height of *Olympias* in the Trial Condition

John Coates

Repeated reference in the literature to drying out fleets of triremes and the implied importance of preventing fleets 'becoming heavy in the water' before a battle have been discussed recently to improve our understanding of the qualities and operational limitations of the trireme. In *The Athenian Trireme*, Appendix I, the writer argued that the effect of absorption of water by hull timbers could not of itself have increased the displacement of a trireme by more than about 1 tonne, and that as a worst case the weight of bilge water in a leaky but heavily manned ship was not likely to be more than about 6 tonnes (Morrison, Coates and Rankov 2000, 276–9). Such an increase would not reduce maximum speed by more than 2%, whereas loss of speed through fouling would commonly have been five times as much. It could, however, have been loss of agility that was mainly meant by ancient authors, rather than simply speed and the writer indicated in the above reference that an increase in mass of 1+ 6, or a total of 7 tonnes, *i.e.* 15% of the dry mass of a trireme, would reduce acceleration by that proportion and time to turn by about 8%.

These considerations show that a proper appreciation of this important aspect of naval operations with triremes, namely the effects of added weight and bilge water on their operational effectiveness, cannot be much advanced without experimental simulation of the condition in a reconstruction of the ship. Such an experiment should therefore be a prominent part of any further sea trials of a trireme reconstruction.

Deliberately letting water into the manned ship is a step which should not be undertaken without adequate previous estimation of its effects on flotation and stability, and the purpose of this paper is to indicate the nature of those effects and their magnitude. First, to estimate the greatest loss of stability, the effect of the greatest likely amount of crew movement is considered so that it could be added to that of the free surface of bilge water in reducing stability to arrive at an upper limit to that loss. Then the effects of the presence of two amounts of bilge water *i.e.* up to the tops of the hull floors and then of a larger amount, 0.2 m above the tops of the floors, are estimated.

The calculations upon which these estimates are based are themselves based on the data obtained from the inclining experiment carried out on *Olympias* in 1990 to find the height of her centre of gravity. The calculations are at the appendix to this paper and show that:

i) in the trial condition with a substantial crew, each weighing 80 kg and sitting or standing vertically when the ship rolls, the metacentric height of the ship (GM), dry, is 1.13 m and displacement is 42.25 tonnes;

ii) if, in the same condition, the crew rolled with the ship as if solid, the vertical centre of gravity (VCG) would rise by 0.14 m, reducing GM by the same amount, *i.e.* 12%; if the crew were to lean over with the roll to twice its angle, the loss of GM would double, to 0.28 m. or 25%, reducing it to 0.85m;

iii) bilge water up to the tops of the floors would add 7.42 tonnes to displacement, and reduce the height of VCG by acting as ballast low in the ship as much as it reduced the height of the metacentre (M) owing to the effect of its free surface about 2 m wide, so stability would not be affected; the ship would sink under the added weight by 6.7 cm, which would not greatly affect rowing apart from reducing the height of waves in which rowing could be effective by about twice that amount, 0.13 m; loss of energy through the bilge water sloshing about would have to be found by trial;

iv) bilge water 0.2 m above the tops of the floors would add 50% to the displacement, making it 69 tonnes, and cause the ship to sink 25 cm making rowing ineffective in any but near calm conditions; the effect of the free surface of the bilge water would be nearly double that of the water as ballast, owing to the breadth of the free surface being 3 m, and the net loss of GM would be 33%, a loss which is limited by the flare of the cross section of the trireme; the increase in displacement would render the hull in danger of severe straining and structural damage in a swell.

A depth of bilge water up to the tops of the floors would be able to be readily bailed and may be judged therefore to have been about the depth most likely to have been tolerated in leaky triremes in need of drying out, restopping, cleaning and recoating underwater. These estimates of the effects of bilge water indicate that trials with water admitted into the ship to demonstrate the need for a leaky ship to be dried out could be carried out safely with relatively little loss of stability because the upper limit of the amount of water that could be sensibly admitted for trial would be set by the effect of sinkage on rowing and by straining of the hull in a swell owing to increased displacement.

It is therefore considered practicable and safe to carry out trials to find out what effects bilge water has on trireme operations provided that swell is avoided.

Appendix

The report of the inclining experiment carried out in July 1990 by British Maritime Technology (Defence Services) Ltd – Report TR01/R1952 – found for the light ship condition:

Displacement   25.798 tonnes
(assuming specific gravity of sea water to be 1.025)
VCG above underside of keel (USK)   1.575 metres
LCG from Displacement Station 23   17.521 metres
Yards were hoisted with sails furled and both rudders were in the stowed position.

The trial condition

Added weights on board in the operational state during trials are shown in Table 25.1.

From the hydrostatic curves:

Metacentre above USK (KM)
at displacement 42.25 tonnes   2.90 metre
VCG above USK (KG)   1.77 metre
therefore Metacentric height (GM)   1.13 metre

Effects on stability of bodily movements of people and of bilge water

In view of the large proportion of the ship's weight in the trial codition being that of people, and the possibility of hull leakage, consider the effect of

i)   all bodies leaning rigidly with the the ship instead of standing or sitting vertically and freely as assumed above, and
ii) 0.36 m depth of water in the bilge, measured from the top of the keel at the main mast (*i.e.* amidships) giving a free surface of mean breadth 2.00 m.

i) 'Solid' people in dry ship

The rise in VCG may be estimated as shown in Table 25.2.

KM at displacement 42.25 tonnes   2.90 metres
KG   1.91 metres
therefore GM   0.99 metres,
a loss of 0.14 metre.

If people swayed towards the down side of the ship when she heeled so that they heeled twice as much as the ship, the loss of GM would be doubled, reducing it to 0.85 metre, a total loss of GM of **0.28 metre, or 25%.**

Table 25.1.

Item	Weight tonnes	CG above USK metres	Vertical Moment tonne metres
TR01/R1952 (includes 9 men)	1.1717	2.50	2.93
54 Thalamian oarcrew @ 80 kg	4.320	1.32	5.7024
54 Zygian oarcrew @ 80 kg	4.320	1.82	7.8624
62 Thranite oarcrew @ 80 kg	4.960	2.28	11.3088
21 Deck crew on canopy @ 80 kg	1.680	3.66	6.1488
The light ship	25.798	1.575	40.63185
Total, trial condition	42.2497	1.765	74.58425

Table 25.2.

Item	Weight tonnes	Rise in VCG metres	Added vertical moment tonne metres
Thalamians	4.320	0.35	1.512
Zygians	4.320	0.35	1.512
Thranites	4.960	0.35	1.736
Deck crew	1.680	0.90	1.512
State with crew sitting and standing freely	42.25		74.584
State with rigid crew	42.25	1.91	80.856

ii) Effect on stability of bilge water

i)   Assuming a depth of 0.36 metre of bilge water in the ship, volume of added water may be estimated to be not more than depth × breadth of water × 2/3 × length:

$$0.36 \text{ m} \times 2.00 \text{ m} \times 0.67 \times 18 \text{ m} \times \frac{(0.444 - 0.074)}{0.444} = 7.24 \text{ m}^3$$

(to allow for volume of floors)

Increased displacement will be 42.25 + 7.24 × 1.025 = 49.67 tonnes, an increase of 17.6%.

The added water's VCG is 0.54 m above USK, *i.e.* 1.91 – 0.54 or 1.37m below the ship's VCG, so the addition of the water will reduce KG by $\frac{7.24 \times 1.025 \times 1.37}{49.47} = 0.205$ m

The moment of inertia of the free surface of the bilge water is approximately

$$1/12 \times 2.0^3 \times 18 \times \frac{(0.444 - 0.074)}{0.444} = 10 \text{ m}^4$$

Therefore loss of GM owing to bilge water

$$= (10 / 49.67) - 0.205 \text{ m}$$
$$= 0.201 - 0.205 = -0.004 \text{ m}$$

and ship's GM with a 'rigid' crew and 0.36 m depth of bilge water would be

$$0.99 + 0.004 = 0.99 \text{ m.}$$

The loss of GM owing to free surface is compensated by the fall in VCG, so stability will scarcely be affected. The increase in displacement of 7.4 tonnes would cause the ship to sink by 6.7 cm which would not affect greatly rowing as regards wave clearance, but there would be losses of power owing to bilge water sloshing about fore and aft with the stroke.

ii)   If however the depth of bilge water were to increase to, say, 0.6 m, the breadth of the free surface would become 3 m. In that case:

increase in displacement would be substantial, *i.e.* 0.6 × 3.0 × 0.67 × 22 × 1.025 = 27 tonnes, making the displacement 69 tonnes.

The added water's VCG would be 0.7 m above USK, *i.e.* 1.91–0.7 or 1.21 m below the ship's VCG and KG of ship will fall by $\frac{27 \times 1.21}{42 + 27} = 0.47$ m.

The ship's KM would reduce slightly, by 0.08 m to 2.82 m.

Moment of inertia of free surface would become $1/12 \times 3.0^3 \times 22 = 50 \text{ m}^4$, so loss of GM owing to free surface would become substantial, 50/ 69 = 0.72 m and the net GM would become 0.99–0.08 + 0.47–0.72 = 0.66 m, a loss of 33%, which would be noticeable under oar and make it necessary to handle the ship with particular care under sail.

Sinkage however in this latter case would be 25 cm and have more serious effects, making rowing very difficult and ineffective in any but near calm conditions; while the ship would be able to be brought to land for repair, she would be virtually inoperable.

Bibliography

Morrison, J. S., Coates, J. F. and Rankov, N. B. (2000) *The Athenian Trireme: the history and reconstruction of an ancient warship.* 2nd ed. Cambridge, Cambridge University Press.

26. Trireme Life Span and Leakage: a wood technologist's perspective

Paul Lipke, with contributions by John Coates

What follows, written in 1993–94, is perhaps the first detailed exploration of wood-moisture relationships and wood mechanical properties in the context of mortise-and-tenon construction in the building and operation of triremes, and of ancient long ships in general. As a first effort, the author has tried to sketch the main areas of investigation in the hope that others will extend and improve on this modest beginning. Since the author has not been paying attention to maritime archaeology since 1996, there is almost certainly more recent, relevant evidence of which he is unaware, and he apologizes for its omission. An early draft of this document was shared with *Olympias'* naval architect, John Coates, who used some of it with permission in developing his paper, 'Planking tenons in ancient Mediterranean ships built shell first' (Coates 2001).

Certain physical properties of the wood species and joinery used to build triremes had an enormous influence on their operational limits. This paper explores some critical weaknesses and their impacts on trireme construction and life span.

Introduction

The top speeds and life span of an ancient trireme would have been determined to a large extent by the maximum

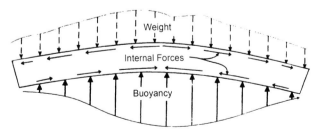

Figure 26.1. Differences in a ship's buoyancy along its length relative to weight distribution create shear forces, causing components of its skin to want to slide past one another. Such forces can lead to the ship sagging at the ends, known as "hogging" (Wooden Boat).

acceptable leakage. The "maximum acceptable leakage" for ancient trireme crews cannot, of course, be quantified. Engineering and common sense tell us the penalty in lost effectiveness due to leakage could be severe, especially when coupled with hull deformation, hull roughness and the difficulties of rapidly removing water from a trireme's bilge – all factors that would go hand in hand with leakage (Morrison and Coates 1989, 69–73; Morrison, Coates and Rankov 2000, 276–279).

Leakage would have resulted primarily from damage by shipworm (see Lipke, above pp. 203–6) and adjacent, submerged planks crushing each other and slipping longitudinally over small distances. This crushing and slippage would eventually destroy any caulking material and/or wood-to-wood, watertight joints between adjacent, moving planks. The planks would slide because:

1. Some of the approximately 20,000 tenons joining the planks together would be installed loose in their mortises, or would become so over time, for reasons explained below (see Figs 26.1, 26.2 26.3, 26.7, 26.8, 26.9).
2. Because the strength of the available wood was inadequate to fully resist the shear forces created under various conditions.

Though ancient shipwrights may not have realized it, there were two aspects of trireme design and mortise-and-tenon construction which combined to form what was most likely the weakest point in the structure (the liability of triremes to shipworm damage is ignored here, as it has been addressed elsewhere in this volume, pp. 203–6). Either aspect could constitute a significant weakness by itself. Since the two weakest features related to the same part of the hull, in combination they can be presumed to have had a great impact on the performance and life span of triremes. Furthermore, these two fundamental weaknesses could have been difficult to understand and resolve, even though the resultant failure was conspicuous.

Because of their long, slender proportions and these two weaknesses, triremes would have drooped at the ends (in nautical terms, "hogged") soon after they were built. For the same reason they would have leaked sooner than

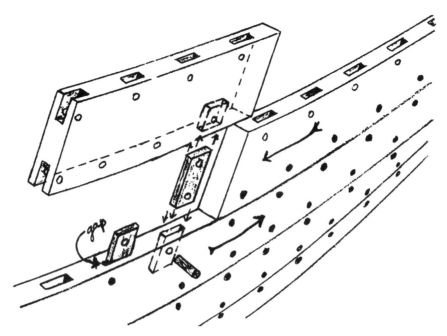

Figure 26.2. Under shear forces, planks will slide if the tenons are too narrow – e.g. there are gaps between the tenon and mortise adjacent to their fore and/or aft faces. Tenons installed tightly can develop gaps over time if the tenon is of insufficient strength relative to the planking. Such gaps and shear forces can lead to the ship sagging at the ends, known as "hogging," which in turn impacts performance (Drawing: Paul Lipke, based on illustrations by John Coates and Scientific American).

other, stouter ships of the period. Hogging and leaking would reduce performance by 1) increasing wetted surface (creating greater friction); 2) increasing displacement; 3) reducing the height of the oar handle relative to the lowest rowers at the ends of the ship during the drive of the stroke, thereby making the stroke less powerful (Morrison, Coates and Rankov 2000, 277). The two root causes of hogging and leaking were:

i)   The tenons in the planks just above the waterline would have gaps between the tenon and the mortises, at least at times, due to moisture cycling and probably from compression set (defined below). These same tenons were located near the area of the hull subject to the greatest shear stress. Therefore the stiffness of the hull was reduced in the area where stiffness was needed most.

ii)   Wood is anisotropic; it has very different stability and strength properties in different directions with respect to a tree's vertical, radial and tangential orientations (Fig. 26.7, 26.8 and 26.9). Wood's maximum shrinkage and swelling averages 0.1% longitudinally, 4% radially, and 8% tangentially. Therefore transverse shrinkage and swelling caused most of the dimensional change problems with plank leakage, especially since triremes were hauled out of the water frequently. Furthermore, no available combination of wood species from which ancient shipwrights made mortises and tenons had closely matched strength properties in the relevant orientations relative to grain. In short, trireme tenon material had insufficient strength in compression perpendicular to the grain. As a result, tenons under shear loading were crushed by the endgrain of the mortise cut in the planks,

and this crushing could have led to increased plank slippage and thereby aggravated the leaking and hogging problems.

In order to resist the above mentioned tendency of planks to slide, a mortise-and-tenon built ship had to have no gaps between the fore and aft faces of the tenons, and the end grain surfaces of the planking that had been exposed within the mortises.

What were the factors influencing tightness of tenons? They were quality of workmanship (proven in excavated shipwrecks to be very high), dimensional change in wood due to changes in moisture content, shear forces crushing tenons, and compression set (each technical term will be defined below as each issue is addressed). After defining the nature of this problem and its ramifications in some detail, this paper will close with a strategy for mitigating these problems.

Wood properties and dimensional change in planks and tenons

Classical shipwrights had to fabricate tens of thousands of tight joints and keep them tight in planking shaped to create complex curves. They had to do this in a material that changes size over time in response to complex moisture cycles.

Most people are aware that a tight joint made of 'green' timber will open up and become very loose if the components are given a chance to dry out. This happens because wood is hygroscopic. It continually gains or loses moisture as necessary to find and maintain a moisture content that is in equilibrium with its surroundings. Once a piece of wood reaches an initial balance point with its surrounding fluid (*i.e.* air or water) the wood will continually gain or lose water in response to subsequent changes in liquid water availability and relative humidity (RH). In many applications this means the wood is constantly shrinking or swelling in response to changes in RH; if the RH changes dramatically, the dimensional changes can be severe.

Generally, the thinner the piece of wood, the faster its overall rate of response. A thin, narrow strip of wood that is going to be cut up into tenons, let alone an individual tenon, will dry very quickly.

The wider and thicker the piece of wood, the greater the dimensional change. Wide, fat tenons and planks will be less dimensionally stable than narrow ones.

A trireme builder had to plan the use and shaping of timber to take advantage both of wood's hygroscopic behaviour and the fact that most woods are much easier to work when they have relatively high moisture contents (wood's moisture content (MC) is defined as 'The weight of the water in the cell walls and cavities of wood expressed as a percentage of oven-dry weight' (Hoadley 1980, 243)). The shipwright needed to work such wood when it was relatively green, but also needed to prevent joints from loosening due to shrinkage. These needs were (and are) in conflict. To deal with the conflict, even in boatyards today, different parts of a planked wooden hull are built using wood in various MC ranges that balance working properties and shrinkage rates against the planned application.

The correct amount of moisture depends on the properties of the particular species of wood being used, the width and plane of cut of the wood being used, the macro and micro-climates in which it will operate, the duties it will perform, and finish to be applied.

Some parts of a ship, such as narrow, relatively straight, radially cut deck planks that are exposed to the weather are best put together with very dry material (MC 6–9%). In this way, even after a summer drought when the decks have been baked by the sun, the joints will ideally still be tight enough that the first rains or seawater on deck will not leak through cracks between the deck planks. But as we will see, material like decking must not be installed too tightly or be laid when it is too dry or compression set can occur. Planking, which tends to be wider and have more shape, is much more easily shaped and bent into place when somewhat green, *i.e.* at an MC of about 17–20%.

These complex considerations have been understood to varying degrees by good woodworkers and shipwrights for millennia, and even some of the more subtle nuances were known to classical shipwrights, as will be demonstrated below. Even so, using the best species and plane of cut at the correct moisture content for a given application is never easy to achieve consistently in real practice.

There have always been delays in and limits on procurement, customer demands for prompt completion, complex drying schedules, the vagaries of the weather, etc. Meiggs has collected numerous accounts of the difficulties ancient shipwrights had with timber procurement, shipping and processing (Meiggs 1982, 330–40).

Wood species and moisture in triremes during construction and operation

From the above it is safe to suggest trireme planking materials like Aleppo and black pine (*Pinus halepensis* and *P. nigra*) and Mediterranean fir (*Abies cephalonica*) (Meiggs 1982, 118) were most probably worked when somewhat green (MC 17–20%). At this moisture content, woodworking is still relatively easy, and enough shrinkage has occurred to permit some very desirable swelling when the ship is launched. Plank stock to be placed high above the waterline might ideally have been fastened in place when fully air-dry (MC 8–14%).

Although the rip saw was known at least as early as the 5th Dynasty in Egypt, in Classical Attica planks and tenons were commonly riven (split radially like pie slices) from a log, (See Fig. 26.4). Today, when stacked to dry under cover, planks of 35–50 mm thickness can go from fully green to air-dry MC of 8–14% in 3–14 weeks (the longest period applies to pieces of 50 mm thickness during slower, winter drying) (Tsoumis and Voulgaridis, 1980; G. Tsoumis and P. K. Kavvouras pers. corr.).

Tenons holding planks together, which were typically made of oak (*Quercus sp.*) or olive (*Olea europaea*), are small enough that they would dry to 8–14% MC very quickly (in days to a week or so) after cutting to shape, and indeed they needed to be as dry as practical so that they would not shrink further after being fitted tightly into mortises. Clearly, it would have been relatively easy for trireme builders to insure tenons would not shrink after fitting.

Given these moisture contents, when first launched, an increase in MC of 14% or more would then occur for the planking below the waterline as MC increased to the fibre saturation point. This increase in MC would cause the planks and tenons to swell. Since they were underwater, they would stay swollen tight until the ship was hauled out, *i.e.* taken off active duty for some weeks or stored for the winter. The planks and tenons would swell different amounts in different directions depending on the species used and grain direction, but the important point is that too much swelling could lead to leakage when planks swelled against planks and crushed themselves, or when tenons swelled against the very strong, stable endgrain of the plank (in the mortise) and essentially crushed itself.

It is necessary at this point to make a brief but important digression concerning tenon species and properties. A number of published archaeological reports of early shipwrecks have specified wreck tenons were made of a particular sub-species of the red-oak group, Turkey oak, *Quercus cerris*. These reports do not state on what basis this identification of the sub-species was made.

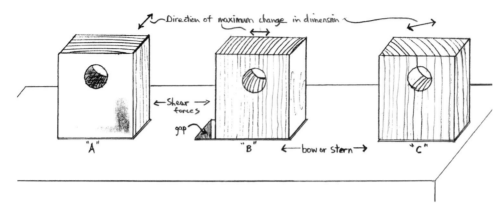

Figure 26.3. Three possible grain orientations for tenons, ranging from pure radial and tangential annual ring orientation to an intermediate one. Tenon "A" has its annual rings oriented to run fore and aft. This is the most stable orientation under moisture cycling, and also provides the most resistance to shear forces, since radial faces of the tenon are the strongest available. Tenon "B" has its annual rings oriented to run inboard and outboard. This is the least stable orientation under moisture cycling, and also provides the least resistance to shear forces, since shear forces are acting on relatively weak tangential grain. It is therefore the orientation most likely to result in gaps between the tenon and the mortise, all else being equal. Tenon "C" has its mixed orientation of its annual rings, giving intermediate stability and strength performance. See also Figure 26.6. (Drawing: Paul Lipke).

Unfortunately, the different sub-species within each of the white and red oak groups cannot be differentiated from each other using the harvested wood alone, even under a microscope or with chemical analysis. Access to twigs, buds or leaves of the tree are necessary in order that, for example, the various red oak species to be identified. Since leaves, buds and twigs from the trees which the tenons came from are no longer available, the attribution of Turkey oak in wreck tenons must be viewed with some scepticism.

Despite this uncertainty, Turkey oak examples are included in this paper for two reasons: 1) the wood was common in the region in antiquity, and so was highly likely to be used for tenons; and 2) Turkey oak is generally slightly more dense, strong and dimensionally unstable than all the other available oak species, and so deserves to be considered, but considered separately.

As it happens, Turkey oak's strength and other properties are closer to the averages for the white oak group, *Quercus robur, pendulata*, etc., than those of the red oak group to which it belongs taxonomically. Unless stated otherwise, this paper uses either the white oak group or Turkey oak, whichever will give the more conservative values for the issue under consideration.

As stated above, wood swells and shrinks about twice as much tangentially as it does radially. Contrary to Coates' assertion in his paper on planking tenons (Coates 1996, 6) stronger, heavier woods such as those used in tenons swell more (not less) than lighter woods (Hoadley 1980, 74; USDA 1987, 3–13 to 3–15). Fig. 26.3 illustrates three possible grain orientations for tenons, ranging from pure radial and tangential orientations to an intermediate one.

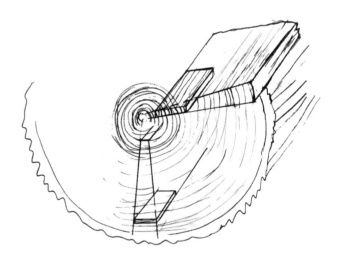

Figure 26.4. Riven boards, which readers can conceptualize as pie slices, can provide tenon material with annual rings in either radial or tangential orientation (Drawing: Paul Lipke).

Tenon "A" has its annual rings oriented to run fore and aft. This is the most stable orientation under moisture cycling, and also provides the most resistance to shear forces, since radial faces of the tenon are the strongest available. Tenon "B" has its annual rings oriented to run inboard and outboard. This is the least stable orientation under moisture cycling, and also provides the least resistance to shear forces, since shear forces are acting on relatively weak tangential grain. It is therefore the orientation most likely to result in gaps between the tenon and the mortise, all else being equal.

To date there is very little archaeological evidence which indicates whether Classical shipwrights consistently fabricated tenons with the tenon's tangential or radial planes oriented fore and aft. The orientation of grain of the tenons was not noted in the Kyrenia Wreck. Personal communication with Honor Frost indicates the Marsala tenons were aligned so shear forces acted on radial faces, as would likely be most common with tenons cut from riven bolts. This author unsuccessfully sought such data from the Ma'agan Michel and Marseille wrecks.

For the purposes of understanding the effect of moisture on the mortise-and-tenon joints of a trireme, it is useful to conceptually divide the hull into three distinct horizontal sections. The first section is the saturated planking at and below the waterline. The second section of planking is just above the waterline, and could experience wide swings in moisture content due to waves, mooring positions relative to the drying effects of the wind and the sun, and so forth. Lastly, the upper topsides will generally stay 'dry.' In reality these zones form a continuous moisture gradient.

Data on plank and tenon moisture contents was collected aboard *Olympias* during 1993 and 1994 (see Table 26.1). They confirm, as indicated above, that moisture contents ranged from well above the fibre saturation point to 'air-dry' at about 12% depending on 1) the height above and below the waterline, and 2) the depth probed in the planking and tenons as measured from the inside surface of the hull. (The fibre saturation point (FSP) is 'The condition of moisture content where cell walls are fully saturated, but the cell cavities are empty of free water. Free water is moisture held in the cell cavities of the wood, not bound in the cell wall' (Hoadley, 1980, 241). Most

Table 26.1. Olympias' Plank and Tenon Moisture Content.

Set A: Starb'd seats 22–23	% Moisture contents at depths from interior plank surface			
Distance above/below the waterline (River Thames, London, 16 June 1993)**				
	depth 5/4"	depth 3/4"	depth 3.4" qv*	depth 3/8"
12" below	30.H	30.H	30.H	30.H
3" below	29.0	30.L	30.H	30.L
6" above, 2nd strake***	17.2	17.0	30.H	21.7
14" above, 3rd strake	12.5	14.9	19.9	13.5
20" above, 4th strake	12.9	15.5	30.L	13.1
Set B: Starb'd seat 15	% Moisture contents at depths from interior plank surface			
Distance above/below the waterline				
	depth 5/4"	depth 3/4"	depth 3.4" qv*	depth 3/8"
12" below	30.H	30.H	30.H	30.H
3" below	30.H	30.H	30.M	27.9
6" above, 2nd strake***	26.4	26.0	30.M	13.5
14" above, 3rd strake	24.2	30.0	30.M	27.5
20" above, 4th strake	21.4	30.5	30.H	24.0
Four days later at the same locations				
Set A: Starb'd seats 22–23	% Moisture contents at depths from interior plank surface			
Distance above/below the waterline				
	depth 5/4"	depth 3/4"	depth 3.4" qv*	depth 3/8"
12" below	30.H	30.H	30.H	30.H
3" below	30.M	30.H	30.H	28.5
6" above, 2nd strake***	28.4	20.2	30.H	21.2
14" above, 3rd strake	16.1	19.1	23.1	16.4
20" above, 4th strake	17.9	16.8	30.H	17.7
Set B: Starb'd seat 15	% Moisture contents at depths from interior plank surface			
Distance above/below the waterline				
	depth 5/4"	depth 3/4"	depth 3.4" qv*	depth 3/8"
12" below	30.H	30.H	30.H	30.H
3" below	30.M	30.H	30.M	21.7
6" above, 2nd strake***	24.4	24.2	30.M	18.6
14" above, 3rd strake	17.2	24.3	30.M	20.6
20" above, 4th strake	16.4	27.9	30.M	16.6

H = well over fibre saturation
M: moderately over fibre saturation
L = slightly over fibre saturation
* Adjusted for Oak, *Quercus*
** Ship had been in the water 7 days, after 10 days exposed to sea air and 2–3 weeks afloat in Greece
*** 1st strake above waterline was inaccessible due to obstruction by wale

Note: Moisture content readings taken in Greece during April, 1994, when the ship had been out of the water at dockside but not under cover all winter were almost all over fibre saturation, except a few in the mid-20s, at random heights and depths of probe (it was not clear of the ship had recently been washed or hosed down).

species have fibre saturation moisture contents of around 28%. Under this condition, all the water in the wood is 'bound' water held within the cell walls. It is the loss or gain of this bound water, at moisture contents below 28%, that results in wood shrinking or swelling. For comparison, 'air-dry' wood in northern temperate climates generally has a moisture content of 12–14%.) *Olympias*, built and launched near Athens, Greece has been exposed to mean relative humidities between 47% and 75%, resulting in moisture contents (MC) for air-dry wood of between 8.3% and 14% (National Climactic Data Center/NOAA Station 16716; Hoadley 1980, 69; Tsoumis and Voulgaridis 1980; G. Tsoumis and P.K. Kavvouras pers. corr.). Any difference between modern relative humidities and those experienced in the forested Mediterranean of antiquity would not be significant in the context of the arguments that follow.

Given these climatic conditions, the likely dimensional changes to a trireme's oak tenons could fall anywhere in the ranges indicated below in Table 26.2a and 26.2b. The ranges for other species which were used for tenons have also been calculated.

How much a piece of wood, such as a tenon, will shrink or swell as a result of shifts in moisture content can be estimated for a given shaped timber for a given species by the following formula. It is important to note that any individual piece of wood can vary as much as 50% from the species' statistical norm.

$D_f = D_i * S(MC_f - MC_i / FSP)$
where:
    D_f = final dimension
    D_i = initial Dimension
S (specified as S_t or S_r) = the percent shrinkage for a particular species in the tangential plane (S_t) or radial plane (S_r) as moisture content is reduced from green to oven-dry
MC_f = final Moisture Content (MC)
    MC_i = initial Moisture Content
FSP = Fibre Saturation Point at which (and above which) dimensions are stable, with FSP typically considered to be a moisture content of 28%.

Here are two examples:

European oaks, *Quercus robur, pendulata*, etc. have tangential shrinkage (S_t) of 7.5% and a radial shrinkage (S_r) of 4.0%. The tenons of *Olympias* are 37 mm wide when air-dry at 12% MC. If MC_i is 12%, and MC_f is 28%, unrestrained swelling along the width of such an oak tenon as a result of a likely maximum MC swing of 26% will be between 1.3 mm and 2.5 mm depending on the plane of cut of the tenon.

Turkey oak has a tangential shrinkage (S_t) of 10.5% and a radial shrinkage (S_r) of 4.5%. Unrestrained swelling along the width of a Turkey oak tenon as a result of a likely maximum MC swing of 26% will thus be between 1.5 mm and 3.6 mm depending on the plane of cut of the tenon. In both cases, such unrestrained dimensional changes are large enough to be highly significant.

Swelling of tenons that are restrained because they are tight in their mortises when initially installed (low MC_i) would be a different matter, and will be discussed below.

Tenons in the planking below the waterline would stay at fibre saturation point while the ship was in the water. The data in Table 26.2a and 26.2b show the only possible way in which they could be loose in their mortises after launch would be if they were undersized by a millimetre or more *and* fully saturated when first fitted.

High above the waterline, equilibrium moisture contents for planks would be fairly stable within an annual mean range of 6%, so unrestrained dimensional change even for the more dimensionally unstable 37 mm Turkey oak tenon would be barely measurable, from 0.36–0.83 mm.

A different picture appears if we apply this formula to the wet/dry zone immediately above the waterline, up to the 1 metre maximum wave height it appears triremes could most probably regularly handle (see Shaw, above p. 73). In this area, annual moisture cycling can be extreme, and changes in MC of 22% could result in unrestrained dimensional swelling of 1.2–2.2 mm for European oak, and 1.3–3.0 mm for a Turkey oak tenon of 37 mm. The MC of wet/dry zone tenons at any given time would depend on:

- the particular tenon's height above waterline,
- size of the waves encountered in recent periods,
- whether it had rained recently (in much of Greece it virtually never rains in the summer)
- relative humidity of the air
- how easily any rain and/or seawater were wicked into plank seams and mortises
- how long a pocket of water in a mortise would take to dry out
- the season of the year.

Table 26.1 indicates, however, that a wide range of moisture content values can be found in the wet/dry zone over time and even at any one period of time. It is quite probable that under the conditions which were likely to exist when triremes were re-launched into service, gaps of 1–3 mm or more between tenon and mortise could be common as little as 6–12 inches (15.2 cm) above the waterline.

Gaps would occur whenever there had been time and dry enough conditions for the water trapped in the pockets of tenons to dry out. The most common, gap-producing conditions were probably 1) the ship had been in a shipshed and thus kept dry; and 2) the ship was hauled out without a shipshed in the dry season.

Such gaps are one of the root causes of weakness in triremes as we have come to understand them. Gaps would probably have greatly reduced the resistance to sliding between planks.

Planks, caulking and leakage

Why is resistance to shear between planks so important? Why would gaps between tenons and mortises have such a strong, negative effect? If the planks of a trireme were to slide back and forth past each other in the fore and aft

Table 26.2a. Dimensional Change and Compression Set in Tenons and Planks.

Species	Tenon width	Grain orientation	Change in moisture content	Dimension change for given change in moisture content (below 28 %)	Max. possible compression set for change in moisture content (under full restraint
Species used for tenons in antiquity	mm		%	mm	mm
Turkey oak, *Quercus cerris*	37	Tangential**	22	3.05	2.68
shrinkage: green to 12 % moisture	37	Radial	22	1.31	0.94
Pure tangential shrinkage = 10.5 %	37	Tangential	13	1.80	1.43
Pure radial shrinkage = 4.5 %	37	Radial	13	0.77	0.40
	37	Tangential	6	0.83	0.46
	37	Radial	6	0.36	none
55 mm oak tenons, Kyrenia Shipwreck	55	Tangential	22	4.54	3.99
	55	Radial	22	1.94	1.39
	55	Tangential	13	2.68	2.13
	55	Radial	13	1.15	0.60
	55	Tangential	6	1.24	0.69
	55	Radial	6	0.53	none
70 mm oak tenons, Marsala Wreck	70	Tangential	22	5.78	5.08
	70	Radial	22	2.48	1.78
	70	Tangential	13	3.41	2.71
	70	Radial	13	1.46	0.76
	70	Tangential	6	1.58	0.88
	70	Radial	6	0.68	none
80 mm oak tenons, Madre de Giens wreck	80	Tangential	22	6.60	5.80
	80	Radial	22	2.83	2.03
	80	Tangential	13	3.90	3.10
	80	Radial	13	1.67	0.87
	80	Tangential	6	1.80	1.00
	80	Radial	6	0.77	none
European oak, *Q. ribur, pendulate, etc.*	37	Tangential	22	2.18	1.81
Shrinkage: green to 12 % moisture	37	Radial	22	1.16	0.79
pure tangential shrinkage = 7.5 %	37	Tangential	13	1.29	0.92
Pure radial shrinkage = 4.0 %	37	Radial	13	0.69	0.32
	37	Tangential	6	0.59	0.22
	37	Radial	6	0.32	none
	55	Tangential	22	3.24	2.69
	55	Radial	22	1.73	1.18
	55	Tangential	13	1.92	1.37
	55	Radial	13	1.02	0.47
	55	Tangential	6	0.88	00.33
	55	Radial	6	0.47	none
	70	Tangential	22	4.13	3.43
	70	Radial	22	2.20	1.50
	70	Tangential	13	2.44	1.74
	70	Radial	13	1.30	0.60
	70	Tangential	6	1.13	0.43
	70	Radial	6	0.60	none

** Tenons might commonly have a mix of tangential and radial grain. In these cases, shrinkage and compression set values would fall between the pure radial and tangential values.

directions, they would eventually destroy or 'spit out' any caulking material that had been inserted between them, or would cause any watertight, wood-to-wood joints to leak from abrasion.

We do not know for certain if triremes were caulked, and if so what materials were used between the plank seams. On one hand, pitch-soaked flax fibre may have been used, or shipwrights may have relied purely on wood-to-wood, watertight fits between planks. If this sounds unbelievable, it is worth noting woodworking of this type and quality could be found in the mid 20th century among some wooden boat builders.

If a shipwright felt that normal swelling between planks would not provide a sufficiently tight joint, he could resort to making a caulked seam between each plank. This generally involves removing a portion of the wood from one edge of one plank along each seam to form a shallow 'Y.'

Morrison and Coates contains an excellent summary of the evidence about caulking in triremes (Morrison, Coates and Rankov 2000, 184–6). Coates and Morrison conclude, quite rightly, that we do not know for certain if caulking was used. However, of all the evidence they review, one piece seems particularly compelling to this author because of his background in wooden ship construction and

Table 26.2b. Dimensional Change and Compression Set in Tenons and Planks.

Species	Tenon width	Grain orientation	Change in moisture content	Dimension change for given change in moisture content (below 28 %)	Max. possible compression set for change in moisture content (under full restraint
Species used for tenons in antiquity	mm		%	mm	mm
European olive, *Olea europaea*	37	Tangential	22	1.89	1.52
shrinkage: green to 12 % moisture	37	Radial	22	1.16	0.79
Pure tangential shrinkage = 6.5 %	37	Tangential	13	1.12	0.75
Pure radial shrinkage = 4.0 %	37	Radial	13	0.69	0.32
	37	Tangential	6	0.52	0.15
	37	Radial	6	0.32	none
	55	Tangential	22	2.81	3.99
	55	Radial	22	1.73	1.39
	55	Tangential	13	1.66	2.13
	55	Radial	13	1.02	0.60
	55	Tangential	6	0.77	0.69
	55	Radial	6	0.47	none
	70	Tangential	22	3.58	5.08
	70	Radial	22	2.20	1.78
	70	Tangential	13	2.11	2.71
	70	Radial	13	1.30	0.76
	70	Tangential	6	0.98	0.88
	70	Radial	6	0.60	none
	80	Tangential	22	2.76	5.80
	80	Radial	22	1.92	2.03
	80	Tangential	13	1.63	3.10
	80	Radial	13	1.13	0.87
	80	Tangential	6	0.75	1.00
	80	Radial	6	0.52	none
Planking species used in antiquity		**Plank width**			
Silver fir, *Abies alba*	148	Tang./Radial	22	7.91	6.43
Shrinkage: green to 12 % moisture	148	Tang./Radial	13	4.67	3.19
Pure tangential shrinkage = 9.2 %	148	Tang./Radial	6	2.16	0.68
Pure radial shrinkage = 4.4 %					
Avg. of radial and tangential = 6.8%					
Pine, *Pinus nigra*	148	Tang./Radial	22	4.92	3.46
Shrinkage: green to 12 % moisture	148	Tang./Radial	13	2.92	1.44
Pure tangential shrinkage = 5.5 %	148	Tang./Radial	6	1.35	none
Pure radial shrinkage = 3.0 %					
Avg. of radial and tangential = 4.25%					

** Tenons might commonly have a mix of tangential and radial grain. In these cases, shrinkage and compression set values would fall between the pure radial and tangential values.

maintenance. A fourth-century speech of Demosthenes (47.20) reads,

> It happened that there was a dispatch of *triereis* and an emergency expedition speedily mobilized. There was not enough gear in the dockyard...What was more there was not available for purchase in Piraeus a supply of sailcloth and *stuppeion* and ropes, all of which are needed for getting a *trieres* ready for sea.

Stuppeion has been translated to mean raw flax or old rope. Raw flax or old rope can be used for caulking. Even today, old natural rope fibre is sometimes teased apart and used for caulking the seams of wooden ships and boats. In considering whether *stuppeion* means caulking material, it is important to ask what other uses essential for getting a trireme ready for sea could be found for fibre that might be purchased in some form other than rope (rope is clearly specified, therefore *stuppeion* is something else). Here are the only other plausible meanings of *stuppeion* the author (by every admission not a Classicist) can conceive of that might fit this context:

i) *Stuppeion* could mean small diameter lines, such as are used for lashing, mending and the myriad odd chores aboard ship. These range from about 1.5 mm to 7.5 mm in diameter, and are known to sailors and riggers today as "marline" and "housline." It is arguable how essential this material is. Furthermore, larger diameter lines can always be unlaid (unraveled) to get smaller material for this purpose, especially in an emergency.

ii) *Stuppeion* could mean chafing gear such as the binding on the shaft of an oar in the area near the thole pin that protects it against chafe. This is certainly not absolutely essential, and leather or cloth will readily substitute.

This author finds neither of these possibilities convincing, and suggests that *stuppeion* might refer to caulking.

John Coates has suggested 1) the absence of caulking in the few classical shipwrecks found to date 'may well be true evidence of its actual absence' and 2) thin planks with many tenons would have very little plank thickness remaining in which to create a seam for caulking (Morrison, Coates and Rankov 2000, 185). This author won't argue with the first point; the second justifies a comment.

Fibre-caulked modern wooden ships typically devote ⅓ to ½ to of their plank thickness to the caulking seam. While the thin planking of triremes would most probably not have been able to accommodate a deep caulking seam, a modest caulking seam could certainly be made, even in much thinner planking. The author has used thin fibre caulking in seams as shallow as 5 mm in planking of just 10 mm thickness in replicas of 19th century working watercraft. *Olympias'* 40 mm thick planks could have been caulked even if her tenons had been made thicker in order to deal with shear problems discussed below. This author does not believe the use of tenons would have prevented the use of caulking.

Whether caulking was used in triremes or not, if the planks were to slide back and forth, the ship would eventually leak. Over time leakage would get worse until the ship became unusable, especially given the difficulties of bailing water in a trireme.

It is hard to imagine any arrangement of the hull bracing and rowing furniture that would not have lots of cross beams, oars and bodies in the way of a crewman trying to toss water up over the side from down in the bilge with a bucket, pumps being as yet unknown. Human chains to pass a bucket up over the side are possible, but the crew needs to be rowing, not bailing, during battle. How easily and quickly would serious leakage and waterlogging occur? As will be shown, poor construction and shipworms aside, it would depend largely on how often a ship was hauled out and how rapidly it was put back into hard service after re-launch. (In considering triremes being slower from being 'heavy in the water' John Coates (Morrison, Coates and Rankov 2000, 277; cf. Coates, above pp. 182–4) assumes 'as a worst case that all timbers in the hull below the water were to be waterlogged...' True waterlogging (*i.e.* to the point where wood will sink if dropped into water) is difficult to achieve in a working vessel. Even so, waterlogging would constitute only one of the seven tons of water Coates adds to a trireme's dry displacement to estimate the effect of 'heavy' hull conditions, the other six tons being free-flowing bilge water that has risen to the top of the floor timbers.)

Plank slippage due to shear and unequal tenon and mortise strength

The mortise and tenon system is the primary means for preventing movement in the face of significant shear forces between planks. The magnitudes of the horizontal shear forces result from the shape, construction and forces exerted upon the vessel. Just as a chain can only be as strong as its weakest link, for a mortise and tenon system to resist these forces for as long as possible, the strengths of the mortises and tenons should be nearly equal. It is apparent in what follows that such equality of strength was not the case in triremes of antiquity. As a result, the mortise and tenon technology that made it possible for ancient shipwrights to fit 170 men into a 120' foot ship was also the vessel's weak point.

In order to understand how well and how long a trireme's tenons might resist such forces, we need to take another look at the materials involved. As stated earlier, anisotropic materials like wood have physical properties that are different in different directions relative to their structure. The difference in radial and tangential swelling mentioned above in respect to moisture cycling of tenons is a good example.

More generally, the different physical properties and resultant behaviours depend on 1) the nature of the forces involved, 2) their directions relative to the grain, 3) the particular anatomical structure of the species under load, and 4) the moisture content of the timber under load. Furthermore, due to variations in growing conditions and parts of the tree used, any given piece of timber may vary by as much as ±50% of the established mean for a given species and strength property. Any assessment of the construction, repairs or mechanics of a wooden structure must take each of these factors into account.

Four other factors must be borne in mind. First, data on certain physical properties is not always available for the exact species under consideration. However, it is common practice in wood science to identify anatomically identical or very similar species and use those figures as a basis for analysis. This has been done here, substitutions being noted in Tables 26.1 and 26.3, which see.

Secondly, in some cases there have been very significant reductions in published strength values for timber as its quality has declined. Reductions, occasionally as high as 40%, can be found in some important species cited in two United States Forest Service Wood Handbooks. These values are based on identical tests conducted and published just 20 years apart.

It is beyond the scope of this work to quantify how much weaker or stronger certain species may have been in ancient times. But ancient vessels were probably (though not necessarily) blessed with timber of considerably better strength and durability (resistance to decay).

Thirdly, due to differences in the proportions of certain types of cells, slow-grown versus fast-grown trees may generate wood with very different properties. For example, slowly-grown conifers are generally stronger, swell/shrink more, and are more durable (resistant to decay) than the same species grown more quickly on open woodland that has been harvested (or burned) in the recent past. The former are like the pines and firs that had to fight for light in the mature forests of the ancient Mediterranean region.

Table 26.3. Wood Strengths Relative to Grain Direction.

Species	Compression perpendicular to grain (fibre stress at proportional limit)8	Compression parallel to grain (maximum crushing strength)**	Compression to grain (fibre stress at proportional limit)	Avg. rad./tang. max. shear parallel to grain
	Psi or N/mm²	Psi or N/mm²	Psi or N/mm²	Psi or N/mm²
American white oak, *Quercus alba*, at 12 %, if green. USDA 1955 edition	1,070 or 7.4	7,440 or 51.3	4,760 or 32.8	2,000 or 13.8
	670 or 4.6	3,560 or 24.5		
European oak, *Q. robur, pendulata, etc.,* at 12 %, if green		7,490 or 27.6		
		4,000 or 27.6		
Live oak, *Q. viginiana* at 12 %. USDA 1974 edition (as in *Olympias*)	2,040 or 14			
	2,842 or 19.6			
True firs, *Abies spp.,* at 12 % USDA 1955 edition		2,800 or 19.4	4,300 or 29.7	
		5,340 or 36.9		
Pacific silver fir, *A. amabilis* = *A. alba* if green		6,410 or 44.2	4,660 or 32.2	
		3,140 or 21.7		
Pine, *Pinus sylvestris*, at 12 %, if green		6,512 or 45.0		
		3,039 or 21.0		
Douglas fir, *Psuedotsuga menziesii*, at 12 %. USDA 1955 edition (as in *Olympias*)		3,560 or 24.6	5,350 or 36.9	
		6,740 or 46.6		

* Applies to tenons restrained from fore and aft movement as the planks slip, or bottom of mortise if tenons rotate as planks slip in shear.
** Applies at the endgrain of the mortise where they contact the fore and aft faces of the tenons, and to the endgrain at the corners of the tenons if the tenons k=jam against the bottom of the mortise if they rotate.
Sources: Handbook of Hardwoods, HMSO; Wood Handbook, USDA 1987; 1974; 1955 editions; WoodenBoats nos 74 and 87.

Conversely (due, once again, to differences in the proportions of cell types) slowly-grown, ring-porous hardwoods like the oaks used for tenons in ancient Mediterranean ships might have been weaker and more dimensionally stable than modern ones that grew more quickly. If in fact ancient conifers were stronger and oaks weaker than they are today, the strength inequality between planks and tenons discussed below would be even worse than that presented, though the likelihood of compression set might be reduced slightly.

Finally, wood is less strong, less stiff and more plastic when it is wet.

Because a chain is only as strong as its weakest link, manufacturers try to make chains in which every link is equally strong. The links' shape, dimensions and processing maximize uniformity and strength. Mortise-and-tenon joints in triremes need to be like well-made chains. Specifically, the surfaces of the mortises and the tenons that bear against each other should have a strength ratio of one to one. In such a case, as adjacent planks try to slide past each other, each part of the system resists equally.

At first glance, the reader might think that the simplest way to equalize strength between tenons and mortises would be to use the same wood oriented in the same direction, *i.e.* fir planking containing fir tenons with the tenon's grain running longitudinally along the hull, in the same direction as the grain of the planks. This would be a good solution if fore-and-aft shear was the main or only significant force tenons had to withstand. But longitudinal shear forces only become an issue after much more common and substantial forces perpendicular to the hull have been dealt with successfully.

Think of it this way. If you build a stone or brick wall, your first worry is not about it falling down in a direction parallel to its length. You are concerned with perpendicular forces, from the side or above. Similarly, trireme tenons had to withstand significant tension perpendicular to the hull:

i) during construction (when planks set at different angles with rows of tenons in their mortises were being driven together)
ii) from the inward thrust of the water against the hull
iii) when coming up against a dock or other side loading of the tenons
iv) during ramming.

Unfortunately, wood is remarkably weak in tension perpendicular to grain and so would be quite incapable of withstanding these forces if the grain of the tenons ran fore and aft.

Since wood is much stronger in shear parallel, compression parallel and compression perpendicular to grain than in tension perpendicular to grain, the next obvious alternative is to rotate the tenons 90 degrees so their grain runs perpendicular to that of the planks. Under this arrangement, sliding planks exert a force on the tenons that creates compression perpendicular to grain.

The planks are massive relative to the tenons and there is a great deal of solid wood left between the mortises. In addition, wood is so much stronger in compression parallel to grain (the loading of the mortise sides, which is acting just like a weight pressing down on a column) compared even to compression perpendicular to grain (the loading of the tenon) that there is virtually no danger of the planks splitting. In fact, in this arrangement it is hard to achieve anything approaching a one-to-one strength ratio without careful species selection.

It is clear from Classical writings about ship timber (Meiggs 1982; Morrison, Coates and Rankov 2000) and studies of the species used for planks and tenons in excavated shipwrecks, that Classical shipwrights understood, at least at some level, the need to make these joints stiff. Dense hardwoods are used for tenons, lighter conifers are used for planking. If a preferred species was not available for a given application they made sensible substitutions. A good example of this is the occasional use of olive (*Olea sp.*) in place of Turkey oak tenons in the Marsala ship. Contemporary wood science can begin to quantify the problem of matching tenon and mortise strength.

Excavated shipwrecks and the writings of Aristophanes, Theophrastus and others identify the species used for planks and tenons. In the worst cases, ancient shipwrights were creating mortise-and-tenon combinations resulting in strength ratios of 4:1 or worse. Triremes built to these standards would very likely have had shorter, less useful life spans. Casson cites triremes lasting 20 years, though from the text it is clear this was exceptional (Casson 1971, 90). From this and the author's experience it is fair to say eight to fourteen years might have been an average working life for a well-maintained trireme in hard service. Badly matched tenons would shorten this period.

Let us consider the worst ratios, mortises and tenons of ancient triremes built of any true Mediterranean fir and white oak respectively. As detailed in Table 26.3, the strength ratio between the mortise's loading in compression parallel to grain and the tenon's loading under compression perpendicular to grain is about four to one. That is, the endgrain of the fir mortise is typically four times stronger than the side grain of the white oak tenon.

With this arrangement the tenons in the hull will give way first when the joint is subjected to horizontal shear loading (or moisture-induced swelling under restraint). Because of this, gaps will form between the tenons and their mortises and reduced resistance to shear will result upon drying or further flexing of the hull. Eventually the ship will appear to sag at the ends and then leak (see again, Figs 26.1, 26.2 and 26.3). Differences in a ship's buoyancy along its length relative to weight distribution create these shear forces, causing components of its skin, such as wooden planks, to want to slide past one another. Such forces can lead to such sagging at the ends, known as "hogging."

Our projections of the ratio experienced in triremes can be refined if we assume the oak tenons are wet during a trireme's operations, and that in better ships they were combined with (wet) Mediterranean silver fir planking. The ratio then increases to 4.7:1. The oak tenons placed in the stronger (but heavier) pine planks would be stressed even more.

In the *Olympias* reconstruction, tenons of live oak, *Quercus virginiana*, were used instead of European oak, *Quercus sp.* because the former is much stronger, and because the project's managers knew the reconstruction was such a large investment they could not take the risk

that its life span and/or performance be prematurely reduced. The use of live oak makes sense in terms of the hull stiffness and longevity of expensive reconstructions like *Olympias*, but its performance should not obscure (as John Coates points out in Morrison, Coates and Rankov 2000, 201–204) the very real crushing problems the ancients had to confront. For the planking Douglas fir, *Pseudotsuga menziiesi*, was used because historically correct species like Mediterranean fir were not available in sufficient quality and lengths. This combination results in a ratio of about 1.7:1

From the above material it is clear mortise-to-tenon strength ratios for *Classically available* woods is estimated to be about 4:1. In general, the sides of tenons get crushed long before the end grain of the mortise is deformed. Hogging and leakage were inevitable; we can now examine the forces involved and how quickly they occurred.

Analysis of shear forces on tenons

Wooden-planked ships are often incorrectly analyzed by engineers and discussed in reference texts as if they were single, simple beams. In fact, a series of flexible beams laid one on top of another (like a leaf spring) has been proven to be a much better model (Evans 1983; Coates 1996).

John Coates developed a mathematical model to explore what this means for *Olympias*: 'In this simplified model of a mortise-and-tenon joint between two planks, subject to shear force, S per tenon, pressure between the mortise and the edge of the tenon is assumed to extend from plank edge to peg-level, i.e. a line bisecting the peg. Linear distribution is also assumed. Forces required for the rotational equilibrium of the plank may be neglected.' In summary, the maximum shear force per tenon is estimated to be 1730 Newtons, and the maximum compressive stress on the tenon 10.9 N/mm2. This maximum compressive load on the tenon is more than twice as great as the proportional limit of compression perpendicular to grain of white oak at the fibre saturation point, and 1.2 times greater at 12% moisture content. By comparison, this force is only half the compressive strength parallel to grain of a wet pine plank mortise, and one quarter when the mortise is dry. Clearly, the tenons will be crushed.

The ash, mulberry and elm to which Theophrastus ascribes special strength for ship parts (Meiggs 1982, 118) do not today exhibit strength values sufficiently greater than the deciduous oaks to make any difference in the crushing problem if tenons were made from these species. It is impossible to offer data supporting Theophrastus' assertion.

It does not seem unreasonable to assert that ancient shipwrights, observing leakage and crushed tenons in triremes under repair, would naturally make the tenons of subsequently-built triremes bigger and more numerous in an effort to reduce the load per tenon. In indirect confirmation, later mortise-and-tenon built merchant shipwrecks generally have proportionally thicker tenons

A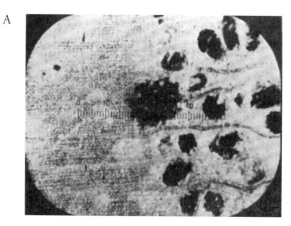

B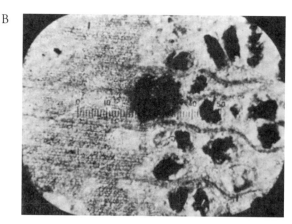

Figure 26.5. Photomicrograph of compression set in catalpa. "A" is before, "B" after swelling under restraint and re-drying. Catalpa has a ring porous cell structure similar to white oak. Note in "B" how the large rays, running left to right, are more bent and curvy than in "A" (Photo: Hoadley, 1969).

spaced more closely than those of earlier periods (see Table 26.2a and 26.2b).

Compression set due to swelling of adjacent planks

'When ships that have been built with green timber sweat out their moisture, they contract and develop cracks. There is nothing more dangerous for sailors.' (Vegetius 4.36)

'For carpentry, the oldest wood is best ... But for shipbuilding, because of the need for bending, it is necessary to use sappier wood (though when it is a case of stopped joints the drier the wood the better). The fact is that (hull) planking shows gaps [between the planks] when it is new, but when the ship is launched the planks absorb water, close up and are watertight, except in the case of timber which has been completely dried out. *In that condition planks do not make a close joint, or not as well as they would if the wood was not completely dried out.*'[my italics] (Theophrastus 4.2.8, Aldine ed.)

John Coates (Morrison, Coates and Rankov 2000, 182) wrote 'The text of the foregoing [Theophrastus] passage is uncertain in places...' but recognized that Theophrastus and Vegetius are clearly defining the need to use planking stock which is dry enough to swell and close up cracks when launched, but not too dry. Modern shipwrights restate the problem by specifying planking stock be conditioned to between 10–18% moisture content (depending on climate, application and species) because such stock is both moist enough to be pliable and sufficiently below fibre saturation point as to be capable of sufficient swelling to close up gaps.

It is the final part of Theophrastus' passage that seems unclear. Coates takes him literally and writes of wood that is 'not so dry that it will not take up water when immersed.' There is no such thing as normal dry wood that is so dry it will not take up moisture. Therefore Theophrastus must mean something else.

A more likely interpretation is that Theophrastus' final comment seems to be the earliest known description of a phenomenon that has plagued woodworkers throughout history and into the present. It is called compression set.

Compression set occurs when wood tries to swell more than about 1% (the limit of elastic strain, i.e. deformation) while the wood is restrained in some way. When the wood tries to swell beyond this limit the cells get flattened and/or displaced so that when the wood shrinks again, the piece of wood has a smaller dimension along the axis of restraint than it had initially. Subsequent re-wetting will not produce as much swelling as occurred in the first moisture increase. More precisely, 'compression set' is that portion of the original dimension that is not recovered. Swelling under restraint is similar to compressing wood. If the elastic limit is exceeded, '...upon re-drying the piece "unloads" itself by shrinking to a smaller than original diameter' (Hoadley 1980, 114).

Swelling under restraint could visibly distort the anatomical structure of ring porous oak, so that the large earlywood pores are squashed and large rays would be 'bent' when viewed transversely. Fig. 26.5 shows before and after photomicrographs of compression set in catalpa, which has a ring porous cell structure similar to white oak. In the 'after' example, the large rays, running left to right, are more bent and curvy. This is mentioned in the hope that investigation of tenons by nautical archaeologists of known and future projects will include examination for this critical evidence of compression damage and standards of ancient ship construction.

Virtually everyone has experienced compression set in the form of loose rungs in wooden chairs. The forces and factors are very similar to those in a trireme's planking or mortise and tenon joints. Imagine a chair with rungs let into sockets in the chair's legs. It has been manufactured during the winter in a modern, heated (dry) furniture factory or woodworker's shop. The air in the shop has low relative humidity, and the joints are machined to fit tightly and glued in place. During storage and/or shipping and/or in your home the chair is cycled back and forth through relative humidities ranging from perhaps 90% to 30% (MC's of 21–6%) during humid summers and dry winters.

During the first exposure to significantly higher relative humidity, the rungs try to swell (increase in diameter, i.e. swelling perpendicular to grain). As they try to swell, the rungs are restrained along the axis of the chair leg. The chair legs behave like columns; they have very high strength in compression parallel to grain, just like the endgrain of the mortises in a trireme's planking. As a result of the great relative strength difference between the rungs and legs due to grain orientation, "weak" rungs are swelling against "strong" legs. The rung's elastic limit can be exceeded if the increase in relative humidity is large enough.

If there are large swings in relative humidity, when the chair dries out during the following winter the rungs shrink to less than their original diameter and the chair is rickety. When the relative humidity increases again, the rungs cannot regain their original dimensions due to the crushed cell structure. Re-gluing with an inelastic adhesive and/or putting a wedge in the gap between the rung and the leg during dry conditions only makes matters worse; the next moisture cycle will lead to further compression set.

Table 26.2a and 26.2b include compression set calculations for different swings in relative humidity for various woods used in triremes.

If a trireme were planked tightly and launched during the dry Aegean summer, it could hit the water with a moisture content as low as 8%. In service, planking moisture contents at and below the waterline would reach fibre saturation at 28%. This ship would not leak the first time it was launched, but thereafter such a ship could have significant leakage problems due to compression set. Table 26.2a and 26.2b indicate that each plank of 148 mm in width could acquire 3–4 mm in compression set (and occasionally more) under such extreme moisture cycling. Thus Theophrastus wrote as he did, that 'planks that are too dry do not make a close joint...'

Compression set in mortise and tenon joints:

Compression set was most probably also a problem in mortise and tenon joints in certain critical parts of trireme hulls. Compression set could create temporary gaps between the tenon and the mortise greater even than John Coates' estimated 1–2 mm slide between planks due to crushing of tenons.

If we assume a very dry, 37 mm wide tenon (MC of 8%) was placed tightly in a mortise near the waterline, it would try to swell when it got wet, but like the chair rung would be restrained by the endgrain of the mortise. When it dried out again, it would return to less than its original size because of compression set and later on would fail to fill the mortise fully upon subsequent swellings.

Let's return to the three zones with different moisture contents (actually a gradient) discussed earlier. As can be seen in Table 26.1, below the waterline and at the waterline, any tenon gaps should not be a problem since the tenons would swell and reach fibre saturation point within a matter of hours of re-launch. Well above the waterline, even with the worst grain orientations, compression sets would be effectively zero, that is only 0.46 mm.

In the intermediate wet/dry zone, each Turkey oak tenon 37 mm wide could swell and then retain between 0.94 and 2.68 mm of compression set if it were eventually hauled out and dried, depending on initial moisture content, number of rings per inch, whether the tenons' grain orientation was aligned radially, tangentially or in some combination of these. If these tenons were created in dry summer months and given a 'crush fit' fore and aft, compression set would be still worse and initial stiffness for re-launch could decrease.

How much and how fast the gaps would close over time after re-launch, as the planks and tenons absorbed seawater, would vary depending on their exact strength, grain orientation, proximity to the waterline, how quickly it rained, etc. With a wider tenon, i.e. like the tenons found in parts of the Kyrenia and Marsala shipwrecks, the compression set figures are much worse, as much as 3–5 mm in each tenon. See again Fig. 26.3.

The values in Table 26.2a and 26.2b show possible unrestrained swelling in *Olympias'* tenons of as much as 2.8 mm, and compression set prior to re-launch could be as much as 2.4 mm for a Live oak tenon in Douglas fir planking. But the designer of *Olympias*, John Coates, has calculated the maximum slippage between planks due to shear to be between 1.0 and 1.8 mm. In short, the gaps caused by compression set could be in excess of the possible sliding between planks. The fore and aft faces of the tenons would then offer no resistance to initial sliding. No wonder *Olympias* has hogged.

Even worse, Coates has calculated *Olympias's* neutral axis to be 1.2 m above the underside of the keel (about 10 cm above the load waterline) at the locations of maximum shear between planks. The wet/dry zone begins just above this height, so any compression set in this area would lead to lower shear resistance in the hull just where it is most needed.

We can now hypothesize with some confidence that for either contemporary or ancient triremes, a drive fit oak tenon in Mediterranean fir planking would swell and 'crush itself' in certain areas of the hull when it got wet. Unless Classical shipwrights understood the nuances of wood's behaviour and compensated for it by allowing for swelling in critical parts of the hull, debilitating gaps would have been created by moisture cycling.

The passage from Theophrastus cited above clearly indicates compression set was recognized. Whether ancient shipwrights understood it well enough to compensate for it in tenons is likely to remain unknown. Given the distorted, waterlogged condition of the wood found in ancient shipwrecks it would be most unlikely that gaps between tenons and mortises would be found in wrecks today. At best it may be possible for nautical archaeologists to determine when compression set had been a problem in a given vessel by studying the anatomical structure of the tenons in some detail.

As illustrated, compression set would most likely appear as visible squashing, crushing or distortion of the wood's microscopic anatomical structure, particularly as viewed in transverse section, and as mirror imaging between the faces of the tenon and the sides of the mortise.

Richard Steffy (1985, 81) has noted that in the Kyrenia wreck, tenons were generally cut 5 mm to 10 mm shorter than the sum of their two mortise depths, but also notes that their widths matched well, and even the end shapes of the tenons somewhat resembled the bottom configurations of their mortises. It is possible that some of these resemblances are due to crushing and compression set of the planking and tenons.

Jay Rosloff of the Ma'agan Michel wreck excavation reports in personal communication that the vessel's oak tenons were very tight in the mortise, with no appreciable gaps.

Unfortunately, it is likely shrinkage and compression set gaps would have occurred near in the most sensitive area in a trireme hull. The behaviour of wooden planked ships is such that the greatest shear forces creating sliding between planks will occur at a distance of one quarter of the waterline length from either end of the waterline at the height of the neutral axis. For *Olympias*, this neutral axis occurs just above the waterline.

The archaeological and mathematical evidence, while slim, strongly suggests there were probably serious compression set problems in the intermediate wet/dry area that coincides with locations of maximum shear along the neutral axis. Compression set gaps could then constitute the 'Achilles heel' of trireme construction. Only the first strake or so above waterline is likely to automatically swell fully (upon re-launch) due to its reaching fibre saturation point. I suggest the second and third strake or so above the waterline could have tenons with significant gaps until they are exposed to big enough waves, heavy rain, or the ship is heeled over to thoroughly wet them.

Launching a thoroughly dried trireme and taking it directly to sea within 24–48 hours could subject it to significant shear loads at a time in the moisture cycle when the hull is least able to resist such loads. This is when hogging is most likely to occur, and when wood-to-wood or caulked watertight joints would likely be damaged by plank slippage, resulting in increased leakage.

Thus in the first few days after re-launch, a trireme could be less stiff. It is also possible the lack of stiffness due to inadequate contact between fore and aft faces of the tenon and mortise walls could be mitigated by a number of factors.

Without tenon to mortise contact, initial stiffness under load could still be substantial due to:

i) caulking-to-plank friction (if caulking was used)
ii) plank-to-plank friction
iii) frictional forces on the corners, inboard and outboard faces of the tenons. A strake 15 m long (*i.e.* in the centre of the ship) with tenons every 0.92 m (as in *Olympias*) has about 163 tenons per seam. With so many joints in a given seam and their probable slight misalignment with respect to each other, the frictional forces alone could significantly 'bind up' adjacent planks
iv) any resistance offered by attachment to internal framing members
v) possible jamming of the end grain of the tenon against the bottom of the mortise as the planking swells and/or the tenon rotates in the slot

Since it would appear the absolute strength properties of wet tenons under compression perpendicular to grain are grossly inadequate for the loads incurred, it must be that friction with sides, rotation against the mortise bottom, and these other factors make a substantial difference.

The author believes only testing on full size models in a proper laboratory would enable researchers to evaluate this assertion and the relative significance of these various factors.

Hogging

John Coates has written:

'Soon after the ship was first operated at sea in 1987, the tenons joining together adjacent shell planks allowed some slip to occur between planks, and the hull hogged by about 6 cm over the length of the oar system. Owing to the way many of the tenons in *Olympias* were fitted during building, this possibility had been anticipated. Several plank seams had been marked with vertical lines drawn across them before the ship was moved from the building berth. By the end of the first sea trials these marks showed that the planks had slipped, relative to their neighbours, by about 1 mm. Since the planks are about 15 cm wide, this slippage was sufficient to be the cause of the amount of hog observed, and shows that the hog was due to shear, not bending, in the hull.

To try to prevent an increase in hogging during future service the tenons in *Olympias* were glued in place by injecting a gap-filling epoxy resin as far as was possible into the gaps between the fore and aft faces of the tenons and their mortises. Before that action was taken, the ship was slipped [*i.e.* cradled on blocks] so that her ends were held up to cause the hull to sag. The injection does appear to have helped in resisting further hogging, though no one can say for certain whether hogging would have increased if no glue had been injected.

The hogging experienced in *Olympias* shows that the hulls of triremes were at the limit as regards their length relative to hull depth. The tenons preventing the side planks from sliding upon each other would have had to be fitted into their mortises very tightly in the fore-and-aft direction. Indeed it is reasonable now to suppose that in antiquity they would have been given a crush-fit to achieve in practice the simultaneous bearing required stiffly to resist sliding between planks. The taper found on the fore and the aft faces of tenons in some excavated wrecks could have been made to facilitate achieving such a crush-fit when the upper plank was driven down over the tenons to close a seam. [But see notes on compression set, caulking, drawboring and other matters elsewhere in this paper.]

The shear strength of the sides of a trireme is also affected by the presence of large oarports, and it now seems likely to me that the side planking in way of them between the lower and middle wales would have been thicker in order to house thicker tenons with greater bearing area to resist shear forces more stiffly.'

After the first period of trials in 1987, the hog in Olympias was about 6 cm measured by eye (Morrison and Coates 1989, 69–73; Coates, Platis and Shaw 1990, 73). In 1992, the hog of the ship was measured to be 9 cm to starboard and 13 cm to port, both with and without the oarcrew on board. If viewed in pure profile, the starboard high spot is about midway between the mast and the stern, on port the high spot is virtually opposite the mast. These measurements confirm the general visual impression that the ship is twisted (a condition which is common to most wooden ships) with the bow lower and rotated to port relative to an arbitrary, level, midships plane.

The hog was measured on a very calm day using a steel measuring tape. The tape was lowered plumb from the outrigger to the water's surface at five locations along the length of the outrigger. The tape length was adjusted until the peaks and troughs of the very slight surface undulations were equidistant from the tape's tip, then the measurement was recorded. Under these conditions the accuracy of this method is estimated to be plus or minus one centimetre.

Operations of *Olympias* in England in 1993 have clarified the factors influencing hog still further. John Coates observed when the ship was pulled from the water after operating on the Thames River, that while the keel was straight, the topwale, outrigger and hull sides displayed some hog. Coates' analysis (quoted from personal correspondence) follows:

I was not able to measure the hog in those parts of the hull but they were certainly hogged to a noticeable degree, as had been observed for some years previously. It is most unlikely that the keel would have straightened out as the ship was lifted out of the water while supported in her cradle, moments before this observation was made at Tilbury.

It follows that there has been some deformation in the transverse sections of the middle-body of the hull by which the rise of floor has increased. If the keel has remained undeformed, this hogging must be confined to the sides of the hull. If the hull sides have risen relative to the keel, the ends of the transverse hull beams would then have to have bent upward so as to decrease their overall camber ['camber' is the convexity upward or curvature of a ship's beams]. The ends of the beams would rise more than the pillars since the pillars are secured to the floors nearer

the keel and the beams would likely be flexible enough to flatten under some tension in the pillars sufficiently to keep the pillars attached top and bottom.

Whether upon building the beams were to any extent bent to their required camber is not known, so the degree to which the beam pillars would now be in tension must be unknown too. Prior to haul out at Tilbury there had been no search to see if the pillars were separating from beams at their heads or from the stringers at their heels, and it was not possible to check for this at Tilbury. We have little idea of what forces might have developed to separate pillars from beams or stringers. The pillars would however be fairly inextensible, compared with the flexibility in the vertical direction of the ship's sides in shear and of the keel in bending. Pillars are attached to the stringers and beams at their bottoms and tops with 74 mm-long tenons locked in place with a spike.

To put some numbers into the question, I estimate that the beams would deflect, at the tops of the pillars, by about 0.240 mm per kg of tension in each pillar, relative to the height of the ends of the beams, and therefore to the sides of the hull. If that is right, then a deflection of 60 mm would call for a tension of 250 kg in each pillar. The locking spikes would be deformed by such a load and some separation from the stringer and beams might be visible.

The keel and its associated planking nevertheless form a substantial longitudinal member on the middle-line of the hull. This has appreciable flexural stiffness with an effective length of only about half that of the hull, owing to the long rising parts of the keel forward and aft. The transverse timbers, following ancient practice, are laid across the shell in several tiers which are not directly connected to each other. In *Olympias* their flexural stiffness in resisting change of transverse shape of the hull, particularly at the curve of the bilge, may have been further reduced. They were cut out of straight lengths of straight-grained iroko timber [instead of curved timbers which would allow the grain to follow the curve of the hull] so that they are cross-grained at the ends of each tier.

The shell of the hull sides forms much the deepest component of the hull structure. It is therefore the stiffest in resisting the vertical shear forces which arise from the longitudinal bending moments acting on the hull. It seems likely that the keel, being a much shallower member, could bear the bending actions placed upon it by the deformation of the hull in an elastic and recoverable manner. In contrast, the inherently stiffer shell of the hull in deforming under the shear forces could only do so by slippage of the tenons, which would not have been elastic and recoverable. There would have been considerable friction between tenons and the long sides of their mortises, tending to hold the hull sides in their sheared (hogged) shape.

In this hogging deformation of the ship it is surprising that the keel structure should apparently be so stiff in bending. It is however likely that it does bend upwards amidships by some amount when the ship is afloat, under the upward pressure of water on the bottom, thereby reducing the tension needed in the pillars to keep everything joined together.

Drawboring of the pegs in mortise-and-tenon joints

Drawboring mortise-and-tenon joints is the practice of drilling the peg holes in shouldered mortises and tenons at slightly offset (*c.* 4 mm) positions. When the peg is driven into place, the tenon is 'pre-tensioned' so that any initial gap or slack is significantly reduced. Typically, the offset serves to draw a shouldered tenon more deeply into the mortise so that the tenon's shoulder is drawn tightly against the shoulder of the mortise (see Fig. 26.6).

Robert 'Ben' Brungraber (1985) showed convincingly that,

> '...the drawboring technique [is] the most influential factor in determining a connection's service load level stiffness against applied axial loads and bending moment. Drawboring, or 'preloading' the peg, ensures that all the components are in solid bearing before any loads are applied to the connection. As a result there is no slack...'

He goes on to show the initial resistance of the joint to being pulled apart, i.e. in tension, is doubled. The initial resistance to collapse, i.e. under compression, is quadrupled with proper drawboring technique. Drawboring in the timber frames of houses, which is what Brungraber studied, has 'very little' effect on shear loads. Given the extra labour and limited effectiveness such a technique would involve for un-shouldered mortise-and-tenon joints in planking, its use in this application in antiquity seems very unlikely.

In contrast, drawboring could have been very useful in strategic locations of a trireme's internal members, such as in the pillars mentioned above, fore-and-aft bracing of the beams upon which the zygians sit, in the rowing furniture, and other part of the ship where initial stiffness against axial loads and bending moments is valuable. It will certainly be worth exploring applications of drawboring in these locations in future trireme reconstructions.

Detection of drawboring in ancient shipwrecks would likely be difficult. The telltale signs would be hard to distinguish in degraded, distorted and waterlogged timbers containing joinery that may also have been deformed during in-service loading. Evidence could include 1) a measurable offset distance between the holes drilled in the tenon and mortise, 2) greater compression set on the 'drawn' side than those found on the 'un-drawn' side of the pin, and 3) crushing or compression of the holes where drawboring generates the greatest loads.

It remains to be seen if drawboring can be detected. The Trireme Trust USA circulated a description of the issue and an offer of assistance to the shipwreck archaeology community in the hope of creating an interest in looking for this and other evidence related to mortise-and-tenon performance. The information we have gathered in response to this inquiry, such as the evidence on grain orientation in the Marsala wrecks sent by Ms. Honor Frost, is included in this report, with many thanks to the contributors. None of the evidence submitted to date has presented evidence related to drawboring.

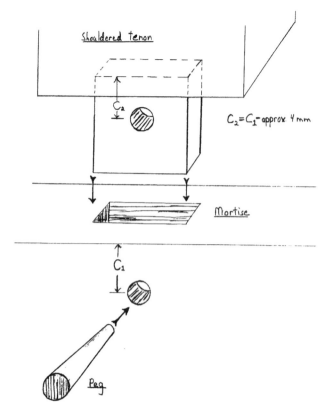

Figure 26.6. Detail of the technique of drawboring pinned mortise-and-tenon joints, which is the practice of drilling the peg holes in shouldered mortises and tenons at slightly offset positions in order to pre-tension the joint by pulling the two parts more tightly together (Drawing: Paul Lipke).

Possible solutions available to Classical shipwrights

The solutions that common sense suggests were most likely to present themselves to trireme builders relate to 1) tenon grain orientation, and 2) tenon thickness and spacing. The labour and material costs of increases in the latter far outweigh those of the former.

For two substantive reasons, better triremes could be built using tenons cut in such a way that surfaces with radial orientations faced fore and aft. As mentioned earlier, this appears to have been done in the Marsala shipwreck, but evidence from other wrecks is lacking.

i)   Radial orientation would reduce swelling against the end grain of the mortise, and therefore compression set, in comparison with tenons that have tangential surfaces facing fore and aft. If the radial surfaces face fore and aft the maximum calculated compression set in a 37 mm Turkey oak tenon is 0.94 mm.

ii) Ring porous species like oak have radial faces that are stronger than tangential faces because the alternating bands of dense latewood are stronger (Fig. 26.7, 26.8 and 26.9) and prevent the large diameter, thin-walled earlywood cells from being readily crushed. Therefore, a tenon with its radial planes facing fore and aft would

Figure 26.7. Planes of wood: T=Tangential, R=Radial, X=cross-section or transverse (Photo: Wilfred Cote).

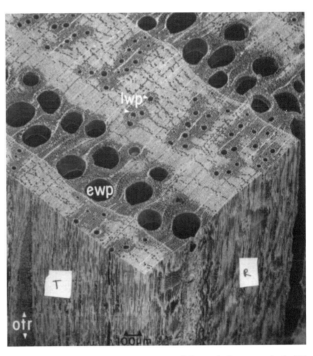

Figure 26.8. Ring porous species like oak have radial (R) faces that are stronger than tangential faces (T) because the alternating bands of dense latewood prevent the large early wood pores from getting crushed (Photo: Wilfred Cote).

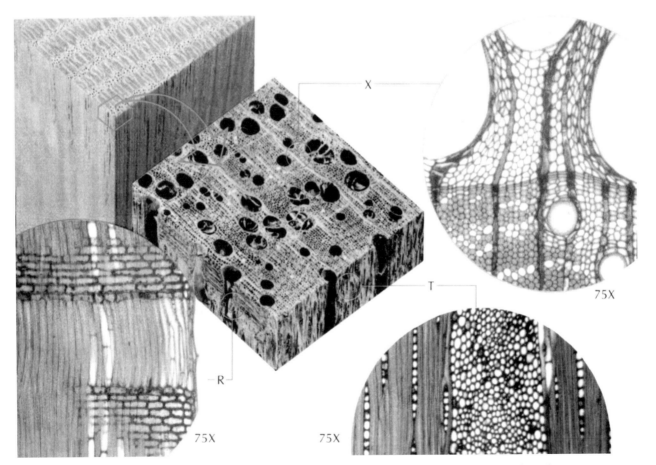

Figure 26.9. Photomicrographs of red oak, showing how dramatically different its structure displays, depending on orientation (Photo: Bruce Hoadley and Wilfred Cote).

be stronger than one with tangential surfaces facing fore and aft.

Given this, crush fitting of radially-oriented plank tenons might prove very helpful in stiffening a hull with much less risk of compression set if this were done near locations of maximum shear.

It is possible to produce tenons with either tangential or radial orientations from boards riven from a log (or cut from logs by quarter sawing). See Fig. 26.4. Thick wedges produced from large-diameter trees can be sawn, axed, or split again to produce radially oriented tenons. Slash-sawn timbers can have radial grain exposed on fore and aft surfaces of tenons almost regardless of the tree size.

As the author can personally attest, riving green timber (especially oak) can be faster and less effort than ripping long planks out of a log, even with a two-man hand saw. Riving can waste a lot of timber, but since tenons are small, this was less likely to be a factor. While wood scraps from other applications could be cut up to make tenons, the need for tens of thousands of tenons per hull would certainly necessitate processing timber specifically for that purpose.

Finally, in considering possible improvements to any trireme reconstruction to follow *Olympias*, Coates (1996, 10) concludes, 'tenons [in the way of the oarports] could sensibly have been 20 mm thick, not 12, and side planking 60 mm [thick as opposed to only 40 mm]. Elsewhere in the hull planks and tenons could have been satisfactory if of the dimensions found in the Marsala ship...'

This author concurs with one caveat, the Marsala tenons were 70 mm wide, nearly double those of *Olympias*, and so moisture cycling and compression set would likely have been a serious problem. This author suggests future efforts experiment with tenons that are thicker athwartships and more closely spaced, especially in areas of maximum plank shear, but not necessarily much wider longitudinally. A more modest increase in width, perhaps to 55 mm would result in maximum compression set in a Turkey oak tenon of 'only' about 1.4 mm.

Conclusion

As complex issues and new understandings in this paper have made clear, there is a great deal we do not yet know about the performance and interactions of the most basic structural elements of a trireme. Further research and experiments are needed. Both this author and John Coates believe an interdisciplinary study of mortise-and-tenon dynamics, involving both wood scientists and naval architects, holds enormous potential for increasing our understanding of the practical limits faced by shipwrights and crews operating triremes and other mortise-and-tenon-built ships of antiquity.

Bibliography

British Standards Institution (1991) *British Standard Nomenclature of Commercial Timbers* Milton Keynes, British Standards Institution.

Brungraber, R. L. (1985) *Traditional Timber Joinery, A modern Analysis*. Stanford, unpublished PhD dissertation.

Henderson, F. Y. (1977) *A Handbook of Softwoods*. London, C. Lockwood.

Casson, L. (1971) *Ships and Seamanship in the Ancient World*. Princeton, NJ, Princeton University Press.

Coates, J. S. (2001) 'Planking tenons in Ancient Mediterranean ships built shell first' in Tzalas, H. (ed.), *Tropis VI. 6th International Symposium on Ship Construction in Antiquity, Lamia, 28, 29, 30 August 1996*. Athens, Hellenic Institute for the Preservation of Nautical Tradition.

Coates, J. S., Platis, S. K. and Shaw, J.T. (1990) *The Trireme Trials 1988*. Oxford, Oxbow Books.

Evans, J. H. (1983) *Ship Structural Design Concepts: Second Cycle*. Centreville, MD, Cornell Maritime Press.

Farmer, R. H. (1972) *Handbook of Hardwoods*. London, Her Majesty's Stationery Office.

Frost. H. (1976) Lilybaeum (Marsala). *Notizie degli scavi di antichità: Serie Ottava 30*.

Hoadley, R. B. (1969) 'Perpendicular to Grain Compression Set Induced by Restrained Swelling', *Wood Science* 1.3, 159–166

Hoadley, R. B. (1980) *Understanding Wood*. Newtown CT, Taunton Press Inc.

Hoadley, R. B. (1990) *Identifying Wood*. Newtown CT, Taunton Press Inc.

Jane, F. W. (1970) *The Structure of Wood*. London, A. & C. Black.

Meiggs, R. (1982) *Trees and Timber in the Ancient Mediterranean World*. Oxford, Oxford University Press.

Mitchell, A. (1974) *A Field Guide to the Trees of Britain and Northern Europe*. London, Collins.

Morrison, J. S. and Coates, J. F. (1989) *An Athenian Trireme Reconstructed*. Oxford, Oxbow Books.

Morrison, J. S., Coates, J. F. and Rankov, N. B. (2000) *The Athenian Trireme. The History and Reconstruction of an Ancient Greek Warship*. 2nd ed. Cambridge, Cambridge University Press.

Rival, M. (1991) *La Charpenterie Navale Romaine*. Paris, Presses du CNRS.

Schweingruber, F. H. (1990) *Anatomie europäischer Hölzer / Anatomy of European Woods*. Bern, Stuttgart, Verlag Paul Haupt.

Shaw, J. T. (ed.) (1993) *The Trireme Project*. Oxford, Oxbow Books.

Steffy, J. R. (1985) 'The Kyrenia Ship: An Interim Report on its Hull Construction', *American Journal of Archaeology* 89, 71–101.

Tsoumis, G. and Voulgaridis, E. (1980) 'Experimental Air Drying of Pine, Fir and Beech Lumber,' *Geotechnica* 1 (Jan–March).

USDA, Forest Products Laboratory (1955) *Wood Handbook: Wood as an Engineering Material* Washington, DC US Government Printing Office.

USDA, Forest Products Laboratory (1974) *Wood Handbook: Wood as an Engineering Material*. Rev. ed. Washington DC, US Government Printing Office.

USDA, Forest Products Laboratory (1987) *Wood Handbook: Wood as an Engineering Material*. Rev. ed. Washington DC, US Government Printing Office.

27. Triremes and Shipworm

Paul Lipke

Introduction

In the Spring of 1995, the planking of *Olympias* was found to be damaged by shipworms, which had riddled the hull when the ship was left in the water with insufficient or degraded bottom paint (Fig. 27.1). Damage was bad enough that extensive re-planking was necessary to make the ship operational. There is a lesson here as to the purpose of hauling triremes ashore for 'drying out' in antiquity. Shipworm attack was by far and away the greatest threat to the viability of the trireme as a weapon. The threat remains so pervasive that even 2400 years later we are re-living the losses faced by the navy of Classical Athens.

Shipworm life cycles

Shipworms (*Teredinidae*) are molluscan, tiny clams with long soft bodies about 30 cm (one foot) in length when mature (though they can get longer). Imagine a worm with a bony head at one end, and siphons for drawing in or expelling water at the other. Adjacent to the siphons, shipworms have two pallets. Under distress (low salinity, adverse temperatures, *etc.*) *Teredinidae* pull in their siphons and plug the entrance hole with their pallets.

As free-swimming, small (1 mm or so) larvae, shipworms find a tiny crack or crevasse in a piece of wood to which they can attach. They change to a burrower, eventually make a tiny hole, and then start eating and growing. Their tunnels can reach several meters in length, and are lined with a calcareous coating. This coating, and their plug-able entrance hole increase their ability to maintain a moist environment in which they can survive when wood they have infested is removed from sea water (Spence 1993; Turner 1996).

Shipworm in triremes

This author suggests that of all the potential weaknesses of the trireme as an expensive, high-tech ship, *e.g.* its dependence on very high quality construction, ease of

damage in battle, impacts of poor crew on performance, *etc.*, none would have been as hard to control, or full of risk to those involved, as its liability to shipworm attack and the resultant poor speed and manoeuvrability due to leakage.

Shipworm infestation can be hard to detect. Once started, damage can progress rapidly; modern wooden hulls have been reduced to worthlessness in a couple of months. The damage cannot typically be patched or caulked; damaged planking must be replaced. In the warm climate of the Aegean, infestation can occur rapidly in any season and at any time a hull is more or less stationary. All the larvae need to get attached is a tiny patch of uncoated planking or a crack in a seam below the waterline.

Modern marine coatings for wood are durable enough to prevent shipworm attack over relatively long periods of immersion (*i.e.* up to 6 months at a time in warm water) but traditional coatings, such as the tar and pitch available to ancient shipwrights, would have to be frequently re-applied to be effective. Fast galleys could not afford, as could merchant ships, the loss of speed that would come with a prophylactic hull sheathing of lead, as was found on the late 4th century BC Kyrenia shipwreck.

Shipworm and mortise and tenon joints

Compared to other, later planking methods, it would appear mortise and tenon built hulls would present conditions under which shipworms could get established more easily and once established could survive various life threats for longer. Slight imperfections in the many plank surface penetrations (made by the pins of the tenons) could provide easy access to planking at the most vulnerable stage in a shipworm's life cycle, when they are seeking wood to which to attach, and making the transition from free-swimmers to burrowers.

In addition, though it would vary with wood moisture content and species, the open endgrain of the tenon pins could absorb more protective hull coating material than

Figure 27.1. Teredo-damaged planking from Olympias. Note the damage in and around the planking mortises (Photo: Paul Lipke).

any adjacent planking. In fact, with tenon pins made out of oak, *Quercus sp.*, unless extra care was taken to apply enough coating material to the thousands of pins to truly seal them up, the large open pores of the open endgrain could provide shipworms with a nearly ideal entrance point.

Furthermore, when a mortise-and-tenon-built ship is hauled out, the mortises create, in effect, little reservoirs that can supply water to dryer parts of the planking. Since established *Teredinidae* infestations of plank-on-frame wooden ships are known to survive haul-out periods of six weeks, it is reasonable to suggest the extra moisture held in reserve in the mortises of a trireme would likely extend that time span (see more on this topic below).

In *The Athenian Trireme*, the authors write of 'caulking of worm-holes' and using 'a coating of pitch' to remedy 'the effects of teredon...provided that the hull is not too much weakened' (Morrison, Coates and Rankov 2000, 186). While this might work in a few cases, shipworm entrance holes are often quite small (1–3 mm) and hard to locate, particularly with the shipworm's siphons withdrawn and pallets in place. It is also likely that any entrance hole conspicuous enough to locate would be connected to a tunnel large enough to significantly weaken a plank (which would therefore need replacement rather than repair).

In Classical literature, to this author's knowledge, shipworms are not specifically mentioned in connection with 'drying out,' but they are clearly a common concern. In Aristophanes' comedy *Knights* (1300–10) the ships are talking to each other and one trireme says, '...I would rather become an old maid here and be eaten by shipworm' [than go to Carthage upon the request of Hyperbolus].

Other marine borers

Theophrastus (5.4.4) wrote that pine is more liable to shipworm attack than fir, and that while 'the damage done by *skolex* and *thrips* is easy to cure, the damage done by teredon is impossible to repair' (meaning teredo-damaged planks must be replaced entirely). Morrison reports the naval inventories frequently list 'worm-eaten' wooden gear.

In Morrison, Coates and Rankov (2000, 293–4), *skolex* and *thrips* are incorrectly described as types of shipworm. If this is true, the passage in Theophrastus makes no sense. '*Skolex*' and '*thrips*' most probably refer to the crab-like gribble of the genus *Limnoria*, which does not burrow in wood but feeds more slowly on the wood's surface. Gribble and shipworm are often lumped together by non-specialists, but the former is far less destructive to ships, and far easier to detect and treat.

Ship worm and 'drying out'

Morrison and Coates summarized the Classical literary evidence for 'drying out' hulls. The work focuses primarily on the hauling and 'drying out' process as a means to remove marine growth, renew hull coatings, and caulk planking seams to reduce leakage. It should be noted that while beaching is thought to be quite common (Blackman, 1968; 1982 note 114; Casson, 1971, 89–90; Foley 1982; Coates and Shaw 1993, 87–90), just how this was accomplished and with what frequency is not certain. The careful analysis of Coates and Shaw (1993; see also Coates, above pp. 134–41) can be contrasted with the completely unrealistic proposals of Steinmayer and Macintosh Turfa (1996, 108), in which the authors write quite unrealistically, 'the crew would begin to pull and also to run. When the ship touched the shore, the momentum would help substantially to beach it.'

It is hard for anyone not intimately involved in the care of wooden ships to truly grasp how critical maintenance like beaching is to the life span of the vessel. Far more sensitive than buildings, under certain conditions a month or two of sloppy attention to detail in a wooden ship can prove disastrous. From more than 15 years as a professional maritime preservationist, the author can attest that some of the best-managed historic ship projects around the world re-discover this fact with dismaying frequency.

Morrison and Coates rightly avoid putting much value on the common misconception that the purpose of hauling a trireme out of the water was to make the ship lighter by reducing the moisture content of the hull. Any reduction in moisture content in planking below the waterline during hauling and 'airing out,' would be undone within a day or so of re-launching.

This is true even if a hull coating of tar and/or wax (Morrison, Coates and Rankov 2000, 187) was heated and applied while still hot to a clean, thoroughly dry hull. Such an application could penetrate the surface and provide a thin, marine growth and water-resistant layer, but submerged planking would still reach fibre saturation point in a matter of hours or, at most, two days. The true benefits of hauling out are as a means of reducing the rate and extent of shipworm infestation by killing off larvae in the first few hours that they attempt to enter the wood.

How long would a trireme have to be out of the water to kill off *Teredinidae*? The answer depends on hull temperature, exposure to direct sunlight, the species of *Teredinidae* involved and the age or extent of the infestation.

If an un-infested trireme could be hauled every few days, (*i.e.* if it was operating in peace-time from a strong naval base with shipsheds) regular, frequent haul-outs and coating touch-ups would probably kill off any shipworms that were just getting attached/established. If the period

between haul-outs lengthened to a couple of weeks or more, then haul-outs would have to last longer and/or involve more exposure to high temperatures, direct sun on the planking, *etc.* to be an effective defence against shipworm.

Similarly, if slightly infested planking was hauled up on a hot summer beach with full exposure to the sun and any marine growth was scraped off, a few days' exposure could effectively kill off any lightly established shipworm. By contrast, a long established colony might last weeks under these conditions and thrive when re-immersed.

If more moderate temperatures were involved and/or if the planking was shaded from the direct sun (*i.e.* storage in a ship shed or the infestation was in strakes below the turn of the bilge, shaded by the topsides) the colony could survive longer still, and would thrive again when the hull was returned to the water.

The different Mediterranean shipworm genera of *Teredo*, *Bankia*, *Lyrodus*, etc. would vary widely in how long they could survive in a given set of haul-out conditions. Those like the *Lyrodus* with strong, thick pallets which could effectively seal off their tunnel opening, would presumably last far longer than those with weak pallets. Imagine a well established colony of *Lyrodus* in a vessel hauled out in the cool, wet fall or spring of Greece; a month or more on the beach would likely not kill off the infestation. Re-immersion would end the hibernation and give the colony the opportunity to thrive.

One good example will suffice to underscore the importance of shipworm and its devastating effects. In Thucydides (7.12.3), Nicias wrote from Syracuse after a year in which his fleet of 'fast' triremes had been at the moorings,

> 'Our fleet was originally in first-class condition, the ships dry and the crews unimpaired, but now the ships are leaky...It is not possible to beach the ships and dry them out because the enemy fleet ... keeps us constantly on the look-out for an attack'

What would make the ships leaky as they sat at their moorings? What are the possibilities?

- In hot, dry weather in calm water, planking seams immediately above the waterline could dry out and open up. Such seams are easily 'choked' with cloth, fibre, any sort of putty *etc.* to reduce leakage, and in any case daily wash-downs with buckets of sea water would prevent this problem from occurring in the first place.
- Fibrous caulking materials, if they were used in triremes, would not deteriorate significantly under such passive conditions.
- Seam-filling compounds of pitch and/or wax would hold up well in stationary ships, and leaks from lost seam compounds are rarely extensive enough to warrant Nicias' complaints. In any case seams could be re-filled while the ship was still afloat in shallow water or under a careening lasting only a few hours. (N.B. such seam touch-ups would probably have little effect on established shipworms).

This author believes the problem lay with shipworm. The long trip from Corcyra to Sicily would create, even in the best-maintained hull seams, plenty of crevasses in which *Teredinidae* could get established. Static storage in warm water is ideal for shipworm. Nicias' fleet at Sicily offered exactly this.

Tunneling along the length of the planking, shipworms would tend to detour around the denser woods used for tenons but would 'happily' consume the softer fir or pine planking around it. Inevitably, tunnel edges would intersect mortises, which would likely increase the numbers of leaks both at the mortise and along adjacent plank seams. These would be impossible to caulk, and the damage could not be repaired without re-planking the infested parts of the hull.

As made clear above, short haul-outs would likely be of no value in eliminating such entrenched shipworms. In fact, with established colonies, brief haul-outs or careening to scrape off marine growth (in order to maintain battle-ready condition) could actually accelerate the consumption of planking by increasing water flow past the siphons (Turner 1995).

Future experiments

Dr. Ruth Turner, the leading world authority on the *Teredinidae*, has said to this author, 'There is so much we don't know [about *Teredinidae*]. There is so much [to learn] about how rapidly they could destroy ancient ships or how well they could survive the ships being hauled out; this is an area which cries out for some simple experimentation (R. D. Turner, pers. comm. (8/27/95)).'

Teredinidae were, in all probability, the most critical weakness in the viability of the trireme as an instrument of political and economic hegemony. The constraints imposed on triremes by the laws of physics have not changed since Classical times, and this fact enabled *Olympias* to be reconstructed, built and tested. In the same way, the life cycles, behaviours and problems generated by *Teredinidae* have not changed in the intervening millennium.

Therefore, to understand triremes day-to-day operations and the challenges faced by Classical shipwrights, scholars might want to focus on conducting experiments on this topic using very economical hull and planking test-sections before any funds are spent on any future reconstruction including:

i)   Out-of-water survival rates of *Teredinidae* in infested mortise-and-tenon-joined planking under different weather conditions and periods of time.

ii) Ability of *Teredinidae* to penetrate (or find voids in) pine tar/wax/pitch hull coatings of mortise-and-tenon planking.

iii) The influence of frequent haul-out, with and without touch-up of hull coatings, on both *Teredinidae* infestation rates, and on rate of destruction of planking after it is infested.

It is hoped such experiments will be carried out in the near future, but not directly on *Olympias* or any of her successors.

Acknowlegdement

This paper would not have been possible without the cooperation and encouragement of the leading world authority on *Teredinidae*, Dr Ruth D. Turner of Harvard University Museum of Comparative Zoology.

Bibliography

Blackman, D. J. (1968) The ship-sheds. In Morrison and Williams (1968), 181–192.

Blackman, D. J. (1982) Ancient Harbors in the Mediterranean. *International Journal of Nautical Archaeology* 11, 79–104 and 185–211.

Bletchly, J. D. (1967) *Insect and Marine Borer Damage to Timber and Woodwork*. Forest Products Research Laboratory. London, HMSO.

Casson, L. (1971) *Ships and Seamanship in the Ancient World*. Princeton NJ, Princeton University Press.

Coates, J. F. (1997) Some comments on the article on shipworm in (and beaching of) ancient Mediterranean warships in *International Journal of Nautical Archaeology* 25.2, 104–121. *International Journal of Nautical Archaeology*, 26.1, 82–83.

Coates, J. F. and Morrison, J. S. (1987) Authenticity in the replica Athenian *trieres*. *Antiquity* 61, 87–90.

Foley, V. *et al.* (1982) A trireme displacement estimate. *International Journal of Nautical Archaeology* 11, 305–318.

Hoadley, R. B. (1980) *Understanding Wood*. Newtown, CT, Taunton Press Inc.

Morrison, J. S and Williams, R. T. (1968) *Greek Oared Ships 900–322 B.C.* Cambridge, Cambridge University Press.

Morrison, J. S., Coates, J. F., and Rankov, N. B. (2000) *The Athenian Trireme. The History and Reconstruction of an Ancient Greek Warship*. 2nd ed. Cambridge, Cambridge University Press.

Shaw, J. T. (ed) (1993) *The Trireme Project*. Oxford, Oxbow Books.

Spence, L. (1993) Shipworms and gribbles: the wooden boat eaters. *Wooden Boat* 111 (March/April).

Steinmayer Jr., A. G. and MacIntosh Turfa, J. (1996) Effects of shipworm on the performance of ancient Mediterranean warships. *International Journal of Nautical Archaeology* 25.2, 104–121.

Turner, R. D. (1966) *A Survey and Illustrated Catalogue of the* Teredinidae. Cambridge MA, Museum of Comparative Zoology, Harvard University.

USDA, Forest Products Laboratory (1987) *Wood Handbook: Wood as an Engineering Material*. Revised edition. Washington DC, US Government Printing Office.

28. *Cordone, contracordone* and *hypozomata*

André Wegener Sleeswyk

1. *Cordone* and *contracordone*

Cordone were structural reinforcements applied to the hulls of Genoese galleys of *c.* AD 1600. A reason for drawing attention to them, apart from the inherent interest of the subject, is that it may plausibly be argued that they were developed from the *hypozomata* of ancient Greek warships such as the *trieres*. These early 17th century devices are briefly described by Joseph Furttenbach in his *Architectura Navalis* of 1629 (Furttenbach 1629, 53-4). His description is elucidated by a schematic illustration of the cross-section of a Genoese galley which is reproduced here as Fig. 28.1.

The *cordone*, sometimes called *centa* (Furttenbach 1629, 30), are wooden beams mounted outboard on each side of the hull along its entire length. They are of approximately semicircular cross-section, have a thickness of 5/12 *palmo* and a width of 2/3 *palmo* (1 *palmo* = 244 mm or 0.8 ft). The distance below the gunwale is a constant 1½ *palmi*. Similar timbers are mounted on the inside of the frames, at the positions marked *m* in the diagram. These beams, of rectangular cross-section, are called *contracordone*.

After presenting his description of both the *cordone* and the *contracordone*, Furttenbach (1629, 54) briefly explains the purpose of this construction in the following terms:

> 'both aforementioned *cordone* cause the ribs of the galley to be gripped together and to be fixed in such manner that none of them can bend, much less have sufficient play to alter its position.'

At first sight, it might seem that it was the bending of the *cordone* around the hull that caused the planking to be pressed against the frames, especially in the middle, having the same overall effect as a cable laid under tension around the hull would have. However, calculation shows that the wooden *cordone* beam is far too flexible for this method to have a significant effect. The 46 m (152 ft) long beam, itself weighing about 3000 N (300 kgf or 660 lbs), when bent around the hull exerted a force of no more than 70 N (7 kgf or 16 lbs), a negligible value.

But if bending the beam around the hull did not produce an appreciable effect, a viable alternative would have been to subject it to tension, just as a cable would have been. A reason for using a beam instead of a cable would be that a wooden beam, when drying out or being wetted, would shrink or expand far less than a laid cable would do. In addition, setting up a tensile force in the beam, *e.g.* by means of wedges, may have been simpler than doing the same in a cable.

A quantitative estimate of the force which could have been exercised athwartships by the beam as it was pulled longitudinally at both ends around the hull can be obtained without difficulty. The cross-sectional area of the *cordone* is approximately 130 cm, and if half of the allowable stress of 5.6 MPa in spruce is taken as the working stress (Beer and Johnston 1992, 702), the force that may be applied to its ends will be 36 kN (8,100 lbs). Assuming that the shape of the hull around which the *cordone* is laid is a section of a circle, the force exercised athwartships can be calculated from the principal dimensions of the hull as 19 kN (4,300 lbs), a few tons, a value which seems of the right order of magnitude.

It appears highly probable that the name *cordone* given to the bent wooden beam on the outside of the hull is historically significant, as the translation of this Italian word is 'thick rope.' The most straightforward explanation is that the appellation must be a relic of the tensioned cable which was presumably originally used instead of a bent wooden beam under tension. Of particular interest is the presence of the two *contracordone*. If they were no more than originally straight wooden beams which had been bent in the same manner as the *cordone*, they would merely have exerted a weak inward force on the frames in the middle of the ship, in the same direction as the planking was being pushed by the *cordone*. But if the *contracordone* were made to exert forces in the opposite direction, i.e. outwards, the frames and the planking would have been pushed together by opposing forces. Moreover, in that case bending of the frames could indeed have been avoided, as

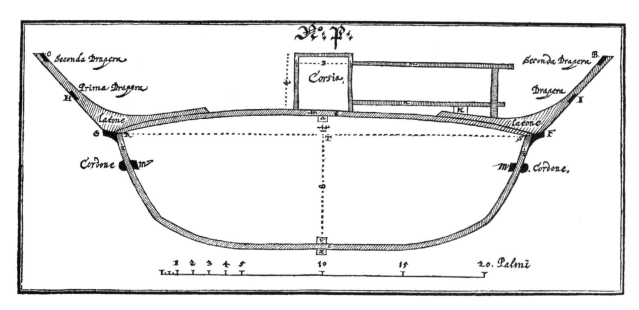

Figure 28.1. Furttenbach's schematic cross-sectional diagram of a Genoese galley of c. AD 1600, showing both the cordone *on the outside of the hull, and the location of the* contracordone *at m on the inside of the frames.*

Furttenbach claims, because if these forces acting on the frames were of equal magnitude, they would have cancelled each other.

It cannot have been difficult to cause the pair of *contracordone* to exert outward-directed forces. If it may be assumed that the *contracordone* were bent in parallel to the *cordone* – as is most probable – application of forces of opposite sign but of the same magnitude as those applied to the ends of the *cordone* would have resulted in a force athwartships having the same magnitude as the opposing force exerted by the *cordone*. The transverse forces on the ends of the pair of *contracordone* would have balanced each other if these ends were made to support each other in the plane of symmetry of the hull. Furttenbach does not offer any indication of how the forces in the *cordone* and *contracordone* were set up. Mechanically, it would seem best if these forces were made to balance each other directly, but this does not exclude the alternative, viz. that the forces in the two were set up separately.

2. Frapping the hull

Although it is clear from the foregoing that the *cordone* were part of a mechanical system for forcefully pressing together the shell and the frames of a Genoese galley in the middle of the hull, this does not tell us why this was done. The explanation must be sought in the dangerous mechanical loading conditions which may prevail in the middle of a ship, where the bending forces acting on the hull are at a maximum. The scale of that maximum depends mostly on the length of the hull and the state of the sea; it tends to be large in a long ship in a seaway. As a result of extreme conditions of this kind, the strakes may start to slide back and forth past each other in the seams as the

ship passes through the waves. Such repeated movement would result in the loss of the caulking in the seams in a ship of the post-classical period, and in an ancient Greek or Roman ship in a gradual increase of the play of the tenons in their mortises in the planking and in working loose the tenon-and-dowel joints. If these effects caused heavy leakage, this would have represented only an initial stage leading to an even worse next stage, in which the coherence of the hull was threatened by working loose of the treenails which joined the frames to the planking.

This danger, which would eventually lead to the hull breaking up, would be greatly enhanced if the planking and the frames ceased to be in contact. It was in particular to counteract the danger of disintegration of the hull of a ship in a gale that measures were taken to prevent the separation of the planking and the frames. 'Frapping,' i.e. winding four or five turns of cable under tension vertically around the middle of a weakened hull as a temporary reinforcement was the commonly applied remedy (Falconer 1815, 158). The principal effect was, of course, to press the planking against the frames. According to Casson (1971, 91), the technique:

> 'is known from at least the first century AD and lasted as long as the wooden sailing ship; the most celebrated example is when St. Paul's vessel was struck by a gale and the sailors "used helps to undergird the ship".'

Other less well-known but also less obscure references make perfectly clear how it was done. Apparently, the effect of the pre-stressed *cordone* and *contracordone* was similar to frapping the hull; they constituted a permanent means of pressing together the planking and the frames in the middle of the ship, in anticipation of conditions where this might be needed to ensure the structural integrity of the hull. In a long and slender galley that necessity would manifest itself much sooner, presumably, than in a shorter and more heavily built merchantman. Moreover, the presence of outriggers may have rendered effectual frapping of the hull in a gale difficult, if not altogether impossible. This would have been a good reason for equipping sea-going galleys with devices which did so permanently.

3. *Hypozomata*

If *cordone* were originally cables instead of wooden beams, as appears most likely, they would not have been vertical, as in the provisional frapping of a ship in a gale, but horizontal above the waterline, just as the *cordone* were. These cables must have been identical to the *hypozomata* mentioned in a number of ancient Greek inscriptions and other sources, which were reviewed by Morrison and Williams (1968, 294–8). They deduced from one such inscription (*IG* 2² 1631 671) that a *hypozoma* 'was long enough to pass round outside the hull of a 120 ft. *trieres* from end to end with something to spare'. They confirmed this finding by data on the oversized *tesserakonteres* of Ptolemy Philopator, from which it follows that the length of a *hypozoma* girdling a hull 280 cubits long was 600 cubits. Referring to this passage of Morrison and Williams, Casson (1971, 91) thought that their 'comprehensive review of the evidence ends a controversy which has raged for over a century.'

However, the fire of the controversy to which Casson referred was rekindled when *Olympias* was designed. Morrison and Coates (1986, 197 = Morrison, Coates and Rankov 2000, 196), ignoring the earlier review by Morrison and Williams, stated that

> 'The position and rigging of *hypozomata* have been a particular mystery in *triereis*, but it is virtually certain that their purpose was to reduce bending stresses which would otherwise damage the hull. ...To protect the hull structure against breaking its back by hogging, the *hypozomata* should be stretched between points forward and aft high in the hull section where they would act like a hogging truss.'

Accordingly, the lightly constructed hull of Olympias was equipped with an internal hogging truss. But, as the author argues elsewhere in this volume (pp. 109–20), there is good reason for believing that the hull of the original Greek trireme was much more heavily built than that of *Olympias*, which in all probability obviated the necessity of having recourse to a hogging truss.

If the *hypozoma* really was a precursor of the *cordone*, the question must be asked whether or not it was applied in conjunction with a *contracordone*. As far as we know, the Genoese galley was the last type of ship to carry a permanent external reinforcement such as a *cordone*; it does not seem probable that at that time the *contracordone* was a recent improvement. It seems more likely that the latter was already used in antiquity. We are thus led to assume, with some confidence, that ancient Greek galleys were equipped with both *hypozomata* and a pair of

contracordone. It does not seem warranted to extend this assumption to the much earlier Egyptian ships which are sometimes depicted as being girdled by *hypozomata*, such as the ships of Sahure of *c.* 2500 BC (Borchardt 1913). We do not know anything about their internal structure, but in general they were of a build different from the Greek vessels, as they commonly consisted of frameless thick shells built up of interconnected planks. Perhaps the Greeks discovered, when applying the Egyptian *hypozoma*, that *contracordone* were needed in their thin-shelled ships.

It may appear to be a problem that the planking of galleys, both ancient and modern, would have been more or less parallel to the gunwale. Consequently, the *hypozomata* or *cordone* could have pressed directly against one or two strakes only. However, in the Greek galleys in which the strakes were edge-joined by dowelled tenons, the force exerted by the *hypozomata* would have been transmitted to the adjacent strakes also. Obviously, the system would have been very effective in ships built in this manner.

At first sight, it would seem that the situation would have been quite different in Renaissance galleys, in which the strakes were not edge-joined. But one must remember that these ships were caulked, which, besides rendering the hull watertight, has the important secondary effect of generating large compressive forces in the plane of the shell of planks. As a result, the strakes are interconnected up to the friction threshold produced by these forces (Culler 1974, 93). Below that threshold, the planking may be considered as being effectively edge-joined. Presumably, the pressing upon the strakes by a *hypozoma* would have been quite effective in this case also, but obviously only up to the point where the seams lost their caulking.

4. Pre-stressing the *hypozomata* and the *contracordone*

How the necessary tension in the *hypozomata* and the large longitudinal compressive forces on the *contracordone* were generated are problems best considered together, because the resulting compressive forces must counterbalance one another. From the foregoing it may be concluded that the forces necessary to bend the *cordone* and *contracordone* beams were approximately equal and negligible in comparison to the longitudinal forces applied to these. As explained above, the desired balance of compressive forces on the shell and the frames results if the forces applied to the ends of the *contracordone* and to the ends of the *hypozomata* also work in opposite directions and are of equal magnitude.

Devices for maintaining the tension in *hypozomata* are mentioned in Greek literature and in inscriptions under the names of *entonoi* or *tonoi*, or even '*tonoi* of *hypozomata*' (Morrison and Williams 1968, 296). There is no doubt that these tightening devices were located inside the hull of the ship, not on the outside, which implies that at least part of each *hypozoma*, or perhaps an extension of it, must have been led into the hull. Neither the *contracordone*, nor the

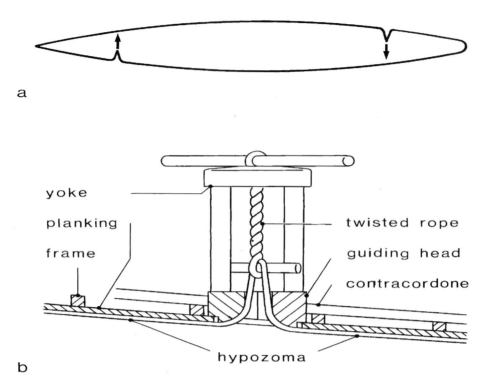

Figure 28.2. a: Schematic diagram of the run of the hypozoma *around the hull of a trireme, with bights for two* tonoi. *The scheme gives one of the many obvious possibilities; b: hypothetical reconstruction of the* tonos, *which fits both the 'well-twisted rope' mentioned in the literature and mechanical exigencies. The means of closing the hole through which the* hypozoma *bight enters is not shown.*

method of pre-stressing them, appears to be mentioned in the ancient sources; it is possible that such references are hidden in hitherto obscure passages in the known literature.

It is not entirely clear how *hypozomata* were fastened to the hull aft, where the gunwale and the stern both sweep up toward the *aphlaston*. In some ancient depictions of oared ships a powerful loop of plaited rope, called *koryphaia*, is shown passing vertically around the stern. It may have provided anchoring points on the outside of the hull for the *hypozomata* (Morrison and Williams 1968, 296; Casson 1971, 91). Presumably, these would have allowed the *hypozoma* to deviate from the line parallel to the gunwale and to pass around the stern at a convenient angle.

Setting up simultaneously a tensile force in the *hypozoma* and a compressive force of the same magnitude in the *contracordone* involves an elementary mechanical principle which may well have been used by ancient Greek shipwrights: it requires the *contracordone* to support the *hypozoma* cable where it is guided sideways at a 90° angle. Several ways of achieving this are possible, but if we take into account that the *hypozoma* loop was somewhat longer than twice the length of the galley, it seems most probable that a length of half-loop of the *hypozoma* cable was drawn through a hole in the hull, as shown schematically in Fig. 28.2a, and passed through a gap in the *contracordone* too. The ends of the latter should each have been fitted with a

head rounded off so as to guide the cable over the quarter turn. The tensioning device, *tonos* or *entonos* – the word does not indicate on what principle it operated – should have been made to act on the middle of the half-loop inside the ship; the force it exerts should have been equal to at least twice the tension force in the cable. The mechanical system would have been completed by a transverse pillar or beam supporting the *contracordone*, or the head fitted to it, for taking up the force component athwartships exerted by the cable guided around the head on the *contracordone*. That support system would have been duplicated for the other end of the *contracordone*. If the two supporting pillars or beams were interconnected by a third beam to which the end of the *tonos* was fastened in the middle, as shown in Fig. 28.2b, the three beams would have formed a yoke to which the large transverse forces exerted by the *tonos* were confined; only the forces aligned alongships would have been transmitted to the *hypozoma* and the *contracordone*.

The purpose of the *hypozomata*, and the run of the cable as explained above, appear to fit surprisingly well Apollonius Rhodius' description (*Argonautica* 1.367–9) of the fitting out of the *Argo* prior to launching:

'they girded it by a well-thought out plan, putting a tension on each side with a well-twisted rope from within, so that the planks should fit well with the dowels and withstand the opposing force of the sea'.

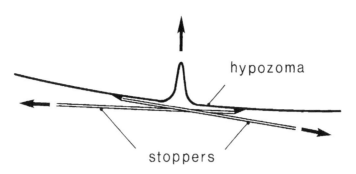

Figure 28.3. Diagram of the arrangement of the stoppers attached to the hypozoma *when these are mounted. While the* tonos *inside the hull exerts a force on the bight in the* hypozoma, *two crews of men pull on the stoppers. When the men ceased pulling, a large extra force upon the* hypozoma *would have been locked in by friction.*

As Morrison and Williams (1968, 297) comment, 'The "well-twisted rope from within" sounds just like the *tonos* or *entonos.*' One may add that the passage actually specifies its working principle, and that 'putting a tension on each side' may be readily be understood by referring to Fig 28.2b, where it is shown how the tension generated by the *tonos* is transmitted to both ends of the *hypozoma*. In the interpretation illustrated, the 'well-twisted rope' is taken as referring to an auxiliary rope led through an aperture in the middle of the wooden yoke.

That some sort of yokes were, in fact, carried by Greek warships is suggested by a curious passage in Thucydides (1.29.3) to which Morrison and Williams (1968, 295) refer: 'When in 435 the Corcyraeans were threatened by a Corinthian fleet they "yoked [*zeuxantes*] their old ships to make them seaworthy." This practice is probably that of fitting *hypozomata* to ships which are not on the active list.' To this may be added that, at least according to the reconstruction presented here, fitting the *hypozomata* implied fitting yokes as well.

The magnitude of the allowable tension in the *hypozomata* may be estimated as follows. Morrison and Williams established that these consisted of 'eight-finger' rope, *i.e.* rope with a circumference of 160 mm. The average fracture force of hempen rope of three *pouces* (81.2 mm) was determined by Duhamel du Monceau (1783, 385) as 4,500 livres, 21.8 kN (2,200 kgf or 4,900 lbs). The fracture force of the eight-finger *hypozoma* may then be estimated at 84.0 kN (8,600 kgf or 19,000 lbs). Assuming, as is customary, that the allowable force would be ⅑ of the breaking strength of the rope, one would obtain 9.3 kN (950 kgf or 2,100 lbs). Normally, two *hypozomata* were used, but under certain circumstances there were four. The total tensile forces to which they would have been subjected would have been 18.6 or 37.2 kN. The closeness of the agreement of latter value to the 36 kN for the allowable force in the *cordone* of a Genoese galley is surely fortuitous, but that these forces were of comparable magnitude does indicate that they served the same purpose, and it confirms the idea that *cordone* were derived from the *hypozomata* used in antiquity.

So far, we have neglected friction, but leading ropes at an angle of approximately 90° over fixed heads must have caused a substantial amount of frictional loss of the forces exerted by the tensioning devices on the ends of the *hypozoma* girding the hull. The maximum loss is a fraction of the original force; estimating the value of the friction coefficient at between 0.1 and 0.25, it would have been about one quarter to one half of the applied tension.

However, while the ship was on the slipway, a stratagem, which would have suggested itself readily to anyone routinely handling ropes under tension, could have been employed to increase the tension in the *hypozoma* on the outside of the hull. It consists of 'helping' the *tonos* while it was being tensioned, by temporarily applying extra tensile forces to the *hypozoma* near to the point where it was led into the hull. The extra tension, produced by two crews of men pulling in opposite directions tangential to the hull, would have been transmitted by stoppers applied temporarily to the *hypozoma* (Fig. 28.3). The *tonos* would then have taken up the extra elongation of the *hypozoma*, such that when the men ceased pulling, the extra tensile force would have been locked in by friction.

Provided that the extra tensile force was large enough, a reversal of the ratio between the force exerted by the *tonoi* and the force transmitted to the *hypozoma* on the outside of the hull could have been achieved. As a result, a substantial tensioning force would have been locked in and added to the force in the part of the *hypozoma* outside the hull. Consequently, the total force would have been much larger than that which could have been produced by the *tonos* alone.

A procedure of this kind for bringing additional tension to bear on the *hypozoma* would explain the otherwise cryptic text of an Athenian inscription (*IG* 1² 73, cited by Morrison and Williams 1968, 305) from the beginning of the Peloponnesian war. It prescribes that a minimum number of fifty men is needed to fit a *hypozoma* around the hull of a trireme. These men would have constituted two crews of twenty-five men, each of which pulled on one of the two stoppers temporarily fastened to the *hypozoma*, as explained above. A crew of 25 men would have exerted a force of about 3 kN (about 300 kgf or 660 lbs), each man being able, on the average, to pull with a force of about 120 N. The latter value is not more than that established by 18th-century French engineers, who determined it as between 24 and 27 *livres*, as reported by Belidor (1782, 43–45). The minimum value of the friction coefficient deduced from the values of the various forces discussed above is 0.16, which is in agreement with our earlier estimate.

5. Conclusions

The conclusions from the foregoing discussion may be summarised as follows:

1. The *cordone* on the early 17th century Genoese galleys described by Furttenbach in 1629 were timbers under mechanical tension. They were mounted parallel to the gunwale and pressed the planking and the frames together.
2. Fitting the *cordone* was a preventive measure to protect the ship if she was hit by a gale: it provided a permanent means of frapping the hull.
3. Bending of the frames by the force exerted by the *cordone* was prevented by a timber under compression, the *contracordone*, mounted on the inside of the frames. It exerted an outward force balancing the force exerted by the *cordone*,
4. The term *cordone* indicates that originally the tensioned element on the outside of the hull was a heavy rope rather than a wooden beam, which must have been identical to the *hypozoma* of the oared ships of antiquity. Calculation shows that the allowable tension forces on the *cordone* and on the *hypozomata* were of the same magnitude.
5. As in the Genoese galleys, the forces exerted on the frames by *hypozomata* in ancient Greek ships were probably balanced by means of *contracordone*.
6. It is shown that a hypothetical but simple mechanical method of simultaneously pre-stressing the *hypozomata* and the *contracordone* in ancient oared ships accords with some otherwise obscure passages in the known descriptions of *hypozomata* and their manner of fitting.

7. A number if men pulling on the *hypozomata* outside the hull while the *tonoi* were tensioned inside would have produced a substantial amount of additional tension which was permanently locked into the *hypozomata* by friction.

Acknowledgment

The author is much indebted to Prof. F. J. A. M. Meijer for discussing the problems and ambiguities in the Greek texts upon which part of this work is based.

Bibliography

Beer, F. P. and Johnston, E. R. (1992) *Mechanics of Materials.* London, McGraw-Hill.

Belidor, B. F. de (1782) *Architecture Hydraulique.* Paris, Charles-Antoine Jombert.

Borchardt, L. (1913) *Das Grabdenkmal des Konigs Sahu-re.* Bd. II. Leipzig, J. C. Hinrichs.

Casson, L. (1971) *Ships and Seamanship in the Ancient World.* Princeton, Princeton University Press.

Culler, R. D. (1974) *Skiffs and Schooners.* Camden ME, International Marine.

Duhamel du Monceau, H. L. (1783) *Encyclopédie Méthodique Marine.* Paris., Panckoucke. Facs. ed. (1987) Nice, Editions Oméga.

Falconer, W. A. (1815) *A New Universal Dictionary of the Marine*, ed. Burney, W. London, J. Murray. Facs. ed. (1974), London, Macdonald and Jane's.

Furttenbach, J. (1629) *Architectura Navalis. Das ist: Von dem Schiff-Gebäw Auff dem Meer und Seekusten zugebrauchen.* Ulm. Facs. ed. (*c.* 1980) Lindau, Antiqua-Verlag.

Morrison, J. S. and Williams, R. T. (1968) *Greek Oared Ships 900–322 B.C.* Cambridge, Cambridge University Press.

Morrison, J. S. and Coates, J. F. (1986) *The Athenian Trireme. The History and Reconstruction of an Ancient Greek Warship.* Cambridge, Cambridge University Press.

Morrison, J. S. and Coates, J. F., and Rankov, N. B. (2000) *The Athenian Trireme. The History and Reconstruction of an Ancient Greek Warship.* 2nd ed., Cambridge, Cambridge University Press.

Part 6

Recent Research

29. Collision Damage in Triremes

Robin Oldfield

Introduction

This study seeks to begin shedding some technical light on the area of trireme combat, by better understanding the engineering aspects of a deliberate collision. This broad objective has been separated into three specific aims;

i)   Analyse the damage caused at different speeds and headings;
ii) Analyse the amount of damage required to disable a trireme;
iii) Consider how analysis of the previous two aims might influence trireme tactics.

Trireme structure

Triremes were designed to be as light as possible, thus the hull structure was a lightly stiffened shell which was "little thicker in relation to its curvature than a plastic bucket" (Morrison *et al.* 2000, 210). This study has considered the *Olympias* a representative trireme. The wooden shell is made up from planks butted up flush against each other (Fig. 29.1) and fastened together with a series of wooden tenons. Longitudinal stiffness is provided by the keel, top wale, three inboard stringers, and a length of taut rope, the *hypozomata*, between the bow and stern. Transversely there are two frames, the top timber and the futtock, which hold the shape of the shell. The shell is also supported by a beam, spanning the width of the ship between top timbers, at the level of the middle wale. In should be noted that the lower thalamian beam provides no transverse support to the shell. The beam sits on top of the thalamian stringer, instead of being built into either of the frames at the level of the lower wale.

The structural elements at the waterline are the top timber, futtock, lower wale, planks and the joining tenons (Fig. 29.2). The tenons are regularly spaced along the shell planking, allowing any load on a single plank to be spread to adjacent planks. For the trireme shell to fail, these tenons would have to shear before planks would bend and fail.

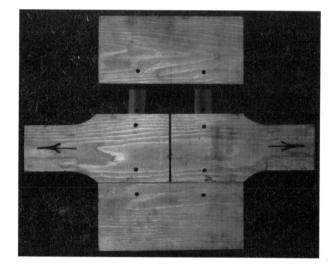

Figure 29.1. Mortice-and-tenon planking (Photo: John Coates)

Materials

Analysis of the timbers recovered with the Athlit Ram (Casson *and Steffy* 1991, 17) suggests that the wales and planking, the majority of the hull, were a red pine. The tenons, which held the planks and wales together, were oak "possibly of the live oak group". Other historical evidence (Morrison *et al.* 2000, 179–181) suggests that fir was extensively used for much of the hull. In the case of the *Olympias* reconstruction, the selected materials were Douglas Fir for planks and Greenheart for the tenons, principally for their decay resistance.

Unlike modern ship materials (*i.e.* steel), wood is not homogeneous and has different material properties in different directions: an orthotropic material. This is due to the cellular structure of wood, which has a grain (fibres) running through it in a single direction. The orientation of the wood to loads is therefore particularly important, with wood exhibiting its greatest strength longitudinally, along

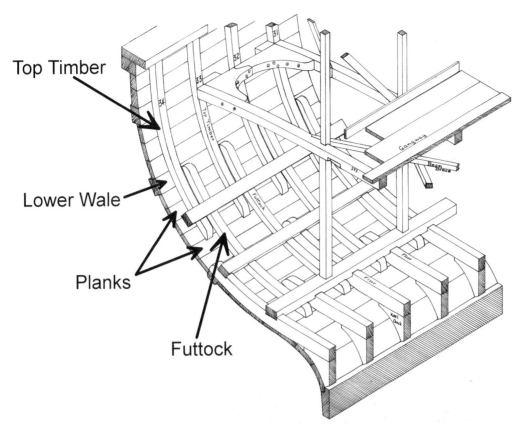

Figure 29.2. Isometric view of Olympias' *structure (Drawing: John Coates).*

the grain/fibres. In the radial and transverse directions, the timber can fail at loads several times smaller than when longitudinally loaded along the grain.

The moisture content of the wood also affects the mechanical properties. As the wood dries out, the cells contract causing shrinkage. Typically, mechanical properties data is given for green wood (freshly cut, so very moist) and wood which has been dried to a moisture content of 12%.

Tactics

Historians believe that triremes were designed to be as light and as fast as possible with a view to outmanoeuvring their opponents. A skilled crew in a fast and agile trireme would allow the commander to quickly "strike the [opposing] vessel where it was most vulnerable, preferably in the sides or stern" (Casson and Steffy 1991, 78). This speed and manoeuvrability was also the trireme's principal means of defence, facilitating evasive manoeuvring to dodge incoming opponents.

The Athlit Ram, on which *Olympias'* replica ram was based, had "a striking head that concentrated enormous forces into a very small contact area, but which was prevented by a sufficiently widespread grid from penetrating too far into the hull" (Casson and Steffy 1991, 38). The commander wanted to strike with only sufficient force to have "opened seams or broken planks over meters of

length" (*ibid.*). A pointed ram, or a high energy collision, which fully penetrated the opponent's hull could be just as damaging to the ramming vessel. The ships might remain ensnared, leaving the attacker impotent and susceptible to boarding. In the worst case the ensnared ram could be ripped off, damaging the attacker and rendering them 'toothless'. Ultimately the objective of the attack was to inflict sufficient damage to disable the opposing triremes, by causing them to take on so much water that they were too heavy to row and difficult to steer. Accounts suggest that at the end of an engagement damaged triremes "continued to float and were towed away" (Morrison *et al.* 2000, 165) as opposed to completely sinking.

Collision modelling methods

There is a range of methods available to model structural damage from ship collisions. These are generally energy-based and vary in complexity from basic one-dimensional models to three-dimensional time-domain simulations (Brown 2001).

Minorsky method

The simplest of the current methods is the 1D Minorsky method, which is based on conservation of momentum. This method assumes the following:

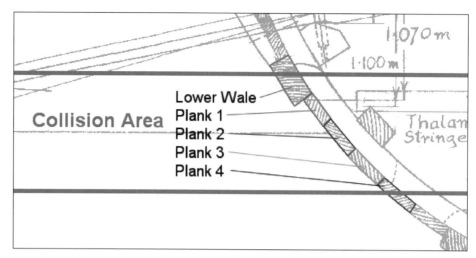

Figure 29.3. Collision area (Drawing: John Coates/Robin Oldfield).

i) The collision is completely inelastic;
ii) The collision energy has little effect in the target ship's longitudinal direction;
iii) Rotations of the two ships are negligible.

Damage

Developed by the Massachusetts Institute of Technology, the DAMAGE program is also based on conservation of linear momentum, as well as angular momentum and energy. The program incrementally calculates the energy absorbed in hull deformation until all of the collision energy is used. The level of detail within this program allows it to take into consideration the materials and the structural features of the rammed ship's side structure.

Three degrees of freedom models

Two 'three degrees of freedom' collision models are the Hutchison model and the expressions derived by Pedersen and Zhang. The Hutchison model expanded on the Minorsky method to consider surge, sway, yaw and hull membrane resistance. The assumptions which apply to this model are:

i) The distribution of mass does not change after the initial collision;
ii) Changes in headings and rotations are small and as such are neglected for parts of the model;
iii) The ships coalesce after impact.

Pedersen and Zhang examined the impulses and motions in the locality of the impact point to obtain the collision energy, which is calculated uncoupled from internal mechanics. Their assumptions were:

i) Rotations are small during the collision;
ii) The ratio of absorbed plastic deformation energy is constant throughout the collision for the longitudinal and transverse directions.

Method of analysis

For this study it was decided to split the analysis into two parts. First, to calculate the minimum energy required to cause failure of a representative section of the trireme hull. Secondly, to calculate the kinetic collision energy for given ship speeds and headings. If the calculated collision energy is greater than, or equal to, the energy calculated to cause structural failure then it would be assumed to be a successful attack.

Hull failure

The principal problem to be solved in this study was the means of calculating the failure of the trireme hull. The structure of the hull shell meant that, through the connecting tenons, planks adjacent to the contact point provide support in addition to the transverse framing. It was observed that a ram would not strike the whole surface of the hull in a single instance. Assuming a ram similar to but slightly smaller than the Athlit Ram (which came from a *tetreres*/quadrireme or *penteres*/quinquereme) and a flat calm, the lower wale would be contacted first. If sufficiently deflected, or in the case of failure, the ram would then strike the first plank of the four within its path; and so on until all kinetic energy has been absorbed. This is illustrated in Fig. 29.3.

To simplify the problem it was desirable to consider each plank individually. As previously noted, the tenons connecting the plank to those adjacent would first need to shear. The stages of analysis are summarised below:

i) Calculate the force required to shear all tenons along damage length;
ii) Use this force to calculate the elastic deflection of the plank;
iii) Check force is sufficient to produce the same deflection of the frames; if frame deflection is insufficient, calculate the force that achieves the required frame deflection;
iv) Check the deflection and failure mode of the plank for

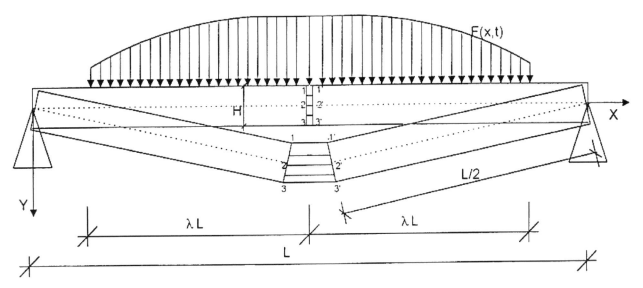

Figure 29.4. Elasto-plastic beam model.

the greatest force determined at step 3, increasing the force if the plank has not failed or deflects a distance less than its thickness.

Assumptions

The assumptions applied to these calculations are as follows:

PLANKS ARE FIXED BEAMS SPANNING 0.668 METRES

The length of 0.668 m is the equivalent of two frame spacings (Fig. 29.4), and was selected because a single frame spacing is less than the width of the Athlit Ram scaled down to fit a trireme. The ends of the beams are considered fixed because it is assumed unlikely that there would be longitudinal displacement of the frames at the ends of the beams. These frames' connections with intact planks away from the contact area and support from longitudinal stringers should ensure that they retain their longitudinal positions.

CENTRALLY LOCATED UNIFORMLY DISTRIBUTED LOAD

The loading is uniformly distributed along the width of the ram, at the central point of the planks and wales. This is primarily because the elasto-plastic calculations are set up for this.

EFFECTIVE WIDTH OF PLANKING IS 60% OF FRAME SPACING

Referred to as the effective width of plating when dealing with modern steel ships' frames, the same principles apply to wooden planking and frames (assuming the joining between the two is satisfactory). When a frame is loaded it deflects, but part of the planking is deflected with it. This planking acts as if it is a flange on the frame, increasing the inertia of the frame and therefore the stiffness. Just how much of the planking behaves as a flange is unknown. Application of Faulkner's method (Chalmers 1993) proves unfeasible, so a nominal percentage has been assumed.

CAULKING BETWEEN PLANKS IS NEGLECTED

It has been assumed that any caulking material would provide negligible resistance to any impact.

COLLISION ENERGY IS WORK DONE.

The energy required to cause failing of the shell would be the sum of the ramming force multiplied by the displacement caused on each component part.

MIDSHIP SECTION'S STRUCTURE IS REPRESENTATIVE OF THE WHOLE HULL.

The section shown in Fig. 29.2 is representative of the majority of the *Olympias*. It is only at the very extremities of the ship that there appear to be notable differences.

TIMBER IS NOT GREEN.

The moisture content of wood affects the mechanical properties. The use of 12% moisture content data is in line with the design work of the *Olympias*.

TIMBER IS FREE OF SIGNIFICANT DEFECTS.

Defects in the wood such as knots, decay and grain irregularity are ignored. The mechanical data used has come from test results with defect-free samples. It is also assumed that timbers used for trireme construction would have been checked for major flaws.

Material properties

Data on the material properties of the wood used were sourced from Forest Product Laboratory of the United States Department of Agriculture's Forest Service. This single source provided the greatest range of data for all the material types of interest. It should, however, be noted that quoted mechanical properties of wood can vary significantly from source to source. The material properties used for the analysis are presented in Table 29.1. The origin of the tested timber is indicated. Varieties grown outside

Table 29.1. Material properties.

	Planks, Frames and Wales		Tenons
	Douglas Fir, Coastal *	Red Pine *	Greenheart †
E – Longitudinal (MPa)	13,400	11,200	22,400
σ_y (MPa)	5.5	4.1	-
τ_y (MPa)	-	-	5.9

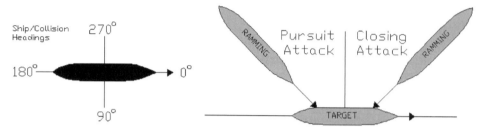

Figure 29.5. Collision headings.

the Mediterranean may not be wholly representative of the indigenous trees.

Elasto-plastic beam calculations

The elasto-plastic properties of wood means that it will not fail when the elastic limit is reached. One suitable means of calculating the elasto-plastic behaviour for the planks and wales was put forward by Yankelevsky and Karinski (2000). Their model has a symmetrically loaded beam split in half, with an infinitely small gap between the two half lengths. It is within this small gap that the plastic deformation occurs. With symmetrical loading conditions, only half the beam has to be analysed.

Frame calculations

The frames are considered as having fixed ends, where they are built into other structural elements (Fig. 29.2); for the top timber this is the end at the top wale, and for the futtock the end below the inner stringer. It is noted that the free ends of these frames are very close to the ramming contact area, suggesting that they will offer little restraint against collisions.

Collision modelling

The collision modelling utilises the Minorsky method. This simplistic model is easier to apply as other methods require terms, such as added mass, which are unknown for the *Olympias*.

Assumptions

The following assumptions have been made;

COLLISIONS OCCUR IN FLAT CALMS

There are no ship motions other than the forward velocities of the ships. The performance of triremes is dependant on weather and sea state (Morrison *et al.* 2000, 278), as crews experience difficulty drawing clean strokes with increased ship motions. As a starting point, this study models the optimum conditions.

IF THE X-AXIS RELATIVE SPEED <0 THEN THERE IS NO COLLISION

It has been assumed that the target trireme outmanoeuvres the ramming trireme when the latter has insufficient speed in the x-axis to catch its target.

THE ABSORPTION OF KINETIC ENERGY IS NON-IDEAL

It is unknown just how much collision energy would be lost as heat and noise. It is assumed that the collision is 90% efficient.

THE ENERGY OF A 90° COLLISION IS REPRESENTATIVE OF ENERGY REQUIRED AT OTHER ANGLES

The beam calculations used to determine the energy required to cause hull failure only consider a right-angle collision. It has been assumed that this failure value is broadly acceptable to apply to collisions at other angles.

Collision calculations

The modelled collision uses a co-ordinate system relative to the forward heading of the target ship (Fig. 29.5). The longitudinal positions of the top timbers were recorded, and the tangent of the hull at the waterline was measured at each of these locations. The model calculates kinetic energy absorbed at each of the top timber locations, having considered the angle of the hull and the angle of the ramming attack, and the ramming speed.

The deceleration experienced by the ramming ship has also been simply calculated, with a view to appreciating some of the crew's human factors. The deceleration calculation assumes that only the component of the collision speed that is at right-angles to the hull is relevant; at acute angles the ramming ship would lose little forward speed as it rebounds off the target's hull.

Table 29.2. Douglas Fir hull analysis results.

	For Calculated Deflection				
	Elastic Deflection (mm) Under 4,165N	Top Timber Force (N)	Futtock Force (N)	Condition Under 4,165N	Condition Under 4,942N
Lower Wale	0.050	2.19	0.66	Plastic	Collapse
Plank 1	0.156	5.81	3.18	Collapse	Collapse
Plank 2	0.145	4.34	3.53	Collapse	Collapse
Plank 3	0.120	2.81	3.74	Collapse	Collapse
Plank 4	0.104	2.11	4.34	Collapse	Collapse
Work Done (J)	-	-	-	802	829

Table 29.3. Red Pine hull analysis results.

	For Calculated Deflection			
	Elastic Deflection (mm) Under 4,165N	Top Timber Force (N)	Futtock Force (N)	Condition Under 4,165N
Lower Wale	0.192	1.75	0.53	Collapse
Plank 1	0.597	4.64	2.54	Collapse
Plank 2	0.555	3.46	2.82	Collapse
Plank 3	0.457	2.24	2.98	Collapse
Plank 4	0.398	1.68	3.47	Collapse
Work Done (J)	-	-	-	727

Findings

Hull failure

Tenons

During the design of the *Olympias* the tenons had been sized, and the material selected, to withstand "a load per tenon of about 2 kN" (Morrison *et al.* 2000, 203). Comparative calculations with Greenheart showed that the shear force through the width of a tenon was 1.8 kN; a good match. This, however, is only appropriate for loads applied longitudinally through the ship. The force calculated to shear a tenon through its thickness is much lower, at only 595 N. Across the damage length of 0.668 m there are approximately seven tenons, roughly spaced 0.092 m apart. Therefore, the ramming force required to shear all seven tenons would be 4,165 N.

Frames, planks and wales

Two materials, Douglas Fir and Red Pine, were examined in the analysis of the frames, planks and lower wale. For both materials the low shear force produced very slight mid-span elastic deflections of the planks and wales (Table 29.2 and Table 29.3). It is unsurprising that the forces to similarly deflect the frames were also very low; it should be remembered that both the top timber and the futtock frames end, unsupported, in the contact region, a clear weakness.

For the Fir and Pine, the force required to shear the tenons was well in excess of the force required to deflect the frames. For the Douglas Fir, the 4,165 N force is insufficient to cause the lower wale to fail, or deflect it by its thickness. It was therefore necessary to increase to applied force to a level where the lower wale deflected at least 74 mm or completely failed. As greater force was

applied, the Douglas Fir did not deflect a sufficient distance before failing at 4,942 N. All elements of the Red Pine structure failed at the tenon shear force.

The increased load bearing of the lower wale increases the force required to cause failure for Douglas Fir. The lower wale primarily appears to serve, along with the other wales, as reinforcement for the oar ports. The locations of the wales in the *Olympias* had been influenced by the Lenormant Relief, but the lower wale has been placed nearer the waterline on the reconstruction (Morrison *et al.* 2000, 199). Perhaps the trireme represented in the Lenormant Relief would have been more vulnerable to attack than the *Olympias*.

Collision modelling

A range of collision scenarios was analysed for both the Douglas Fir and Red Pine triremes. One historical source (Xenophon *Anabasis* 6.4.2) suggests that the average speed of a trireme was around 7.37 knots (Gardiner *et al.* 1995, 57; cf. Shaw above, pp. 63–7), and it can be assumed that the typical combat speed would be higher than the average speed. The greatest sprint speed attained momentarily during the *Olympias'* sea trials was 8.9 knots (Morrison *et al.* 2000, 264). In discussion with the Trireme Trust's Boris Rankov, it was suggested that a maximum speed for a modified (*i.e.* Mark IIb; see Part 2 of this volume, pp. 76–91) trireme of similar construction to *Olympias* might have been nearer 9.75 knots with a full complement of fit and competent oarsmen. Based on this information the following collision cases detailed in Table 29.4 were examined.

Analysis of a successful collision at right-angles to a stationary hull indicated that the minimum ramming speed

Table 29.4. Collision cases.

	Ramming Speed (knots)	Target Speed (knots)	Comment
A	8.25	8.00	Minor advantage to attacker
B	8.50	8.00	Advantage to attacker
C	9.00	8.00	Large advantage to attacker
D	8.00	8.25	An opportunity attack
E	9.75	9.00	A very high speed attack and evasion

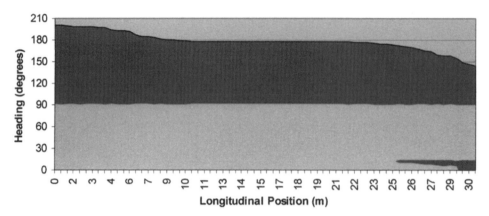

Figure 29.6. Case A: collision headings for Douglas Fir.

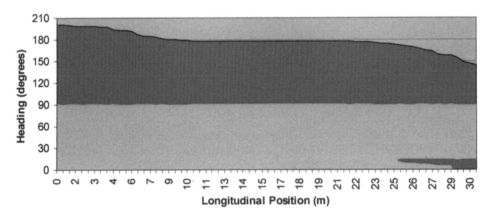

Figure 29.7. Case A: collision headings for Red Pine.

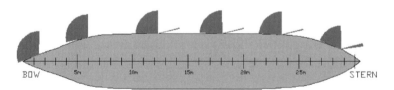

Figure 29.8. Case A: headings diagram for Douglas Fir.

to cause failure was 0.37 knots for Douglas Fir and 0.32 knots for Red Pine. Despite the ~15% extra energy required to cause failure in Douglas Fir trireme, there were negligible differences between any of the cases. All closing headings produced identical results, and every heading in every case succeeded. Without a doubt a closing attack is certain to have a greater chance of success, because the speed of the target only increases the magnitude of the collision speed.

The pursuit results were of far greater interest. Case A, with the small 0.25 knot speed advantage, demonstrated that a pursuing attacker had insufficient speed to realistically inflict damage on the target. Successful headings were found (Fig. 29.6, Fig. 29.7 and Fig. 29.8) along the parallel sides of the target, but these were 1° arcs. It would be remarkable for any helmsman to be so accurate. At the aft end, the angle of the hull reduces the deflection angle

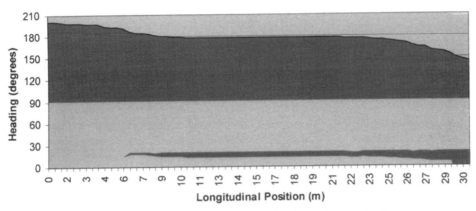

Figure 29.9. Case B: collision headings for Douglas Fir.

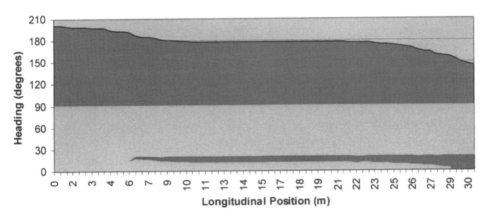

Figure 29.10. Case B: collision headings for Red Pine.

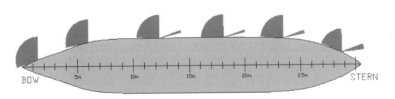

Figure 29.11. Case B: headings diagram for Douglas Fir.

between the ramming heading and the hull, providing a cleaner strike which can transfer more energy into the target's hull. Despite this advantage, the increased arcs of success were concentrated in such a small area that skilful targeting would still be required. The assumptions behind the structural model also break down at the extremes of the target; the keel would offer additional strength.

As the relative speeds increased in Case B (Fig. 29.9, Fig. 29.10 and Fig. 29.11) and Case C (Fig. 29.12 and Fig. 29.13), the pursuit arcs opened up. This was particularly evident at the aft end. Along the parallel sides, the arcs of success began to become increasingly viable. With a speed difference of 1.00 knot these pursuit arcs increased to ~15°, from ~7° at 0.50 knots. It thus appears that small speed improvements can greatly improve the attacker's options.

Case D was envisioned to simulate an attack of opportunity by a slower trireme against a faster opponent, which has unwittingly become a target. As expected, the slower speed of the ramming trireme prevents it from conducting a pursuit attack. The ramming trireme's only option is to close head-on with its target, resulting in arcs of success identical to those seen in all other cases.

Deceleration

The simple deceleration analysis produced some significant decelerations. It was observed again that there was negligible difference between the two hull materials. Unlike the collision headings calculations, it is the speed of the triremes, not simply the difference in speed, which determines the magnitude of deceleration. Case A

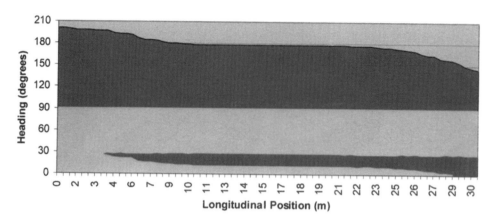

Figure 29.12. Case C: collision headings for Douglas Fir.

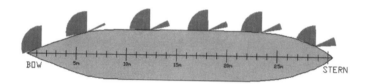

Figure 29.13. Case C: headings diagram for Douglas Fir.

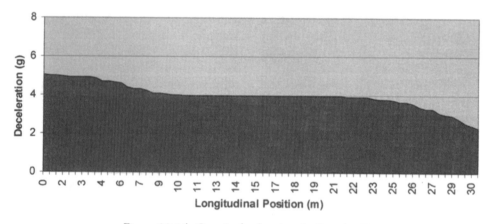

Figure 29.14. Case A: deceleration for Douglas Fir.

(Fig. 29.14) involves a ramming trireme at 8.25 knots and a speed difference of 0.25 knots. With Case C (Fig. 29.15), the attacker is now at 9.00 knots and there is some increase in the maximum calculated deceleration. The deceleration limits for Case E (Fig. 29.16) increase further, but the speed difference is only 0.75 knots; the increased deceleration levels result from the greater speeds of both vessels.

Discussion

Hull Structure

The energy required to cause failure of the hull is so low that it was initially quite surprising. Historical sources, however, say that triremes were built to be light, fast and manoeuvrable; there is no suggestion that they were designed to resist attacks and continue the fight. The results of the study correlate strongly with this. The energy required to cause failure has been found to be low, but would be even less were it not for the lower wale.

The increased thickness of the lower wale helps the hull to resist the ramming force, but its placement in the *Olympias* reconstruction may be a fortunate circumstance. Literature makes no mention of the lower wale functioning as a protective belt of wood around the trireme. Replacing the lower wale with a standard plank reduces the energy to cause failure by 31 J to 798 J. This small decrease would not greatly change the heading range for successful collisions. The wale would thus not offer any significant additional protection.

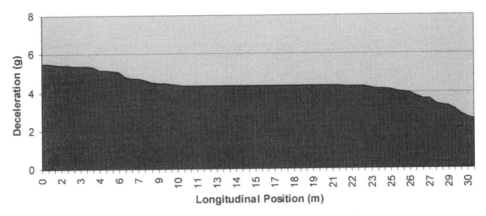

Figure 29.15. Case C: deceleration for Douglas Fir.

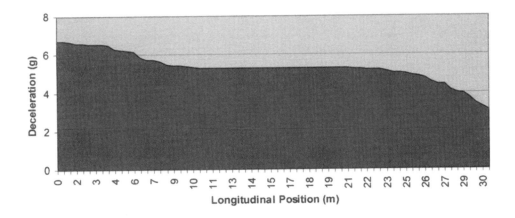

Figure 29.16. Case E: deceleration for Douglas Fir.

It had been assumed that "starting the seams" involved deflecting timbers further than their thickness, but before they completely failed. The *Olympias'* lower wale was the first timber struck in modelled collisions. The lower wale would have to be overcome before other timbers were struck, but the required force was found to subsequently fail the thinner inboard planks. A structure with no lower wale still failed before a plank deflected further than its thickness, due to the tenon shear force.

Materials

The results with the more ductile Red Pine were little different from Douglas Fir, despite the Pine planks failing at the lower tenon shear force. Both materials require so little energy to cause structural failure that the difference in collision speeds, which determines the kinetic energy in the collision, is negligible. Once again the historical evidence (Morrison 2000, 180) appears to support this finding, as the Greeks only compared the two on the basis of weight and decay resistance.

Collision Headings

The results support the logical assumption that the greater the speed advantage of the ramming vessel, the more freedom for selecting a suitable collision heading. On the other hand, increased magnitudes of speed are undesirable as they potentially result in greater deceleration being experienced by the ramming trireme crew, depending on the relative collision angle. Decelerations have been simplistically calculated at magnitudes many times greater than gravity.

Despite the maximal collision arcs for closing attacks such approaches would be highly undesirable. The results show that these attacks have higher collision speeds and therefore there is greater kinetic energy in the collision. It should be remembered that the energy calculated in this analysis has been the minimum to cause damage; increased energy would result in the ramming trireme continuing into the target until all the kinetic energy had been absorbed. Increased kinetic energy would thus be a double-edged sword, easily damaging the target but resulting in the ramming trireme striking deeper into the opponent's hull, an undesirable situation for a hit and run attacker. Furthermore, the deceleration would be greater for closing attacks, causing discomfort and possible injury to the crew of the ramming trireme.

More preferable are pursuit attacks. Whilst the range of possible collision angles is often very limited, this is a function of the difference in ship speeds. The greater the speed advantage of the ramming ship over the target, the greater the range of collision angles. Targeting the fuller face of the stern improves the range of viable pursuit headings. Inspection of the results suggests that it would probably be unrealistic to expect a trireme commander to successfully attack with a speed advantage less than 0.50 knots (*i.e.* less than Case B). In such an instance, the arcs of success are typically less than 15°. To strike the target within such an arc, particularly in a fluid combat environment, would be tremendously challenging.

Further benefits of an astern attack are the smaller decelerations and the reduced level of penetration, as the relative speed difference is small. Even if there was a penetration, the forward speed of the target trireme would help the ramming trireme extract itself as it backed water (reversed). An attack on the stern also has further benefits in that the ramming vessel is well clear of the target's ram, and can probably make a good escape well before the target can manoeuvre around (if it is still capable of moving).

Conclusions

The key findings produced by the analysis can be summarised as:

i)   The trireme structure is not designed to withstand ramming attacks;
ii) The lower wale can increase the force required to cause failure, but does not offer any significant protection;
iii) The greater the attacker's advantage in speed, the larger the arcs of successful collision headings;
iv) The greater the speeds of the triremes, the greater the deceleration;
v)   There are negligible differences in collision headings between a trireme constructed of Douglas Fir and one of Red Pine;
vi) Pursuit attacks require a speed advantage of at least 0.50 knots.

Many of these findings are supported by logic and historical evidence: triremes are light with minimal structure and therefore vulnerable to collisions. Greater collision speeds result in greater kinetic energy, and a faster collision over a fixed distance experiences higher deceleration. The tactical considerations drawn from the findings are similar to those implied by the historians (at least for the Classical period), principally that attacks on the stern and sides were preferred to head-on collisions. Attacks from astern require a speed advantage of at least 0.50 knots, to provide a helmsman with a sufficient arc of success.

It is encouraging that this analysis has provided seemingly satisfactory results, however it is recognised that more information and understanding can be obtained through more thorough analysis in further work.

Bibliography

Brown, A. J. (2001) *SCC-1400 Draft Report: Modelling Structural Damage in Ship Collisions.* US Department of Commerce.

Casson, L. and Steffy, J. R. (1991) *The Athlit Ram.* College Station, Texas A&M University Press.

Chalmers, D. W. (1993) *Design of Ships' Structures.* London, HMSO.

Gardiner, R. *et al* (1995) *The Age of the Galley: Mediterranean Oared Vessels since Pre-Classical Times.* London, Conway Marine.

Morrison, J. S., Coates, J. F. and Rankov, N. B. (2000) *The Athenian Trireme: The History and Reconstruction of an Ancient Greek Warship.* 2nd ed. Cambridge, Cambridge University Press.

Yankelevsky, D. Z. and Karinski, Y. S. (2000) Dynamic elasto-plastic response of symmetrically loaded beams. *Computers and Structures* 76, 445–59.

30. The Dimensions of the Ancient Trireme: a reconsideration of the evidence

Boris Rankov

In establishing the dimensions of the *Olympias* trireme reconstruction, the architect of the ship, John Coates, began with the oarsystem and the accommodation of the 170 rowers (Coates and McGrail 1984, 51–70; Morrison, Coates and Rankov 2000, 131–50). The naval inventories indicated that a fourth century Athenian trireme would have had 170 oars, of which 62 were thranites, 54 zygian and 54 thalamian (*IG* 2² 1615–18), while a passage of the Roman architect Vitruvius implied that the distance between each thole-pin (*interscalmium*) and therefore the 'room' for each oarsman was two cubits long (Vitruvius *De Architectura* 1.2.4, cf. Morrison, Coates and Rankov 2000, 133–5). Based on an Attic cubit of 0.444 m and therefore an *interscalmium* of double that distance, the oarsmen on each side of the ship would therefore take up a length of 31 × 0.888 = 27.53 m in the central portion of the ship. Moreover, as an hypothetical reconstruction of an Athenian vessel of the 4th century BC, the ship had to fit within the dimensions of the best-known shipsheds of that period, excavated by Iakob Dragatsis and Wilhelm Dörpfeld in the eastern part of Zea harbour in the Piraeus in 1885 (Dragatsis 1886). Dörpfeld's plan and sections (Figs 30.1 and 30.2) were interpreted to indicate that the sheds each had a maximum dry length of around 37 m and a maximum clear width of 5.94 m (Morrison and Williams 1968, 181–6 (by D. J. Blackman); Morrison, Coates and Rankov 2000, 132–3). Taking this, other evidence and naval architectural requirements into consideration, Coates' design resulted in a ship which had an overall breadth of 5.45 m and overall length of 36.8 m (see Frontispiece) (Morrison and Coates 1989, 17–25, esp. 20). After the ship was launched in 1987, new evidence was published for an alternative cubit of 0.49 m in use in Attica at the same period, based on a metrological relief discovered on the island of Salamis in 1985 and now in the Piraeus Archaeological Museum (Dekoulakou-Sideris 1990), and of a corresponding foot-unit of 0.327 m apparently employed in the newly-discovered naval arsenal of Philon in the Piraeus (Steinhauer 1989). Consequently it was proposed that the design should be modified in a

notional *Olympias* Mark II to incorporate the longer cubit. This would result in an *interscalmium* of 0.98 m and an overall increase in breadth to 5.62 m and in length to 39.6 m (Morrison 1993; Coates 1993; Morrison, Coates and Rankov 2000, 267–73).

Since the publication of this last proposal, new excavation and survey of the Zea harbour sheds from 2001 onwards by the Greek-Danish Zea Harbour Project has revealed that the lower end of the sheds has been submerged by a rise in relative sea level since antiquity, and that their original dry length was much longer than had been thought. The sheds have now been traced as far out as 58.51 m from the interior of the back wall of the complex (Lovén 2011, 100 and pl. 16), and it has become clear that there were at least three phases on the site, apparently consisting of open slipways in Phase 1, a normal-length group of sheds in Phase 2, and a group of sheds built on the foundations of the latter but extending *c.* 13 m backwards up the shore; it is Phase 3 which is the clearest on Dörpfeld's plan and sections, but features of Phase 2 are also visible on these and in the sea (Lovén *et al.* 2007, 63–6, esp. 65 and figs 4 and 5; for the interpretation of these finds, see Blackman and Rankov *et al.* forthcoming). The present paper is based on a close reconsideration of the plan and sections, on what they can tell us about the architectural layout of the sheds, and about what this implies about the ships which they housed.

The Phase 3 sheds were divided by alternating colonnades in which the columns, according to the measurements shown by Dörpfeld (Figs 30.1 and 30.2), were set 3.38–3.39 m and 2.16 m apart respectively, measured interaxially. It was deduced from this by Dragatsis and Dörpfeld that a single gable roof covered each pair of sheds, with the widely-spaced colonnade supporting the ridge beam and the narrowly-spaced colonnades supporting the heavy guttering on either side. My starting point is the observation that there was a precise ratio between the two interaxial distances of 11:7. This implies the use of a modular layout for the sheds, based on a module of 30.8 cm (11 × 0.308 m = 3.388 m and 7 × 0.308 m =

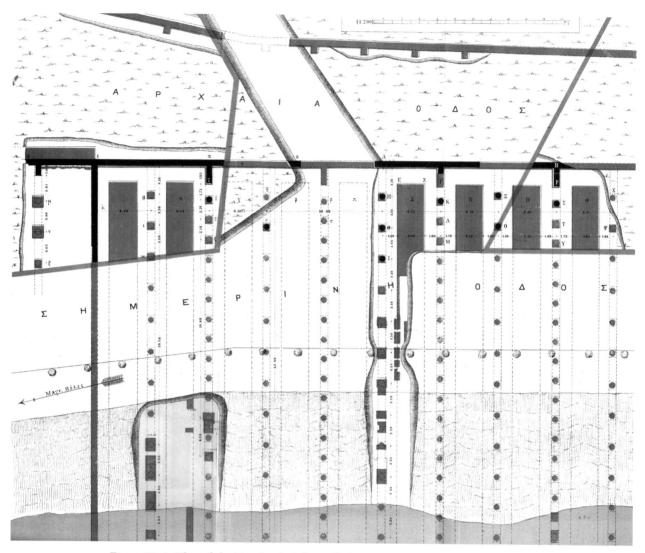

Figure 30.1. Plan of the Zea shipsheds by Wilhelm Dörpfeld (Dragatsis 1886, pin.2).

2.156 cm) (Dörpfeld gives measurements to the nearest centimetre only, which produces a margin of error for all calculations from them; the figure of 30.8 cm for the proposed module is that which best fits the numerous relevant measurements on the plan and sections).

This 30.8 cm figure corresponds to a known foot-module of between *c.* 30.6 cm and 30.8 cm, usually referred to as a 'common' foot. This foot-module has been detected in a number of major Greek buildings, including the theatre at Epidauros (30.58 cm: Rottländer 1991–2) and the Parthenon (30.7 cm: De Waele 1984; cf. Wilson Jones 2000, 79–80, 88–91), and a 30.7 cm version has now been recognised also on the Salamis metrological relief. This relief, of which only the right-hand half survives, shows the top half of a human figure with arms outstretched, together with a separate forearm (*pechus*) to show a cubit, a straight foot-rule, a footprint (*pous*), and a hand with fingers spread to show digits (*daktyloi*) and a span (*spithame*). It is only the second such relief to have been discovered, and it has been the focus of considerable scrutiny in recent scholarship

(the other relief, which was discovered in the 17th century and is now in the Ashmolean Museum at Oxford, has measurements of a different standard and is thought to have originated in the western part of Asia Minor). The original publication by Dekoulakou-Sideris measured the units from the recessed parts of the relief and gave the cubit as 48.7–48.8 cm, the foot-rule as 32.2 cm, and the footprint as 30.15 cm (Dekoulakou-Sideris 1990). Then, in 2000, Wilson Jones made a reassessment and argued that the units should be measured from the surface of the relief, and that the correct figures should be 49.1–49.2 cm for the cubit, 32.75–32.8 cm for the rule, and 30.6–30.7 cm for the footprint (Wilson-Jones 2000). It may be, in fact, that both sets of measurements are correct, and that by bevelling the cutting of the units from the surface to the bottom the relief is actually showing alternative measures, like the builder's rule (*kanon*) recently found in the Ma'agan Mikhael shipwreck off the coast of Israel: the lower and upper surfaces of the latter offered its user alternative foot-units of 33.3 cm (the 'Philetaerian' foot)

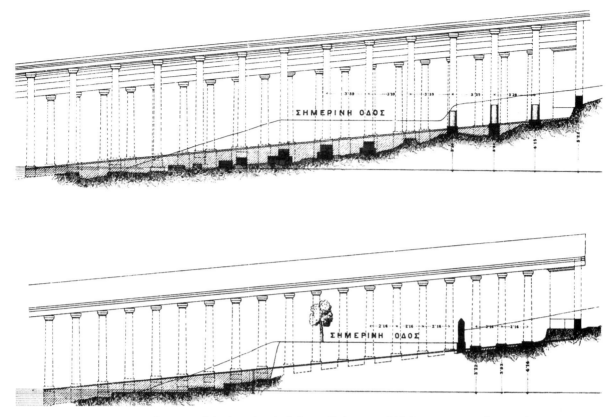

Figure 30.2. Sections of the Zea shipsheds by Wilhelm Dörpfeld (Dragatsis 1886, pin. 3).

and 32.75 cm (the 'Doric' or 'Solonian' foot, as on the Salamis relief) respectively. Moreover, Stieglitz has recently argued, partly on the basis of this rule, that the 30.7 cm footprint on the Salamis relief represented a 'common' foot of 15 *daktyloi* compared to the 'Doric/Solonian' builder's foot of 16 *daktyloi* (Stieglitz 2006).

The recognition that a particular foot-module was being employed for proportional layout of the Phase 3 Zea sheds allows us to make much more sense of the architectural plan. The next step is to note that the overall width of the individual sheds, given by Dörpfeld as 6.49, 6.54, 6.50 (?), 13.03 (for two sheds), 6.53, 6.50, 6.49 and 6.47 m respectively from north to south, appears to be three times the length of the interaxis of the narrowly-spaced colonnades at 2.16 m. Although at first glance, it would appear that the average width of the sheds at around 6.50 cm is a little too long for this, it should be remembered that the purpose of the sheds was to take Athenian triremes, and that the significant figure was not their average but their *minimum* width. Dörpfeld's figures interpreted in the light of the 30.8 cm foot-module fit this perfectly (2.156 m × 3 = 6.468 m), and the designed overall width of the sheds may therefore be recognised as 21 'common' feet.

The most important figure from the point of view of accommodating a trireme was, however, the clear width at the ship's widest point, the outrigger at the top of the hull. This depended on the diameter of the columns at that height. Dragatsis gives the diameter of the column drums he found at Zea as 58 cm (Dragatsis 1886, 67), although Dörpfeld appears consistently to have drawn them on his plan and sections at around 70 cm (3.5 mm at 1:200). Meanwhile, thirteen column drums, almost certainly from ship sheds, which were dredged up in the north-western part of the harbour in 1964, have been measured by the Zea Harbour Project, and a column of three drums made up from these would have had a lower drum tapering from *c.* 67 cm diameter at the bottom to *c.* 63 cm at the top, a middle drum tapering from *c.* 63 to *c.* 58 cm, and an upper drum tapering from *c.* 58 to *c.* 53 cm (Lovén 2011: 89–97, esp. tables 6.9; 6.10, 6.11); the famous Deutsches Archäologisches Institut photograph of the Zea sheds shows tapering columns from the Dragatisis/Dörpfeld excavation which are of similar proportions to these. Given the evidence presented here for modular design in the sheds, these figures are consistent with a designed column diameter at around outrigger height (roughly one third of the way up the middle drum, depending on the height of the ramp), of around two 'common' feet (61.6 cm). It is thus reasonable to suggest that the intended clear width of the sheds was 21–2 = 19 feet (5.852 m), and it would certainly have been very close to that figure.

If the shed was designed to provide a minimum clear width of 19 feet, then we must assume that the ships for which they were built would themselves have been constructed to a maximum width in order to fit inside them. As Graser realised when he made the first detailed survey of the sheds in 1871 (Graser 1872, 22–3), the intended fit would have been tight, both to save space and in order to reduce the potential danger to the sheds from accidental toppling of a ship; the smaller the distance over which a ship could topple, the less the force with which it could strike the columns (cf. Coates, above pp. 135–6). It was for precisely this reason that John Coates, working to his estimated clear width at Zea of 5.94 m, designed *Olympias* to be 5.45 m wide, allowing a space between outrigger and column of 24.5 cm on either side; in his modified design based on the cubit shown in the Salamis relief, the ship's width was increased to 5.62 m, allowing a space of only 16 cm on either side (Morrison, Coates and Rankov 2000, 133, 272). The most obvious figure for the maximum width of the ship would therefore be only about a foot less than the clear width, *i.e. c.* 18 feet, which would allow a space of 15.4 cm on either side of the outrigger. One attraction of this particular figure is that 18 feet is the equivalent of exactly 12 cubits, and as Basch (1983) has pointed out, our literary and epigraphic evidence suggests that ships were normally laid out in cubits rather than feet (cf. the dimensions given for Ptolemy IV's 'forty' in Athenaeus (5.203e–204b), for the *Isis* freighter by Lucian (*Navigatio* 5), and for the 9 and 9.5-cubit oars listed in the epigraphic inventories from the Piraeus; from this, Basch has also argued that the dimensions of the Athlit ram were based on an Attic cubit of 0.444 m.).

This figure is attractive for another reason. As already noted, the epigraphic naval inventories record that triremes had 170 oars, of which 62 were thranite probably at the top level, 54 were zygian, probably at the middle level, and 54 were thalamian, probably at the lower level (*IG* 2² 1615–18). This means that in modern terms there would have been 31 'rooms' for the thranite rowers on each side of the ship, 27 for the zygians, and 27 for the thalamians, and it was the maximum length of these 'rooms' around which John Coates built his design for *Olympias.*. As already noted, however, Vitruvius refers to the space for each rower as an *interscalmium*, which literally means 'between the thole-pins (Lat. *scalmi*, Gk. *skalmoi*)' and says that the Greek expression for this was *dipeciaca* (for *dipechiake* or *dipechuia*), *i.e.* a two-cubit space (Morrison and Williams 1968, 181–6 (by D.J. Blackman); Morrison *et al.* 2000, 132–3). The terms were clearly shipbuilding expressions and taken together suggest that this distance was used as a design module. It is thus reasonable to deduce that the oarsystem would itself have been part of the modular design of the ship, and that it would have been measured between the thole-pins at each end. Certainly, at the beginning of the 18th century, Jean Antoine de Barras de la Penne, one of Louis XIV's galley captains, proposed that the dimensions of a contemporary galley should be proportional to the sum of the *interscalmia*, known as the *longueur de vogue* (Jean Antoine, Marquis de Barras de la Penne, *Description Abregée d'une Galère Moderne* in *La Science des Galères* (Paris *c.* 1693–1727), Bibliothèque

Nationale Ms. Fr. 9177, 146ro–172ro, cited by Lehmann 1995, 110). Between the bowmost and sternmost thranite thole-pins there would have been 30 spaces, and 26 between the corresponding zygian and thalamian pins. The maximum length of the oarsystem for an Athenian trireme of the late fourth century BC would thus have been 30 × 2 = 60 cubits, which is of course exactly five times the ship's width proposed here.

If there was indeed such a proportionality between the ship's width and the oarsystem in the central section of the hull, one would also expect a proportionality between the width and the overall length of the ship. It has in any case usually been assumed that ancient galleys had hulls which were approximately seven times as long as they were broad, compared with merchant vessels which were only three or four times as long (cf. for instance McGrail 2001, 153), and clearly this figure would fit very well with a central section of the ship which was five times as long as the width (*i.e.* the bow:oarsystem:stern proportions would be 1:5:1). If so, the Zea sheds are likely have been designed to take triremes which were 12 cubits (18 feet) wide and 84 cubits (126 feet) long, *i.e.* 5.54 m by 38.81 m. These would have been the architect's 'ideal' triremes, based likewise on a 'common' foot of 0.308 m and therefore on a cubit of 0.308 × 1.5 = 0.462 m and an *interscalmium* of 0.462 × 2 = 0.924 m, although ships of similar or smaller dimensions could also have been accommodated. It may be noted incidentally that such triremes could still have incorporated a canted oar system such as that proposed by Shaw and Coates (above pp. 76–91).

A ship of 38.81 m, with its stern exactly level with the upper end of the ramp, would have the tip of its ram level with both the 12th long-interaxis column and the 18th short-interaxis column from the top. If the ship had been horizontal, it would have reached to the lower end of column bases in each case. This is because the top end of the ramp was laid out to begin where the base of the putative short-interaxis column which was replaced by the spur wall would have ended, so that there were 18 spaces of 7 common feet each. On the other side, this equated to 11.45 interaxial spaces of 11 feet each, but significantly the columns of the long-interaxis colonnades were laid out to line up with those of the short-axis colonnades at precisely this point. This is one of only two places on Dörpfeld's plan where the long-interaxis and short-interaxis columns align (Lovén 2011, 159–61 with table 8.4) and are directly over the bases of Phase 2 columns (see below and Fig. 30.1); the other is at the 5th long-interaxis and 7th short-interaxis column from the top, located over the Phase 2 column bases situated alongside the top end of the Phase 2 ramp (see Dörpfeld's upper section in Fig. 30.2). It is very likely, in fact, that the Phase 3 sheds were laid out over the Phase 2 sheds from precisely these architecturally significant alignments (Blackman and Rankov *et al.* forthcoming). The sheds were, of course, planned horizontally, but because the ships within them would have been on a gradient of 1:10.5 they would, if they were precisely 84 cubits/126 feet long, have reached *c.* 17.5 cm less far horizontally than the lower end of the column bases, so that the tips of their rams would have been level with parts of the columns themselves. Visually, of course, the effect would have been that the ships appeared to be housed in a demarcated upper section of the sheds.

Comparison with the small complex of six sheds of roughly the same period found at Oiniadai in Western Greece (Sears 1904) provides a strong corroboration of the proportions proposed for the Zea triremes. The Oiniadai sheds are of particular value for this because they are the only sheds of which the lower ends can be firmly identified. The colonnades here are evenly spaced and have an average interaxis of 2.25 m or 2.2575 m. These can be equated with 7 feet of 0.3214 m or 0.3225 m respectively. Meanwhile, their clear width is reported as 6.76 m or 6.78 m, which would equate to 21 feet or 0.3219 m or 0.3229 m respectively. These are in fact tiny discrepancies with a total range of only 1.5 mm, and the module looks very like the Salamis foot-rule foot of 0.322 m, which can also be detected in cubit form in the Phase 3 long-interaxis colonnade at Zea (see below). Column drums are recorded at between 0.75 m and 0.60 m in diameter, which is again consistent with a diameter of around 2 feet (= 0.644 m) at outrigger height, again giving a clear width of 19 feet (= 6.12 m) The lower end of the shed is marked by a strong stone pier of T-shaped plan in place of a column, to support the ship as it is launched or comes out of the water, and there are 18 further columns and an engaged half-column at the top of each colonnade, with a total of 17 interaxial spaces of *c.* 2.2575 m with a further 2 averaging 2.135 m each at the top. The upper end of each ramp is situated between the engaged half-column and the uppermost column, at a distance which can be calculated as *c.* 41.54 m = *c.* 129 feet from the lower end of the shed (Sears 1904; Kolonas 1989–90; Blackman and Rankov *et al.* forthcoming.).

At first glance, the Oiniadai sheds would appear to have been designed for ships of the same proportions as the Zea sheds but built to a Salamis foot-rule foot module of 0.322 m, and therefore slightly broader at 5.80 m and slightly longer at 40.57 m. The reasons for suspecting that the situation is not quite so simple is firstly that such a ship would leave very little room for movement and restrict lines of sight across the sheds at the bottom of a 41.54 m ramp, and secondly that the piers of T-shaped plan at the lower end of the sheds appear to be of the same width as the rock-cut bays which took the actual column bases. These bays are shown on Sears' plan as 1.00 m wide, probably the equivalent of 3 feet (*i.e.* 0.966 m). If so, this would have reduced the actual mouth of the sheds to a width of 21–3 = 18 feet, which would be too tight for a ship of that width. Since the Oiniadai complex may have been an Athenian naval outpost (Xen. *Hell.* 4.6.14, referring to 389 BC), the explanation could be that the sheds were built, using a larger foot-module, for ships such as those housed in the roughly contemporary Zea Phase 3 sheds

of the same proportions. One may compare the shed at the northern end of the Zea complex which was laid-out differently from and probably slightly later than the Phase 3 sheds to the south on the other side of the dividing fire-wall. This northern shed is otherwise of the same dimensions as one of the Phase 3 sheds, but its colonnade had an interaxis of 3.43 m according to Dörpfeld's plan. This would equate to 7 cubits of 0.49 m, corresponding to Wilson-Jones' interpretation of the Salamis cubit as a Doric cubit of 0.491–0.492 m. This shed thus uses a different type of module to achieve similar internal dimensions.

Finally, it may be suggested that a slightly differently-proportioned type of trireme may originally have been housed in the Phase 2 sheds at Zea. It has been argued here that the Phase 3 sheds at Zea had colonnades with interaxes of 7 common feet (2.156 m) and 11 common feet (3.388 m) respectively, but the latter figure would also be equivalent to 7 cubits of 0.484 m based on a foot of 0.3226 m, which would be very close to the length of both the Salamis foot rule and the foot-module employed at Oiniadai. This is unlikely to be a coincidence, both because of the proposed 1:7 ship ratio and because an interaxis of 7 cubits would have practical value for the establishment of the gradient of the shed. This gradient could most easily have been achieved by surveying a drop of a certain number of feet or cubits between the appropriate column bases. Thus, for Zea Phase 3, where Dörpfeld's levels suggest a gradient of around 1:10.5, the architect could have used a drop of 2 feet/2 cubits over three interaxial spaces of 7 feet/7 cubits each (2 ÷ 21 = 10.5) (Blackman and Rankov *et al.* forthcoming). The northern shed, as we have seen, was laid out using an interaxis of 7 slightly different cubits. Given the proposed significance for shipbuilding of the figure seven, it is no surprise to find interaxial modules which are seven feet or cubits long. The Phase 2 colonnades at Zea, however, do not correspond to this pattern, since their interaxes can be scaled from Dörpfeld's plan at more or less exactly 4.00 m, which would correspond to 13 of the Zea common feet (13 × 0.308 = 4.004 m) (Blackman and Rankov *et al.* forthcoming).

If the interaxis did relate in some way to the proportions of the trireme being housed, then it may be suggested that the breadth:length ratio of the latter could in this case have been 1:6.5, even though the clear width of the Phase 2 sheds was identical with that of the Phase 3 sheds, and indeed must have determined it. Such a trireme would have been 12 cubits wide and 78 cubits long, and the length could have been based on taking the *longueur de vogue* not from the thranite level of 30 *interscalmia* but from the zygian or thalamian level of 26 *interscalmia*. The central section of the ship would thus have been regarded as being 26 × 2 = 52 cubits in length, and the designed longitudinal proportions of the ship would have been 1:4:1, *i.e.* 13 cubits at the bow, 4 × 13 cubits in the centre, and 13 cubits in the stern, whilst the breadth would have been 12 cubits as with the later vessels. The overall dimensions of such a ship would then be 12 cubits (18 feet) = 5.54 m by

78 cubits (117 feet) = 36.04 m. The ramp of the Phase 2 sheds was probably 128 common feet (39.42 m) in length (very similar to the foot-length at Oiniadai) (Blackman and Rankov *et al.* forthcoming), so that such a ship would have sat comfortably upon it with plenty of space to pass at the lower end. If, however, there was a subsequent move in shipbuilding fashion towards a 1:7 ratio, producing an 84-cubit (126-foot) ship of 38.81 m in length, this would have created a much tighter fit, resulting in difficulties with movement and lines of sight across the shed at the lower end. This tight fit might eventually have led to a decision at Zea to extend the sheds backwards to provide easier movement and more storage space, leading to the demolition of the Phase 2 sheds and their replacement with the much longer Phase 3 sheds.

The arguments presented here have sometimes been somewhat tentative but are based on the observed dimensions and proportions of three different layouts of shipshed at Zea and a fourth at Oiniadai, and the ship dimensions proposed all have the merit of fitting comfortably and logically within their respective sheds:

Zea Phase 2:	Ratio 1:6.5	12 cubits (5.54 m) × 78 cubits (36.04)
Zea Phase 3:	Ratio 1:7	12 cubits (5.54 m) × 84 cubits (38.81 m)
Zea northern shed:	Ratio 1: 7	Same as Zea Phase 3 (?)
Oiniadai:	Ratio 1:7	Same as Zea Phase 3 (?)

For comparison, *Olympias* as built has a ratio of 1:6.75 and dimensions of 5.45 m × 36.80 m, and the *Olympias* Mark II design (Morrison, Coates and Rankov 2000, 267–73) has a ratio of 1:7 and dimensions of 5.62 m × 39.6 m. The most significant conclusion here, however, lies not in the dimensions themselves, but in the evidence presented which suggests that triremes, like the sheds which housed them, were built according to modular and proportional principles. What is also clear is that the sheds and the ships would have been built in such way that the former could receive the latter, but that this could be achieved by the architects in a variety of different ways.

Bibliography

Basch, L. (1983) The cubit as a nautical unit of measurement in Antiquity. *The Mariner's Mirror* 69.3, 248–9.

Blackman, D. J. and Rankov, N. B. *et al.* (forthcoming) *Shipsheds of the Ancient Mediterranean*. Cambridge, Cambridge University Press.

Coates, J. F. (1993) Development of the Design. In Shaw (1993), 71–4.

Coates, J. F. and McGrail, S. (eds) (1984) *The Greek Trireme of the Fifth Century BC: Discussion of a projected reconstruction at the National Maritime Museum, Greenwich.* Greenwich, Trustees of the National Maritime Museum.

De Waele, J. (1984) Der Entwurf des Parthenon. In Berger, E. (ed.), *Parthenon-Kongress Basel: Referate und Berichte, 4. bis 8. April 1982.* Mainz, Verlag Philipp von Zabern, 99–114.

Dekoulakou-Sideris, E. (1990) A metrological relief from Salamis. *American Journal of Archaeology* 94, 445–51.

Dragatsis, I. Ch. (1886) Ekthesis peri ton en Peiraiei anaskaphon. *Praktika tes en Athenais Arkhaiologikes Hetairias tou etous 1885*, 63–68.

Graser, B. (1872) Meine Messungen in den Altathenischen Kriegshafen. *Philologus* 31, 1–65.

Kolonas, L. (1989–90) Anaskaphe Oiniadon: ta neoria. *Archaiognosia* 6, 153–9.

Lehmann, L. Th. (1995) *The Polyeric Quest. Renaissance and Baroque Theories about Ancient Men-of-War.* 2nd ed. Amsterdam, De Gouden Reaal.

Lovén, B. *et al.* (2007) The Zea Harbour Project: the first six years. In Hallager, E. and Tae Jensen, J. (eds), *Proceedings of the Danish Institute at Athens V*, 61–74.

Lovén, B. (2011) *The Ancient Harbours of the Piraeus. Volume I.1 – The Zea Shipsheds and Slipways: Archaeology and Topography.* Athens, Danish Institute at Athens.

McGrail, S. (2001) *Boats of the World from the Stone Age to Medieval Times.* Oxford, Oxford University Press.

Morrison, J. S. (1993) *Trireis*: the evidence from Antiquity, In Shaw (1993), 11–20.

Morrison, J. S. and Coates, J. F. (eds) (1989) *An Athenian Trireme Reconstructed. The British Sea Trials of Olympias, 1987.* BAR International Series 486. Oxford, Archaeopress.

Morrison, J. S. and Williams, R. T. (1968) *Greek Oared Ships 900–322 B.C.* Cambridge, Cambridge University Press.

Morrison, J. S., Coates, J. F. and Rankov, N. B. (2000) *The Athenian Trireme. The History and Reconstruction of an Ancient Greek Warship.* 2nd ed. Cambridge, Cambridge University Press.

Rottländer, R. C. A. (1991–2) Eine neue aufgefundene antike Massenheit auf dem metrologischen Relief von Salamis. *Jahreshefte des Österreichischen Archäologischen Instituts in Wien* 61, 63–8.

Sears, J. M. (1904) Oiniadae VI. The Ship Sheds. *American Journal of Archaeology* 8.2, 227–37.

Shaw, J. T. (1993) *The Trireme Project. Operational Experience 1987–90. Lessons Learnt.* Oxford, Oxbow Books.

Steinhauer, G. (1989) Excavations: Piraeus: Philon's Arsenal (in Greek). *Arkhaiologikon Deltion (Khronikon)* 44, 50–5.

Stieglitz, R. R. (2006) Classical Greek measures and the builder's instruments from the Ma'agan Mikhael shipwreck. *American Journal of Archaeology* 110.2, 195–203.

Wilson-Jones, M. (2000) Doric measure and architectural design 1: the evidence of the relief from Salamis. *American Journal of Archaeology* 104.1, 73–93.

31. Battle Manoeuvres for Fast Triremes

Andrew Taylor

1. Introduction

In the accounts of ancient authors, it is common to find triremes operating in multiples of five or ten. Trireme fleets that were acknowledged as slow seem to have formed squadrons in multiples of 5, while fast formations operated much more frequently in multiples of 10. The minimum frontage occupied by five triremes in line abreast, spaced as closely as plausible, would have been of the order 100 m, based on the 10.8 m width of *Olympias* from oar-tip to oar-tip and allowing a similar sized gap between ships. This space roughly matches the minimum-radius turn reported for *Olympias* (a diameter of 62 m: Coates *et al.*, 1990, 30) plus an extra margin for the width of the ship and some clearance from any neighbours. This provides a possible explanation for the multiple of five associated with slow fleets. This tightest reported turn resulted in a halving of the ship's speed during the turn, and hence has in this paper been termed a 'slow turn' or 'tight anastrophe'. Turns where *Olympias* maintained a higher proportion of its initial boat speed on entering the turn had minimum diameters ranging from 107 to 120 m. Allowing for the width of the ship and clearance from neighbours, the space required for these 'fast turns' is thus approximately double that of the tightest possible turn, and matches the frontage that would be occupied by ten ships in a closely-spaced line abreast. Exploring this convergence between the numbers of ships reported by ancient authors and the reported turning diameters and speeds from the sea trials of *Olympias* was a major motivation for the detailed modelling work reported here.

This paper first seeks to demonstrate how the results of a series of six trials with *Olympias* were applied to produce a model of her movement through the water, and how that model was adapted to take account of the modifications proposed in this volume for the construction of a Mark IIb 'fast trireme' (above, pp. 76–91). The model is then used in the latter part of the paper to investigate a variety of tactical scenarios involving both individual vessels and squadrons arranged in multiples of five and ten, and thus to establish some quantitative parameters for fleet manoeuvres in battle. Finally, a tactical paradigm is offered for engagements between ancient trireme fleets.

1.1. The dynamics model

For the purposes of this paper, a dynamics model was developed to model the manoeuvres of *Olympias* reported by Lowry and Squire (1988), Coates *et al.* (1990, 20–31, 69–89) and Shaw (1993, 45–7). The parameters of this model were then adjusted to fit the proposed changes for a hypothetical Mark IIb Trireme that incorporates the design and operational lessons from *Olympias* (see pp. 76–91 above). The resulting model thus provides a plausible hypothetical estimate of the dynamics of a fast ancient trireme. In the final part of the paper, the model will be used to evaluate the space and time constraints associated with the types of manoeuvres which triremes seem to have undertaken when approaching and operating in close proximity to an enemy force.

The mathematical models for the dynamics of *Olympias* and a proposed Mark IIb fast trireme were developed using Excel spreadsheets. The physical parameters considered within the model are discussed in what follows and the related numerical values are tabulated in Table 31.1. Since the model was developed and tested against the observed motions of *Olympias*, these parameters will be discussed first. In detail, the turns fitted are those presented by Coates *et al.* (1990, 87–88) in their tables F and G. Here the turns are labelled F1–F6 and G1–G5 as sequentially listed in their tables.

2. Parameters for *Olympias*

2.1. Linear forward motion

The linear acceleration of the ship allows for an apparent mass 10% larger than the ship's actual assumed displacement. The drag measured in towing tests with *Olympias* is given by Coates *et al.* (1990, 54) in the form of parametric

Table 31.1. Model parameters used to fit the observed performance of Olympias *recorded during sea trials and to extend the model to predict the dynamics possible for an optimised fast, Mark IIb trireme design:*

Model Parameter	Olympias	Fast trireme	Units
Mass of vessel	42.0	44.0	tonnes
Apparent dynamical mass for forward linear motion	46.2	48.4	tonnes
Drag for bare hull up to 6.7 knots (v in knots) 6.7–9.0 knots over 9.0 knots	$40.2\ v^2$	$44.7\ v^2$ $83.6\ v^2 - 1733$ $98.4\ v^2 - 2933$	N
Drag from straight rudders	$(79.6-40.2)\ v^2$	$10\ v^2$	N
Effective lateral cross-section deflecting water in a turn	35	39	m^2
Waterline length	32.2	35.2	m
Draft	1.1	1.1	m
Height of centre of gravity above Keel (KG) for ship plus 200 crew	1.94	1.9	m
Distance (along centre line) from centre of mass to the rudder	14.9	16.5	m
Lever arm from centre of mass to the centre of the oar race	4.8	5.4	m
Moment of inertia about vertical axis	4×10^6	5×10^6	$kg\ m^2$
Coefficient for resistance of water to angular velocity	5×10^6	6×10^6	$kg\ m^2$
Vertical lever arm from C of M to lateral resistance of water on ships hull	1.46	1.42	m
Vertical lever arm from C of M to middle of rudder's lateral resistance	1.16	1.12	m
Metacentric height	0.97	0.9	m

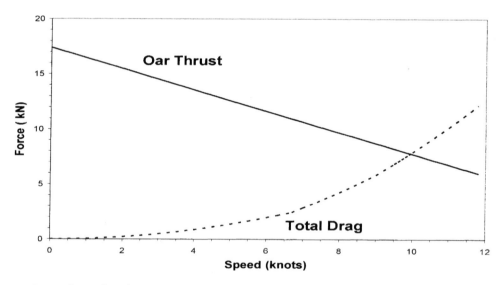

Figure 31.1. Force relationships for an optimised Mark IIb fast trireme. The drag curve is based on the parameterised summary provided by Shaw (1990) for Olympias *but with increased surface drag and less disruptive rudders. The oar thrust assumes a skilled crew operating an optimised oar rig with more room per rower and increased separation of their blades. The adopted linear relationship follows a line that would drop to zero thrust at a speed of 18 knots.*

equations as a function of speed in three separate speed bands. These produce a relationship broadly similar to that plotted for a Mark IIb trireme, as in Fig. 31.1.

An extra increment of linear drag equal to 1.4 times the straight rudder drag is included to allow for the extra turbulence associated with an applied rudder angle of 67.5 degrees. This is reduced to 0.6 for a rudder angle of 45 degrees and 0.2 for the 22.5 degrees rudder angle when modelling the reported Kempf Manoeuvre. Once entered into a turn, the linear drag on the ship will increase as a result of drift angle, the angle between the ship's heading and its forward linear motion. This increased resistance is calculated assuming that the water's resistance acts at an angle (of half the drift angle) from forward of the perpendicular to the ship's track. The adopted value for the effective lateral cross section deflecting water during a turn is very close to the actual cross section of the wetted hull. The sum of the longitudinal drags compares reasonably well with the expected oar thrust from measured power outputs on rowing machines and estimated efficiency factors. The thrust generated by the oar-crew has been matched to the sum of the hull and straight rudder drags for *Olympias* at the entry speed given in the reported turn data, thereby providing a steady-state entry speed. Since these values are well below the maximum reported capabilities of the crews they are assumed to have remained constant throughout the turn if both sides continued rowing, or halved if the inside oar-bank stopped rowing.

2.2. Turning motion

The lateral force on the hull provided by the reaction force of the water deflected as it flows past the hull is the main factor in determining the turning diameter for the ship. The water, with a density of 1025 kg m^{-3}, is deflected by the drift angle and its change in momentum gives the magnitude of the impulse changing the direction of the ship's track through the water. The turning force, perpendicular to the motion of the ship, due to the rudder has been estimated as a fraction of the rudders' along-track drag, typically ranging from 40 to 80%. The actual fraction used was determined from a polynomial fit of the rudders angle, Φ, with respect to the ship's track through the water.

$$\text{Coefficient} = 0.14 + 0.020 \, \Phi - 0.00015 \times \Phi^2$$

The torque applied by the rudder on the ship has been determined using the distance from the rudder to the centre of mass of the ship. Several of the turns were achieved by getting the oar-crew on one side of the ship to stop rowing. This turning moment has also been considered with a lever arm running from the centre-line of the ship to halfway between the outer oar tips and the inner edge of the thalamian oar-blades. The resistance of the water to rotation of the ship about its centre of mass has been determined by multiplying the moment of inertia by the angular yaw rate squared. This decision to model rotation about the vertical axis through the centre of mass of the ship, rather than rotation about the centre of lateral resistance is a principal difference from the UCL model discussed below. The resisting torque for rotation (yaw rate) was modelled as a simple function of the angular velocity (ω) squared with a suitable constant, Ω, that has an order of magnitude similar to that of the moment of inertia of the ship.

$$\text{Resisting torque} = \Omega \, \omega^2$$

2.3. Angle of heel

A key constraint for maintaining boat speed with *Olympias* in a turn is the extent of heel experienced (see Taylor, pp. 50–7). A heel angle of the order of 3° leads to problems for rowers on the inside of a turn with getting their oars into the water, and for those on the outside with getting their oars out. The oar-rig in *Olympias* was designed to work with a heel of up to 3°. Within the model the heel was calculated by balancing the tipping moments of the rudder and the lateral resistance of the water in a turn

with stability implied by treating the ship as a simple pendulum with a length equal to the metacentric height. The actual height of the centre of gravity above the under side of the keel (USK) was used to determine the response of the ship to the lateral resistance of the water while the effective height, 0.2 m lower, was used in determining the metacentric height, since the crew will tend to lean during a turn putting their effective centre of mass at the height of their seats. The maximum heel angles generated within the model calculations match the 3° constraint reasonably closely and therefore did not require any extra reduction in the oar thrust due to this factor to be included in the model.

3. Actual turns fitted by the model

The actual turn data fitted are summarised by Coates *et al.* (1990, 87–88). Some observations about fitting those data are included here for those interested in the detailed development of the model.

In general the Trust Crew, G1–G5, had a distinctly flat set of measured oar-thrusts for speeds 4 to 7 knots. It therefore seems reasonable to assume that the crew maintained their effective thrust throughout the turns, or at least something near it provided the ship did not heel too much. The entry speeds for the G2 and F2 turns were unusually low and I have assumed that the crew increased their output in the turn to more closely match those achieved in the other turns. Since the G3 turn did not get completed it is not so useful for analysing the drift angle during a turn. The lower average true speed also suggests that oar thrust dropped during the turn.

The various estimates of yaw rate suggest that steady state turning is occurring well before the ship has turned to 90° from its initial heading. The difference in time between the ship's head and ship's track turning to 90° therefore gives a good estimate of the steady state drift angle. These values have a fairly large uncertainty but match the expectations for drift angle, as required by the centripetal force needed for the turns, rather better than some of those stated in the text of the 1988 Report (Lowry and Squire 1988). For example, the drift angle stated for the G1 and G2 turns with full rudder applied and the full oar crew rowing is 15° ± 2°. This does not relate very well to the 3-second delay between the ship's head and the ship's track going through 90 degrees to the starting bearing. That is, the delay times the yaw rate = 3 × 2.6 = 7.8° for the drift angle. Presumably the stated drift angles were measured over a wider variety of turn angles; however, we should probably assume the lower value.

The turn data reported for the Hellenic Navy crew, F1–F6, include a much wider variety of applied rudder angles in addition to data with a lower oar thrust with only the thranites rowing in several trials. These data were particularly relevant in constraining the model prior to fitting the data recorded in the Kempf manoeuvre. The implied oar thrust on entry to F1, the turn with the smallest applied rudder angle, is difficult to reconcile with the total drag figure. The long duration of the timed turn is a possible cause for the reduction in oar thrust. Measurement uncertainties might account for the rest of the discrepancy but would need to be fairly extreme, while increasing the rudder drag significantly would cause problems for the 45° rudder-angle turns. Turns F5 and F6 had slightly low entry speeds compared with that prior to their other turns. The half crew rowing in each case could easily have increased their efforts to produce oar thrusts more similar to half that on previous turns with the full crew rowing.

The Kempf or Zig-Zag manoeuvre data provided key data on how rapidly *Olympias* entered and came out of turns, *i.e.* both the moment of inertia and the drag associated with rotation of the ship about its vertical axis. The advance and transfer of the various reported turning curves provided extra data in how the quickly the ship responded to an unbalanced torque applied by the rudder or as a result of half the oar-crew stopping rowing.

4. Comparison with other modelling

The results of the model articulated in the manoeuvres presented in this paper were compared with similar output from a modelling project undertaken by the Mechanical Engineering Department of University College, London (Prof. Simon Rusling and Dr Tristan Smith, pers. com. 2006). Although the work at UCL used a more conventional approach in modelling the trireme, the results were in close agreement, principally as a result of fitting the parameters to the same original data set from sea trials with *Olympias*.

5. Changes from *Olympias* to a hypothetical fast Mark IIb trireme

One significant outcome from the trireme project has been a series of proposals about how to improve the performance of a vessel conceived along the lines of *Olympias* but based on the operational experience obtained with *Olympias* and more recent archaeological evidence. The principal modifications incorporate a modest lengthening in the design, the slight canting or skewing of the rowers' seats, and an increase in the lateral separation of the oar blades by further refining the 'wine-glass' cross section of the hull. Allowing the crew to reach past the rower next astern and therefore deliver a 50% longer stroke would significantly improve the efficiency with which the oar-crew convert their power output to an effective thrust driving the ship. The design and operational experience gained with *Olympias* suggest that these changes could be achieved with only minor changes in the other dynamic parameters of the manoeuvring model discussed here (see above pp. 76–91 and the references there for a much more detailed discussion of these issues). Key parameters used to model the dynamics of a hypothetical fast Mark IIb trireme are included in Table 31.1.

5.1. Physical dimensions for Mark IIb

To accommodate the extra room for the rowers on the proposed Mark IIb fast trireme, the overall length of the ship is assumed to be increased by 3 metres. Combined with some lightening of the structure it is envisaged that the displacement would increase by just two tonnes to 44 tonnes. It is assumed that the main mast, yard, sail and associated gear would have been landed prior to battle and these are not included in the mass balance. Increased confidence in the stability of the ship should allow a slight reduction of 0.1 m in the metacentric height. This also allows for a slight increase in the width of the ship, separating the oar blades laterally, whilst still ensuring that the design could fit between the pillars of the surviving remains of ancient ship sheds.

The increase in the wetted surface area of the hull would lead to an increase in the frictional drag of the hull, in direct proportion to the increased length; the draft is assumed to remain the same as for *Olympias*. No attempt has been made to model the change in wave making resistance associated with the increased length since this is a relatively minor component in the overall hull resistance for *Olympias*. Although it might have a greater influence at the higher speeds discussed for a Mark IIb trireme the assumptions about the magnitude and duration of the total possible effective oar thrust will probably dominate these subtleties. Based on the Froude number, peaks in the wave-making resistance for the Mark IIb hull would occur at 6.5, 8.2 and 10.6 knots; peaks that comfortably bracket the expected range of maximum speeds of from 9 to10 knots postulated for a fast trireme and provide another window of low resistance for the sorts of cruising speeds, around 7.6 knots, required to match the long day's row reported in Xenophon (see Shaw, 1993, 64 and above pp. 63–7). The actual formulae used to calculate the hull drag are based on the parametric equations from Coates *et al.* (1990, 74) and presented in Table 31.1.

The drag from fully immersed straight rudders on *Olympias* is of the same order of magnitude as that for the whole of the rest of the hull. This model assumes an optimised rudder design with a minimum drag one quarter of the full value measured for *Olympias*; a value near that assumed for the minimum drag achieved with partially immersed rudders during maximum speed runs with *Olympias*. The increased along-track drag associated with an applied rudder varied by a factor between 0.6 and 3.25 times the straight rudder value; broadly in line with that assumed for the *Olympias* modelling. The relationship of drag with boat speed can be seen in Fig. 31.1.

5.2. Oar thrust for Mark IIb

In separate sets of sea-trials with widely different oar-crews in terms of numbers, levels of fitness and skill, *Olympias* demonstrated a consistent 40% efficiency in converting power delivered by the rowers to the oar handle, as measured by fixed-seat ergometer tests, into the power

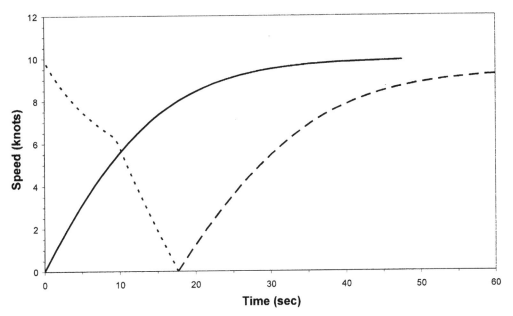

Figure 31.2. Speed/Time graphs for an optimised Mark IIb fast trireme. The acceleration curve (solid line) directly uses the force relationships from Fig. 31.1. The deceleration curve (dotted line) is initially the result of fully applied rudders, set in opposite directions to ensure maximum drag but no turning. During this time the crew is assumed to be turning in their seats, taking the oar of the person behind and at 10 seconds placing their oars into the water to increase the braking force, assumed to be equivalent to the maximum thrust at zero speed (see Fig. 31.1). Once the vessel comes to a halt, the crew continues to pull the ship backwards (dashed line) with an effective oar thrust equivalent to 80% of their maximum forward thrust at the same speed.

needed to overcome the resistance of the water to the passage of the hull and rudders. These were achieved in bursts with durations of a few minutes designed to achieve a maximum possible boat speed; Taylor (above pp. 50–7) found a figure of 43%, with Shaw (1993, 58–68) quoting 39% for previous trials.

Shaw (1990, 29) projects that the 1988 Trial's Crew could 'probably' have delivered an effective power of 200 W per rower on the thranite and zygian levels for a maximal sustained 6-minute effort, *i.e.* a total of 23 kW for 116 rowers. The Mark IIb design was proposed to ensure that all rowers deliver effective power, especially those on the thalamian level, and perhaps at a higher efficiency. An improvement in the effective efficiency of the oar-rig for a Mark IIb design to a figure closer to 60% should allow this effective power value to increase to 300 W per rower; 51 kW for full 170 oar-crew. A more modest total effective power of 40 kW, capable of being delivered at maximum speed and sustained for a few minutes, has been assumed for this modelling project. The durations of the manoeuvres discussed in this paper are all less than two minutes. Matching power output with the estimated drag gives a maximum speed of 9.9 knots with an effective oar thrust of 7.8 kN at that speed; see the intersection point of the two curves in Fig. 31.1.

A variety of measured acceleration runs with *Olympias*, including some from standing starts, led Shaw (1990, 25) to conclude that the effective thrust of the oar crew decreased, in a linear relationship, with increasing speed.

A similar relationship has been adopted here and this is also displayed in Fig. 31.1.

Thrust (kN) = 17.4–0.967 × speed (in knots)

6. Manoeuvrability for a fast trireme

The dynamics model, extended to incorporate the likely improvements in a Mark IIb design based on *Olympias*, has been used to investigate the expected manoeuvrability of an ancient fast trireme.

6.1. Speed changes

Fig. 31.2 provides a graph comparing the speed of two fast triremes, one initially at maximum speed, 9.9 knots, and the other stationary. The acceleration curve for the stationary ship uses the force relationships discussed above; it reaches 5.5 knots in the first 10 seconds, 9 knots at 24 seconds, and is effectively at full speed within 40 seconds.

The second curve illustrates a deceleration profile where the oar-crew stop rowing at the start time (zero seconds), turn in their seats to take over the oars of the oarsman behind them in the first 10 seconds and then begin rowing the ship backwards, initially providing additional braking until 18 seconds and then accelerating the trireme sternwards. Throughout the deceleration phase of this manoeuvre the rudders are assumed to be fully flared, *i.e.* turned 67.5° in opposite directions, providing the maximum possible additional drag but no net turning effect.

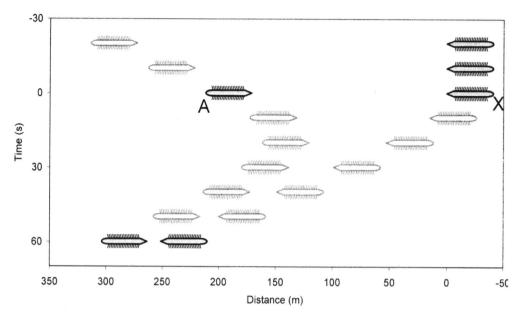

Figure 31.3. Backing away. A trireme approaching an enemy ship decides to stop and then back away from the encounter: an anakrousis. The aggressor, trireme A, is a fast vessel moving from left to right at its maximum speed of 9.9 knots. At 170 m from the stationary enemy it enters a full braking routine: rudders fully flared in opposite directions with the crew taking 10 s to turn in their seats then applying an additional braking force equivalent to the maximum thrust that they generate when stationary. Trireme A reaches a full stop after just under 20 seconds. Subsequent acceleration assumes backing away with a thrust that is 80% of what the crew can develop moving forward, with the ship reaching a maximum speed backwards of 9.4 knots after 60 seconds. Simultaneous with the onset of trireme A's braking, the reacting ship X (also modelled as a fast trireme) begins to accelerate attaining its maximum speed of 9.9 knots at around 40 seconds. The diagram shows the relative positions of the two triremes at ten-second intervals. After 60 seconds, trireme A has still avoided contact and is travelling, backwards, at a maximum speed of 9.4 knots.

This method of rowing a ship backwards proved to be the most effective with *Olympias* despite the fact that she was very far from optimised for such work. Secure places to brace the rowers' feet and more sustained practice with taking timing from rowers in the bow of the ship would both have improved the speeds obtained (see Taylor, above pp. 50–7 for a more complete discussion). An oar thrust equal to 80% of that possible with the crew rowing the ship forward has been assumed for the subsequent acceleration backwards from 18 seconds on. A final speed of 9.4 knots backwards is obtained with the hull drag being assumed to be the same as for forward motion. This speed therefore gives a plausible benchmark for a possible slow ancient trireme. The remainder of the manoeuvres discussed in this paper all compare fast triremes interacting with each other.

Incorporating distance travelled into the simulation allows for the comparison between a fast trireme, at full speed, approaching an initially stationary one. Fig. 31.3 illustrates a moving ship approaching to within 170 m of a stationary enemy and still being able to stop, then back away with relative immunity.

6.2. Turning circles

Turning a ship inevitably involves increasing the drag forces acting against the direction of motion, both from increased

rudder drag and the deflection of water by the hull. In a rowing boat the increased heel associated with turning also acts to reduce the oar thrust available to continue to overcome this drag. *Olympias* was designed to allow for a maximum heel of 3 degrees and there is clear evidence that boat speed was significantly affected by changes even smaller than this (Taylor, above pp. 50–7). At a projected maximum speed of 10 knots the tightest turn that a trireme with dimensions similar to *Olympias* (or any other vessel constrained by the dimensions of trireme ship sheds, *e.g.* Mark IIb), whilst allowing a maximum heel of 3 degrees, has a diameter of 140 m. This calculation also requires some mitigation by the non-rowing deck crew of the trireme moving to the inside beam of the ship, rather in the spirit of the passenger of a racing motorcycle sidecar combination.

Fig. 31.4 illustrates two possible turning circles where a trireme turns back to reverse its course, an *anastrophe*. The first, a 'fast' turn, where the trireme maintains maximum possible boat speed, 9.5 knots, with the full oar crew rowing and a modest, 22.5°, applied-rudder angle. This gives a turning diameter of 145 m. The alternative, a 'tight' turn, involves one side stopping rowing and the application of full rudder to achieve a turn diameter of 80 m, but with a consequent drop in boat speed to 6.5 knots during the manoeuvre. A tighter turn is possible, closer to the tightest 62 m diameter turn recorded with

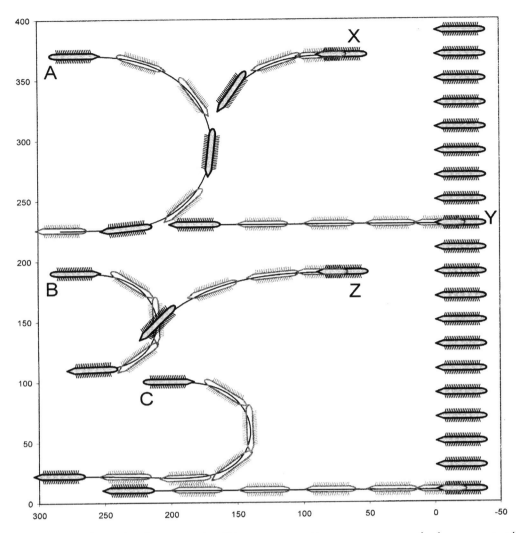

Figure 31.4. Fast anastrophe and tight anastrophe. Triremes approaching an enemy turn back, an anastrophe, to avoid contact with a counter-attacking enemy. In each case the approaching ships are moving at 9.9 knots whilst the responding ships (assumed fast) are stationary; the onset of the turn of the attacking ship and the start of acceleration by the responding ship are simultaneous. The image of a trireme is overlaid at 10–second intervals with closely interacting pairs of ships shaded and marked in bold where they occur at the same instant. Dimensions are in metres

Trireme A enters a fast turn, with a minimum speed of 9.5 knots in the turn and an effective diameter of 145 m. The maximum heel during the turn is 3.5 degrees, which with some remedial action by the deck crew to provide some counter balancing should allow the rowers to maintain full thrust throughout; as has been assumed here. The isolated ship X accelerates and turns to follow reaching 8.2 knots after 30 seconds but does not manage to ram trireme A. After 50 seconds trireme A has completed its turn and is still clear of ship Y. Provided an approaching trireme reacts promptly, they can safely approach to within 160 m of an isolated ship or within 250 m of a rank of stationary enemy vessels before turning away with a fast anastrophe.

Employing a more aggressive turning strategy, trireme B applies full rudder with only the port oarcrew continuing to row in the turn. This does not significantly decrease the minimum safe distance for approaching an isolated ship, trireme Z, largely because the speed in the tight anastrophe is reduced to 6.5 knots and it takes another 20 seconds or so to accelerate back up to full speed. The minimum safe distance from a rank of enemy triremes does, however, drop to 180 m for trireme C when entering this sort of tight turn.

Olympias, with, for example, the oar crew on the inside providing some braking but with the boat speed dropping even lower during the manoeuvre. A lower entry speed would also allow a tighter turn.

To estimate how closely a ship might safely approach an enemy whilst still being able to turn away safely and

escape the immediate threat, a set of initially stationary, fast triremes have been modelled interacting with the approaching vessel. The image of a trireme, drawn to scale, is overlaid at ten second intervals with the initial positions and closely interacting pairs of ships shaded and outlined in bold. In a straight-ahead approach, a ship that begins

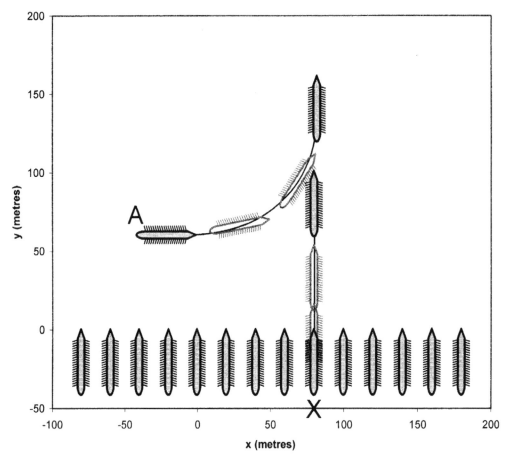

Figure 31.5. Encirclement. One response to a fleet forming a defensive circle, a kuklos, is to row around them in an encirclement, e.g. the Athenians at the first Battle of Naupactus, 430 BC (Thucydides, 2.84.1). Provided that trireme A is about 60 m away from the stationary enemy ships, and it responds immediately, it can turn away and escape from any ship that accelerates out to ram it. Just such an event is reported to have been initiated by the Greeks breaking out of their circle at the Battle of Artemisium, 480 BC (Herodotus 8.11.1). Here and for the rest of the scenarios the dynamics of the counter-attacking ship have been modelled as those of a fast trireme.

turning 160 m away from an isolated, facing, stationary ship will be able to remain clear. The threat zone increases to 180 m if approaching a rank of stationary fast triremes. More subtle approaches can significantly reduce these distances and they are discussed in the next section.

7. Battle manoeuvres for ancient triremes

7.1. Closing the gaps

A trireme rowing at right angles across the front of a rank of stationary triremes at a distance of 60 m would be relatively immune from being rammed provided it responds promptly by turning away if one of the enemy ships begins an attack run: see Fig. 31.5. On reaching the end of an enemy line the moving trireme could row around the end of the line, a *periplous*, as in Fig. 31.6. In this case the end ship has been modelled accelerating away in pursuit although it is still unable to catch the initially moving vessel. The presence of another vessel following the lead ship provides a considerable additional threat to any

antagonistic response from the stationary ships. This sort of additional threat would provide a considerable incentive for the stationary fleet to adopt the sort of formation described as a *kuklos*, a defensive circle, without any ends to be rowed around, one portion of which might be as illustrated in Fig. 31.5.

Fig. 31.7 illustrates a trireme rowing through a gap in the enemy line, a *diekplous*. A prompt response by the stationary ship on the far end of the gap would make it extremely dangerous to attempt the *diekplous* if the gap was less than 150 m, in this case. More aggressive turning strategies following the sort of approach course steered in Fig. 31.8 indicate that this gap could be reduced to at least 130 m: see Fig. 31.9. The presence of following vessels would further constrain options for the stationary defensive fleet and might allow this minimum gap to be reduced still further. If the oars of any of the stationary ships were afoul of their neighbours then a yet smaller gap would suffice.

Fig. 31.8 illustrates how a ship, initially approaching an enemy rank head on as in Figs 31.3 and 31.4, could

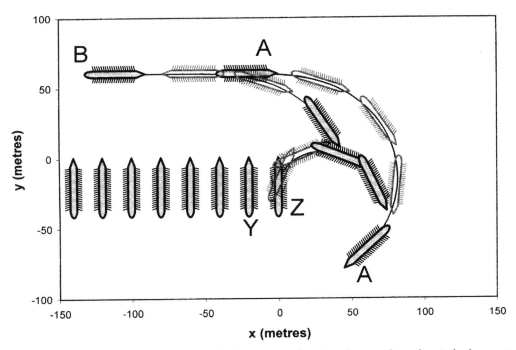

Figure 31.6. Periplous. On reaching the end of a rank of stationary ships that has not formed a circle the moving trireme A could row around the end of the line, a periplous, and attack the enemy from the rear. If the end ship Z turns and accelerates in pursuit, then the following trireme B is in a perfect position to ram Z provided that ship Y does not react too promptly; e.g., moving out as in Fig. 31.5.

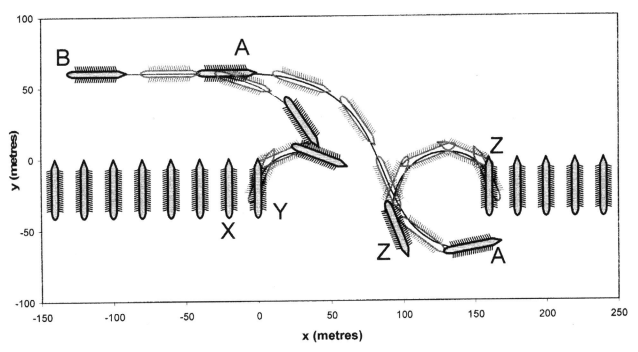

Figure 31.7. Diekplous with following trireme(s). A gap of width 150 m is sufficient to allow a trireme to row through, a diekplous, with immunity provided that the defending ships do not react until the aggressor begins his turn. If the defending ships react earlier they will increase their vulnerability, as depicted in Fig. 31.11. Again, the threat of the following ship B may well dissuade Y from attempting the plotted turn, which would narrow the safe gap needed for a diekplous, although ship X could also react as in Fig. 31.5 and join the counter attack. Fifty seconds into the manoeuvre trireme A is inside Z's turning circle and a threat to ships further down the line. If the oars of the triremes in the rank were entangled and therefore unable to be worked, then the gap required for a successful diekplous would be considerably narrower.

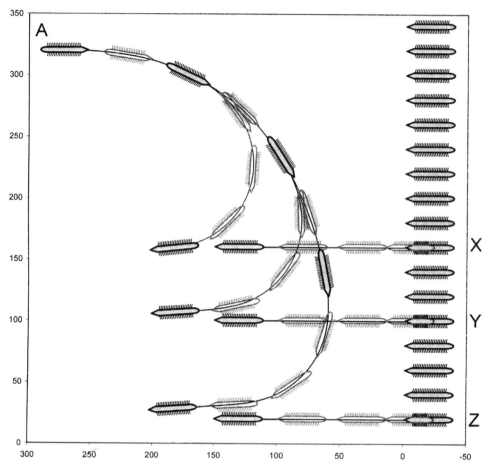

Figure 31.8. Steering for anastrophe or diekplous. By steering judiciously it is possible to approach an unbroken rank of enemy ships much more closely than is evident in Fig. 31.4, whilst at each point still being able to turn back and complete an anastrophe without being rammed. In this example ships, X, Y and Z begin their counter-attack 20, 40 and 60 seconds into the approach of trireme A, i.e., concurrent with the bold icons on the approach curve. The initially stationary ships moving out of the line accelerate as a fast trireme, whilst trireme A reacts instantly to enter a fast anastrophe. In each case trireme A manages to get clear.

steer a course that would eventually have it moving across the front of the enemy rank at a range of 60 m as in Figs 31.5, 31.6 and 31.7. Providing that the approaching ship turns away promptly in response to any threatening moves, then the illustrated track represents a path that allows a turn away to safety at any point in the approach.

7.2. Maintaining and disrupting more complex formations

A close-packed rank of triremes is a very effective defence against attacking fast vessels, with near neighbours providing protection against triremes following a leading attacker. However, it is very vulnerable to being disrupted by any sort of crosswind. Such disruption is certainly attested at the First Battle of Naupactus (Thucydides 2.84.3) and in the initial stages of the Battle of Salamis (Diodorus Siculus 11.18.4). Therefore, waiting for a fast

fleet to close would require a formation that allowed more room for station keeping whilst avoiding falling foul of neighbours, but also one that could quickly be converted into the more defensive closely-spaced rank.

The starting formation in Fig. 31.10, illustrating twenty triremes deployed in four files of five ships, is proposed as having these requisites. This is exactly the formation adopted by the 20 triremes of the fast squadron deployed on the Corinthian right flank at the beginning of the Second Battle of Naupactus, 430 BC (Thucydides 2.90.1–2). Each ship has sufficient room to turn in place without disrupting its neighbours whilst still being able to maintain position against a wind blowing from any direction. The 100 m spacing between files allows the formation to turn internally to redeploy to the rear whilst keeping the separation less than that indicated as vulnerable to a *diekplous*, as in Fig. 31.9. An error in files closing up to the left or right of the leading ships, for example as a result of miscommunication

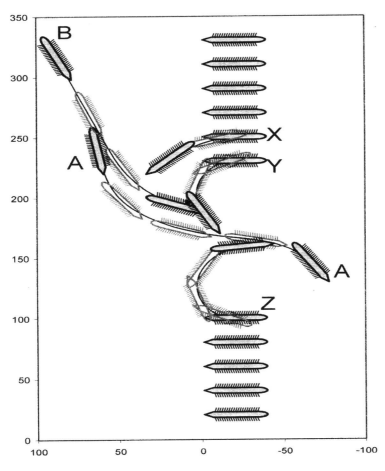

Figure 31.9. Diekplous of a rank. Triremes nearing the end of the arc rowed in Fig. 31.8 and following a slightly more aggressive turning strategy than in Fig. 31.7 can penetrate a gap in the defensive rank of triremes that is as narrow as 130 m. Forty seconds into the diekplous trireme A, moving at 7 knots, is inside the turning circle of Z, itself moving at 6 knots, and clear of its ram. Ship Y is vulnerable to the threat of B which in turn must be wary of ship X. A formation organised to defend against a diekplous should ensure that the ships in a front rank are more closely spaced than this gap.

at the junction between two squadrons, could leave a gap of this size accidentally unfilled, emphasising the importance of this consideration.

Individual files are also shown moving into a single close-spaced rank of ships, taking up to 70 seconds to do so. The rear ships in a file containing more than about five triremes would not be able to react quickly enough to fill any vulnerable gaps in response to any incoming threat; the entire approach phase in Fig. 31.8 takes just 60 seconds, and this is less than the time for the fifth ship in a file to reach the front rank. Maintaining files with more than five ships in a slow stationary fleet would probably therefore be a waste of resources. Deploying from column to line is frequently implied in the accounts of ancient battles. Iphicrates in 372 BC got his fleet to practice just such manoeuvres on their voyage to Corcyria (Xenophon *Hellenica* 6.2.28). Switching between file and rank in this way would be natural to those trained to fight in a hoplite phalanx. The similarity of such trireme manoeuvres to those performed by hoplites in a column

is directly alluded to in Xenophon's *Constitution of the Lacedaemonians* 11.10.

A fleet that remained in this phalanx-like formation of files spaced at 100 m intervals would still remain vulnerable to an attacking squadron of fast triremes. Fig. 31.11 shows that a fleet in such a defensive formation might well be pinned in place with just 30 seconds to react to any attempted ramming attack. The more concentrated attack on a single file shown in Fig. 31.12 provides a yet stronger attacking option.

A squadron of 10 fast triremes in a single file could be organised to ensure an almost continuous stream of ships approaching the slow, defensive fleet. Assuming that the file in Figs. 31.11 and 31.12, ships A to D was extended to include ships E to J, then while the first ships were turning away and repositioning the second half of the file could be making the sort of threatening runs illustrated there. The ships would be conducting a series of turning-back or *anastrophe* manoeuvres whilst looking for a vulnerable point at which to execute a breakthrough, a *diekplous*

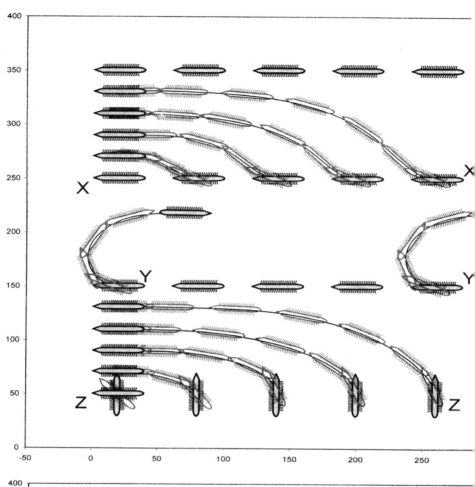

Figure 31.10. Close formation of a slow fleet. In this formation twenty triremes are arrayed in a grid with four files of five ships. In this case the second file, X–X is shown forming a close-spaced rank with ships arriving between 30 and 80 seconds after the start of the manoeuvre. File Y–Y illustrates that the 100 m spacing between adjacent files provides just sufficient room for the triremes to turn through 180 degrees without running foul of their neighbouring files if required to be redeployed to the rear. In a crosswind blowing from the top of the page it would be easier to maintain formation with the trireme's bows into the wind, as in file Z–Z. Deploying from this orientation into a rank sees ships arriving between 20 seconds for the lead ship to 70 seconds for the last.

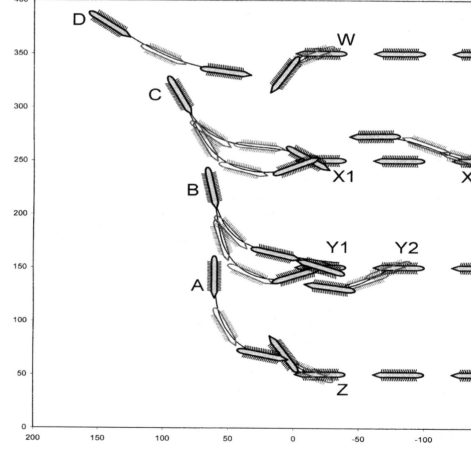

Figure 31.11. Attacking files, multiple threats. A squadron of fast triremes which have steered in such a way as to complete an anastrophe or undertake a diekplous are rowing across the front of a stationary array of files. In the case of both trireme B and trireme C about 5 seconds separates the tracks leading to the opposite sides of X1 and Y1, respectively. If the lead ships reacted before the illustrated start points for B and C then they could end up turning in the wrong direction to counter the attacking ship. Within 25 to 30 seconds of this decision point the attacking ships, B and C could be ramming either side of X1 or Y1. Provided that there is near-perfect coordination between Y1 and Y2 the 30–second interval ought to be sufficient to protect the lead ship of the file, i.e. Y1. The ships further down the file are too far away to affect the outcome of the initial encounter, e.g., X3 arrives too late to help protect X1 from C. Triremes A and D would preclude the lead ships from the neighbouring files W and Z from intervening.

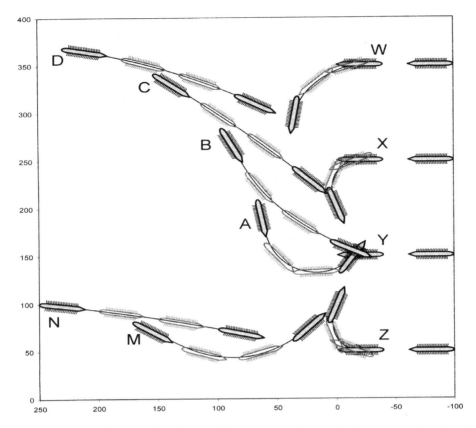

Figure 31.12. Concentrated attack on a file. Two neighbouring squadrons of triremes, each in line ahead, are shown approaching a fleet in an open phalanx-like formation; their positions are shown over the next 30 seconds. The lead ships A and B simultaneously threaten both flanks of ship Y. The following triremes C and D preclude the ships from neighbouring files from intervening immediately. Conversely, if W and X do not move immediately to intercept C and D, then the concentration on file Y will continue to escalate rapidly. The approaching trireme N from the neighbouring squadron will give the lead ship from file Z pause, whilst M and those following N could continue to concentrate at the break-through point.

(cf. Phormio's speech before the Battle of Naupactus in Thucydides, 2.89.8).

8. Conclusion: a tactical paradigm

Based on the above modelling, a tactical paradigm of the contact phase of a trireme conflict may now be proposed. A fast fleet will approach a defensively-deployed slow fleet in order to force them into a more secure close-spaced rank. The slow fleet will delay this as much as possible to avoid ships being blown foul of each other and creating the conditions that would make them especially vulnerable to a *diekplous*. They would nonetheless need to close up to a single defensive rank to avoid an attacking concentration on a relatively isolated file leader. If there was not an appropriate opening to press home the attack then the fast triremes could complete an *anastrophe* and turn back to await further developments. An attacking file of ten triremes could probably maintain an almost continuous succession of vessels approaching the slow fleet. A squadron near the end of the enemy line might instead undertake a *periplous* and row around the enemy force. To avoid exposing their sterns, the defensive fleet would need to

form a *kuklos*, a circle, or attempt to match the *periplous* with a similar movement towards the flank.

The initial stages of the fighting would continue with the slower fleet trying to maintain formation and the fast fleet aiming to break it up. Aside from exploiting openings, this might extend to trying to tempt the slow fleet into moving out of their formation to launch a counter-attack. So the fighting would first be with "their ships in a mass and then scattered" as at the Battle of Arginusae in 406 BC (Xenophon *Hellenica* 1.6.33). The splitting of the Athenian force at the Second Battle of Naupactus, leading to two separate pursuits (Thucydides 2.90–91), and at Cynossema (Thucydides 8.104–105), provide possible examples of just such tactical thinking; the Battle of Notium, 407 BC, perhaps provides an example that was less successful (Xenophon *Hellenica* 1.5.12–15).

Bibliography

Coates, J. F., Platis, S. K. and Shaw, J. T. (1990) *The Trireme Trials 1988*. Oxford, Oxbow.
Lowry, I. J. and Squire, T. M. (1989) *Trireme Olympias Extended Sea Trials Poros*, 1988. Cardiff.
Shaw, J. T. (ed.) (1993) *The Trireme Project*. Oxford, Oxbow.